Special Edition

Using
PageMaker® 6
for Windows 95

Special Edition

Using
*P*ageMaker® 6
for Windows 95

Rick Wallace

que®

Special Edition Using PageMaker 6 for Windows 95

Copyright© 1996 by Que® Corporation.

This book is sold *as is*, without warranty of any kind, either express or implied, respecting the contents of this book, including but not limited to implied warranties for the book's quality, performance, merchantability, or fitness for any particular purpose. Neither Que Corporation nor its dealers or distributors shall be liable to the purchaser or any other person or entity with respect to any liability, loss, or damage caused or alleged to have been caused directly or indirectly by this book.

98 97 96   6 5 4 3 2 1

Interpretation of the printing code: the rightmost double-digit number is the year of the book's printing; the rightmost single-digit number, the number of the book's printing. For example, a printing code of 96-1 shows that the first printing of the book occurred in 1996.

All terms mentioned in this book that are known to be trademarks or service marks have been appropriately capitalized. Que cannot attest to the accuracy of this information. Use of a term in this book should not be regarded as affecting the validity of any trademark or service mark.

Screen reproductions in this book were created using Collage Plus from Inner Media, Inc., Hollis, NH.

Composed in *Cheltenham Light* and *Univers Condensed Bold* by Que Corporation.

CREDITS

President
Roland Elgey

Vice President and Publisher
Marie Butler-Knight

Editorial Services Director
Elizabeth Keaffaber

Managing Editor
Michael Cunningham

Director of Marketing
Lynn E. Zingraf

Senior Series Editor
Chris Nelson

Acquisitions/Development Director
Stephanie Gould

Production Editor
Lisa M. Gebken

Editors
Charles K. Bowles II
Rebecca Mounts
Christine Prakel
Paige Widder

Assistant Product Marketing Manager
Kim Margolius

Technical Editor
John Cornicello

Technical Specialist
Nadeem Muhammed

Acquisitions Coordinator
Tracy M. Williams

Operations Coordinator
Patty Brooks

Editorial Assistant
Carmen Krikorian

Book and Cover Designer
Ruth Harvey

Illustrator
Nathan Clement

Production Team
Steve Adams
Brian Buschkill
Jason Carr
Bryan Flores
Trey Frank
Jason Hand
Sonja Hart
John Hulse
Daryl Kessler
Stephanie Layton
Clint Lahnen
Michelle Lee
Laura Robbins
Bobbi Satterfield
Michael Thomas
Kelly Warner
Paul Wilson
Jody York

Indexer
Carol Sheehan

To the kids—who make me more proud than a father has any right to be. Cyndi has started her career as a graphic artist in Raleigh-Durham, N.C. Melanie teaches autistic kids in Boston, Mass.

And to Karen, who helped me go on a diet in the middle of a book!

ABOUT THE AUTHOR

Rick Wallace spent 20 years as an award-winning reporter, investigator, and news director in the radio and television news business before discovering computers. In the years since then, curiosity and an interest in information design have taken him on a path that has involved computers in many ways:

▶ Associate at a crisis management and political campaign firm, using computers to create strategy documents, presentations, television commercials, and print advertising

▶ President of a company that produced video tutorials on computers and software

▶ Author of a series of books on computer-aided law practice management

▶ Producer of training materials and documentation for many of the largest companies in the computer industry

▶ Publishing newsletters on a wide range of subjects, often full of computer tips and company news

Throughout most of this voyage, beginning with its earliest version, PageMaker has been his constant companion.

Acknowledgments

The book you are holding in your hand, in a sense, was not completely written by me. Sure, I thought up the words and I've worked with the software for years. But throughout this process of bringing this edition another step forward from the last one, there were a number of people working right alongside me on what I think of as "our" project. So, this is my chance to make sure you know about the part they played. Frankly, I'm only worried—because there were so many who played an important role—that I'll unintentionally leave someone out.

There are even more people to thank than you might expect, because this edition was produced in two versions, one for Macintosh PageMaker and one for the Windows version of the program. (Maybe I'm not supposed to mention this business about dual platforms, but it is the way of the future for desktop publishing, and I believe both books are all the stronger for their dual platform heritage.)

I have always appreciated my relationship with the folks on the CompuServe Desktop Publishing and Adobe forums. I appreciate it even more now, after completing this book.

I met John Cornicello online, for example. He's the best technical editor you could imagine—full of accurate answers and creative suggestions. And John helped set up a unique online discussion group consisting of more than 2,000 messages. We actually had a private forum all to ourselves for a group of experts who have become friends and confidants over the months of creating the books. All these people made suggestions, reviewed chapters, and just generally became advisors to the book as we explored the new versions of PageMaker together, and in several cases you will find their names in the Learning from the Pros chapters as well. Their bios are included in the parts of the book where we meet them:

- ▶ Moe Rubenzahl
- ▶ Dave Saunders
- ▶ Rik Bean
- ▶ Kathleen Tinkel
- ▶ Ray Robertson
- ▶ Phil Gaskill
- ▶ Jim Dornbos
- ▶ J.B. Whitwell

Three people at Que have been intimately involved—"every day" involved—with this book, including all its inevitable crisis points:

- ▶ Lori Lyons worked until midnight many an evening making deadlines as she managed production for the Macintosh book.
- ▶ Lisa Gebken did the same for the Windows book with great verve, even though in some ways she was given the most stringent of all our deadlines.
- ▶ Stephanie Gould cooly, calmly, and enthusiastically brought order to chaos, even when it did not seem possible for anyone to do so.

Finally, for appearing in or helping to arrange the Learning from the Pros section (as well as contributing to the CD-ROM that comes with this book), thank you to:

- ▶ Larry Miller, Daddy Desktop
- ▶ Carlos Segura of [T-26] type foundry
- ▶ Joe Treacy of Treacyfaces
- ▶ Brenda Newman of Precision Type
- ▶ The software developers you will find listed in Appendix F for contributing all the software on the CD-ROM

We'd Like to Hear from You!

As part of our continuing effort to produce books of the highest possible quality, Que would like to hear your comments. To stay competitive, we *really* want you, as a computer book reader and user, to let us know what you like or dislike most about this book or other Que products.

You can mail comments, ideas, or suggestions for improving future editions to the address below, or send us a fax at (317) 581-4663. For the online inclined, Macmillan Computer Publishing has a forum on CompuServe (type **GO QUEBOOKS** at any prompt) through which our staff and authors are available for questions and comments. The address of our Internet site is **http://www.mcp.com** (World Wide Web).

In addition to exploring our forum, please feel free to contact me personally to discuss your opinions of this book: I'm **73602,2077** on CompuServe, and I'm **sgould@que.mcp.com** on the Internet.

Thanks in advance—your comments will help us to continue publishing the best books available on computer topics in today's market.

Stephanie Gould
Acquisitions/Development Director
Que Corporation
201 W. 103rd Street
Indianapolis, Indiana 46290
USA

CONTENTS AT A GLANCE

Introduction   1

I   ▲   Getting Started   9

1   Touring PageMaker   11
2   Exploring What's New in PageMaker 6.0   43
3   Personalizing PageMaker Preferences   55
4   Getting an Overview of the DTP Process   69

II   ▲   Working with Text   79

5   Typing In Your Type   81
6   Formatting Paragraphs   115
7   Designing a Text-Style System   161
8   Pouring Text into PageMaker   181
9   Editing Copy with the Story Editor   203

III   ▲   Working with Graphics   231

10   Drawing with PageMaker   233
11   Placing Images   247

IV   ▲   Creating Page Layouts   271

12   Setting Up a New Publication   273
13   Designing a Master Page Grid   285
14   Precisely Positioning Graphics and Text   319
15   Creating Special Effects   359
16   Formatting Forms, Tables, and Databases   405
17   Building Many Pages   439

V   ▲   Making Pages Colorful   489

18   Creating Colors   491
19   Applying Colors   517
20   Meeting Color Challenges   527

VI ▲ Publishing   551

    21   Producing Mechanicals   553

    22   Proofing Your Publication   603

    23   Working with the Print Shop   619

    24   Master Checklist for Desktop Publishing   647

VII ▲ Supercharging PageMaker   669

    25   Developing a System for Managing Your Type   671

    26   Completing Your Own PageMaker System   685

    27   Leaping Across Platforms   695

    28   Automating PageMaker   707

VIII ▲ Riding the Cutting Edge   741

    29   Publishing Electronically: The Web or Acrobat   743

    30   Linking and Other File Connections   765

IX ▲ Learning from the Pros   781

    31   Thinking On-Screen   783

    32   Setting Grunge Type: Point and Counterpoint   795

    33   Designing for the Web   807

    34   Putting PageMaker 6.0 to Work   817

X ▲ Appendixes   827

    A   Installation   829

    B   Rescue!   837

    C   Keyboard Shortcuts   845

    D   PageMaker's New Tagging Language   863

    E   Resource Guide   871

    F   What's on the CD?   877

▲ Index   883

Contents

Introduction   1

What Special Features Does This Book Contain?   2
Where Do I Start?   3
    I'm a Brand New Desktop Publisher. Help, Please?   3
    I've Gotta Do This, But Do I Have To?   3
    I'm Already a Designer. Could You
       Just Tell Me About PageMaker?   4
    I'm a Power PageMaker User; Where's the Good Stuff?   4
How Is This Book Organized?   5
    Part I: Getting Started   5
    Part II: Working with Text   5
    Part III: Working with Graphics   5
    Part IV: Creating Page Layouts   5
    Part V: Making Pages Colorful   6
    Part VI: Publishing   6
    Part VII: Supercharging PageMaker   6
    Part VIII: Riding the Cutting Edge   7
    Part IX: Learning from the Pros   7
    Part X: Appendixes   7
    CD-ROM   7

I GETTING STARTED   9

1 Touring PageMaker   11

Taking the Quick Tour   12
    Creating a New Publication   12
    Loading a Publication   15
    Navigating   17
    Magnifying Your View   18
    Turning On Rulers and Guides   19

Stopping by the Master Pages   21
Storing Objects on the Pasteboard   23
Opening Up the Toolbox   24
Formatting Text   27
Editing in the Story Editor   28
Printing   30
Flying the Control Palette   31
Applying and Defining Colors   35
Taking In Some Special Sights   36
Managing Guides   37
Aligning Objects   37
Grouping Objects   38
Weaving the World Wide Web   38
Building Paperless Hypertext for Acrobat   39
Getting More Help   40
Adobe   40
Newsletters and Magazines   41
Online   41
Where to Go from Here   42

2   Exploring What's New In PageMaker 6.0   43

Designing Pages   44
Setting Type   46
Publishing In Color   47
Printing and Prepress   48
Publishing Electronically   50
Running and Automating PageMaker   50
Integrating PageMaker into a Complete
    Publishing Environment   51
Understanding Programming Improvements   52
Working Around What's Still Missing In PageMaker 6.0   53
Where to Go from Here   53

3   Personalizing PageMaker Preferences   55

Understanding the PageMaker Default Scheme   56
Using PageMaker's Default Brain   56
Understanding the Four-Way Matrix of
    PageMaker Defaults   56

Key Concept: Two Types of PageMaker Defaults   56
Key Concept: Two Ways to Set Defaults   57
Using the Preferences Command   58
Setting Measurements   58
Highlighting Layout Problems   59
Setting Graphics Display   60
Managing the Control Palette   60
Choosing a Save Option   61
Setting Guides   61
Choosing More Preferences   61
Substituting Fonts   64
Managing Color   65
Accessing Express Preferences   65
Setting Mini-Defaults   65
Where to Go from Here   68

4   Getting an Overview of the DTP Process   69

Planning   70
Defining the Goal and Audience   70
Setting a Budget and Deadline   71
Developing a Core Creative Concept   71
Testing the Concept and Getting Preliminary Approvals   72
Collaborating with the Printer and Service Bureau   72
Making Up Your Pages   73
Perfecting Your Elements   73
Setting Up Your Publication   74
Placing Text and Graphics   74
Fine-Tuning, Producing Special Effects, and
Coloring Your Pages   75
Generating Contents and Index   76
Publishing   76
Trapping   76
Separating   76
Final Output   76
Imposition, Proofing, and Approvals   77
Going to Press, Folding, and Binding   78
Where to Go from Here   78

II ▼ WORKING WITH TEXT   79

5   Typing In Your Type   81

Using the Text Tool   82

Setting Text Attributes   82

Setting Attributes by Selecting Existing Text   83

Typing New Text at the Insertion Point   83

Setting a Mini-Default Without Clicking an
Insertion Point   83

Selecting Type Attributes   84

Making Multiple Type Decisions with the Type
Specifications Dialog Box   84

Doing Simple Formatting Using the Type Menu   85

Experimenting with Type Effects Using the
Control Palette   85

Selecting a Typeface   86

Choosing a Typeface In the Type Specifications
Dialog Box   86

Choosing a Typeface from the Font Submenu   87

Choosing a Typeface with the Control Palette   87

Choosing a Type Size   88

Sizing Type with the Type Specifications Dialog Box   88

Making a Fast Type Sizing Decision with the
Type Menu   89

Sizing Type with the Control Palette   89

Key Concept: Measuring Type Size: Picas, Points,
and Ems   90

Spacing Lines with Leading   93

Key Concept: Understanding PageMaker's
Double-Location Leading Scheme   94

Setting Leading   95

Automating Your Leading Design Decisions with
Autoleading   96

Giving Your Type Weight and Style   97

Automating Capitalization   99

Adjusting Letter Space Using Kerning, Tracking,
   and Width   100

   Spacing Pairs of Letters with Kerning   100

   Tuning Overall Letter Spacing with Tracking   103

   Editing Tracks   104

   Adjusting the Width of a Type Selection   106

   Using Line End to Hold Words Together   107

Setting Subscripts, Superscripts, and Baseline Shifts   108

   Raising and Lowering Letters with Baseline Shift   108

   Using Superscript and Subscript   109

Using the Control Palette to Set Type   111

Where to Go from Here   113

6   Formatting Paragraphs   115

Key Concept: Understanding the Nature of a
   PageMaker Paragraph   116

Choosing Different Text Alignment Options   117

   Aligning Text Using the Dialog Box, Menu, and
      Palette   118

   Justifying Text: Word and Letter Spacing,
      Automatic Kerning   120

   Key Concept: Understanding PageMaker's Special
      Spacing Power   121

   Hyphenating Words   126

   Tactics Recipe: Setting Up a Justification System   131

   Force Justifying   135

Applying Tab Stops and Indents   136

   Using the Indents/Tabs Ruler   136

   Setting a Tab and Choosing Tab Alignment   137

   Setting Tabs for Multiple Rows of Data   138

   Using the Position Box for Precision Tabbing   139

   Dotting a Leader Tab   139

Setting Precision Multiple Tabs with the
Repeat Command   140
Making New Default Tabs and Resetting
the Built-In Ones   140
Indenting Paragraphs   141
Indenting Paragraphs with the Menu
and Control Palette   145
Controlling the Flow of Lines and Paragraphs   146
Forcing a New Line with Shift+Enter   146
Controlling Paragraph Flow Using the Paragraph
Specifications Dialog Box   146
Setting Off Paragraphs with Spacing and Rules   150
Spacing Before and After Paragraphs   150
Adding Rules to Paragraphs   151
Choosing Your Leading Method   155
Using the Leading Method Radio Buttons   155
Key Concept: Understanding the Three
Leading Methods   156
Deciding Which Leading Method to Choose   157
Where to Go from Here   159

7   Designing a Text Style System   161

Key Concept: The Advantages of Paragraph Styles   162
Applying Styles   162
Styling with Palettes and Menus   163
Augmenting and Overriding Styles with
Local Formatting   165
Identifying Styles and Their Status   167
Defining or Redefining Styles   168
Exploring the Styles Definition Dialog Boxes   168
Cascading, Mimicking, Merging, Copying, and
Importing Styles   171
Tactics Recipe: Developing Your Personal Style   176
Where to Go from Here   180

8   Pouring Text into PageMaker   181

Key Concept: Understanding Text Blocks, Stories,
Threads, and Windowshades   182
Using the Place Command and Pouring Text onto
the Page   184
Using the Place Command to Load Your Text Icon   184
Understanding the Three Text Placement Icon Types   185
Pouring Text   187
Sizing and Positioning Text Blocks   189
Unthreading and Rethreading Text Blocks   190
Importing Text   192
PageMaker Filters   192
Using Style Tags   195
Importing Microsoft Word Text   196
Using the Text-Only Import Filter   198
Using the PageMaker Story Importer   199
Linking and Unlinking Text   200
Where to Go from Here   202

9   Editing Copy with the Story Editor   203

Learning Story Editor Basics   204
Opening a Story and Changing Views   205
Managing Story Editor Windows   209
Enhancing the Story Editor Display   210
Editing Text in the Story Editor   212
Selecting Text and Navigating   212
Cutting, Copying, Deleting, and Pasting   214
Styling and Formatting Type and Paragraphs   215
Checking Your Spelling   215
Accessing and Using the Spell Checker   215
Editing Your Dictionary   217
Finding and Changing Text   222
Accessing and Starting Find and Change   223
Defining Your Search-and-Replace Parameters   224
Finding, Changing, and Finding Again   227
Where to Go from Here   229

III ▼ WORKING WITH GRAPHICS   231

10   Drawing with PageMaker   233

Drawing Lines and Shapes   234
  Drawing Simple Lines   234
  Key Concept: Constraining Graphics   235
  Drawing Shapes: Rectangles and Ovals   235
  Rounding Corners   236
  Drawing Shapes: Polygons   236
Moving and Sizing a Drawn Object   238
  Moving an Object   238
  Sizing an Object   239
Customizing Lines and Shapes   240
  Choosing Quick Lines   240
  Choosing Quick Fills   242
  Using the Comprehensive Fill and Line Menu   242
  Key Concept: Understanding Layers and the
    Colors None and Paper   243
Where to Go from Here   246

11   Placing Images   247

Key Concept: Reviewing Resolution-Dependent and
    Resolution-Independent Images   248
Placing Graphics   251
  Using the Place Command for Graphics   252
  Replacing an Existing Graphic   253
  Placing Inline Graphics   253
  Storing Graphics In or Out of a Publication   255
  Editing the Original Graphic   255
  Clipboarding Graphics   256

Organizing and Inserting Graphics with the
Library Palette   257
Sizing and Cropping Graphics   257
Sizing with Click and Drag   258
Sizing Proportionally and Using Magic Stretch   258
Cropping with the Cropping Tool   259
Viewing and Compressing Graphics   260
Viewing Graphics at High Resolution   260
Setting Compression for a Graphic   261
Tuning and Manipulating Resolution-Dependent Images   263
Using Image Control   263
Applying Image Filters   266
Using Special Tools for Importing Scanned Images   266
Scanning Images Directly into PageMaker   266
Importing Photo CD Images   268
Where to Go from Here   269

IV ▼ Creating Page Layouts   271

12   Setting Up a New Publication   273

Tactics Recipe: Starting a New Publication   274
Using the Document Setup and Numbers Dialog Boxes   277
Setting Page Size and Orientation   277
Setting Number of Pages and First Page
Number Options   278
Printing on Both Sides of the Page   279
Setting Margins and Gutters   279
Indicating Printer Resolution   280
Specifying Page Number Style   280
Changing Document Setup (Beware!)   281

Opening Templates   283
  Opening a PageMaker Template   283
  Making a New Template   283
  Using a Previously Saved Template   284
Where to Go from Here   284

13   Designing a Master Page Grid   285

Guiding the Grid   286
  Setting Margin Guides   287
  Setting Column Guides   288
  Setting Ruler Guides   289
  Manually Managing Guides   290
Setting Guides Automatically: The Guide Manager   292
  Creating a Library of Grids   292
  Defining Grids Of Guides   295
  Copying and Deleting Guides   297
Setting Snap Constraints   298
Measuring a Layout Grid   298
  Moving and Locking the Zero Point   299
  Setting Up Rulers   299
Understanding Master Pages   299
  Navigating Between Master Pages   300
  Master of All: The Document Master   300
  Applying Master Pages   300
  Setting Up a New Master   302
  Editing A Master   303
  Basing a Master Page on Existing Pages   303
  Making a Master of None   304
Putting Master Page Grids to Work   304
  Adding Standard Master Page Elements   306
  Key Concept: Understanding Grid Terminology   308
  Tactics Recipe: Powering Up the Layout Grid   309
Fitting Copy   316
  Establish Horizontal Copy-Fitting Controls   316
  Work Out the Automatic Vertical Copy Fit Parameters   317
  Tune Each Page Manually   317
Where to Go from Here   317

14 Precisely Positioning Graphics and Text 319

Undoing and Reverting 320
  Undo 320
  Revert 320
  Mini-Revert 321
  Backing Up as a Safety Net 321
Displaying Your Pages at Optimum Accuracy 321
  Toggling Magnification 322
  Managing Screen Resolution and Screen
    Redraw Time 324
Positioning by Eye and Snap Guides 325
  Getting a Readout 325
  Constraining Moves with the Shift Key 326
  Snapping To Guides 327
  Positioning Tiny Objects 329
  Nudging with the Arrow Keys 330
Getting Ultra-Precise with the Control Palette 330
  Taking Action with Nudge Buttons and
    Text-Entry Boxes 331
  Understanding the Apply Button 333
  Selecting a Reference Point with the Proxy 333
  Setting the Proxy Action Mode 334
  Understanding the Center Proxy Point 336
  Moving with Multiple Objects Selected 337
  Moving an Object with the X and Y Coordinates 338
  Reviewing Scaling and Cropping Basics 338
  Sizing an Object with Scaling and Cropping 339
Skewing, Flipping, and Rotating Graphics and Text 340
  Skewing 340
  Flipping 341
  Rotating 343
  Editing Skewed, Flipped, or Rotated Text 345
Grouping Objects 345
  Making a Group 346
  Understanding Group Idiosyncrasies 346
Aligning and Distributing Objects 348
  Getting the Basics of Aligning and Distributing 348
  Getting the Ins and Outs of Alignment 349
  Making the Most of the Distribution Options 349

Pasting for Placement   350
  Pasting Multiples   350
  Power Paste Precision   351
Locking Graphics to Text as Inline Graphics   352
  Keeping an Inline Graphic on the Leading Grid   352
  Making Space for the Inline Graphic   353
  Controlling an Inline Graphic's Text Slop   354
Locking Graphics to the Page   355
Masking   355
Where to Go from Here   357

15   Creating Special Effects   359

Hanging Type and Graphics   360
  Hanging Multidigit Numbers   360
  Companion Column Graphics   360
  Hanging Punctuation   362
  Simultaneous Forced Left and Forced Right   363
Casting Headlines   364
  Cross-Column Headlines   364
  Cut-In Headlines   366
  Companion Column Headlines   369
  Decorating Headlines   376
Setting Fractions   379
Wrapping and Molding Text   381
  Using the Text Wrap Command   381
  Customizing Your Text Wrap   383
  Molding Text into Shapes with Text Wrap   384
  Text Inside a Shape   386
Cutting in Initial Caps   388
  Raised Cap   388
  Hanging Cap   388
  Drop Cap   389
Twisting and Mangling Type   392
  Spinning and Skewing Type   392
  Playing with Baselines and Kerning   393
  Stacking Up Drop Shadows   394

Building Boxes, Backgrounds, and Screens   395
   Using Keyline and Other Boxing Methods   395
   Creating Vertical Rules   398
   Inserting Screens and Other Backgrounds   399
   Taking Full Advantage of Masking and Grouping   401
Where to Go from Here   403

16   Formatting Forms, Tables, and Databases   405

Building Tables into Your PageMaker System   406
Managing an OLE Table   407
   Starting a New OLE Table   407
   Opening an Existing OLE Table   407
   Updating, Closing, and Saving Your OLE Table   408
Managing Your Table as a Standalone Graphic   408
   Opening the Adobe Table Program   408
   Exporting and Saving a Standalone Graphic Table   408
   Importing an Adobe Table as a Standalone Graphic   409
   Updating a Standalone Adobe Table Graphic   409
   Working with Other Table Editor Files   409
Making Page Breaks for Long Graphic Tables   410
Constructing an Adobe Table   410
   Setting Up the Table   411
   Entering Data   412
   Navigating and Selecting Cells   412
   Shaping, Sizing, Adding, and Deleting Cells   414
   Setting Table Type   417
   Setting Borders and Fills   418
   Establishing Table Preferences   420
Importing Databases and Spreadsheets   421
   Key Concept: The Nature of PageMaker Database and
      Spreadsheet Info   421
   Tactics Recipe: Setting Up Tables and Forms   422
Importing Data   423
   Raw Databases   423
   Spreadsheets and Databases   424
   Importing Word Processor Tables   426

Formatting Data Tables and Forms   426
   Cleaning Up Data   427
   Setting Tabbed Columns and Hanging Indents   428
   Emphasizing Data with Paragraph Rules   429
   Laying in Vertical Rules   431
Precoding Data Tables for Maximum Efficiency   432
   Prestyling Your Data   433
   Coding Paragraph Styles In Plain Text   434
   Supercharging Table Coding with Tagging   434
Creating Lines and Check Boxes on Forms   435
   Setting Check boxes   435
   Setting Fill-In Blanks   436
Where to Go from Here   438

17   **Building Many Pages   439**

Building a Book List   440
   Using the Book Command   440
   Organizing Your Book Files   442
   Organizing Chapters with Prefix Style Numbering   443
Manipulating and Navigating Pages   444
   Inserting Pages   444
   Removing Pages   445
   Sorting Pages   446
Constructing Tables of Contents   448
   Defining TOC Entries   448
   Compiling the TOC Entries   449
   Placing and Tuning the TOC   450
   Composing Chapter-Level Tables of Contents or
      Specialty Lists   452
Coding Indexes   453
   Key Concept: Understanding Indexes and Index
      Entry Types   454
   Tactics Recipe: Composing a Book Index:
      A Tactics Recipe   455
   Importing a Master Topic List   457
   Coding Your Index Entries   458
   Doing a Basic Index Entry (Existing Topic)   460
   Adding a New Topic from Text   465
   Making a Cross-Reference Entry   466

Indexing Every Occurrence of a Word   468
Indexing Names   469
Editing Your Index Electronically   470
Creating, Placing, and Styling Your Index   474
Managing Book Special Effects   477
Making Running Headers and Footers   477
Tactics Recipe: Coding Page Cross-References   482
Tactics Recipe: Setting Footnotes   484
Tactics Recipe: Creating Bleeder Tabs   485
Where to Go from Here   487

V ▼ MAKING PAGES COLORFUL   489

18   Creating Colors   491

Key Concept: Your Screen Doesn't Match
the Printing Press   492
Working with Spot Color   494
Spot Color Means Accurate Color   494
Spot Color Overlays and Press Plates   495
Working with Process Color   496
Understanding Traditional Process Color   496
Considering High-Fidelity Color   497
Deciding Between Spot and Process Color   498
Converting Between Color Systems   500
Defining Colors in PageMaker   503
Adding/Editing a Color on Your Colors Palette   504
Specifying Overprint and Knockout   511
Making Color Definitions Consistent Within and
Between Publications   512
Merging Colors   513
Removing Colors   513
Copying Colors Between Publications   514
Adopting Colors from Imported or Clipboarded
Objects   514
Using Color Templates and Mini-Defaults   515
Installing and Making Your Own Color Libraries   515
Where to Go from Here   516

19   Applying Colors   517

Exploring the Colors Palette   518
    Colors List   518
    Coloring with Line, Fill, and Both   519
    The [None], [Paper], [Black], and
        [Registration] "Colors"   519
Coloring Text   520
Coloring PageMaker-Drawn Objects   522
    Colors Palette   522
    Fill and Line Dialog Box   522
    Assigning Overprint Status   524
Coloring Imported Objects   524
    Moving an Imported Object to an Overlay
        or Separation   524
    Deciding Which Imported Graphics Can and Can't
        Be Colored   525
    Restoring Color   525
Where to Go from Here   526

20   Meeting Color Challenges   527

Collaborating with Your Printer and Service Bureau
    on Color   528
Understanding Color Management   530
Setting Up Color Management   532
    Establishing Basic Color Management Settings   533
    Ad Hoc Color Management Settings   534
    Optimizing Your Color Viewing Environment   536
Trapping   537
    Key Concept: What Is Trapping and Why
        Do I Need It?   537
The Way It Used to Be: Mechanical Trapping   539
Object Trapping   540
Raster Trapping   541
Deciding Whether to Do Your Own Trapping   541
Consider Running with No Trapping: Kiss Fit   542
Design Away the Need for Trapping   543
    Overprinting Black   543
    Sharing CMYK Colors   544

Frame the Untrappables   544
Design Away Trapping Nightmares   544
Putting PageMaker's Automatic Object Trapping to Work   547
Getting Together the Technical Info   547
Understanding How PageMaker Traps   548
Setting Trapping Parameters   549
Where to Go from Here   550

VI ▼ PUBLISHING   551

21   Producing Mechanicals   553

PostScript or Not?   554
Selecting and Setting Up Your Printer Driver   554
Making Your Setup Choices   555
Customizing Your Printer Setup   556
Printing to a Laser Printer   558
Setting General Print Parameters in Document Mode   558
Selecting Paper Size, Scaling, and Tiling   561
Customizing Graphics Handling, Printing to Disk,
and Overall Efficiency   565
Selecting Features   568
Non-PostScript Printer Differences   569
Comping and Imagesetting Color   570
Optimizing Your Laser Printer Output Results   574
Poor Person's High-Resolution Output   574
Adjust Toner Amount   575
Rock It and Clean It   575
Fixative Spray   575
Warm Up with All Black Pages   575
Print to Rented 11" x 17" for Imposition and Bleeds   576
High-Resolution Laser Is Not the Same as
Phototypesetter   576
Laser Photos on Copiers   576
Use Special Papers   576
Laser Shirts, Foil Embossing, and More   577
Give the Landfill a Rest   577
Using Printer Styles   577

Using the Build Booklet Plug-in   579
   Taking the Imposition Risk   579
   Getting Ready   580
   Building a Booklet   580
Preventing the Output Time Blues   583
   Use Checklists and Consultations   583
   Buff That File   583
   Size and Crop Graphics Before Placing Them   584
   No White Boxes, Please   585
   Complex Graphics Can Choke the Output Device   585
   Paste Inside Masks Can Be Problems   586
   Avoid Embedding Text in EPS Files   586
   Rotate Graphics Before Placement   587
   Avoid TrueType Fonts and WMFs (Imagesetter)   587
   Compute Blend Steps to Avoid Banding   587
Packaging Up Your Service Bureau Job   590
   Deciding on a Tactic   590
   Negotiating Lower Rates with a Service Bureau   591
   Specifying Your Service Bureau Run   592
   Using the Service Bureau for More PrePress Services   599
Where to Go from Here   600

22   Proofing Your Publication   603

Checking Copy   604
   Run the Spelling and Grammar Checkers   604
   Spot Check with an Index and a Table of Contents   605
   Hire Professional Proofreaders   605
   Use In-House Proofing Tricks   606
   Get Formal Sign Offs   606
Laser Proofing   606
   Thumbnails   606
   Composites   607
   The Proof Check Box   607
Running Pre-Service Bureau Proofs   607
   Listen to Your Laser Printer   607
   Check for Problems On-Screen   608
   Use a PostScript Error Checker   608
   Turn Your Laser Printer into an Imagesetter Proofer   608

Proofing Color at the Service Bureau   610

Test Separations on a Laser   610

Inexpensive Color Printer Comps   611

Set a Color Goal   611

Focus on the Memory Colors   611

Evaluate Colors In Controlled Light   612

Choose Between Composite and Laminate Proofs   612

Checking Your Publication at the Print Shop   613

Swatches of Ink and Varnish   613

Printer Inspection of Films   614

Blueline   614

Dummy   614

Press Check   615

Where to Go from Here   616

23   Working with the Print Shop   619

Running a Preflight Check   620

Which Comes First: Preflight or Bidding?   621

Preparing for Your Preflight Meeting   621

Beginning the Collaboration   623

Developing Tactics   624

Bidding the Job   627

Developing a Bid Form   628

Specifying Paper   628

Arranging for Bindery Services   631

Inspecting Your Finished Job   632

Key Concept: Understanding Halftones and Screens   632

Choosing a Line Screen with Your Print Shop   641

Understanding the Effects of Dot Gain   641

What To Do with the Line Screen Information   641

Some Line Screen Guidelines   643

Compensate Scans for the Press   643

Where to Go from Here   645

24   Master Checklist for Desktop Publishing   647

Planning   648

Defining the Goal and Audience   648

Setting a Budget, Deadline, and Schedule   650
Developing Your Core Creative Concept   652
Testing the Concept and Getting Preliminary
   Approvals   654
Collaborating with the Printer and Service Bureau   655
Making Up Your Pages   658
Perfecting Your Elements   658
Setting Up Your Publication   661
Placing Text and Graphics   663
Fine-Tuning, Producing Special Effects, and
   Coloring Your Pages   664
Generating Contents and Index   664
Publishing   664
Submitting Files to the Service Bureau   665
Proofing and Final Approvals   666
Going to Press: Imposing, Folding, and Binding   668

VII ▼ SUPERCHARGING PAGEMAKER   669

25   Developing a System for Managing Your Type   671

Key Concept: Windows Type Technology and
   Adobe Type Manager   672
Tactics Recipe: Organizing Your Fonts   675
Managing PANOSE Font Substitution   679
Getting an Overview   679
Getting the PANOSE Greeting   680
Setting PANOSE   681
Setting PANOSE Defaults   682
Recognizing Fake Font Signals   683
Where to Go from Here   683

26   Completing Your Own PageMaker System   685

Managing Your Plug-ins   686
Installing Plug-ins   686
Finding Out What You've Got   686
Running Plug-ins   686

Using the Plug-ins That Come with PageMaker   687
Adding Third-Party Plug-ins   688
   Shopping for Plug-ins   688
   Basic Plug-in Recommendations   689
   Plug-ins That Manipulate Objects   689
Editing the Uneditable   692
   Going Native for Editing   692
   ArtSPREE and Transverter Pro   692
Text and Type Management Utilities   693
   Tagging Text   693
   Making Book Features   693
   Proofing   693
Converting Files   693
Compression Tools   694
Where to Go from Here   694

27   Leaping Across Platforms   695

Getting the File Across the Gap   696
   Slipping a Disk   696
Connecting Directly   697
   Connecting One-on-One   697
   Connecting via Telephone   697
   Connecting More Permanently by Networking   698
Translating Foreign Page Element Files   699
   Stick to Platform Agile Graphics Formats   699
   Making Words Flow Across the Gap   700
   Decoding Cross-Platform Compressed Files   701
Making PageMaker Jump the Gap   701
   Setting Up PageMaker   701
   Making Transfer Decisions   702
   Understanding Linking Effects   703
   Jumping the Font Hurdle   704
Where to Go from Here   705

28   Automating PageMaker   707

Key Concept: Scripts and Tags Are Just Fancy
   To-Do Lists   708

Using the Scripts Palette 710
    Running a Script 710
    Managing Scripts in the Palette 711
    A 20-Second Solo Flight 712
Pushing the Script Envelope with Ray 713
    Trying Out the CD-ROM Scripts 713
    Supercharging Find/Change with Scripting 717
    Setting a Fraction 719
Scripting Survival Guide 720
    Grammar and Syntax 720
    Tips and Gotchas 725
What PageMaker Scripts Can't Do 727
Taking the Next Step: Conversing with Your Computer 728
    Key Concept: Tagging Your Text 730
    Tactics Recipe: Working Through the
        Tagging Process 732
Getting Tagged 733
Tagging Survival Guide 734
    Tagging Language Grammar 734
    Tag Tricks and Insight 735
    Take My Graphic, Please! 736
    Make PageMaker Work for You: Macros 737
    Batching It 738
If You Don't Want to Bother 739
Where to Go from Here 739

VIII ▼ RIDING THE CUTTING EDGE   741

29   Publishing Electronically: The Web or Acrobat   743

Key Concept: Making Electronic Publishing Choices 744
Tactics Recipe: Paper-based to Web-based
    Document Work Flow 747
Converting and Re-Linking 750
A Web Layout Survival Guide 751
Running HTML Author 754

Getting a Problem Spotter Report   754
Establishing Content and Web Pagination   755
Lining Up Your Styles   756
Making Your Links   758
Export to HTML   759
Acrobat and PDF   760
Font Issues   761
Install and Manage Distiller   761
Managing Automatic Hypertext Links   762
Page Structuring   763
Where to Go from Here   764

30   Linking and Other File Connections   765

Assessing the Link Strategies   766
Why Do We Link in the First Place?   766
Linking Is Mostly for Graphics   767
Why Two Choices?   768
Understanding the Differences   769
Making and Managing Links   772
Controlling Your Links   772
Editing Originals   776
Making a PageMaker Link   777
Linking and Embedding with OLE   778
Where to Go from Here   780

IX   LEARNING FROM THE PROS   781

31   Thinking On-Screen   783

32   Setting Grunge Type: Point and Counterpoint   795

33   Designing for the Web   807

34   Putting PageMaker 6.0 to Work   817

X ▼ APPENDIXES   827

Appendix A Installation   829

System Requirements   830
  Official Specifications   830
  Making Yourself More Efficient   831
Installing PageMaker   831
  Installation Options   832
  Performing the Installation   832

Appendix B Rescue!   837

Preventing Problems In the First Place   838
When PageMaker Goes Bad   839
  Performing a Diagnostic Recompose   840
  Other Things to Try Inside PageMaker   840
  Try File Operations at the Desktop Level   842

Appendix C Keyboard Shortcuts   845

Help   846
Tools   846
Express Preferences   847
File and Program Management   847
Layout   848
Graphics   849
Adjusting Graphics or Text Blocks   849
View, Layout   850
View, Story Editor   850
View, Selecting and Redrawing Page   851
View, Scrolling   851
Control Palette   851
  Power Nudging   852
  Selecting a Style, Font, or Track   852
Styles Palette   852
Colors Palette   853
Type Formatting   853
  Font Size   853
  Alignment   853

Leading, Width, Track   854
Case   854
Position   854
Type Style   854
All Character Attributes   854
Paragraph Formatting   855
Text Editing   855
Selecting   855
Insertion Point   855
Search and Replace (Story Editor Only)   856
Indexing   856
Kerning   857
Special Characters   858
Metacharacters   859
Power Shortcuts   860
Special Commands   860
Compressing TIFFs In Place Dialog Box   860
Recomposing Text   861

Appendix D PageMaker's New Tagging Language   863

Character Level Formatting Tags   864
Paragraph Level Formatting Tags   866
Special Character Tags   869

Appendix E Resource Guide   871

Appendix F What's on the CD?   877

PhotoDisc   878
Precision Type   878
[T-26]   879
Treacyfaces   879
Scripts By Ray   879
SNR   879
ZIP and StuffIt   880
Graphics Converters   880
Web Editing Tools   881

Index   883

Introduction

MY OBJECTIVE IN this book has been to gather every bit of information I could on PageMaker 6.0—even stuff that isn't in the manuals—and put that information into a deeply pragmatic context. If I've succeeded, and I sincerely hope I have, all the usual information about the PageMaker commands is here, but it has also been focused by a lens of practicality. The information has been glued together with hard-won experiences gained through day-to-day usage. ▶ ▶ ▶

What Special Features Does This Book Contain?

There are several special features that organize the information in this book:

▶ *Master Checklist.* Producing a publication can be pretty intimidating—there are so many details to handle. In addition to bullet point checklists scattered throughout the book, Chapter 24 has a nearly 300-point master checklist for the entire desktop publishing process.

▶ *Tips.* Of course, every computer book has tips, but there's been a special effort to tune these to the working world of desktop publishing. Tips have been constructed on a foundation of the practical.

▶ *Tactics Recipes.* The Tactics Recipe sections throughout the book work sort of like extended tips, giving you a complete "cookbook" to a particular desktop publishing task. These sections set out all your choices and leave the final decision up to you, while making a guiding recommendation.

▶ *Key Concepts.* Key Concepts sections explain basic information, giving you the background you need to understand such fundamental topics as the basic nature of a paragraph in PageMaker, the technology of computerized type, paragraph styles, and various types of graphic file formats.

▶ *Learning from the Pros.* If one working pro can give you good advice, how about a whole gaggle of them? The "Learning from the Pros" chapters contain extended interviews, with work examples. You'll get solid tips and insight into the creative process.

▶ *Design Notes.* There's no sense having PageMaker unless you get a good-looking page out of it. To help, Design Notes are placed at strategic points in the midsection of the book, where the features you use to put the design elements onto your pages are discussed.

▶ *Keyboard shortcuts and special characters.* If you are someone who stretches a program right out to the limit, you'll love all the tiny little nuggets in the charts of keyboard shortcuts and special characters, located in Appendix C.

▶ *Really useful appendixes.* Speaking of the appendixes, these have some valuable stuff. There's a new appendix for this edition called Rescue!. It'll help you pull a file back from the brink of death when, inevitably, things go horribly wrong. There are other appendixes on installing PageMaker, the new tagging language, and the already mentioned keyboard shortcuts and special characters.

▶ *Surfing the Web.* The new burst of interest in electronic publishing has been covered in two places. There's a chapter devoted to the electronic publishing capabilities of PageMaker 6.0, including the generation of Web pages in HTML language, and the ability to generate Acrobat PDF files. In addition, there's a Learning from the Pros interview with a Webmaster, containing design tips for attracting and keeping your Internet audience.

▶ *A 4-color section.* PageMaker 6.0's color potential is illustrated in an exciting 32-page, 4-color section of the book. The concepts and color effects demonstrated in these pages are referenced and explored in-depth throughout the book's chapters.

Where Do I Start?

There's no way you are going to read every page of this book. Well, maybe eventually, but it's not exactly a mystery-thriller-adventure-spy novel, is it? Here's a guide to help you find your way and to help you focus your exploration of PageMaker's power.

I'm a Brand New Desktop Publisher. Help, Please?

You have not only never used PageMaker, but you've never published anything, either. Start with Chapter 4 to get an overview of the whole process of publishing a document.

After you have that holistic view, jump into the Chapter 1 tour. That'll deepen your overview and give you a context for everything that follows.

Part IX, "Learning from the Pros," has a lot of important conceptual information and insight. That section also has some great material on the nature of the creative process—the basic way you get a design going in your head before you move it to PageMaker.

From there, you have as many routes to follow as there are types of publications. Your best approach may be to decide what kind of publication you want to create first, and follow through each chapter one-by-one. They're roughly in the order you need them to build a publication.

I've Gotta Do This, But Do I Have To?

Maybe you have been "volunteered" to do the church newsletter. Perhaps the boss said somebody has to do the new marketing brochure—and it ended up that you are that somebody. Or, everybody else took one step back and left you in the limelight when the academic council asked who'd like to be advisor to the yearbook club.

Believe it or not, you might consider starting with Chapter 24, "Master Checklist for Desktop Publishing." You have a specific goal for your work in PageMaker, so use that checklist and its cross references to all the chapters in the book to build your publication and learn PageMaker at the same time.

I'm Already a Designer. Could You Just Tell Me About PageMaker?

Start out with the tour in Chapter 1 to get a quick introduction to how the program works. You'll notice that it gives you an electronic Pasteboard, just like the one you have used in traditional X-acto knife paste-up. That's one reason PageMaker has been immensely popular among designers who are coming over to the computer for the first time.

Next, you may enjoy the foundation experience of hearing how other designers use PageMaker. That's Part IX, "Learning from the Pros." They'll share with you how they make use of the program in their everyday work.

Most designers seem to have a particular working style. Some start with text and some start with graphics. Pick your style and use it to lever yourself into the intensive coverage of PageMaker commands in Part II, "Working with Text," and Part III, "Working with Graphics."

From there, you'll want to move into Part IV, "Creating Page Layouts," including the electronic Master Page Grid concept in Chapter 13. Use any special needs you have to drive you on into PageMaker from that point. There are special chapters and sections on special effects, forms and tables, book building, and color.

Finally, to help you relate digital design to traditional design, use Chapter 24's Master Checklist to back you up so that you don't let any details drop.

I'm a Power PageMaker User; Where's the Good Stuff?

Check out the tips that appear throughout the text. This special hot information is set off in shaded boxes so that you can find it easily as you flip pages. And Chapter 2 lists every single new feature for Version 6.0.

You'll be tempted to skip the Chapter 1 tour, but it's worth a look even if you don't want to actually take the tour. It acts as a visual cross reference to the rest of the book so that you can see where to go to find out about features of specific interest.

There's a lot of tweaky thoughts on pushing the contours of the PageMaker interface in Chapter 15, "Creating Special Effects."

With Version 6.0's new color facilities, including color management and trapping, you'll want to spend some time in Part V, "Making Pages Colorful."

Power users tend to gravitate towards scripting and other means of reducing job tedium, and that's in Chapter 28, "Automating PageMaker." That's also where you'll find coverage of the new tagging language.

You'll probably appreciate the Master Checklist in Chapter 24. It'll act as a fail-safe double-check as you hit the frenzy of deadline time.

See how your views match up with other professionals in the "Learning from the Pros" section.

How Is This Book Organized?

Overall, you'll probably notice that information flows in building block style. For example, Part II (the section on text) begins with individual characters, moves on to paragraphs and then to stylesheets, text importation, and high-end text editing.

Part I: Getting Started

This means getting started for everyone, no matter who you are and what your background might be.

There's a quick-start tour in Chapter 1, the new features of Version 6.0 in Chapter 2, setting up your PageMaker working style in Chapter 3, and a global view of the desktop publishing process in Chapter 4.

Part II: Working with Text

Type and building type into blocks of text has to be the major strength of the first desktop publishing program for personal computers. It remains so in Version 6.0.

You'll start with single letters and build them up into whole stories. Look particularly for the text formatting information that begins in Chapter 5, including the Tactics Recipe in Chapter 7 on stylesheets.

Part III: Working with Graphics

Check out Chapters 10 and 11 for drawing and importing images. Note that much of the information on linking graphics files has been pulled out into Chapter 30, "Linking and Other File Connections." Likewise, color info has been pulled together into its own section, Part V.

Part IV: Creating Page Layouts

Here's where you pull the pieces together, and it's probably the heart of the book.

In building block style, you start in Chapter 12 with setting up a standard page, building a Master Page grid in Chapter 13, and positioning your elements on the page during electronic paste-up in Chapter 14.

Next, Chapter 15 covers the tune-up stage where you create such special effects as specialized headlines, initial capital letters, rotation, the skewing of text and graphics, and so on.

The headaches of building forms and tables and working with spreadsheets and databases have hopefully been eased by the dozens of working tips in Chapter 16. This chapter includes complete coverage of PageMaker's new-from-the-ground-up table editor.

If you assemble books, all the PageMaker long form document features have been pulled together for you in Chapter 17. There's also an extensive Tactics Recipe on the process of book building.

Part V: Making Pages Colorful

You'll get basic information on spot color and process color here, as well as details of using the PageMaker color commands.

Note especially Chapter 20, "Meeting Color Challenges." There's a complete explanation of the new color management system and built-in trapping.

Part VI: Publishing

You ultimately will need to produce mechanicals and get your project printed or otherwise reproduced.

Chapter 21 covers all the ins and outs of the PageMaker Print command, a complex (and it is indeed complex) of four powerful dialog boxes.

Chapter 22 bridges its bookend chapters with a complete treatise on methods of proofing your project, from text to color accuracy and the press check.

Chapter 23 gives major guidance on how you can work for optimum results with your print shop.

A central focus of the book resides in Chapter 24. That's a Master Checklist with nearly 300 items on it, covering every aspect of the desktop publishing process from idea to bindery. It's a companion to Chapter 4, the DTP Process Overview chapter.

Part VII: Supercharging PageMaker

Chapter 25 helps you crunch text. It pulls together all the font technology stuff, including a Tactics Recipe for managing your myriad of fonts.

Chapter 26 will give you a roundup of all the top utilities you need to help PageMaker help you.

In Chapter 27, you can find out all about sharing PageMaker files, and others, across the Macintosh and Windows platforms.

Chapter 28 will set you free. Read it to find out all about scripting to automate your primary desktop publishing tool, PageMaker. It also tells you all about how to use PageMaker's new tagging language.

Part VIII: Riding the Cutting Edge

There's coverage of electronic publishing in Chapter 29, both with the Acrobat technology and creating pages for display on the World Wide Web.

In Chapter 30, the mysteries of file linking with PageMaker's classic Place and Link technology and its OLE alternative are all explained.

Part IX: Learning from the Pros

A group of professional designers tells you how they put PageMaker to work.

Daddy Desktop Larry Miller describes how he does thumbnails on-screen, but then lets his intuitive finger range the sketch pad.

Carlos Segura of [T-26], and Joe Treacy of Treacyfaces, make point and counter-point conversation about working with the exciting and controversial experimental—some say grunge—type.

Moe Rubenzahl gives design tips and work flow suggestions on building World Wide Web pages, using PageMaker's new power to do so.

A whole raft of PageMaker experts got together online to talk about making PageMaker 6.0 work hard for you. Their "top 10" feature of PageMaker grew into a full chapter with a couple of "favorites."

Part X: Appendixes

You'll discover a resource guide to products mentioned in this book, a guide to installing PageMaker, detailed compendiums of keyboard shortcuts and special characters, and a reference for the tagging language. Plus, there's Rescue!—a step-by-step guide to digging yourself out of the hole when your digital design process caves in on you.

CD-ROM

Included with this book is a CD-ROM with high-quality stock photos, useful pre-built scripts, free fonts and font encyclopedias, and a collection of the software you'll need to produce Web pages.

PART 1

Getting Started

1 ▲ Touring PageMaker

2 ▲ Exploring What's New In PageMaker 6.0

3 ▲ Personalizing PageMaker Preferences

4 ▲ Getting an Overview of the DTP Process

Chapter 1

Touring PageMaker

This chapter tours you through the following topics:

Creating a new publication.

▼

Understanding the master page concept and multiple master pages.

▼

Pasting up page elements with PageMaker's production artist metaphor, the Pasteboard.

▼

Editing copy in the Story Editor.

▼

Controlling graphics and type using the Control palette.

▼

Putting the new Guides Manager to work.

▼

Accessing PageMaker's new electronic publishing capabilities—Internet Web pages and Acrobat paperless hypertext documents.

THIS CHAPTER WORKS as a sort of gateway into the PageMaker world—a hands-on, self-guided tour that you can follow "hands-on" or simply read as you like.

Whether or not you take the tour, use this chapter as a visual index. The illustrations direct you to the chapters where each item on the tour gets more in-depth coverage.

If you're new to PageMaker, this is where you can pick up confidence and some familiarity of how PageMaker works.

If you're a grizzled PageMaker veteran, this tour serves as a quick introduction to the new attractions of PageMaker 6.0. ▶ ▶ ▶

Taking the Quick Tour

This little spin has been designed to take maybe 30 minutes, just to give you an overview. If you want more detailed information at any point, check the illustrations for cross-references to the appropriate in-depth chapters. So, grab the mouse (or just read along, if you prefer) and sample the high points of PageMaker 6.0.

One more thing before we start. Some of this tour makes use of the templates provided with PageMaker 6.0. If you didn't install the templates, you may want to stop now and do so. For more help on installation, see Appendix A, "Installation."

Creating a New Publication

Begin as you would with any other program. Click the Start button, maneuver to the Programs section of the pop-up menu, and click the Adobe PageMaker 6.0 program listing, as shown in figure 1.1.

Fig. 1.1 ▶

Selecting PageMaker 6.0 from the Start menu.

Chapter 2, "Exploring What's New In PageMaker 6.0"

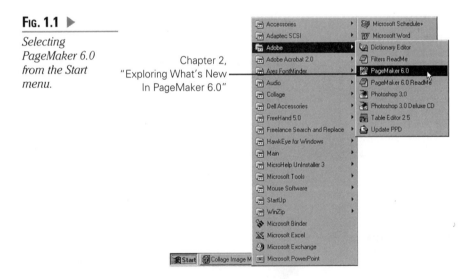

After the opening PageMaker "splash" screen has flashed by, pull down the File menu and choose the New command (see fig. 1.2).

You get a Document Setup dialog box, like the one you see in figure 1.3.

In the Document Setup dialog box, you establish basic document information such as page size, margins, and number of pages. The Numbers button enables you to set up the page number style of your publication (for example, Arabic or Roman numeral).

FIG. 1.2 ▶

*Beginning a new
publication with the
New command.*

In Chapter 14:
"Undoing and Reverting"

Chapter 11,
"Placing Images"

Chapter 8, "Pouring
Text into PageMaker"

In Chapter 32: "Linking and
Other File Connections"

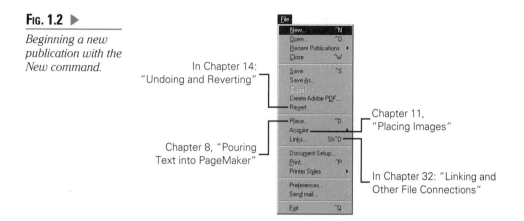

FIG. 1.3 ▶

Chapter 12,
"Setting Up a
New Publication"

*The Document
Setup dialog box.*

In Chapter 12:
"Specifying Page
Number Style"

In Chapter 11:
"Sizing Proportionally and
Using Magic Stretch"

Chapter 21,
"Producing
Mechanicals"

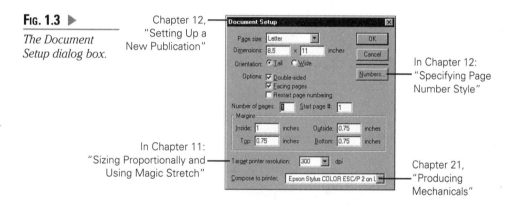

The Target Printer Resolution setting helps PageMaker optimize image quality when you resize one-bit graphics (Magic Stretch, it's called) or import Photo CD images (resolution selection). Set the Target printer to the resolution of your final output device—an imagesetter resolution such as 2450 if you will be sending your file to a service bureau or a much lower resolution such as 300 or 600 if your final product will be output on your local laser printer.

It's critical that you set a final destination printer when opening a new document. Set Compose To Printer to the device that will be last in your production workflow. For some situations it will be a laser printer, but for many projects you will be sending your files out to be run at a service bureau on a high resolution image separator. In either case, selecting the printer here tells PageMaker such vital information as which fonts will be available and whether the device has special features such as color capability. Changing this setting after you have started composing your new document could change all sorts of things, including page breaks and line endings.

Click the OK button to create a new document from scratch. You get a blank, un-titled page, as in figure 1.4. Your margins are marked by the box running around the inside rim of the page. (By the way, your Toolbox and other palettes may be in different spots compared to the figure.)

FIG. 1.4 ▶

*A blank
PageMaker page.*

In Chapter 13:
"Setting Margin
Guides"

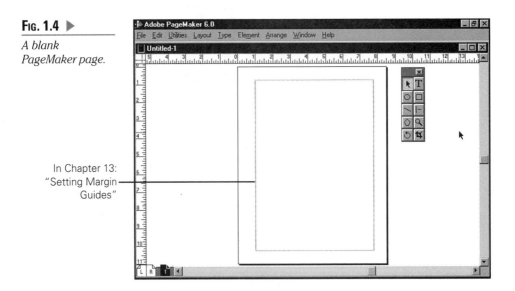

Save your publication via the standard Windows dialog box in figure 1.5. To get the Save dialog box, choose the Save or Save As commands from the File menu, or use the keyboard shortcut Ctrl+S. Because this is a brand-new publication, you get a dialog box asking you to assign the file a name. Naturally, you can store your file in any folder or hard disk you like. After you save the publication for the first time, the Save command performs its work without the dialog box in-terruption. You can always change a new version of the file under a new name by using the Save As command.

Take a second to pull down the Save As Type list. Yep. That's right. You see a his-toric first for PageMaker—backward compatibility. You can save your work in Version 5.0 format. Of course, as you'd expect going back to an earlier version, you'll lose a few Version 6.0 features if they exist in your file.

You can select Template from the Save As Type list to save a publication as a pattern for future publications, recycling your work with big savings of time as a result.

The Files Required for Remote Printing and All Linked Files buttons help you package your publication for output at a service bureau.

Okay, we'll tour on.

Fig. 1.5 ▶

Saving a new publication.

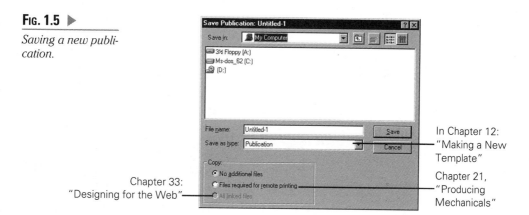

Chapter 33:
"Designing for the Web"——

In Chapter 12:
"Making a New
Template"

Chapter 21,
"Producing
Mechanicals"

Loading a Publication

Now that you've created a new publication, it's time to bring up an existing one. Don't worry about closing the one you already have open. You can have as many documents open as you like, memory permitting.

If you've been driving that computer of yours for any length of time at all, you already know how to use a File Open dialog box. PageMaker's looks just like every other one you've ever seen. That's old hat, so we'll skip it.

Something new has been added, however, to the File menu. You'll notice in figure 1.2 a Recent Publications item on the File menu. The submenu for this item gives you rapid access to the last eight publications you've worked on, without the need for a dialog box.

Let's head on over to the templates stop on this quick tour. Templates let you recycle your own work or reuse shared work from other designers—in this case one of the templates included in PageMaker 6.0.

Ordinarily, you would open a template through the File Open dialog box. You'd get a new publication, an untitled copy of the template. In this case, however, the templates that come with PageMaker 6.0 have been packaged in a special way, as PageMaker scripts, to save space on the distribution disks. To access the script, go to the Utilities menu and choose Open Template from the PageMaker Plug-ins list.

The template script will lay out a new publication with placeholders for your graphics and text boxes you can fill with your own copy. Some templates also give you options to customize your new publication, choices of paper size and so on.

You can manage screen clutter, if you keep many publications open at once, by using the Tile and Cascade commands in the Window menu. Tile gives you a mosaic of all the open publications, with no overlap. The Cascade command, shown in figure 1.6, gives you maximum viewing area of each publication but overlaps the views, leaving their title bars showing, so you can click them to navigate between publications.

FIG. 1.6 ▶

PageMaker publica-tions, cascaded.

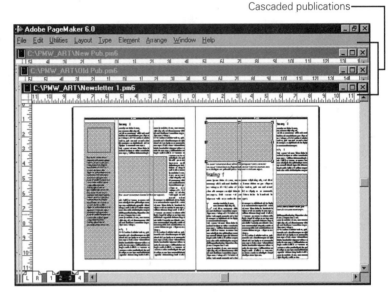

Cascaded publications

Take a second and try out drag-and-drop copying between two publications. Use the Pointer tool to click an object and drag it from one publication to the other, as shown in figure 1.7. You get a four-arrow cross type pointer when you start dragging.

FIG. 1.7 ▶

Making a drag-and-drop copy between two publications.

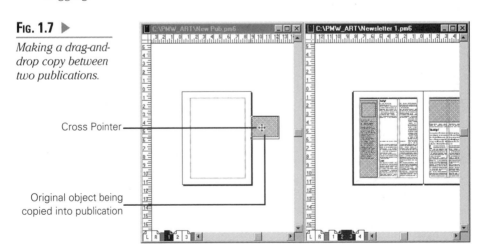

Cross Pointer

Original object being copied into publication

When you run up against the boundary edge of the originating publication, you hit a point of resistance. Just bump right through it and your drag-and-drop object will appear on the other side. When you have the object over the empty document, release the mouse button. Now you have the object in both places. Of course, you can also use regular Copy, Cut, and Paste to transfer objects from one publication to another.

You're done with the new publication you created, so you can close it now, using the Close command under the File menu. PageMaker gives you the chance to save your changes, or you can just click No and move on to the next stop on the tour.

Navigating

You can use three techniques to move between pages in PageMaker.

If you need to jump more than a few pages at a time, use the Go To Page command (see fig. 1.8). With this command, you can type in any page number you want or move to one of the master pages. Use the Ctrl+/ shortcut to get Go To Page, or choose it from the Layout menu.

TIP ▷ See a Slide Show of Your Publication

Flip through all your pages automatically. Use Shift+Go To Page, and PageMaker will go instantly to the first page of your publication and leaf through each page, until you make a mouse click to tell it to stop.

FIG. 1.8 ▷

Using the Go To Page command.

The fastest way to turn the page in PageMaker is a convenient keyboard shortcut: press F12. You flip forward one page. To move back one page, use F11. If you hit these keys fast enough, you can quickly flip through several pages to the page you want without any delays for redrawing the screen. This method works well for moves of one to half-dozen pages at a time. You can't, however, use this method to reach Master Pages.

If point-and-click is your style, you may prefer the most intuitive of the ways to maneuver in PageMaker. In figure 1.9, look at the page icons in the lower-left corner of your publication window. On the left end are the master page icons; regular pages are strung out along the bottom of the publication window. Click any one of the icons, except the one for your current page, just to see how it works.

FIG. **1.9** ▶

Navigating with the page icons.

Chapter 13, "Designing a Master Page Grid"

Magnifying Your View

You have three ways of pulling in for a closer (or wider) look at your pages. You can use a menu, a combination of keys and mouse clicks, or custom magnification.

First, go to the Layout menu and pull out the View submenu (see fig. 1.10). Try the 200% view first.

In Chapter 13: "Setting Column Guides"

In Chapter 14: "Displaying Your Pages at Optimum Accuracy"

FIG. **1.10** ▶

Menu-driven magnification.

In Chapter 17: "Manipulating and Navigating Pages"

In Chapter 13: "Manually Managing Guides"

In Chapter 8: "The Autoflow Text Icon"

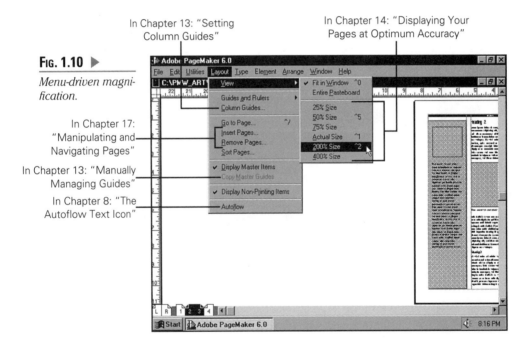

If you hold down the Alt key as you select one of the views on the View submenu, all the pages in your publication will be displayed at that magnification. Otherwise, each page "remembers" its last magnification setting.

Whenever you jump from view to view using the menu, PageMaker centers the current page (or pages if you are in Facing Pages mode). If you have an object selected at the time, however, it stays centered in the publication window.

You have a choice of magnification commands available through keyboard and mouse click commands (listed in detail in Appendix C, "Keyboard Shortcuts").

One of the most popular methods for setting your view is available on your right mouse button. A right mouse click gets you 100 percent view. Add the Shift key to the right mouse click, and you get 200 percent. Once at a magnified view, you can right-click again to toggle back to the Fit in Window view.

Hold down the Ctrl+spacebar keys, and you get a magnifying glass with a plus sign in it (see fig. 1.11). Every time you click with the magnifying glass, you jump up one level of magnification, and your view is centered on wherever you clicked. Use Alt+Ctrl+spacebar to get a minus sign magnifying glass to go the opposite direction.

You can make a custom magnification view with a click and drag of the magnifying glass to frame the area you want to magnify. When you release the mouse button, your view jumps to a full-screen close-up of your defined area, up to a top limit of 800 percent magnification.

You can also use the magnifying glass from the Toolbox. By the way, double-clicking the magnifying glass tool gives you 100 percent view, centered on the page. Alt+double-click gives you Fit in Window view.

Fig. 1.11 ▶

Dragging out a custom magnification close-up view.

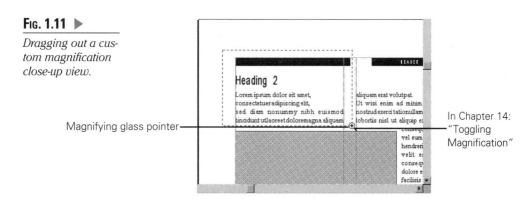

Magnifying glass pointer

In Chapter 14: "Toggling Magnification"

Turning On Rulers and Guides

You need rulers to do any kind of precision layout work. Use the Layout menu's Guides and Rulers command to load the rulers (see fig. 1.12). You can customize the measurement system for your rulers in the Preferences command.

Fig. 1.12 ▶

Calling up the rulers.

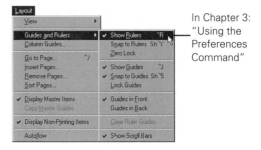

In Chapter 3: "Using the Preferences Command"

All those lines you see on the page are guides provided as part of the template, to help you organize objects on the page. You can easily create your own guides. To pull out a ruler guide, you use a click-and-drag move. Click with whatever tool you have currently selected on the ruler and drag towards the center of the page. As in figure 1.13, a dotted line comes along with the pointer, controlled by a double-headed arrow pointer. You can slide it to any spot you like on the page.

Fig. 1.13 ▶

Creating a ruler guide.

Double-headed arrow pointer

In Chapter 14: "Positioning by Eye and Snap Guides"

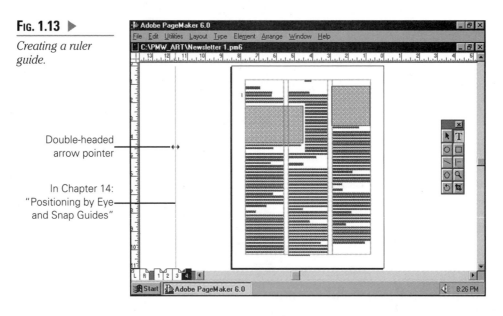

The Snap commands on the Layout menu's Guides and Rulers submenu allow you to pop objects into predetermined positions on your page. When the corresponding Snap command has been turned on, ruler markings or ruler guides act as magnets. When you get close enough for the "magnet" to take hold, any object on the page you are click-dragging will be snapped into alignment with the ruler tick mark or guide.

Stopping by the Master Pages

By now you've heard that PageMaker 6.0 finally includes multiple master pages.

Before we get into the nuts and bolts, have a glance at the page in figure 1.14. It helps illustrate why master pages are so essential as a work tool to increase efficiency and help maintain publication consistency.

You can see, there are quite a number of standard items on this page. There are a lot of guides—margin guides, column guides, ruler guides. Other standard items appear on almost every page—page numbers and header and footer rules, for example.

It would be a pain to put each of these items separately into place for each of the many pages in a document. That's why PageMaker has master pages. Master pages allow you to set up repeated page elements in one location so they automatically repeat on many pages.

Navigate to the master page. You can click the Master Page icon in the lower-left corner. And you can now see where the guides in figure 1.14 originated (refer to fig. 1.13).

Fig. 1.14 ▶

The master page.

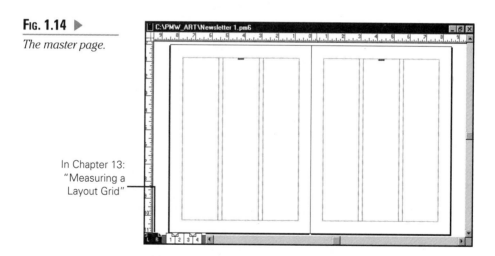

In Chapter 13: "Measuring a Layout Grid"

Now, about the new multiple master pages. Unless you tell it to do otherwise, PageMaker assigns each new page the standard Document Master master page, a required component for each publication. You can change it any way you want, but it will be the default master page, which pretty much behaves just like the old PageMaker master pages.

But a typical publication has many kinds of pages—body text, chapter breaks, index, reference sections. You can create and name additional master pages through the Master Pages palette. Using its pull-out submenu, you can access the Create New Master Page dialog box (see fig. 1.15). Also, using the Master Pages palette submenu, you can create a master page from scratch or copy an existing one.

Fig. 1.15 ▶

Master Pages palette, the Create New Master Page dialog box, and the Master Page Navigation pop-up.

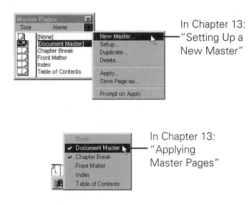

In Chapter 13:
"Setting Up a
New Master"

In Chapter 13:
"Applying
Master Pages"

To navigate to one of your additional master pages, right-click the master page icon in the lower-left corner of your screen, as shown in figure 1.15. A list will pop up in a second, so you can then select the master page you want.

Once you've set up your master pages, you can assign them to pages. You can use the palette's submenu to apply a master to many pages at once, or you can navigate to a page and simply click the desired master page title in the palette. You can also use an existing layout page as a model for a master page.

Storing Objects on the Pasteboard

When PageMaker was first introduced, it caught on right away in the design community. That's because PageMaker works just like those designers did, using the Pasteboard.

To have a look at PageMaker's Pasteboard, use the Y̲iew command's Entire P̲asteboard subcommand from the L̲ayout menu to pull back to a wide view.

The Pasteboard is that big white area all around your pages and inside the rectangular line. Use the Pasteboard to store things, just as a graphics artist would put typesetting output and clip art and such off to the side on a make-up table (see fig. 1.16).

Fig. 1.16 ▶

*Storing an object
on the Pasteboard.*

Object being dragged
onto Pasteboard

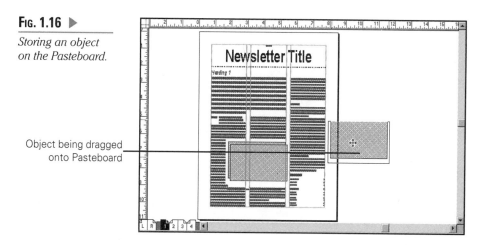

To see how the Pasteboard works, select an object (maybe a block of type or one of the gray placeholder boxes) and use the E̲dit, C̲opy menu or Ctrl+C to copy it. Now paste the object and drag it out over the Pasteboard and drop it. Use F11 to flip to the next page and View Entire Pasteboard again. The object is right there where you left it on the Pasteboard, even on a new page. (That is, it will be there if it was entirely on the Pasteboard. For this to work, the object can't touch any part of a page.) Objects stored on the Pasteboard are available to all the pages, and for that reason, it's a good place to keep standard objects that you use over and over again. (The Library palette has even more extensive capabilities to perform this function, but the omnipresent Pasteboard may be easier to use for quick work.)

Opening Up the Toolbox

If your Toolbox isn't showing already, choose the Toolbox command from the Window menu to turn it on (see fig. 1.17).

Fig. 1.17 ▶

The PageMaker Toolbox.

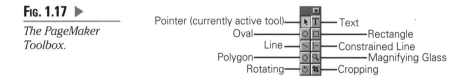

Pointer (currently active tool)———Text
Oval——————————————Rectangle
Line————————————Constrained Line
Polygon—————————————Magnifying Glass
Rotating————————Cropping

Notice the new look. Instead of signifying your tool selection by blacking the tool, the Toolbox has a new 3-D look with the currently active tool indented like a push button. You may also notice there are now ten tools, arranged vertically instead of eight laid out horizontally. The new ones are the Magnifying tool mentioned earlier in the tour and—yes, it's true—the new Polygon tool:

▶ The Pointer tool selects objects.

▶ The Text tool enables you to type text.

▶ The Oval tool draws circles and ovals. You get circles if you draw with the Shift key down.

▶ The Rectangle tool draws boxes, square ones if you hold down the Shift key.

▶ The Line tool draws a straight line at any angle.

▶ The Constrained Line tool limits you to drawing only lines at the 45-degree points on the compass, although lines can be changed to any angle after they are drawn.

▶ The Polygon tool lets you draw many-sided objects, flat-sided or star-shaped. They can be constrained or stretched just like ovals and rectangles.

▶ The Magnifying Glass is the same tool you get with the Ctrl+spacebar keyboard shortcut.

▶ The Rotating tool rotates objects.

▶ The Cropping tool trims the view of imported graphics.

Give the new Polygon tool a workout. Start by setting the number of sides. Do that by double-clicking the Polygon tool to get the Polygon Specifications dialog box (or use Polygon Settings in the Element menu). In addition to ordering up the number of sides, you can set a star effect. The steepness of the star effect's V-shaped sides can be adjusted using the percentage slider for Star inset (see fig. 1.18).

As you draw, notice that you have a crosshair cursor to aid precision placement, and the location of your cursor is tracked by the tick mark locators on both of the rulers. Like the Oval and Rectangle tools, holding down the Shift key will constrain your polygon to a symmetrical shape.

FIG. 1.18 ▷

Drawing a polygon and the Polygon Specifications settings that produced it.

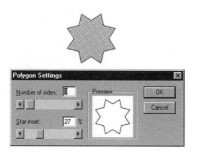

Next, give the Text tool a spin. To type some text, first get to a magnified view like 200 percent, with the area where you want to work centered. (By default, PageMaker comes set with 12-point type, and you need to get it blown up a bit to read it easily.) Press Ctrl+spacebar and click with the resulting plus magnifier to get to the magnified view.

Select the big "T" Text tool and drag out a text block rectangle (see fig. 1.19). When you release the mouse button, you have an insertion point blinking in the block, and you can start typing.

FIG. 1.19 ▷

Dragging out a text block with the Text tool.

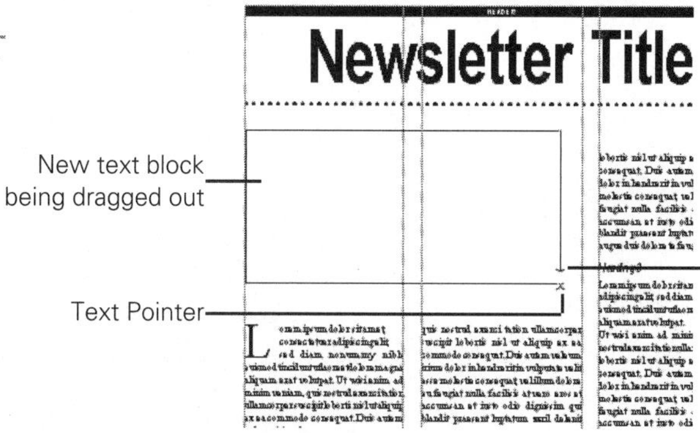

New text block being dragged out

Text Pointer

In Chapter 5: "Using the Text Tool"

After you type your text, use the Pointer tool to click anywhere on your text. The box you see, with the windowshade tabs at the top and bottom, is a text block—an object which holds text (see fig. 1.20). You can move the block and cut and paste it just like any other PageMaker object.

Fig. 1.20 ▶

Selecting a text block.

In Chapter 8: "Sizing and Positioning Text Blocks"

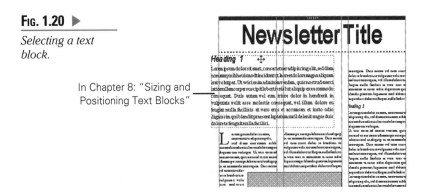

Take some time now to experiment with each of the tools. Use the Pointer to select an object and shift it around the page. Doodle a bit by drawing a box and a circle and a line. Get the feel of it.

TIP ▶ **Toolbox Express Access to Defaults**

The Toolbox has a new feature—express access to a set of dialog boxes that can be used to set publication level defaults. Double-clicking almost any of the tools will deselect whatever object you were working on and will give you a dialog box that goes with that tool. The Rectangle tool, for example, yields the Rounded Corners dialog box. But the main attraction is the Pointer tool which accesses the main Preferences dialog and its subsidiary dialog boxes.

Oh, while you are doodling, be sure to rotate something (see fig. 1.21). Just select the Rotation tool and click the object you want to spin.

Fig. 1.21 ▶

Rotation in progress.

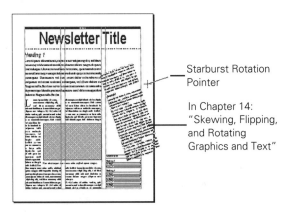

Starburst Rotation Pointer

In Chapter 14: "Skewing, Flipping, and Rotating Graphics and Text"

Click the starburst rotation pointer somewhere near your object and drag away from the object. The resulting line is your rotation lever; the longer the line you have, the more subtle the movement. You'll be rotating around the crosshair point where you originally click down with your Rotation tool, so that's the fulcrum. You need to experiment a bit to get a feel for how it works.

Try one more rotation trick. Before clicking down to begin rotation, hold down Ctrl. This constrains the rotation so that the pivot point is always the center point of the object, no matter the initial click down location of your starburst Rotation tool.

Formatting Text

Go back to the Text tool and click anywhere in a text block. Use the Edit menu's Select All command (Ctrl+A) to select all the text.

Pull down the Type menu. Figure 1.22 should look pretty familiar even if you are new to PageMaker. It looks a great deal like something you'd see in a regular word processor, right? Use the Font or Size submenus to select whatever font and type size you like, and you've experienced basic typesetting in PageMaker.

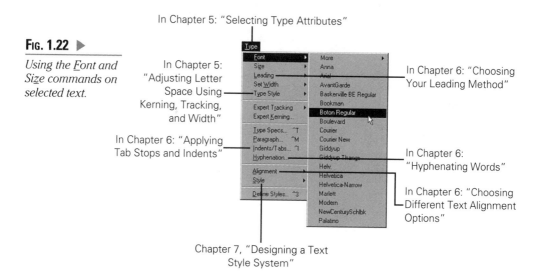

Fig. 1.22 ▶

Using the Font and Size commands on selected text.

While you have some text selected, take a glance at PageMaker's heavy-duty text formatting tools—the specification dialog boxes.

Choose Type Specs from the Type menu (see fig. 1.23), or use the Ctrl+T keyboard shortcut. You can control pretty much anything about an individual character of type using this dialog box.

In Chapter 5, "Making Multiple Type Decisions
with the Type Specifications Dialog Box"

Fig. 1.23 ▶

*A look at the Type
Specifications dia-
log box.*

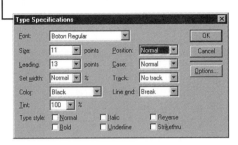

For setting paragraph justification or centering, and much more sophisticated
paragraph attributes, try out the Paragraph Specifications dialog box (see fig.
1.24). Choose Paragraph from the Type menu, or use the Ctrl+M keyboard
shortcut.

Fig. 1.24 ▶

*The powerful Para-
graph Specifications
dialog box.*

Chapter 6,
"Formatting
Paragraphs"

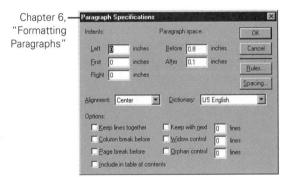

Most of the power of these text-formatting tools, as well as the capability to
manipulate graphic objects and text blocks, can also be found in the Control
palette, which we'll visit in a bit.

Editing in the Story Editor

PageMaker has a text editing mode, usually much faster to use for major editing
or text entry than working in the Layout view you've been using so far. Flip to a
page with a good bit of text, choose the Text tool, and click in a text block. Call
up the Story Editor using the Edit Story command under the Edit menu or the
Ctrl+E keyboard shortcut. You can also triple-click a text block with the Pointer
tool. Figure 1.25 shows the Story Editor window.

FIG. 1.25 ▶

*Accessing the Story
Editor for text
editing.*

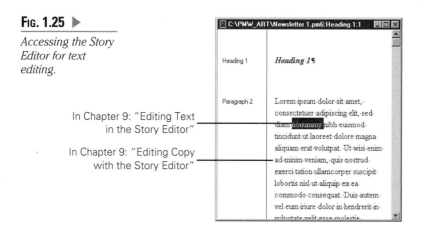

In Chapter 9: "Editing Text
in the Story Editor"

In Chapter 9: "Editing Copy
with the Story Editor"

Scan across the menu line at the top of the screen to see how the items have changed from Layout view. For example, the Element menu has disappeared because you can't work with graphic objects in the Story Editor. Instead, the Story Editor view has a new menu called Story.

Also, as you move around using the arrow keys and your mouse to select text and see how things work, you notice that the Story Editor isn't as much like a word processor as it first appears. It really acts more like a text editor. The text is in nearly raw form, and much of your text formatting won't be fully displayed in the Editor. To format text, you want to use Layout view so you can see the effects of your typesetting decisions.

The Utilities menu (see fig. 1.26) has a powerful search and replace capability, which includes the capability to Find and Change type and paragraph styles. A new feature in PageMaker 6.0 is the ability to search and replace colors and tints. There's also a spelling checker. Note that Find, Change, and Spelling are only available in Story view, not in Layout view.

FIG. 1.26 ▶

*The Find/Change
and Spell check
commands.*

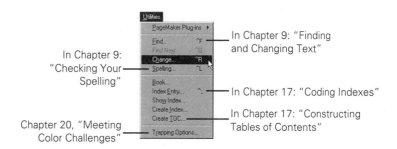

In Chapter 9:
"Checking Your
Spelling"

In Chapter 9: "Finding
and Changing Text"

In Chapter 17: "Coding Indexes"

In Chapter 17: "Constructing
Tables of Contents"

Chapter 20, "Meeting
Color Challenges"

To return to Layout view from the Story Editor, use the Ctrl+E shortcut again. It pops you back to the exact same spot in Layout view where you had your cursor in the Story Editor. You can also use the Close Story command in the Story menu (Ctrl+W), not to be confused with the Close command on the File menu. The Close Story command puts you back in Layout view on the same page where you were last working before opening the Story Editor.

Printing

Ultimately, you will want to put your design on paper or on a printing press. (Unless you are headed for the Web or Acrobat, but we'll get to that in a bit. You'll still need to print proofs, right?) Check out the latest version of the Print dialog box, accessed from the File menu (see fig. 1.27).

Chapter 21, "Producing Mechanicals"

Fig. 1.27 ▶

The main Print dialog box for PageMaker 6.0.

Chapter 22, "Proofing Your Publication"

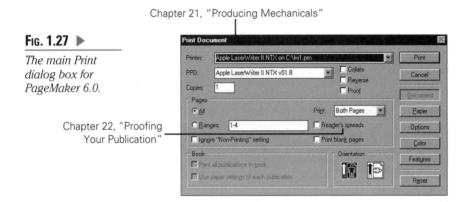

This dialog box and its subsidiaries give you rich power over your final output. It has been improved, even, over the robust changes rung in by PageMaker 5.0. Notice that you can control whether objects designated with the new non-printing attribute are allowed through to the printer. You can also print side-by-side pages—reader's spreads.

The version of the Print dialog box shown here is the one you see when you are printing to a PostScript printer. Some of the following features won't be available if you are going to a non-Postscript device.

The companion dialog boxes can be reached by clicking the appropriate item from the vertical row of buttons on the right side of the dialog box. In the Paper menu, if you are printing to a PostScript printer, you get a new visual interface for determining page fit. The Features menu gives you control over special features of your printer, like choices of specialized paper for inkjet printers and access to Color Management System (CMS) Setup.

PageMaker 5.0 introduced a Printer Styles add-on, but in the new Version 6.0 it has been integrated into the program, where it lives on the File menu, much easier to access (see fig. 1.28).

Getting Started

Fig. 1.28 ▷

The Printer Styles dialog box.

As you can see in the lower portion of the Printer Style dialog box, this feature lets you set any of the parameters available through any of the Print dialog boxes. Once you have assembled all your instructions into a defined style, you can specify them for final output by selecting them from the File menu. This not only makes for efficiency; it also makes for accuracy when working on a deadline situation where it could be disaster to blow printing specifications.

Flying the Control Palette

The Control palette gives you centralized control—no access to menus required—for almost all of PageMaker's positioning and text formatting commands.

When the Control palette first arrived in PageMaker, everyone understood that it was a powerful new tool that would make work easier and more precise. But at the same time some people unfortunately just felt intimidated by it. Many still do, even several years after it was introduced.

It's so rich in features that it looks a bit like the cockpit of a 747. It takes a bit of time to get the most out of it. So, here's a start. Jump in and try out the Control palette. You won't be sorry you did.

Controlling Objects

Click the Pointer tool on any object, maybe one of the gray placeholders if you are following along in a template. Bring up the Control palette (see fig. 1.29) using the Window menu or the keyboard shortcut Ctrl+' (apostrophe).

Apply   Proxy

FIG. 1.29 ▶

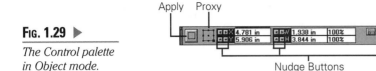

The Control palette
in Object mode.

Nudge Buttons

The Control palette has two basic modes—Text mode and Object mode. Your current selection determines which of these two modes will be in effect in the Control palette. If you select an object, you get the Object mode as you see here. If you click a text insertion point, you get the Text mode. Text mode can be further divided into Character and Paragraph formatting subsets, which we'll get to in a few seconds.

This will be a walk-through tour and not a full tutorial. You can pick up the details of working with the Object mode of the Control palette in Chapter 14.

First, activate the Control palette by clicking it. If the palette obstructs your view of the page, move it by clicking and dragging the short skid bar at the extreme left end of the palette.

The Apply button, the first button on the left, will show any one of about a dozen symbols. It not only tells you what kind of object is selected by displaying those symbols, but clicking it applies whatever action you've just defined.

The next button over to the right is the Proxy. Click the center and note how the tiny square bullet turns into a larger one, indicating that it has been selected. You've just anointed an anchor point for any moves you make from the Control palette. PageMaker uses this anointed point of the chosen object as the anchor point for whichever moves you elect to make, including sizing and rotation moves.

Which brings us to the main command section of the Control palette. Click the nudge buttons there and get the feel of jockeying an object into place by adjusting the "X" (horizontal) and "Y" (vertical) coordinates. Nudge buttons are those small triangular arrows located next to most of the text entry items.

TIP ▶ **Snap To Commands Can Affect Nudge Button Action**

If you don't get any action out of the buttons, you may have one of the Snap To commands turned on in the Layout, Guides and Rulers command. This would keep a selected object sort of "glued" to the guide or ruler tick mark, preventing the small moves produced by the nudge buttons. Turn the command off and try again.

In addition to using the nudge buttons, you can also type an action directly into the text-entry boxes. Press the Tab key until the "Y" box has been selected. That's the vertical coordinate of the anointed anchor point on the object you have selected.

You are probably set up to measure things in inches, which is the way PageMaker comes from Adobe. So let's say you want to move your chosen object down by one inch. Tab or click to the "Y" box and literally add one inch to the coordinate by typing **+1** after the existing entry.

To put your move into effect, click the Apply button. You can also press Enter. Do whichever one you like, and watch the object move vertically by one inch.

You can also size your object using the width and height adjustments. And, buttons and entry boxes on the far right end of the Control palette give you rotation, skewing, and mirroring. You can use nudge buttons, or you can type adjustments directly into the text entry boxes. There's much more on object moves with the Control palette in Chapter 14.

Controlling Type Formatting

Now select the Text tool and click anywhere in a text box. The Control palette will change to Character mode (see fig. 1.30).

Fig. 1.30 ▶

The Control palette's Character mode.

"A" button highlighted
in Character mode

Within Text mode are two submodes: Character mode and Paragraph mode. You are probably in the Character mode with the "A" button highlighted.

Triple-click some text to select an entire paragraph. Now try clicking the tiny "B" button just under the typeface name. That's "B" for bold, and your text turns bold. Even though most of the other Control palette actions require you to implement them with the Apply button or by pressing Return, when you click a button, the action takes affect immediately.

You can control many other aspects of your document's typography using the Control palette. For example, you can choose from a list. Click the arrow just to the right of the font name (in this case, Times), and you see a list of fonts you can try (see fig. 1.31). (Although, you undoubtedly have a different list of fonts installed on your computer.)

Fig. 1.31 ▶

Picking a typeface with the Control palette.

Instead of picking from the font list, you can also use the speedy direct entry and look-up technique. Tab (or Shift+Tab for reverse) to the entry box. Say you want to change to Avant Garde. Just start typing out the font name. By the time you type the first few letters, the Control palette finishes the word for you and makes Avant Garde ready for your formatting action. Press Enter, and the text shifts to the new typeface.

So now you have a hands-on feel for direct entry boxes, choosing from a windowshade type list, nudge buttons, and formatting buttons. These are all skills you can use to fly any of the Control palette modes, including the next one, the Paragraph mode.

Controlling Paragraph Formatting

Click the paragraph symbol, and go to Paragraph Formatting mode (see fig. 1.32).

Fig. 1.32 ▶

The Paragraph Formatting mode.

Paragraph symbol highlighted
in Paragraph mode

Try centering the paragraph text. From the icons just to the right of the paragraph symbol, click the third one over, the one that visually suggests centered alignment. All your text will shift into centered alignment.

The desktop publishing strategies we suggest in this book rely heavily on the powerful paragraph styles capability available in PageMaker. A paragraph style defines, with a single move, all the text formatting for the paragraph where you clicked the Text tool. (You don't need to select the entire paragraph, just have your cursor located anywhere inside it.) These style definitions can include all sorts of text attributes, including typeface, type size, paragraph alignment, indents, leading, tab settings, and so on.

You can apply paragraph styles to text in the paragraph mode of the Control palette. To see a list of styles, click the arrow to the right of the style box, as shown in figure 1.33. Select a new style from the list and watch all the text in your selected paragraph change to the new paragraph style definition.

Fig. 1.33 ▶

Selecting a para-graph style.

The styles you see here were predefined as part of this template. You can create your own styles by using the Define Styles command in the Type menu. You can also define a style by formatting some text and typing the new style name into the style selection box in the Control palette.

Applying and Defining Colors

Have a look at the Color palette. Choose it from the Window menu or press Ctrl+K (see fig. 1.34).

Fig. 1.34 ▶

The Colors palette for PageMaker 6.0.

Assign any of the colors in this palette, including any that you define for yourself, by selecting an object and then clicking your chosen color in the palette. You must use the Text tool to select text before applying color. You can't apply color to text by selecting a text block with the pointer.

The icons at the top of the palette determine how your color selection will be applied to the chosen object. If you have clicked the diagonal stripe prior to clicking a color, the color will be applied only to the line aspect of a PageMaker-drawn object. If the solid square has been clicked, the color will be applied to the fill of the object. The next icon, the square within a box, tells PageMaker to apply color to both line and fill. If you click the arrowhead in the upper-right corner of the palette, you will get a pull-down list of object-level tints that you can assign on an object-by-object basis. You no longer are required to define a special color to get a tint, a new feature in PageMaker 6.0.

Go ahead. Select an object, or draw one, and try it out.

You decide what colors to have available to you on your palette as you work in a publication. In this way the Colors palette resembles the way an artist works, by daubing tubes of paint onto an artist's palette.

To put a color of your own design on your Colors palette, use the Define Colors command on the Element menu and click the New button. Or for a shortcut you can Ctrl+click the [Registration] color in the Colors palette. Either way, you end up at the dialog box in figure 1.35 where you can access one of the many color libraries available in PageMaker 6.0.

FIG. 1.35 ▶

Picking your spot color library standard.

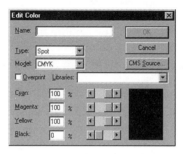

Select a library, Pantone ProSim for instance, and select a color swatch, as you see in figure 1.36.

FIG. 1.36 ▶

Selecting a new color from the swatch panels.

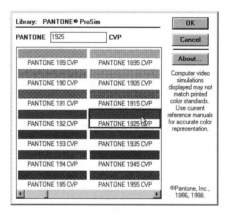

Click OK until you get back to Layout view, and your new color selection will be added to the Colors palette.

Taking In Some Special Sights

Now that you have an overview of the fundamentals, I'd like to show you where to find some of the more out-of-the-way new features of PageMaker 6.0. Just a quick introduction, okay?

Managing Guides

Enter the new Guide Manager Plug-in for PageMaker 6.0 (see fig. 1.37).

In the old days, if you had a bunch of ruler guides on a page, you'd have to move all those guides around on a page, one at a time. If the guides were on a specially constructed layout page, not on a master page, it was a major project to copy them to another page. Here's the welcome solution.

Fig. 1.37 ▶

The Guide Manager dialog box.

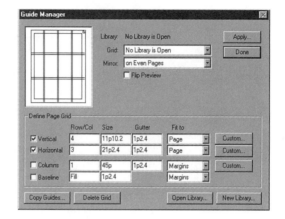

Like all Plug-ins (yep, they used to be called Additions), you reach the Guide Manager through the Utilities menu PageMaker Plug-ins command.

Use this dialog box to establish a grid of rows and columns on your page or to copy existing guides to other pages. Among many other things, you can also set guides for irregular distances using the Custom buttons and store sets of guides in a guides library.

Aligning Objects

For a few years it has been possible to bolt on to PageMaker alignment tools available in various forms through outside developers. But PageMaker 6.0 now has a fully integrated Align command. In fact, it is the same excellent tool that was formerly offered by the folks at Zephyr Design (see fig. 1.38). You access the dialog you see in figure 1.38 by choosing Align Objects from the new Arrange menu, or with the Ctrl+4 shortcut.

Fig. 1.38 ▶

Aligning several selected objects.

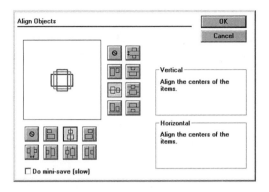

Naturally, you must select two or more objects before the Align command will become active. In the dialog box you can mix and match the icons to align or distribute the chosen objects.

Grouping Objects

The new Group command goes way beyond the old PS GroupIt Addition that came with PageMaker 5.0. As you would expect from a Group command, it collects into a single unit all the objects selected when you implement the command. More importantly, Group does its job much faster and with less fuss. Just select two or more objects and choose the Arrange, Group command (see fig. 1.39).

Fig. 1.39 ▶

Grouping some objects with the new Group command.

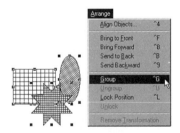

Weaving the World Wide Web

You can use PageMaker to construct Web pages. Have a look at the HTML Author Plug-in, reached through the Utilities menu, PageMaker Plug-ins command. We'll talk more in Chapter 29, but as an introduction for this tour look at figure 1.40. It shows what may be the most significant feature of this plug-in. It allows you to convert styles in a PageMaker document to the standard set of styles used in the Web page language, HTML. That may be a bit much to swallow right now if you aren't a Web-head, but trust me, this is a really good thing.

Fig. 1.40 ▶

The HTML Author Plug-in.

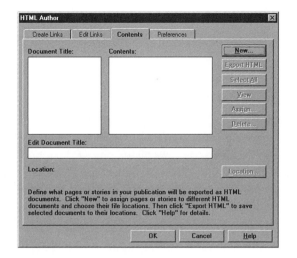

HTML Author Plug-in doesn't provide the full language set used by some Web browsers—seems like it's a moving target that's evolving all the time anyway—but it has the minimum tools to get you started. Maybe the biggest use of this Plug-in will be the "re-purposing" of existing paper-based PageMaker documents for electronic use on the Internet. The Plug-in even analyzes pages and gives you a report about where they violate the Web page standards, so you can make the needed adjustments.

Building Paperless Hypertext for Acrobat

You can also make PDF files from PageMaker publications. That's Adobe's Acrobat format for paperless, hypertext linked documents that can be distributed electronically. You reach this dialog box through the Create Adobe PDF command in the File menu (see fig. 1.41).

Fig. 1.41 ▶

Creating an Acrobat electronic file of a PageMaker publication.

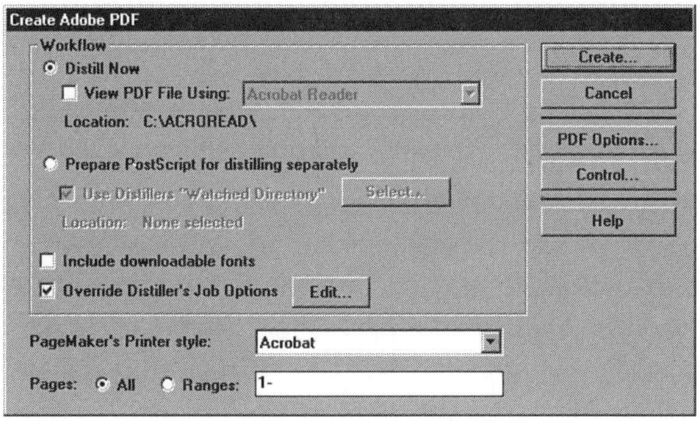

This PDF generator will automatically establish hypertext links between your table of contents and index and their referenced locations in the body of the publication.

Getting More Help

So here you are, just cracking one of the thickest books you'll probably ever buy, and I'm telling you where to get more help. Well, fact is, the desktop publishing business evolves and grows all the time. Think about it. We've just been discussing electronic publishing! Hopefully your knowledge and skills will grow as the business does. Anyway, this book on PageMaker doesn't pretend to be a comprehensive source for quality typography and design—maybe a few hints, but not the last word by any stretch of the imagination.

Anyway, here are some information and help resources you may want to check out. Contact numbers and addresses are listed in Appendix E, "Resource Guide."

Adobe

Just for starters, a lot of help comes built right into PageMaker, backed by other resources from the folks who cut the code:

▶ *Context-sensitive help and the Help Command.* Context-sensitive help is just a Shift+F1 keyboard shortcut away. Use the resulting question mark pointer to choose the command that's puzzling you. If you have an extended keyboard, the dedicated Help key works just like the Ctrl+? key combination.

For more powerful facilities to search out a help subject, use the Help command under the Window menu.

▶ *Tech support.* All the standard tech support offerings are available, including some initial free support for new purchasers. The phone numbers are in your documentation.

▶ *Adobe Magazine.* When you register PageMaker, you can opt to have yourself put on the subscription list for the Adobe magazine, which comes out every two months. You can't beat it for coverage of all the Adobe products, including the latest on Acrobat, Illustrator, and ATM.

▶ *Disk-based training.* Check out the Welcome program on the PageMaker CD. Adobe experts, many of them actually involved in creating the program and its new features, explain how to get the most out of PageMaker. There's also a tutorial chapter in the User Guide, with files to help you work with the program's features. Actually, the presence of the disk-based training and the tutorial are the two reasons why this chapter's tour was designed as a hands-on walk-through. There was no sense duplicating already excellent work.

▶ *Manuals.* Of course (gasp), you could seek information from the printed manuals that come with PageMaker. It seems like a bizarre concept, but it's occasionally of assistance. The *Print Publishing Guide*, particularly, does a good job of demystifying the business of actually publishing your electronic design on paper.

Newsletters and Magazines

For applying PageMaker to the real-world process of design, consider subscribing to any of the following excellent newsletters and magazines:

▶ *Step-By-Step Graphics & Step-By-Step Graphics Electronic Design.* The Step-By-Step publications provide project-oriented case studies of project techniques. The two publications are put out by Dynamic Graphics, a company that also runs a professional designer clip art service and conducts an active schedule of training seminars conducted around the country.

▶ *Before&After.* John McWade publishes *Before&After.* He was the first beta tester for PageMaker and has been exploring the program ever since. The subtitle of the newsletter is "How to design cool stuff," and that's what it's about—recipes for putting together designs.

▶ *Publish.* This monthly magazine combines case studies and product reviews with articles on technological developments as well as reader letters, tips, and makeover columns.

▶ *ThePage.* This newsletter has been taken over by the Cobb Group from its founder, David Doty. There's lots of good stuff on PageMaker as well as articles on PageMaker's primary competitor, QuarkXpress.

▶ *The Flash.* Walter Jeffries and the people at *The Flash* must know just about everything about laser printers and how to get the most out of them. Plus, there's info on all sorts of tweaky stuff like iron-on laser toner for T-shirts, to fancy metal foil you can use in your laser printer to put a ball gown on otherwise plain Jane laser black pages.

Online

The online explosion of information about almost anything still has not birthed anything that can compete with the number one general information source on this business—the CompuServe Desktop Publishing Forum. Type **GO DTPFORUM** to reach this haven of DTP knowledge.

Adobe also runs a forum on CompuServe, and there's no better place to get straight talk about PageMaker. Type **GO ADOBEAPP**—it's official.

In both of these online locations, you'll meet some of the great names in the DTP industry, including several of the folks featured in Part IX, "Learning from the Pros."

Where to Go from Here

▶ The next chapter, "Exploring What's New In PageMaker 6.0," has a comprehensive list of the new features in brisk, list form.

▶ Now that you've had the tour, you will want to customize PageMaker to your particular taste. For instructions on customizing, turn to Chapter 3, "Personalizing PageMaker Preferences."

▶ To fit PageMaker into the way you perform work on a day-to-day basis, check Chapter 4, "Getting an Overview of the DTP Process."

▶ This entire chapter has been a visual index to the chapters that follow. Full detail on actually putting PageMaker 6.0 to work begins with Chapter 5, "Typing In Your Type."

Chapter 2

Here are a few of my favorite PageMaker 6.0 improvements, all of them covered in this chapter:

Guides Manager to quickly set guides among pages.
▼

Sophisticated color management.
▼

Trapping integrated into the program.
▼

Electronic publishing for Web pages (HTML) and Acrobat (PDF) files.
▼

Tagging codes for high volume text formatting.
▼

Table Editor that's much improved over the old one.
▼

Masking lets you use Page-Maker shapes to crop objects right inside the program.
▼

High-fidelity color prepress support.

Exploring What's New In PageMaker 6.0

BOY, A FEW of these things have been on the request list for quite awhile. Real Group and Align/Distribute commands must have been near the top of the list . And for years, PageMaker has suffered under a reputation of not being color capable, but now it has the most flexible color management system anywhere. And for those of us who need to do high volume—but high quality—production typography, there's now a tagging language that beats QuarkXPress.

So, let's explore what's new. ▶ ▶ ▶

Designing Pages

It's this area where PageMaker Version 6.0 has done the most to come even with long-standing expectations about what the program should include in the way of layout features. Multiple master pages, alignment, grouping—all these will make for drastic speed-ups in your layout productivity:

▶ *Multiple master pages.* It may have taken a while for PageMaker to grow this master page feature, but it was worth it. This is a major conceptual advance for this feature, long a source of gloating from QuarkXPress users. From the Master Page palette you can create a new master, duplicate one, and assign it to multiple (and even noncontiguous) pages.

▶ *Guide and grid management.* Coupled with the ability to build multiple master pages you now have a Guide Manager Plug-in. In it you can set up column, vertical, and horizontal guides and save standard sets for future use. Here too, you can apply your guide specifications across multiple pages, even noncontinguous ones, and to master pages as well. You can even set up horizontal guides to match your leading grid.

▶ *Alignment and distribution.* Center on centers, align on sides or tops, distribute with an automatically calculated spacing, or type in the spacing you want. The alignment and distribution tool that pioneered this functionality for PageMaker, from Boyd Multerer at Zephyr Designs, has now been welded seamlessly into the PageMaker 6.0 Arrange menu, elevated from its old bolted-on Addition status. If you've been using Extensis Page Tools for alignment and distribution, this feature has essentially the same functionality as that tool, which was bundled into thousands of PageMaker 5.0 upgrades in 1995 (see fig. 2.1).

Fig. 2.1 ▶

Lining up multiple objects is easy with the new Align/Distribute command.

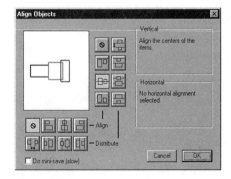

▶ *Grouping and ungrouping.* Forget PS Group It. Now there's a real grouping function, also on the Arrange menu, which will probably remind you of Adobe Illustrator (for some strange reason, given the Adobe/Aldus merger). And this next part is really hot. You can modify any of the group items, including text or object tints and colors, by holding down the Ctrl key while clicking the item to select it first. You can even move individual items around within the group by Ctrl +double-clicking the individual object.

▶ *Position locking and unlocking.* Lock a letterhead logo or any other object, including a text block, to a precise spot on a page—particularly helpful for use in templates that carry standard elements.

▶ *Masking.* Use the Polygon tool, or any other shape, to mask an object. Now you put a circle mask on an imported graphic right in PageMaker. Or you can put it in a starburst. You can also mask text blocks.

▶ *Polygons.* Now you can draw multi-sided objects. You can draw your creation out in a distorted way, as if it was drawn in a funhouse mirror. Or, as with the Ellipse and Rectangle tools, hold down the Shift key and you get a symmetrical object. You can also use a slider to adjust the "star inset," a starburst effect.

▶ *One layer forward and backward.* Much better than simply sending items all the way to the back or all the way to the front, now you can adjust stacking layers one at a time. In a stack of many items, you can put the object of your choice exactly where you want it without rotating through a bunch of send all the way to the back moves.

▶ *Preserve stacking/layer order.* Even better, when you click an object and drag it to a new position, it does not automatically come all the way to the front. It remembers its proper layer in the stacking order as you slide it into place.

▶ *TIFF clipping path support.* Transparency for imported graphic objects is still pretty much a fantasy, but here's a good step in the right direction. In the past if you brought in a vignetted object, carefully outlined and edited, it still lived in an opaque block on the page. Even if the area surrounding the actual visual *looked* clear, it wasn't. The work-around was to build a clipping path and save the item as an EPS file.

With PageMaker 6.0, there's no need for an EPS conversion. PageMaker now recognizes Photoshop clipping paths, even if they are embedded in TIFF files. This means more flexibility for you, and less complicated files. This should mean easier output at the service bureau, since the file structure will be inherently less complex. Those EPS files with embedded TIFFs tend to choke imagesetters.

▶ *Zoom tool.* The Click+spacebar custom magnifying glass now has a home in the Toolbox as well. Just drag out a marquee, and you'll get a new window that contains exactly the portion of the page you want to see, magnified up to a maximum of 800 percent.

▶ *Headers and keylines.* The Running Headers and Create Keylines Plug-ins have new interfaces, making them more straightforward and easier to use and therefore better aids in laying down pages.

Setting Type

PageMaker already had about the most robust typesetting features of any desktop publishing program out there—everything from true tracking for type to paragraph-by-paragraph settings for hyphenation/justification. Now, with Version 6.0, there's more:

▶ *Table creation.* Ahhhh, at last! A decent Table Editor for PageMaker. It's the same solid Table Editor that comes with the Persuasion presentation production program.

It's good, and it's flexible. It even has word wrapping within columns so it will be a useful tool for typesetting. Although you don't get kerning, you do get an otherwise fairly complete representation of PageMaker's main type and paragraph formatting controls, including a sort of mini-Control palette. You can export your table as EPS for placement in PageMaker, a much more solid format than available with the old Table Editor. For further insurance against problems, the fonts you used in creating your table can be embedded right in the EPS.

The new editor will even read files produced by the old Table Editor.

▶ *Finer kerning.* PageMaker has always had very fine typographical controls, with kerning to 1/100 of an em space. Now, however, using the Control palette you absolutely *can* kern finer than a gnat's eyebrow—1/1000 of an em space.

▶ *Expert kerning.* The Expert Kerning utility that was an Addition in PageMaker 5.0 now lives right on a menu, the Type menu.

▶ *Free fonts.* If you buy the CD-ROM version of PageMaker 6.0, you get Type On Call, the Adobe fonts CD-ROM. You can call 24 hours a day to purchase any of the typefaces on the disk. They give you an unlocking code over the phone. Your first call to the Type On Call center will be to unlock—at no charge — the 220 font "Illustrator" set, so called because the original offer was included with Adobe Illustrator. This font set is a good beginning set of fonts suitable for a wide variety of design purposes—and it's free!

Publishing In Color

A flexible color management system, object level tints, high fidelity color—all major advances in functionality for color publishing and all part of PageMaker 6.0:

▶ *Color management.* You get color management of a very comprehensive sort. The Kodak Precision Color Management System comes in your package, but you can install and use almost any of the other competing CMSes. And you can control CMS attributes such as the source device at a number of points in PageMaker, including Preferences, Image Control, and the Print dialog box. You can even use different setups for different objects, so you can be sure you've matched the creation source.

▶ *Photo CD.* Photo CDs are nearly perfectly suited to intensive production work, the kind you do when putting dozens or even hundreds of images into a catalog. But up to now, before putting PCD to work in PageMaker, you had to open your PCD image in Photoshop or some other image editing program in order to convert the image from PCD format, and to conduct sharpening operations. Now the most sophisticated Photo CD filter available lives right inside PageMaker. It also permits saving the PCD image to your hard disk in the device-independent color Lab TIFF format, not only a convenience, but potentially a contributor to greater color accuracy.

▶ *Object-level tints.* You don't have to define a new color name just to be able to apply a tint anymore. Just assign an object-level tint on-the-fly to any object, text, or rule. (A *tint* is a "screened" version of a solid color, expressed as a percentage, with 100 percent being solid color, thus diminishing its intensity by reducing the amount of ink applied to the paper.)

▶ *Remove unused colors.* It is now simple to rid your publication of defined but unused colors. As you work on a project, it's common to build up unused colors on your Color palette. They may be the result of experiments or perhaps leftover from now-deleted imported graphics that were themselves the results of experiments further upstream in the production process.

▶ *Color editing.* You can simply Ctrl+click on a color in the Color palette to open it up in the Edit Color dialog box—and you can even edit colors brought in from an outside source, such as an EPS graphic.

▶ *[None] color.* To remove color from a PageMaker object, there's a new "color" called [None]. It, like the other default colors of [Paper], [Black], and [Registration], is a quick access to creating a new color using the Ctrl+click shortcut.

▶ *RGB to CMYK.* PageMaker now will convert RGB TIFF images to the CMYK color model (if you have color management activated). Most scanning devices produce RGB output, and now you can keep graphics in RGB form until just before output time. This has two advantages. First, it saves disk space because a CMYK TIFF, with its additional "layer" of color information, takes up more disk space than the RGB version of an image. Second, this flexibility could mean more accurate color at the end of your publishing process. The fewer times you transform from one color space to another, the less chance you will introduce color error.

▶ *Expanded color libraries.* More color libraries have been added, including the Pantone version of high-fidelity color, Hexachrome. Pantone specialized inks—metallics, pastels, fluorescents—have also been included. Dainippon Ink and Chemicals (DIC) Color Guide Spot also are included. I don't believe any other page layout or graphics program on the market offers such an extensive selection of color library options.

▶ *High-fidelity color.* PageMaker 6.0 fully supports high-fidelity color. High-fidelity color adds inks to the four CMYK inks. Some experts estimate that within the next year, high-fidelity color printing technology will grow to occupy as much as 10 percent of the color printing market.

Printing and Prepress

Really powerful built-in trapping will get a lot of the attention in PageMaker 6.0. But it's more likely that the major productivity improvements for most users will be reader's spreads, printer styles enhancements, and nonprinting item designation:

▶ *Trapping.* Trapping—real trapping—has now been built into PageMaker. Mid-way through the release cycle for PageMaker 5.0, Aldus released an acclaimed Addition called TrapMaker, but it was only available for Macintosh users. Now this functionality has been built in as a menu item for the Windows version of PageMaker. You get the basic Trapwise technology of raster style trapping, much better than the object trapping offered in QuarkXPress. The new Trapping Plug-in offers sophisticated controls such as trap width, trapping thresholds, black-ink attributes and auto-overprint black text, lines, and fills. You can set neutral ink density values if your job requires departure from the published Neutral Density standards. The color pair override function has been removed, however.

▶ *Nonprinting objects.* This feature controls whether an object prints or not. The most obvious use is adding production notes to publications for your work group colleagues or for your service bureau.

But the ability to make an object "invisible" in this way has many more uses than that, and many a trick will be born from this feature. For example, you could create a nonprinting item and set a standard text wrap for it, then place it on a master page to hold a companion column, or one of those type slash effects the grunge designers like to set up. By the way, you can literally make nonprinting items invisible on-screen, with the Layout menu's Display Non-Printing Items option.

▶ *Font scanning.* In addition to the PANOSE font matching system, which can be set so that it will warn of missing fonts, there's a new EPS Font Scanner Plug-in. If you try to print a publication that contains an EPS calling for an uninstalled font, you'll get a warning and an option to stop and install the missing font before trying again.

▶ *Reader's spreads.* Lovely and long-awaited, the click of a mouse in the Print dialog box gives us reader's spreads, so we can have a look at the way facing pages work together.

▶ *Print fit view.* Will your publication and all its trim marks fit onto the paper you have chosen? You can know at a glance by checking the Fit section of the Print command's Paper subdialog box. You can see the fit evaluated pictorially, and with a double click on the Fit Image preview box, you can see the actual measurements being used by PageMaker to make the evaluation.

▶ *Printer styles.* We got printer styles, actually, in PageMaker 5.0. But now they are an easy-to-use actual menu item. And once you have your settings all stabilized, you can now create an instant new printer style so the settings can be used again and again. Simply hold down the Ctrl key, and the OK button turns to Style.

▶ *Open prepress interface.* OPI connections are more robust with a new OPI Reader and Writer. OPI comments buried deep within imported EPS graphics are now more secure and less likely to cause problems at output time. (There actually have been a few reports of problems with these more rigorous OPI comments. If you have printing troubles with an imported graphics file, try holding down Shift when you click OK in the Place command dialog box. You'll get a special dialog box where you can turn off OPI commenting.)

▶ *Prepress standards.* In addition to compatibility with OPI, a number of other Prepress standards are supported, including DCS 2.0, Scitex CT, Lab, TIFF, and JPEG.

▶ *Access to features.* The entire Print dialog box has been updated to include many of the new items listed here. You can, for example, get to the color management system through the Print dialog box. And now there's a Features button that will allow direct access to printer-specific features such as multiple paper trays and duplex printing.

▶ *Building books.* The functionality of the familiar Build Booklet Plug-in has now been extended to booked publications—ones that consist of multiple files that are compiled through the Book command.

Publishing Electronically

Whatever perceptions you may have about PageMaker pages only being printed on paper, it is time to reconsider them. Version 6.0 has strong tools for electronic publishing for the World Wide Web and for electronic document sharing and viewing:

▶ *Create Acrobat PDFs.* Right on the File menu, there's the Create Adobe PDF command. It's easy. PDF stands for Adobe's Portable Document Format, and it makes it possible for you to share files with anyone who has a copy of the free Acrobat Reader program. The PDF facility can even generate clickable hypertext links from your table of contents and index references.

▶ *Create Web pages.* A new HTML Author Plug-in will scan your existing PageMaker document and give you a list of locations where your publication mismatches with the HTML standard. Once the problems are cleared out (multiple columns, object crossing column boundaries), the HTML Author generates solid code for your World Wide Web page.

▶ *Acrobat Distiller and Reader.* You get a special limited addition of Distiller and a full edition of Reader right on the CD-ROM that comes with PageMaker. The personal edition of Distiller will only work with PageMaker 6.0 files. Distiller will be a vital tool if you want to create electronic versions of your files.

Running and Automating PageMaker

PageMaker is just flat-out easier to run, thanks to a number of interface improvements. And it has new strength for building shortcuts thanks to enhancements to the scripting facility:

▶ *Last eight publications.* Go directly back to work, no waiting. The refurbished File menu in PageMaker 6.0 has a Recent Publications item, with a pull-out submenu listing the last eight publications that you have saved within the program.

▶ *Palette memory.* Most of the palettes—styles, colors, tools, master pages—remember their locations from session to session. If you move your Toolbox palette to the lower-right corner with just the Pointer and Text tool showing, that's where the palette will be when you open PageMaker the next time. (The Scripts palette isn't sticky, unfortunately, because it is actually a Plug-in rather than an integral part of the program.)

▶ *Scripts palette.* The new Scripts palette (see fig. 2.2) makes scripting practical, finally. It was always a drag to have to go to the Utilities menu and select the Play Script Addition to automate your work—kind of contrary to the concept, you know? Now there's a palette right there in view, a click away. You can add scripts to the palette and perform other management duties with a pull-out palette menu, including script editing and tracing.

Getting Started

Fig. 2.2 ▶

*The convenient
new Scripts palette.*

▶ *Ready-made scripts.* Several dozen pre-constructed scripts ship with PageMaker 6.0, including all sorts of productive tools, and some just for fun. In many cases, these scripts will be a good source of scripting code so you can steal snippets for your own scripting.

▶ *Story Editor scripts and Plug-ins.* One place that most needed automation was the Story Editor, the place where you do your intensive text editing inside PageMaker. Now you've got it. Scripts and Plug-ins can access Story Editor features and content.

▶ *New keyboard shortcuts.* To put it mildly, a few things have changed. For example, if you are in the habit of triggering a screen redraw or recentering the page with Ctrl+W, start breaking the habit now. That's the keyboard shortcut for PageMaker 6.0 to close the publication and has been replaced by Ctrl+0 for Fit in Window. There are, of course, new shortcuts for such new features such as Alignment, Lock, Group, Bring Forward, and Send Backward. Find and Find Next have changed as well.

Integrating PageMaker into a Complete Publishing Environment

PageMaker puts pieces of pages together, and those pieces are likely to come from a variety of sources. Import filters and backward compatibility with previous versions of PageMaker will aid in the assembly job:

▶ *Filters.* We've already mentioned the powerful new Photo CD importation and editing filter. There's also the tagging language filter that not only reads PageMaker's own tagging language, but also interprets the QuarkXPress language. A new filter has also been included for CorelDRAW! 5.0. (And there's a conversion utility for QuarkXPress files.)

▶ *Photoshop effects.* A new Plug-in will let you manipulate TIFF images right inside PageMaker. It may not yet be time to toss out your copy of Photoshop, but being able to conveniently make adjustments on images in the same program where you are setting type and arranging page elements is a very attractive notion indeed. Among others, you'll be able to apply Gallery Effects.

▶ *Backward compatible.* If you need to work with someone who has not yet upgraded to Version 6.0, not only can you open a Version 5.0 file, but you can also save a publication back into 5.0 format, although that will cause the loss of some effects only available within Version 6.0.

▶ *PageMaker 5.0 custom settings.* In addition, you can bring forward into PageMaker 6.0 all your custom settings in PageMaker 5.0 using a utility that ships with the program. It's PM5FILES.EXE in the PM6\RSRC\USENGLSH\ UTILITY folder. It will help you save your settings for dictionaries, custom color libraries, and tracking values.

▶ *OLE 2.0 client.* The Object Linking and Embedding protocol has full support in Version 6.0, at least for inbound publication elements. PageMaker can only be a client, however, not a server—meaning you can't create a layout in PageMaker and link it into another application.

▶ *Goodies included.* The batteries may not be included, but plenty of other things are in the PageMaker 6.0 package if you buy the deluxe CD version. There's Type On Call, with 220 fonts free for the asking when you register, and Acrobat Reader and Distiller. Plus, some of the Photoshop filters you'll want to use from within PageMaker.

Understanding Programming Improvements

A number of program code improvements have been made. Here are a few that are visible to you when you run the program, although they are certainly not the only improvements:

▶ *Plug-in power.* Assuming PageMaker 6.0 sells well, look for third-party developers to build some Plug-ins that provide major functionality to the program. Not only is the basic Plug-in programming more robust, but Plug-ins can now maintain private data. That means, for example, the Guides Manager can keep its own library of guide settings for you.

▶ *Slug redraw.* Remember constantly forcing screen redraws because PageMaker draws slugs, not whole pages? That's fixed now. It means even Baseline leading will work.

▶ *EPS performance.* Printing performance for EPS graphics has been improved, and you should experience shorter print times.

Working Around What's Still Missing In PageMaker 6.0

Some things are still missing in 6.0. Here are some thoughts on what you can do to make up for their absence. The list, by the way, is much shorter than the one in the last edition, covering Version 5.0:

▶ *Character level styles.* You still can't designate a style at the character level. It's only available as a paragraph-wide attribute. Some search-and-replace techniques can help you make up for the deficiency, which you find in Chapter 9, "Editing Copy with the Story Editor," in the "Search and Replace" section.

▶ *Page cross references.* There's no facility for automating troublesome long-document page cross references, as in *See Chapter 8, page 214.*

There's a work-around that still involves a lot of labor, but will be easier than doing it completely by hand and will be more accurate as well. It's in Chapter 17, "Building Many Pages," in the Tactics Recipe section "Coding Page Cross References."

▶ *Footnotes.* There's no automation (such as you have in Microsoft Word) for endnotes, level notes, or footnotes. The only recourse is to use manual layout techniques with separate story blocks, augmented by the Column Break paragraph attribute. Check Chapter 17, in the Tactics Recipe section.

Where to Go from Here

▶ Multiple master pages and Guide Manager are primarily covered in Chapter 13, "Designing a Master Page Grid."

▶ Grouping, alignment, and masking are elements of some of the effects in Chapter 15, "Creating Special Effects," and are described in detail in Chapter 14, "Precisely Positioning Graphics and Text."

▶ PageMaker 6.0's newly enhanced color capability is covered in considerable detail in Part V, "Making Pages Colorful," especially in Chapter 20, "Meeting Color Challenges."

▶ All of the new printing and prepress features are explained in Part VI, "Publishing," particularly in Chapters 21 and 22 on outputting your publication for a laser printer and a service bureau.

Chapter 3

Personalizing PageMaker Preferences

You can change virtually every facet of PageMaker so it defaults to suit the specific needs of your publishing environment. This chapter on preferences covers the following information:

Understanding the concepts behind PageMaker defaults.

▼

Choosing between setting a default for the entire program or merely your current publication.

▼

Setting custom PageMaker defaults using two methods—the Preferences command and the menu-based mini-defaults.

▼

Using the Preferences command dialog boxes.

▼

Setting PageMaker functions as mini-defaults.

▼

Managing sets of defaults for different project needs.

LIKE A CHOPPED '32 Ford roadster, a perfectly fitted designer original, or a hand-fitted tennis racket, you can customize PageMaker into the most personal of desktop publishing tools, tuned to every intimate whim of your personal working style.

As you may already know, a *default* is a permanent or semi-permanent setting of a particular function in a software program. This chapter is about setting the PageMaker defaults so they suit your personal working methods. ▶ ▶ ▶

Understanding the PageMaker Default Scheme

First, let's clarify how PageMaker keeps track of your decisions about defaults.

Using PageMaker's Default Brain

All the decisions you make on PageMaker's defaults are kept in one place. You can think of this place as the PageMaker default brain. It's a file—the PM6.CNF file—that is located inside your main PageMaker folder. This file "remembers" when you make a change in the Preferences command dialog boxes or set a mini-default as described later on in this chapter.

TIP ▶ **Resetting Your PageMaker Defaults**

If you ever want to get your copy of PageMaker back to the way it was when you first installed it, right out of the box, close PageMaker and find the PM6.CNF files in your main PageMaker folder. Delete the file. When you next open PageMaker, the program creates a new PM6.CNF file, using the original defaults, which are coded directly and permanently into the program itself.

Understanding the Four-Way Matrix of PageMaker Defaults

You have four basic options for setting PageMaker defaults, sort of a matrix of options. You have a choice between program-level defaults and publication-level defaults. You can use two different techniques to set either of these default types—you can use the Preferences command or set a mini-default.

Using these four factors in various combinations gives you flexibility and power to control your work environment, but it can get a bit confusing. That's why you need to understand the two Key Concepts on the next few pages.

✂ KEY CONCEPT:
Two Types of PageMaker Defaults

Keep one central principle in mind. What you see on-screen when you set a default tells PageMaker which of the following levels of default you are trying to set:

▼ *Publication level.* If you have a publication open as you set a default, that choice applies to all the ensuing work in your current document (until you change it, of course).

However, your choice does not affect any other documents created with PageMaker—past or future. Some people refer to this kind of default as a temporary default, because it is in effect only while a particular publication is open.

This level of default overrides any program-level default.

▼ *Program level.* In contrast, making a default setting choice with no document open sets a program-level default for all your future publications. Program-level defaults are sometimes called permanent defaults because of their future effects on new documents. Of course, program-level defaults are no more permanent than the publication-level default, because you have the power to easily change them.

KEY CONCEPT:
Two Ways to Set Defaults

PageMaker gives you two techniques for setting a default:

▼ *Preferences method.* To set a default using the Preferences method, you fill in blanks or click check boxes in the Preferences dialog box. It's as simple as that.

   If you use the Preferences command with a publication open, you set a publication-level default. If you go to Preferences with no publication open, you set a program-level default.

▼ *Mini-default method.* To set a mini-default, simply choose any of the available options in the PageMaker menus. Make sure you have no objects selected.

   Mini-defaults are based on a key PageMaker design concept. The program tries to help out by remembering your actions for the next time you want to take that action.

   Take note as you work among the menus and dialog boxes of the PageMaker command structure. Many of the items you see are linked to the PM6.0 Defaults file in your Prefer-ences folder. You might say these items are default-sensitive. The section "Setting Mini-Defaults" later in this chapter lists all the dialog boxes and menu items that are default-sensitive.

Mini-defaults are so easy to set that many people do it by accident without re-alizing it, then wonder why their program is acting so crazy. For this reason, if Page-Maker exhibits weird behavior—for ex-ample, the Rectangle tool seems stuck on drawing only fuchsia fills with 12 percent tints—check for an accidentally set mini-default.

   The main thing to remember about mini-defaults is the point about having something selected. If you have something selected, no default is set and your action takes effect in the normal way. Otherwise, if you have no objects selected and you are in a menu or a dialog box that's de-fault-sensitive, you are setting a default. That's how people usually accidentally set defaults. They inadvertently deselect their target object and make the formatting move they intended for the object, setting a mini-default.

These tips can help you set mini-defaults:

▼ If you want to be sure you are setting a mini-default, double-click the Pointer tool. You also can click the Pointer tool at a vacant spot, such as an unoccupied portion of the Pasteboard. Just make sure you don't have anything selected.

▼ If you want to reset one of your mini-defaults back to the original setting, simply change the current setting to your new desired status. PageMaker has no reset command for individual items.

TIP ▶   Palettes Have Defaults, Too

New to PageMaker 6.0 is a much-requested feature. PageMaker remembers how you set up your palettes from session to session. The position and size of your Control, Style, Color, and the other palettes are program-level defaults. (The Scripts palette isn't "sticky" like this, but it's the exception.) Because the palettes are not visible unless a publication is open, they do behave differently from all other program defaults in that you must have a publication open to set them up. The default setting for which palettes you want to be active when you open a publication is a program default, set via the Window menu with no publication open.

Using the Preferences Command

This section covers the dialog boxes reached via the File, Preferences command. Figure 3.1 shows the top level Preferences dialog box.

FIG. 3.1 ▶

*The main Prefer-
ences dialog box.*

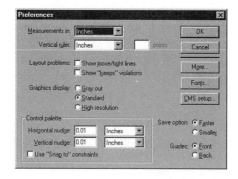

Setting Measurements

At the very top of the dialog box you can set your preferences for the measurement system you want PageMaker to use. Just click the drop-down menus for the horizontal and vertical rulers.

The first Measurements choice establishes the measurement system used throughout PageMaker for the Control palette and all the dialog boxes (see fig. 3.2). Keep in mind, however, that you can override the default measurement system on an ad-hoc basis by using the chart of direct entry codes shown in Chapter 14, "Precisely Positioning Graphics and Text," in the section titled, "Getting Ultra-Precise with the Control Palette."

Fig. 3.2 ▶

The measurement system choices.

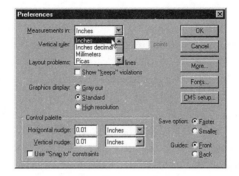

Whatever choice you make in the first Measurements In option is also used for the horizontal ruler at the top of your PageMaker publication window.

You can set your vertical ruler along the left side of the publication window with a different measurement system than the horizontal ruler. You may, for example, want different settings if you prefer to measure type in picas but are used to thinking about page sizes and indents in inches. Because type is primarily measured in character height and line spacing, you could set up the overall measurement system in inches but set the vertical ruler for picas.

The vertical ruler has one extra choice that is not included on the measurement system list you see in figure 3.2. You can have a custom ruler, marked off in the number of points you enter in the Points box. You use this custom ruler in a Snap to Rulers and Align to Grid situation, where these PageMaker facilities interact to force all your lines of type to line up on a grid. You can read more on this technique in the "Automating Your Layout Grid" Tactics Recipe in Chapter 13, "Designing a Master Page Grid."

Highlighting Layout Problems

In the Preferences dialog box, use the two Layout Problems check boxes to ask PageMaker to highlight in Layout view any justified lines that are violating your spacing and "keeps" rules. Layout problems are highlighted in gray or yellow, depending on your setup.

These settings tie back to the Paragraph Specifications command where you can control the spaces between letters and words and the number of lines to "keep" together across a page break. These two Preference choices alert you when PageMaker hasn't been able to hold the line on your paragraph settings, as described in Chapter 6 in the Key Concept section "Understanding PageMaker's Special Spacing Power."

Setting Graphics Display

Drawing complicated imported graphics takes time and computing power. You can save time by setting the Graphics Display buttons to provide something short of a high-resolution display of your imported graphics. The Gray Out option displays a gray box for position only. The High Resolution setting seeks out the original copy of a high resolution bit-mapped graphic (such as a color TIFF) and uses that file—often a very large one, hence the time delay in display—to paint a high resolution, fine-grained display. The default setting and the one most people use is Standard. This setting enables you to see the graphic on-screen, but at a speedier, low resolution. For the Standard setting, the quality of the on-screen resolution is determined by another Graphics setting box that you can reach through the More preferences button.

TIP ▶ **Get a Temporary High-Quality Graphics Display**

You can temporarily display graphics at high resolution, regardless of the setting in Preferences, by holding down the Ctrl+Shift keys while triggering a screen redraw. You can do that, for example, by selecting a view from the menu with the mouse or toggling the view with your right mouse button.

Managing the Control Palette

This section of the Preferences dialog box manages the behavior of the Control palette. The amounts and measuring system you set here for Horizontal Nudge and Vertical Nudge are operative whenever you use the nudge arrow heads in the Control palette.

These settings also set amounts and measuring systems for ordinary arrow key nudging. That's the kind of nudging you use when you select an object and then move it in tiny steps by simply pressing the arrow keys in the appropriate direction.

When you make your Control palette moves, you may or may not want those moves to be controlled by your Snap To settings. The Use "Snap To" Constraints check box is tied to the Snap to Guides and Snap to Rulers settings in the Guides and Rulers command in the Layout menu. If either of these snap settings is turned on, a click in this check box makes all your Control palette and arrow key nudges work the same way mouse moves do. That is, objects snap to guides or rulers when you nudge them.

Choosing a Save Option

PageMaker comes set up to do fast saves whenever you use the Ctrl+S or Save command. Faster saves work out fine sometimes, especially if you are working fast on deadline. However, fast saves can severely bloat the size of your file because PageMaker keeps every change you make to your publication in an add-on section of the file. It's a little like eating a sandwich and forgetting to swallow. Eventually PageMaker files swell up with all the bite-size changes that the program hasn't had a chance to swallow yet. To consolidate and slim down your files, choose Smaller in the Save option. Your saves take longer, sometimes much longer, but your files will be smaller.

The Smaller preference default has the same effect as the Save As command, except that the Smaller option is much less trouble. It's automatic, and you don't need to go through a dialog box that asks you for the new file name.

Setting Guides

Working on a page crowded with objects and many guides can be difficult. You keep accidentally grabbing the guides rather than the object you are trying to position. To combat that problem, you can use the Guides option in the Preferences dialog box to set guides so they display in back of page elements, instead of the usual front display. You can get more information about setting guides in the section, "Managing Your Guides," in Chapter 13, "Designing a Master Page Grid."

Choosing More Preferences

The More button takes you to the More Preferences dialog box (see fig. 3.3).

Making Text Specifications

The first option in the Text section of the More Preferences dialog box deals with greeking. Greeking looks like figure 3.4. Gray bars appear in the place of lines of text when you are viewing your publication at small magnification. The higher the number you specify in the Greek Text Below box, the more greeking you get and the faster your screen display runs because the software can quickly slug in some gray bars instead of trying to accurately draw characters on-screen. On the other hand, a more detailed representation helps you make an evaluation of page layout when you zoom out to an overall view. Greeking, by the way, only happens when you are at a view below 100 percent.

FIG. 3.3 ▷

*The More Prefer-
ences dialog box.*

FIG. 3.4 ▷

Greeked text.

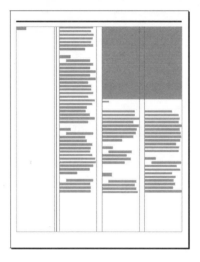

The Turn Pages When Autoflowing option tells PageMaker to show you new pages when they are added as you pour new text into your publication. Page-Maker works faster if you leave this option unchecked and let Autoflow work behind the scenes and out of view.

Check Use Typographer's Quotes if you want curly quote marks rather than the ugly straight-up-and-down typewriter style quotes. Checking this box applies to any new text you type in Layout view or Story view. It doesn't affect text that's already present in your publication. If you need the straight-up-and-down marks (called *primes*) for inches and feet, see the section "Setting Fractions" in Chapter 15, "Creating Special Effects."

Optimizing the Story Editor View

As you know from your tour in Chapter 1, "Touring PageMaker," and other references, you don't get a complete view of your text in Story Editor. Story Editor is a lean and mean text editor. You can, however, optimize your Story Editor view using the settings in the Story Editor section of the Preferences dialog box.

Pick a comfortable viewing font for Story Editor use. You may want to select the same font you use for your body copy type.

Some people like to set the type display in Story Editor to a large size so it's easy to read. A 14-point size usually works well. Type the size you want in the Size box.

Use the Display Style Names and Display ¶ Marks check boxes to further optimize your Story Editor view. Making style names visible when you are working in the text-only Story Editor mode helps you know what the page will look like when you go back to Layout view. Being able to see symbols that show you where spaces, paragraph breaks, and tabs are located helps you spot problems such as double carriage returns between paragraphs or double spacing after periods.

Defining Graphics Resolution

You can define the level of resolution you want to see on-screen when you choose Standard graphics display in the main Preferences dialog box. You have two options for setting resolution: display by Size or display by Resolution percentage.

The Size option sets a fixed upper limit on the low resolution copy of the imported image stored in your publication files. It controls the file space devoted to representation of the actual high-resolution graphic. The default is 64K. Or you can set the size of the internal graphics file on a percentage basis.

Working in standard resolution and storing smaller-than-original-size placeholder images inside your publication saves disk space because they aren't stored twice on your hard drive disk (once inside PageMaker and once for the original image).

Aside from these display resolution issues, you can give PageMaker an upper limit on storing graphics files within the publication. Type a limit in the box titled Alert When Storing Graphics Over. If this upper limit is exceeded, PageMaker displays an alert box that asks how you want to proceed. You can choose to store the graphic entirely within PageMaker, or you can tell PageMaker to create an internal lower resolution representation of the graphic for display purposes only. Again, the latter method saves disk space because you aren't storing the same image twice. On the other hand, storing the full graphic in the PageMaker file increases your display speed and quality considerably.

Managing Memory for PostScript Printing

Very large EPS graphics can swamp the memory of your printer or the service bureau's imagesetter. PageMaker 6.0 now includes this graphics memory management setting that helps in those situations. If you set Memory Freed for Graphics to Maximum, PageMaker temporarily flushes unneeded fonts from the printer's memory. Don't use this option unless you absolutely need it, though, because it can significantly increase printing time by requiring the program to download the same fonts over and over again to the printer.

The Display PPD Name option enables you to select the way your printer information file appears in PageMaker's dialog boxes. By default, the displayed name is the descriptive nickname for the printer, usually a spelled-out manufacturer's name and model number. To see the actual file name of the PPD, select this check box.

Substituting Fonts

The Fonts button helps you determine the way PageMaker applies its universal font technology tool, called PANOSE (see fig. 3.5).

FIG. 3.5 ▶

The Font matching dialog box.

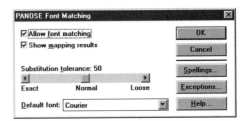

PANOSE, built into PageMaker 6.0, substitutes an existing full-fledged font that comes as close as possible to the missing font. PANOSE is different from the SuperATM technology you hear about from Macintosh users. SuperATM draws on a database of font approximations, which it adjusts chameleon-style in an attempt to ad-lib a new pretend font on-the-fly. PANOSE, on the other hand, simply draws on the fonts you have installed, picking the one that comes as close as possible to the one that's missing.

PANOSE enables you to continue working on a publication, even if someone sends you a document that requires some fonts that you don't have installed on your system. Using this tool, you can at least edit the document.

Generally the substitutes provided by PANOSE are not of sufficient quality to achieve the effect of the originally specified font. They are okay for editing in a pinch, but it isn't a good idea to rely on this technique for a final high-quality publishing job.

Success as a desktop publisher has much to do with understanding the fundamental font technology of your operating system, and with your working methods for organizing your fonts. Many desktop publishers have hundreds of fonts they must organize and regularly install and uninstall. Because of this interaction and the need to explain some basic background, all the font technology information is located in Chapter 25, "Developing a System for Managing Your Type," in the "Supercharging PageMaker" section. That's also where you can find a Tactics Recipe for managing your fonts.

Managing Color

In the main Preferences dialog box, the letters on the CMS Setup button stand for Color Management System. Take it from me, color needs managing. And PageMaker 6.0 has taken some major leaps forward in helping you to achieve color accuracy. As with the font technology discussion, the best way to explain the mechanics of CMS in PageMaker is to put it in context. You can find coverage of how to use the settings behind this button in Chapter 20, "Meeting Color Challenges."

Accessing Express Preferences

New with PageMaker 6.0, you can double-click the items in the Toolbox to obtain express access to publication defaults. The double-click deselects any currently selected objects (hence the publication default) and opens a dialog box that matches the tool. Figure 3.6 illustrates these express linkages, leading off with the most important one, the Pointer connection to the main Preferences dialog box.

Fig. 3.6 ▶

Double-click the Pointer to reach the default Preferences dialog box.

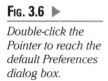
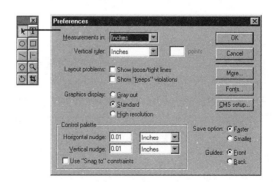

Setting Mini-Defaults

As described earlier in this chapter, you can set mini-defaults by simply making choices from the PageMaker menus with nothing selected. If you are ever in doubt about what you can set as a mini-default, just open up PageMaker (with no publication loaded) and scan all the menus. Almost any menu that's black (not grayed) can set a mini-default.

TIP ▶ During Setup, Use the Menus as Reminders

When you are first setting up PageMaker or beginning a new publication from scratch, go through each of the menus and have a look at every single item. Use the black items as a reminder list for choosing your mini-defaults.

Here's a complete list, organized by menu headings, of all the items you can set as mini-defaults. Keep in mind that you can set each of the following items as a default for all new publications or a default for your current publication only.

File
▶ All the items in the Preferences dialog box.
▶ Each function of Document Setup, including the Numbers subdialog box.

Edit
▶ The number and spacing attributes in Multiple Paste.

Utilities
▶ The Create Index check boxes.
▶ Create Table of Contents choices.

Layout
▶ Guides and Rulers submenu items.
▶ Column Guides.
▶ Display Non-Printing Items.
▶ The Autoflow toggle, not to be confused with the Autoflow page display setting in Preferences.
▶ Although the View menu is black when a document is open (they are gray if there isn't one open), none of the View menu choices will take a mini-default setting.

Type
▶ Virtually every item under the Type menu can take a mini-default. That includes the express formatting items such as Font, Size, Leading, Set Width, Type Style, Expert Tracking, Alignment, and Style. Where an item has an arrowhead, indicating a submenu of choices, all the choices can be set as mini-defaults.

▶ All the items in the Type Specifications dialog box can be set as mini-defaults. The Type Specification defaults override any of the settings established in the express menu items under the Type menu, such as Font, Size, and Leading.

▶ All the items in the Paragraph Specifications dialog box can be set as mini-defaults. But if you set a default style, the settings associated with that style override most of the default settings you establish in the Paragraph Specifications dialog box.

▶ The Define Styles menu item establishes the styles that appear in the Style palette for a new publication.

Element

▶ Fill, Line, and Fill and Line.

▶ Polygon Settings and Rounded Corners.

▶ Text Wrap.

▶ Link Options.

▶ Although Image is black, all the choices in the submenu are grayed out and cannot be set as mini-defaults.

▶ Define Colors sets which colors will appear on the Color palette.

Arrange

▶ None of the items on the Arrange menu can be set as mini-defaults.

Window

▶ You can set all the palettes to open as soon as you open a publication. In fact, these choices are not really mini-defaults. They are program-level defaults, even though you set them with a publication open. PageMaker remembers the location and size of the palettes when you close a session and restores them to those same locations and sizes the next time you open the program.

▶ When you set the Library palette to open as a default, it presents you with a dialog box in which you select a default library file.

TIP ▶ Keep a Backup of Your Defaults File

After you have your preferences and other defaults all tuned, make a backup copy of the PageMaker defaults file (PM6.CNF, stored in the main PageMaker folder). Name it something like PM6CNF.BAK and keep it in the same folder with the real file. Then if you ever totally screw up your carefully adjusted personal PageMaker defaults, you can revert to this backup by trashing your main defaults file and making a copy of this one, renaming it PM6.CNF.

TIP ▶ Keep Sets of Defaults for Different Types of Projects

Extend that backup tip into a major element of your working environment. Design sets of personalized defaults for all your different needs and swap them in and out as needed, using this renaming technique. You might, for example, have a set of default settings suitable for book layout and another set of defaults more suitable for brochures. The ruler and nudge preferences in particular would be different for those two publications, not to mention things like margin settings. You can also accomplish this goal by saving a standard file as a PageMaker template, an option available when you use the Save As command.

Where to Go from Here

The various Preferences command options and the mini-default items touch almost every other location in this book. You may want to explore these special points of linkage:

▶ You can learn much more about the practical purposes of Preferences and mini-defaults in Chapter 12, "Setting Up a New Publication," and Chapter 13, "Designing a Master Page Grid."

▶ All the various Story Editor options are discussed, with some background, in Chapter 9, "Editing Copy with the Story Editor."

▶ Because it has such a variety of powers, the Control palette is covered in several locations. Try Chapter 5, "Typing In Your Type," and Chapter 6, "Formatting Paragraphs," for text management with the Control palette. For graphics object position, look in Chapter 14, "Precisely Positioning Graphics and Text." You can find a quick reference pull-out card on the Control palette in the back of the book.

▶ PANOSE and Multiple Master font issues are covered along with more basic font management considerations in Chapter 25, "Developing a System for Managing Your Type," in the "Supercharging PageMaker" section of the book.

Chapter 4

Getting an Overview of the DTP Process

This chapter on getting an overview of the DTP process touches on the following concepts:

Planning a project for audience, budget, and practicality.

▼

Executing your design once the project has been planned.

▼

Publishing your publication, from creating final art for your printer to the actual press run.

THE COMPLEX PROCESS of getting a publication to the printing press could require an entire college curriculum, much less a book chapter. This chapter just gathers the threads together into a quick overview discussion. Chapter 24, "Master Checklist for Desktop Publishing," helps you think of all the decisions you need to make. The list of questions, issues, and "to-do" items in Chapter 24 has been structured around the three basic steps of desktop publishing in this chapter. ▶ ▶ ▶

Planning

Your desktop publishing process doesn't begin with doing a layout using Page-Maker. It begins with a major injection of reality in the form of advanced planning. What's the budget? What audience must be reached, and what message will be communicated? After a creative concept has been developed, use that as a communication enhancement and a consensus builder to make sure everyone involved in the project has reached an agreement before spending a lot of time in front of your computer.

Defining the Goal and Audience

Every publication has a communication goal and a target audience. Your first task must be to sort out those issues and define them, preferably in writing. It might be on the back of a napkin over lunch with the client, or jotted down while sipping a cup of coffee during a quick break from the "real" work at your company. Or, in large companies or for huge projects you may develop a formal, written goals statement for approval by a committee.

This initial thinking really can be quite informal, as long as the thinking part happens. Figure 4.1 shows the roughed-out goals and target audience for a four-color flyer for some hats.

Fig. 4.1 ▶

You'll make creative notes like these, your first statement of goals and audience, during the original client meeting and creative session.

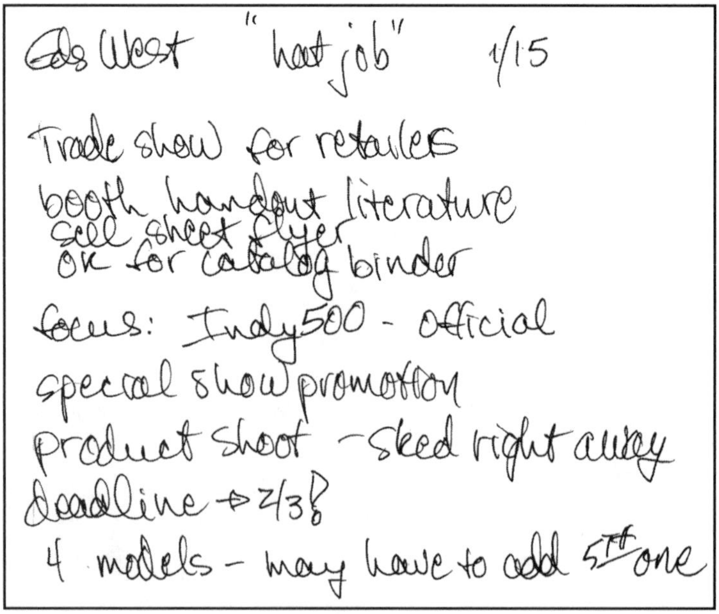

No matter how unsophisticated your first statement of goals and audiences is, your planning truly begins with where you want to end up. Drive your entire creative and development process by keeping the needs and purposes of the project in mind. You have a problem to be solved or a goal to be achieved. Make everything else a slave to that. You are not writing ad copy. You are not making artfully designed graphics. You are not getting something printed. Those are merely means to the real end—fulfilling the needs represented by the communication goal and the target audience.

Setting a Budget and Deadline

After you know your goal and audience, you (or your client or boss) can reasonably evaluate the importance of the project. That, and the practical limits of life, leisure, and lucre will dictate your decisions about how much money to spend as well as the number of resources that ought to be committed in order to deliver the project by a particular deadline date.

There's no sense building a four-color, 20-page, perfectly bound book if you can't spend more than $100 on photocopying presentations for a monthly committee planning meeting. On the other hand, if you are introducing a product at a trade show and several million dollars in resources have been risked in creating the product, you'll want to recoup your investment. To do so, it'll probably take more than spending $1.98 on your trade show handout brochures.

After you know what they are, draw up your budget and scheduling goals in writing and get total agreement before proceeding with your work.

Developing a Core Creative Concept

Start with the main thrust of your creative approach. After you have focused on a core creative concept for your project, most of the other design elements just naturally slip into place.

Ask yourself some questions, such as the following:

- ▶ What will actually be the main visual element on my pages?
- ▶ How will that help me get to the single driving creative pulse of my publication?
- ▶ Will my design be driven by copy?
- ▶ Has a slogan leaped out of the communication goal process?
- ▶ Does the product or theme have some compelling visual power?
- ▶ Can I focus around a beauty shot of the new pewter toaster oven, or on the flashy colors of that new line of house paint?

You'll probably end up with several creative thoughts that need development. Spend some time with each thought—they'll sort themselves out as you keep re-visiting your target, using the audience and message goal to steer your creative doodling.

Testing the Concept and Getting Preliminary Approvals

It's time to make sure everyone you need to satisfy will, in fact, be satisfied. That includes yourself!

↘Show your concept sketches, like the ones in figure 4.2, to anyone who counts. Show them to your intended audience. Get feedback from colleagues. Do some revisions, always keeping in mind your target audience and communication goal.

Fig. 4.2 ▶

Create concept sketches for preliminary approvals. Start with thumbnails (right), and proceed to a full-size conceptual sketch (left).

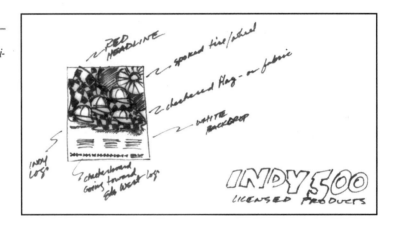

Finally, when the concept has been tested, go to the preliminary approval stage. Once again, sum up the target audience and the communication goal, and use that as a touchstone as you serve up the sketches to your approver. It may be the boss. It may be a client or a committee. It may be you, if your project has been created to serve some in-house need. Whoever it is, create a formal, final sign-off process for the core creative approach of the project before you spend time and dollars to do the actual detail work.

Collaborating with the Printer and Service Bureau

You still don't get to open up PageMaker. It's time to develop final specifications for the project and be sure that they fit your budget. But you don't do this in a vacuum. You go meet with the printer and ask the person who works the print-ing press what kinds of problems your concept might present. You may be able to save money and ensure the proper results for the job by making small design changes to be more practical for the press.

Using the master checklist in Chapter 24, ask every possible question of the printer so that you can nail down issues such as type of paper, how many colors, what type of art to supply for burning the plates, size of print run, color proof responsibility, press check requirements, who does the trapping, and what kind of final art (for example, film or positive mechanicals) would be best for your job. Pin down every possible detail. Chapter 23, "Working with the Print Shop," includes a sample "Bid Request & Specification" form that will help a lot.

It's particularly important at this juncture to decide on issues that influence your handling of graphics. Your screen frequency for halftones, for example, will be based on your printer's recommendation, and that's a collaborative decision between you and the printer, based mostly on the type of paper you'll be specifying for your job. Newsprint won't hold as fine a screen as slick stock.

After you know what the printer wants, you may also need to meet with your prepress provider, the service bureau. Many technical issues may require resolution, and this could be especially important if the service bureau will be doing the trapping, so you can deliver final film that meets the print shop's requirements. It may even be necessary—on complex jobs—to get the printer and the service bureau together on the phone in a conference call to work out such technical issues as the amount of trapping required, dot gain, undercover removal, and gray component replacement. We'll talk more about some of these technical issues in the Part V, "Making Pages Colorful." For now, the important thing is to understand the need for collaboration with your printer and service bureau.

Making Up Your Pages

Here's the execution stage of assembling your pages after all your careful planning. This stage may possibly seem anticlimactic—and that's the way it ought to be. The detailed arena of points, picas, and page layout should by this stage be precise and decisive. All the preliminary decisions should already be behind you.

Perfecting Your Elements

Most projects are constructed as elements which are then brought together in PageMaker for final positioning and typesetting. Get your copy in perfect proofreader shape. Scan your photographs and proof them for color correction. Draw illustrations. Compose tables and graphs.

Even though much of the work at this stage will be accomplished outside PageMaker with a supporting cast of desktop publishing tools, all of the elements must be managed with an eye to how you'll be working when they come into the layout environment.

Setting Up Your Publication

Finally, you get to start really putting PageMaker to work. You'll use a template, or start from scratch and perform all the foundation moves of creating a new publication. Page margins, a layout grid, master page elements, basic type design, paragraph formatting in style sheets, creating the color palette—you need to manage all these elements.

You'll especially use the information in Chapter 5, "Typing In Your Type;" Chapter 6, "Formatting Paragraphs;" Chapter 7, "Designing a Text Style System;" Chapter 12, "Setting Up a New Publication;" Chapter 13, "Designing a Master Page Grid;" Chapter 16, "Formatting Forms, Tables, and Databases;" and Chapter 18, "Creating Colors."

Placing Text and Graphics

Using all the capabilities, you pour in your text and import your graphics and get them positioned on the page just right, as the desktop publisher is doing in PageMaker in figure 4.3. In the end, there's a fair amount of poking, prodding, and trimming to get the text and graphics adjusted to their proper relationships.

Fig. **4.3** ▶

With basic decisions in place, you begin by laying out your text and graphic elements onto the page.

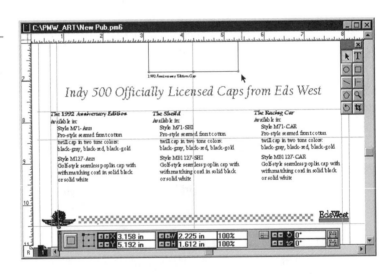

Chapter 8, "Pouring Text into PageMaker;" Chapter 11, "Placing Images;" Chapter 14, "Precisely Positioning Graphics and Text;" and Chapter 16, "Formatting Forms, Tables, and Databases," have a lot of the information you will need at this point in your publishing process.

Fine-Tuning, Producing Special Effects, and Coloring Your Pages

You'll tune up text kerning, page breaks, display heads, and other headline treatments, initial caps, rotated type and graphics, text wraps around graphics, page and column breaks, and dozens of other page layout details (see fig. 4.4). Color issues will get finalized at this stage as well.

Fig. 4.4 ▶

Next, tune up your pages. Make them look slick.

Indy 500 Officially Licensed Caps from Eds West

The 1992 Anniversary Edition
Available in:
Style M71-Ann
Pro-style seamed front cotton
twill cap in two tone colors:
black-gray, black-red, black-gold

Style M127-Ann
Golf-style seamless poplin cap with
with matching cord in solid black
or solid white

The Shield
Available in:
Style M71-SHI
Pro-style seamed front cotton
twill cap in two tone colors:
black-gray, black-red, black-gold

Style MB1127-SHI
Golf-style seamless poplin cap with
with matching cord in solid black
or solid white

The Racing Car
Available in:
Style M71-CAR
Pro-style seamed front cotton
twill cap in two tone colors:
black-gray, black-red, black-gold

Style MB1127-CAR
Golf-style seamless poplin cap with
with matching cord in solid black
or solid white

Product Availability: March 1, 1992
For Further product and ordering information, please call Eds West at 1-800-325-7229

EdsWest

For this stage, you will use many of the techniques in Chapter 15, "Creating Special Effects," as well as the fine points of type management, paragraph formatting, and color management in Chapter 5, "Typing In Your Type," Chapter 6, "Formatting Paragraphs," and Part V, "Making Pages Colorful."

Generating Contents and Index

After you have your pages locked into place, if you're producing a long form document, you'll want to compile your table of contents, illustration lists, and index. Ideally, you will have preplanned for those elements by constructing a good style sheet system and by precoding the index entries using the techniques in Chapter 17, "Building Many Pages."

Publishing

This stage includes both the prepress and actual on-press work of translating your electronic page paste-up into a physical form.

Trapping

If you are producing a color publication, there will probably need to be some trapping. To oversimplify, *trapping* is slightly overlapping the elements on the page to compensate for the inevitable inaccuracies in registering multiple colors on the fast-moving printing press. Without trapping, you might get unsightly white lines, or gaps, between abutting colors.

The question is, who should do the trapping? Should it be you, your prepress service bureau, or your printer? PageMaker 6.0 has new trapping power built into it, although you may want to think over the obligations you take on when you decide to do your own trapping. Turn to the "What is Trapping and Why do I Need It?" section in Chapter 20, "Meeting Color Challenges."

Separating

Producing separations means breaking down an electronic layout into layers of color, one for each ink to be used on the press. Each layer produces an individual plate devoted to one ink color, and when the press rolls, it superimposes all those colors to create the final color image.

All the chapters in Part V, "Making Pages Colorful," have information on how to manage the conversion of your digital computer design into color on the printing press.

Final Output

Whether or not you have color in your publication, you'll probably be sending it to some kind of printing device. It might be your 300 dpi laser printer, or it might be a 2,450 dpi high-resolution imagesetter like the one shown in figure 4.5.

With PageMaker 6.0, you also can produce an electronic publication for the Internet World Wide Web, or for paperless distribution using Acrobat. Although this chapter has been constructed to match the traditional printing process, there's information on electronic publishing in Part VIII, "Riding the Cutting Edge."

Fig. 4.5 ▶

This illustration shows the steps in publishing a four-color project, from layout on the computer to imagesetter output of film for each of the four colors to four plates on the printing press.

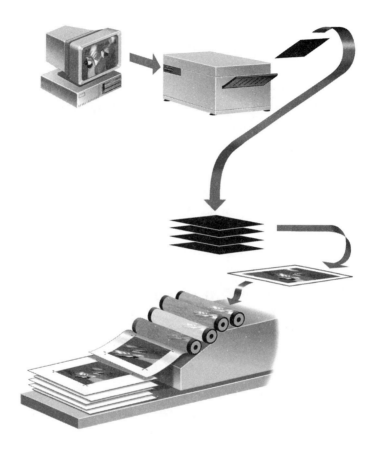

For the final output stage, you'll want to lean on the information in Part VI, "Publishing," especially Chapter 21, "Producing Mechanicals;" Chapter 22, "Proofing Your Publication;" and Chapter 23, "Working with the Print Shop."

Imposition, Proofing, and Approvals

After you have color-separated films, you can have them sandwiched together so that the service bureau or the printer can shoot a proof. If you are working in color, this is a vital step to avoid costly reruns on the press.

Imposition is to arrange all your pages into signatures so that the printer can run large format paper through the press (it saves lots of money to print multiple pages to one large sheet of paper) and then fold the large paper into intricate folds and cut all the pages apart as if it were some kind of origami figure. This can be quite confusing, and if you are working with a large form document—color or not—you'll want the proofs assembled into a mock-up so you can show the printer how all your pages fit together.

With these proofs in hand, get everything officially signed off. If the project is for you, the service bureau and the printer will ask for your signature. Otherwise, it'll be the client or the boss—whoever's paying the bills.

You'll use your checklist security blanket to take you through the last of the proofing, approval, and printing process, following the detailed steps and questions in Chapter 24, "Master Checklist for Desktop Publishing."

Going to Press, Folding, and Binding

Time to roll the press. You may want to be there so that you can conduct a final press check, the ultimate proof. Finally, the paper has been kissed by the ink, your electronic page design has been turned into real pages, and the printer will handle the final stages of manufacturing. Varnish, scoring, folding, and binding are some of the final steps.

Where to Go from Here

▶ Well, of course, you go to work. The next chapter, "Typing In Your Type," starts out with the most fundamental page element of all—type.

▶ This overview chapter ties closely to Chapter 24, "Master Checklist for Desktop Publishing."

▶ To take the first advice in this chapter—know where you want to end up—it's important that you understand the mechanical process of prepress and printing, so you'll want to spend some time with Part VI, "Publishing," even as you work your way through the type, paragraph, story, and page building blocks between here and there.

PART II

Working with Text

5 ▲ Typing In Your Type

6 ▲ Formatting Paragraphs

7 ▲ Designing a Text Style System

8 ▲ Pouring Text into PageMaker

9 ▲ Editing Copy with the Story Editor

Chapter 5

Typing In Your Type

In this chapter, you learn about these topics:

Using the PageMaker Text tool.

▼

Formatting your type in three ways.

▼

Using each of the basic text attributes, including typeface, type size, leading, styling, setting text in uppercase and small caps, kerning and other spacing methods, subscripts and superscripts, and baseline shift.

▼

Setting type with the Control palette.

THIS CHAPTER DELVES into the fundamental building blocks of desktop publishing.

In this chapter, you too begin by putting characters on a page. Then, as you move through the rest of Part II, "Working with Text," you build up to paragraphs, text blocks, and stories.

If you are not already a PageMaker person, take 15 minutes for the tour in Chapter 1, "Touring PageMaker." You get a basic grounding in the PageMaker way—the Pasteboard, navigation through pages, magnified views, and the Control palette, as well as the creation, loading, and saving of publication files. ▶ ▶ ▶

Using the Text Tool

Okay, get the Toolbox out. You need your Text tool to do anything at all concerning type in PageMaker.

If the Toolbox isn't on your screen, you need to open it. Select the Window, Toolbox command. (By the way, if you were a PageMaker 5.0 person, a shortcut no longer exists to call up the Toolbox.)

In the upper-right corner of the Toolbox, you see the Text tool icon. If you click the icon, you get the I-beam Text pointer (see fig. 5.1). The Text pointer looks and acts much like any other text editing pointer. You use a Text pointer when you edit file names on the desktop or when you use your word processor.

Fig. 5.1 ▶

*The Text tool and
Text pointer.*

You can select the Text tool from the Toolbox using any one of these methods:

▶ Click the *T* symbol in the Toolbox.

▶ Press Shift+F2.

▶ If you have the Text tool selected, you can toggle between the Text tool and the Pointer tool by pressing Ctrl+spacebar. Notice that you use this same key combination to get the Magnifying Glass pointer. To tool toggle, tap the spacebar. To get the Magnifying Glass, hold down the two keys for a few seconds until the glass appears, and keep holding them while you make your magnification adjustment.

Setting Text Attributes

PageMaker has three basic text formatting modes. The mode you are in depends on what you have just been doing with the Text tool.

If you've ever used a word processor, there are no surprises here. You have three possibilities to format text:

▶ Select a range of text using the Text tool.

▶ Click an insertion point with the Text tool, and you are ready to type some new text.

▶ Set formatting before selecting text or clicking an insertion point.

Setting Attributes by Selecting Existing Text

Most commonly, you start by using the Text tool to select some text, as in figure 5.2. You drag the tool across a range of type, selecting anywhere from a single character to an entire story. You also can click an insertion point and then Shift-click at a new spot; the range of text between the two click points is selected. Or you may press Shift+arrow to select text.

Fig. 5.2 ▶

Use the Text tool to select a range of text.

A select few have been chosen to become PageMaker experts. More power to us.

After you have a range of text selected, you can use any of the type formatting commands to format your selected text just the way you want it.

Typing New Text at the Insertion Point

Another option for formatting text is to click the Text tool where you want to put some new text. Then use the text formatting menus to set up the formatting for the text you type from that point on (see fig. 5.3). If you choose Palatino Bold, for example, the text you type from that specific insertion point will be Palatino Bold.

Fig. 5.3 ▶

Click an insertion point so you can type text with new formatting.

Be aggressive. In order to click with the world you must insert your words.

Text insertion point

These attributes are temporary. After typing your text, if you click somewhere else and begin typing again, the Text tool reverts back to its last mini-default.

Setting a Mini-Default Without Clicking an Insertion Point

If you select the Text tool but don't click anywhere in the publication, you can make text attribute decisions before you actually put the Text tool to work. This technique creates one of the mini-defaults described in Chapter 3, "Personalizing PageMaker Preferences." From that point, any text you type has the attributes you chose for font, size, and so on, until you change the attribute again.

To set a mini-default for the Text tool, make text-formatting decisions with no text selected. You don't even need to have the Text tool active to do this.

Selecting Type Attributes

You want to design type that has snap, which means picking various type attributes to fit the needs of your publication. Maybe you want to use Bauhaus demi for a special headline, and perhaps you want the letters twice as big as the body copy. Or maybe you want some of the key words in a quote to be bold for emphasis.

These examples are type *attributes*. In any one of the three text tool modes just described, you can select a number of type attributes.

PageMaker gives you three ways you can set type attributes. Your choices are:

▶ You can use a dialog box (in this case the Type Specifications dialog box).

▶ You can select from a main menu item or one of its submenus (the Type menu for text).

▶ You can make many decisions from the Control palette.

Making Multiple Type Decisions with the Type Specifications Dialog Box

The Type Specifications dialog box is the most comprehensive of the three methods to set type attributes. This dialog box contains or connects to all the possible text attributes. This method may not be the most direct way to accomplish something in PageMaker, but it's the old reliable common denominator.

For making complex type attribute decisions, you can access the Type Specifications dialog box from the Type menu, or use the shortcut Ctrl+T (see fig. 5.4). This option has the main advantage of permitting you to select more than one attribute in a single move. You also can indicate text attributes that aren't available through any of the other methods, such as assigning colors and tints to type, and setting the percentage levels for superscripting and subscripting.

Fig. 5.4 ▶

The Type Specifications dialog box enables complex formatting in a single move.

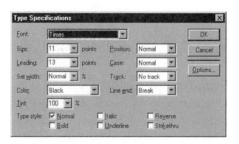

Doing Simple Formatting Using the Type Menu

Making formatting choices from the Type menu often is simpler and faster than using the Type Specifications dialog box. Type submenus provide direct express access to the most-used formatting choices, without getting into the more comprehensive Type Specifications dialog box.

As you see in figure 5.5, you can call many of the type attributes on the Type menu and its submenus using various keyboard shortcut keys.

FIG. 5.5 ▶

The Type menu for quick, simple formatting of text.

Experimenting with Type Effects Using the Control Palette

Virtually all of PageMaker's typesetting power is available to you from the Control palette (see fig. 5.6). Really, you have no more direct way of making these decisions.

FIG. 5.6 ▶

Control palette for experimenting on-screen with type attributes.

You can operate the Control palette hands-on (mouse-on) like a PageMaker cockpit, or you can use the keyboard. Open the Control palette with the Window menu's Toolbox command or the Ctrl+' (apostrophe) keyboard shortcut.

Because the Control palette is such a comprehensive instrument, with an entirely different working style from the usual dialog box and menu approach, table 5.2 (shown later in this chapter in the section "Setting Type with the Control Palette") summarizes all the Control palette navigation commands relating to type. For palette navigation commands relating to paragraphs, see Chapter 6, "Formatting Paragraphs."

II

Working with Text

All the Control palette modes (character, paragraph, and object positioning) are covered together in one quick reference page in Appendix C.

Selecting a Typeface

Selecting a typeface for your text is easy, no matter which of the three text formatting methods you choose. Each method has something in common—a scrolling menu for making your selection.

The typeface scroll menus list all the fonts you have installed in your system, and only those fonts. Occasionally, you may see a typeface name grayed in the list. The grayed typeface means that the currently loaded publication has some text formatted in a typeface you haven't loaded into your system.

You can select a typeface using any of the three methods just discussed—the Type Specifications dialog box, the direct access Type menu, and the on-screen Control palette.

Choosing a Typeface In the Type Specifications Dialog Box

Figure 5.7 shows how you can select a typeface from the scrollable Font list box in the Type Specifications dialog box. Highlight the typeface you want and release the mouse button.

Fig. 5.7 ▶

The scrollable type-face list in the Type Specifications dia-log box.

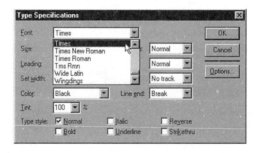

Design Note
Choose a Typeface Mood

Try to fit your typeface choice to the mood of your publication or story. Typefaces, like human faces, are humorous, serious, warm. You may think assigning personalities to type a little quirky, but which of the typefaces in figure 5.8 would you choose for the annual report of a Fortune 500 company? What if the company made athletic shoes? Distributed imported Italian furniture? Manufactured computers?

FIG. 5.8 ▶

Selecting a type mood for your publication.

Bauhaus

Optima

Times New Roman

Lubalin

Palatino

Zapf Chancery

Choosing a Typeface from the Font Submenu

For the most direct access to typeface selection, go right to the typeface list by way of the Type, Font command, shown in figure 5.9. Then move through the list until you highlight the font you want. Release the mouse button to put your choice into effect.

FIG. 5.9 ▶

The Font submenu of typeface choices.

Choosing a Typeface with the Control Palette

For the fastest and most direct text formatting of all, use the Control palette. If the Control palette isn't on-screen, you can bring it up by choosing it from the Window menu or by pressing Ctrl+' (apostrophe).

You can switch from your layout to the Control palette by clicking anywhere on the palette. To return to your layout, click the layout. Or you can get the same toggle effect by pressing the key combination Ctrl+` (grave).

Figure 5.10 shows the typeface selection list, as accessed through the Control palette.

FIG. 5.10 ▶

The typeface selection portion of the Control palette.

With the Control palette activated, you have two choices for selecting a typeface. Just click one on the list with the mouse. Or, if you are a keyboard person, use the Tab key to move through the fields to the typeface field. Just start typing the name of the typeface you want, and PageMaker throws up guesses until you provide enough letters for PageMaker to match your request.

Whichever method you use, put your choice into effect by pressing the Enter key, or tabbing to the next field, or Shift+tabbing to the previous field. You also can click the Apply button.

TIP ▶   For Service Bureau Material, Choose PostScript Fonts

If your publication will be run on a type-imaging machine at a service bureau, don't use TrueType fonts. Stick to PostScript fonts. Imagesetters are built to chew PostScript, and the TrueType technology emerged well after PostScript was adopted as the standard way to get high-quality type. Things have improved some in the last few years as service bureaus have developed techniques for dealing with the problem, but you still hear of big glitches where a TrueType font caused problems and blew a lot of very expensive imagesetter output, usually on deadline. Your job may turn out okay. But on the other hand, who needs to risk it when you can choose from thousands of PostScript fonts covering almost every conceivable need? Learn more about how to make sure your job will run okay at the service bureau in Chapter 21, "Producing Mechanicals."

Choosing a Type Size

In PageMaker, you can have type sizes from 4 to 650 points, in increments of a tenth of a point.

You choose one of these type sizes using the same three methods you use to select a typeface: the Type Specifications dialog box, the Type menu, or the Control palette.

For an explanation of typesetting measurements in points and picas, see "Key Concept: Measuring Type Size: Picas, Points, and Ems" later in this chapter.

Sizing Type with the Type Specifications Dialog Box

In the Type Specifications dialog box shown in figure 5.11, you can enter a type size, specified within a tenth of a point. Or you can select from a list of type sizes in whole numbers by clicking the arrow just to the right of the type Size field.

Don't forget, you can bring up the Type Specifications dialog box on-screen without using a menu by pressing the keyboard shortcut, Ctrl+T.

Fig. 5.11 ▶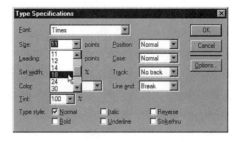

The Type Specifications type Size selection box and drop-down list.

Making a Fast Type Sizing Decision with the Type Menu

You can select a whole-number type size from the Type menu by using the Size submenu (see fig. 5.12). Select the Other option to open a dialog box where you can type a fractional point size. Personally, if I need an "other" size of type, I use the Control palette or Ctrl+T to access the Type Specifications dialog box—it's much faster. (Try this. Ctrl+T, press Tab, type your point size, tab again, type your leading size and press Enter. Very fast!)

Fig. 5.12 ▶

The Type menu's Size submenu.

Sizing Type with the Control Palette

The Control palette has all the type-sizing power of the Type Specifications dialog box, and you can see it right on-screen in front of you without pulling down a menu.

Use the mouse or the Tab key to navigate to the type size option (see fig. 5.13).

Fig. 5.13 ▶

The Type Size option of the Control palette.

Type the precise type size you want, or use the arrow key to the right of the type size field to select from a short list of possibilities.

Don't forget, if the Control palette comes up in Paragraph view, you can toggle to Character view by using Ctrl+Shift+` (grave). Use the same command to toggle back to Paragraph view in the Control palette.

TIP ▶ Make Real-Time Type Size Adjustments Using the Keyboard

There's nothing like experimentation—trying out your design ideas to see if they work. Experiment with your type size choices directly from the keyboard using the Ctrl+> or Ctrl+< shortcut. As you may expect, the combination using the greater-than symbol increases type size, and the one using the less-than symbol shrinks the type. This command skips among the type sizes you find listed in the Size submenu of the Type menu—a limited range of "standard" sizes. If you want to jump type size in smaller increments, add the Shift key to the chord (Ctrl+Shift+> for bigger sizes in one-point jumps and Ctrl+Shift+< for one point smaller). This shortcut only takes you up or down in whole numbers—no decimals.

This shortcut also doesn't work if you have the Control palette activated. However, you can use a variation on this shortcut in the Control palette. If your cursor is in the type size field and you press Ctrl+> or Ctrl+<, it will adjust the type size as you would expect, just like the layout view shortcut. However, the move doesn't take effect instantly. It only takes effect when you press Enter or otherwise implement the Control palette setting.

KEY CONCEPT:
Measuring Type Size: Picas, Points, and Ems

Traditionally, typography has used picas and points as measures.

There are 72 points in an inch, 6 picas in an inch, and 12 points in a pica. For type, use points as a measurement. You usually use picas to delineate page-sized specifications such as margins. Check out the PageMaker ruler in figure 5.14 to see how picas compare to inches.

A confusing fact exists about point sizes of type. For any given size of type, expressed in points, the apparent visual size of the characters varies—sometimes by quite a lot. Type in 24-point Bauhaus is different from 24-point Avant Garde and different from 24-point Lubalin (see fig. 5.15). This difference occurs because type is designed to look good on a certain height of line. The design takes into account all the parameters of the type such as the relative height of the round tummy of the lowercase letter *b*, compared to the height of the vertical stem (the staff of the *d*) or the descender (the tail of the *g*).

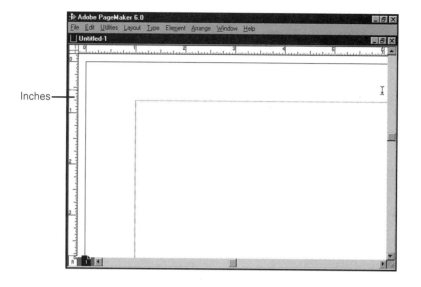

Inches

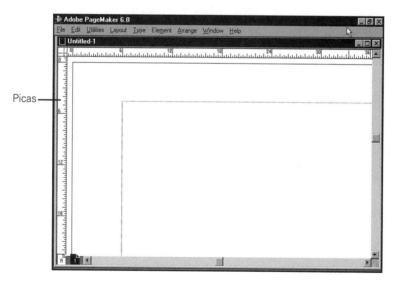

Picas

Fig. 5.14 ▲

PageMaker rulers set one above the other to compare picas and inches.

II

Working with Text

Hi, I'm in 24 point Bauhaus

Hi, I'm in 24 point Palatino

Hi, I'm in 24 point Palatino Bold

Hi, I'm in 24 point Avant Garde

Hi, I'm in 24 point Lubalin Graph

Hi, I'm in 24 point Times

Fig. 5.15 ▲

Typefaces vary in apparent height, even though they are the same point size.

Using this traditional measuring system of picas and points has no particular advantage, except it may help you in communicating with designers and others who work in the publishing and printing trade. Picas and points also help you understand the size relationships between type and other page elements, such as margins.

You can set PageMaker's measuring system to picas, inches, millimeters, or whatever you like using the Preferences command. See Chapter 3, "Personalizing PageMaker Preferences."

Some letter-spacing moves (such as kerning and baseline shift) are measured in *em spaces.* The name comes from the width occupied by the letter *m.*

Now you may be saying to yourself, "If different typefaces are different sizes, even though they carry the same point value, how do you know the size of an em space? Or an en space?" The answer is, you don't know the size of an em because it varies, and that's the point. It is all relative.

You may think a character should always be the same width, like an inch or a mile or a pica. However, each font has a slightly different-sized character *m,* depending on the point size and what the designer had in mind when creating the letter.

You use ems for measuring kerning, because in that situation the goal is to improve the appearance of the type. You do that by adjusting the *relative* space between individual letters. It's terribly important to make the adjustment in context—in proportion to the size of that particular font. Using the em width as a measure of adjustments to letter spacing means the tiny kerning adjustment increments are automatically in proportion to that font's characters.

An em for any given typeface, by wide understanding among typographers, almost always equals the point size of the typeface. So 10-point type has a 10-point-wide em.

For trivia freaks, PageMaker's internal software code can handle a measurement of one twip, which is 1/1440th of an inch. A twip? Yes. It stands for *tw*entieth of a *p*oint.

DESIGN NOTE
Evaluate Readability of Your Typeface and Size Decisions

Trying out wild typefaces can be so much fun that you lose sight of the goal—to communicate. Before committing to a design, print out a sample page and hold it up at full arm's length. If you can't read the type easily, maybe even with your reading glasses removed, try to figure out why and consider tweaking the design. You simply may need to make the type larger or give the lines of type more space (leading). Some typefaces are harder to read than others. You probably would never use Zapf Chancery for body text, for example, because it's designed to be used as display (headline) type in large type sizes. (Some designers wouldn't use Zapf Chancery under any circumstances, but it has the advantage of coming free with most PostScript laser printers!)

Spacing Lines with Leading

The term *leading* comes from the old days when typesetters set type by hand. The line spacing was achieved with strips of metal (actually lead or brass) that fit between the lines of type. In those days, adding two points of leading to a section of type meant inserting a two-point-thick shim of metal to space out the type on the page.

In the DTP world, leading has generally come to mean something slightly different than the traditional definition. The Leading command in PageMaker sets the total space occupied by the line of type—the point size of the type plus the amount of leading as expressed in the old days. Using PageMaker, a typographer might say that type has been set "11 on 13," meaning 11-point type in 13-point leading (11 points of type plus 2 points of old fashioned leading).

You may understand this point more easily by looking at figure 5.16, which shows a series of PageMaker slugs with different amounts of leading. In each case, some type has been highlighted using the Text tool to reveal the height of the slug. (The term *slug* comes from the days of hot metal typesetting with a Linotype, where the type was cast in strips, called slugs.)

II

Working with Text

*PageMaker slugs,
showing different
amounts of leading.*

When the typesetter punched out this slug,
he was slugged by the editor. This was no
surprise, since the typesetter had made this
type 14 points on 14 points leading.

When the typesetter punched out this slug,
he was slugged by the editor. This was no
surprise, since the typesetter had made this
type 14 points on 16 points leading.

When the typesetter punched out this slug,
he was slugged by the editor. This was no
surprise, since the typesetter had made this
type 14 points on 20 points leading.

When the typesetter punched out this slug,
he was slugged by the editor. This was no
surprise, since the typesetter had made this
type 14 points on 24 points leading.

KEY CONCEPT:
Understanding PageMaker's Double-Location Leading Scheme

Unfortunately, PageMaker's leading scheme spreads the leading functions between two locations in the menu system. You set the amount of leading in the Type Specifications dialog box (for example, 13 points, 14 points, autoleading). However, you set the *method* for calculating that amount of leading (proportional, baseline, top of caps) in the Paragraph Specifications dialog box.

Even more confusing, if you select Autoleading in the Type Specifications dialog box, you must go to the Paragraph Specifications dialog box to adjust the percentage used to compute the autoleading amount.

This inconvenience ultimately turns out not so badly. Day to day, you make most of your leading adjustments in only one location—the type-formatting section of PageMaker. You probably will select a leading scheme one time and stick with it for an entire publication. The leading method is a fundamental decision, which has to do with your working style and the general nature of the work you usually perform in PageMaker.

As just mentioned, you have a choice of three types of leading in PageMaker. Top of caps, proportional, and baseline leading are explained in full detail in Chapter 6, "Formatting Paragraphs."

Setting Leading

With that background out of the way, let's talk about actually setting the amount of leading for your type.

Again, you have the choice of using one of the big three—the Type Specifications dialog box, the Type menu with its Leading submenu, or the Control palette (see fig. 5.17).

FIG. 5.17 ▶

The three access methods to get to PageMaker's leading functions.

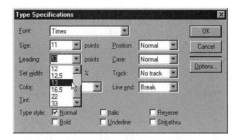

As you can see, the Type Specifications dialog box enables you to type your leading setting or choose from a scrolling list. Like the type size function, you can set leading in increments of a tenth of a point. You also may choose from a pop-up list of PageMaker's best guesses based on the point size of the type you select.

With the same degree of precision, you can set leading from the Control palette, by typing in the amount you want or by using the arrow just to the right of the leading box to get a list of best-guess choices.

Under the Type menu is a direct-access submenu for Leading, where you can choose quickly from among PageMaker's best guesses for leading settings. Also, like the type Size submenu, you have a choice for Other that gives you a box where you can type a more precise amount of leading. If you know you need a custom leading setting, it's usually quicker to use the Control palette or use the Ctrl+T shortcut to get the Type Specifications dialog box.

Automating Your Leading Design Decisions with Autoleading

Notice that each of the leading lists includes an option for Autoleading. Autoleading is the PageMaker factory-set default, which is what you get unless you specifically tell the program to use fixed leading.

Here's how autoleading works. PageMaker multiplies the point size of your text by 120 percent and uses that leading. PageMaker makes this autoleading calculation based on the largest type in a line of text.

Actually, the percentage of autoleading may be something other than 120 percent. That's simply the amount of autoleading PageMaker applies as a default. You can adjust this autoleading calculation by clicking the Options button in the Paragraph Specifications dialog box.

TIP ▶ It's Best to Use Fixed Leading, Not Autoleading

Autoleading is convenient and easy, but you almost always should use fixed leading. For one thing, you usually want to have all the lines in a paragraph spaced evenly. Check figure 5.18 to see what happens when you put a bit of large type into a paragraph formatted with autoleading rather than fixed leading.

For another thing, who says that 120 percent leading is the right thing for your publication? Leading is a design decision and a big part of your control over how your type looks. Do you want your type to look dark and dense? In that case, use a small amount of leading compared to the point size. Do you want an open and airy look to your type? That format usually makes for improved readability, so you may want to use more than 120 percent leading, depending on the typeface you've chosen.

Fig. 5.18 ▶

The potentially evil side of autoleading when combining point sizes of type. The second paragraph has been formatted with fixed leading instead of autoleading.

Even now, the lurking aardvark crept forward across the desert sands. Its belly scraped along on the cool grit, providing an unnecessary reminder that hunger gnawed at the edges of its dim existence.

Even now, the lurking aardvark crept forward across the desert sands. Its belly scraped along on the cool grit, providing an unnecessary reminder that hunger gnawed at the edges of its dim existence.

Giving Your Type Weight and Style

In table 5.1, you can see that PageMaker has many options for weighting and styling your type—bold, italic, underline, and strikethrough. You also may use a reverse style to etch out the shape of your type against a contrasting background, letting the underlying paper show through.

TABLE 5.1   PageMaker Type and Styling Options

Type Styling	Keyboard Shortcut
Normal	Ctrl+Shift+spacebar
Bold	Ctrl+Shift+B
Italic	Ctrl+Shift+I
Underline	Ctrl+Shift+U
~~Strikethrough~~	Ctrl+Shift+S
Reverse	Ctrl+Shift+V

When typographers talk about the *weight* of type, one of the things they mean is whether the type is bold or italic. Italic is generally considered lighter than normal type, and bold is heavier. Typefaces often include other weights (such as demibold or black), but the weights generally are not accessible by keyboard shortcuts.

TIP ▶ Adjust Spacing When Mixing Italic and Roman Type

When setting italic type, notice how the letters lean over to the right. In some typefaces, italic styling may look as if you left out the space after an italicized word as your text switches back to normal (Roman) type. The degree of the problem depends on what typeface you have chosen, because of the tremendous variation in designs. Try these techniques and pick one that suits your design:

▶ As a rule, you probably want to format the space following the italicized word (the *word space*, as typographers say) in normal type. That space generally is more suitable than the italic word space.

▶ In headline type especially, try kerning the space between the italicized and Roman typeset words. Kerning is covered later in this chapter's section "Spacing Pairs of Letters with Kerning."

▶ As a last resort, try using an em space or an en space after the italic text. These special spaces tend to be wider than regular spaces. Type an em space with Ctrl+Shift+M and an en space with Ctrl+Shift+N. You can even try a thin space, which is Ctrl+Shift+T.

The three standard techniques for accessing PageMaker commands hold true for applying all the type style keyboard shortcuts you see in table 5.1.

In the Type Specifications dialog box, you have a series of check boxes to select or deselect each option.

Under the Type menu, the Type Style submenu lists the same options, which you can select in the usual way.

In the Control palette, use the buttons below the typeface name field. You can remember which button does what from the first initial on the buttons and the appearance of the labeling letters. Use the arrow keys to move between the options; turn them on and off using the spacebar.

TIP ▷ **Use Keyboard Shortcuts for Type Attributes**

Style type using keyboard shortcuts. You don't need to use a menu or a Control palette button. If you need memory prompting, the shortcuts are displayed beside their matching commands in the Type menu and submenus, and the shortcuts are listed beside their respective text styles in table 5.1. For example, Shift+Ctrl+B sets type in bold and Shift+Ctrl+I italicizes your text.

Of the styles shown in table 5.1, the reverse attribute isn't technically a type style or weight. Reverse styling doesn't change the shape or thickness of a letter's strokes. It simply sets the type to the color of the paper. You can put a black box behind the type, and the reversed type "cuts" through the black to the paper behind. Why not assign the color white to the type? That wouldn't work if one of the printing plates had white ink. Reversing also avoids confusion if you are working on non-white paper. What if the paper was ecru or light violet or you were using a light-colored ink on black paper?

TIP ▷ **Special Setup Required for Reverse Type in Non-PostScript Printers**

Laserjet printers (PCL types, as opposed to ones that use PostScript) have trouble printing reverse type. The trick is to go to Windows' Printer Setup dialog box and turn on the setting to print text as graphics.

Design Note
Underlining Marks You

Try to restrain your urge to use underline except in special cases. The underline habit comes from the old typewriter days, when no other typographical tool was available to give emphasis to words. PageMaker offers bold and italic type styles that are more professional than underline.

Automating Capitalization

You can use the case attribute to set the case of your text. The advantage of this setting comes from its temporary nature—you have the flexibility to switch case without retyping the text. If some design change requires you to go back to normal uppercase and lowercase letters, just change the styling back to normal case.

Figure 5.19 shows the effect of these different case options.

Fig. 5.19 ▶

Effects of the All Caps and Small Caps commands.

Normal Case
Small Caps
ALL CAPS

Use the Case command in the Type Specifications dialog box to automate your capitalization. Just click the box next to the Case item, and you get a list of Normal, All Caps, and Small Caps.

You also can set case with the Type Style option buttons in the Control palette, right under the typeface box.

Finally, you can set case from the keyboard. Use Ctrl+Shift+K for all caps.

The case style doesn't appear in the Type Style submenus.

If you want to adjust the relative height of the small caps and big caps in the Small Caps Case styling option, click the Options button in the Type Specifications dialog box. The Type Options dialog box appears, and you can adjust PageMaker's default figures. You use this same dialog box for baseline shift and for customizing settings for subscript and superscript.

Design Note
Learn Design by Observation

Good type design generally boils down to a lot of experience mixed in with some natural talent for understanding the relationship between visuals and communication. You can do a great deal to train your design sense just by keeping your eyes open. You gain this experience in your everyday world without sitting in front of your computer. Notice the graphics on a billboard, the typeface for the ending credits on a TV show, the colors in the latest newsletter from the Royal Beekeeping Society—these are all design lessons.

This suggestion may seem utterly basic and obvious, but we all do tend to overlook the obvious in our daily lives. Of course, you tune your powers of observation by

II

Working with Text

experimenting with your own work to see what looks best. Absorb design insight wherever you can find it. Consider some of the newsletters or other desktop publishing resources listed in Chapter 1, "Touring PageMaker."

Adjusting Letter Space Using Kerning, Tracking, and Width

Three PageMaker type attributes have to do with the space your type occupies on the page. These attributes are kerning, width, and tracking. It's important not to confuse width or tracking with kerning, although they have some similarities.

Kerning sets the space between specific pairs of letters.

Tracking is an automated way to adjust letter spacing over a range of text and to make that adjustment in proportion to the size of the type.

Width adjusts the horizontal width of letters without changing the space between them and without changing their vertical size.

Spacing Pairs of Letters with Kerning

With PageMaker, you can use kerning to make extremely fine adjustments to the space between letters. In fact, PageMaker 6.0 now enables you to trim or add space between letters in increments of 1/1,000 of an em. The old limit was 1/100 of an em.

Why would you want to kern a pair of letters? Aside from using kerning to create special effects, you use kerning to make spacing adjustments that you believe will make your type more readable and more visually attractive. Kerning is pretty subjective stuff.

Kerning most often comes up when you are designing headlines or other displays of large type. Larger-than-life type deserves greater care on its appearance because headlines are in a feature role and therefore attract more of a reader's visual focus.

You almost always adjust letter kerning by pairs. For example, making some adjustment on the letters T and O is common, as you can see in figure 5.20. Letters are different shapes and therefore appear to take up different space on the line, assuming you aren't using a monospace typeface such as Courier. The crossbar of the T in unadjusted type ends completely before the circle of the O begins on the line. Because of this quirk in the shapes of the letters, more space seems to appear between this specific pair of letters than between others in the surrounding text. Using kerning, you can adjust a pair of letters so they nestle together visually without encroaching on one another.

Fig. 5.20 ▶

*An example of
kerning a letter
pair.*

TO
TO
TO

It's possible to select many letters and kern the whole range of them, but that's a little like performing surgery with an ax. When you must adjust the overall space occupied by a group of letters, assign tracking or width attributes—not kerning.

For large masses of text (a book maybe), you probably should let PageMaker's automatic pair kerning take over. Few people have the time or money to manually kern every clumsy pair of characters in 300 pages of 11-point type.

Design Note
Kerning Should Equalize the Apparent Space Between Letters

When kerning, aim for this objective: the reader's eye should be able to leap the small space between two letters easily, without impairing readability by getting the letters so close together that they look cramped. Instead of being broken up by the differences in apparent spacing between letters, the letters become a single comfortably spaced mass of visual information. This point may be easier to understand if you remember that speed readers often read entire lines of type in one glance. If type has been tuned to optimum spacing, a word is perceived as one smooth group, rather than individual letters.

Manual Kerning

When you are kerning manually, you need to see what's happening to your letter pairs as you work. For that reason, you are best off using PageMaker's keyboard commands to perform fine-kerning work. You can use the numeric keypad or the Backspace key to kern letters.

Using the numeric keypad (with Num Lock off):

▶ Remove space with Ctrl+– (4/100 em) or Shift+Ctrl+– (1/100 em)

▶ Add space with Ctrl++ (4/100 em) or Shift+Ctrl++ (1/100 em)

Using the Backspace key:

▶ Remove space with Ctrl+Backspace (4/100 em)

▶ Add space with Ctrl+Shift+Backspace (4/100 em)

You also can kern with the Control palette, using your mouse and the nudge buttons in the same way you do keyboard kerning. These nudge button moves take effect instantly, giving you real-time visual feedback on the effect of your changes. However, if you are a touch typist, reaching out to grab the mouse probably is slower than using the keyboard.

You also can type a kerning amount in the kerning text box of the Control palette, as indicated in the navigation chart in table 5.2. However, your changes aren't visible until you apply them by using the Apply button, pressing the Tab key, or pressing Enter. The Control palette does come in very handy if you know the precise amount of kerning you want to apply. In that case you can simply type the amount. The Control palette is your only access to the new 1/1,000 of an em kerning capability of PageMaker 6.0.

You can select a range of text and use the Control palette or keyboard commands to kern it *en masse*, by brute force. Except for special purposes, however, using this method generally isn't a terrific idea. Kerning is intended for fine adjustments of type spacing between a couple of letters. Instead of using this method to squeeze letters, consider using a tighter tracking setting. The width command may also help, if you are working on fitting copy into a limited space.

Remove all your manual kerning by selecting the text and pressing Shift+Ctrl+0 (zero, not on numeric keypad). Or, using the Control palette, highlight the text and enter a zero in the kern box.

TIP ▷ **Use Adobe Type Manager for Fine Adjustments to Type**

Assuming you are using PostScript fonts, don't even think about making really fine adjustments to type without installing Adobe Type Manager (ATM). ATM uses the PostScript outline fonts to draw type on your screen—the same PostScript fonts that will be used in your printer or the service bureau imagesetter. For that reason, ATM makes your on-screen view of type adjustments more accurate, more likely to match your final output precisely.

TIP ▷ **Use Kerning to Create Art Out of Type**

Kerning can help you turn plain text into a fancy logotype. You use kerning to intentionally distort the type. For more details on creating all sorts of special effects with text, see Chapter 15, "Creating Special Effects."

Automatic Kerning

PageMaker comes set to make automatic kerning adjustments to any type larger than four points. Most fonts come with built-in kerning pairs coded into them, and PageMaker seeks out those designated kerning combinations and uses them to make automatic adjustments. This automatic kerning setting is in the Spacing option of the Paragraph Specifications dialog box.

Expert Kerning

You can have an expert do your kerning for you by using the Expert Kerning command on the Type menu to open the Expert Kerning dialog box (see fig. 5.21). Expert Kerning uses a special set of rules to look at every pair of letters in your selected text and tune them to optimum spacing.

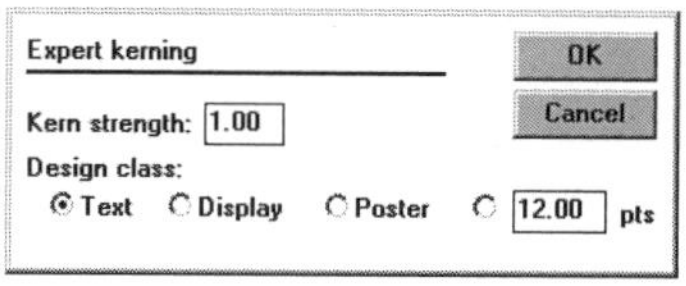

Fig. 5.21 ▶

*Expert Kerning,
ready to go to
work.*

Expert kerning

Kern strength: 1.00

Design class:
⊙ Text ○ Display ○ Poster ○ 12.00 pts

OK

Cancel

To perform Expert Kerning you must, of course, have some text selected. This text must be formatted in a PostScript Type 1 font, and you should have tracking and automatic kerning turned off in the paragraph where the text is located.

Choose the Type, Expert Kerning command, then type your kerning strength in the range of 0.00 to 2.00, with 2.00 being the tightest setting.

Using the Design Class options, you can give the Expert Kerning function more information about the kind of type you are kerning. The rules try to take into account the basic design of the type, in several different classifications. You also type in a type size, which should indicate the type size on which the original design was based.

Here's what this Design Class business is all about. The Expert Kerning Plug-in bases decisions on what the font designer seemed to have in mind when constructing the font. Usually a design is aimed at a particular use, which means a certain range of sizes are the optimum for that type. For example, Times was designed as body copy type. So, when working with Times, your Expert Kerning results will probably be better using the Text setting, even if you are going to set the type at a point size larger than a normal body copy size of 9 to 12 points.

Tuning Overall Letter Spacing with Tracking

People sometimes refer to tracking as track kerning. This term tends to grate on typographers, because kerning is something you do on a letter-by-letter basis. Tracking adjusts the spacing of large expanses of text and does it with no regard to the individual pairs of letters. It's main advantage is that it adjusts letter spacing as you change the size of the type. Tracking doesn't care if it's squeezing together a combination of T and O or the space between an O and an A. So, just use the term *tracking*, and you minimize your danger of some typographer smacking you up side the head with an old-fashioned rack of metal type.

II

Working with Text

You can see why someone may mix up the three techniques of tracking, kerning, and width setting. Figure 5.22 shows how tracking adjusts the space between letters. The technique is sort of like simultaneously kerning a bunch of letters. Also, you can see that the tracking setting makes a big change in the width that a selection of type takes up on the line.

Fig. 5.22 ▶

The effect of various tracking settings.

Tracking set very loose on 12 point type

Tracking set normal on 12 point type

Tracking set tight on 12 point type

Tracking set very loose on 9 point type

Tracking set normal on 9 point type

Tracking set tight on 9 point type

PageMaker's tracking table system makes spacing adjustments on the basis of the point size of the selected type. The tracking table tries to keep the adjustment in proportion to the type. A tracking scheme applied to 6-point type may actually spread it out a bit to make it more readable. On the other hand, that same tracking setting may tighten up 18-point type quite a bit because large type can tolerate the space squeezing better while maintaining its readability.

Tracking choices range from no tracking at all, to very loose, to very tight. You choose tracking from a list in the Type menu, the Type Specifications dialog box, or the Control palette. The tracks are individually tuned for each font, with many standard Adobe font settings included with PageMaker. If a font isn't in the PageMaker tracking database, a generic tracking setting kicks in.

Editing Tracks

You can edit your own tracking settings, either by changing the tracking for one of the fonts in the database, or by adding your personal tracking design to the database for a font that wasn't included in the database. Choose the Edit Tracks command from the Type menu's Expert Tracking submenu to get a graphics adjustment table like the one in figure 5.23.

Fig. 5.23 ▶

The Edit Tracks adjustment box.

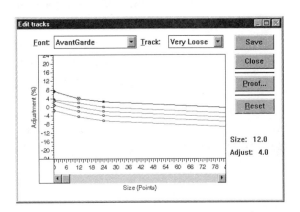

This table really helps to graphically illustrate how tracking works, doesn't it? Notice how spacing adjusts as the point size of the type increases from very small to quite large.

To edit tracks, choose the font you want to edit from the pull-down list in the upper-left corner. Then adjust the small boxes, or *handles*, that are strung along each track. Make the adjustment by clicking and dragging any handle on a track, sliding the handle point up or down to adjust the amount of space expansion or reduction. Slide the handle horizontally to adjust which point size of type the space adjustment affects.

Using the arrow keys to make adjustments may be more precise than using the mouse. Use the up and down arrows to raise or lower a handle after you have selected it.

You can add more handles by Alt+clicking the track line. Subtract handles by Alt+clicking the handle you want to delete.

Adjust an entire track line by selecting it, pressing Ctrl, and using the up or down arrows to move the line in 1/10 percent increments.

When you are satisfied, click the Proof button. The dialog box shown in figure 5.24 walks you through printing out a proof of the effect of your adjustments. You can choose between short or long sample text, and you can change the sample text if you like by editing the text shown in the sample text boxes at the bottom of the dialog box.

FIG. 5.24 ▶

Creating a proof of your tracking edit session results.

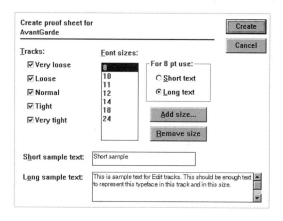

You may want to share your tracking edits among several different fonts. Simply choose the Copy command while viewing the tracks you want to adopt, select the destination font, and Paste. This step copies the entire set of tracks. You cannot copy individual tracks.

All this tracking information is stored in the file TRAKVALS.BIN, which is kept in your main PageMaker folder, inside the USENGLSH folder, which is nestled inside the RSRC folder.

Unfortunately, the Save command in Edit Tracks doesn't have a Save As option, so you can edit only the Tracking Values copy, which resides in the Adobe folder. If you want to create a special purpose custom Tracking Values file, use these steps:

1. Copy the TRAKVALS.BIN file, renaming the copy as a backup.
2. Perform your tracking edits.
3. Copy the edited TRAKVALS.BIN file to your publication folder and rename the original back to its proper title.

TIP ▶ Use Special Care for Track Edits Going to a Service Bureau

When you edit tracking and send your publication to a service bureau, you must send your edited type tracking information with your file, or the imagesetter results will not be what you expect. Make sure to send along your Tracking Values file. Fortunately, the Tracking Values file is one of those that PageMaker automatically collects if you use the Files For Remote Printing option in Save As when you bundle up your publication for transmission to a service bureau. Chapter 24, "Master Checklist for Desktop Publishing," includes a special checklist in the section "Submitting Files to the Service Bureau," designed to help you track such details.

TIP ▶ Track Editing May Be Just for the Experts

The Edit Tracks Plug-in is easy to use; what's not so easy is getting the most out of it. Unless you have special training in typography or want to achieve some special effect, chances are you'll do quite well with the tracking settings as they come from the PageMaker factory.

Adjusting the Width of a Type Selection

The Width command expands or reduces the horizontal size (the width) of every letter in your text selection, which is a lot like the condensed and expanded effect you find in many word processors. In other words, width changes the total line space that a group of words occupies, but it does not achieve this effect by changing the space between the letters, as you can see in figure 5.25. (This feature *does* change the width of the space character, and therefore has an effect on word spacing.)

Fɪɢ. 5.25 ▷

The effect of various Width command settings.

A width setting of 80%

A width setting of 90%

A width setting of 100%

A width setting of 110%

A width setting of 120%

You adjust the width of your text selection by giving it a percentage, with 100% being normal. To do so, access the width attribute through the Type menu, the Type Specifications dialog box, or the Control palette. Do keep in mind that folks who pride themselves on producing fine typography rarely, if ever, use this setting. It bastardizes the shapes of the letters.

Using Line End to Hold Words Together

One common reason people make some of these typographical adjustments (width, tracking, kerning) is to fit text properly on a line or page. The Line End function helps with this copyfitting task. You also may use the function for special text such as numbers or names that you want to keep together on one line, with no break.

Highlight some characters you need to glue together. In the Type Specifications dialog box, and only there, you find the Line End function. Choose No Break—referring to the fact that PageMaker holds the selected words together, not allowing them to break at the end of a line. You can see the effect in figure 5.26.

Fɪɢ. 5.26 ▷

Applying the No Break character attribute to a line end.

Type and graphics firm Gin, Key & Lime announces a major breakthrough in creativity.

Type and graphics firm Gin, Key & Lime announces a major breakthrough in creativity.

II

Working with Text

Setting Subscripts, Superscripts, and Baseline Shifts

The baseline of your type is an imaginary line drawn across the base of the letters. The descenders—tails of letters such as *y* and *g*—fall below that baseline.

Another thing that can descend below the baseline is a *subscript*. A *superscript* rises well above the baseline. These *scripts* are simply automated combinations of baseline shifting and smaller point sizes relative to the rest of the type around them.

Keep in mind that the baseline of a line of type rides high or low within its slug depending on your choice of leading method (proportional, baseline, top of caps). However, the baseline and the text always have the same relationship when they start. The text sits on the baseline with the descenders hanging below it. You can change that relationship with the baseline shift attribute.

Raising and Lowering Letters with Baseline Shift

Figure 5.27 demonstrates the baseline shift effect. You can apply it through the Type Specifications dialog box or Control palette techniques. Unlike type size and leading, baseline shift is not available through the T̲ype menu.

FIG. 5.27 ▶

Baseline shift raises and lowers letters in a line of type.

A hair ^{raising} experience may be $_{demoralizing}$

Your fastest access to PageMaker's baseline shifting powers comes in the Control palette. It has all the capability of the Type Specifications dialog box with less dialog box hassle. In the Control palette, the baseline shift is available in character mode, at the extreme right end of the palette (see fig. 5.28).

FIG. 5.28 ▶

The Control palette baseline shift field and setting arrows.

Baseline shift

If you decide to set baseline shift using the Type Specifications dialog box, you must burrow a layer deeper in the dialog box by using the O̲ptions button. The dialog box in figure 5.29 appears.

Fig. 5.29 ▷

*Access the Type
Options dialog
box from the Type
Specifications
dialog box.*

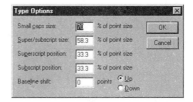

At the bottom of the Type Options dialog box, you can see the field and button combination you use to shift letters up or down against the baseline by whatever amount you choose (-1600 to +1600 points!).

TIP ▷ **Make On-the-Fly Changes to Measurement System in Control Palette**

The measurement you see in the Control palette baseline shift function matches whatever measurement system you set for the vertical ruler (see Chapter 2, "Exploring What's New In PageMaker 6.0"). You can, however, toggle through the measurement systems available in PageMaker. After you have clicked or tabbed into the baseline shift field, each time you press Shift+F12, you rotate to a different unit of measurement.

TIP ▷ **Close All Dialog Boxes Using Shift+Click**

When you get layers deep into a dialog box, it's a pain to click OK or cancel repeatedly to back out of it. (Wait till you get to setting rules in paragraphs, where you have dialog boxes three deep. You'll love this tip then.) When you are done making decisions in your dialog box, hold down the Shift key as you click OK or press Enter (or click Cancel or press Esc). The current dialog box and all the dialog boxes above it cascade close all at once. Of course, you may not even need this tip. In most cases, why not just use the Control palette in the first place and avoid the dialog box ordeal?

Using Superscript and Subscript

You've seen superscripts and subscripts before, of course. They're the hard-to-read little numbers that refer to footnotes at the bottom of the page.

Superscripts and subscripts combine baseline shift with an adjustment to a smaller type size. PageMaker automates this dual function for you. With one formatting command, you simultaneously raise or lower the type on the baseline and make the type smaller (or bigger, if you like). All you need to do is choose the sub- or superscript type attribute. (You can customize the degree of sub- or superscripting. More on that in a bit.)

As with many text attributes, the most direct ways to create the scripts are through a keyboard shortcut or the Control palette.

For subscripts, use Ctrl+\. For superscripts, use Ctrl+Shift+\.

On the Control palette, use the position buttons right below the font selection field—the buttons with the letter *S* and a choice between an up or down arrow for super or sub.

You also can set the scripts from the Type Specifications dialog box, using the Position option. Just click the box and a windowshade drop-down list gives you a choice of Normal, Subscript, or Superscript.

The sub- and superscript options are not available from the Type submenus.

You can customize the appearance of your sub- and superscripts. Refer to figure 5.29 to see the dialog box you get when you choose the Options button in the Type Specifications dialog box.

Type the percentage values, relative to the size of the type, that you want PageMaker to utilize for shrinking or growing the scripted character. Also indicate in the Baseline Shift box how far to position the type above and below the baseline.

DESIGN NOTE
Use Professional Typesetting Conventions: Part I

Many of us have fallen into nasty computer typesetting habits, based on the days when we learned to type on a cranky old manual typewriter. The following guidelines can help you make your publications look professional:

▼ Don't press the Enter key twice to space paragraphs. Instead, use leading and paragraph spacing settings. Paragraph spacing settings are discussed in Chapter 6, "Formatting Paragraphs."

▼ Don't use underlining for emphasis in text; use bold or italic.

▼ Use the professional curly quotation marks rather than the straight ones that look like inch marks. You can specify this setting in Preferences so PageMaker applies curly quotes automatically.

▼ Instead of using a double hyphen, use the character that the double hyphen is usually imitating, an em dash.

▼ Type only one space after sentence punctuation such as the period, question mark, and exclamation point. Most fonts have extra space built into the period character.

Using the Control Palette to Set Type

You can display the Control palette (or turn it off) by choosing it from the <u>Win</u>-dow menu or, faster yet, by using the keyboard shortcut Ctrl+' (apostrophe).

Figure 5.30 shows all the type attributes you can control from the Control palette when it's in character editing mode. In this figure, you can see that the palette is in the Character view because, just to the right of the Apply button, the letter A is highlighted, not the paragraph symbol.

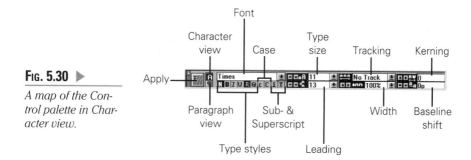

FIG. 5.30 ▶

A map of the Control palette in Character view.

The Control palette contains virtually every command you find in the first layer of the Type Specifications dialog box (except the Line <u>E</u>nd Break/No Break command.)

You already know the navigation principles for the Control palette from Chapter 1, "Touring PageMaker." Table 5.2 gives you a specialized navigation chart for the Control palette when it's in Character mode.

TABLE 5.2   Control Palette Navigation Chart

Action		Keyboard	Notes
Activate palette		Ctrl+` (grave)	Puts Control palette into gear so you don't accidentally type characters into your text.
Choose a command		Tab or Shift+Tab	Tabs from field to field in the palette (Shift+Tab goes backward).
Apply	![icon]	Tab, Shift+Tab, Enter	Implements any changes ordered in the Control palette.
Palette view	![icon]	Ctrl+Shift+` (grave)	Appears when the Text (Paragraph or Character) tool is selected. Switches between formatting type and formatting paragraphs.

TABLE **5.2**   **Continued**

Action	Keyboard	Notes
Font	Select from list or type the font name	PageMaker looks up the name from list as you type in characters.
Type styles, Case, Sub/Superscript	Arrow keys and spacebar	Use the arrow keys to make selection and spacebar to turn the option on and off.
Type size	Type a number or select from list	Accepts 4 to 650 points in 1/10 point increments. Nudge buttons make 1/10 point moves.
Leading	Type a number or select from list	Accepts 0 to 1300 points in 1/10 point increments. Nudge buttons make 1/10 point moves.
Tracking	Type the track name or select from list	Looks up name after you've typed a few characters.
Width	Type a number or select from list or click the nudge buttons	Accepts 5 percent to 250 percent from reference of 100 percent. Nudge buttons make 1 percent moves.
Kerning	Type a number or click nudge buttons	Ranges from -1 to +1 em.
[10] Baseline shift	Use Shift+F12 to rotate through measurement	Uses measurement chosen through the Preferences command within a range of -1600 to +1600 points from a base of zero.

TIP ▶   **Before Typing, Check Control Palette Activation**

Make certain you activate the Control palette before using the keyboard to run the Control palette in Text mode. Otherwise, you end up typing a lot of tabs and returns in your text by accident. If no highlight is visible in the Control palette, it isn't active.

Where to Go from Here

▶ Be sure to read Chapter 6, "Formatting Paragraphs." That chapter is especially important in context with this chapter because so many of the text and paragraph-formatting commands cross over these rather arbitrary boundaries.

▶ You can automate virtually every text attribute discussed in this chapter by including it in a paragraph style, the subject of Chapter 7, "Designing a Text Style System."

▶ You can use many of the text attributes in this chapter to build spectacular special effects, as discussed in Chapter 15, "Creating Special Effects."

▶ The Tactics Recipe on "Organizing Your Fonts" in Chapter 25, "Developing a System for Managing Your Type," is extremely helpful, especially if you, like most of us, manage to collect more fonts than you can remember you have.

Chapter 6

Formatting Paragraphs

This chapter on formatting paragraphs tells you all about:

The fundamental nature of a PageMaker paragraph.

Aligning text flush left, flush right, centered, justified, and force justified.

▼

Adjusting word and letter spacing for maximum readability in justified text.

▼

Tuning hyphenation.

▼

Creating tab stops, including special tabs that insert leaders, center columns, or align on decimal points.

▼

Setting paragraph indents and hanging indents.

▼

Aiding paragraph flow with page and column breaks

▼

Preventing widows and orphans.

▼

Developing a strategy for leading type.

AFTER TYPE, THE PARAGRAPH comes next in the hierarchy of PageMaker pages. It's a design element with text formatting power.

The paragraph visually organizes your type. Without paragraphs, your pages would be blobs of unbroken, and often unformatted, characters. Paragraphs do more than organize thought and provide grammatical structure. They visually contain and decorate—serve up your writing—making it inviting, pleasant to see, and easy to read. ▶ ▶ ▶

KEY CONCEPT:
Understanding the Nature of a PageMaker Paragraph

Hey, everybody knows what a paragraph is, right? This is too easy.

Well, okay then, multiple choice time. Choose the right answer and the winner gets the rest of the day off…unless you have a home office. If you work at home, you get to take out the trash, wash the car, or pay the paper boy instead.

A paragraph is which of the following?

▼ A collection of sentences dealing with a single, sharply focused idea, thought, or subject.

▼ A passage of text with the first line indented, visually marking it off as a paragraph.

▼ Any place with one of those funny-looking ¶ thingies.

If you went with the first definition, you probably are a terrific writer, but you may not understand the fundamental nature of a PageMaker paragraph. Not surprising, because the concept of a paragraph trips up more new PageMaker users than almost any other aspect of the program. So here's the key to understanding paragraphs in PageMaker (bear down hard on this thought—it has cosmic significance).

Every time you press the Enter key, you put one of those funny-looking ¶ thingies into your text. And that marks a PageMaker paragraph.

You can't see paragraph markers in the Layout view of PageMaker, but you can see them in PageMaker's Story Editor view. The Story Editor is covered in Chapter 9, "Editing Copy with the Story Editor," but here's a picture of what it looks like, just so you can get a graphic idea of how these paragraph markers work. Figure 6.1 shows some text in Story Editor view. Notice that each paragraph has a ¶ symbol at the end of it. Headlines, bulleted items, body copy—every time you press the Enter key, you make a PageMaker paragraph. I recommend turning on the Show Paragraph option in the Story Editor (or in Preferences). Spotting formatting issues is much easier if you can see exactly where each paragraph break occurs.

Indents, centering, justification, tabs, leading scheme, paragraph rules, control for widows and orphans, hyphenation scheme—these features and more are paragraph-based attributes. You cannot apply tabs or indents or any other paragraph-level attributes to a few characters or words in a paragraph. PageMaker doesn't let you do it. Unlike type attributes such as kerning or bold and italic, these typesetting moves apply to the entire paragraph. It's an all or nothing situation.

On a good note, because of this behavior, you can apply a paragraph-based formatting attribute by clicking anywhere in the paragraph. The formatting applies to the whole paragraph. Instead of selecting all the text in the paragraph, just click anywhere in the paragraph text.

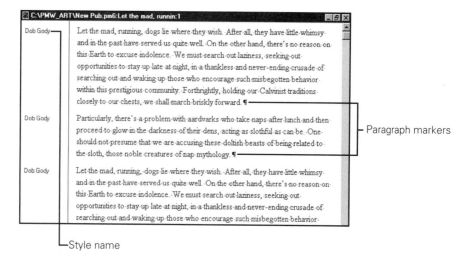

Fig. 6.1 ▲

PageMaker's paragraphs all have paragraph markers at the end.

Also, the paragraph-based formatting attributes move with the paragraph marker. You can copy and paste a paragraph marker from one paragraph to the other, and all the attributes in the first paragraph transfer to the second paragraph. Think of the paragraph symbol as a storage bin for the formatting of any particular paragraph.

Choosing Different Text Alignment Options

You probably are already familiar with left and right alignment, centering, and justification from using your word processor. PageMaker, however, takes type alignment beyond the word processor level.

Check figure 6.2 for examples of the five basic kinds of text alignment you can have in PageMaker: left, right, center, justified, and force justified.

The following list describes each type of alignment and lists its keyboard shortcut:

  ▶ *Flush left text* (Shift+Ctrl+L) is flush against the left side of the column, making a straight line of text along the left side. Sometimes you hear flush left alignment called *ragged right*, referring to the ragged edge you get along the right side because you are aligning only the left side of the column.

II

Working with Text

FIG. 6.2 ▶

Samples of flush left, flush right, centered, justified, and force justified text.

Type Plucker Forced To Retire ———— Centered

The right honorable Henry Slugbinder took his leave today of
the printing shop where he has worked for nearly three decades. He began plucking type as a boy, choosing letters from
among the type bins at the village weekly. He never missed a ── Flush Left
deadline and the paper's pages were always filled with elegantly set type, however the financial difficulties at the
Village Au Courant finally left the management no choice.

— *Special To The Au Courant From Philadelphia* ── Flush Right

Type   Plucker   Forced   To   Retire ── Force Justified

The right honorable Henry Slugbinder took his leave today of
the printing shop where he has worked for nearly three decades.
He began plucking type as a boy, choosing letters from among
the type bins at the village weekly. He never missed a deadline
and the paper's pages were always filled with elegantly set type, ── Justified
however the financial difficulties at the Village Au Courant finally left the management no choice.
— *Special To The Au Courant From Philadelphia*

▶ *Flush right* (Shift+Ctrl+R), or *ragged left*, is the opposite of flush right—
aligned along the right side of the column.

▶ *Centered text* (Shift+Ctrl+C) is just that—centered. PageMaker automatically calculates the space occupied by the letters on the centered line,
divides that distance in half, and places the center point of each line of text
precisely on the horizontal midpoint of the column of type.

▶ *Justified text* (Shift+Ctrl+J) aligns both ways, presenting a straight line down
both the left and the right side of the column. When it comes to justified
type, any comparison between word processing and PageMaker typesetting quickly screeches to a dead stop. It may not be apparent at a quick
glance, but PageMaker offers real typographic sophistication compared to
any of the word processors (adjustable everything, from hyphenation to
word and letter spacing).

▶ *Force justification* (Shift+Ctrl+F) uses a sledge hammer to splatter your text,
forcing it to stretch all the way across a column, even if that means putting
a half-inch of space between two words on the line. Force justification is
for special effects.

Aligning Text Using the Dialog Box, Menu, and Palette

Setting text alignment works about the same as all the other PageMaker text attributes. You have three methods from which to choose: the standard PageMaker
trio of dialog box, menu, and palette.

Setting Alignment with the Paragraph Specifications Dialog Box

You can use a comprehensive tool, the Paragraph Specifications dialog box, to
set alignment (and all the other paragraph attributes for that matter).

To bring up the Paragraph Specifications dialog box in figure 6.3, you can use the keyboard shortcut Ctrl+M, or you can pull down the Type menu and choose Paragraph.

FIG. 6.3 ▷

The Paragraph Specifications dialog box.

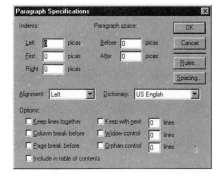

Setting Alignment with an Express Menu

You can align text express menu style by using the Alignment hierarchical submenu from the Type menu (see fig. 6.4). The keyboard shortcuts for each of the alignment methods are listed right in this menu.

FIG. 6.4 ▷

You can use the Alignment sub-menu commands to align type.

Setting Alignment with the Control Palette

The Control palette gives you instant on-screen access to alignment. The alignment icons are located just to the right of the paragraph indicator, as shown in figure 6.5.

II

Working with Text

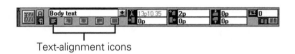

Text-alignment icons

The Control palette's text-alignment icons duplicate the alignment functions in the Type, Alignment menu.

D<small>ESIGN</small> N<small>OTE</small>
Flush Right or Centered Type Is Text with an Attitude

Any time you see text aligned to the right side of the column, you can bet that the designer made a bargain with the very tempting devil of design and ignored the angel of readability.

Keep in mind when making alignment decisions that you are probably trading off readability for design when you use any alignment other than flush left or justified type. This isn't to say you shouldn't use these valuable design techniques. But you should regard the techniques as special purpose tools to be used in moderation when you are trying for some special effect. In other words, flush right and centered text have an attitude. Figure 6.6 shows some examples of centered and right-aligned type so you can see how these alignments affect the readability of body copy.

F<small>IG</small>. **6.6** ▶

Flush right and centered type samples—the design/readability trade-off.

Gwimbling Prohibited Here!

Skinks, being despicable creatures, have been irrevocably prohibited from gwimbling in this location. Beach use has been restricted to the loitering hours of dawn. Until such time as conditions improve, this official decree shall be as ineffective as it ever were.

—— Centered body copy

**Art Monger Proclaims "Gwimbling"
Performance Art, Completely Legal**

"Following the avant garde performance art traditions of the early Nineteenth Century skink has not been easy," shouted the art monger, playfully.

—— Flush right body copy

"However, gwimbling gives me a chance to dig my roots into the fertile soil of these nearly ancient traditions of protest, posturing and peskiness!" he continued.

Justifying Text: Word and Letter Spacing, Automatic Kerning

Selecting justified text alignment is easy. But PageMaker, in order to justify your type to the exact width of your column, must go through each line and tweak the spacing between every word and letter. PageMaker also must factor in all your other elements of spacing and line breaks, such as automatic and manual kerning, consecutive hyphens limit, and tracking.

So on the surface, justification may seem to be the simplest of maneuvers, but quite a bit of computer power churns away in the background dealing with all the interacting variables. This section covers those variables and how you can manage them.

KEY CONCEPT:
Understanding PageMaker's Special Spacing Power

Comparing PageMaker to a word processor may help you understand the rich, powerful, and complex nature of PageMaker's justification.

In a word processor, the justification turns out to be just as simple as it seems to be when you choose the justification option on a menu. You don't get much control, just what the program hands you. Word processors have built-in and permanently locked programming formulas called *algorithms*, which calculate how much space to add or subtract between words to make lines come out evenly on both the right and left margins. It's pretty primitive stuff compared to PageMaker's typographical potential.

You could simply use PageMaker's factory settings for justification—the same way you use your word processor—ignoring PageMaker's capacity for fine typographic adjustments. The things that go into calculating justification, including word and letter spacing, are set to be suitable for basic everyday layout work. Really, you could work a very long time in PageMaker without ever knowing how to fine-tune all these attributes for setting justified text. Many people do.

On the other hand, typesetting power ranks among PageMaker's great benefits, perhaps one of the primary reasons to buy it. So, to get the most out of PageMaker, delve deeply into its standard settings for word and letter spacing. Text justification—done well—requires special attention to PageMaker's word and letter spacing power. Not only does PageMaker enable you to adjust these settings to compensate for the special requirements of your publication, but it also has a potent set of internal algorithms working in the background to put your adjustments to work.

Word spacing, letter spacing, kerning, hyphenation, width, and tracking all affect each other and must be changed with care. You can really screw up typesetting quality if you don't carefully monitor the collective, interacting effects of these settings as you work. When you punch up one factor, you generally need to shave down another related one.

Here's a contextual index to help you pull together all the factors that have an influence on justification in PageMaker:

▽ For an overall strategy for handling all these interrelated factors, check this chapter's section called Tactics Recipe: "Setting Up a Justification System."

▽ Like word and letter spacing, automatic kerning is controlled in the Spacing Attributes dialog box under Paragraph Specifications. You find automatic kerning information in the section "Adjusting the Automatic Kerning Trigger Point."

II

Working with Text

▼ Manual kerning, width, and tracking are covered in Chapter 5, "Typing In Your Type," in the section, "Adjusting Letter Space Using Kerning, Tracking, and Witdth."

▼ Hyphenation (assuming you have hyphenation turned on) particularly affects justification. For all the details, look to "Hyphenating Words" later in this chapter.

▼ Using paragraph styles greatly en-

hances your ability to quickly and consistently control all the attributes that go into quality line justification. Paragraph styles are covered in Chapter 7, "Designing a Text Style System."

▼ Also, for some special context on the design issues associated with justified type, check out this chapter's "Design Note: Flush Left Versus Justified Type Readability."

Setting Paragraph Spacing Attributes

Word and letter spacing, along with hyphenation, are PageMaker's primary justification tools. You control them through the Spacing Attributes dialog box, which you access by clicking the Spacing button in the Paragraph Specifications dialog box (see fig. 6.7). Don't forget—you can call the Paragraph Specifications dialog box with the keyboard shortcut, Ctrl+M.

FIG. 6.7 ▶

The Spacing Attributes dialog box.

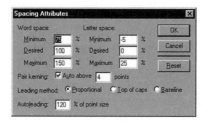

When you first install PageMaker, the program comes with values already entered in each field of the Spacing Attributes dialog box. You can set these items to suit your own readability standards and sense of design. That's the purpose of the next few sections—to describe how each of these spacing settings works.

Setting Word Spacing

You have three Word Space settings you can adjust: Minimum, Desired, and Maximum. To understand what these settings mean, you need to know that every font comes with a built-in standard allowance for the *space band*. This typographer's term refers to the amount of space allotted to the space character inserted between words when you press the spacebar. In justified text, PageMaker narrows or widens the space based on these Word Space percentage settings. The result, along with the other spacing attributes, is a line that completely fills the column.

You usually set Desired at 100 percent, meaning that PageMaker attempts to provide exactly what the font designer intends for space between words. When you are working in a justified text paragraph, the Minimum and Maximum settings specify a range on either side of your desired setting. PageMaker then uses this range as it makes line lengths work out correctly so it can justify your text.

PageMaker comes with factory defaults for a Minimum setting of 75 percent and a Maximum setting of 150 percent. This means that PageMaker, when creating justified lines, is allowed to reduce spacing between the words on a line to as little as 75 percent of what the designer felt was optimum and increase space to a maximum of 150 percent.

Figure 6.8 shows the effects of two different word spacing settings, with no other justification factors in place (hyphenation turned off, no kerning, letter spacing in neutral).

FIG. 6.8 ▶

The effect of different Word Space settings.

As they swam toward the setting sun, the shark and the platypus drove their sleek bodies into wave after wave, streaming with the phospherescence of the tiny food chain members who had volunteered to be the plankton of the evening. The sea urchin offered a bottle of crisp chardonnay. They sipped, and enjoyed the filet of kelp flotation bulbs. A subtle discernment of pleasure seeped through their aura of invincible seaworthiness.

—— Word spacing = 100/125/150 percent

As they swam toward the setting sun, the shark and the platypus drove their sleek bodies into wave after wave, streaming with the phospherescence of the tiny food chain members who had volunteered to be the plankton of the evening. The sea urchin offered a bottle of crisp chardonnay. They sipped, and enjoyed the filet of kelp flotation bulbs. A subtle discernment of pleasure seeped through their aura of invincible seaworthiness.

—— Word spacing = 50/75/100 percent

TIP ▶ Get PageMaker to Alert You to Questionable Spacing

Sometimes it's just plain impossible to do a perfect job of juggling all these justification variables. PageMaker will alert you to the situation if you ask it to do so. In the Preferences dialog box (under the File menu), check the Show Loose/Tight option. A band of gray or yellow (depending on your hardware and software setup) will then highlight any text locations where PageMaker could not quite implement your spacing settings. Often this happens because the column is too narrow for the type size or because the line has a lot of technical words that can't be hyphenated because they are not in PageMaker's dictionary.

These helpful alerts actually trigger a lot of tech support calls to Adobe because people don't realize that PageMaker is trying to help, and they wonder why these bars of yellow or gray are running behind their text.

II

Working with Text

Setting Letter Spacing

If you tell it to do so, PageMaker can adjust letter spacing to justify a line.

As with word spacing, the designer of a font builds into the design an optimum space between letters, called the *side bearings*—the spaces on either side of the actual character.

Another technical term relating to letter spacing is the *pen advance*, sort of like the horizontal distance a calligrapher's pen advances in the process of drawing a new letter. The pen advance distance runs from the left edge of one letter to the left edge of the next one, including the character and its left side bearing.

The defaults for the Letter Space settings are Minimum –5%, Desired 0%, and Maximum 25%. That means PageMaker tries its best to make zero changes to letter spacing, but if it must, it tries to remove no more than 5 percent of the letter spacing in a line and add no more than 25 percent.

Of course, you can type values that better suit your needs. You may even want to put 0 percent in each of these boxes. Many highly respected typography experts feel strongly that anything other than 0 percent is wrong because letter spacing is usually created by a typographer, who intends the type to look a particular way with a particular amount of space—with the side bearings designed into each letter.

In figure 6.9, you see how letter spacing settings can influence the look of a line. These letter spacing examples are set with no other justification factors affecting the type.

TIP ▶ **Setting for Desired Word and Letter Spacing Affects Unjustified Text**

The range settings for Minimum and Maximum word and letter spacing come into play only with justified text paragraphs. However, the Desired settings are always in effect and do have an impact on line breaks even when you are setting unjustified text. You can increase word or letter spacing by putting more than 100 percent in the Desired Word Space box and more than 0 percent in the Desired Letter Space entry. You need to be conscious of this fact if you have set some non-default desired spacing and then switch from justified to unjustified text. In fact, you could use the desired spacing to adjust line length in unjustified text, although tracking, width, and hyphenation settings are probably more precise, easily adjusted, and predictable ways to do the job.

FIG. 6.9 ▶

The results of two alternatives for letterspacing settings.

As they swam toward the setting sun, the shark and the platypus drove their sleek bodies into wave after wave, streaming with the phospherescence of the tiny food chain members who had volunteered to be the plankton of the evening. The sea urchin offered a bottle of crisp chardonnay. They sipped, and enjoyed the filet of kelp flotation bulbs. A subtle discernment of pleasure seeped through their aura of invincible seaworthiness.

—— Letter spacing =
0/5/10 percent

As they swam toward the setting sun, the shark and the platypus drove their sleek bodies into wave after wave, streaming with the phospherescence of the tiny food chain members who had volunteered to be the plankton of the evening. The sea urchin offered a bottle of crisp chardonnay. They sipped, and enjoyed the filet of kelp flotation bulbs. A subtle discernment of pleasure seeped through their aura of invincible seaworthiness.

—— Letter spacing =
−20/−5/0 percent

Adjusting the Automatic Kerning Trigger Point

PageMaker typesetting shines in this area—automatic kerning. Most fonts are designed so that several hundred pairs of letters (and sometimes many more) are predefined for kerning whenever they appear together in a line of type. These designs assume the software is programmed to take advantage of the built-in *kern pairs*, as they're called. Generally, a word processor is deaf to auto-kerning and unable to take advantage of these built-in kerning pairs. However, PageMaker recognizes the designers' specifications and puts them to work when you turn on the Pair Kerning option.

The question is, at which type size should this automatic kerning trigger into operation? The smaller the type, the more difficulty the eye has in discerning any kerning effect, which represents a point of diminishing returns. PageMaker comes set so that automatic kerning takes effect on all justified type of sizes above four points. I recommend leaving kerning set right there. If, however, you want to get rid of automatic kerning for some reason, simply click off the Pair Kerning box next to the A̲uto Above label.

One point needs emphasis: kerning pairs are not the same as letter spacing. *Kerning* refers to adjustments made to better fit specific pairs of letters together whenever they occur in text. That's *pairs*, as in kerning pairs. Letter spacing (or pen advance) adjusts the spacing for each individual character and ignores the adjacent characters.

If you are wondering about the leading options you see in the Spacing Attributes dialog box, that topic is coming up later in this chapter in the section "Choosing Your Leading Method."

DESIGN NOTE
Flush Left Versus Justified Type Readability

At the Annual Typographers' Ball, this controversy sets off more fist fights on the dance floor than anything else—even cutting in on somebody else's date. I don't want

II

Working with Text

to get popped in the mouth, so I'll just lay out some of the issues, and you can decide for yourself.

Because English speakers read the language from left to right, pretty much everybody agrees that body copy should be set either flush left or justified. That way, your eye always knows where to go when it moves down the page because everything is lined up on the left side of the column. The controversy concerns what to do with the right side of the column—should you line it up (justified type) or rag it (flush left/ragged right)?

Because it has a ragged edge along the right side, flush left alignment gives your text an informal feel. The bumps of white space along the non-aligned edge have the effect of opening up the copy.

On the other hand, justified text fills all the space in a column. It therefore looks darker, and because both ends of each line are evened up along the column edges, justified type has a formal feel.

As for readability, some designers argue that the ragged space bumps down the right side of the column provide the reader with "landmarks" as the eyes scan down the page. Others contend that justified type is easier for people to read because the strict edges provide a better guide for the eye, so every line is the same length and the reader always knows what to expect.

On the other hand, justified type has more hyphenation and, if poorly set, may have uneven word and letter spacing, which may reduce readability. The width of a column influences these factors a great deal, as does hyphenation, word spacing, and letter spacing settings. In other words, your quality of execution has a big impact on the readability of your justified type. Also, much depends on other readability issues such as size of type, typeface, leading, space before and after paragraphs, column rules, and on and on.

As usual with most design issues, both sides of the argument have a good deal of merit. Rather than settle on always using justified or left aligned type, you can experiment with both on every project to see what's best for that particular situation. It's the only way to account for all the variables.

Hyphenating Words

With PageMaker, hyphenation seems so simple at first. You cruise along, and the software handles the whole thing for you. As a matter of fact, you could do a lot worse than simply letting PageMaker run the way it comes from the factory. If, however, you want to fine-tune for optimum hyphenation performance, check out "Tactics Recipe: Setting Up a Justification System" later in this chapter.

Using the Hyphenation Dialog Box Options

Use the dialog box in figure 6.10 to control hyphenation in your publication. You access the dialog box by choosing Hyphenation from the Type menu. In PageMaker 6.0, the old keyboard shortcut to reach Hyphenation is not available. That shortcut is used for the Master Pages palette instead. (Not a bad trade, would you say?)

FIG. 6.10 ▷

The Hyphenation dialog box.

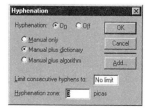

After you arrive at the Hyphenation dialog box, you have the following options:

▷ *Hyphenation: On/Off.* You can turn off hyphenation so it doesn't work, even if you attempt to manually hyphenate the text with soft hyphens. (They are hyphens you type into text, as opposed to hyphens inserted by PageMaker. These hyphens are soft because they take effect only at the ends of lines and are otherwise invisible. More on soft hyphens later.)

▷ *Manual Only.* PageMaker does not actively perform any hyphenation but permits you to insert manual hyphenation (soft hyphens).

▷ *Manual Plus Dictionary.* Stepping up in hyphenation assistance, PageMaker can use the spelling dictionary to hyphenate words at syllable breaks.

▷ *Manual Plus Algorithm.* PageMaker can calculate where to break words by using an algorithm (an internal mathematical formula) in addition to its spelling dictionary.

▷ *Limit Consecutive Hyphens To.* You can tell PageMaker how many lines in a row can have hyphens. (You can enter a number from 1 to 255, or type **No limit**).

▷ *Hyphenation Zone.* You can set up a hyphenation zone, the strip of territory at the right side of your column where PageMaker makes its hyphenation decisions. If a word starts within this zone and can't fit on the line, it will be moved to the next line. For that reason it's sometimes more helpful to think of it as the no-hyphenation zone. This function does not work in justified text.

II

Working with Text

Hyphenation is all about line length. Whatever alignment you have chosen—ragged right or left, centered, or justified—you want to get the lines as near as possible to the same length, unless you are trying for some special effect. Figure 6.11 shows how the hyphenation zone setting can affect PageMaker's work on left-aligned type. In both examples, the hyphenation dictionary has been used, but no algorithms. All spacing attributes have been turned off or set to have minimum effect.

FIG. 6.11 ▶

An extreme example of hyphenation zone settings, just to demonstrate the effect of the zone on the right hand side of the column.

As they swam toward the setting sun, the shark and the platypus drove their sleek bodies into wave after wave, streaming with the phospherescence of the tiny food chain members who had volunteered to be the plankton of the evening. The sea urchin offered a bottle of crisp chardonnay. They sipped, and enjoyed the filet of kelp flotation bulbs. A subtle discernment of pleasure seeped through their aura of invincible seaworthiness. ——— 12-pica hyphenation zone

As they swam toward the setting sun, the shark and the platypus drove their sleek bodies into wave after wave, streaming with the phospherescence of the tiny food chain members who had volunteered to be the plankton of the evening. The sea urchin offered a bottle of crisp chardonnay. They sipped, and enjoyed the filet of kelp flotation bulbs. A subtle discernment of pleasure seeped through their aura of invincible seaworthiness. ——— 3-pica hyphenation zone

Manually Hyphenating Your Text

To take over from PageMaker and do all the hyphenation yourself, turn on manual hyphenation in the Hyphenation dialog box. Do *not* turn off hyphenation. This may seem a bit confusing, but if you turn off PageMaker's hyphenation, you turn it completely, absolutely, and utterly off. PageMaker then loses its capability to "read" the special soft hyphens you insert for manual tuning of hyphenation breaks.

The primary tool of manual hyphenation is the *discretionary hyphen* or *soft hyphen*, which you enter with the Ctrl+ - (hyphen) key combination.

If a line falls so that your hyphenated word would rest in the hyphenation zone, as defined in the Hyphenation dialog box, the line will break at your soft hyphen mark. Soft hyphens have priority over PageMaker's hyphenation dictionary or algorithms when the program is making hyphenation decisions.

If the column width changes, or if you change the hyphenation zone or edit the line (never happens to us, of course), the soft hyphen disappears from view when it shifts up into the midst of the line. The soft hyphen comes back into effect if further editing slides it back into the hyphenation zone.

When the inevitable happens and someone edits the copy after you've performed your elegant hyphenation magic, you will deeply regret having used regular hyphens to break words. These hard hyphens are pulled into the middle of a line and there they stay—a stupid and glaring typo. You could do a search and replace to find all the hard hyphens in your 250-page book, going through each hyphen to see if it's used for a hyphenated word or a hyphenated line. Or you can just use soft hyphens in the first place and save yourself the trouble.

Adding, Editing, or Removing Hyphenated Words in the Dictionary

Notice the <u>A</u>dd button in the Hyphenation dialog box? You use the <u>A</u>dd button to add words to your custom PageMaker dictionary, your User Dictionary (see fig. 6.12). Fortunately, PageMaker uses the same dictionary for spelling and hyphenation, so adding a word in hyphenation also customizes and expands your spelling dictionary.

Fig. 6.12 ▶

The Add Word dialog box with a word prioritized for hyphenation.

When you add a word to the dictionary, you can preset your hyphenation for that word and even prioritize your hyphenation breaks. You use the tilde (˜) key when you type the word into the Add Word dialog box.

You assign each hyphenation break a priority by the number of tildes, you insert at each possible break. When trying to adjust line length, PageMaker first attempts to hyphenate that word where you marked it with a single tilde, then two tildes, and then three.

Take maximum advantage of the Add Word feature by first highlighting your word before going to Hyphenation. The dialog comes up with your word already entered in the text box, with tildes marking possible hyphenation points. Of course, you can also type a new word directly into the text box without preselecting it.

To change the hyphenation of a word in the dictionary, type the word into the text box and click OK. If the word already exists in the dictionary, PageMaker may open a dialog box to double-check that you mean to insert the new word over the one already there.

II

Working with Text

Be doubly certain that you have spelled the new word correctly. If you make a mistake, you need to use the dictionary editor program to go into your dictionary to remove the error.

The section on "Checking Your Spelling" in Chapter 9, "Editing Copy with the Story Editor," also talks about dictionary-related matters, including the use of PageMaker's Dictionary Editor. This editor enables you to adjust spelling and hyphenation of individual words and easily build your own large custom dictionaries.

DESIGN NOTE
Avoid the Algorithm Hyphenation Function

When turning on hyphenation, most designers choose the middle level, Manual Plus Dictionary. The third level, Manual Plus Algorithm, gives you a tighter right rag or justified line, but it tells PageMaker to figure word breaks based on its hyphenation guess engine, instead of going strictly by the dictionary. Most editors prefer to hyphenate at syllable breaks as listed in a dictionary. Actually, many veterans prefer to do all their hyphenation manually, not using the electronic dictionary at all.

The algorithm hyphenation can be handy, though. If a particular paragraph is giving you line break trouble, temporarily turn on hyphenation for the paragraph and let the algorithm show you some breaks you may be missing.

TIP ▶ **Use Multiple Dictionaries In the Same Publication**

Your hyphenation specifications are a paragraph-based attribute, which means that theoretically you can have a different dictionary for every paragraph in your publication, limited by the amount of RAM in your computer and the number of dictionaries you own. More likely, you may use a technical or foreign language dictionary in certain passages to get the best possible hyphenation and spell-checking in those specialized areas. Tell PageMaker which dictionary you want to use in any given paragraph by selecting the dictionary from the list in the Paragraph Specifications dialog box.

Preventing Hyphenation of Specific Words

To prevent hyphenation, you can still use the traditional PageMaker move, the easy keyboard-direct standby of inserting a discretionary hyphen Ctrl+- (hyphen) directly in front of the non-hyphenated word.

You also can permanently lock specific words by using the Add Word dialog box to unhyphenate them in your dictionary. Type the word you want to lock in the Add Word dialog box. Or highlight the word in text and open the dialog box. Then simply place one tilde directly in front of the word and remove any other tildes.

TIP ▶ Use No Break "Glue" to Prevent Hyphenation

You also can lock a word from hyphenation by highlighting it and then formatting it with the Line End No Break attribute in the Type Specifications dialog box (Ctrl+T). No Break glues together both single words and multiple word passages.

Tactics Recipe:
Setting Up a Justification System

All these line length options interact with one another. After a frustrating day of attempting to create finely tuned lines of type, you may feel as though you've been punching your fist into a big block of gelatin—push in at one spot, and you displace another glob of goo in another spot.

Summing Up the Differences Among Various Line Length Options

To cut frustration and get the most out of the PageMaker type adjusting tools, keep in mind how these tools differ. Table 6.1 summarizes all the various line length options. The character-based attributes are covered in Chapter 5, "Typing In Your Type," and the paragraph formatting elements are covered here in Chapter 6.

TABLE 6.1   Line Length Options

Option	Base	Line Length Effects
Width	Character	Width doesn't change letter spacing. It changes the width of the letters and therefore affects line length.
Tracking	Character	Tracking adjusts the space evenly among all letters where it's applied, and does so by different amounts, depending on the size of the type.
Manual kerning	Character	You can customize the spacing of specific pairs of letters or a range (heaven forbid) of letters using the PageMaker kerning command.

continues

II

Working with Text

Table 6.1   Continued

Option	Base	Line Length Effects
Automatic kerning	Paragraph	PageMaker applies automatic pair kerning, if you turn it on, based on the built-in kerning pair settings that are part of most commercially available fonts.
Word spacing	Paragraph	Word spacing tunes the space between words; it's covered in this chapter. The range of minimum and maximum spacing works on justified paragraphs only, although the desired setting affects unjustified text.
Letter spacing	Paragraph	Letter spacing reduces or expands spacing between characters, adding to or subtracting from whatever other changes have been made, such as kerning. The minimum and maximum spacing settings do not work on unjustified text.
Hyphenation	Paragraph	Hyphenation splits a word in two across a line break if PageMaker's other spacing and line length options can't make the line length work out properly. Hyphenation zones do not have any effect in justified text.

The Priority Order of the Line Length Options

PageMaker uses a "pecking order" to implement your various settings for word and letter spacing. Here's a rundown of the steps in PageMaker's process of composing a line of type:

▼ PageMaker first applies all manual and pair kerning, tracking, and set width attributes.

▼ The program then uses your settings for Desired Word and Letter Spacing to lay text onto a line until a word won't fit. Focusing on that overset word, it then figures out the closest word break and hyphenation point opportunities on either side of the right margin.

▼ Hyphenation is temporarily disabled while PageMaker takes further measures.

▼ It tries to fit the entire overset word on the current line by reducing word spaces to the minimum value. PageMaker always begins with the smallest increment when it is reducing or expanding word or letter spacing, and stops as soon as it finds a solution, although it will go all the way to the Minimum or Maximum value if that's necessary.

▼ Next, it tries to expand word space to the Maximum value to try to push the overset word to the next line.

▼ Hyphenation comes back on.

▼ The program tries to fit the hyphenated word by reducing word space.

▼ Next, word space is expanded to try to fit the hyphenated word.

▼ PageMaker tries out a combination of letter and word space to attempt to fit the hyphenated word.

▼ If all these steps fail, PageMaker gives up and applies your maximum letter spacing setting to the line, expanding word space beyond the maximum if necessary.

▼ PageMaker will virtually never go outside your minimum/maximum letter spacing settings. The only exception to that rule would be a situation where it must fit text with no word space (a very long word, for example) onto a line. It might, in that situation, reduce letter spacing below the minimum.

The Show Loose/Tight Lines alert bars will trigger on if PageMaker can't fit the line by using your spacing settings, assuming you've turned on that feature in Preferences.

It takes a lot more time to talk about all this than to watch it take place. Your computer whips through it in a few gnat blinks, so fast that you don't even see it happening.

Cooking Up Your Own Justification Settings

With that background information in mind as you begin a new project, you need to do some creative thinking about the look you want to achieve with all this justification power. Once made, decisions about word and letter spacing fundamentally influence your project. So, take a deep breath and take some time for

experimentation—a basic investment that helps you create great-looking type. This educated playing will ultimately save you much time, serving as insurance against having to backtrack and re-do work that doesn't look quite right. The examples of spacing settings in this section are just that, examples only. They may make sense in many situations, but you should develop your own sensibilities about justification.

Use the following steps to experiment your way to a justification solution for your project:

1. *Load some sample type.* Begin by loading some sample type into your new publication. Hopefully you have already made some basic decisions about column width, typeface, and type size. They may be tentative decisions, but you need some sort of starting point.

   The average word lengths in your sample type should be about the same as you can expect when you actually begin work. Light magazine fare with shorter words, set on a three-inch column, justifies more smoothly than a three-inch column of dense copy containing many multi-syllabic words for an academic journal. All these parameters make a big difference in your justification adjustments.

2. *Establish the neutral point for your text.* At this point, allow the basic nature of your type to come forward by setting your spacing and hyphenation to neutral. That means you turn on justification, and you set your first line paragraph indents, if any. But turn off hyphenation completely. Set tracking to None (not normal). Force word spacing to neutral by entering 100

percent in all three boxes. Likewise, neutralize letter spacing with a 0 percent setting. Turn on automatic kerning for all type above four points.

Now look at your type, and you probably see something like figure 6.13. (Notice how loose and sloppy the spacing is with this setup.) This figure shows Times, set 12 points on 14-point leading, in a 21-pica-wide column (about 3 1/2 inches).

Let the mad, running, dogs lie where they wish. After all, they have little whimsy and in the past have served us quite well. On the other hand, there's no reason on this Earth to excuse indolence.

We must search out laziness, seeking out ——— Sloppy spacing opportunities to stay up late at night, in a thankless and never-ending crusade of searching out and waking up those who encourage such misbegotten behavior within this prestigious community. Forthrightly, holding our Calvinist traditions closely to our chests, we shall march briskly forward.

Particularly, there's a problem with aardvarks who take naps after lunch and then proceed to glow in the darkness of their dens, acting as slothful as can be. One should not presume that we are accusing these doltish beasts of being related to the sloth, those noble creatures of nap mythology.

Fɪɢ. 6.13 ▲

Type loaded into PageMaker with all spacing options in neutral.

3. *Balance spacing and hyphenation.* This step is the most important in the experimentation process—achieving a balance between spacing and hyphenation. The more hyphenation you allow, the better PageMaker can implement your spacing settings. On the other hand, a narrower range of spacing settings makes it harder for PageMaker to hyphenate without creating ladders. *Hyphen ladders*, that is—when a series of hyphens line up along the right edge of your column, looking like the rungs of a real step ladder.

After you have your neutral text in place, play around with this balance between your spacing settings and your consecutive hyphenation settings.

Figures 6.14 and 6.15 show two different approaches to balance, one reined in and the other somewhat loose. Both samples depart from the PageMaker standard settings of 75 /100 /150 percent and –5 /0 /25 percent. Neither sample is ideal, of course, but they demonstrate the range of effects these tools can have.

The tighter of the two samples, figure 6.14, has hyphenation settings that permit as many as three hyphens in a row (a ladder in almost anyone's book). Word spacing is set at

65/100 /110 percent and letter spacing at −15 /0 /0 percent.

The looser setting in figure 6.15 permits no adjacent lines to have hyphens (only one hyphen in any group of three lines). Word spacing is more liberal at 85 /100 /125 percent, and letter spacing is 0 /0 /5 percent. Readability is better, don't you think?

Let the mad, running, dogs lie where they wish. After all, they have little whimsy and in the past have served us quite well. On the other hand, there's no reason on this Earth to excuse indolence.

We must search out laziness, seeking out opportunities to stay up late at night, in a thankless and neverending crusade of searching out and waking up those who encourage such misbegotten behavior within this prestigious community. Forthrightly, holding our Calvinist traditions closely to our chests, we shall march briskly forward.

Particularly, there's a problem with aardvarks who take naps after lunch and then proceed to glow in the darkness of their dens, acting as slothful as can be. One should not presume that we are accusing these doltish beasts of being related to the sloth, those noble creatures of nap mythology.

Consecutive hyphens

Spacing too tight

FIG. 6.14 ▲

A tighter set of spacing settings, giving the text a darker and denser look.

Let the mad, running, dogs lie where they wish. After all, they have little whimsy and in the past have served us quite well. On the other hand, there's no reason on this Earth to excuse indolence.

We must search out laziness, seeking out opportunities to stay up late at night, in a thankless and never-ending crusade of searching out and waking up those who encourage such misbegotten behavior within this prestigious community. Forthrightly, holding our Calvinist traditions closely to our chests, we shall march briskly forward.

Particularly, there's a problem with aardvarks who take naps after lunch and then proceed to glow in the darkness of their dens, acting as slothful as can be. One should not presume that we are accusing these doltish beasts of being related to the sloth, those noble creatures of nap mythology.

No consecutive hyphens

Overall even spacing of word and letters

FIG. 6.15 ▲

A more open combination of spacing and hyphenation

Force Justifying

The term *force justification* qualifies as justification only in the most literal sense. Force justification does make the first and the last letters in a line sit flush against their respective column edges—but it does so even if only two letters are on the line! Flushing the text left and right is the only characteristic that resembles justification; the concept of force has much more to do with what happens. Keep in mind that hyphenation and all other line length adjustment options are overridden when you choose the force justification text alignment method. This method simply divides the line length by the number of characters and then applies brute force to space everything out evenly, putting most space between words, spreading all the characters over the entire line.

You'll probably use force justification (Ctrl+Shift+F) only for special effects, as shown in figure 6.16. In this example, en spaces, which have a fixed length, are inserted between each character; several more en spaces are placed between the words and bullet points.

FIG. 6.16 ▶

*Using force justifica-
tion for a special effect.*

The · Honor · Of · Your · Presence · Is · Requested
At · The · Retirement · Party · For
The · Right · Honorable · Henry · Slugbinder

Applying Tab Stops and Indents

Indents and tab stops shape your PageMaker paragraphs into columns and other structures, shaping the container of your words. Plus, they perform that work easily and in an easy-to-replicate way. Instead of trying to remember to press the Tab key to indent the first line of a paragraph, you can use the first line indent function, setting it so every paragraph you type has the same indent. In tables of information, you can set your tabs one time for the first row of information and make those tab settings line up the rest of the data columns beneath the first row.

Using the Indents/Tabs Ruler

The ruler-style dialog box you see in figure 6.17 is the basic PageMaker tool for setting indents and tabs. Choose Indents/Tabs from the Type menu, or use the keyboard shortcut Ctrl+I.

FIG. 6.17 ▶

*The Indents/Tabs ruler
dialog box.*

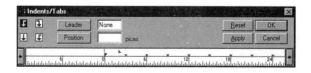

The PageMaker ruler-style interface probably reminds you of your word processor. This ruler operates in much the same way.

Unlike a word processor, however, this ruler operates in a dialog box you must open each time you want to set tabs; you can't set the ruler to stay at the top of the window all the time. This side effect is a result of PageMaker's pasteboard metaphor. PageMaker cannot use a fixed, page-oriented ruler like the ones you see in word processors such as Microsoft Word. Word processors don't have pasteboards, so they can simply hang a ruler at the top of the page. But in PageMaker, the text can be anywhere on-screen, perhaps even completely off the page. Therefore, having a fixed-position ruler like in word processors is impossible.

PageMaker stretches the ruler across the entire screen, even if you have a super-wide monitor. This wide view means you get great access without scrolling the ruler back and forth. In addition, you get a better perspective on your entire column of text, even at super-high magnification views and even with extremely wide columns of data.

The ruler attempts to line up its zero point with the left edge of your column, assuming the left column edge is in your page view. Then you can visually estimate your tab locations. PageMaker also adjusts the scale of the ruler to whatever view magnification you were using when you called up the Indents/Tabs dialog box.

Setting a Tab and Choosing Tab Alignment

To set a tab, first click one of the tab icons on the left side of the Indents/Tabs dialog box. You have a choice of four tab alignments: left aligned, right aligned, centered, and decimal. In figure 6.18, you see examples of all four alignments.

Fig. 6.18 ▶

A sample table showing all four types of tab alignment.

Leftie	Center	99.99	Rightedge
Leftie	Center	99.99	Rightedge
Leftwise	Center	100.99	Rightup
Leftkowitz	Center	1999.99	Rightie
Lefton	Center	10000.99	Rightface
Leftie	Center	99.99	Rightedge
Leftwise	Center	100.99	Rightup
Leftkowitz	Center	1999.99	Rightie
Lefton	Center	10000.99	Rightface
Leftie	Center	99.99	Rightedge
Leftwise	Center	100.99	Rightup
Leftkowitz	Center	1999.99	Rightie
Lefton	Center	10000.99	Rightface
Leftie	Center	99.99	Rightedge
Leftwise	Center	100.99	Rightup
Leftkowitz	Center	1999.99	Rightie
Lefton	Center	10000.99	Rightface

After you choose a tab style, click anywhere on the ruler; your tab symbol is planted where you click. You can then click and drag the tab to the position you like, or you can type an exact position in the Position box.

II

Working with Text

Tabs take effect when you click the Apply button or the OK button. The Apply button really helps when you try to set up a complicated table, because you can view your changes without repeatedly opening and closing the ruler dialog box.

The new tabs apply to any PageMaker paragraph you highlighted (even partially, with a simple insertion point) when you opened the Indents/Tabs dialog box.

It's critical you understand that tab settings aren't the same as tab characters. *Tab characters* are what you get when you use the Tab key on your keyboard. If you open up Story Editor you can see the characters, just like you could see the paragraph markers in figure 6.1 at the beginning of this chapter.

When you type tab characters into your text, they force your words to line up on the tab settings. If you haven't created any tab settings, your words line up on the default tab settings built into PageMaker. PageMaker comes with tab settings every 1/2 inch, but you can set your own default settings using the techniques described in Chapter 3, "Personalizing PageMaker Preferences," and in this chapter's later section "Making New Default Tabs and Resetting the Built-In Ones."

Setting Tabs for Multiple Rows of Data

When you create a table like the one in figure 6.18, you can use several ways to propagate your first-row tab settings throughout the rest of the table.

The most intuitive way to format tabs for a table-style list is to enter all your data, highlight all of it, and experiment with your tab settings. Use the Apply button to evaluate the effects of your moves as you proceed. After you have all the columns set at the right width to accommodate their data, click OK and you're done.

An even better method is to set up a paragraph style for your table and tweak it. Check Chapter 7, "Designing a Text Style System," for complete details on why you should use styles for all your paragraph formatting, including tabs and indents.

You also can use PageMaker's tab adoption technique to set all the tabs in a group of rows, using the first row as a model. To adopt tabs, follow these steps:

1. Set the tabs for the first line and get them just right.
2. Close the Indents/Tabs dialog box.
3. Highlight the entire table of data, and open and close the ruler dialog box again. The settings in the first row are adopted by all the rows you highlighted.

For some situations, the best way to set multiple rows of tabs is to set them all as one paragraph. Instead of breaking the paragraphs at the end of each row, use a new line character (Shift+Enter) at the end of each line. This technique works well when you have multiple lines in one column of a table, but all the other columns are single-line entries. Chapter 16, "Formatting Forms, Tables, and Databases," discusses the topic in more detail. In particular, read about the new Table Editor included with PageMaker 6.0, probably a better option for this situation than setting tabs.

Finally, keep in mind that PageMaker passes paragraph formatting on to following paragraphs. If you are typing columnar information directly into PageMaker, get the first row of data arranged with tabs and press the Enter key at the end of the line. PageMaker carries all those paragraph attributes, including the tabs, to the new paragraph below. Each newly typed paragraph that follows also assumes the formatting. This method has one drawback. It doesn't take into account that the paragraphs following the first one may have wider columns of data. You may need to go back through the table and tune the tab settings. If you use style definitions for the table, however, performing this tuning operation should be easy.

Using the Position Box for Precision Tabbing

You may have difficulty placing a tab exactly where you want it by using the click-and-drag method. The Indents/Tabs Position box offers the most precise way to add or move a tab. To add a new tab in an exact spot, type into the Position box your location information and click the Position button to get a list of possible tab moves where you can choose the Add option. To move an existing tab, select it by clicking its "tail," type your location point into the Position box, and then click the Position button, selecting the Move option from the Position box list.

Dotting a Leader Tab

You can set a leader for any of your tabs. Using leaders is a great technique for lists like tables of contents, where the eye needs to follow from one entry over to the next (see fig. 6.19).

To set a leader, in the Indents/Tabs dialog box you select the tab that should have the leader by clicking its "tail," and then click the Leader button. You'll get a list of leader options. Choose from dots, dashes, a solid line, or a custom job. The solid line leader works well for drawing precise lines on an order form. You may also type any two characters and create your own custom leader.

Fig. 6.19 ▶

A variety of tab leaders.

Analyzing Handwriting 1
   Loops   5
   Descenders   18
   Connections   37
Samples **62**
   John Hancock   66
   Henry Butterworth   67
   Saul Leifkowitz   68
Ego Revealed To Us By The Pen ▱▱▱▱▱▱▱▱▱▱▱▱ **62**
   Heavy Hitter   66
   Golden Beanie   67
   Empress Jeanine   68

> **TIP ▶** **Preceding Space Determines Tab Leader Formatting**
>
> If you formatted your paragraph for bold type, like the first heading in the sample table of contents in figure 6.19, the tab leader also is bold. The result is a very coarse leader. A solution does exist, however. The tab setting takes on the font styling of the character immediately preceding the tab character. In the second heading of figure 6.19, a thin space (Ctrl+Shift+T) is inserted and formatted as non-bold type. You also can set your thin space at a small point size, making the leader very delicate. As another example, the third heading has a funky custom leader. The thin space right before the tab is formatted with the Zapf Dingbat typeface, and a + character (the Zapf Dingbat hand) is entered into the leader box in the Indents/Tabs dialog box and then clicking the Leader button to choose the Custom leader option.
>
> For this trick to work, you must use a hard space immediately prior to the tab character. A thin, em, en, or fixed space will do the job.

Setting Precision Multiple Tabs with the Repeat Command

PageMaker can set up to 40 different tabs in any paragraph. To set precision multiple tabs, use the Position box and the Repeat function to set a series of regular spaced tabs. Make sure that your first tab is selected by clicking its "tail," because that is the beginning reference point for your new repeating tabs. Then type a number in the Position box to tell PageMaker how far apart you want each of these new tabs. Pull down the Position box arrow list and select Repeat. You get a series of tabs across the ruler at the interval you specified.

Making New Default Tabs and Resetting the Built-In Ones

As you probably noticed, default tabs (the small inverted triangles) are set every half inch on the Indents/Tabs ruler line. In fact, you get these tabs back if you click the Reset button.

If you set no other tabs, these defaults are present. As you set tabs, you wipe out the default tabs as you move across the ruler from left to right. In figure 6.20, notice that all the small inverted triangles have disappeared to the left of that first tab set.

Fig. 6.20 ▶

Tabs you set take precedence over default tabs.

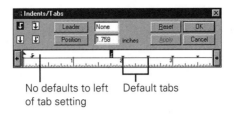

No defaults to left   Default tabs
of tab setting

To set your own default tabs, use this standard procedure:

1. Make sure you have the Pointer tool selected (not the Text tool), and open the Indents/Tabs dialog box.

2. Set up your tabs.

3. Close the box and save your publication. Now if you start a new paragraph that has no tabs inherited from a previous paragraph, you get these publication-level default tabs.

To set default hard tabs for all future PageMaker publications, follow the same steps but with no publication open. (Note that the Reset button will always take the Indents/Tabs dialog box back to its pristine condition, with tabs every 1/2 inch.)

Both these techniques follow the general principles of setting PageMaker defaults, outlined in Chapter 3, "Personalizing PageMaker Preferences."

Indenting Paragraphs

What if you want to indent the left and right margins of a quoted passage of text? Or maybe you want to indent the first line of one (or many) paragraphs. To perform this chore back in the typewriter days, you would spend all afternoon typing a line, hitting the carriage return, and tabbing over to the indent point. Now you can set the indents as part of your paragraph formatting and let PageMaker do the work.

Setting Indents with the Indents/Tabs Ruler

If you understand how the Indents/Tabs ruler dialog box works, you have paragraph indents licked. The ruler has left and right indent markers; the left marker even has a split in it like the indent markers in Microsoft Word.

When you have some text selected, open the Indents/Tabs dialog box. Don't forget the Ctrl+I keyboard shortcut; or you can use the Type menu for access.

In figure 6.21, notice the black sideways triangles at each side of the ruler, where the column edges sit. Vertical dotted lines also act as place markers for the column edges.

Fig. 6.21 ▶

*The indent markers on
the Indents/Tabs ruler.*

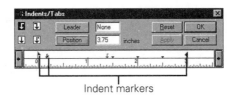

Indent markers

When these two indent markers sit right on the column edges (where the dotted lines are), the column has no indent at all. However, you can click and drag the markers wherever you like on the ruler, as long as you stay inside the column margins.

Setting a First Line Indent

You can give the first line an indent different from all the other lines in that paragraph by unlocking the two halves of the left indent marker. Normally, these two pieces are locked together and move as a unit.

To unlock the two pieces of the left indent marker, simply hold down the Shift key before you click the bottom half of the split marker. If you want to move the top marker (the one that controls the first line of the paragraph), you can just click and drag it without using the Shift key.

To create a first line indent, for example, hold down the Shift key and slide the top half of the split indent marker over to the right by the amount of your indent.

DESIGN NOTE
Begin by Using the Standard Paragraph Indent

Every design presents its own challenges, but it's a good idea to begin with a guideline and work from there. For first-line paragraph indents, try starting with an indent of one em. How big is an em? The measure is relative and is not on the Indents/Tabs ruler. Figure that one em equals the point size of your type. Twelve-point type usually has an em space about 12 points wide, for example. Feel free to use your own favorite amount for a first-line paragraph indent, but this one em guideline gives you a starting point.

Hanging an Indent: Bullets and Numbers

A *hanging indent* "hangs" out to the left of the main body of a paragraph. In other words, the hanging indent has a negative indent compared to the indent set for the rest of the paragraph.

Look at figure 6.22, which shows text before a hanging indent is applied. The figure shows the text and the Indents/Tabs ruler dialog box that produced it. A tab follows each bullet point character. However, notice that the bullet and the left edge of the text are lined up. This example is not yet a hanging indent.

Fig. 6.22 ▶

Text before setting the hanging indent.

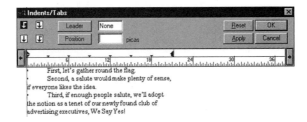

In figure 6.23, the lower half of the left indent marker is unlocked by holding down the Shift key and, with a click-and-drag move, sliding the lower half of the marker over to the right. A left tab is then clicked onto the ruler and slid over to the new bottom half indent marker. The top half of the indent marker, the first line indent, hangs out to the left. This example represents a hanging indent.

Fig. 6.23 ▶

Text after setting the hanging indent.

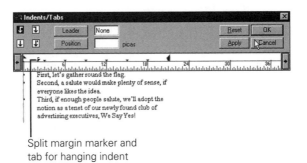

Split margin marker and
tab for hanging indent

Putting the Bullets and Numbering Plug-in to Work

Instead of bullet points, like the list shown in figure 6.23, a hanging indent often leads to a numbered list. Either way, the Bullets and Numbering Plug-in can be very helpful. Click an insertion point at the beginning of the first hanging indent, pull down the Utilities menu, choose PageMaker Plug-ins and select Bullets And Numbering. You get the dialog box in figure 6.24.

This Plug-in remembers whether you used it to make bullets or numbers the last time you had it open. If you want numbers and the Bullets mode is showing, click the Numbers button.

Fɪɢ. **6.24** ▶

Adding numbers with the Bullets and Numbering Plug-in.

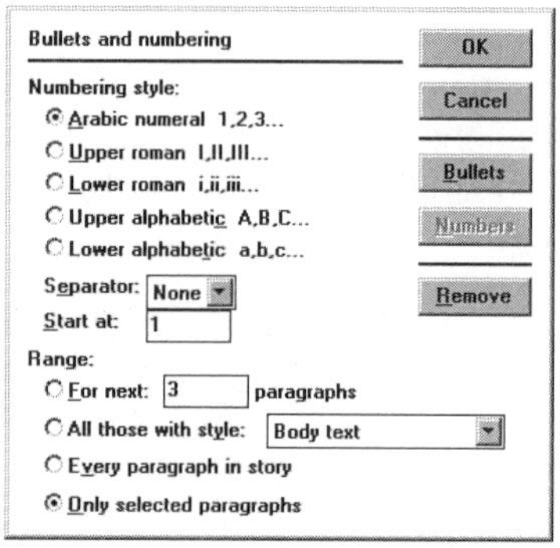

In this example, the dialog box calls for Arabic numbers, starting at one, with a period after. The dialog box asks for numbers to be added to the three paragraphs following the cursor. The result appears in figure 6.25.

Fɪɢ. **6.25** ▶

Text after using the Bullets and Numbering Plug-in.

1. Gather round the flag.
2. Salute, if everyone likes the idea.
3. If enough people salute, adopt the notion as a tenet of We Say Yes!

Remember one crucial detail about the Bullets and Numbering Plug-in. It does not update automatically. If you move the paragraphs, they are not renumbered, so apply this Plug-in after you have locked the text.

Besides numbering paragraphs, this Plug-in gives you a powerful facility for setting bulleted paragraphs. Click the Bullets button for a choice of five bullets, along with all the Range options you had in Numbers mode (see fig. 6.26).

Fɪɢ. **6.26** ▶

Bullet creation mode of Bullets and Numbering Plug-in.

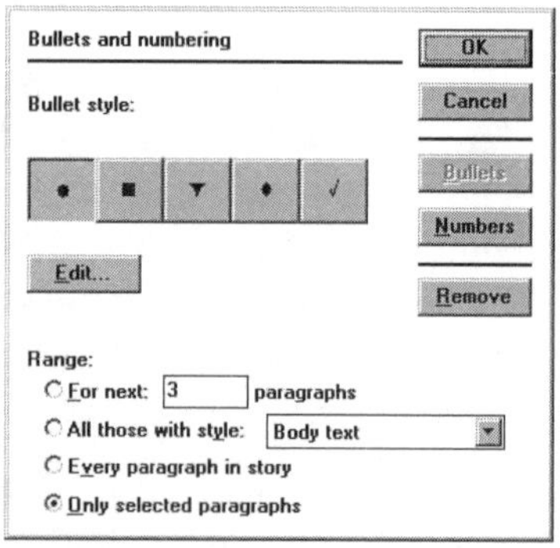

If the bullet styles aren't to your taste, select one of the five positions and click the Edit button to choose a different character for that spot. As you see in figure 6.27, you can select your bullet's typeface and point size from the Edit Bullet dialog box. Tell PageMaker which bullet character you want by selecting it from the grid of characters. (To get a better look, temporarily choose a very large point size so you get a bigger example view. Don't forget to change the point size back to what you really need.)

FIG. 6.27 ▶

Editing your bullet options in the Bullets and Numbering Plug-in.

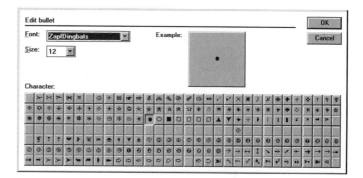

Indenting Paragraphs with the Menu and Control Palette

As intuitive as working with the Indents/Tabs ruler is, sometimes using a menu or the Control palette to set indents makes more sense. (You cannot set tabs any other way except by using the ruler.) For example, if you have several paragraph formatting options to set, using the one-stop-shop capabilities of the Paragraph Specifications dialog box may be easier than working in the ruler.

Figure 6.28 shows both the Paragraph Specifications dialog box and the Control palette for the bulleted paragraphs used in the preceding hanging indent example (refer to fig. 6.25).

You can set left and right indents and first line indents right from the keyboard using the Paragraph Specifications dialog box and the Control palette. Using these methods isn't as intuitive because you don't get the visual feedback of lining up margin markers in the ruler. But if you know the exact settings you need, the keyboard entry method can be much more precise and possibly faster.

Open the Paragraph Specifications box with Ctrl+M. Then tab from field to field to fill in the indent information.

As discussed in Chapter 5, "Typing In Your Type," you open the Control palette with Ctrl+' (apostrophe) and activate it with Ctrl+` (grave). You can toggle between Character and Paragraph view with Ctrl+Shift+` (grave). In Paragraph view, to select a Control palette function you tab from field to field, just as you do in the Paragraph Specifications box.

Fɪɢ. 6.28 ▶

*Creating indents using
the Paragraph Specifi-
cations dialog box or
the Control palette.*

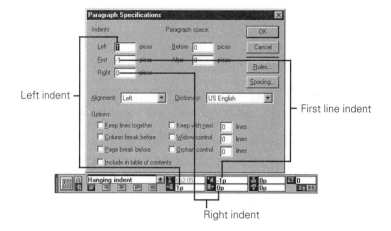

Left indent

First line indent

Right indent

Controlling the Flow of Lines and Paragraphs

PageMaker can help you control the way your paragraphs and lines fit together
and even where they appear on the page. By using the keyboard or the Options
section of the Paragraph Specifications dialog box, you can do the following:

▶ Force a line to break at a certain point.

▶ Command adjacent paragraphs to stay together on the same page.

▶ Tell a paragraph to force itself to the top of the next page or the next
column.

▶ Prevent the typographical embarrassment of widowed or orphaned lines.

Forcing a New Line with Shift+Enter

The simplest control you have over where a line breaks is a brute force technique—the new line character. Insert this character in text by clicking an insertion point and pressing Shift+Enter. Instead of creating a new paragraph, you
force the line to break and start over again on the next line. Like the tab character and the carriage-return character, this new line character is visible in the
Story Editor but not in Layout view.

Controlling Paragraph Flow Using the
Paragraph Specifications Dialog Box

Have another look at figure 6.28 and take note of the Options section at the bottom of the Paragraph Specifications dialog box. Each Options command works
directly on the way a paragraph relates to the page, controlling the location of
page breaks and the way paragraphs break between pages. The following sections cover each of the Options items (except Include in Table of Contents,
which is covered in Chapter 17, "Building Many Pages").

Keep in mind that these options are all paragraph level attributes and you can apply them via styles or by clicking anywhere in the paragraph you want to assign the attribute.

Keeping Lines Together

Use the Keep Lines Together command whenever you want all the lines of that paragraph to stay together on one page. You might use this command to prevent a multiline headline or a multiline row in a table of data from breaking across to a new page.

Forcing Page and Column Breaks

To force a paragraph to snap to the top of the next page or the next column, choose Column Break Before or Page Break Before in the Paragraph Specifications dialog box. You may want to use this option with first- and second-level headlines in books, where you want a chapter or major new section to begin on a new page. This attribute is especially useful if you set it where appropriate for inbound text paragraphs when you pour new text into a PageMaker publication. Then your most vital page breaks are automatically set up for you, saving considerable time when you do your page-break tuning. Chapter 8, "Pouring Text into PageMaker," discusses pouring text.

Keeping Adjacent Paragraphs Together

Tell a paragraph to stick on the same page with the following paragraph by choosing Keep With Next. This option is great for headlines; if you use it, you will never see a lonely headline sitting at the bottom of a page or column, mourning the text it is supposed to be introducing.

Preventing Widows and Orphans

Academics have actually written weighty monographs on the definition and origin of the terms *widow* and *orphan*. Nobody seems to know for sure when typesetters and art directors first began using these terms, but they've been talking about widows and orphans since the late 1600s. You'd think by now somebody would have worked out a definition that everybody could agree upon.

Because this book is about PageMaker, what really counts here is what PageMaker thinks about widows and orphans. PageMaker looks at widows and orphans like this:

▶ A *widow* is the first line of a paragraph that is isolated from the rest of its paragraph by being stuck all alone at the bottom of a page or column.

▶ An *orphan* is the last line of a paragraph stuck at the top of a page or column, with the rest of the paragraph left behind on the previous page or column.

To see an example of each, look at figure 6.29.

These blasted widows and orphans will be the death of me yet. I simply can't decide what they ought to be. For example, some slug rackers contend that a single word as the last line of the last paragraph in a column would be tolerable but they will not abide a hyphenated fragment being left to stand alone.

While you may focus your worries on ———————————————————— Widow

this nuance, you should know that PageMaker defines these typographical oddities in terms of lines not words. Really, the situation is hard to figure and even harder to manage when laying out a page. We propose this solution. Let them eat their words.

These blasted widows and orphans will be the death of me yet. I simply can't decide what they ought to be. For example, some slug rackers contend that a single word as the last line of the last paragraph in a column would be tolerable but they will not abide a hyphenated fragment being left to stand

alone. ———————————————————— Orphan

While you may focus your worries on this nuance, you should know that PageMaker defines these typographical oddities in terms of lines not words. Really, the situation is hard to figure and even harder to manage when laying out a page. We propose this solution. Let them eat their words.

Truth be told, your most expedient cure for widows and orphans is to edit the copy until it fits. But that's usually not an option on a project by the time it reaches layout. So, if you want PageMaker to assist you by exerting widow or orphan control, type a number from 0 to 3 in the Widow Control or Orphan Control boxes in the Paragraph Specifications dialog box.

You could go through each paragraph, setting widow and orphan control where needed in a document. However, you'd be better off setting these items one time and forgetting about them. The point is for the computer to do the work, not you. For that reason, you probably want to incorporate this setting in your paragraph styles.

A couple of examples may help explain how your entries influence PageMaker's behavior.

If you enter **2** in the Widow Control field, you give PageMaker a definition to follow as it paginates your text into columns. If PageMaker finds a paragraph breaking across two pages, it checks your Widow Control definition. If you have at least two lines in a portion of the paragraph at the bottom of the page, PageMaker allows the page break. Otherwise, PageMaker tries to adjust the paragraph break to conform to your definition.

You can put that example into the context of orphan control. When PageMaker is about to break a paragraph between pages, it looks at your Orphan Control definition. PageMaker adds the number you entered in the Orphan Control option field to the lines at the top of the page. If the number of lines falling at the top of the page is equal to your definition, PageMaker takes action and adds a line from the previous page to avoid the problem.

Design Note
Decide About Widow and Orphan Limits

In designing your publications, what should you do about the centuries-old debate over widows and orphans?

Most of the arguments are over how many words (not lines, as PageMaker defines the concept) are permitted to remain behind on the last line of the last paragraph on a page. Typesetters have widely varying opinions on the minimum width to allow for that last line, with most agreeing that a full-length line is always the optimum result. Because a full-length line is not possible 100 percent of the time, the major controversy usually rages around the issue of whether it's okay to leave a single word or even part of a hyphenated word alone on the last line of a paragraph.

A consensus doesn't exist, but most typesetters probably would tell you that (on deadline and struggling to get the publication out) it's generally okay to leave two words alone in the last line of a paragraph, but not so good to leave a single word on the last line, and very bad to leave part of a hyphenated word.

On the other hand, some designers insist that these widow/orphans are acceptable because they put white space into the column of type, making it more readable.

Perhaps the most important thing for you to keep in mind for this issue and other style decisions is this: make style decisions consistent throughout your publication, whatever they are, and strive for the best typography possible in context. In other words, perfection becomes a relative term defined by deadline and budget. Do the best you can under the circumstances.

TIP ▶ Turn On the Show Keeps Option In Preferences

To target the spots in your type where PageMaker subverted your paragraph option commands (Keep Lines Together, Keep With Next, and so on), go to the Preferences command in the File menu and turn on the Show Keeps option. It's in the same location as the Show Loose/Tight Lines command. Any violations are highlighted (in gray or yellow, depending on your setup). In those spots, you may want to tweak a line by adjusting paragraph spacing settings, or by kerning.

Setting Off Paragraphs with Spacing and Rules

PageMaker provides two major tools for framing your paragraphs. You can allow extra space above and below them, or you can set a line (a rule) above or below a paragraph.

Remember that in PageMaker, not all paragraphs are prose text. Paragraphs are any text followed by a carriage-return character. Headlines are paragraphs. So are captions.

Primarily, rules visually set aside your headlines or other special paragraphs by emphasizing and separating them from your body copy. You also can use the paragraph spacing attribute for setting off headlines, but spacing has much broader purposes.

Spacing Before and After Paragraphs

You find the Paragraph Space settings in the upper-right corner of the Paragraph Specifications dialog box. You can access the same settings toward the right end of the Control palette in its Paragraph view. Both these paragraph spacing options are shown in figure 6.30.

FIG. 6.30 ▶

Two ways to set space before and after a paragraph: the Paragraph Specifications dialog box and the Control palette.

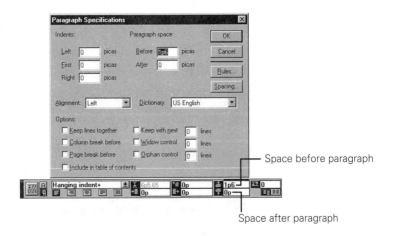

Space before paragraph

Space after paragraph

You may be asking yourself, why not just press the Enter key a couple of times to space out paragraphs? That method locks you into paragraph spacing that exactly equals your leading or multiples of it. No finesse. No flexibility. Precisely defining space between paragraphs is much more elegant. In figure 6.31, notice how you gain tremendous flexibility using this method—flexibility that helps when you need to juggle vertical spacing of a piece of copy so it fits on a page just right.

FIG. 6.31 ▶

Experimenting with paragraph spacing.

No Space After This Headline
The backbone of great design will often be experimentation and flexibility. Without the ability to quickly try out your ideas and to try them out with precision, your cause may be lost.

2 Points After This Headline
The backbone of great design will often be experimentation and flexibility. Without the ability to quickly try out your ideas and to try them out with precision, your cause may be lost.

5.5 Points After This Headline
The backbone of great design will often be experimentation and flexibility. Without the ability to quickly try out your ideas and to try them out with precision, your cause may be lost.

9 Points After This Headline
The backbone of great design will often be experimentation and flexibility. Without the ability to quickly try out your ideas and to try them out with precision, your cause may be lost.

TIP ▶ Space Before Setting Vanishes at Top of Pages or Columns

If a paragraph formatted with space before happens to fall at the head of a column, PageMaker ignores the space command and slips the first line right up to the top of the column with no space preceding it. PageMaker 5.0 has been around long enough to take this feature for granted, but in earlier versions of PageMaker this was a major issue. You would get a rude gap if a paragraph with spacing before happened to fall at the top of a column or page. This effect was particularly ugly when you were working on a multicolumn page and one of the columns had extra space at the top, but the columns beside it didn't. Thank heavens for historical perspective, huh?

TIP ▶ Enter Your Choice of Measuring Units In Dialog Boxes

No matter what measurement system you choose in the Preferences dialog box, you can enter any of PageMaker's standard measuring units in its dialog boxes. Personally, I almost always work completely in picas. However, at times you may need to express yourself in a different measure. Suppose that you entered picas as your measurement system in Preferences, and you want to make a quick adjustment in inches. Type the number of inches in decimals, followed by the letter *i*, and PageMaker makes the conversion when you click OK. For millimeters, use *m*, for picas, use *p* after the number, and for points, use *p* before the number. Oh yes, almost forgot ciceros. Use *c* for ciceros. (Nope. Don't know a single soul who measures stuff in ciceros. It's a Euro-thing.)

Adding Rules to Paragraphs

You add rules (lines) to paragraphs for one big reason: to make them stand out. Figure 6.32 shows a few ways you can use rules to compose attention-getting headlines, and the method to create each example is described in this section.

*Some examples of
paragraph rules.*

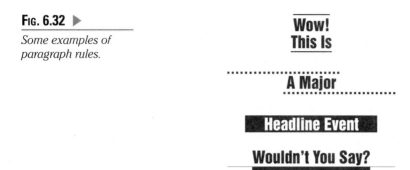

Your tools for setting paragraph rules are two supporting dialog boxes that
supplement the Paragraph Specifications dialog box. You reach the basic Paragraph Rules dialog box by clicking the Rules button; that box has its own supporting dialog box with further options for controlling paragraph rules. You
access this dialog box by clicking the Options button (see both dialog boxes
in fig. 6.33).

Fᴵɢ. **6.33** ▶

*The Paragraph Rules
dialog box and its
Paragraph Rule Op-
tions dialog box.*

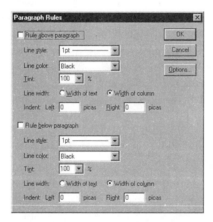

The rule lines available to you are nearly identical to those offered for drawing
purposes under the PageMaker Element menu. You have several thousand variations of spacing, thickness, style, and color that you can put together by using
these check boxes, text-entry boxes, and drop-down lists.

You can color your rules using the Line Color list in the Paragraph Rules dialog
box. You even can assign rule a tint using the object-level Tint control. Top and
bottom rules are independent from one another, which means you can choose a
shocking pink top rule and a lime-green bottom rule. (Take my advice. Never eat
watermelon while writing late at night with "Miami Vice" reruns on the tube in
the background.)

Chapter 15, "Creating Special Effects," spends more time on the design potential of paragraph rules. For now, see how the Rules and Options dialog boxes function by looking at the settings used for each of the examples in figure 6.32. All these headline examples are set in Helvetica Inserat, 30 points on 32 points of leading, using the baseline leading method. You can find more on baseline leading toward the end of this chapter in the section "Deciding Which Leading Method to Choose."

Figure 6.34 shows some ordinary, plain vanilla headline rules.

Fig. 6.34 ▶

Ordinary 2-point rules, set above and below the paragraph.

Wow!
This Is

The word "Wow!" is set with a 2-point rule above, with the <u>W</u>idth of Text button clicked. In the Options dialog box, the baseline spacing is left as Auto.

The phrase "This Is" has also been set with a 2-point rule, but below the paragraph this time. Because I used baseline leading, I went into the Options dialog box and set the rule 8 points below baseline so it stayed clear of the letters.

Now here's the trick. Both lines of this headline are in the same paragraph (with a new line Shift+Enter character to force a new line), so you get simultaneous above and below rules used on a multiline paragraph.

Figure 6.35 shows that you have a choice of line styles to choose from in the Line <u>S</u>tyle list box; you can manipulate the line width in the column.

Fig. 6.35 ▶

Simultaneous above and below paragraph rules with indents.

A Major

I used the 4-point dotted line from the drop-down list of lines and set the rules to run the width of the column. Then I indented the top rule 9 picas in from the right, and the bottom rule an equal amount in from the left. In addition, because of the baseline leading, I adjusted the bottom rule down 10 points so it wouldn't cross the hook of the *j* in Major.

In figure 6.36, I used a custom rule to reverse the type.

II

Working with Text

Fig. 6.36 ▶

Headline Event

*Reversed-out type
headline using a cus-
tom rule.*

Because the type was set on 32-point leading, I set a 32-point top rule, using the Custom item from the Line Style list. Then, to vertically center the black rule and the reverse-styled type, I used the Top text box in the Options dialog box to set the line 2 picas and 4 points above the baseline. I set the rule to the width of the text and then applied a –3 pica indent on both the left and right so the rule ends would float well outside the edges of the text.

Notice that the indents can take negative as well as positive numbers. A negative indent on a rule set to text width makes the line stick out from the outer edges of the text by the amount indicated. A negative indent on a rule set to column width causes the line to stick out past the column edges.

Believe it or not, figure 6.37 shows simultaneous above and below paragraph rules.

Fig. 6.37 ▶

Wouldn't You Say?

*Superimposed above
and below paragraph
rules.*

The top rule is set at zero points above the baseline, which actually puts it down below the phrase "Wouldn't You Say?" The top rule is a .5 point rule set to the width of the column. The bottom rule is set to the text width, 8 points wide and 8 points below the baseline so that the two lines just match up.

TIP ▶ Paragraph Rules Can Throw Off Paragraph Spacing

Paragraph rules may have a big effect on the way your paragraph sits vertically in a column of type. If you use the Auto setting in the Rule Options dialog box, PageMaker tries to keep the rule inside the paragraph space by extending the top rule down from the top edge of the slug for the first line of the paragraph. The bottom rule creeps up into the paragraph from the bottom edge of the slug for the last line. Of course, your Paragraph Space settings add space outside the rule and the type slug, but as long as you specify rules that fit within the paragraph's total slug, you won't change the position of the paragraph when you are in Auto mode.

As soon as you set a distance in the Paragraph Rule Options boxes, you change the behavior. As with most things "Auto" in PageMaker, any fixed setting entered in place of Auto makes the program act in a more rigid manner. (Think of the effects of auto leading versus fixed leading.) If you tell PageMaker that you want a rule placed 5 picas above the baseline, and you are dealing with an 18-point single line headline, you force that rule way up above the paragraph. In turn, this placement shoves any paragraphs above the headline way up in the column (or shoves your headline down, depending on how you look at it).

This situation can seriously affect your leading grid and align-to-grid strategy (see Chapter 13, "Designing a Master Page Grid").

Choosing Your Leading Method

PageMaker's methods of calculating leading may remind you of the old saying about moving the sun. Assuming that you have a pry bar millions of miles long, where would you stand to use it? And where would you find your lever point? A pry bar is no good without those two things. Measuring something—leading in this case—is no different. It's impossible unless you have a reference point.

PageMaker offers you three choices of reference points for calculating leading. All of them use the slug and the baseline as answers to our moving-the-sun question. You stand on the slug and you use the baseline as the pry point.

Using the Leading Method Radio Buttons

As discussed in the preceding chapter, you set the amount of leading using the Type menus. However, you choose the type of leading using the Spacing button from the Paragraph Specifications dialog box; the Spacing Attributes dialog box appears (see fig. 6.38).

Simply click the leading method you want to use. To help you make your decision, use the following "Key Concept: Understanding the Three Leading Methods."

Fig. 6.38 ▷

The Spacing Attributes dialog box, showing the Leading Method buttons.

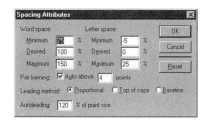

KEY CONCEPT:

Understanding the Three Leading Methods

First, take a look at the leading slug in figure 6.39. It's a slug of type in PageMaker, with the height of the slug revealed by selecting the text with the Text tool. The height of a slug, in PageMaker parlance, is the vertical space taken up by a line, as defined by the largest amount of leading in that line. If you specify 14-point leading, you get a slug 14 points tall.

FIG. 6.39 ▲

A slug using proportional leading.

The baseline of your text runs along the bottom of the letters (except where their descender, their "tails," fall below the basline), as you see in figure 6.39. In proportional leading, the standard method in PageMaker, the top of the line slug measures up 2/3 from the baseline, and the bottom floats down 1/3 of its thickness from the baseline. So, to carry out the analogy introduced at the beginning of this section, if the slug is where you stand, the baseline is the pry point.

Figure 6.40 shows baseline leading. Notice that the baseline of the text always rides in the same position in reference to the type, running along the bottom of the lowercase letters. But the slug shifts up and down in relation to the baseline (the pry point). In baseline leading, the leading slug measures up from the baseline. This method is more like traditional leading, where the typesetter inserted a narrow strip of lead or brass above the strip of type, adding the point size of the type and the leading.

FIG. 6.40 ▲

A slug using baseline leading.

The final PageMaker leading method is top of caps, as shown in figure 6.41. With the top of caps leading method, you inject a note of uncertainty about where the baseline of the text will sit. That's because the baseline floats down from the top of the slug by the height of the tallest character on the line. The baseline isn't at the bottom of the slug—it's 2/3 the way down from the top. The baseline floats inside the height of the line's leading slug. (Really, this option is there simply to maintain compatability with the very oldest versions of PageMaker. Don't use it unless you have some very special reason to do so.)

Top of caps
leading slug

Baseline

Fig. 6.41 ▲

A slug using top of caps leading.

TIP ▶ Screen Redraw Is Fixed in PageMaker 6.0

Good news! PageMaker has made a major breakthrough in the way it redraws the screen. You no longer lose the descenders on letters when you make adjustments on a line formatted with baseline leading. Gone are the weird artifacts of shattered letters that used to hang around on the screen. The problem was never more than peevish, but it did keep many people from using baseline leading.

From its early days, PageMaker has been built around the slug, so much so that the program drew the screen in slug-by-slug fashion. This procedure was such a fundamental aspect of the program's code that it has taken quite awhile to work out a solution.

Screen redraw offers another big benefit discussed in Chapter 15, "Creating Special Effects." Negative leading situations get properly redrawn, which means some of the tricks developed to build side-by-side heads now work much better. At least you can see the heads on-screen. Helps with the editing, you see.

Deciding Which Leading Method to Choose

Chances are you want to use baseline leading. However, if you are a longtime PageMaker user, you may want to stick to proportional leading because you already fought your way up the learning curve and have all sorts of publication templates that rely on that method. You certainly don't want to standardize on the top of caps leading method.

The paragraphs that follow give some pluses and minuses for the three methods.

Proportional Leading

PageMaker comes standard set for proportional leading. Everyone in the PageMaker design community knows how to use it.

On the other hand, proportional leading can be confusing. You are constantly grabbing the calculator to figure what's 1/3 of 16-point leading so you can precisely locate the baseline and stick to your leading grid. That's not even counting what happens when you put an unusual paragraph rule together and you must figure the distance to set the line off the baseline. There you are again, furrowing your brow at the calculator.

Baseline Leading

Working out the spacing for a paragraph rule is easier if you use baseline leading. You need to compute only one direction rather than two, because the baseline sits right on the bottom of the slug. If you are working on an 18-point type headline, you can pretty well figure that the descenders are out of the way within 6 points. So you simply set the paragraph rule a little more than 6 points below the baseline, which nestles along the bottom of the slug. Likewise, working out a leading grid can be much less confusing if you use baseline leading. (Chapter 13, "Designing a Master Page Grid," covers leading grids.)

When you choose between proportional and baseline leading, no major technical advantage exists for either approach. They are equally accurate. Your decision may depend simply on which method you find easier to use.

Top of Caps Leading

Much of the PageMaker measuring system (rules for one example, Baseline-Shift for another) depends on knowing where the baseline rides in a slug. With top of caps leading, you can't be sure how far down into the slug the baseline is riding. Big problem. Unless you are striving for some sort of special effect, you probably should cross top of caps leading off your consideration list.

TIP ▶ Set a Mini-Default for Your Chosen Leading Type

When you know what you want to do for leading method, set it into PageMaker permanently. If you decide on proportional leading, you don't need to make a change because PageMaker comes set up with proportional leading. If you want to use baseline leading, you probably should stick with this decision across all the documents you do. To establish baseline leading as your default leading method, open PageMaker, but don't open a document. Open the Paragraph Specifications dialog box, click the Spacing button, and click the button for your chosen leading method. Quit PageMaker, and the next time you start the program, your default is in place.

Where to Go from Here

▶ Maybe some of the discussion on leading left you spinning a bit. You may want to read the material on leading in Chapter 5, "Typing In Your Type."

▶ To make paragraph formatting super easy, check out Chapter 7, "Designing a Text Style System." All the formatting attributes discussed in this chapter can be set up as a style and applied in one easy step from PageMaker's Style palette.

▶ We hope the discussion of paragraph rules was a turn on, because that's just a taste of the design fun you can have if you sample Chapter 15, "Creating Special Effects."

▶ Your process of laying out pages is affected a great deal by this chapter's information on controlling paragraph flow. You can put this information to use in Chapter 8, "Pouring Text into PageMaker"; Chapter 14, "Precisely Positioning Graphics and Text"; and Chapter 17, "Building Many Pages."

II

Working with Text

Chapter 7

Designing a Text Style System

In this chapter on designing a paragraph styles system, you find out about:

Why styles work for you, a Key Concept section.

▼

Applying styles using the Styles and Control palettes.

▼

Overriding styles with local formatting as needed.

▼

Defining styles from scratch and by adopting existing formatting.

▼

Editing style definitions.

▼

Interlinking cascading styles to make editing easier.

▼

Building your style definitions by copying in styles from other documents.

▼

Developing your own style working method, a Tactics Recipe.

PARAGRAPH STYLES MAKE one step do the work of dozens. They keep design implementation consistent. And they enable your creative mind by making experimentation easy.

By putting the power of styles to work, you can implement a dozen formatting commands with a single mouse click, paragraph after paragraph. You get design consistency with none of the tedium of repetitive detail. All this, coupled with the design consistency you get by using paragraph styles, empowers you to do your best design work. ▶ ▶ ▶

KEY CONCEPT:
The Advantages of Paragraph Styles

Think of a *style* as a collection of formatting commands, conveniently gathered up into a set of instructions that you can apply in a single keyboard or menu move. You can perform a dozen—or even more—formatting commands with the click of a mouse.

The entire collection of styles for a publication is sometimes called a *style sheet*, a term left over from years ago when word processors first came out with styles, which at the time were maintained outside the document in a separate file called the style sheet. These days PageMaker, like modern day word processors, keeps style information inside the main publication file.

Usually, taking the time to set up a style for even a short passage of text is worthwhile. And, of course, you often won't be talking about formatting a couple of paragraphs—you'll be formatting hundreds of them. Defining the style requires you to do the formatting just once. From then on, you can apply this collection of formatting commands with one click of the mouse on the Styles palette (or you could choose the style from the Styles menu).

Clearly, saving time is motivation enough to use styles. But that doesn't say the half of it. How creative can you be if you know your decision to make a change requires a tedious process of reformatting every paragraph in a publication? You don't make that kind of work for yourself on a whim. With styles, however, you can fool around to your heart's content, knowing that a change will simply require you to redefine a style.

Applying Styles

Styles apply to entire PageMaker paragraphs. That's a critical point.

You can use a style to create a headline with bold type, but you can't use a style to selectively format just a few words in the headline. (One day character-level styles will be part of PageMaker, but not yet in Version 6.0. However, this situation isn't as painful as it once was thanks to PageMaker's new tagging language, more robust scripting capabilities, and new power for developers who write Plug-ins. You can find out more about all these things in Chapter 28, "Automating PageMaker.")

Styling with Palettes and Menus

You can choose from four methods of applying styles. You can use the Style palette, the Text mode of the Control palette, or the <u>S</u>tyle submenu in the <u>T</u>ype menu. In each case, you must use the Text tool and click an insertion point in the paragraph you want to format or select multiple paragraphs if you like. To apply paragraph formatting, such as a style, it isn't necessary to highlight the entire paragraph, just click anywhere in the paragraph text.

Styling with the Styles Palette

The Styles palette ranks as the easiest of the methods to apply PageMaker styles.

When you bring up the Styles palette (press Ctrl+Y or use the <u>W</u>indow menu), the palette will be ready to go to work assigning styles to your text (see fig. 7.1).

FIG. 7.1 ▶

The Styles palette.

After you select the paragraph you want to style, move the Text tool over to the Styles palette, where the tool changes to a pointer. Click the style you want to apply, simple as that.

If you always want the Styles palette to appear when you open a new publication, set it as a default, as described in Chapter 3, "Personalizing Pagemaker Preferences."

TIP ▶ **Stretch Out the Styles Palette for Maximum Access**

When it first appears, the Styles palette is tiny, and you must scroll up and down to access your list of styles. Luckily, the Styles palette operates like any other window, so you can size it larger for easier access to all your styles. You can also click and drag the title bar and put the Styles palette anywhere you want on the page. I usually stretch the Style palette into a tall vertical shape and keep it along the right side of the Pasteboard, so my styles are completely available without scrolling—just a mouse click away.

Styling with the Control Palette

With the Control palette in Paragraph mode, as shown in figure 7.2, you can select a style from the menu list at the left end of the palette.

You can also have the Control palette look up your style for you by typing the first few letters of its name. It will jump to the style that most closely matches what you type, and as you keep typing, it will keep guessing at where you are headed (the same way you can look up a font in Character view). Once the style has been selected, just Tab to the next field or press Enter, and the style is assigned to whatever text you selected for formatting.

FIG. 7.2 ▶

The Control palette style assignment section.

Styling with the Style Submenu
You can also use the Style submenu, located under the Type menu (see fig. 7.3). As with the other methods of assigning a style, you must first select the text to be styled and then use the menu to pick which style you want to use.

FIG. 7.3 ▶

The Style submenu method of applying a style.

TIP ▶ Undo Doesn't Undo Styles

When you assign a style, keep in mind that you can't undo your move. PageMaker's Undo command doesn't have any power over styles.

Automatic Styling by Inheritance and Cascading
When you are typing new text into PageMaker, you can automatically assign styles to new paragraphs, and you can do it in two ways. Both of the following

methods work by passing on a style assignment from one paragraph to the next as you are typing:

▶ *Inherited style assignment.* When you press Enter at the end of a paragraph, the previous paragraph's formatting carries on to the new paragraph. Think of it as the new paragraph inheriting its style assignment from the preceding one.

▶ *Cascading style application.* If you defined a Next Style attribute within the original paragraph's style, your new paragraph will not inherit the previous style. It will be formatted with your Next Style designation. The method of defining a Next Style function is discussed in the later section "Cascading, Mimicking, Merging, Copying, and Importing Styles."

Augmenting and Overriding Styles with Local Formatting

You don't need to feel restrained by the style process. Any time you like, you can override a style by imposing what PageMaker calls *local formatting.* In fact, right there's an example of local formatting. The italic styling on the words "local formatting" has been applied on top of the body copy style definition for this paragraph. (This entire book has been composed in PageMaker.)

Why call it local formatting? It's because you are applying the formatting on an ad hoc spot basis, as opposed to the global, document-wide formatting defined by a paragraph style. You'll occasionally hear the alternate term *hard formatting* used for local formatting.

In figure 7.4, you can see how it's possible to emphasize parts of a paragraph and still have all the benefits of the style formatting technique. The style definition has created all the formatting for this sample paragraph (the type face, indent, type size, and so on), and local formatting has been used to draw additional attention to the word `emphasis` by setting it in italic type wherever it occurs in the text.

Fig. 7.4 ▶

Local formatting for emphasis within a styled paragraph.

Sometimes, even though there's a style in place on a paragraph, you will want to put *emphasis* on a word or two. This *emphasis* can be applied, such as the use of italic styling here, right over the top of the style definition for the paragraph. So, *emphasis* can be said to be local formatting, as opposed to the global formatting achieved through the use of style definitions.

As you read the next few paragraphs, it's critical that you keep in mind one confusing fact about PageMaker terminology. Type styles are not the same as paragraph style definitions. The term type styles refers only to the typographic attributes available in the Type Style command under the Type menu. Those are normal, bold, italic, underline, strikethrough, and reverse. Paragraph styles are the collections of text and paragraph attributes that you define and then apply to paragraphs through the Type menu's Style command, the Control Palette's list of styles, or the Styles palette. Type styles and paragraph styles do interact with one another, however, and you need to understand how that interaction works.

You might think that applying a new paragraph style or reapplying a paragraph's current style would completely reformat a paragraph to comply with the new style definition. However, that's not true. Some kinds of local formatting are more permanent than others. Type styling attributes, such as bold or italic, stay put when you apply a new paragraph style. So does case formatting (all caps or small caps) and position formatting (super- and subscripts). Remember I mentioned that some folks call local formatting by the alternative name of hard formatting? This characteristic of permanency for some of the text attributes explains why.

To help you remember which type attributes have this diehard behavior, you have a built-in list right in the Control palette—the buttons right beneath the typeface name help you keep in mind which of the type attributes are retained even when you apply a new paragraph style.

There's a twist to this interaction of paragraph styles and type styles. If you apply a paragraph style to some text, and the text has some local formatting for type styling, and the paragraph style contains the same kind of type styling, your move has the same effect as assigning the type style twice. It reverses your old type styling because it toggles it off. For example, applying a paragraph style that calls for bold type reverses any existing local formatting for bold type.

TIP ▶ Keyboard Shortcuts for Keeping or Tossing Local Formatting

You can take control over this interplay between local formatting and your paragraph styles with a couple of keyboard shortcuts. If you want to preserve all local formatting (for any text or paragraph attribute) as you apply a new style, hold down the Shift key as you click in the Styles palette.

You can remove type styling (returning it to what PageMaker calls the Normal type style) by selecting the text you want to normalize and pressing Shift+Spacebar. PageMaker considers "normal" to be a type style just like bold or italic or underlining, and that's why it is listed on the Type Style submenu. (Don't confuse this item on the Type Style submenu with the defined paragraph style "Normal" used by Microsoft Word.)

Case (all caps and small caps), superscript, and subscript aren't listed on the Type Style submenu; therefore, you can only reverse these by reapplying the type style, which toggles it back off. Case and the "scripts" do not respond to the normal type style key shortcut.

You can apply styles on huge passages of complicated text if you can identify a pattern that links all the paragraphs you want to style. For example, perhaps all your first level headlines have the word "chapter" in them with a punctuation mark, such as a colon. The point is to search on some unique combination of characters.

Search for the unique character combination, applying the headline style as you go so that you replace both the style and your search criteria. This feature is discussed more in Chapter 9, "Editing Copy with the Story Editor." Because scripting now works in Story Editor, you can even automate this tip. Check Chapter 28, "Automating PageMaker," for more information on using scripting.

Identifying Styles and Their Status

With PageMaker, you have several ways to determine what style you assigned to a particular paragraph; you can also determine whether the style has been given any special additional formatting.

In simple documents with just one or two headline styles and some body copy, you can easily sort out one style from another just by looking at them. Headlines are usually bold, and body copy appears in plain type. But in larger documents, it's not so easy to sort things out. Figure 7.5 shows the style status clues you can use to keep your style assignments straight.

FIG. 7.5 ▶

The style status clues.

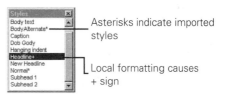

Asterisks indicate imported styles

Local formatting causes + sign

In plain view on your screen, you can see what style has been applied to a paragraph by glancing at the Styles palette (if it is in paragraph mode) or the Control palette. The style name will be highlighted in the Styles palette, and in the Control palette, the style will be the one showing in the selection box.

You can also view style assignments when you pull out the Style submenu under the Type menu. The style in power will be checked.

If you are working in the Story Editor, you can tell Preferences to display style names alongside each paragraph down the left edge of your editor window.

In addition to all these clues to the exact style that's been assigned to some text, you will sometimes see a plus sign (+) or an asterisk (*) next to a style name.

The plus sign means that the style has some local or hard formatting assigned somewhere in that paragraph. The entire paragraph is not consistent with the body text style, and so the plus sign indicates that you have overridden the style.

The plus sign also shows if the cursor is over the "inconsistent" characters in the paragraph.

An asterisk tells you that the style has been brought in from outside and, strictly speaking, isn't yet a PageMaker style. This often happens when you edit a document in a word processor, assigning styles to make it easier to work with your text when you bring it into PageMaker. PageMaker lists the word processor style, but doesn't fully adopt it until you edit it for the first time in PageMaker. Chapter 8, "Pouring Text into PageMaker," provides you with more detail on this process.

TIP ▶ **Generate a Style Reference List**

Applying styles in a complex document can be much more manageable if you keep a printed reference list of all your styles and how they relate to one another. The overview you get from this master list of styles helps you use the styles more effectively and consistently. (This never happens to you or me, mind you, but some people have been known to create a duplicate style, losing track of the fact that they had already defined one for that job.) The Pub Info Plug-in can do this style reference list job for you.

Defining or Redefining Styles

The real power of PageMaker styles comes from defining your own. When you apply the styles you've defined, that's just the payoff. This section covers the basics of defining styles. The section "Tactics Recipe: Developing Your Personal Style" then builds on this section to help you put styles to work.

Exploring the Styles Definition Dialog Boxes

Figure 7.6 gives you a map of the Define Styles and Edit Style dialog boxes. As simple as they are, these dialogs are among the most powerful of all the components of the PageMaker user interface.

Fig. 7.6 ▶

The Define Styles and Edit Style dialog boxes.

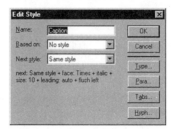

Understanding the Define Styles Dialog Box

You get to the main Define Styles dialog box (as opposed to its subordinate Edit Style dialog box, covered in the next section) by using the Define Styles command on the Type menu.

To edit an existing style, scroll through the list of styles in this dialog box and choose the style you want to edit, clicking the Edit button to modify it.

For information on keyboard + click direct access to both of these functions see this chapter's tip "Express Access to Style Editing."

After you are in the Define Styles dialog box, in addition to editing an existing style, you can make up a completely new style. Just click the New button. You get the Edit Style dialog box with no name entered into the Name field. Fill in the name of the new style definition, and make any changes you want to PageMaker's assumptions about text and paragraph formatting.

PageMaker bases the initial entries in the New Style dialog box on an existing style if you happened to choose one before clicking the New button. Or, if you click the [Selection] option at the head of the scrolling list, the new style will be based on whatever text you had selected prior to going to Define Styles. If you did not have any text selected, the new style will be based on the current mini-defaults for character and paragraph formatting.

When you are done, click OK to adopt your finished style.

You may have noticed the Copy button. Discussion about copying styles is in the upcoming section "Cascading, Mimicking, Merging, Copying, and Importing Styles."

The Remove button does just what it sounds like it would do—it removes a style. This option cannot be undone. If you remove a style by mistake and catch your error in time, however, you can click the Cancel button and back out of the situation without making an irrevocable change. Also, if you do a Save immediately before removing a style and then realize you made a mistake in the Edit Style dialog box, you can use Revert in the File menu as a rescue path to get back to where you were.

TIP ▶   Delete a Style to Convert Text to Local Formatting

Whenever you remove a style, any text tagged with that style acquires a "No style" identification in the style application lists. However, all the text's style-assigned formatting is retained as local formatting attributes.

TIP ▶   Create Instant Styles with the Control Palette

Use the Control palette to make an instant style. First, format some text, experimenting until you've got just the look you want. Then highlight the text. Activate the control palette and tab to the style list section. Type in the name of your new style and press Enter. Presto, instant new style. Note that if you duplicate an existing style name, PageMaker will respond as it normally would, offering to assign the existing style to the highlighted text.

Extra added bonus! This Control palette technique performs a two-step procedure in a single powerful move. When you use the Style menu command, you need to first define the new style and then use the Styles palette to apply the style. The Control palette style definition routine simultaneously defines the style and applies it to the selected text.

Editing Existing Styles and Formatting New Ones

If you click the Edit button in the Define Styles dialog box, you gain access to all the text formatting functions of PageMaker in the Edit Style dialog. Notice the four buttons that appear on the lower right side of the dialog in figure 7.6.

These four buttons—Type, Paragraph, Tabs, and Hyphenation—take you directly to the corresponding dialog boxes you reach through the Type menu (which are covered in detail in Chapters 5 and 6). The Type button gets you to the familiar

Type Specifications dialog box; <u>P</u>aragraph to Paragraph Specifications; T<u>a</u>bs to Indents/Tabs; and <u>H</u>yphenation to the Hyphenation command's dialog box. Each of these dialog boxes, when reached through Edit Styles, works almost exactly the same way it does when reached through the Type menu, with one major difference: the actions that you perform when you access the dialog boxes through these four buttons are recorded as style definition information. Unfortunately, there's one minor exception to this behavior. The Apply button doesn't work in the Indents/Tabs dialog box when you are defining a style.

The next section, "Cascading, Mimicking, Merging, Copying, and Importing Styles," covers the <u>B</u>ased On and Next <u>S</u>tyle pull-down lists in the Edit Style dialog box.

Notice the space directly below the <u>B</u>ased On and Next <u>S</u>tyle functions. All your style decisions are reflected here in the form of a style definition that spells out the character and paragraph attributes in the definition.

When you arrive in the Edit Styles dialog box, the <u>N</u>ame field will be filled out differently, depending on what you selected from the scrolling list of styles before you clicked the <u>E</u>dit button.

If you highlighted the [Selection] item, the <u>N</u>ame area is empty because you will be creating a new style.

If you chose a style name from the list, the existing style name will be automatically entered in the <u>N</u>ame field. Your style definition actions will modify the existing style.

TIP ▶ Express Access to Style Editing

You can zoom right to the Edit Style dialog box. Hold down the Ctrl key and click in the Styles palette. What you get depends on what you clicked. If you clicked an existing style, you will be in Edit Style for that existing style. If you clicked [No Style], you will be delivered to the Edit Style dialog box but you will have a blank name field, and the formatting entries will be based on the currently selected text or on the current mini-default. You'll be creating a new style. (You can also use the keyboard shortcut Ctrl+3 to directly access the Define Styles dialog box without having to reach for the mouse.)

Cascading, Mimicking, Merging, Copying, and Importing Styles

Once you design a style, you can amplify and extend that work into other styles and other publications. Use the following techniques to recycle your style definitions:

▶ Cascade from one existing style to another using the Next Style features of the Edit Style dialog box.

▶ Mimic an existing style in your current publication with the Based On function from Edit Style.

▶ Merge two styles in your current publication.

▶ Copy the styles from another PageMaker publication.

▶ Import styles when you bring in text from another document.

Cascading Styles by Using Next Style

When you use the Next Style pull-down list, you are telling PageMaker which style to assign to a following paragraph (see fig. 7.7) as you are typing text into your publication.

This Next Style function befuddles a lot of people, so here's the important thing to remember. The Next Style only works when you press Enter to start a new paragraph (starting it with the next style, see?).

The Next Style attribute won't change any paragraphs that already exist in your document, only ones that you type new. Also, it won't assign the next style to paragraphs as they are being imported. It only operates when you are working in text and type Enter.

Fig. 7.7 ▶
_____

The Next Style list in the Edit Style dialog box.

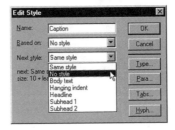

Mimicking Styles with Based On

The Based On style definition attribute, unlike Next Style, forms a parent/child link between two styles (see fig. 7.8). When a style has been subordinated to another style through the Based On pull-down list, any change to the parent style (the style the child is "Based On") ripples down through all its subordinate paragraphs. The ripple can go many layers deep if you allow a number of paragraphs to be dependent on one another.

This Based On attribute can be powerful indeed, but use caution or you could get some pretty wild and unexpected effects. For example, if you have a subhead style subordinate to a major headline and change the typeface, you'll change the typeface of the subhead as well. About the only text attribute that doesn't change when you make one of the "based on" moves is the size of the type. Practically everything else changes though—bold, italic, typeface, superscript, and so on.

FIG. 7.8 ▷

The Based On list of choices from the Edit Style dialog box.

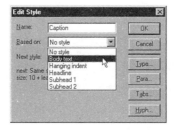

Merging Two Styles

This usually comes up when you've been using local formatting to experiment with a new version of a style and you now want to adopt the experiment as the new style definition. Or, in the heat of deadline time, maybe you inadvertently created two similar styles and want to combine them.

You might be tempted to use the search-and-replace function of the Story Editor to accomplish a style merger, but merging through the Define Styles dialog box is usually easier and faster.

To merge two styles, you must first decide which style contains the formatting information you want to keep. When you merge, you replace one style with the other. We'll call the one you want to keep the survivor style.

Next, Ctrl+click the survivor style's name in the Style palette. The Edit Style dialog box comes up, with the name of your survivor style showing in the name field.

Edit the name of the survivor style to exactly match the name of the style being replaced. Click OK. You get a dialog box like the one in figure 7.9, asking whether you want to replace the old style with the new style.

FIG. 7.9 ▷

The Replace Style dialog box—the critical point in the merger of two styles.

II

Working with Text

This is your last chance to cancel because you cannot undo the move. If you aren't sure about your decision, click Cancel. Assuming you're ready to go ahead, click OK.

Throughout your publication every instance of the old style will be replaced with the survivor style formatting. The merged style will have the name of the old style, but you can, of course, rename the new merged style to anything you like.

TIP ▶ **Faster Style Merge/Editing Using Control Palette**

You can perform this style merge process right from the Control palette. I think it's faster this way.

When you want to merge two styles, follow the procedure I've just described—except when you've decided which style is the survivor style, you can Ctrl+click the style name in the Control palette. This will take you to the Edit Styles dialog box where you can do your style renaming and all the rest of the style merging procedure.

After the merge is complete, you can Ctrl+click again to edit the name of the combined styles if you like.

Of course, you can also use Ctrl+click in the Control palette style name area to edit an existing style, just as you can access the Edit Styles dialog box with a Ctrl+click on a style name in the Styles palette.

Copying Styles from Another Publication

You can use the Copy button in the Define Styles dialog box to "borrow" style sheets from other publications.

The Copy button brings up the dialog box in figure 7.10. It's a standard Open File dialog box. Simply select the source publication that contains the style sheet of definitions you wish to copy and click OK.

Fig. 7.10 ▶

The Copy Styles dialog box.

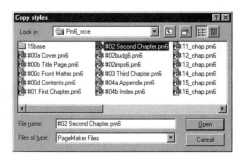

This style copying operation behaves a lot like the style merge discussed in the last section, except it operates on a large scale. It takes in the entire style sheet from the source publication. You can't pluck just one style from a complex source style sheet. You must adopt the entire sheet of style definitions. There's only one possible exception to that rule—duplicate style names.

If even one style on the inbound style sheet already exists in your current publication, you get a dialog box asking whether you want to copy over existing styles:

▶ If you reply yes, all the inbound styles that are named exactly the same as styles in the current publication will merge over the top of those existing styles. In other words, the inbound duplicate styles will be the survivor styles.

▶ If you say no, PageMaker preserves your old styles as the survivor styles and does not copy any of the inbound styles that have duplicate names.

In either case, all the non-duplicated styles from the inbound style sheet are added to the style sheet of the current publication.

TIP ▶ **Use the Copy Button for Style Consistency Across All Chapters of a Book**

The text throughout a book should have consistent formatting. It wouldn't do to set Palatino body text in one chapter but specify Times New Roman body copy in another chapter, for example.

Use the Copy Style command to help achieve this consistency when laying out a multi-chapter book. Select one chapter to be the benchmark for the publication (usually the first chapter). Whenever you make a style adjustment, perform the adjustment in that style leader chapter. Then copy the styles from the style leader chapter into each of the other chapters, one by one. (Unfortunately, there's no book copy command for styles.)

Importing Styles with Inbound Text

Any time you bring styled text into PageMaker, you can make those styles part of your PageMaker style sheet. In order for PageMaker to incorporate the inbound styles, the source must be coming into PageMaker via one of three possible ways:

▶ Paste, following a Copy or Cut.

▶ Drag and drop from another PageMaker publication or the Library palette.

▶ Imported, through PageMaker's Place command.

PageMaker first checks the inbound text for style information. If any new styles are coming in, PageMaker adds those styles to your existing style sheet putting an asterisk (*) next to the name to indicate that it is an imported style.

If any of the inbound styles have duplicate names to those in the destination document, PageMaker gives the destination document styles the leading role. The existing style attributes always come out on top over the inbound styles. In this way, the style import operation works exactly the reverse of the Copy command in Edit Styles.

For much more information on how text importing works, see Chapter 8, "Pouring Text into PageMaker."

TACTICS RECIPE:
Developing Your Personal Style

Style sheets methodically specify your publication design, and at the same time they embody your creative vision. Think of them as the key to consistently and easily bringing to life your personal sense of style in a publication. Here's an overview of how this Tactics Recipe guides you through the process of developing your own personal approach to style sheets:

▶ Decide whether you will take a structured approach to working with styles or will opt to use a sort of "scratch pad" technique.
▶ Plan a basic list of styles.
▶ Design your style-naming system.
▶ Define your styles, using a cascading style approach.
▶ Build a style library using the Library palette.
▶ Be consistent in applying your styles.

Deciding on Your Working Style for Designing Styles

There are two basic methods for developing style sheets:

▶ In the structure method, you plan everything meticulously in advance.
▶ With the scratch pad technique, on the other hand, you improvise your styles as you work and organize them only after you have a good idea how your publication will work.

Here's the crux of this work style issue. Consider this point: To what extent will you design the structure of your publication before you begin designing its pages? Will you define every style or just the major ones? The greater your craving for knowledge of where you will end up with your design, the more you will favor the structured approach to styles.

Probably the best approach combines a little of both, starting with some structure and then experimenting with it as you go.

For example, you probably already know something about the structure you need (three major kinds of type for heads and body copy, three levels of heads, one kind of body copy, captions for graphics, special headlines for sidebar material, and so on).

With these basic styles defined (or imported from your style library or a PageMaker template), edit them in scratch pad fashion, refining your design choices and adding any special purpose styles as you work.

This combined approach delivers all the basic advantages of PageMaker styles. You get consistency because you have a structure, and you gain the creative edge of being able to casually experiment with design options without the drag of tedious reformatting.

But this part's up to you. Some people like to jump in and go for it. Others like to meticulously specify the type for the whole project before starting.

Fundamental Tactic

Whether you choose a structured approach or go with a scratch pad ad hoc style, one fundamental tactic will be essential. Format every paragraph—no exceptions—with a style. It's the only way to achieve the full power of styles in PageMaker.

Planning Your Basic Style Needs

Here's a great way to get started. Outline your document. That's the best way to examine how your styles should relate to one another. The outline makes clear your style requirements. For example, you will probably start by creating a headline style for every level of the headline. When you know how many headline styles you need, you also have a handle on how your body text styles would best fit into the holes beneath each style of headline. Then you can decide what special purpose styles you will need for captions, illustration callouts, bulleted lists, and so on.

II

Working with Text

TIP ▷   Rid Yourself of PageMaker's Default Styles

PageMaker comes with some built-in styles. They almost certainly will not match your style sheet system. When you do build your own styles, the initial PageMaker styles will just be confusing clutter in the Styles palette. One of the first things I do when setting up a new installation of PageMaker is to delete these styles using the Program default technique described in Chapter 3. With no publication open, use the Define Styles dialog box to remove them.

TIP ▷   Make a Plan for Styling Structured Elements Such as Forms

If you know that your publication will have order forms or database-type material, it's a good idea to sketch out a structure for those elements before you begin a layout. If you plan ahead like this, it will be easier for you to design styles so they can be shared between similar structured sections of your project.

You will also want to try to plan ahead for tables and decide whether the Table Editor will do the job in your particular situation. It may be better for you to build tables using one of the style-based techniques discussed in Chapter 16, "Formatting Forms, Tables, and Databases."

Naming Your Styles

Name your styles by their function instead of by their appearance. Rather than call a style by its dominant type attribute, use its function in the name. Instead of "Bold Helvetica," name it "Headline One," signifying that it's a level one headline style.

Make sure that you name your styles in a way that fits your word processor working method. If you use Microsoft Word and use the outline function, you'll want to name your headlines for the built-in outline heading styles of Word. That way you can import your heads with styles already assigned right from your Word document, and the heads can easily be set up for your table of contents and for page breaks.

PageMaker always lists styles in alphabetical order. For that reason, try to name special purpose or little-used styles so that they are out of the way, down at the bottom of the list. That saves you a lot of scrolling.

TIP ▶ Style Major Heads for Page Breaks and Table of Contents

Build page breaks and table of contents specifications into your styles. Your major headlines for starting chapters, for example, will probably need a page break so they always begin on a new page. Likewise, build your table of contents structure into your basic list of styles. Usually headlines would be in your table of contents, for example. This will save tons of time when you pour text into your publication. Chapter pages will automatically break to a new page. Your table of contents can be quickly built.

Defining Styles with the Cascade Approach

By using the Based On attribute in the Edit Style dialog box, you can really link your styles into a system and can create a few fundamental character styles and base all your other styles on them. Headlines would share a common base style. Body copy would be based on another common style. This enables you to make massive changes in a complex style sheet by adjusting a single base definition.

Here's how to set it up. Establish a "base head" style for your headlines, including typeface and paragraph alignment and any other attributes that are going to be common to all of your headlines. Use this base head style as the beginning point for all your headline styles. Then, if you decide your headlines would look better in Helvetica instead of Franklin Gothic, make the change in the base head style, and it will be automatically incorporated in all the headline styles upon which it is based.

You would do the same thing for your body copy, perhaps sharing the base body style among the main text and bulleted text styles.

You might also want to set up a special text base style if your captions, callouts, page numbers and other special page elements will share a common typeface.

Be conservative about linking too many styles together. It's easy to completely twist your style sheet system by making a small tweak in a base style. For that reason, the "base body" and "base head" styles ought to be reserved for simple character formatting. For example, I make changes to table of contents, page break, column break, and indent attributes in the individual styles rather than the "base" styles.

Building a Library of Styles

When you have created a particularly useful style, you should save it to recycle it for future use in other publications. Your options for building style libraries include:

▶ Individual styled paragraphs stored in the Library palette, ready to be dragged and dropped into your publication. The individual style will automatically be incorporated into your style sheet.

▶ PageMaker templates with sets of styles that would be common to certain kinds of publications (books, advertisements, brochures, newsletters). Use the Copy styles command to bring them into your publication.

▶ Scripts written to add styles to your publication, available at the click of a button from the Scripts palette.

▶ Tagging language files that can be placed into your publication, bringing their style definitions in with them.

Selecting a technique will be up to you. The important thing is to build a style library. Any investment in time to do so will be more than compensated for by the time you will save by pulling a ready-made style into a publication with a mouse click or two.

Maybe the easiest method would be the Library palette one. The Library palette can be easily searched so you could have 50 or 100 styles in it and be able to find them easily. If you want to use the Library palette method, here's a run-down:

1. After you go to all the work of creating a ground-thumpingly great style, copy and paste a paragraph of the style into a text block.

2. In the text for the paragraph, include the name of the style and a brief description so you'll be able to remember it in the future when you call on it.

3. Switch to the Pointer tool and select the text as a block.

4. Call up the Library palette from the Window menu if it isn't already open and click the big plus sign in the upper-left corner of the palette. Your item is added to the list of objects in the Library palette.

5. Name your library entry for easy searching. Double-click the untitled item and fill in the dialog box blanks with the name of your entry, your notes, and with keywords so that you can search it out in the future by using the palette's search feature.

6. When you want to pull one of these styles out of your library, simply drag and drop it into your publication from the Library palette. The style name will appear like magic in your Style palette. You can then delete the little text block because it has served its purpose.

Note that the Library drag-and-drop method follows the same style dominance rules as cut and paste or inter-publication drag and drop. The style is adopted only if it is new.

PageMaker's own styles dominate whenever there are duplicate style names.

Where to Go from Here

▶ You won't get the most out of styles unless you know the major elements of formatting text. Chapters 5 and 6 cover type specifications, paragraph specifications, the indents/tabs ruler, and hyphenation.

▶ You will want to spend a lot of time with Chapter 8, "Pouring Text into PageMaker." Writing documents with styles built into them at the word processor can automate much of your typesetting process, particularly for building long documents.

▶ Chapter 9, "Editing Copy with the Story Editor," helps you get a leg up on the power of styles in that environment. You will be really excited about the ability to do massive text formatting with the Story Editor's search and replace capability.

▶ Are you formatting forms, tables, and databases? This book has a chapter by that very name—Chapter 16. Styles are an essential part of one strategy for getting those jobs done.

▶ If you are constructing books or other long documents, Chapter 17, "Building Many Pages," outlines style strategies particular to that process.

▶ New to PageMaker 6.0 are two forces for automation. The new Tagging language and the Scripts palette are covered in Chapter 28, "Automating PageMaker." Both of them have the potential for being major boosts in getting the most out of the style feature.

Chapter 8

Pouring Text into PageMaker

In this chapter on pouring word-processed text into PageMaker, you learn about:

The PageMaker text block object, the story, the concept of a text blocks threading together to make up a story, and the text block windowshade.
▼

The three text placement icons.
▼

The three techniques for pouring text onto the page (drag and place, page by page, and AutoFlow).
▼

Sizing, unthreading, and rethreading (merging) text blocks.
▼

PageMaker filters for converting and importing text from several dozen word processor formats.
▼

Linking and unlinking text for updating.

FRANKLY, PAGEMAKER DOESN'T rank as the best word processor on the face of the planet. Its designers never intended that it be used that way, although many people do so.

For most projects, PageMaker works best when used to assemble the elements of pages—when it is used to combine type and graphics. And nine times out of ten those elements come from outside PageMaker. In the case of text, the usual source is a word processing program such as Microsoft Word. And that's what this chapter is all about—bringing in that outside text. ▶ ▶ ▶

KEY CONCEPT:
Understanding Text Blocks, Stories, Threads, and Windowshades

Think of a block of PageMaker text as an object instead of text. Even though *text blocks* contain text, you can move and size them as you would move and size graphic objects. The text block simply acts as a container for your text. Fix this critically important fundamental concept firmly in your mind—you'll use it many times a day when working with text blocks and stories.

Text block objects combined make up a complete PageMaker *story*. The text blocks are connected by an invisible connection that links them like beads on a thread. They are *threaded* together from top to bottom, beginning to end. As blocks are expanded or reduced, the text thread flows freely between them, trying to fill each block with text.

A story may have one text block, or it may have hundreds. The thread of text blocks in a book will probably be pretty straightforward, running from page 1 to page 300 in serial order. But the thread in a newsletter, newspaper, or magazine may be a little more complicated. For example, a story on page 1 may be continued on page 23, with a dozen other stories located on the intervening pages. Even though separated by those pages, the text blocks of the page 1 story are threaded together, and text flows between them as the blocks are expanded and contracted during layout. Together the text blocks constitute a thread that makes up a complete story.

Figure 8.1 shows three text blocks, poured into three adjacent columns.

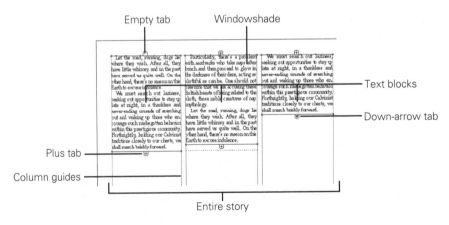

Empty tab   Windowshade

Text blocks

Down-arrow tab

Plus tab

Column guides

Entire story

FIG. 8.1 ▲

Here is the complete anatomy of a PageMaker story with three text blocks in three adjacent columns.

The horizontal lines across the top and bottom of each text block are called windowshades. You can pull the tabs attached to each windowshade up or down so that they roll and unroll portions of the story's text like an old-fashioned, roller-type windowshade. As the text block expands and contracts in this manner, the text inside the block squeezes in and out of the other blocks in the thread.

Each windowshade tab contains a symbol that indicates the condition of the text just outside your view. A plain, empty windowshade tab at the top or bottom of a text block indicates that no text is left to be rolled out. A plus sign tab shows that there's more text, but it's located in the next (or previous) text block in the thread. A down arrow indicates there's more text, but it hasn't been placed.

In figure 8.2, notice what happens when the bottom windowshade of the second text block is moved upward. The move leaves less room in that text block for the text (less room in the container). As a result, the excess text in that block spills down the story thread into the next text block in the thread.

Here's one last thing you need to know about—the vertical lines you see are called *column guides*. When you are placing text on a page and click near a column guide with a loaded text placement icon, the text pours between the column guides, stopping at the bottom margin. For more information on column guides, see Chapter 13, "Designing a Master Page Grid."

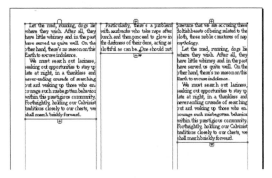

Fig. 8.2 ▲

Text slides up and down the thread among the three text blocks.

Using the Place Command and Pouring Text onto the Page

The metaphor that you pour text into PageMaker comes from the way you import text by filling a PageMaker text placement icon (also sometimes called a *text bucket* or a *text gun*). You then use your filled text icon to pour the text into a text block object, either between column guides or by dragging out a space on the page to define an ad hoc text block.

Before you can pour any text onto your pages, you must first load your text placement icon.

Using the Place Command to Load Your Text Icon

Choose File, Place (or the keyboard shortcut Ctrl+D). The Place dialog box pops up on-screen (see fig. 8.3). It's a standard File Open dialog box, and you simply select the file you want to import. You can have any of PageMaker's pointer tools in use when you choose this command. The tool doesn't matter because as soon as you implement the Place command, your pointer automatically changes to a text placement icon.

FIG. 8.3 ▶

The Place dialog box as it appears when ready to pour in some text.

When you select your file and double-click it or click OK, PageMaker brings the file into memory, conducts whatever file translation may be needed, and loads the text from the file into a text placement icon.

Additional sections of this chapter talk about the other options in the Place dialog box (retaining format, converting quotes, and reading style tags).

PageMaker 6.0 now has a powerful new tagging language that resembles para-graph style tags. Chapter 28, "Automating PageMaker," has complete information about PageMaker 6.0's new tagging language, which relies on using the Place command.

Understanding the Three Text Placement Icon Types

Figure 8.4 shows the three different types of text placement icons. Each acts differently when you click the icon on a page.

FIG. 8.4 ▶

The three text placement icons—Manual, Semiautomatic, and AutoFlow.

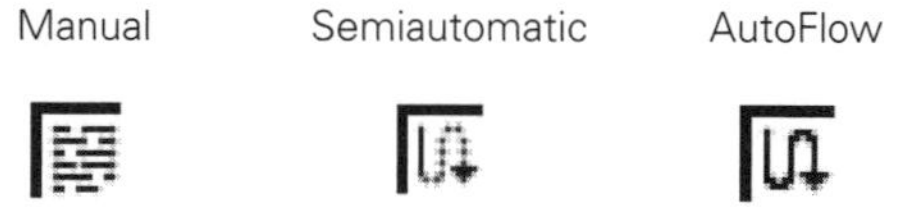

Manual   Semiautomatic   AutoFlow

The Manual Text Icon

The Manual text icon looks like a tiny page of text. Manual text placement works on a one-shot basis, so you must reload it every time you dispense some text onto the page.

Reload your Manual text icon by clicking a down-arrow windowshade tab at the end of a story thread that has not been completely placed.

You can also reload your Manual text icon by clicking a plus windowshade tab at the top of a block. This will add a new block in the middle of a story; it doesn't place the same text twice, but simply creates a new empty container that sucks text back from the next text block in the thread.

The Manual text icon is best for placing text a column or page at a time, or for drag-placing text. That's where you click the text icon and drag out a box to size the text block to hold your poured text. Use drag-placing for intricate work where you are fitting text around graphics (captions, drawings placed across columns) or placing text across columns (a page headline).

If you click anywhere between two column guides without dragging out a text block, the Manual icon fills that column from the click point on down until it butts up against a lower margin or another text block.

To access the Manual text icon, turn off AutoFlow mode in the Layout menu or hold down the Ctrl key to temporarily convert the AutoFlow icon to a Manual icon.

The AutoFlow Text Icon

The curvy line of the AutoFlow text placement icon suggests the way text blocks thread together on a page to create a story.

That's an apt association, because that's how the AutoFlow icon functions—by placing an entire story at a time, automatically jumping from column to column and from page to page, placing text between empty column guides as it goes. If the AutoFlow text icon gets to the last page of your publication and needs more room to finish placing a story, it even adds pages to finish the job.

To use the AutoFlow text placement icon, turn on AutoFlow under the Layout menu. Or you can have the AutoFlow icon on a temporary basis by pressing the Ctrl key when the Manual icon is showing.

AutoFlow works best for the initial placement of a large story that will take many pages, such as all the pages of a book chapter or a technical report.

The Semiautomatic Text Icon

The Semiautomatic icon lets you fire single shots of text, but it automatically re-loads itself after each bit of text placement. This icon looks like a modified form of the AutoFlow icon, and that's just how it acts.

Use this icon if you need to place text into defined spaces that don't fall one right after the other, as they do when you autoflow text. This icon is terrific for rapid-fire placement of text—spotting bits of text on a single page, placing text into multiple columns on double-facing pages, clicking text onto a page, and then jumping to the next spot where you continue the story thread and alternating column placement with drag placement.

Like the other text placement icons, after you "let go" of the text and it is pouring into a column or page, placement continues to the bottom of a column or page, or until it runs up against another text block. Semiautomatic will not add pages.

You can't lock in the Semiautomatic text icon as you can with the Manual or AutoFlow icons; it's a temporary measure only. You access the icon by holding down the Shift key while either of the other two icons are showing.

TIP ▶ **For Maximum Flexibility, Leave Autoflow Turned Off**

Many people, including tech editor John Cornicello, do most of their text placement with Autoflow turned off. That way you are in Manual most of the time and can get to Automatic (Ctrl) or Semiautomatic (Shift) with easy keyboard access. This will vary depending on your project and working style, but Semiautomatic has the advantage of always coming back to you with a loaded text placement icon if there's more text to place. Manual and Automatic come back with a Pointer, requiring you to go back and click on the windowshade if you still have unset text.

Pouring Text

After you have a loaded text placement icon, you can pour the text onto the page in one of two ways:

▶ You can drag-place text within a text block that you draw in freehand style.

▶ You can simply click the text icon to pour your text within column guides or page margins.

Placing Text In a Custom Text Block

Sometimes you want to place text in freehand fashion instead of within formal column guides. You don't need to automate your text placement; you just need text poured into a container of a particular size and shape. Use the drag-place move to pour text in this customized way. You "draw" the confines of the text block onto the page using a click-and-drag movement, which gives you a text block container shaped to your specifications. Of course, like any other Page-Maker object, you can click and drag on the text box handles at the corners of the windowshade to adjust the shape of the text block.

To drag-place, use any of the three text icons, but you will probably use Manual most of the time. Simply click and drag down and to the right from the upper-left corner of your text location (see fig. 8.5). Drag-place ignores column guides.

FIG. 8.5 ▶

With this drag-place in progress, the Manual text icon is used to drag out a text box for the in-bound text.

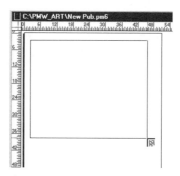

C:\PMW_ART\New Pub.pm6

TIP ▶ **Draw a Text Box with the Text Tool**

You can perform a click and drag with your Text tool, just as you can drag-place with a text placement icon. If you aren't placing text but you know where you want your text to go as you type it in, click the Text tool where you want your text placed and drag out until you get a box the size you want. The box seems to disappear after you draw it, but as you type, your text wraps from line to line as each line reaches the right edge of the text block you've drawn. Of course, if you have much text to create, you are much better off doing your typing in the Story Editor. Even though it has the advantage of what-you-see-is-what-you-get, Layout mode is a lot slower for text entry than the Story Editor.

Working with Text

Placing Text within Column Guides

If you simply click your text icon pointer inside a pair of column guides, the text automatically flows perfectly onto the page inside your defined column.

As the text flows into the column, it interacts with barriers placed in its way (such as a bottom margin, or a graphic with a text wrap boundary). The behavior depends on which of the three text placement icons you have been using:

▶ With the Manual icon, PageMaker stops and waits for further orders when it hits the bottom of a column or another text block. Text flow stops, and the bottom windowshade has a down-arrow tab, indicating that you must reload your Manual text icon by clicking the tab in order to place the next text block in the thread.

▶ The Semiautomatic icon acts like the Manual icon, stopping at a column bottom or text block. However, because you are working with the Semiautomatic icon, the icon automatically reloads and can repeatedly place new text blocks without requiring you to reload by clicking again on the down-arrow tab of the windowshade.

▶ In AutoFlow, the text placement doesn't stop at all. PageMaker lays text into place up to the lower margin or the Text Wrap graphic and skips to the next available open spot in the current column or the next column.

You can slow down the AutoFlow process so that you can see each page as it fills with text. To do that, before you start the text placement process you go to the Preferences dialog box, under the File menu and click the Other button. Then click the button for Display All Pages.

TIP ▶ Put Unplaced Text on Hold

If you want to pause your text placement for a bit, but still have some unplaced text in your icon, you have a couple of options. If you have already placed at least one block on the page, click any tool in the Toolbox to switch off the text placement icon. If you have not yet placed any text, drag-place a text block on the Pasteboard to give yourself a temporary placeholder text block. In either case, the last text block you placed displays a down arrow. To resume, click the down arrow to reload your text placement icon.

If you have not yet created any sort of text block, and this is a fresh load of text, and you click something in the Toolbox, you will completely cancel the Place operation. You'll lose all your text and will have to use the Place command again to restart.

Sizing and Positioning Text Blocks

Because text blocks are objects, they can be sized and positioned just like graphic objects. To adjust the size of a text block to fit it into a column, use the Pointer tool to grab one of the four handles at each end of the upper and the lower windowshades. The Pointer tool turns into a double-headed arrow resizing pointer, like the one in figure 8.6. Click and drag on a handle. The text block changes to a box (the handles disappear), and you can pull the text block into your desired shape and size.

FIG. 8.6 ▷

You can size a text block with the Pointer tool.

Pointer tool

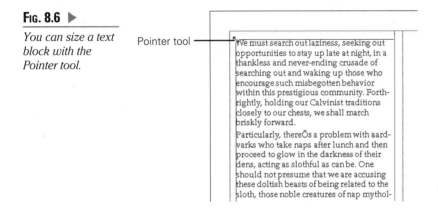

By the way, you don't need to worry about distorting the horizontal or vertical shape of the type inside the text block, as you would in some paint or draw programs. Type specifications are assigned internally; all you are doing is changing the shape of the container.

You can also use the windowshades to change the vertical size of a text block without changing its width. By unrolling (or rolling up) text using the windowshades, you can fine-tune the way paragraphs break between columns and pages. To pull a windowshade up or down, click and drag on a handle and adjust the text break as shown in figure 8.7.

Notice how the pointer turns into a sort of vertically-oriented double arrow? Also, notice the dotted line directly below the lower windowshade—you see that dotted line marker every once in a while when PageMaker can't quite place all the text it thinks it ought to. This line is PageMaker's way of telling you that your widow and orphan controls or other paragraph formatting is preventing it from filling the text block you have set up. Try dragging the windowshade handle past the dotted line to see if the material will fall into place anyway, or if you can tweak the line breaks to optimize the layout solution.

Fig. 8.7 ▶

*Adjust the vertical
size of a text block
by unrolling or
rolling up a
windowshade.*

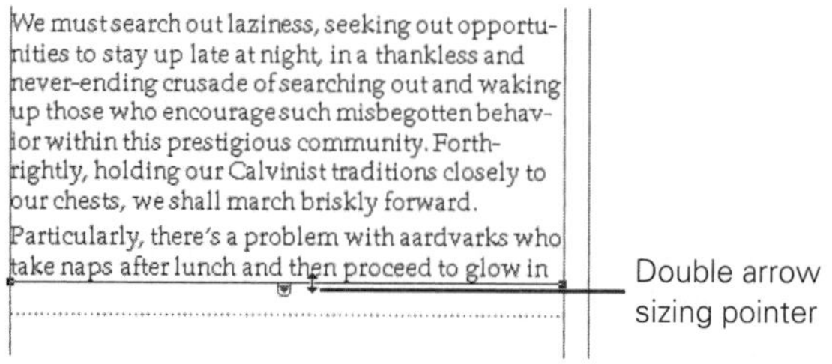

We must search out laziness, seeking out opportunities to stay up late at night, in a thankless and
never-ending crusade of searching out and waking
up those who encourage such misbegotten behavior within this prestigious community. Forthrightly, holding our Calvinist traditions closely to
our chests, we shall march briskly forward.
Particularly, there's a problem with aardvarks who
take naps after lunch and then proceed to glow in

Double arrow
sizing pointer

TIP ▶ **Place Centered Text Blocks Completely Across Columns or Pages**

You might be tempted to try centering text by eye, just by sliding the text block
around on the page. Instead, size the text block completely across the area you are
centering on (a column or page, for example). Then center align the text (using the
Control palette, or the Paragraph or Alignment commands on the Type menu). This
lets PageMaker do the work for you—probably more precisely than your eyeball could
do it—by automatically centering your text in your target area.

Unthreading and Rethreading Text Blocks

Text blocks have special properties when it comes to cutting and pasting them,
and you can use these properties to your advantage when you need to unstring
or restring a bunch of text blocks in a thread.

Unthreading Text Blocks

The top of figure 8.8 shows three text blocks. Notice that each one has a
windowshade tab showing a plus, indicating that the block is a part of a thread.
At times you may need to unlink (or unthread) blocks like the ones in this illustration, so that they become discrete stories on their own.

The bottom part of the figure shows the same text blocks after the middle block
has been unthreaded from the other two. The middle text block now has an
empty tab at the top and bottom windowshade, indicating that as a story it is
completely placed and has no threaded connections to other blocks. It has been
completely unthreaded from the two other text blocks. The other text blocks
remain threaded to each other, however. You can tell by their plus tabs at the
bottom of the left-hand column and the top of the right-hand column.

To unlink a text block, select it using the Pointer tool, and then cut it and paste it
right back in place. Use the shortcuts for the Cut command (Ctrl+X) and the
Paste command (Ctrl+V).

If you want the unlinked text block to be pasted back into the exact same position it held before it was cut, use the power paste trick. Paste it back with the
keyboard combination Ctrl+Shift+P.

FIG. 8.8 ▶

This before and after view shows the middle text block in its threaded and unthreaded condition.

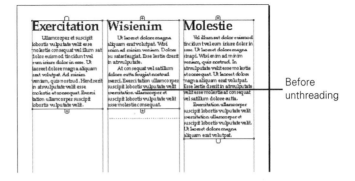

Before
unthreading

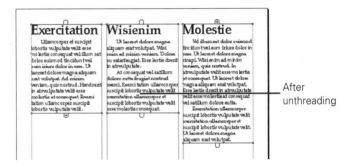

After
unthreading

II

Working with Text

Rethreading Text Blocks

You can reassemble unthreaded text in a couple of ways: by using the Text tool method or the Pointer tool method.

Using the Text tool, click in a text block and choose <u>E</u>dit, Select <u>A</u>ll (or Ctrl+A) to select all the text in the unthreaded text block. Then you <u>C</u>opy (Ctrl+C) or Cu<u>t</u> (Ctrl+X) the text, and <u>P</u>aste (Ctrl+V) it in the text block where you want it. That action merges the text into the same thread using the same basic approach as you might use in your word processor.

If the text block you are rethreading has unplaced text (a down-arrow tab on the bottom windowshade), that unplaced text is inserted along with the visible text at the Text tool insertion point of the threaded text block.

The Pointer tool method tends to be faster than the Text tool technique. Instead of selecting the text inside the text block, simply select the text block as an object by using the Pointer tool, then cut or copy the text block. After you have the text block on the Clipboard, you use the same technique as the Text tool method. Switch to the Text tool, click in the text block where you want the unthreaded text block to go, and choose the Paste command. The unthreaded text block merges into the target text block.

Using this Pointer method, only the visible text is copied into the other story, and any overset (unthreaded or unplaced) text will be lost.

TIP ▶ **Use Standard Text Selection Tricks In Layout View**

Most of the text selection moves you know from your word processor also work in PageMaker, both in Layout view and in Story Editor view. Here are some reminders of a few favorites:

▼ Double-click with the Text tool to select a word.

▼ Triple-click to select a paragraph.

▼ Ctrl+right arrow and Ctrl+left arrow move the insertion point backward and forward one word at a time.

▼ Ctrl+End moves the insertion point to the end of a sentence.

▼ Ctrl+Home moves the insertion point to the beginning of a sentence.

▼ Ctrl+up arrow moves the insertion point up a paragraph at a time.

▼ Ctrl+down arrow moves the insertion point down a paragraph at a time.

TIP ▶ **Searching for a Lost Text Block**

It can be really easy to lose a story that you dragged off onto the Pasteboard, especially if it's Reverse text or a small block that inadvertently got dragged into a corner of the Pasteboard. Here's one approach to finding the missing block, assuming it doesn't show up in overset text. Just go to Entire Pasteboard view. Make sure you have the Pointer tool selected, and choose Edit, Select All (or the keyboard shortcut Ctrl+A). With everything selected, you should be able to spot the lost text block.

Importing Text

This latest version of PageMaker has even more text import filters than before. This should make the process of importing most kinds of text nearly painless. The only problem will be the next round of word processor upgrades with new versions that don't work with the existing filters, but there's a way to handle that as well.

PageMaker Filters

When you use the Place command to bring in text from outside PageMaker, you are bringing it in through a filter. A *filter* is software that interprets the text from a word processor or other source, converting it into a form that PageMaker can understand while, hopefully, retaining your formatting.

In almost every case, PageMaker gives you a sturdy and practical translation. Most common text and paragraph formatting attributes (bold, italic, indents, line spacing, paragraph spacing, and so on) are translated successfully. Fancier features, such as indexing, tables of contents, paragraph borders, and rules, are variable, depending on the feature set of the word processor. Of course, any word processor that doesn't use style sheets (gasp and shudder!) won't have styles assigned to its paragraphs when it comes into PageMaker (unless you use style tags—see "Using Style Tags" later in this chapter).

You may have been thinking, "How will I know which filter to pick?" Relax, you're in luck. PageMaker does a pretty good job of figuring out which filter it should use. It looks at the standard file name extensions, so files ending in DOC get the Microsoft Word filter, and files ending in WP6 get the WordPerfect 6.0 filter, for example.

Looking at Your Installed Filter List

To find out which filters you have, hold down the Ctrl key as you select the About PageMaker item under the Help menu. You get a window like the one in figure 8.9. It lists Plug-ins first, and if you scroll down past those, you see a list of all your filters (for both text and graphics files).

Fig. 8.9 ▶

List your installed filters by holding down the Ctrl key while selecting About PageMaker.

All the obvious word processing options come with PageMaker 6.0, including a complete set of filters for all the Microsoft Word and WordPerfect varieties, a plain text filter (Smart ASCII), filters for various multipurpose integrated Works-type programs, XyWrite, several interchange formats such as RTF (Rich Text Format) and DCA, and so on.

To see exactly which filters were shipped with your PageMaker package, as opposed to which ones you've installed, check the PageMaker online help and the Readme file that came along on your PageMaker distribution disks. Try searching for the words "format" or "import."

TIP ▶ Use Shift Key to Access Special Import Features

Several of the import filters have options for enhancing the text as it is being imported. Hold down the Shift key as you click on Open in the Place dialog box, or while
you double-click on a document in the Place dialog box's file list box. To get details on
which word processor filters have these preferences dialog boxes, see your online
help. Try the topic "Importing format-specific text options."

Keeping Up-to-Date on Your Filters

This filter business seems to be changing constantly. The word processor market
is so competitive that new versions of the leading packages hit the market all the
time. So, you may need to add a filter or two to your set of installed filters as time
goes on. Normally, you get these new filters direct from Adobe or online services
such as CompuServe and America Online. Adobe also has a Web page where
you can pick up files (**html://www.adobe.com**).

TIP ▶ Tagging Language Finally Arrives for PageMaker

The most important new filter with PageMaker 6.0 is the Tagging filter. At long last
PageMaker includes a tagging language similar to the one in QuarkXPress. As with
QuarkXPress, the tagging functionality comes into PageMaker through the importation
and exportation of text, made possible by the tagging import and export filters. In fact,
the filter for the tagging language can digest QuarkXPress tags as well as the enhanced tagging codes that PageMaker includes. Full coverage of the tagging language
has been included in Chapter 28, "Automating PageMaker."

TIP ▶ Import Spreadsheets and Databases

PageMaker, especially with this latest release, has strong capabilities for importing
database files and spreadsheets. If you do much of this kind of work, especially if
you compose tables of information, install these filters. For more information, check
Chapter 16, "Formatting Forms, Tables, and Databases."

Exporting Text

Just as you can import text into PageMaker, you can export text back out of it. To
export text, click the Text tool anywhere in the story that you want to export (or
select the specific text you want to export), and choose Export from the File
menu. The Export Document dialog box appears (see fig. 8.10).

Choose which format you want to use for exporting the file (Tagging, Rich Text
Format, ASCII plain text, Microsoft Word, and so on) using the scrolling list
labeled Save as Type at the bottom of the dialog box. Depending on your
choice, you will have various options to consider, such as whether to export
with style tags.

FIG. 8.10 ▶

The Export Document dialog box.

Using Style Tags

Style tags are "hard" codes that you type into your text. PageMaker reads these tags (filters them) and uses them to assign styles to the paragraphs that are being exported or imported. This style tag concept was a precursor to the new tagging language and now functions almost as a subset of the full-blown tagging language. However, style tags assign paragraph styles to paragraphs in many text filter situations, not merely with the tagging filter.

If you use Microsoft Word, the purpose of style tags may be a bit puzzling to you. The PageMaker filter for importing Word text translates styles beautifully, hardly missing a lick. However, if you aren't using Word and you do want to preassign styles to your text (you do, you do, you do), your only route may be to use style tags. Figure 8.11 shows a sample of style tag-coded text.

FIG. 8.11 ▶

A sample of style tag-coded text.

```
<head>Style Tag Test Text Runs Wild!
<body>Let the mad, running, dogs lie where they wish. After all,
they have little whimsy and in the past have served us quite well.
On the other hand, there's no reason on this Earth to excuse
indolence.
We must search out laziness, seeking out opportunities to stay up
late at night, in a thankless and never-ending crusade of searching
out and waking up those who encourage such misbegotten behavior
within this prestigious community. Forthrightly, holding our
Calvinist traditions closely to our chests, we shall march briskly
forward.
```

Notice that there are only two style tags in the sample—one for the headline and the other for the body text. You don't have to code every single paragraph because the style tags act as a toggle. A style tag stays in effect for every paragraph until you insert a different style tag, which then takes over.

Style tags will save you hours of work if you are bringing text in from a text source that does not support styles (an Optical Character Recognition scan or plain ASCII text, for example).

Do keep in mind that your tags must exactly match the style names. That includes capitalization. If you have a style in PageMaker called "Body," but the style tag reads body with no capital letter, you won't get a match.

Who puts the style tag coding into the text before you bring it into PageMaker? Whoever you can talk into doing it, that's who. Get someone else (anyone else but you) to style the text they are submitting for layout. That's the whole idea of style tags. If someone insists that they can't provide you with true style sheet-type word-processor output (Microsoft Word as a leading example), go to work with your powers of persuasion. Give them a list of standard style names and tell them to use the correct style tag codes in front of their headlines or body text paragraphs (or captions, or secondary headlines, and so on). Otherwise, you'll end up styling it yourself. And if you have to do it yourself, why bother with style tags? Just do the styling in Word.

TIP ▶ Combine Local Formatting with Style Tags

The Place dialog box (refer to fig. 8.3) has a couple of special features: R̲etain Format and Read Ta̲gs. If you choose both of these options, you can import text with paragraph styles, and the filter will also attempt to keep intact simple local formatting such as bold and italic.

Importing Microsoft Word Text

Why this special focus on Microsoft Word? Well, PageMaker and Microsoft Word look and act so much alike that they could be siblings; their approach to paragraph styles matches very closely. It's a relationship that was born in the early days of the desktop publishing revolution.

Back then, Microsoft Word was the leading heavy-duty word processor for the Macintosh, and PageMaker was just being developed—the beginning of DTP. Both Microsoft and Aldus, the developer of PageMaker that has since merged with Adobe, were located in Seattle. Aldus settled on the use of the Microsoft interchange format (RTF) as the fundamental common ground for getting text in and out of PageMaker. Later on when PageMaker added the capability of style sheets, Word had plowed pioneering ground on style sheets in the days of processing text on DOS machines with glowing green text-only monitors.

If you select a Word document in the Place dialog box and then hold down the Shift key while double-clicking (or clicking OK), you get the special dialog box you see in figure 8.12. PageMaker remembers the settings you make in this box for the remainder of your work session. That means, once you close and restart PageMaker, you will need to set the import preferences again.

FIG. 8.12 ▷

The special customization dialog box for importing Word text.

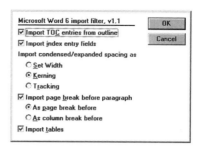

Word has two ways of generating a table of contents, but PageMaker has only one. With this dialog box, you can choose which way to build table of contents information into PageMaker. You can base it in your paragraph by paragraph TOC coding (the .C. codes), or you can base it on Word's outline-based table of contents method. PageMaker codes individual paragraphs (.C. method) or style names (outline method) with a paragraph specification designating them as TOC entries. The outline style table of contents is preferable because it gives you a ready-made structured approach to document building and because it's based on styles (heading 1, heading 2, heading 3, and so on).

Your index codes in Word are imported into PageMaker if you click the Import Index Entry Fields option. This option can be a great tool for starting an index, a topic which is covered in Chapter 17, "Building Many Pages."

Word doesn't have tracking, kerning, or width typographic tools. Word does have condensed/expanded type formatting. The Set Width option is generally closest to what's intended by condensed/expanded type.

The next option in the Word custom import filter box is a choice of how to break specially designated paragraphs. Both programs allow you to format paragraphs so they break to a new page, but in PageMaker, you can format paragraphs in another similar way, so they break to the top of a new column.

Finally, the Custom Filter box allows you to import tables from Word. However, before you get too excited about the possibilities of this command, you should understand that it does not import a fully formatted table (with row and column rules, for example). It imports only the text from the table. However, this can be a significant head start on getting a table set up because the text will retain any special formatting (italics, bold, and so on) and the tab settings will match the column widths in the Word table.

II

Working with Text

TIP ▶ **Adopt Asterisk-Marked Imported Styles**

Asterisk-marked styles are styles that are new to PageMaker, brought in with imported text such as Word or with style tags. PageMaker considers these asterisk-marked styles as just visiting until you open each style for editing and okay it. Over the years, these adopted styles have been potential file-corruption problems. The play-safe approach is to consolidate the asterisked styles. To open each style, use Ctrl+3 to get to the Styles Definition box and then double-click each of the marked styles in turn, clicking OK to adopt them.

TIP ▶ **Save As Before Importing Word Text**

Word has a quick-save function similar to PageMaker's Save Faster mode. It saves recent changes in a special temporary spot in the Word file. When PageMaker tries to import a file that has been put together in this temporary fashion, the filter gets confused, and some pretty strange things can happen. You might only get part of your file, for one thing. Because this quick-save behavior only occurs during ordinary Save operations in Word, there's a remedy. To make sure that your file has been saved in cohesive order, use Word's Save As command right before importing the file in Page-Maker. Even better, go into Word's Preferences command and deselect the Allow Fast Saves option.

Using the Text-Only Import Filter

ASCII stands for *American Standard Code for Information Interchange*. It might also be called the lowest common denominator or the *lingua franca* of computerized text. ASCII text contains no bold text, no italic, no paragraph indents, and it very often turns every single line of a document into an individual paragraph.

In figure 8.13, you can see PageMaker's answer to dumb ASCII text—a filter designed to remove or change many of the things about ASCII that make it look and act so ugly. The ASCII filter works like a search-and-replace engine (removing carriage returns, replacing spaces with tabs, and so on).

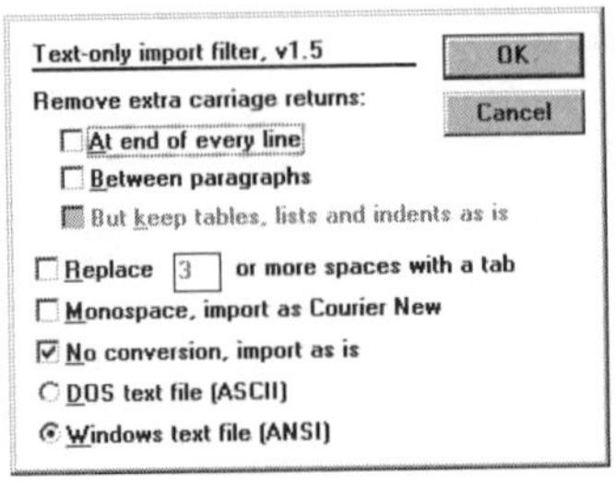

FIG. 8.13 ▶

PageMaker's ASCII filter for plain text.

Text-only import filter, v1.5   OK

Remove extra carriage returns:
- ☐ At end of every line
- ☐ Between paragraphs
- ▨ But keep tables, lists and indents as is

☐ Replace 3 or more spaces with a tab
☐ Monospace, import as Courier New
☑ No conversion, import as is
○ DOS text file (ASCII)
◉ Windows text file (ANSI)

For example, much ASCII text has a carriage return, forcing a line break for every line so that it can be read under the most ordinary of computer circumstances. The PageMaker filter tries to detect where these carriage returns should be removed. If you check the appropriate options, the filter also filters out double carriage returns provided to space out paragraphs and tries to preserve the formatting of any special tables or lists it manages to recognize.

ASCII files often have multiple spaces to take the place of tab characters because there are no tab settings in ASCII text. You can adjust the sensitivity of the filter for space and tab replacement. The default is to replace every three spaces with a tab. However, you may want to replace every five spaces since that's a more common tab approximation (one that almost everybody seems to have learned in high school typing class).

Monospaced type doesn't look elegant, but it does preserve column-style formatting that otherwise would look like gibberish in proportional-spaced type. If you want to have PageMaker format the incoming text with a monospaced font (such as Courier), check this option.

Finally, you can shut off all conversion and bring the ASCII text into PageMaker in its original form with no modifications.

Using the PageMaker Story Importer

With all this filter power, it only makes sense that you'd get a filter to bring in stories from other PageMaker publications. It's called the PageMaker Story Importer.

Figure 8.14 shows the Story Importer dialog box and a view window showing some text that's about to be imported.

FIG. 8.14 ▶

*The PageMaker
Story Importer filter.*

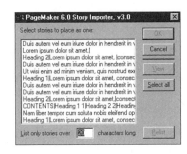

The dialog box lists the stories in the PageMaker publication chosen by the Place command. They don't have titles, of course, so the stories are listed by their first few words of text. Select a story for placing or viewing by clicking it. You can select all the stories in the list with the Select All button.

You can tune the Story Importer filter so that it will only show stories of a certain length. The default is 20 characters, but in a complex document you may want to set the sensitivity figure much higher. If you are trying to bring in a number of large stories, you can use this story length option to tune out footers and other short elements so you can use the Select All button in a more selective way than might otherwise be possible. Use the Relist button when you change the length sensitivity of the Story Importer filter, and the filter will search the publication again and rebuild the list.

The list of stories can be pretty obscure, so click the View button to see what you'll be getting. A view window will appear on-screen showing you the text from that story, as an aid to your selection process.

Unfortunately, the Story Importer does not preserve inline graphics from imported text, although they are preserved if you drag and drop text blocks between publications. It also imports but unrotates any rotated text. Pair-kerning settings get dropped in the import process, and the pair-kerning information of the destination document or paragraph is used instead. Index entries are truncated in that cross-references are not imported.

TIP ▶ **Use the Story Importer to Save a Damaged Publication**

The Story Importer may be the only way to save a PageMaker publication that somehow can't be properly opened or accessed in any other way. Even if you can't import the stories out of the damaged publication in the normal Story Importer fashion, you may be able to copy the stories into a new publication by selecting the text from the view window. You'll lose most of your formatting that way, but it's better than nothing if it works. At least you won't need to retype your text.

Linking and Unlinking Text

Any time you import a text file into PageMaker, the placed text is linked back to the original file (unless you unlink it). This feature sounds really great because it means you can update a placed story that somebody has reedited in the old word processing file. However, this feature may not be nearly as great as it sounds. More on that in a bit.

You can see these links in several places—in the Element menu, under Link Info and Link Options, and in the File menu, under Links. Figure 8.15 shows the Link Info dialog box.

Assuming that someone has been working away to edit copy in the original word processing file, you can automatically update your PageMaker text by selecting the file in the scrolling list and clicking the Open button in this dialog box.

Basically, this process of updating performs the Place command again, shortcutting the file selection process you associate with the Place command.

FIG. 8.15 ▶

The Link Info dialog box. Use the Open button to update a file.

Much of the time, re-linking a text file turns out to be a very bad idea because you lose your detailed typography (kerning, for example) and all of your inline graphics. For text files, you almost certainly don't want to choose Update Automatically in the Link Options dialog box, because you will lose any control over the update process. The file is also replaced every time you open your PageMaker publication.

This link process and some similar strategies can be a vital advantage, however, when doing massive workgroup-style publishing, which tends to come up when working with long documents (books, journals, newspapers, and technical documentation). That's why there's more discussion on linking in Chapter 17, "Building Many Pages." There's also some information on linking in Chapter 11, "Placing Images," an environment where linking has a more practical application. You'll find the major coverage on all the technologies for establishing relationships between imported files and PageMaker in Chapter 30, "Linking and Other File Connections."

Where to Go from Here

▶ Styles are vital if you are working on imported text, and you can get much more information on style sheets and getting the most out of them in Chapter 7, "Designing a Text Style System."

▶ Placing stories usually means you are to the stage of production where you are beginning to lay out pages. Page layout is covered in Chapter 13, "Designing a Master Page Grid."

▶ Working with lists of data? That process usually involves importing spreadsheets, databases, or PageMaker 6.0's new Table Editor. You've got a special chapter devoted to the topic—Chapter 16, "Formatting Forms, Tables, and Databases."

▶ Are your documents long—really long? And complex to boot? For the special needs of large documents (meaning tons of text) and group-written projects, there's Chapter 17, "Building Many Pages."

▶ Placing stories also means that you are dealing with linking in some way. For more on that, see Chapter 30, "Linking and Other File Connections." This includes information on PageMaker Linking and OLE.

Chapter 9

Editing Copy with the Story Editor

This chapter on editing copy with the Story Editor talks about:

The basics of accessing and navigating in the Story Editor.

▼

Using the Story Editor to edit text.

▼

Checking your spelling.

▼

Using the Story Editor's powerful search and replace features.

▼

A Tactics Recipe for cleaning up text.

IF YOU ARE on deadline, you don't have time to mess around, but you know you absolutely do not want to do much copy editing in PageMaker's Layout view. Recomposing text after every move and redrawing a screen that's packing precision type and graphics takes time.

Such are the circumstances of creative impulse and deadline terror. Fortunately, PageMaker has a built-in text editor (as opposed to a word processor) that's fast and capable. For all these situations where you need to massage some text inside PageMaker, use the Story Editor. ▶ ▶ ▶

Learning Story Editor Basics

Think of the Story Editor as always being available. The Story Editor is simply a different view (quite a different view) of your publication, in contrast to the elegance and sheen of the Layout view.

When you see the Story Editor for the first time, you know right away that you're no longer in Layout view. The Story Editor may even seem a bit ugly, with its plain, unadorned look. Figure 9.1 shows the difference between the two types of views.

FIG. 9.1 ▶

A comparison of the same text in Layout view and Story Editor view.

Section shown in
Story Editor window

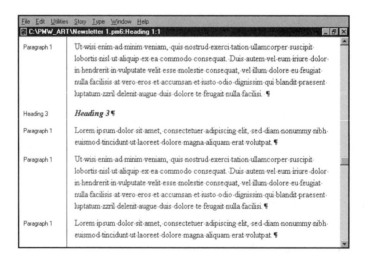

Forget line wrap. Don't even think about seeing your graphics. You don't even get to see your text in the correct font. Story Editor's job is to put you in direct contact with your text. Remember, the Story Editor is not a word processor—it's not that fancy. Story Editor is more like a text editor. In that way, the Story Editor has a lot more in common with a typewriter than a fancy word processor.

Opening a Story and Changing Views

To open the Story Editor view of your text (working from the Layout view), you have a whole list of choices, which are discussed in the sections that follow.

Starting at a Particular Spot in a Story

If you are in Layout view and want to edit a specific point in a story, use the Text tool and click an insertion point or select some text. Now use the Ctrl+E keyboard shortcut or the Edit Story command in the Edit menu. The Story Editor opens, ready to go to work at that point in the story.

Triple-Clicking into Story Editor

One of the easiest ways to switch to the Story Editor is to use your Pointer tool and triple-click any text block belonging to the story you want to edit. The Story Editor pops up with the edit cursor at the top of that text block.

Only the Pointer tool can open a story with a triple-click. If you triple-click with the Text tool, you merely select a paragraph instead of opening the Story Editor.

You get the same result as the triple-click method by using the Pointer tool to select the text block and then choosing Edit Story from the Layout view's Edit menu; or you can use the Ctrl+E keyboard shortcut. The Story Editor opens with the insertion point at the top of that text block.

Returning to Layout View

You can get back to Layout view by three different routes, depending on where you want to end up.

The simplest way back to Layout is so obvious, it seems almost silly to mention it. Simply do what comes naturally—point and click at what you want. Click the Layout window, and you return to where you were before you opened the Story Editor with all your Story Edit windows remaining open in the background.

You can also use the keyboard to return to Layout view at the same page you left. Close your story by using the Close Story command on the Story menu, pressing Ctrl+W, or by simply clicking in the "X" close box in the upper-right corner of the Editor. If you left an insertion point blinking in text and had the Text tool chosen, that's where you are when you return, although you won't have an active text cursor when you get back to Layout view. Instead, your Pointer tool will be active. Even if you sashayed all over your story in the Editor, when you close the Editor window you return to your Layout view starting point.

If you have several stories open in the Story Editor, you can close them all by holding down the Shift key, which will give you a Close All Stories command in the Story menu.

Finally, you can toggle back and forth between the Story Editor and Layout view so you can examine the effects of your editing. Just use the Ctrl+E key combination, assuming you have the Text tool active and an insertion point clicked in the text. After you edit the copy, press Ctrl+E again to return to Layout view. The cursor positions match up between the two views. This technique works well when you are slamming through a bunch of pages and get to a point where you need to tromp on a section of text in the Story Editor.

TIP ▷ **Yes, You Can Do Page Flips In Layout View**

PageMaker doesn't automatically turn a page if your insertion point butts up against the bottom of a text block at the end of a page spread. QuarkXPress users have long gloated about the Quark feature that scrolls right to the top of the next page. But those Quark folks don't get the benefits of PageMaker's built-in text editor, and because no page barriers exist in a story thread when you are in Story Editor, page breaks don't matter quite so much.

You sometimes may need to edit in Layout view, however. Have page-flip envy no more; instead, try this technique. When you are at the very last character on the page, press Ctrl+E to open the story, then press the right-arrow key once or twice to advance the insertion point into the text on the adjacent page. Press Ctrl+E again to toggle back to Layout view. Do the same with the left-arrow key at the first character on a page to go to a previous page.

Do this step fast enough and it takes no more than a blink, thanks to PageMaker's automatic interruptible-screen-redraw feature. The technique is not as slick as scrolling pages, but it's a lot better than the old Ctrl+Tab-and-reach-for-the-mouse technique. You can do this task right from the keyboard, and after the page turn you have an insertion point already in place.

Returning to an Open Story Window

If you have a story already open, you can reach it no matter what tool you have chosen and whether or not you have clicked somewhere in the story. Choose the Window menu in Layout view and select your story from the list at the bottom of the menu, as shown in figure 9.2. Only stories that are open in Story Editor are listed on the submenu at the bottom of the Window menu. You'll find them in the submenu you can pull out from the file name of the publication you have open.

Fig. 9.2 ▶

*Using the Window
command to open
a Story Editor view.*

Creating an Unplaced New Story or Pre-Editing Your Imported Text

With nothing selected, you can start a new story using the Edit Story menu command or the Ctrl+E shortcut. Either command gives you a blank Story Editor window. Instead of the title bar indicating the first few words of the story, the label is `Untitled`.

After you are in the Story Editor view, you can import a new story for editing before you place it on the page. When you have the Story Editor open, use the Place command to bring in a file. The result looks like the Place command in Layout view, except for the Story Editor dialog box title in the upper-left corner (see fig. 9.3).

Fig. 9.3 ▶

*The Place com-
mand dialog box,
Import to Story
Editor.*

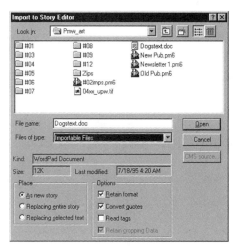

TIP ▶ **Use Edit Original to Access Word Processor**

If you maintain the link between PageMaker and your original word processor file, you can have express access to the original. Use the Edit Original command in the Edit menu. There's more on Links in Chapter 30, "Linking and Other File Connections."

II

Working with Text

Returning to Layout View with Unplaced Text

This section covers what happens when you want to return to Layout view with unplaced text in the Story Editor. Perhaps you've created a new story in Story Editor or have imported text directly into the Story Editor by using the Place command.

If you use the Ctrl+E method to return to Layout view, you return with a loaded text icon, all set to place your new text. The story window remains open in the background. You can use Ctrl+E to pop back into the Story Editor if you need to. Or, you will also be returned to your unplaced story in the Story Editor if you get rid of the text icon (by clicking a tool in the Toolbox, for example).

You do not get a loaded text icon in the following situations:

▶ If you simply click the Layout view, leaving the Story Editor without a formal good-bye, your new story remains open in the background as unplaced text; you come back to Layout view without a loaded text placement icon. If you Quit with PageMaker in this condition, when you reopen the publication next time, PageMaker will open showing the unplaced story in Story Editor.

▶ If you Quit in Story Editor view, your new text is left unplaced in the Story Editor. When you reopen a PageMaker document with unplaced text in the Story Editor, that story is the first thing you see when you begin your next work session.

▶ If you close the story window using Ctrl+W or the Close box in the upper-left corner, you get the dialog box shown in figure 9.4. You need to negotiate the dialog box before you can return to Layout view. If you select the Place option, the story window closes, and you have a loaded text icon. Or you can discard the story. Or you can click Cancel to remain in the Story Editor.

Fig. 9.4 ▶

The dialog box for resolving unplaced text when closing the Story Editor.

TIP ▶ **Export a Backup of Text Created In PageMaker**

When you type your copy into the Story Editor (or Layout view, for that matter), you have no backup text file. Therefore, when you finish editing, use the File, Export command to dump a text copy to disk for backup purposes. (You are keeping backups of your publication development as you go through a project—aren't you?) Outboard text files don't contain your PageMaker typographical magic. But at least these text files are crude backups that can save you a lot of retyping if something goes desperately wrong with your main PageMaker document file.

Getting PageMaker to Load with an Open Story

When you quit PageMaker, all the story windows shut down. Therefore, when you open PageMaker, you need to reopen any stories you want to work on using Story Editor—with one exception. As mentioned earlier, the exception to this rule is any story you have not yet placed on a page. In that case, the unplaced story immediately appears in the Story Editor when you reopen the publication.

TIP ▶   **Quit and Open PageMaker as a Tool to Resolve Unplaced Stories**

This behavior of opening the Story Editor on unplaced stories can be helpful in some situations. In older versions of PageMaker, you could lay some real land mines for yourself by accidentally scattering unplaced stories around. These stories tended to confuse PageMaker pretty badly and occasionally caused some horror stories of file corruption. At the very least, the stories wasted disk space.

In more recent versions of PageMaker, you can find entire unplaced stories by quitting PageMaker and then reopening the program. Any unplaced story comes up in Story Editor, ready for your action. If you try to close the story, you are given the options of discarding the vagrant story or placing it on a page.

Managing Story Editor Windows

The PageMaker world can get pretty crowded. Figure 9.5 shows the results of one way you can manage all those windows (four are open in the illustration). It's the Cascade command under the Window menu.

Rather than view a cascade of title bars, you may want to see what's in all those windows simultaneously. In that case, you want a Tile view, which you also reach through the Window menu (see fig. 9.6).

If you have more than one publication open, with more than one Story Editor view open, you can cascade or tile all the stories if you like. Hold down the Shift key while choosing the Tile or Cascade commands. The commands change to Tile All or Cascade All.

If the view really gets obscured and cluttered, you can call up the story of your choice by selecting it from the Window menu, where it's listed in a submenu of the Layout view that owns it.

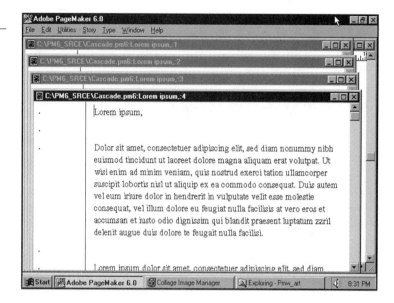

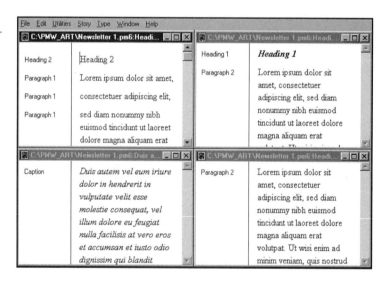

Enhancing the Story Editor Display

As plain as the Story Editor looks, you can dress it up a bit and make it more
useful at the same time.

FIG. 9.7 ▶

Setting the display options for the Story Editor.

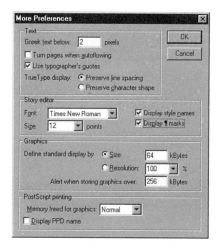

Under the File menu, buried deep within the Preferences command, are three options you can set for the Story Editor. Set all of them—you won't regret it. Figure 9.7 shows the dialog box you get when you click the More button in the main Preferences dialog box. Notice the Story Editor section.

You probably want to select your favorite, most readable font for use in the Story Editor text display. Many people use their body text font for whatever project they happen to be working on. That way, the Story view looks somewhat like the Layout view. On the other hand, some PageMaker users prefer to view stories in a font that's distinctly different from their body copy, as a visual reminder that they are in the Story Editor, not Layout view.

While you are at it, consider setting your Story view display font to a larger size—say, 14 points. That size is just plain easier to read, which is important if you are spending hour after hour in front of that screen.

Finally, you may find editing your text easier if you can see it—all of it. Turn on the Display ¶ Marks option, and you can see more than your carriage returns. You also see all the symbols shown in figure 9.8 for new line characters, tabs, and spaces.

Assuming you are using the style sheet techniques from Chapter 7, "Designing a Text Style System," turn on the display of styles along the left edge of the Story View window, as you can also see in figure 9.8.

II

Working with Text

FIG. 9.8 ▶

The Story Editor display set up for optimum viewing.

New line character

Paragraph mark

Style names

Tab

Spaces

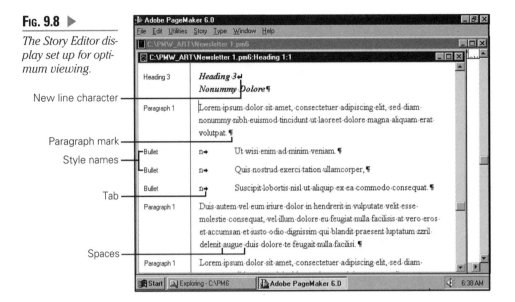

Editing Text in the Story Editor

So, like, when do we actually edit with this Story Editor?

Right exactly about now. First you'll need to know how to select text and navigate within a story. Then we'll move on to cutting, copying, pasting, and other editing techniques.

Selecting Text and Navigating

Navigating in Story Editor works a great deal like your word processing program. You point and click with the mouse and you use your arrow keys. And in Story Editor, you can use the numeric keypad for all your navigation.

Using the Numeric Keypad and Dedicated Cursor Keys

Most of PageMaker's non-mouse text-editing power is concentrated in the keypad—assuming you have the Num Lock key off. You can use the arrow keys and other dedicated cursor-movement keys such as Home and End, but the keypad does it all. You may want to use the numeric keypad as your primary text navigation center.

Table 9.1 shows your text selection and insertion point navigation options for the numeric keypad and the dedicated cursor-movement keys on the keyboard.

TABLE 9.1   Keyboard Shortcuts for Text Selection and Navigation

Type of Text Selected	Action to Perform
Word	Double-click with Text tool
Paragraph	Triple-click with Text tool
Range	Click insertion point in text, hold Shift, and press a keyboard cursor-movement shortcut

Insertion Point Movement	Action to Perform
Up one line	Up arrow or keypad 8
Down one line	Down arrow or keypad 2
Up one screen	Page Up or keypad 9
Down one screen	Page Down or keypad 3
To beginning of line	Home or keypad 7
To end of line	End or keypad 1
To beginning of sentence	Ctrl+Home or Ctrl+keypad 7
To end of sentence	Ctrl+End or Ctrl+keypad 1
To beginning of story	Ctrl+Page Up or Ctrl+keypad 9
To end of story	Ctrl+Page Down or Ctrl+keypad 3
Left one character	Left arrow or keypad 4
Right one character	Right arrow or keypad 6
Left one word	Ctrl+left arrow or Ctrl+keypad 4
Right one word	Ctrl+right arrow or Ctrl+keypad 6
Up one paragraph	Ctrl+up arrow or Ctrl+keypad 8
Down one paragraph	Ctrl+down arrow or Ctrl+keypad 2

Selecting Text with the Shift Key

PageMaker follows the convention of selecting text using the Shift key. To select text instead of merely moving your cursor, hold down the Shift key while performing any of the text navigation keystroke maneuvers.

II

Working with Text

Selecting Large Amounts of Text

You can select the entire story, even unplaced text, by choosing the Select <u>A</u>ll command from the <u>E</u>dit menu. Better yet, just press the key combination Ctrl+A.

To select a paragraph, triple-click it with the Text tool. Or click the paragraph's style name in the left margin of the Story Editor if you have that feature turned on.

Double-click a word with the Text tool to select it. Your double-click highlights the word plus its trailing space. You can type over the top of the selection or delete it (or apply formatting commands).

TIP ▶ Watch for Trailing Space when Overwriting a Double-Clicked Word

Keep in mind that PageMaker, unlike many word processors, overwrites the trailing space when you type over a word selected with a double-click. You could easily end up with two words jammed together with no space.

Scrolling to the Beginning or End of a Story

If you want to move the cursor to the very beginning or end of a story in Story Editor view, hold down the Ctrl key when pressing the Page Up or Page Down keys or their keypad surrogates, numbers 9 and 3.

Cutting, Copying, Deleting, and Pasting

The usual Cu<u>t</u> (Ctrl+X), <u>C</u>opy (Ctrl+C), <u>P</u>aste (Ctrl+V), and C<u>l</u>ear (Del) commands work from the keyboard or from the <u>E</u>dit menu.

Your Backspace key acts as you might expect, deleting one character to the left.

The dedicated Delete and the keypad Del (.) keys remove one character to the right of the insertion point.

The regular Insert key and the keypad Ins (0) key perform the Paste command, as expected.

PageMaker works in what some folks call *insert mode*. If you select some text and then insert the Clipboard text or just start typing, the new material replaces the old.

Even though PageMaker has drag-and-drop copying, it's only for working with objects in Layout view and then only between two open publications or between the Library palette and a publication. Story Editor has no other drag-and-drop copying feature.

Styling and Formatting Type and Paragraphs

The Control palette works in Story Editor, in both Character and Paragraph views. So do all the commands on the Type menu, except for Hyphenation, Expert Kerning, and the Indents/Tabs commands. Perform text formatting with caution, however, because for the most part you work blindly in the plain text Story Editor view and can't gauge the effects of your moves.

The only exceptions to working blindly are bold and italic type. You can see that formatting. Also, Story view indicates paragraph indentations by bumping the first line of a paragraph in from the left edge of the Story Editor, but the indents aren't displayed with any accuracy.

TIP ▷ Use Find and Change for Mass Production Styling and Formatting

You can do high-volume type and paragraph formatting in Story Editor using the Find and Change commands. This chapter's section, "Finding and Changing Text," gives more detail on how to use the commands for this purpose. With PageMaker's capability to search through all open publications, this Find and Change formatting gives you exceptional power for managing large book-type publications.

Checking Your Spelling

The Spelling command works only in the Story Editor. The command uses the same dictionary as the Hyphenation command, so you may want to check out the hyphenation dictionary discussion in Chapter 6, "Formatting Paragraphs."

Accessing and Using the Spell Checker

To access the spell checker, use the keyboard shor tcut Ctrl+L or the Spelling command under the Utilities menu. Either action gives you the Spelling dialog box (see fig. 9.9).

Fig. 9.9 ▷

The Spelling dialog box.

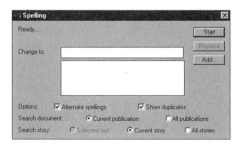

First, tell PageMaker how big an area you want to spell check. If you highlighted some text before giving the Spelling command, the Selected Text option is automatically selected when the dialog box opens. You also can check an entire story, every story in a single publication, and every story in every open publication.

You can turn off the option for Alternate Spellings. PageMaker then locates words it doesn't recognize, but it doesn't take the time to suggest alternatives. This option is faster—if you are a great speller and just need to be alerted to problems but don't need actual spelling help.

The spell checker finds duplicate words words. This option is great. Just check Show Duplicates. Show Duplicates does not, however, detect duplicated phrases duplicated phrases.

When you are all set, just click the Start button or press Enter and the spell check begins. When the spell checker finds a problem word, you see the dialog box change to resemble figure 9.10.

Fig. 9.10 ▶

PageMaker has found a problem word.

Misspelled word

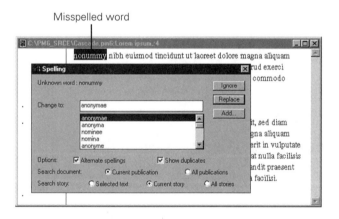

You probably want to move the Spelling dialog box down the screen to expose as much as possible of the story. That arrangement gives a clearer view of the text and enables you to see your spell check in context, because PageMaker highlights each detected word as it moves through the story.

Click the Replace button to replace the misspelled word with the suggested spelling. Better yet, just double-click the suggested word.

If you click Ignore (or press Enter to accept the default Ignore response), Page-Maker moves on and ignores the detected word for the rest of that particular PageMaker work session.

TIP ▶ You Can Check Spelling In Layout View (Sort of)

Even though the Spelling command isn't available in Layout view, you still can get to it very quickly to check the spelling of a specified word or a short passage of text. Select your text and call the Story Editor with Ctrl+E. Don't wait for the screen to redraw. Press Ctrl+L to call the spell checker. This technique works well for checking a single word or a couple of paragraphs.

Make sure you have Selected Text turned on, not All Publications, otherwise you will be off on a wild chase and lose your spot in Layout view. Press Enter to put the spell checker in motion. You have a single-word spell check in no time.

One reason this works so well is the fact that the spell checker remembers its setting from use to use. You can set it up for Current Publication and Selected Text in advance for rapid spell checking when you're flipping back and forth between Layout and Story view.

TIP ▶ Load Story Editor and Spell Checker into Memory for Faster Response

The preceding spell-check-from-Layout tip works even faster if you make a habit of opening the Story Editor and the spell checker at the beginning of every PageMaker session. Go back to Layout view without closing the spell checker and Story Editor, and you have faster access, because they are already loaded into memory.

Editing Your Dictionary

From the spell checker you can perform ad hoc editing of your Spelling/Hyphenation dictionary. Or, using the Dictionary Editor utility, you can perform large-scale surgery and even create and import dictionaries.

Understanding PageMaker's Dictionary Setup

Keep in mind that the dictionary you edit is not the big, mainstream dictionary that comes with PageMaker. You edit your own personal dictionary, which augments the big one. PageMaker doesn't permit you to edit the standard Proximity dictionary.

You can have more than one custom dictionary for each language, but only one installed at a time. True, you can have different language dictionaries assigned to different paragraphs, but only one custom dictionary per language.

TIP ▶ Set Up a Start Button Shortcut for Dictionary Editor

When something (such as the PageMaker dictionary files) has been buried deep in folders, use the shortcut technique. Choose the Settings command from the Start menu. Use the Start Menu Programs tab to add the Dictionary Editor to your menu. You can also drag an application onto the Start button to add it to the menu.

TIP ▶ **Share Your Dictionaries**

If you're working with a group on a project, create a standard user dictionary that you all use (and outlaw any individual customizing). You can put special project-oriented words in the dictionary so they are all spelled, hyphenated, and capitalized consistently. Just copy this customized and shared user dictionary onto everyone's hard disk. You should put this UDC dictionary file into the PM6/RSRC/LINGUIST/PRX/ USENGLSH folder, where PageMaker will know to look for it.

Adding or Editing a Single Word

You're only a button away from easy ad hoc editing of your personal dictionary. Notice the Add button in the Spelling dialog box, which takes you to the Add Word dialog box (see fig. 9.11). This feature works just like the Add button in the Hyphenation command.

Fig. 9.11 ▶

Adding a word to your personal Page-Maker dictionary.

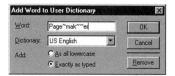

If you are using more than one dictionary, be sure to check that the proper one is chosen in the Dictionary list box.

If capitalization is an issue for the word you are adding, check the Exactly As Typed option. The other option, As All Lowercase, allows PageMaker to take into account all the likely capitalization variations (such as capitalization for the first word of a sentence). You most often use this option when you add a word to the dictionary.

As with the hyphenation Add button (the hyphenation and spell check features share this dictionary), you can control hyphenation by inserting tilde symbols (~) before or within the word. A tilde before the word prevents hyphenation (for a company name, for example) and tilde symbols inserted within the word tell PageMaker where to break the word. One tilde marks your optimum break point, two tildes for the next priority for hyphenation, and three for the least favorite option.

If you misspell a word when you add it to the dictionary, you can remove it by misspelling it again in exactly the same way (as in the Hyphenation dialog box). Or, even better, you can use the Dictionary Editor utility and pick the word you want to delete from a list. That step may be much easier than the hit-and-miss technique of trying to misspell the word intentionally.

Adding, Fixing, and Removing Words with the Dictionary Editor

The Dictionary Editor will be loaded onto your Start menu during installation. In figure 9.12, a personal dictionary has been opened for editing.

FIG. 9.12 ▶

The Dictionary Editor opening dialog box.

Use the Dictionary Editor's File menu to access all the usual commands, such as New, Open, Close, Save, Save As, and Print.

You can use the Print command to print out a copy of your personal dictionary for editing and proofing, with the name of the dictionary stamped on every page.

The major benefit of using the Dictionary Editor is that you can find a word you need to fix on the list and remove it or modify it. Older versions of PageMaker required you to play guessing games of misspelling a word just right to remove it from the dictionary.

To edit your dictionary, choose the File, Open command. Look in the language-specific folder inside the PROXIMITY folder for the file with the UDC extension and double-click it. You get a list of all the words in the dictionary, ready for editing and hyphenation.

To put a word in the edit box, double-click it; then do your editing. If you are doing a lot of hyphenation, you may get tired of reaching over to press the tilde key all the time. Try Ctrl+Y to let the Dictionary Editor guess the best hyphenation points. Finish all your editing, then click Replace.

If you are adding a word, enter it in the Edit Word box and then click Add. You can remove misspelled words by selecting them (single click) and clicking the Remove button.

If you have a big dictionary, you may need to use the Find command from the Edit menu. You get the standard Find dialog box you see in figure 9.13. You even get Whole Word and Match Upper/Lowercase options.

Fig. 9.13 ▶

Finding a word in Dictionary Editor.

Importing, Exporting, Expanding, and Installing Dictionaries

You can use the Import command to bring in a text-only (ASCII) file of words and make them into a personal dictionary or add to one that already exists. Import, under the Dictionary Editor's File menu, gives you the dialog box in figure 9.14. The Export command (also under the File menu) can create an ASCII text file.

Fig. 9.14 ▶

Importing a dictionary for editing or installation.

Use the Import command for converting a dictionary or to expand one that you already have loaded in the Dictionary Editor. Choose whether to allow duplicate words or whether you want the inbound dictionary list to overwrite any duplicated words it finds. This smart (or dangerous, depending on how you look at it) overwrite feature replaces any words that have the same spelling but different hyphenation.

When importing a dictionary, you can choose to let PageMaker attempt to hyphenate the incoming words using an algorithm (as opposed to actual dictionary syllable breaks).

TIP ▶ **Avoid Hyphenation by Algorithm**

Algorithm hyphenation has some pitfalls. At the very least, you should hand check the results for words that you have subjected to the algorithm process. The PageMaker software engine (algorithm) for creating hyphenation is a good one, but if you are a strict hyphenarian or work for one, the results may not match your expectations.

For both the Import and Export commands, each word has its own line, separated by a carriage return. (Actually, that format is the PageMaker file format. Some outside dictionaries may separate each word by a space or tab character; the PageMaker Dictionary Editor can read those formats, although it exports in carriage return delimited format.) Tilde symbols indicate hyphenation, just as you would expect from using the Add button in the spell checker.

When you finish using the Import command, combining it with your existing personal dictionary and performing any fine editing, you are ready to install the new word list. Use the Install command. You must use this command before PageMaker can see your new dictionary. Figure 9.15 shows the Install command's dialog box.

Tell the Dictionary Editor which language folder is to be the storage place for your new personal dictionary, and you're done.

FIG. 9.15 ▶

Installing a new dictionary with Dictionary Editor.

TIP ▶ Save That Old PageMaker 5.0 Dictionary

PageMaker 6.0 comes with a utility that can easily and quickly put your valuable dictionary to work in the new version. Use the *Use PM5 Custom Settings* program (PM5FILES.EXE). Follow the directions on-screen and you can bring that old dictionary into the new version with just a few mouse clicks. The program also enables you to adopt into PageMaker 6.0 many other items, including custom color libraries and tracking values.

TIP ▶ Manage Multiple-User Dictionaries with a Disable Dictionary Folder

Remember, if you already have established a user dictionary, the Editor asks where to store the old user dictionary when it puts the new one in place. Create a new folder just to store your disabled dictionaries. That arrangement enables you to easily find a dictionary if you want to swap it back in, and it helps to organize your attempts to keep old and new dictionaries tracking parallel with one another.

Converting Non-PageMaker Dictionaries

Before you can import a word-processor dictionary (or other non-PageMaker dictionary), you must find a way to convert it to text (ASCII) format. If your word processor permits, the easiest way is to open the dictionary in your word processor and use the Save As command to save the file under a new name as ASCII or Text Only. (You could also use PageMaker's Story Editor as your word processor and then export the file as Text Only.) You may need to consult the manual for your word processor to discover where it stores your personal dictionary files.

Many outboard dictionaries don't use tildes to signify hyphenation. Have a look at your dictionary. If it uses a regular hyphen or some other symbol, do a search-and-replace on the file to convert to a tilde.

When you have your dictionary in ASCII all-text format (with every word delimited by a carriage return, space, or tab), you are ready to import it using the PageMaker Dictionary Editor.

Finding and Changing Text

For some weird reason, many people are scared of their search-and-replace tools. Maybe they feel they would need to spend too much time learning how to use the features. Maybe it's masochism. Who knows? The point is this: Invest some time in learning about the Find and Change commands in PageMaker. These commands don't cost you time; they save it. Use the commands and you'll quickly recover the investment. Learning the tools is easy because virtually all search-and-replace commands work roughly the same way (some more powerful than others, granted). Your investment pays off in all your work. Heck, even spreadsheets have search-and-replace these days.

Maybe the fact that computers are so darn literal is the major boggle about search-and-replace. You're afraid that if you don't get that search-and-replace command just right, you may wreak major mayhem on your precious publication file. To allay those fears, check out the insurance you can obtain by using the following Revert and Mini-Revert tip.

TIP ▶   Revert or Mini-Revert When the Change Command Goes Wrong

Unlike many word processors, the Undo command in PageMaker doesn't work after you make a Change move. Keep a mistaken Change operation from ruining your day by always saving right before your Change command. Then you can revert to the last saved version by choosing File, Revert. Just check your results right after your search and before taking any other action, or you stand a chance of losing your opportunity to make a rescue.

If you forgot to save before using the Change command, you can do a Mini-Revert, which returns your publication to its appearance at the last time the program did an automatic mini-save. To do a Mini-Revert, hold down the Shift key when issuing the Revert command. (PageMaker does a mini-save every time you change the page, insert or delete a page, print, switch between Layout and Story view, use the Clipboard, click the active page icon, or change anything in Page Setup.)

Accessing and Starting Find and Change

To use Find or Change, you need to get to the Story Editor. The feature doesn't work in Layout view. So triple-click your story or use Ctrl+E. Then choose the Change command from the Utilities menu to open the Change dialog box (see fig. 9.16).

Fig. 9.16 ▶

The Change dialog box.

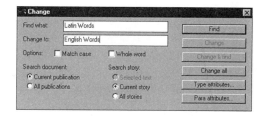

Find looks and works the same way as Change, from the Utilities menu, except you see only the Find part of the dialog box (see fig. 9.17). You can search the same territory with the same options, except you cannot replace what you find.

Fig. 9.17 ▶

The Find dialog box.

As an alternative to using the Find or Change command, you can use Ctrl+F (Find) or Ctrl+H (Change, as in Replace). You may have only one of the two commands up and running; they cannot both be operative at the same time.

TIP ▶ Pre-Load the Find or Change Commands for Faster Access

Like the Spelling command, you get faster response if you have the Story Editor and either the Find or Change command up in the background. (You can't have both Find and Change running simultaneously.) Then you don't need to wait for these

continues

II

Working with Text

TIP ▶ **Continued**

commands to load into memory when you need them. Just open them at the beginning of a session and return to Layout view without closing them. Most of the time, I use the Change command because I can keep it open in the background ready for use, and it can perform both the Find and Change functions.

Defining Your Search-and-Replace Parameters

Think of the search process as an exercise in narrowing things down. The process starts with all your text available. Then you limit the nature of your search, say, to the current story as opposed to the entire publication. With the Match Case or Whole Word options you further define (or limit) your search. Then you get really specific by typing whatever text you want to find in the Find What text box (or by setting formatting attributes with the Attributes button).

Tuning the Search Bandwidth

Like a radio receiver searching for signals, you must set the bandwidth of your Find or Change receiver. You can search just the text you have selected, the current story, the current publication, or all the stories in all the open publications. This option works just like it does in the Spelling command.

Searching for Text

Type the characters you want to find in the Find What box, and if you are doing a Change operation, type the characters you want to use for replacing that found text in the Change To box.

Computer science majors from Stanford or MIT call the text you put in the Find What and Change To boxes *strings* or *literals*. The text represents strings of characters that the computer takes literally. Searching for text is one of those times you face the cosmic truth about telling computers what to do. The computer performs the step exactly, nothing more and nothing less. Everything you say, the computer takes literally.

So, if you want to find *cat* and you enter *cats* in the Find What box, you won't find *cat*. You may get *cats* and *catsup*, but you won't get *cat*.

One computer trainer I know says computers are so frustrating because "they always do what you tell them to do, not what you want them to do."

Locating Special Characters

You can find and change a ton of characters besides the alphabet and the numbers. These characters are listed in a chart in Appendix C for ready reference. A tab, for example, is ˜t, and a paragraph ending (carriage return) is ˜p.

If you need to find some character that's not on the chart, you can use the usual technique for typing such characters. Click in the Find or Change box. Then hold down Alt and type its ANSI character number. That's a four-digit code (usually a zero followed by three other numbers) that's assigned to every key on the keyboard.

You can find the ASCII character for any character in any font by using the Character Map that comes with Windows 95. Access the map through the Start button, navigating through the Programs submenu to Accesories. There you'll find a Character Map.

Another helpful tool for finding special characters is the character map template, CHARSET.PT6, which you can find in your PageMaker folder.

TIP ▶ Use the Change Command to Index a Word

If you need to add a word—every occurrence of it—to the index, search for the word with the Change command. In the Change To box, type the index entry marker search character, which is **^;** (a caret and a semicolon). Do the Change operation, and you're all set. That exact word is indexed every time PageMaker finds it in your search area.

Limiting the Search to Whole Words

If you check the Whole Word option, you are telling PageMaker you want to find only text that exactly matches what you entered in the Find What box—nothing else. PageMaker then turns up a match if your characters stand alone as a word, meaning the letters are set off by spaces or punctuation.

To continue with the earlier cat example, if you type *cat* in the Find What box and check the Whole Word option, *cat* is the only word PageMaker finds. If you don't check the Whole Word option, PageMaker also finds occurrences of *catch, catapult, cats, catsup, and Pocatello.*

Matching Capitalization

You can limit PageMaker's search to words that exactly match the capitalization you have typed in the Find What box (and replace them exactly as you have typed them in the Change To box). Checking the Match Case option defines your search as case-sensitive to whether each character is uppercase or lowercase.

For example, I probably use the word *story* in this book about 1,011 times, give or take 50 or so. About half of those times I talk about a story, and the other half I talk about the Story Editor or Story view. Suppose Adobe suddenly changed the name of Story view to Editor view. With the Match Case option, I could limit my search to the specific spots where I used *Story* (as opposed to *story*) and replace those occurrences with the word *Editor*.

Searching for Formatting Attributes

PageMaker can find many of the text attributes you set with the Type Specifications dialog box, as well as any of the paragraph styles you have defined. More importantly, when PageMaker finds these attributes, it can change them.

You reach this function by clicking one of the two attributes buttons—Type or Para—to get the dialog boxes you see in figure 9.18.

FIG. 9.18 ▶

The Change Attributes dialog boxes.

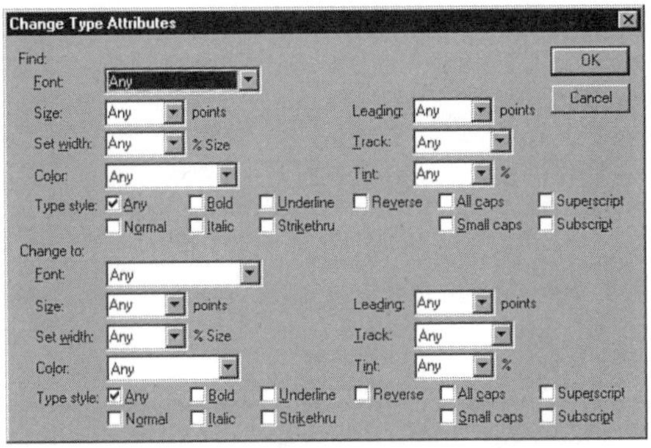

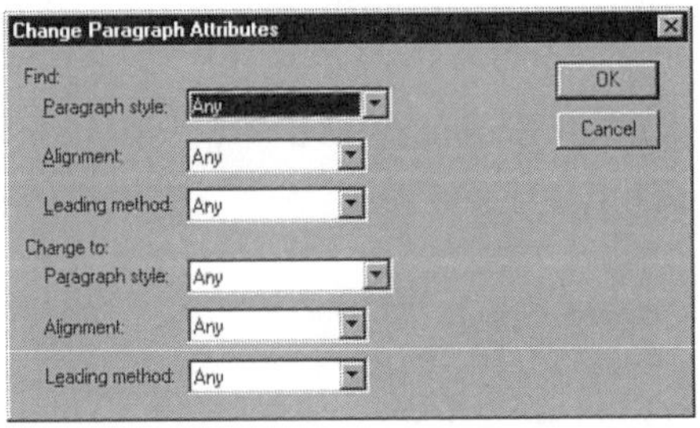

New in PageMaker 6.0 is the ability to search for leading method and leading amount, colors and object-level tints, width, track, and alignment. You also can change to any of these attributes.

Carried over from PageMaker 5.0 is the ability to search for paragraph styles, a specific font, the size of that font, and type styles.

For example, if you wanted to change all the occurrences of boldface type to italic type, you could set those attributes in the Find What and Change To boxes and then use the Change command to implement the change.

For another example, suppose you want to format all your hanging indent bullets with a Zapf Dingbat bullet. You might have used the letter *o* followed by a tab to mark all your dingbat locations. When you are ready to apply the Zapf Dingbat font format, search for your bullet marker **o^t** in the Find What box. Set the Change To box by entering the same text. The Attribute button setting, however, would be for Zapf Dingbats. The letter **o** plus the tab character are used for the bulleted checklist you see in figure 9.19.

FIG. 9.19

A practical use of attributes in the Change command—Zapf Dingbats for a bulleted checklist.

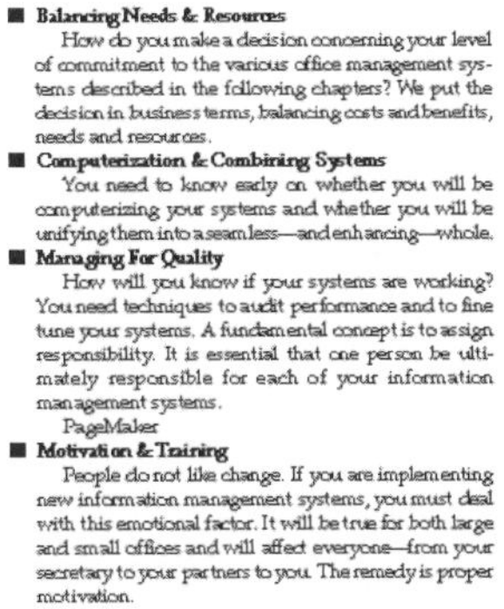

- **Balancing Needs & Resources**
  How do you make a decision concerning your level of commitment to the various office management systems described in the following chapters? We put the decision in business terms, balancing costs and benefits, needs and resources.
- **Computerization & Combining Systems**
  You need to know early on whether you will be computerizing your systems and whether you will be unifying them into a seamless—and enhancing—whole.
- **Managing For Quality**
  How will you know if your systems are working? You need techniques to audit performance and to fine tune your systems. A fundamental concept is to assign responsibility. It is essential that one person be ultimately responsible for each of your information management systems.
  PageMaker
- **Motivation & Training**
  People do not like change. If you are implementing new information management systems, you must deal with this emotional factor. It will be true for both large and small offices and will affect everyone—from your secretary to your partners to you. The remedy is proper motivation.

After you have set attributes for your search definition, click OK and you return to a slightly modified Change dialog box. The dialog box labels Change To and Find What are underlined. The underlining is your visual clue that attribute settings are in place.

You need not go to the Attributes settings to get rid of these underlines and their underlying Find or Change attributes settings. A simple Alt+click on the Attributes button clears the attributes settings.

Finding, Changing, and Finding Again

When you have set all your options and defined your search, click the Find button to set things into motion. Both the Find and Change dialog boxes have a Find button.

You also have the option of choosing Change All, which immediately implements your change operation for the entire area you have chosen (the bandwidth), perhaps your entire publication or selection. Use caution with this option, because the only way back to your original text is a Revert or Mini-Revert.

TIP ▶ **Use the Change Button to Test Your Move Before Using Change All**

If you choose Change All, you don't have anything further to say about it—no checking to see if you're sure you want to take this drastic step. If you mess up, your only way out is a Revert or Mini-Revert command to reverse the Change. Instead, you may feel more secure if you use the Find button first. When you get a potential change hit, use the Change command. Unlike Change and Find, Change stays right there so you can see if you have done the right thing. Try the Find and Change cycle a couple more times, and when you feel confident that you have programmed your search-and-replace correctly, you can click Change All.

The Find and Change boxes are like the Spelling command's dialog box in that you can move the dialog box around on the page. Moving the box enables you to see the context of your found target text because the text is highlighted.

Also, you can click the Story Editor box and leave the Find or Change box open in the background. Software engineers call this dialog box behavior *non-modal*. With the Find or Change box open, you can do the Find Next command on the Utilities menu. It's easiest to get to, however, if you use its keyboard shortcut, Ctrl+ G. Suppose you spot something that needs fixing as you are working through a search-and-replace operation. Rather than closing the dialog box, you can make your edit right then and easily return to the change process. This one feature can change the quality of your life. It will reduce the smog level in major metropolitan areas and aid in the biodegradable and environmentally acceptable breakdown of garbage in landfill sites.

DESIGN NOTE
Use Professional Typesetting Conventions, Part II

Chapter 5, "Typing In Your Type," discussed a number of professional standards for type. The following professional conventions are added here because the Find and Change capabilities of PageMaker aid in their use:

▼ Rather than use a double hyphen, use the em dash.

▼ Put some space around your em dashes, but not the usual big, fat space from the spacebar. Do a search-and-replace operation on your em dashes (or any double hyphens that crept into your text) and put thin spaces on either side of each em dash location. This technique has the great advantage of preventing a dash from starting a line, because the thin space character is a non-breaking space.

▼ Use styles for paragraph spacing rather than double carriage returns. Use leading and paragraph spacing settings in a paragraph style.

▼ Replace underlining with bold or italic.

▽ Search out double spaces after punctuation.

▽ Outlaw those straight, typewriter-type quotes. Use the professional, curly quotes instead. Set this option in Preferences so you don't type the typewriter quotes in PageMaker.

TIP ▶ Inch and Foot Marks Aren't Converted In the Text Import Filters

Any single or double quote marks that follow a number are not converted by the Convert Quotes function in the PageMaker text import filters. The filters are designed to assume those marks are intended as inch or foot marks. You may need to do a search and replace to put the proper inch and foot marks (primes) in your text. These characters are found in the Symbol font that comes with Windows (TrueType) or ATM (PostScript) or in the Universal News and Commercial Pi font. You can type them with Alt+0130 (double prime) and Alt+0162 (single prime).

Where to Go from Here

▶ Much of this chapter ultimately connects up to text and paragraph formatting and styles, which were covered in the first three chapters of Part II. Chapter 5, "Typing In Your Type;" Chapter 6, "Formatting Paragraphs;" and Chapter 7, "Designing a Text Style System," give you more insight into what you can edit with the Story Editor.

▶ Spreadsheets and databases are a special sort of text translation issue, and you get much more on the subject in Chapter 16, "Formatting Forms, Tables, and Databases."

▶ PageMaker's capability to spell check and do search and replace across many open publications greatly enhances your task of "Building Many Pages," Chapter 17.

▶ Above all, combine Story Editor's power into a dynamic toolbox of text and type massaging power. Check out the Tactics Recipe on "Cleaning Up Your Text" in Chapter 25, "Developing a System for Managing Your Type." You also can find information on PageMaker 6.0's new tagging language.

PART III

Working with Graphics

10 ▲ Drawing with PageMaker

11 ▲ Placing Images

Chapter 10

Drawing with PageMaker

This chapter on drawing with PageMaker covers the following information:

Creating graphics using PageMaker's drawing tools for lines, rectangles, ovals, and polygons.
▼

Constraining those objects into symmetrical squares, circles, and polygons, or into perpendicular or 45-degree angle lines.
▼

Rounding corners on rectangles.
▼

Moving and sizing a PageMaker graphics object.
▼

Selecting and customizing lines, and filling in shapes.
▼

Understanding stacking order and layers, the PageMaker "colors" called *none* and *paper*, and how all these attributes interact on the page.

JUST AS YOU HAVE a choice between creating type right in PageMaker or pouring text in from outside, you have a choice in drawing objects. You can use PageMaker's drawing tools, or you can create your graphic in a draw or paint program and then place it in PageMaker.

Also, just as with PageMaker's text block objects, you can select, copy, cut, and paste graphics objects. ▶ ▶ ▶

Drawing Lines and Shapes

Drawing in PageMaker is easy. Just click the tool you need and drag out the object you want. The object you get depends on the tool you select, as you see in figure 10.1.

FIG. 10.1 ▶

PageMaker-drawn objects and the tools that create them.

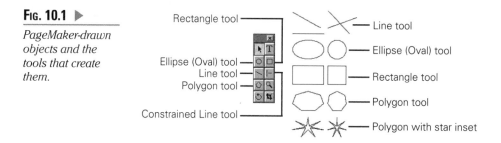

It's worth noting that old-timers call all the objects you draw in PageMaker *LBOs* (pronounced *elbows*). LBO stands for lines, boxes, and ovals. Technically, now that PageMaker 6.0 is out, these objects should not be LBOs, but LREPs. The official documentation calls these tools the Line, Rectangle, Ellipse, and Polygon tools—lines, rectangles, and ellipses.

You can use these shortcuts to select tools from the Toolbox:

Tool	Shortcut
Oval tool	Shift+F3
Rectangle tool	Shift+F4
Line tool	Shift+F5
Constrained Line tool	Shift+F6
Polygon tool	Shift+F7

Drawing Simple Lines

You have a choice of two tools when drawing lines. Both tools create the same kind of line when you're done, but the issue is the angle of the line. You can choose between a tool that draws a straight line at any angle or a tool that's constrained to draw the straight line at 45-degree angle increments (0, 45, 90, 135, 180, 225, 270, 315, and 360 degrees). In either case, after you draw your line, you can adjust it to any angle.

Notice that you can't draw a curved or bent line with either line tool—just a straight one. Look at figure 10.2 for some examples.

Fig. 10.2 ▶

Examples of simple lines drawn in PageMaker.

TIP ▶ Lines Are Positioned and Measured by Their Edges

When you position a line on the page, it may look as though you should be adjusting the line based on its center, but that's not true. In PageMaker, lines are positioned by their outer edge. The outer edge varies, depending on how you draw the line on the page—as a horizontal, vertical, or diagonal line. Only diagonal lines are drawn by their centers. Vertical and horizontal lines flip to one side or the other of the line tool instead of riding the center. For more on this issue, check the section "Flipping Lines and the Pixel Edge Effect" in Chapter 14, "Precisely Positioning Graphics and Text."

Key Concept:
Constraining Graphics

This word *constrain* comes up a lot when you draw and manipulate graphics in PageMaker. You constrain an object when you hold down the Shift key. The Shift key generally limits in some way the operation of whatever tool you are using at the time. With lines, for example, you can choose between the Line tool (Shift+F2) or the Constrained Line tool (Shift+F3). However, you can constrain the regular Line tool to get the same effect as the Constrained Line tool by simply holding down the Shift key while you use the regular Line tool. Why have a special Constrained Line tool when you can duplicate it with the Shift key? Why not also have constrained rectangle, oval and polygon tools? Beats me. Go figure.

Drawing Shapes: Rectangles and Ovals

Use the Rectangle and Oval tools to create the rectangle and oval shapes (see fig. 10.3). By holding down the Shift key as you draw, you can constrain rectangles and ovals to squares and circles.

FIG. 10.3 ▶

*PageMaker rect-
angle, square,
ellipse, and circle
drawings.*

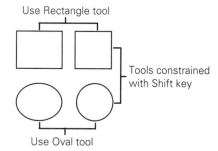

Rounding Corners

After you draw a box, you can round its corners by using the Rounded Corners
command from the Element menu. Figure 10.4 shows examples of rounded corners. You can also get this dialog box by double clicking the rectangle tool, except in that case you will be deselecting all objects and setting a mini-default for
rounded corner rectangles. The mini-default does not affect the box you have
selected, only boxes you draw from that point on.

FIG. 10.4 ▶

*The Rounded Cor-
ners dialog box
and an example
of using rounded
corners.*

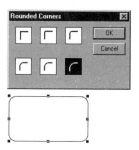

Drawing Shapes: Polygons

You can't round the corners on a polygon, but you can see stars. To draw a polygon you use the Polygon tool. No surprise there. You also should know about
two main controls—the number of sides and the percentage value of the star
inset.

Both of these controls are in the Polygon Settings dialog box, which you access
from the Element menu (see fig. 10.5). You can also set a polygon mini-default
by double-clicking the Polygon tool in the Toolbox palette.

FIG. 10.5 ▶

The two options available in the Polygon Settings dialog box, along with the Preview box.

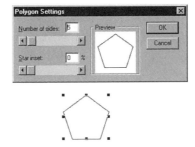

You can set the number of sides from 3 to 100, as you can see in figure 10.6.

FIG. 10.6 ▶

A range of polygon settings for the number of sides— 3, 5, 8 and 20.

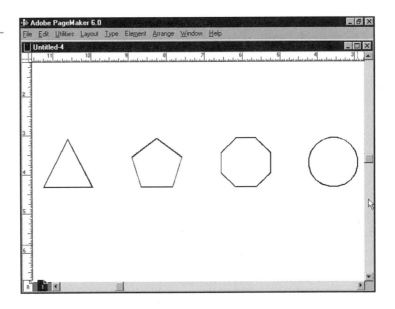

The star inset adjusts the distance between the center of the polygon and the mid-point of each side of the polygon. You get flat sides with a 0 percent setting, a star shape at the mid-way point, and radial spikes at 100 percent, where the mid-way points on the sides actually coincide with the middle of the polygon (see fig. 10.7).

FIG. 10.7 ▶

Setting the star inset for a polygon— 40%, 15%, 100%, 20%.

III

Working with Graphics

Moving and Sizing a Drawn Object

Using the Pointer tool, you can place a drawn object anywhere on the page, and you can make it almost any size you want. Manual positioning of an object, "eyeballing" it in, requires some experimenting. Use the Edit, Undo command (Ctrl+Z) to retract an experimental move that doesn't work out. Also, to keep your options completely open, save right before you begin a series of experiments so you can use the File, Revert command to get back to the original state if necessary. To put an object precisely where you want it, check the techniques in Chapter 14, "Precisely Positioning Graphics and Text."

Moving an Object

To move an object, click it with the Pointer tool and drag it. You will get a four-arrow cursor like the one you see in figure 10.8, and you can slide the object around on the page or Pasteboard.

Fig. 10.8 ▶

Click and drag to move an object.

Four-arrow cursor

When moving a PageMaker-drawn object, avoid the handles around the edges of the object because they resize the object instead of moving it. Also, if the object has a fill attribute of None, PageMaker's Pointer tool doesn't have anything to grab to make the move unless you click an edge (without getting a sizing handle). If the object is filled, you can click inside the object to grab it for a move.

Holding down the Shift key during a move constrains the move to the first 90-degree direction you take. For example, if you first move left or right after you get the four-arrow cursor, even a tiny bit, PageMaker seizes that direction as your constraint for the move, and the object slides only along that horizontal axis.

TIP ▶ **Pick Your Animation During the Move**

You get two kinds of visual representations—animations—of the move when you click and drag any PageMaker object. If you immediately move the object after you click it (before the four-arrow cursor appears), you see a simple outline frame that shows only the box shape occupied by the object as you slide it to its new position. You get a box (with the sizing handles at the corners) even if you are moving an oval or a circle. On the other hand, if you click the object and wait for a moment before dragging it, you get a picture of the object in full detail. Although the frame animation is faster, the detailed view is potentially more accurate, depending on what you are trying to accomplish with the move.

Sizing an Object

You size your graphic using the handles around your object's edges (again see fig. 10.8). A line sizes in only one direction, so it has only two handles, one at each end.

To resize an object, click and drag any of the handles. The handles in the middle of a side enable you to change the width or height of a graphic, limiting the move to one dimension. The corner handles draw the object out along that corner's axis (from the center of the object), simultaneously changing the size of two sides of the object.

In figure 10.9, you see a corner-handle click-and-drag move.

Fig. 10.9 ▶

Sizing an object using a corner handle.

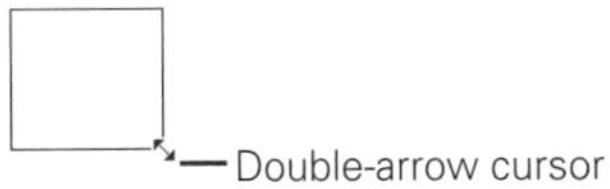

— Double-arrow cursor

You can constrain a size move. However, the constraint works a bit differently than in most other graphics programs. Holding down the Shift key changes a rectangle to a square, an ellipse to a circle, and a polygon to a symmetrical object. The Shift key keeps a line from straying away from the perpendicular axis or some multiple of a 45-degree angle. Instead of a *proportional* size constraint, it immediately transforms your object to a constrained *shape*.

You do get proportional moves in the Control palette. You also can size LBOs around their centers, rather than their sides or corners. You can find more on Control palettes and PageMaker-drawn objects in Chapter 14, "Precisely Positioning Graphics and Text." That's also the chapter where you can learn more about positioning, sizing, skewing, rotating, and flipping all kinds of objects, including imported ones.

You are probably aware that PageMaker has a cropping tool, but it doesn't have any effect on PageMaker-drawn objects. You simply need to resize those objects. You can, however, crop any imported graphic, a topic covered in Chapter 11, "Placing Images." The masking tool can be used for some of the same purposes, and there's coverage on it in Chapter 14, "Precisely Positioning Graphics and Text," and in Chapter 15, "Creating Special Effects."

III

Working with Graphics

Customizing Lines and Shapes

PageMaker-drawn objects work sort of like your kids' coloring books, except you have no way to go out of the lines. Actually, if you're one of those high-end, cutting-edge designers, I guess you could say that PageMaker objects work like your very own coloring book.

Of course, lines are simply lines; they aren't filled in. But shapes can have both lines *and* fills, which means that shapes may or may not be filled, and the lines around the edges can be assigned different types of lines, including no line at all. Also, unlike a coloring book, lines and shapes can be stacked in layers so they create special effects by either blocking out the underlying layered objects or allowing them to show through. The Key Concept, "Understanding Layers and the Colors None and Paper," later in this chapter, explains these special effects in more detail.

Choosing Quick Lines

You have a nearly infinite choice of lines to use for, well, lines, as well as for the outlines of PageMaker-drawn objects. The choices range from no line at all on the edge of an object to a line 800-points thick. For line styles, you can choose from plain, dotted, dashed, and special double and triple rules (sometimes called *Scotch rules*).

A Fill and Line command enables you to handle both attributes of an object at the same time. However, because you cannot fill lines, you may just as well use the rapid-access Element, Line command when you set up the look of a simple line object. The Line choices shown in figure 10.10 are nearly the same choices you get when you use the Line drop-down list in the Rules dialog box, in the Paragraph Specifications dialog box.

If you choose None from the Line submenu, you get a line or a shape perimeter that has no weight. In other words, the object doesn't appear on the page and doesn't print, but it acts as though it's there.

Before PageMaker 6.0, a common technique was to use lines with no weight as invisible objects for special effects. For example, you may have created a shape with no-weight lines and no fill, but with a text wrap setting to keep text from flowing into a particular area of a page. However, PageMaker 6.0 has nonprinting objects, which make this sort of trick a lot easier to perform.

You can set a Transparent or Reverse line directly from the quick Line submenu; alternatively, you can access those attributes by choosing the Custom line choice from the submenu, which gives you the Custom Line dialog box shown in figure 10.11.

Fig. 10.10 ▷

The selection of lines available through the Element, Line command.

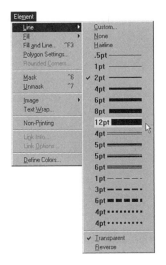

With the Custom Line dialog box, you can set a line as slim as 0 points and as wide as 800 points for any of the line styles, including broken lines and Scotch rules. You can set any of these weights with an even $^1/_{10}$ of a point accuracy.

Fig. 10.11 ▷

The Custom Line dialog box.

A transparent line allows whatever is behind it to show through; a reverse line in PageMaker has the official color of paper, meaning that the line is a knockout and prevents any ink or laser toner from being applied to the page. The terms *reverse*, *knockout*, and *paper* are different ways of saying the same thing, which can cause confusion. See the later Key Concept section, "Understanding Layers and the Colors None and Paper," to better understand these terms and the practical aspects of using these line settings.

TIP ▷ Use Care When Designing with Extremely Fine Lines

A hairline-weight line has nearly no weight; technically it is 2/10 of a point wide. Using PageMaker's custom line weight, you can get down to 1/10 of a point or even to zero. You probably conceptualize your designs on a video monitor that can't resolve a line any finer than one point or so. Anything finer just looks like a one-point line, no matter its setting. By the time you run your piece through a high-resolution imagesetter, the

III

Working with Graphics

line may be nearly invisible. It almost certainly will be thinner than you imagined it would be, judging from the view on your computer monitor.

You may want to consult your print shop before using hairlines. Some presses and papers simply won't hold that fine a line. Newsprint, for example, blots up ink voraciously, and a hairline rule is likely to come off the press looking considerably wider.

Choosing Quick Fills

In addition to adding a line around a shape, you can use the Element, Fill command. You can fill in a shape with one of the PageMaker cross-hatching patterns. Figure 10.12 shows the Fill submenu.

FIG. 10.12 ▶

The Fill submenu.

TIP ▶ **Use the Colors Palette to Set Color for Lines and Fills**

The Colors palette enables you to set colors on lines, fills, or both. A detailed discussion of working with color is in Part V, "Making Pages Colorful."

Using the Comprehensive Fill and Line Menu

If you really want control over the look of a shape or line, use the Fill and Line dialog box, which you access from the Element, Fill and Line command (see fig. 10.13).

FIG. 10.13 ▶

The one-stop Fill and Line dialog box.

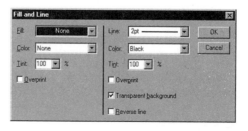

In the comprehensive Fill and Line dialog box, you get the same drop-down lists that you get when you use the individual Line and Fill submenu commands. Also, the Transparent Background and Reverse settings work the same way here as they do in the Line and Fill submenus. The difference is that you get control of everything in one dialog box. You even get a keyboard shortcut: Ctrl+F3.

A new feature for this dialog box in PageMaker 6.0 is object-level tints. Not only can you select any of your defined colors from this one location, you also can select on-the-fly the intensity (the percentage) of that color to apply.

The Overprint settings deal with the interaction of layers of color and are explained fully in Chapter 18, "Creating Colors," in the section "Specifying Overprint and Knockout."

✂ KEY CONCEPT:
Understanding Layers and the Colors None and Paper

Each time you draw a new object, PageMaker assigns it to a new, top layer. Each object on the page—including text blocks, imported graphics, and drawn graphics—occupies a unique layer. If you don't do anything to change this order, these objects stack up on one another, with the most recently created or placed object on top, and the oldest object on the bottom. This effect is sometimes called the *stacking order*. In general, unless you use the Overprint color attribute, the objects on upper layers block out the objects in the rear layers.

Using the Send to Back (Ctrl+B) and Bring to Front (Ctrl+F) commands under the Arrange menu, you can change the stacking order of objects. The box on the left in figure 10.14 is placed on top of the circle. On the right, the layers are reversed by selecting the box and applying the Send to Back command.

New with PageMaker 6.0 is the ability to manipulate stacking order from layer to layer, not just all the way to the front or back. Use the Ctrl+8 keyboard shortcut to move an object towards the front by one layer, and Ctrl+9 to move it back one layer. (On the Arrange menu, it's Bring Forward and Send Backward.)

Another new feature is that PageMaker respects the stacking order of selected objects. (This concept will take getting used to.) If you click and drag an object, it stays

FIG. 10.14 ▲

Two objects stacked in layers. On the left, the box is brought to front; on the right, it's sent to back.

on its own layer. In previous versions, the simple act of selecting an object would bring it all the way to the front layer.

The two objects in figure 10.14 block one another because they are filled. Filled shapes are opaque and can't be set to transparent; filled objects, by default, completely blot out whatever sits behind them. *Lines* can be transparent, but filled objects can't be.

You can set an object to have no fill; in effect, you make the object transparent. To set an object to have no fill, choose the None attribute from the Fill command or from the fill side of the Fill and Line dialog box. Don't confuse the None attribute with the terms *paper, reverse,* or *knockout*. None means the absence of ink in the selected object (the absence of a fill) and its layer. Paper, reverse, and knockout, on the other hand, all mean the prevention of ink on any layer *beneath* the object where the effect is applied. The terms are confusing because they all mean the same thing. *Paper* and *reverse* are used in PageMaker dialog boxes in various locations; *knockout* is the general graphic-arts term for the effect.

The sandwich of objects in figure 10.15 and the text below it show how layering and the "colors" of paper and none work on one another.

The gray box in figure 10.15 is set to 60 percent black in the Fill menu; the box is sent to the back to show how the none and paper colors react against it.

The oval shape has a fill color of none (so you can see through it); the line defining the oval is set at 2 points of black.

The knockout type is set to a color of Reverse from the Type Styles submenu. (If you check the Type Specifications dialog box, you see that clicking the Reverse check box automatically switches the color of the type from black to paper. *Paper* and *reverse* mean the same thing, even though the designers of PageMaker chose to use two different names in different dialog box locations.)

In figure 10.15, the knockout text has knocked out—removed, defeated, prevented—the ink of the gray box. In fact, the knocked-out text takes precedence over anything that resides in a layer underneath it, including the black line of the ellipse. If you bring the black ellipse line forward, however, it takes precedence over the knockout text.

It would probably be less confusing if PageMaker used one term in all dialog boxes for reverse, paper, and knockout situations. Perhaps the standard term should be knockout rather than reverse or paper. Knockout describes what happens pretty well. The reverse or paper options "knock out" any application of ink by any objects behind the knockout object.

In figure 10.16, four dashed lines are superimposed on a gray box. The gray box has been sent to the back, and the lines are on layers in front of the box. Several

Fig. 10.15 ▲

A sandwich of layers showing the "colors" [none] *and* [paper].

combinations of Transparent and Reverse attributes are shown so you can see how their effects interact.

As you go through the following descriptions for each of the four lines in figure 10.16, keep in mind the explanations in this section for the "colors" of [None] and [Paper].

The left line in figure 10.16 shows a PageMaker dashed line with both the Transparent and Reverse attributes turned off. The line is neither transparent nor reversed. This dashed line ends up being an alternating stripe of blocks of black (or some other color of ink) and paper. Because the underlying paper is white, you see a stripe of black and white overlaid on the gray box. If the paper were bright turquoise, you'd get alternating blocks of black and turquoise because the paper would show through between the black dashes.

For the second line, it's important to understand that lines can be set to transparent (with objects like rectangles and ovals, you use the [None] attribute). How is the transparent attribute for a line different from the fill attribute of [None] for a two-dimensional PageMaker object? Actually, they aren't terribly different. [None] means that the object has no fill. Transpar-

ent means that nothing is filling in the spaces between the elements of a Scotch rule or a broken line. You can't say the line has the hypothetical color of [None] because the lines still get ink even though the spaces between don't.

For the second line, the Transparent setting is on and the Reverse setting stays off. The black dashes stay, overriding the underlying gray box. But the spaces between the dashes now allow the gray to come through. Unlike the first line, the spaces are not knocking out the gray to let the paper show through because the line has been made transparent.

For the third line, the Reverse setting is on, and the Transparent setting is off. The spaces between the dashes are painted with ink (black in this case), and the dashes are reversed to the color of the paper, knocking out the gray beneath the line, allowing the underlying paper to show through.

The fourth line has both the Transparent and Reverse settings on. What you see here is gray showing through between the dashes (the spaces are not the color paper and don't knock out the gray), and the dashes are reversed, meaning that they now are paper-colored rather than ink-colored.

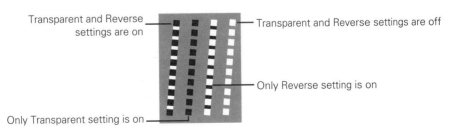

Transparent and Reverse settings are on — Transparent and Reverse settings are off

Only Reverse setting is on

Only Transparent setting is on

FIG. 10.16 ▲

A dashed line on top of a gray box, with combinations of Transparent and Reverse settings.

Where to Go from Here

▶ There's more to graphics life than drawing simple boxes, circles, and lines in PageMaker, as you see in Chapter 11, "Importing Images."

▶ When you have objects on the page, you need to put them in the right spot; check out Chapter 14, "Precisely Positioning Graphics and Text."

▶ The Control palette can be great for managing precision objects; Chapter 14 has information on this topic.

▶ The last Key Concept on how objects work between layers may have tantalized you with some special-effects possibilities. Chapter 15, "Creating Special Effects," offers many practical examples of how to put these concepts to work.

▶ The issues of layers, knockout, and overprint are important when you work with color, a subject extensively explored in Part V, "Making Pages Colorful."

Chapter 11

Placing Images

This chapter on importing images covers these topics:

Understanding the basic types of graphics files: resolution-independent and resolution-dependent.

▼

Importing graphics with the Place command.

▼

Replacing an existing graphic, putting a graphic into a line of text, and saving file space by compressing graphics.

▼

Using the Library palette database for PageMaker objects to make layout more efficient.

▼

Sizing and cropping graphics.

▼

Setting various views for graphics and controlling how images print on the press.

▼

Taking advantage of PageMaker's special new power for importing Photo CD images.

PAGEMAKER'S CAPABILITY TO draw lines, rectangles, and ovals gives you some graphics power, but for real story-telling you often need to include illustrations and photographs in publications. Those elements most likely are created and fine-tuned outside PageMaker. Your resources may include a clip art collection, a collection of stock photography, a drawing from Illustrator or FreeHand, or a digital painting from Photoshop, to name a few.

In PageMaker, importing graphics has a great deal in common with importing text. For one thing, you use the Place command. You can also negotiate a variety of file formats (graphics formats rather than word processor formats) using the filters you install in PageMaker. ▶ ▶ ▶

KEY CONCEPT:
Reviewing Resolution-Dependent and Resolution-Independent Images

You encounter two kinds of graphics in this world—resolution-dependent and resolution-independent. I chose these terms over the traditional computer-industry terms for these file types to suggest the practical results you achieve with each sort of graphics image. Traditionally, resolution-dependent graphics have been called *bit-mapped*, *paint*, or *raster* images. Resolution-independent graphics have been called *object-oriented*, *draw*, or *vector* images.

Preventing Jaggies with Resolution Independence

If you run a resolution-independent graphic through an imagesetter, you get a smooth reproduction with no jaggies, no matter how much you magnify the graphic. As you can see in figure 11.1, object-oriented images yield resolution-independent results.

You produce resolution-independent files when you work with drawing programs such as Illustrator and FreeHand. (PageMaker-drawn graphics also are resolution-independent.)

Resolution-independent images are not stored as a bunch of dots; they are stored on disk as a set of equations, sometimes called vectors because the equations describe vectors—lines that add up to arcs, circles, or boxes. The equations for each intricate line, curve, and angle in the image can be sent right to the printing device to appear on paper or film at the device's maximum resolution. So, when you enlarge a resolution-independent graphic and then use PageMaker's Print command to send the result to the imagesetter or laser printer, the output device uses these resolution-independent vectors or equations to draw a new and resized version of the graphic. This whole process takes place in the background, so you never see it except in the form of printer output.

FIG. 11.1 ▲

A resolution-independent eye at two magnifications.

The main resolution-independent format in desktop publishing is the *EPS file*, which stands for Encapsulated PostScript. EPS files contain PostScript code. Adobe, the company that merged with Aldus and now owns PageMaker, invented PostScript. The PostScript page-description language virtually dominates the desktop publishing market and provides the central technology for most laser printers and imagesetters.

Please take note that you *can* bundle up a resolution-dependent image inside an EPS file. The part of the EPS file that is resolution-dependent stays that way. It's just that the EPS format was designed primarily for the purpose of containing resolution-independent PostScript descriptions of graphic information.

When you see an EPS file placed in PageMaker, the image you see on-screen isn't the same as the vectors transmitted to the laser printer or imagesetter. The EPS contains, encapsulated within the file, a second representation of the image that you see on-screen.

This screen version of the image enables you to see what you are doing when you position the graphic on a page. The screen image is there because your computer can't use the PostScript graphic itself to create a screen image.

In Windows, the screen image is a TIFF file, or perhaps a WMF file. For the Macintosh, the EPS contains a PICT version of the image. This difference in screen previews is why EPS graphics exchanged between Mac and Windows platforms often look like a plain gray box on-screen, but print just fine. The PICT preview is usable only on a Mac, and the WMF preview works only in Windows. Many graphics problems give you the option to save an EPS with a TIFF preview, a format that tends to be portable between the Macintosh and Windows platforms, assuming you are using a PostScript printer on both types of machines.

If you are printing to a non-PostScript printer, PageMaker tries to print your page using the screen preview, a poorer quality, resolution-dependent file format. If you are printing an EPS PostScript image to a PostScript printer, the preview image is purely for on-screen display and isn't used for printing.

Working with Resolution Dependent Images

Scanners create resolution-dependent graphics. So do paint programs such as Photoshop and Fractal Painter. These programs produce files made up of dots rather than vectors. The total number of dots making up any particular resolution-dependent image is fixed and constant. Therefore, when you magnify the image, the dots get bigger and farther apart.

For this reason, resolution-dependent images produce quite different results from EPS graphics. If you blow up resolution-dependent graphics into larger sizes, their fixed-resolution dots can look lumpy and ugly, like a badly damaged tile mosaic. Take a look at the eye in figure 11.2—and then at the accompanying close-up. Both images have the same number of dots devoted to the eyeball, but as you might expect, the magnified image reveals those dots to the…well, to the naked eye.

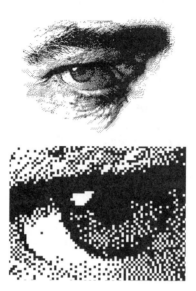

FIG. 11.2 ▲

A resolution-dependent eye, from a paint program graphic.

The main resolution-dependent files in desktop publishing are TIFF files. TIFF stands for Tag Image File Format. Most scans are saved in TIFF. High-end painting and photo-retouching programs such as Photoshop commonly use TIFF for graphics. TIFF files are capable of conveying simple black-and-white picture information, more complex shades of gray, and colors. Gray-scale files have up to 256 levels of gray. Color TIFF files are, well, colored.

TIFF files, although resolution-dependent, are capable of extremely fine resolution if you are willing to pay the price in hard disk space (highly detailed TIFF images create huge files). The more visual information (resolution, gray scales, colors), the bigger the files.

Often, resolution is expressed in dots per inch. This business of dots per inch can confuse you in a hurry. In this Key Concept section, we're discussing the resolution of a file when it arrives in

PageMaker. That's not the same as the dots you get when you put the pages containing these graphics onto paper.

Somewhere along the line (maybe in high-school science class), you've probably heard the old magnifying-glass-and-magazine-picture explanation. The ink dots that make up the printed picture fool the eye into thinking that the picture is a real photograph with smooth shades of gray or smooth gradations of color. The magazine dots are different from the ones we refer to in defining resolution-dependent graphics, although the two kinds of dots are related.

The dots in a magazine picture or illustration are called *halftones*. That topic is another discussion, involving line screens and frequencies, dots, pixels, cells, and dot gain. All these topics are covered in Chapter 23, "Working with the Print Shop," in the Key Concept section "Understanding Halftones and Screens."

TIP ▶ Use EPS or TIFF Files for Professional Results

No matter the source for these images or how they are created, you want to use EPS and TIFF graphics files wherever possible. Since the last edition of this book, these two formats have become even more solidly entrenched as the standards for professional desktop publishing. You may encounter a virtual alphabet soup of other file formats (PNT, PCX, WMF, and CGM to name a few). The main thing to remember is that PageMaker works best when outputting PostScript language to a printer or imagesetter. PageMaker has been optimized to do that job and you can't reliably depend on getting the expected result if you don't use PostScript.

This guideline has a few exceptions. For example, Desktop Color Separation (DCS) files are high-end scanned images (usually extremely large files) that your service bureau separates into the four process colors (cyan, magenta, yellow, black). The bureau keeps the high-resolution file to save transporting such a large file and provides you with a low-resolution version of the file for positioning in your publication. The DCS positioning image is then automatically replaced at output time by the high-quality image. Likewise, Scitex Continuous Tone (SCT) files are high-quality, large-file images that your prepress service bureau produces. However, for the vast majority of situations, use EPS or TIFF for graphics files. This advice is especially important if you must exchange files with other people during a project, or hand off your publication to a service bureau when your design is complete.

Placing Graphics

To import graphics, you use the same command you use to import text—the File, Place command. The placement icons change, depending on the file format of the graphic you are importing into PageMaker. Table 11.1 lists the graphics placement icons and the file types they represent.

TABLE 11.1   Placement Icons and Associated Graphics Files

Icon	File Type
	EPS
	TIFF
	Paint or Bitmap
	Vector or Draw

Using the Place Command for Graphics

The Place dialog box changes depending on which tool you have selected when you choose the command. Figure 11.3 shows the dialog box that appears if you choose the Place command with the Pointer tool selected. This dialog box enables you to place independent graphics (as opposed to inline graphics, covered in an upcoming section). Notice that all the choices dealing with text, such as the Convert Quotes option, are dimmed because you are importing a graphic. Also, you see some information about the file, a new feature with Version 6.0.

Fig. 11.3 ▶

Specify which file to place, and view the file type, size, and date of modification.

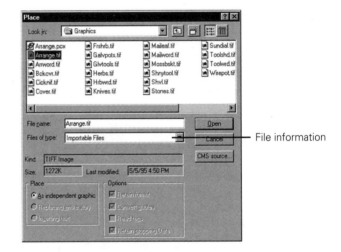

— File information

TIP ▶   **Solve Printing Problems for EPS Files with Embedded TIFFs**

At press time, there was a problem with PageMaker 6.0 when placing EPS files from Macromedia FreeHand 5.0 which had TIFF files placed in them. At printout time, PageMaker was simply ignoring the TIFF files.

If you experience this problem, here is a way to solve the problem. Hold down the Shift key when you are double-clicking the EPS file name in the Place dialog box. Instead of getting a loaded EPS placement pointer, you get the EPS import filter dialog box. Click off the check box labeled Read Embedded OPI Image Links. Then click OK, and everything will go fine from there.

Unfortunately, at least at release time, this filter did not remember the setting from session to session in PageMaker, so you need to reset the check box on the first occasion you use the filter after opening PageMaker. Actually, by the time you read this information, this whole thing may be moot because new filters and other fixes could already be developed. Check the usual online sources for updates.

Replacing an Existing Graphic

If you select a graphic by clicking it before opening the Place dialog box, things look a bit different (see fig. 11.4). The Replacing Entire Graphic option is selected. This option enables you to replace the existing graphic with the new one.

Fig. 11.4 ▶

The Place dialog box set to replace a graphic and retain cropping information.

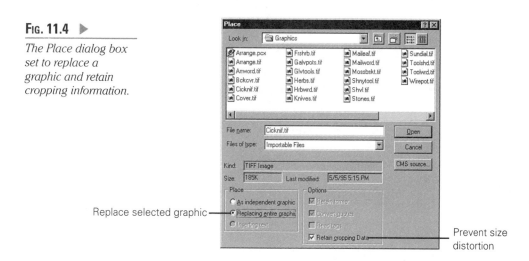

Replace selected graphic ⟶

Prevent size distortion

Watch out here. If you don't check the Retain Cropping Data option, PageMaker squeezes the new graphic inside the box represented by the old graphic, regardless of the fit. Figure 11.5 shows how this option works. Both of these images were imported with the Replacing Entire Graphic option checked, but the check box to retain cropping information was selected for the image on the right.

Fig. 11.5 ▶

A squeezed graphic on the left; cropping data retained for the image on the right.

Placing Inline Graphics

If you place a graphic in your text, the graphic becomes an inline graphic and locks into that location just as if it was a text character. This has the huge advantage of allowing you to do all sorts of editing above and below the graphic and have the graphic retain its position in the text. You can't do that if you place the graphic as an independent element.

III

Working with Graphics

To place an inline graphic, you select the Text tool before choosing the Place command. See how the Place dialog box changes in figure 11.6.

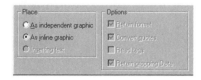

The Place dialog box with the Text tool selected and options set for an inline graphic.

Figure 11.7 shows two examples of inline graphics.

Fig. 11.7 ▶

Inline graphics used as a reverse head and as a text-alert icon.

Inline graphic ——————

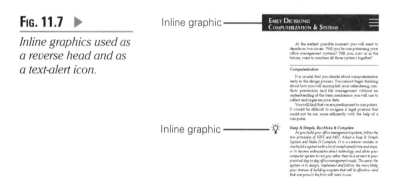

Inline graphic ——————

The reversed head at the top of the page in figure 11.7 was created using an EPS graphic drawn in FreeHand. The head sits in its own paragraph, assigned a style with very small leading. The graphic is pulled down with the Pointer tool so it appears behind the text (your pointer turns into an icon that looks a bit like an elevator, indicating you can move the graphic up or down in relation to the baseline); the text is styled as reverse so it shows up against the black graphic.

The second EPS graphic, the icon in the narrow left column, appears in a specially styled subhead used throughout the book to highlight text. Tabs are part of the style; they center the icon in the companion column.

The inline graphics capability has all sorts of practical applications for laying out pages, as you do in Part IV, "Creating Page Layouts." Also, these two examples (and more) are presented in detail in Chapter 15, "Creating Special Effects." Some special mechanics are involved in precisely positioning inline graphics on a page and within text; those issues are covered in Chapter 14, "Precisely Positioning Graphics and Text."

Storing Graphics In or Out of a Publication

As you import graphics, you may see a dialog box like the one in figure 11.8, asking whether you want to store the graphic in or out of your publication. If you store the graphic inside the publication, you use twice the disk space, because you store it twice (the original, plus a copy embedded in the publication). On the other hand, storing graphics internally makes the publication file complete and potentially more convenient to send to someone else. And the graphic may possibly display faster on-screen.

Fig. 11.8 ▷

This dialog box asks whether to store a graphic in or out of the publication.

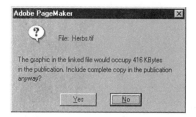

You can set a size limit on Placed files you normally want to store in your publication file. The Preferences command under the File menu has an option labeled Alert When Storing Graphics Over. You can set PageMaker's decision point for the size of graphics automatically stored in or out of a publication (see Chapter 3, "Personalizing PageMaker Preferences").

The capability to store a file outside a publication stems from PageMaker's capability to maintain connections between a publication and a file's originating program:

▷ PageMaker's linking technology has been in the program since Version 4.0, and is PageMaker's own technology for file updating and tracking.

▷ With PageMaker 6.0, OLE (Object Linking and Embedding) is enhanced in Version 2.0.

Both of these linking technologies are covered in greater detail in Chapter 30, "Linking and Other File Connections."

Editing the Original Graphic

If a graphic has been imported through the Place command, in most cases, you can open the element in its original command for editing purposes—from right within PageMaker. Use the Edit Original command on the Edit menu. This technique is hot stuff—it saves a lot of trouble and basically extends PageMaker's power to include any program in your graphic toolbox.

III

Working with Graphics

Suppose that you want to change a FreeHand EPS graphic. First select the object. Then choose the Edit Original command to open the original illustration file right in FreeHand. When you finish editing, save the file and quit FreeHand; the illustration is re-exported as an updated EPS graphic and re-placed, bringing you automatically back to PageMaker with the newly updated graphic already in position.

You don't need to know much about PageMaker's links to use this command. Just select the object and choose the Edit Original command. Windows may detect which program originated the graphic element, but if not, PageMaker will display a dialog box so you can select the program of your choice to make your edit.

Although the Edit Original command works well for editing graphics, in most cases, you do not want to use this command for text files. With text files, you usually don't want to re-import your file because you lose text formatting and other special layout work (such as kerning, baseline shift, inline graphics, and so on). Re-importing graphics files doesn't present the same kind of problems, because you generally don't edit them inside PageMaker as you do text.

Clipboarding Graphics

You can cut, copy, and paste graphics in PageMaker. You also can drag-and-drop between two open PageMaker publications, which really is a special form of copy and paste.

If you use the Clipboard to bring in graphics, PageMaker automatically tries to pick the optimum format for you. The process works so transparently that many people don't realize that an object often exists on the Clipboard in several formats. Therefore, it's good that you have a choice of using an enhanced Paste command, called Paste Special. This command appears on the Edit menu.

Figure 11.9 shows how the new command enables you to override PageMaker's best guess for special purposes. PageMaker's recommended choice appears first on the list in the dialog box, followed by the alternative Paste formats.

Fig. 11.9 ▶

*The Paste Special
dialog box.*

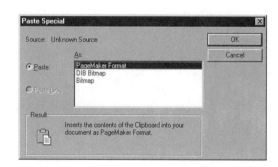

Organizing and Inserting Graphics with the Library Palette

You also can drag-and-drop from the Library palette to a publication. To add an item to the Library, select an object in the publication and click the large plus sign in the upper-left corner of the Library palette (see fig. 11.10).

Fig. 11.10 ▷

The Library palette and its menu.

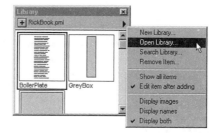

Items are listed in the Library palette as thumbnail sketches with names you designate yourself. You can have a different view of your data by switching your view to thumbnails only or text entries only.

After you load an item into the Library, you can double-click the item to assign key words and make notes that are searchable. This feature is especially useful if you must search through a big Library palette to find certain objects.

Place a Library palette item in PageMaker by clicking it and then dragging-and-dropping it into the publication.

You may use the New and Open commands to establish new libraries and open up alternative libraries.

Sizing and Cropping Graphics

PageMaker provides you with two ways to adjust the size of your illustrations:

▶ You can change the actual size of the image on the page by clicking and dragging a handle with the Pointer tool.

▶ You can leave the image the same size and cut away portions of it with the Cropping tool.

You can perform both of these moves using the Control palette, as described in Chapter 14, "Precisely Positioning Graphics and Text."

TIP ▶ **Size and Correct Graphics Before Importing**

The next couple of sections cover sizing, cropping, and correcting graphics. Although you sometimes may need to perform adjustments from within PageMaker after importing a graphic, for best results you ought to do major graphics editing before importing into PageMaker. This advice is especially true for cropping, sizing, or rotating an image.

Cutting down a graphic before importing it saves file space. You may prevent a crash-and-burn crisis at deadline time when your megafile chokes at the service bureau. Plus, programs such as Photoshop or FreeHand are much more powerful for image editing than PageMaker, so you stand a better chance of getting the desired effect by editing before the import step.

Sizing with Click and Drag

Sizing an imported graphic works just like drawing an object with one of the PageMaker tools. (Well, there's one difference: if you use the Shift key to proportionally size a PageMaker drawn object, it constrains by snapping to a square or circle shape.) Use the Pointer tool to click and drag one of the eight handles of the graphic. Figure 11.11 shows an EPS graphic before and during a corner move and a side-handle move.

Fig. 11.11 ▶

Sizing a graphic with the Pointer tool.

Double-arrow sizing cursor

Sizing Proportionally and Using Magic Stretch

Unfortunately, the graphic in figure 11.11 doesn't look right. It has been badly distorted. The graphic needs to be sized proportionally so that the sizing maintains the relative lengths of the sides, retaining the proper shape of the object. To size proportionally, constrain the move by holding down the Shift key and then performing the click and drag. The Shift constraint move works on all imported graphics objects.

Another form of constrained sizing can help prevent printing defects when sizing black-and-white (as opposed to gray or color) resolution-dependent (bit-mapped) graphics. This sizing is called *magic stretch*. You get the effect by holding down the Ctrl key while performing the click and drag. Figure 11.12 shows what happens if you don't apply this magic. Notice the plaid cross-hatching on these solid gray boxes, which have been resized without using magic stretch.

FIG. 11.12 ▶

Mismatched resolution cross-hatching caused by not using magic stretch when resizing a graphic.

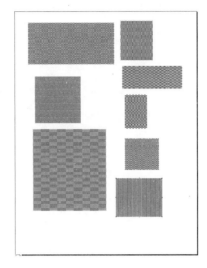

This cross-hatching happens because your printer can't print a half dot. When you stretch a graphic to an odd size—one that's not an exact multiple of your destination printer's resolution—the printer leaves cross-hatch lines where it cannot print the dot properly.

The operation of magic stretch depends on the resolution setting for the target printer in the Page Setup dialog box. This setting enables you to tell PageMaker the output resolution of the device you eventually will use to produce mechanicals. (That output resolution may differ from the resolution of the printer you are using as you lay out and proof the publication.) For example, it is common to set the target printer resolution at 2,450 for an imagesetter, even though you use a 300 dots-per-inch laser printer for proofing chores.

With the magic stretch constraint turned on, the cross-hatch problem is solved. The image refuses to adjust smoothly to any size you might pick, making jerky jumps from size to size. That's because the magic stretch constraint causes the graphic to adjust only to a multiple of the target printer. Hence, no half dots and no white cross-hatch lines.

Cropping with the Cropping Tool

After the graphic is in the document, you may want to trim the edges. Use the Cropping tool, which you can select from the lower-right corner of the Toolbox

III

Working with Graphics

or with the Shift+F11 shortcut. Figure 11.13 shows a graphic in the process of being cropped.

FIG. 11.13 ▶

Cropping an image.

Cropping an image seems a bit like putting a window around it, a window you can adjust to any size as long as it's smaller than the original object. After you crop an object, you can click it with the Cropping tool and slide the object around within that window. Figure 11.14 shows how the Cropping tool turns into a grabber hand for the sliding move.

FIG. 11.14 ▶

The grabber hand adjusting a graphic within its cropping window.

Grabber hand

You may size cropped graphics after you crop them. The proportional and magic stretch constraints work just fine on cropped objects as well. Remember that the magic stretch move applies only to monochrome bit-mapped graphics.

Viewing and Compressing Graphics

Using some nooks and crannies of PageMaker, you can customize the way the program works with graphics and the way some graphic images print.

Viewing Graphics at High Resolution

In the Preferences dialog box, in the Graphics section, you may choose to see graphics three different ways:

▶ You can display on-screen graphics as *gray boxes*. This method works best if you don't need to see the image, just its location on the page. This graphics viewing mode is fast because the computer doesn't need to redisplay the image on-screen every time you make a move.

▶ You can view graphics in *normal resolution*. Normal resolution looks, well, normal. All but the smallest graphics files are replaced for display purposes by a lower resolution screen-only image.

▶ You can view graphics in *high resolution*. High resolution uses the actual graphic image file (the embedded or the linked one) to draw the screen image. This process can take all day if the file is big, but it works great if you must accurately see what's going on. High-resolution viewing mode applies only to resolution-dependent images such as TIFFs. The best PageMaker can do for screen display of an EPS file is to use the EPS format's built-in preview image, which doesn't have near the quality as the final output resolution.

To temporarily display a graphic in high-resolution mode, hold down Ctrl+Shift as you place the graphic or as you force a screen redraw. For example, you could press Ctrl+Shift+F12.

TIP ▶ **Screen Resolution Makes a Difference in Non-PostScript Output**

Ordinarily the viewing resolution does not have any influence on the look of your printed output. However, if you are printing on a non-PostScript device, the printer uses the actual screen display as its main source for the graphic. If you have a low-resolution image on-screen, that's what your printer gets. Don't forget that you can adjust the resolution PageMaker uses for your Standard Graphics Display setting by working with the Define Standard Display command in Preferences, as described in Chapter 3, "Personalizing PageMaker Preferences."

Setting Compression for a Graphic

PageMaker has a powerful way to save real estate on your hard disk. You can compress any TIFF file as you place it. After the compression operation, you can toss the old TIFF file and save the disk space. PageMaker works with the compressed version as if it were the original, but you accomplish significant savings in disk space.

You can always order the compressed version to be decompressed if you ever need to do so. (However, you should be aware that compression can potentially lose some of the data out of a file, particularly if you are applying maximum compression. It's a good idea to keep a backup of the original copy of the image on hand.)

Please note that this technique applies only to TIFF files you store outside the publication. Compression doesn't save space used by TIFFs embedded in the document file.

Here's how compressing works. When placing your TIFF file, hold down one of the key combinations from table 11.2. Depending on your choice of keys, the file is compressed, either maximally or moderately.

So that you can identify compressed files and their degree of compression, PageMaker makes a copy of the original file and slightly changes its name, as noted in table 11.2. For example, if you use the key combination to apply maximum compression to a full-color TIFF file (Shift+Ctrl+Alt+OK), you end up with a file name something like PANDA_M.TIF.

As PageMaker 6.0 must still work with Windows 3.x, it can't put a space in the name, so it cuts off the last two digits (in an eight-digit file name) and replaces them with _X (underscore and then code letter) then TIF. In the example PANDA_M.TIF, the _M indicates maximum compression on a full-color or grayscale TIFF. A_U embedded in the file name, on the other hand, would signify that the TIFF file has been decompressed.

TABLE 11.2   Key Combinations and File Identifiers for TIFF Compression

Type of TIFF	Moderate (Ctrl+Alt)	Maximum (Shift+Ctrl+Alt)	Decompressed (Ctrl)*
Monochrome	_P	_L	_U
Palette color (16 or 256 color)	_P	_L	_U
Grayscale or full color	_D	_M	_U

* Select graphic first if already placed.

PageMaker uses a type of compression called LZW for this process. Any other program that comprehends LZW can read your compressed TIFF files with no trouble.

PageMaker 6.0 has a new graphics compression tool. JPEG has become an increasingly popular alternative to LZW compression schemes, and now 6.0 has a JPEG import filter. However, PageMaker has no keyboard-quick JPEG compression, unlike the arrangements for using LZW compression. Photoshop, for one example, saves a graphics file using JPEG compression. JPEG does have the disadvantage of being a type of compression that can inherently involve throwing out data to achieve its reductions in file size. In most cases this issue is not significant unless a file is subjected to multiple JPEG compression operations.

Tuning and Manipulating Resolution-Dependent Images

PageMaker 6.0 has significantly enhanced its power to make edits to your graphics. The Image Control command has been augmented—and to some degree supplanted—by the new capability to use Photoshop-compatible filters to manipulate images.

Using Image Control

PageMaker's Image Control command (on the Element menu) provides you with some simple controls over how your resolution-dependent images print. The Image Control dialog box shown in figure 11.15 does not work on EPS or color TIFF graphics. It does work on bit-mapped graphics (paint and noncolor black-and-white or grayscale TIFFs).

Fig. 11.15 ▷

*The Image Control
dialog box.*

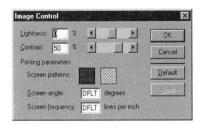

III

Working with Graphics

In the Image Control dialog box you can make gross adjustments of brightness and contrast. Also, if you are printing to a PostScript printer, you can adjust the screen parameters and perhaps achieve some special effects through your choices.

TIP ▷ **Line Screens Are a Touchy Business**

You may want to back off from using the line screen settings in the Image Control dialog box. It's generally best to set line screens in consultation with your service bureau and your printer, and to set them for an entire project rather than for individual images. Therefore, you should adjust the overall line-screen setting for the publication in the Print dialog box. Even in that case, it is almost always best to accept the defaults. For more information on line screens and their impact on the printing process, see Chapter 23, "Working with the Print Shop," especially the Key Concept section, "Understanding Halftones and Screens."

TIP ▷ **Monitors Are Liars**

Do not depend on your monitor to tell you how an image will look when it's printed. You can tweak an on-screen picture until it seems absolutely perfect, and get poor results just because the cleaning lady dusted your monitor overnight and accidentally set it a notch darker than you normally keep it. Aside from this kind of adjustment problem, monitors are inherently liars because they act as projectors of light, shining the image into our eyes. On the other hand, we see images on paper through reflection of light off the surface, so a monitor has no way to truly convey how the image will look on paper. You can find out only by running the image on press.

Few of us have the time or money for experimentation on the printing press during a project, but over time you gain a feel for what works and what doesn't. Short of actual testing on a printing press, your best bet is to run a proof and take it to the printer who will do the job. Part VI, "Publishing," contains more detail on taking care of this gap between your proof and the printing press.

Design Note
Use Image Control to Set a Graphics Backdrop

Use the Image Control dialog box to gray down a visual; then place some bold type over it. The Image Control's simple image-adjusting capability doesn't compare to special-purpose programs such as Photoshop for detailed photo retouching, but it really can shine when creating this kind of special effect. You can gauge the effect pretty well on your monitor if you have a gray-scale or color screen. You can see a similar effect in Chapter 15, "Creating Special Effects." (As with most PageMaker graphics effects, you'll get your most reliable results when using a PostScript printer.)

TIP ▷ **Improve Photocopying with Custom Line Screens**

One situation exists where you may want to set a special line screen for a graphic, but not for the entire project. When you know that your output will be photocopied, you may get better results by experimenting with the line-screen frequency and angle. Experiment to see what works best with your office copier. Sometimes, the default line-screen setting (the DFLT letters in the line-screen boxes in the Image Control dialog box) work fine. Sometimes, a photocopier can benefit from a coarser line-screen setting. Run your test by placing an image on a single page several times and trying several settings and image-control manipulations. Then photocopy the page to assess results.

Design Note
Use Weird Line Screens to Achieve Special Effects

Check out the pretty sailboat race in figure 11.16. It was photographed by John Menihan for the Kodak Photo CD sampler. The image was produced for this example in 256 grayscale TIFF format with no special effects manipulation.

Fig. 11.16 ▷

Pretty sailboats, the starting point for the mezzotint effect in figure 11.17.

Now have a look at what you can do by manipulating the image using PageMaker's Image Control dialog box. In figure 11.16, the image was screened using the default 45-degree dot screen, but with only 25 lines per inch. These settings produced the effect of a mezzotint. The brightness settings were adjusted to kill lots of detail by turning all the gray-scale values into pure black and white (emphasis on the white). Then the contrast control was tweaked until it was possible to see the clouds in the sky and a number on the sail. This process left a lot of mud at the bottom of the shot where the water lacked detail, so the shot was cropped slightly from the bottom. At points in the process, the image looked like Granddad's screened porch on the farm in Kansas—complete with fly specks—but it ended up looking pretty good, didn't it?

continues

III

Working with Graphics

Design Note
Continued

Fig. 11.17 ▶

A digital mezzotint version of the sailboat shot, heavily screened in the Image Control dialog box.

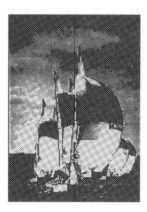

Applying Image Filters

The primitive special effects attainable with the Image Control dialog box are outdone by PageMaker's new ability to do filter manipulations with Photoshop-compatible filters. You can apply these filter manipulations to TIFF images, whether they are RGB or CMYK types.

You reach the Photoshop Effects command via the Element menu's Image command. Basically, this command works by saving a new copy of the file; the application of a filter manipulates the new copy.

When you choose the command, PageMaker asks you to name this file copy. If you want to preserve the original, don't name the file by the same name, or PageMaker saves the filtered copy over the top of the original, wiping it out.

Using Special Tools for Importing Scanned Images

PageMaker gives you two special techniques for bringing scanned images into your publications—Photo CD and direct image scans.

Scanning Images Directly into PageMaker

Some of your best opportunities to control the look of an image come as you scan the item. Because PageMaker includes TWAIN technology, you can scan photographs and other art directly into a publication. You access this capability through the File, Acquire command. Your scanner manufacturer must provide a TWAIN module so you can put this feature to work. Depending on the approach your scanner maker uses, you may be able to have full image controls when you import the scanned image (including control of contrast, cropping, dodging, and so on). What you see when you call the TWAIN driver for your scanner is entirely up to the scanner manufacturer. PageMaker has nothing to do with the interface; the program merely provides the slot to enable your scanner's innate TWAIN talents.

After you have completed the scan and saved it in whatever file format you choose (probably TIFF), you shift into the standard PageMaker Place command mode and have a loaded graphic icon so you can pour the graphic onto the page.

Keep in mind that a better strategy may be to scan the graphic outside PageMaker and edit it with a full-fledged photo-retouching program (such as Photoshop) that may have more powerful capabilities than your scanner's TWAIN module.

TIP ▷ High Scanning Resolution May Waste Disk Space and Memory

You may think that you should scan images at the highest possible resolution for maximum detail. You want to see every strand of hair on that model's head, every line on the company logo—no jaggies. However, you can get only so much information onto the printed page by the time your graphic is subjected to the printing-press process. The image must be screened into dots and burned into metal plates; then the ink soaks into the paper, fuzzing out the dots (a process called *dot gain*).

For all of these reasons, don't scan until you know what your screen frequency will be. This is a subject for considerable discussion with your printer, who knows what the press will produce given all the variables of your particular job, including such details as your choice of paper. When you know the line screen, do your scanning at a dots per inch of *twice* the line screen. Many folks scan even rougher images and save more file space (1.5 times the line screen). If you are printing a 133-line screen, your best scanning resolution may be 200 dpi. If you are laser printing and then photocopying, the screen may best be set at 60 lines per inch. That means your scanning dpi ought to be no lower than 90 dpi and no more detailed than 120 dpi.

You will need to adjust your scanning resolution upwards if you are blowing up the original image. If you are scanning a 2-inch square original to be reproduced at 4-inch square size, you'll need to scan at 1.5 times the line screen times 2, the amount of magnification.

Importing Photo CD Images

Photo CD, once touted as filmless camera technology for consumers, has not taken off in that market but has grown to become a major force in desktop publishing. In just a few years, Photo CD has gone from being a bit on the exotic side to being a normal way of managing large numbers of images—especially for people who publish catalogs.

PageMaker has a special high-end Photo CD filter that makes it even easier to get the most out of Photo CD in a production environment (see fig. 11.18). Until now you had to open the Photo CD image in Photoshop to fine tune it before importing it into PageMaker.

Fig. 11.18 ▶

Choosing a Photo CD file in the Place command opens this dialog box for controlling the process.

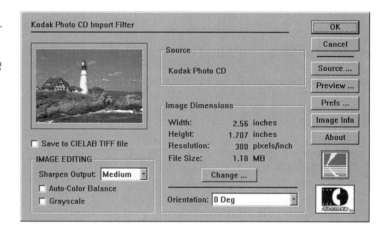

Here's a quick guide to using the Photo CD import filter:

▶ Notice the image preview in the upper-left corner. You can crop the image by selecting the part of the image you want with a mouse drag move.

▶ Choose the image size and resolution by clicking the Change button. Photo CD's come in multiple resolutions on the same CD.

▶ The image enhancement section offers sharpening, color balance, and grayscale conversion. Choose your level of sharpening from the pop-up list. Balance color representation by setting the lightest part of the image as white. Don't use the color balance option unless white is actually in the image.

▶ Photo CD images are scanned in horizontal (landscape) mode, so you can use the orientation attribute to rotate an image.

▶ Clicking the check box to save a CIE Lab TIFF copy of the image may be very helpful when you take your publication to a service bureau.

▶ The Save option enables you to send just a few graphics files (they will be large files) rather than your entire Photo CD. Using this feature, you will also be able to give the image a descriptive file name instead of using the Photo CD standard format of something like IMG012.PCD.

▶ Converting from the native Photo CD color format to the CIE Lab TIFF format puts your graphic in the device-independent color method that forms the basis of the Kodak Precision Color Management System. Making the conversion from the Kodak-supplied Photo CD filter has the advantage of possibly improving the color accuracy of your Photo CD image in the final publication.

Where to Go from Here

▶ Positioning your graphics amidst text requires precision. Take a look at Chapter 14, "Precisely Positioning Graphics and Text."

▶ Will your document be in color and use color images? You can color almost any element of a publication and, of course, import color graphics. Most of the specifics on working with color graphics, such as separations and trapping, are in Part V, "Making Pages Colorful."

▶ Your graphics decisions may depend on such variables as the line screen your printer advises, choice of paper stock, and whether the publication will be output on a laser printer or a high-resolution imagesetter. For a discussion of these sorts of issues, plus information on halftones, look at the chapters in Part VI, "Publishing."

III

Working with Graphics

PART IV

Creating Page Layouts

12 ▲ Setting Up a New Publication

13 ▲ Designing a Master Page Grid

14 ▲ Precisely Positioning Graphics and Text

15 ▲ Creating Special Effects

16 ▲ Formatting Forms, Tables, and Databases

17 ▲ Building Many Pages

Chapter 12

Setting Up a New Publication

This chapter on setting up a new publication covers the following topics:

Using a step-by-step process to get a new publication going.

▼

Putting the Document Setup and Numbers dialog boxes to work.

▼

Managing the often evil and generally unexpected results of changing your document setup after you begin doing your layout.

▼

Working with templates to recycle your work.

LET'S SEE…TYPING in type, check. Formatting paragraphs, okay. Designing styles, right. Pouring text and editing copy, uh-huh. Drawing and importing graphics, covered. It's time.

PageMaker makes pages, and that's the next topic. Once you've got the concepts of setting type, formatting paragraphs, designing styles, pouring text, editing copy, and drawing and importing graphics—it's time to create page layouts. And we begin with the first steps in setting up a new publication. ▶ ▶ ▶

The preceding chapters have covered typing in type, formatting paragraphs, designing styles, pouring text, editing copy, and drawing and importing graphics.

Now it's time to create page layouts—the primary purpose of PageMaker. This chapter begins with the first steps in setting up a new publication.

TACTICS RECIPE
Starting a New Publication

You have a lot to think about when you set up a new publication. This Tactics Recipe pulls all the various tasks together to give you an overview of new publication logistics. This section also directs you to locations where you can find more information on each aspect of the setup process. (For a fine-grained view of the entire process of getting your publication published, don't miss Chapter 24, "Master Checklist for Desktop Publishing.")

Using a Template or Starting Fresh
You can start a new publication fresh from scratch, or you can open a template.

Starting fresh begins with the File, New command. This command takes you straight to the Document Setup dialog box, covered in detail in this chapter.

Starting from a template—if you have one available—is easier, and the "Opening Templates" section in this chapter will help you choose between two options. You can choose to use one of the script-based templates that came with PageMaker or one you developed from a previous page layout job.

When you work with a previously built template, it opens fully formed, so

you can skip many of the steps in this section. A major advantage of templates is not having to go through the many steps of setting up a publication from scratch.

Whether you design your layout from a template or from a fresh start, you establish the basic parameters in Document Setup. Then you save the untitled document under the publication name of your choice in a folder you set aside to collect the new publication.

Setting Your Measurement System and Other Working Preferences
Everyone has their own working style, including such issues as whether you like to work in inches or picas, and how you like ruler guides to behave on the page. Therefore, to make your work efficient, spend some time setting up your working preferences as you start a new publication. You begin by using the Preferences command and the default setting techniques described in Chapter 3, "Personalizing PageMaker Preferences."

Here's the short version on how defaults work (more details are provided in Chapter 3). First, you must understand that defaults come in two flavors: program-level defaults or publication-level defaults. Set or change *program-level defaults* (also called *application defaults* or *permanent defaults*) by making choices in menus and dialog boxes when no publication is open. These defaults become permanent (until you change them again) for any new future publications. (Well, technically they don't become permanent until you quit PageMaker. That's when the default will be recorded in PageMaker's DEFAULTS file.)

You set or change *publication-level defaults* (also called *temporary defaults* or *mini-defaults*) with a document open but no object selected; these defaults affect only that specific document.

Consider these major issues when setting your working preferences:

▶ Will you use picas or inches for your measurement system?

▶ Do you want a special invisible alignment grid that requires a custom vertical ruler?

▶ Do you want to tell PageMaker to alert you to layout problems (loose/tight spacing/kerning and keeps violations)?

▶ What graphics display resolution will you use?

▶ Should guides sit in front or in back of the document work area?

▶ Will you use PageMaker's fast or smaller Save mode?

▶ What setting do you want to use for the Control palette's nudge sensitivity?

▶ What size limit do you want to set for storing imported graphics in or out of the publication?

▶ Should text flow automatically when you are using the Place command?

▶ Do you want to turn on typographer's quotation marks?

▶ Should text greeking be set to match the size of the monitor (below 4 or 6 pixels for a large monitor; a higher number for a small monitor)?

▶ Do you want to set up the display font and size for the Story Editor and set the Story Editor to display style names and paragraph markers?

Many of these items are already set when you open a new publication, either by the template or by PageMaker's built-in defaults. Chances are slim, however, that whoever set up the template or defaults worked exactly the way you do, so you probably want to customize them.

Describing Page Formatting

You handle all the page-formatting items like size and orientation in the Document Setup dialog box (described later in this chapter). Think about these things as you use the dialog box to set up a new publication:

▶ What format do you want for your publication? Will it have a vertical or horizontal page?

▶ What size are the pages?

▶ Will you print on both sides of the page? If so, you need to set up PageMaker so that you see facing pages for best results in designing your spreads.

▶ What style of page numbers do you want (Arabic, Roman, and so on)?

▶ How many pages do you plan to create and at what number should the page numbering begin?

▶ You want your magic stretch moves to match your final printout device; what's the target resolution of your printer or imagesetter? Include the name of your ultimate destination printer to be sure all your color and text formatting decisions make it through the entire work flow of the project.

Designing a Layout Grid and Planning Master Page Elements

Chances are, you will want to use a *layout grid*, a non-printing set of guidelines that rests underneath the document pages. This grid provides underlying structure and consistency for such issues as the number and size of columns of type.

Chapter 13, "Designing a Master Page Grid," talks about creating a layout grid and how to set up the Layout menu choices to make the grid most effective. The options include displaying rulers and using rulers and guides to snap PageMaker objects into place. Also, by using a master page, you can design one page to guide many subsequent pages.

Aside from the layout grid, you may want to set up page numbers in a footer or header. You may want column rules or other graphic elements to appear on most of your pages.

PageMaker 6.0 now has two more powerful features that help with designing the layout grid. You can have multiple master pages, and the new Guide Manager plug-in makes it easy to save standard grid arrangements and copy them between various pages.

Setting Type and Graphics Defaults

Create a system of styles and set up your Type menu defaults to match the most commonly used style (probably the body text style). At this point in the design process, you make basic decisions about fonts. You design font sizes and spacing by setting up styles for your various type needs, including leading, tracking, spacing, and hyphenation.

If you plan to make extensive use of PageMaker-drawn elements, you can create mini-defaults to eliminate the need for manual parameter setups for every new object you draw. In addition to line and fill, pre-set text wrap and rounded corners.

The techniques for setting mini-defaults are given in Chapter 3, "Personalizing PageMaker Preferences." Styles and other text issues are covered in Part II, "Working with Text." Graphics issues relating to the Elements menu are discussed in Chapter 10, "Drawing with PageMaker."

Loading and Defining Palettes

Your layout design probably involves some specific duties for the Library and Color palettes. If you plan to use certain colors again and again, define them in your Color palette. If you want to bring frequently used graphics or text onto your publication pages, load them into the Library palette. That process is described in Chapter 18, "Creating Colors."

TIP ▷ **Set Default Positions for Palettes in PageMaker 6.0**

PageMaker now remembers locations for most of your palettes from session to session. Get those palettes where you want them, and they'll be waiting in those spots when you begin your next work session. One exception is the Scripts palette, which will return to the screen if you had it turned on when you were last working, but will not remember its last position.

Add into the Scripts palette any scripts you will need for the publication. If the project is a big one, you may even want to write a script to automate some tedious aspect of the layout job. You can find more information on scripting in Chapter 28, "Automating PageMaker."

Do you even want some of these palettes on-screen, obstructing the view? If you are working on a black-and-white publication, you may want to set a mini-default that leaves the Color palette closed. Or perhaps you aren't a Control palette fan and want to use a default to close it so the palette doesn't take up screen space.

You can make ad hoc changes to all the items in this Tactics Recipe as the work on your publication evolves, but taking care of these housekeeping chores at one time is usually more efficient. You spend less time on back-and-fill details and more time on your design. Plus, you get more consistent results because your publication is set up to conform to your standard working style.

Using the Document Setup and Numbers Dialog Boxes

You can open the Document Setup dialog box by using that command on the File menu. Usually, however, you first encounter this dialog box when you choose the File, New command. Check out figure 12.1 for a view of the Document Setup dialog box.

Fig. 12.1 ▶

PageMaker's Document Setup dialog box.

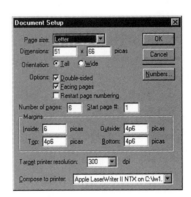

Setting Page Size and Orientation

To set page size, choose from an automatic menu of standard sizes, or manually enter your dimensions. Use the Page Size drop-down list to choose one of the standard page sizes (for example, Letter or Legal). This works like most any word processor or spreadsheet program you have ever used.

For nonstandard page sizes, enter measurements in the fields you see in the Dimensions portion of the dialog box; the reference in the Page Size drop-down list shifts from one of the standards (such as Letter) to Custom.

For page orientation, PageMaker gives you terms that are more descriptive than portrait and landscape. Tall orientation is, well…tall. Use Wide for horizontal-format pages.

TIP ▶ Consider the Post Office and Other Page-Size Bureaucracies

Did you know that the Postal Service charges an extra dime if you use an envelope that is 8 1/4 inches on a side? I found out the hard way. Think about this drawback plus other rules and considerations about page size. Before you print 10,000 of that dandy new brochure, before you even design it, talk to everyone who will be in contact with the publication as it is manufactured and distributed. The folks at the Postal Service may have some suggestions that save you time and aggravation. Your printer may be able to show you how an odd-sized page saves you a nickel a copy because it's a perfect trim size for some paper left over from the last job.

Setting Number of Pages and First Page Number Options

Use Document Setup's Start Page # and Number of Pages boxes to tell PageMaker how many pages your publication will have and what number to use for the first page.

Many folks don't mess with setting the number of pages, particularly for big publications. If you use Autoflow to place the text from your word processor, PageMaker automatically adds pages as needed when it pushes the text into your columns.

If you are creating a book publication and combining multiple documents into a book system, you may want to check the Restart Page Numbering box in the Options section of the Document Setup dialog box. Read about this option in Chapter 17, "Building Many Pages."

TIP ▶ Turn Off Numbering for Title Pages

Many PageMaker versions ago, you could put a negative number in the Start Page # box. That maneuver was wonderful, because PageMaker then put no number on the first pages in the document, and after running through the specified number of "negative numbered" pages, it began numbering on the first "positive numbered" one. Sadly, you no longer have that option. You can achieve the same effect, however, in a couple of ways:

▶ Put the title pages at the end of the document, out of order, and give them a different master page that does not contain page numbers. At the rear of the publication, they don't affect the proper numbering of your pages; the unnumbered pages are at the back, and the text pages start properly from number 1.

▶ Use the Book command and put the title pages in their own unnumbered document file. Chapter 17, "Building Many Pages," explains how to use the Book command and covers many other aspects of working with complex publications.

TIP ▶ Add or Delete Pages Quickly

As a rule, you use the Layout, Insert Pages command to add pages to your publication. If you need to add a bunch of pages to the end of a publication, however, open the Document Setup dialog box and increase the number in the Number of Pages box. In milliseconds, you have added pages to the end of the document. You can also cut pages from a document quickly by putting a smaller number of pages in the Number of Pages box. Remember that this method of adding and deleting pages works only on the pages at the end of the document. You must use Insert Pages to perform such surgery in the middle of the publication.

TIP ▶ Use the Keyboard Shortcut for Snap Page Insertion

Snap a new page into your document with a keyboard shortcut that's new to PageMaker 6.0. Ctrl+Shift+' (apostrophe) inserts one page at the end of the publication.

Printing on Both Sides of the Page

In the Options section of the Document Setup dialog box, click Double-Sided if you want to print on both sides of each page of your publication. Clicking Facing Pages shows you the *spread*—the way the two pages look together in a double-sided publication.

Setting Margins and Gutters

Margins are the distance from a paper's edge to the live layout area. Just enter the measurements in the Top, Bottom, Left, and Right boxes. If you decide to display facing pages, you have Inside and Outside margins rather than Left and Right margins. Inside and outside margins provide a gutter to allow for binding. For example, allow 6 picas (one inch) on the inside and 3 picas (1/2 inch) on the outside.

Indicating Printer Resolution

In the box for Target Printer Resolution, you can type the resolution directly into the text box or choose from a drop-down list of the most common resolutions. PageMaker uses this setting when you import Photo CD images and when you use Magic Stretch. (Magic Stretch is described in Chapter 11, "Placing Images.")

In the early days of PageMaker, the Magic Stretch function was controlled by the printer selected in the Print dialog box. A project headed for Lino had to be swapped constantly between the proof printer and the high-end imagesetter. With Target Printer Resolution, you are saved from this mind-numbing and mistake-generating tedium, because you can set your eventual target resolution for a high-resolution imagesetter (maybe a Linotronics machine) in the Document Setup dialog box. You select your proofing printer (such as a laser printer) in the Print dialog box.

You must still tell PageMaker the name of your ultimate output device destination. The program depends on knowing about the device so it can optimize certain functions.

Specifying Page Number Style

Click the Numbers button in the Document Setup dialog box to open the dialog box shown in figure 12.2.

Fig. 12.2 ▶

The Page Numbering dialog box.

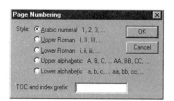

Click the page number style you need (Arabic is the most common). If you are using the Book command from the File menu to assemble a multiple-file publication, you can combine more than one numbering system in different sections of your document by setting this option differently for each file. For example, you may want to use Lower Roman for the front and backmatter, and Arabic for the body of the book.

You also can create chapter-level numbering by making an entry in the TOC and Index Prefix text box then clicking Restart Page Numbering in the Options section of the main Document Setup dialog box. Look for more details about this type of page numbering in Chapter 17, "Building Many Pages."

Changing Document Setup (Beware!)

After you open a publication, organize it, and place some objects on the pages, some evil things can sneak up on you if you change the Document Setup dialog box information. Table 12.1 lays out the possible results for you.

If you must change any of the Document Setup dialog box settings, make a backup copy of the file first. Then check the results of your changes throughout the document *before* you work any further. You don't want to invest a lot of time in a document that has been hit hard by a Document Setup change; you rescue yourself from the situation by dumping the file and going back to a previous version of it—your backup.

Another way to go back to a previous version is to use the Revert command. Save the document right before changing the Document Setup settings and then use the Revert command if you don't like the results.

TABLE 12.1   Results of Changing Document Setup Options

If You Change This	You Get This (Possibly Evil) Result
Page size	PageMaker attempts to center the objects in relation to the edges of the page. Your objects, both text and graphics, hold their position in relation to one another. If you shrink to a smaller page, your stuff may end up leaking off the edge of the page. A major resize move may even throw an object completely off the page and onto the Pasteboard.
Tall/Wide	Objects hold their positions in relation to the edges of the Pasteboard; some objects probably end up off the page.
Number of Pages	You can add or subtract pages using this box, but keep in mind that it works on the end of the document. As with any page deletion, you could have the evil effect of inadvertently and forever destroying pages that contain vital information if you subtract live pages from the end of the document.
Broken spread graphic (Odd pages to Even) (Even pages to Odd) (Start Page Number) (Double-Sided to Single)	There are several changes you can make in the Document Setup dialog box that make a mess of a graphic placed to cross over between two facing pages (a *spread graphic*). Be alert for any change that swaps odd pages to even pages or vice versa. Whenever this change occurs, PageMaker tries to keep the spread graphic with its original left (even-numbered) page. That means the page

continues

TABLE 12.1   Continued

If You Change This	You Get This (Possibly Evil) Result
	ends up as a right (odd-numbered) page with much of the graphic sticking out to the right onto the Pasteboard.
Start Page # (Double-Sided)	In a double-sided publication, PageMaker uses the starting number information to decide which pages are left or right pages. If you change this starting number from even to odd or vice versa, you cause all the pages in a double-sided publication to trade between the left and right positions.
Single-sided to double-sided	In a single-sided publication, all the pages are considered right pages. Turning on Double-Sided converts every even-numbered single-sided page into a new left page with the old right margin converted to the new inside margin. That move may shift the position of graphics and text in relation to the new inside margin.
Double-sided to single-sided	This move converts all even-numbered, double-sided pages from left pages to right pages. The inside margin of the even-numbered pages turns into the new right margin. You may see graphics and text shift on the page to adjust to the new margins.
Margin size	Changing margin size doesn't affect the layouts of any pages already set (this change is not retroactive). On the other hand, if you want to change the margins on existing pages, you must go to each page and readjust graphics and text to the new margins.
Numbering style	Naturally, changing the numbering style gets you a different page number display. The same thing goes for the TOC and Index Prefix box. However, unlike margin changes and single-sided or double-sided pages, this function is dynamic. The change isn't irrevocable, and you can simply change it back.
Target Printer Resolution	As with margins, changing the target resolution doesn't affect any black-and-white graphics you have already placed, but it does affect any future magic stretch moves. For this reason, you may want to go back and redo the magic stretch for any previously placed graphics.

TIP ▶ Inline Graphics Protect You During Major Page Structure Changes

Placing illustrations as inline graphics gives you some margin of safety from unexpected results caused by Document Setup changes. Inline graphics, placed directly in the text instead of on the page, lock themselves in position in relation to text. When the text moves as a result of adjustments to the page structure, the inline graphics move right with the text.

TIP ▶ You Can (Sort of) Undo Page Removal

The Undo command in Version 6.0 now works when you remove (or insert) pages. That is, it works—like all Undo moves in PageMaker and in most other application programs—if you take advantage of it *immediately* after you make the move you need to undo. If you so much as turn the page, you will lose your chance to Undo. Problem is, you may need to flip through some pages to see if the layout has shifted in a bad way (as listed in our table). So, to be safe, you should still make a practice of saving before removing or inserting pages.

Opening Templates

You can use two kinds of templates: PageMaker templates and templates you create yourself. After you have them open, both kinds of templates work pretty much the same: you save the resulting untitled publication with a name of your choice in the hard disk location you prefer. However, the methods you use to open the two types of templates differ.

Opening a PageMaker Template

Adobe saves disk space by shipping its templates as scripts, rather than sending them out as normal PageMaker template files. Scripts, as discussed in Chapter 28, "Automating PageMaker," are small programs written in the PageMaker scripting language. The scripts describe what the templates look like down to the finest detail, but scripts take up less space than the actual publication files they generate.

To open one of these templates, go to the Utilities menu and choose the PageMaker Plug-in called Open Template. This will yield a dialog box so you can select the template file from the list. Some of the templates offer you different options about your preferences for such things as page size or language.

Making a New Template

When you set up a document just the way you like, you don't need to do the chore again. Create a template to recycle your creative labors.

Use the File, Save As command and click the Template radio button to save a publication as a template (you also can take this step to save the results of a template-editing session).

Using a Previously Saved Template

You open a previously saved template the same way you open any other PageMaker publication, except you get an untitled document that you must save and title. You can double-click the template or access it through the File, Open command. If you want to edit a template, click the Open Original button.

Where to Go from Here

▶ If any of the information about the Pasteboard and opening and saving files seems a bit mysterious, you can find help in the Getting Started tours in Chapter 1, "Touring PageMaker," and in Chapter 2, "Exploring What's New In PageMaker 6.0."

▶ Because this chapter was designed to pull together many related threads, it contains much cross-referenced information. Perhaps the most important connecting chapter is Chapter 3, "Personalizing PageMaker Preferences."

▶ Your next logical step after opening a new publication and customizing it to your taste is to design a Master Layout grid, which is the subject of Chapter 13, "Designing a Master Page Grid."

▶ The best place to find out more about the Colors palette is Chapter 18, "Creating Colors."

▶ For more on resolution, as in target printer resolution, check out all of Part VI, "Publishing."

Chapter 13

Designing a Master Page Grid

This chapter on designing a master page grid includes our major coverage of the all-powerful grid tools—Guide Manager and multiple master pages—plus all the other fundamental tools of PageMaker order:

Setting up columns, the basic building blocks of a layout grid.

▼

Pulling out ruler guides for special grid elements.

▼

Using the new Master Pages feature to impose a layout grid on all your publication pages.

▼

Automating grid creation using the powerful new Guide Manager Plug-in.

▼

Powering up your layout grid with the Balance Columns Plug-in, snap to rulers, snap to guides, and column-to-column baseline alignment.

SOME PAGES LOOK like somebody used the text and graphics in a Pin the Tail on the Donkey game—scattered and incoherent. Others instill in the reader a sense of confident logic, flowing from one thought to the next—a sense of "rightness."

What distinguishes such designs, makes one seem scattered and the other hung together just right? Often the key success factor will be a layout grid. ▶ ▶ ▶

Setting up a layout grid means thinking ahead about the underlying structure of your pages (the rough equivalent of a composer deciding on the key of a sonata or a painter working out the composition of a still life). With a grid structure in mind, you can hang your text and graphics on its underlying discipline. It helps you to achieve a fluid and nonchalant presentation of your message—while occasionally breaking out of the lines for dramatic effect.

In PageMaker, you impose your layout grid on each of your pages by setting up master pages. You don't have to do it that way, but it will almost always be the most efficient and consistent way to achieve your layout goals. That's especially true now that PageMaker has—please, a hushed moment of reverence here—multiple master pages.

Guiding the Grid

Use guides to lay out pages. These basic building blocks of structure make up your layout grid, as you see from the layout grid and its resulting news-letter pages shown in figure 13.1. The guides are the dotted lines arranged in (oddly enough) a grid. The lines don't print, but you can see them on-screen; PageMaker will, if you want, use them to guide the positioning of objects on the page. (For more about positioning objects, see Chapter 14, "Precisely Positioning Graphics and Text.")

Fig. 13.1 ▶

A layout grid and its sample newsletter pages.

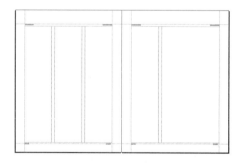

You can set three kinds of guides in PageMaker: margin guides, column guides, and ruler guides. All three of these types are referred to in PageMaker documentation as nonprinting guides. There's a good reason for that. It's because they do not, in fact, show up on your printouts. They are purely for screen display:

▶ Margin guides delineate the margins you set for master pages. Margin guides are both horizontal and vertical; on a color monitor, they are pink.

▶ Column guides are vertical lines. They have special powers to guide text when you flow it onto a page with the Place command. Column guides are blue on a color monitor.

▶ Ruler guides can be either horizontal or vertical. They get their name from the way you create them: by pulling them out from the rulers. You see turquoise ruler guides on a color monitor.

Setting Margin Guides

You set margin guides when you define margins. You can do that in two different places:

▶ For Document Master master pages, the margins are set in the Page Setup dialog box wh⌐n you first create a document, and after that initial step they can be adjusted using the same dialog box.

▶ For all other master pages, set and adjust margins in a similar Setup dialog box reached through the Master Pages palette.

Margin guides are the most basic kind of guide. If you only have one column on your page, the margin guides are, in effect, the column guides. Have a look at figure 13.2. The margin guides run completely around the page, following the settings for the top, bottom, inside (left), and outside (right) margins.

FIG. 13.2 ▶

The simplest layout grid of all: margin guides set from the Page Setup dialog box.

Now here's the secret. Many people believe that vertical margin guides are actually blue, not pink. That's because it does look that way when you first set up a page in PageMaker. The program naturally puts a column guide on the left and right margins of the page. And the column guides, which are blue, coincide with and obscure the location of the left and right margin guides.

In figure 13.3, you can see that the column guides can be dragged into a new position, leaving the margin guides in place. Notice that as you drag, the Pointer tool becomes a double arrow.

Fig. 13.3 ▶

The vertical margin guides are also column guides.

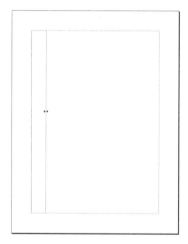

Setting Column Guides

Column guides possess power. Like benevolent control freaks, they tell text where to go.

Put three sets of column guides on a page, and then place some text by clicking on the text icon in the first column. The text threads down the first column to the bottom margin guide, skipping over any graphics that obstruct the way. Then the text fills the rest of the columns on the page, starting at the top of the second column, filling it, and jumping over to fill the third column. If you are in Autoflow mode, the text continues to the first column of the next page.

So, how do you create these magic column guides? Use the Column Guides command, of course, from the Layout menu (see fig. 13.4).

This figure shows the Column Guides dialog box for a double-sided publication, including an option to set different columns for the left and right pages. You won't see that option if you are working with single-sided pages.

FIG. 13.4 ▶

*The Column Guides
dialog box.*

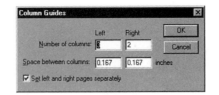

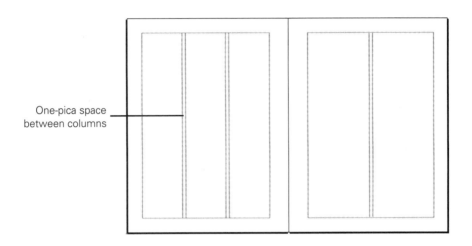

One-pica space
between columns

Figure 13.4 also shows the results when you implement the Column Guides command with those settings. Notice the one-pica (.167-inch) space between columns. If you grab those spaced column guides and drag them to one side or the other, they move together as a pair, maintaining the spacing.

Moving the guides has no effect on text already placed on the page, only on text you place after the guides are repositioned.

Setting Ruler Guides

In addition to establishing your *page geometry* (jargon for "the shape of the page") using margin and column guides, you can set up a third form of guide on an ad hoc basis. These guides are called *ruler guides*; you establish them, as shown in figure 13.5, by simply clicking on the ruler and dragging the guideline down into the page area. As you drag, the Pointer tool becomes a double arrow. (You aren't allowed to have ruler guides on the Pasteboard.)

FIG. 13.5 ▶

*Pulling a ruler guide
down from the hori-
zontal ruler.*

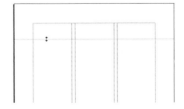

Put horizontal or vertical ruler guides wherever you like, and use them to help line up and position objects on the page. Ruler guides are particularly useful for precise positioning when used in conjunction with the Snap To Guides command, discussed in Chapter 14, "Precisely Positioning Graphics and Text."

Manually Managing Guides

Aside from the multiple master page feature, also covered in this chapter, the new Guide Manager may be one of the hottest bits of news concerning PageMaker Version 6.0. There's nothing like it to set up a grid. However, before we get to the Guides Manager Plug-in, let's spend some time talking about some of the more basic guides management facilities in PageMaker. They've been part of PageMaker since the beginning, and understanding them as fundamentals will build a basis for discussing the latest advances.

Moving Guides

Adjust guides to a new position by clicking and dragging them. When you click on the guide, you see a double arrow, and then you can slide the guide to its new position (see fig. 13.6). You can adjust column and ruler guides, but you can't use a click and drag to move the margin guides.

FIG. 13.6 ▶

Moving a ruler guide.

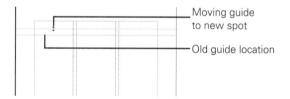

Moving guide to new spot

Old guide location

TIP ▶ **Undo an Accidental Guide Move**

It is easy to accidentally snap a guide and slide it to the wrong spot on the page instead of moving the object you intended to adjust. Immediately after making an accidental guide move, use the Edit menu to Undo the mistake (Ctrl+Z). Also, if you haven't created any local guides for that particular page, you can simply use the Copy Master Guides command on the Layout menu to reset the guides from your assigned master page.

Locking Guides

Set the toggle command Lock Guides on the Guides and Rulers submenu of the Layout menu. When the check mark has been toggled on for the Lock Guides command, you won't be able to click the guides to adjust their positions. They will be locked. This guide locking move is the ultimate protection against accidentally disturbing your guide's setup.

Hiding or Displaying Guides

If you want an uncluttered view of your publication design but don't want to delete your guides, use the Show Guides command on the Guides and Rulers submenu of the Layout menu. If Show Guides has been turned on, a check mark appears next to the command; the check mark is gone if you switch off the guides. Toggling off the Show Guides command makes all three kinds of guides disappear from view throughout your publication. The keyboard shortcut for toggling guides display on and off (Ctrl+J) is handy for forcing a screen redraw as well.

Deleting Ruler Guides

You can make ruler guides go away one by one by pulling them up into their ruler with a click-and-drag move. Or, you can delete all your ruler guides at once on your current single-sided page or double-sided facing pages by using the handy menu command, new in PageMaker 6.0—Clear Ruler Guides.

Imposing Master Page Guides

To delete the guides you've set for the current page or pages and replace them with the guides from the assigned master page, use the Copy Master Guides command from the Layout menu. When you do this, the "local" guides for that page are replaced by whatever guides (margin, column, and ruler type) you built for your master page. This can be really handy after a complex session of fine-tuning a page, in which you used a lot of ruler guides to help position items. It instantly gets you back to your standard grid of guides.

Prioritizing the Guides Display

You can have the guides run in front of or in back of the elements on your page. PageMaker comes set up to have the guides in front. That's great for visibility and maybe that's the way you want the guides most of the time, but on a crowded page it's easy to grab a guide by mistake and move it. If you set the guides to the back, you will be a little less likely to accidentally disturb them.

New with PageMaker 6.0 is a direct access menu command to set guides to front or back. It's right there on the Layout menu's Guides and Rulers submenu, a mouse move away. This new menu command is a treat. It used to be that changing this setting required going all the way into the Preferences menu.

Setting Guides Automatically: The Guide Manager

For a really big treat, have a look at PageMaker 6.0's new Guide Manager (see fig. 13.7). It's a Plug-in, reached like all plug-ins—through the Utilities menu.

FIG. 13.7 ▶

The new Guide Manager.

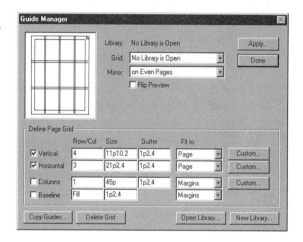

The Guide Manager doesn't do anything you couldn't do slower and more tediously all by yourself, if you insisted on setting guides manually. On the other hand, if you think computers are in this world to make work easier, not harder, you'll love the Guide Manager.

You use the Guide Manager to set up evenly spaced sets of ruler guide grids, custom ruler guides, and column guides. Instead of dragging out guides from the ruler, you type in your settings in one dialog box.

Several guide manager utilities came out following the release of Version 5.0, and the one now included in Version 6.0 has all the functions we've come to expect plus a few handy extras. In fact, the Guide Manager was written by Boyd Multerer of Zephyr Design, who created the original third-party alignment, distribution and guide management utilities for PageMaker. Here's a rundown.

Creating a Library of Grids

With PageMaker 6.0, Adobe built a new, enhanced, plug-in technology—granting plug-ins the ability to keep private data sets called *libraries*. That's the essence of Guide Manager's capability to help you do work—this ability to store up sets of grids like a hamster collecting seeds in a cheek pouch.

In busy-person terms, it means you can create a set of grids once, and then bring the collection back for re-use time after time on repetitive projects. Work once, recycle many times—that's the philosophy.

For example, you might have a set of grids you use whenever working on the Smith account. The library might store grid designs for ad slicks, catalog pages, one sheet flyers, business cards, brochure cover, brochure inside panels, and so on. Another collection of grids might be tucked away in a library for whenever you are doing your monthly newsletter layout for the company personnel office. To call them up, you just switch libraries.

Creating or Opening a Library

You set up one of these libraries by clicking on the New Library button in the lower-right corner of figure 13.7. In the resulting typical File Save dialog box, give the file a name, select the folder location where you want to save it, and click OK.

The name of your currently open library will always be listed at the top of the dialog box.

You open one of your libraries by using the Open button, as you might expect, and using the resulting standard File Open dialog box.

The Guide Manager is "sticky." That means it remembers which library you were working with during your last session and automatically opens with that library open.

Selecting and Applying Grids

Within each library is a collection of grids that you have defined. You can pick from among a list of those grids with the pull-down list you see in figure 13.8.

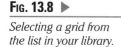

FIG. 13.8 ▷

Selecting a grid from the list in your library.

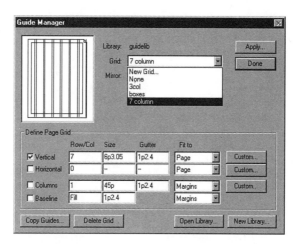

Apply the grid decisions you have made by clicking on the Apply button. The Done button closes the Guide Manager without applying your grid. Figure 13.9 shows your options when you Apply Guides to Page.

Fig. 13.9 ▶

Apply guides options.

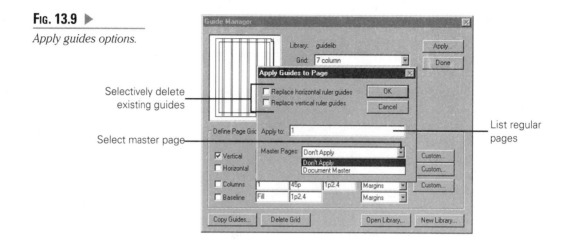

Selectively delete existing guides

Select master page

List regular pages

As you can see, you can choose to add the guides you've designed, or you can replace—delete—the horizontal or vertical ruler guides that are presently in place on your target pages.

Tell Guide Manager where to put the new guides by typing in page numbers in the Apply To box.

You can also apply guides to master pages, selected from a pull-down list, and if the master pages are in a spread, you can choose whether to apply the guides to left or right masters or both.

Mirroring Your Grid

Using the Mirror setting, you can have Guide Manager handle the intricacies of adjusting a grid for left- and right-facing pages. You might choose, for example, to mirror as if the current grid is a right-hand page. The mirror setting would then assume the inside or left-hand margin of the current grid should be the inside or right-hand margin of facing pages, left-hand pages.

You can also mirror the current grid for all pages, regardless of whether they are left- or right-facing pages. Turn mirroring off with the None setting.

Checking and Updating the Preview

You can get a visual representation of your current grid settings by checking out the preview image in the upper-left corner of the Guide Manager dialog box.

The dog ear mark in one of the upper corners of the preview tells you which type of page is being represented. A dog ear in the upper-right corner, the default, means you have a right-hand page or odd-numbered page, and a dog ear in the upper-left corner indicates the outside edge of a left-hand or even-numbered page.

The Guide Manager updates the preview every time you tab from one setting to another, or press the Enter key on the numeric keypad. (In this way, it mimics the update or refresh behavior of the Control palette.)

Defining Grids Of Guides

The middle section of the dialog box helps you do the main work of the Guide Manager—set specifications for various types of grid patterns:

▶ Vertical settings create vertical ruler guides, and thus set columns in the grid.

▶ Horizontal settings create horizontal ruler guides, marking off rows for your grid.

▶ In addition to ruler guides, the Guide Manager can set column guides using the Columns settings.

Keep in mind that the vertical and horizontal rows and columns are ruler guide settings. They may look like column settings, especially if you set up a gutter, but they are simply ruler guides.

Calculating Column and Row Width

Guide Manager automatically calculates the width of your columns or rows for you. Change any of the three parameters—number of rows or columns, size, and gutter—and Guide Manager will change the size setting to accommodate your adjustment. The *gutter*, by the way, is the space between columns or rows.

Determining a Grid Reference Point

Guide Manager's calculations of size and gutter width must be based on some reference point. You can base your guide and column settings on the edges of the page, the margin guides, or any object you select before you open the Guide Manager.

Check figure 13.10 and see how this reference point concept works, using the Fit To settings in the Define Page Grid section of the dialog box.

The selected object reference point concept has a lot of potential. Here are some ways it could be useful:

▶ You begin an ad layout by placing a primary image and a headline in just the right relationship. Select each one in turn and open the Guide Manager to place rules at the edges of each item. They are your primary visual reference points, and with ease you can base an entire page grid on them.

Fig. 13.10 ▶

Picking a grid reference point.

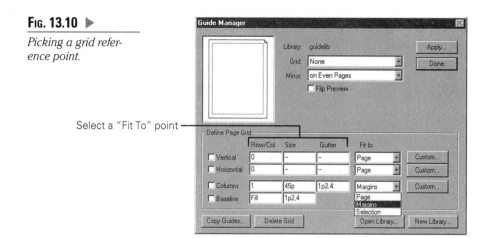

Select a "Fit To" point

▶ You need two columns of text to appear beneath a master headline text block. Select the headline block and go into Guide Manager. Set two column guides based on your selection. Presto—no counting on your fingers—Guide Manager automatically calculates the mathematically precise location for two columns beneath the master head.

▶ You've used the Distribute command to spread three photographs evenly down the left-hand side of a page. You need guides so you can set a text description to the right of each image. Select each one in turn and use the Guide Manager to create a single horizontal guide row on each image. That'll give you guides for the top and bottom of each item.

Setting Custom Guides

The main page grid settings are for evenly spaced grids. If you need a ruler guide or column guide that doesn't match the evenly spaced rows and columns—an independent guide—click the appropriate Custom buttons to reach a dialog box like the one you see in figure 13.11. The advantage here is precision. Instead of trying to eyeball a ruler guide into position, you type in a precise ruler guide setting.

Fig. 13.11 ▶

Making custom ruler guides in the Guide Manager.

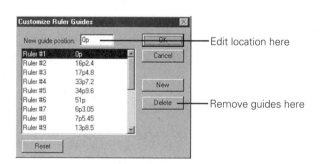

Edit location here

Remove guides here

To change the location of a guide, click its description in the Customize Ruler Guides dialog box and type in the new position information.

Independent or custom ruler guides are positioned based on their distance from the zero point, not from the page edge, margin, or selection. Also, notice that the Customize Ruler Guides dialog box establishes numbers for guides by their order of creation (not in their order of distance from the zero point as you might have expected).

Create new guides or delete old ones using those two buttons. The Reset button returns the settings to what they were when you first opened the dialog box.

Creating Baseline Grids

This specialized part of the Define Page Grid section has been created to help you set up a fine grid of rows—horizontal guides that match the baselines of a text block. Of course, you aren't limited to that purpose. It's suitable for any situation where you need a fine grid of horizontal guides.

The baseline setting has a Fill function not possessed by any of the other grid settings in Guide Manager. Baseline allows you to fill an area with fine horizontal gridlines. It will fill your chosen reference area—page, margin, or selected object—with evenly spaced rows of guides. You can adjust the distance between the guides by typing in an amount in the Size box.

Optionally, instead of using Fill you can type in a specific number of guides. In that case, Guide Manager will count down from the top of whatever reference point you have chosen—page, margin, or selected object.

Copying and Deleting Guides

The Copy Guides command might better be called import guides. The whole concept of the Guide Manager is to let you replicate guides. So far we've mostly talked about typing in precise values for guides, but there are times when you'd rather just doodle on the page to come up with a layout.

That's where the Copy Guides command comes in. Use the Copy Guides command when you want to translate your layout grid to other pages. Copy, or import, the guides into Guide Manager and then you can use the Apply command to send those guide settings out to as many pages—even master pages—as you like. You can also save them as a grid set in a Guide Manager library.

This import or copying process is accomplished by clicking the Copy Guides button, which yields the dialog box you see in figure 13.12. It lets you suck up the column, vertical, and horizontal guides from the current pages. You can even choose whether to bring in the guides from the left or the right page.

Fig. 13.12 ▶

Importing guides using the Copy Guides command.

Selectively import guides

Oh yeah, almost forgot—the Delete Grid button. Click it, and you will wipe out the currently selected grid set from the currently open Guide Manager library. You will see a confirmation dialog box before Guide Manager makes your decision permanent. Simple as that.

Setting Snap Constraints

Guides and rulers are not merely visual alignment tools. When you turn on the Snap to Guides and Snap to Rulers settings under the Guides and Rulers submenu (located in the Layout main menu), you turn these items into magnets. The guides and rulers grab your objects as you move them around the page and pull them into place. You can always tell when these options are on because an object jerks and jumps around as you move it, trying to lock itself into place.

With Snap to Guides, when an object comes within three pixels of one of a guide (all three kinds), the magnet takes hold. Guides snap in one dimension, depending on whether they are vertical or horizontal. An intersection of two guides works together to snap in both dimensions.

If Snap to Rulers has been turned on, the tick marks on the rulers set up invisible criss-crossing lines on the page. This invisible grid of lines (not to be confused with the layout grid you create) sets up hundreds of magnet intersections that grab the corners of objects (or in the case of Align to Grid, the baselines of text). For ruler snap moves, you get two-dimensional snaps to this invisible myriad of intersections.

These snap constraints are a vital tool for PageMaker precision, and that's why we talk about them in greater detail in the next chapter, Chapter 14, "Precisely Positioning Graphics and Text."

Measuring a Layout Grid

A grid would be meaningless unless you could measure your moves. For this purpose, you have a zero point and horizontal and vertical rulers.

Moving and Locking the Zero Point

A ruler measurement must start from a zero data point. In PageMaker, the zero point usually rests in the upper-left corner of a page (the default setting when you open a new document). If you are working with facing pages, the zero point rests on the top edge of the two pages, where they meet, at the upper-left corner of the right page in the spread.

You can move this zero point anywhere you like, including the Pasteboard. Simply click and drag on the zero point icon in the upper-left corner of the window. If you want to revert to the standard zero point position at the upper-left corner of odd-numbered pages, double-click on the zero point icon.

Keep in mind that the Control palette measures everything from the zero point. Also, if you are using Snap to Ruler to help align page elements, the zero point determines the location and intersections of the grid.

To lock the zero point, use the Zero Lock command on the Guides and Rulers submenu of the Layout menu.

Setting Up Rulers

You can eliminate page clutter by turning off your rulers with the Rulers command on the Guides and Rulers submenu of the Layout menu. You can also use Ctrl+J as a shortcut. When the rulers are turned off, you can't see them, but they still are in effect. That means the Snap to Ruler command remains operative even when the rulers aren't visible.

To set the measurement system for your rulers (inches, picas, millimeters, and so on), use the Preferences command. When you set the measurement system, tick marks appear on the rulers. These marks are the visible manifestation of the invisible grid PageMaker creates when you set the Snap to Rulers constraint, using that submenu in the Guides and Rulers command, under the Layout menu.

Understanding Master Pages

For years PageMaker users have begged, cajoled, wheedled, demanded, and otherwise importuned Aldus and then Adobe to include a master page feature in the program. Now master pages have arrived. But the fundamental nature of a master page has not changed one bit.

You'd drive yourself crazy if you tried to manually place column guides and ruler guides and other basic elements on every page of a 300-page book. That's why PageMaker has provided a mechanism to set the layout grid and other common page elements just once for many pages. That mechanism is the master page.

Whatever you put on a master page shows up on all the other pages that have been assigned that master page (unless you command PageMaker to do otherwise by turning off the Display Master Items command).

Our discussion in this section tends to emphasize the use of master pages to carry grids of ruler guides, column settings, and margins. However, before this chapter concludes we'll spend time talking about the fact that you can put anything on a master page—headers, footers, page numbers, graphic elements, and so on.

Navigating Between Master Pages

As explained in the Chapter 1 tour, your master pages are represented by the special page icons you see in the lower-left corner of the PageMaker window, just to the left of the icons for the numbered pages (see fig. 13.13 on the left). Click and hold the master page icons to get a list of all the master pages in your publication. Navigate to any of them by making a selection from this list (see fig. 13.13 on the right).

Fig. 13.13 ▶

Master page icons.

Master of All: The Document Master

One master page dominates your entire publication. Unless you decide otherwise, all your new pages will be formatted with this one master page, the Document Master. You can easily change the setting, but it's the default.

If you add pages using the Document Setup command, the new pages will automatically be assigned the Document Master page.

If you use the Insert Pages command from the Layout menu, however, you will be given the opportunity to choose the master pages to be applied to the new pages, although the Document Master will be the default choice.

Applying Master Pages

The multiple master page feature means you can have a whole list of page designs at the ready to accommodate all the various kinds of pages in your publication—ready to be applied to your pages with the click of a mouse in the Master Pages palette (see fig. 13.14).

You access the pullout menu shown in the figure by clicking on the arrowhead in the upper-right corner of the palette.

Fig. 13.14 ▶

The Master Pages palette—the universal command center for master pages.

If you simply want to apply a master page to one page or spread, move to that location and click the master page of your choice in the Master Pages palette. That's all there is to it.

TIP ▶ **You Can Apply Two Masters to a Spread**

If you hold down the Alt key as you click the Master Pages palette icons next to the master page listing, you will be able to assign a master page to only one side of a two-page spread. The side of the icon you click, left or right, will designate which page of the spread should get that master page. In figure 13.15, you can see from the icons in the Master Pages palette that the left and right pages have different masters assigned. The Chapter Break master page was applied to the right-hand page by Alt+clicking on the right-hand side of the icon next to the Chapter Break master page listing in the palette.

Fig. 13.15 ▶

A tip on how to assign different master pages in a spread.

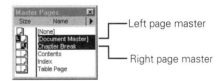

— Left page master

— Right page master

To quickly spread a master page across many pages, use the <u>A</u>pply command, which allows you to build a list of pages to receive a master page assignment. Figure 13.16 shows the Apply Master command dialog box. As you can see from this particular view, you also can choose to apply different master pages to left and right pages. You can list as many pages as you like in the Page Range box, and it works just like the similar function in the Print dialog box. Compose a list using commas and hyphens. For example, **2,4-6,11,20-** would apply the master to the second page, pages 4 through 6, page 11, and page 20 plus all remaining pages in the document.

Fig. 13.16 ▷

Spreading a master page to many pages.

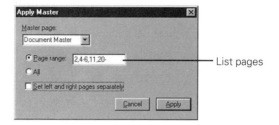

List pages

You might want to turn on the Prompt On Apply setting in the palette menu as a safety measure, so PageMaker will confirm your decision to apply a new master before making it final.

Setting Up a New Master

To create a new master page, select the New option from the pull-out menu. The resulting dialog box, shown in figure 13.17, will help you perform basic setup operations. It combines several of the functions you find in the Document Setup and Column Guides dialog boxes, including page margins and the number and size of columns.

Fig. 13.17 ▷

Setting up a new master page.

Margin settings

Column settings

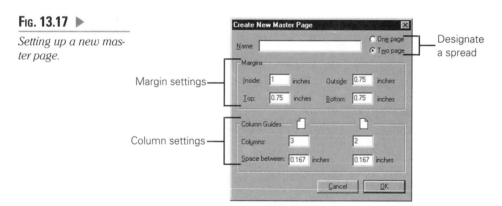

Designate a spread

TIP ▷ **Keyboard Shortcut to Editing or Creating Master Pages**

Like the Colors and Styles palettes, you can Ctrl+click on the items in the Master Pages palette. Using Ctrl+click on [None] starts you out creating a new master page. The same Ctrl+click shortcut used on any of the other master page items in the palette will take you to a Setup dialog box to edit that master page item.

Editing A Master

You have a couple of approaches to choose from when it comes to editing one of your master pages.

You can, of course, navigate to the master page and do your work right on the page, just like the old master page setup in previous versions of PageMaker. This approach allows you to change anything on the page, from column guides to page numbering and graphic elements.

Or, you can use Setup in the Master Pages palette. When you use the Master Pages Setup command, except for the title, you get the same dialog box as the one shown in figure 13.17, which gives you access only to grid elements and does not allow you to edit objects that have been placed on the master page.

The Setup Master Pages dialog box is the only place where you can edit the name of a master page.

The effects of editing a master page are instantaneous. Any items that are displayed on any of your pages based on an edited master page will show the changes immediately. However, unlike most word processors, keep in mind that, in PageMaker, adjustments to margins and columns only affect newly placed text and objects—not items that have already been put on pages.

Basing a Master Page on Existing Pages

To make a new master page but base it on an existing master page, choose the Duplicate menu item (see fig. 13.18). This works great when you need to work a quick variation on a master page, like when you need to tune a text page for a chart layout, or add an advertising hole to a magazine page.

Fig. 13.18 ▶

Duplicating an existing master page using the Duplicate command.

You can also duplicate an existing regular page in the same manner by choosing the Save Page As command. You'll love having this option when you've doodled a new layout into shape and want to capture the look for application to other pages.

Making a Master of None

To remove master page elements at your current page location, you can use the Layout menu commands for displaying master items or copying master guides.

Alternatively, you can use the [None] listing in the master page. It has various effects, depending on how you combine it with various keyboard shortcuts:

▶ Just click+[None] removes objects, leaving column and ruler guides.

▶ Shift+click+[None] deletes everything including objects, column guides, and ruler guides.

▶ Alt+Shift+Click+[None] keeps ruler guides but deletes everything else.

To apply any of the above moves to only one page of a spread, hold down the Alt key and click the single page icon next to [None] instead of on the [None] item itself. You click in the "margin" of the icon, and then the icon will get a R or L in it to indicate which side you are affecting.

▶ Ctrl+Shift+click+[None] retains column guides but removes everything else. (Always applies to both sides of a spread.)

Putting Master Page Grids to Work

Everything we've discussed so far about guides and layout grids can—and should—be applied to your master pages. Put your layout grid on a master page whether you set your grid using Guide Manager, or by using the old manual methods of the Column Guides command and hand-pulled ruler guides.

Figure 13.19 shows thumbnail views for some typical multicolumn layout grids. The vertical lines are column guides, and the horizontal lines are ruler guides.

Fig. 13.19 ▶

A sampling of layout grids.

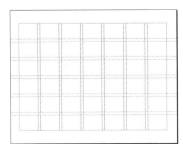
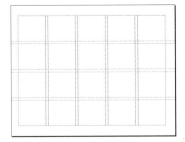

Fig. **13.19** ▶

continued

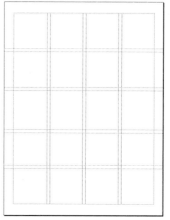

Layout grids need not be symmetrical. For example, you may want uneven columns that leave room for headlines to hang out in a companion column, as shown in figure 13.20.

Fig. **13.20** ▶

The layout grid and a sample page from an instructional book.

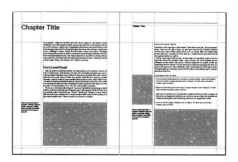

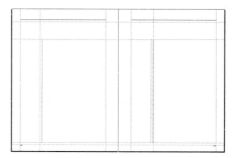

Your layout grid should not be a barrier to your design sense, either. In the layout grid and sample page shown in figure 13.21, the graphics spill across column guide boundaries, but the column guides on the grid are still used to line up the edges. The layout grid still lends the necessary structure by providing a starting point and a set of reference points for the reader's eye.

Fɪɢ. 13.21 ▶

Fɪɢ. 13.21 ▶

Maintaining guide structure while crossing grid column boundaries.

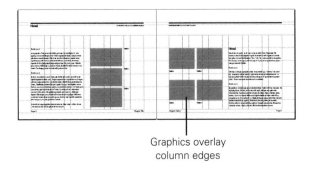

Graphics overlay
column edges

Usually, the more grid cubbyholes you design into your layout grid (with moderation), the better off you are. You have structure, backed by a lot of flexibility. Take the mail-order catalog grid shown in figure 13.22. The designer uses a wide variety of graphics on the page, but averts the danger of a scattered, cluttered, hard-to-read look by setting four rather narrow columns across the master page.

Fɪɢ. 13.22 ▶

Many grid holes lend flexibility to your layout grid structure.

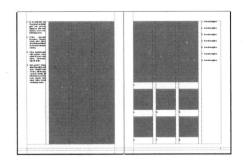

Dᴇsɪɢɴ Nᴏᴛᴇ
White Space Helps Organize the Reader's Eye

White space plays a big part in the success of the mail-order catalog layout grid in figure 13.22. Fairly wide page margins let the elements breathe on the page, and extra wide alleys clearly separate the graphic elements so that the eye can settle on each of them one by one—a critical design criteria for a mail-order catalog. You've probably heard this advice before—it's such a standard and important consideration of good design—but it bears repeating: allow white space in your layout grid. There's no sense jamming words together on one page if the resulting dark, dense mass of type intimidates and discourages the reader from actually reading the copy.

Adding Standard Master Page Elements

After you have arranged your columns, place standard elements onto your master pages. Figure 13.23 shows footers, headers, page numbering, and a top-of-page rule as examples of the kind of elements you may want to design on your master page layout grid.

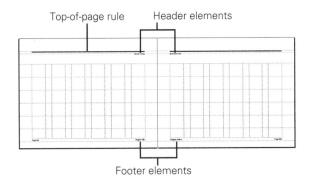

FIG. 13.23 ▶

Standard master page elements take their place on the layout grid.

Top-of-page rule   Header elements

Footer elements

Drawing Page Rules

In figure 13.23, you can see how the top-of-page rules on the master page translate onto a regular page, mixed with copy. These 8-point rules with the book title and major part headers automatically appear at the top of every page—a big work saver and a major aid to consistency. Just think about drawing 600 top-of-page rules for a major book project. Better yet, don't think about it. Just use master pages. You could also place column rules in the column guide alleys on your master page. And now that we have multiple master pages, we can make adjustments for all sorts of layout situations that arise in various sections of a publication—one master page with rules and headers for two-column interior pages, another master page with an entirely different set of rule but a single column for the table of contents pages, and so forth.

Setting Automatic Page Numbers

Master page headers and footers in PageMaker are simply stories. Drag out a text block with the Text tool on the master page. With the insertion point blinking, type the key combination Ctrl+Shift+3 to get the page-number symbol you see in figure 13.24. (Because this one's from a double-sided publication, it shows up as LM—for "left master page.") You can put this page number on any PageMaker page, but a master page is where you will usually use it the most, perhaps preceded by the word Page or the same prefix (section number or chapter number) you entered in the Numbers dialog box when you were in Page Setup. That's an important point, by the way. The Numbers dialog box information isn't included automatically with the page numbering on the master page. You need to typeset it yourself. Of course, you want the two locations to match up so that the index and table of contents page numbering matches the numbering on your text pages.

Fɪɢ. 13.24 ▶

*PageMaker's auto-
page number symbol
in a master page
footer.*

Page LM   Chapter Title

TIP ▶ **Ad-Hoc Master Pages for Selective Use of Elements**

In the last edition of this book, this space listed a complicated tip—listing five different steps—for situations where you might not want to use all the master page elements. That was when we only got one master page publication. Now it's a lot easier. Just use the Duplicate command and create an ad-hoc master page. The Duplicate command takes you right to the duplicate page for editing. Make your adjustments and navigate back to your location in the publication where you can apply your new master page. Of course, you've also built a new master page that can be reused at will.

Key Concept:
Understanding Grid Terminology

Figures 13.25 and 13.26 show a couple of page maps with all their parts identified. These elements are the items you need to take into account when working out the design of your grid—sort of a hit list of decision factors. Besides, if you know all these jargon terms, you'll be able to swap interesting design adventure stories with other PageMaker users. Won't that be fun?

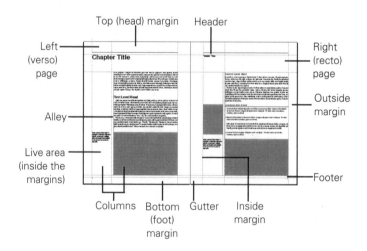

Fɪɢ. 13.25 ▲

Page elements of a book.

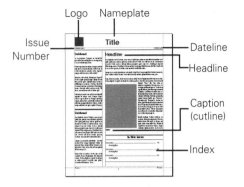

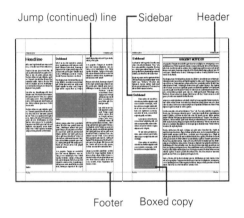

Fig. 13.26 ▲

Page elements of a newsletter.

TACTICS RECIPE:
Powering Up the Layout Grid

In a typical project, there are hundreds—maybe thousands—of lines of text. If you had to perform baseline alignment and other similar chores, it might take you weeks to hand-tune the vertical aspects of your layout grid, making sure that the text columns ran down the page evenly, without leaving ugly holes and blotches in your carefully crafted prose.

You need a way to automate this process. Hence, this Tactics Recipe, which combines the leading grid concept with PageMaker's Align to Grid and Snap to Rulers functions. You'll still need to tune up your pages, but most of the baseline alignment work will be automatically performed for you as you place your thousands—maybe tens of thousands—of lines of text.

In an ideal world, each line of text takes up the same amount of vertical space. Adjacent lines of text on a three-column page all line up, and the reader's eye is never distracted by unevenness. For a sample of unevenness, figure 13.27 should give you the idea.

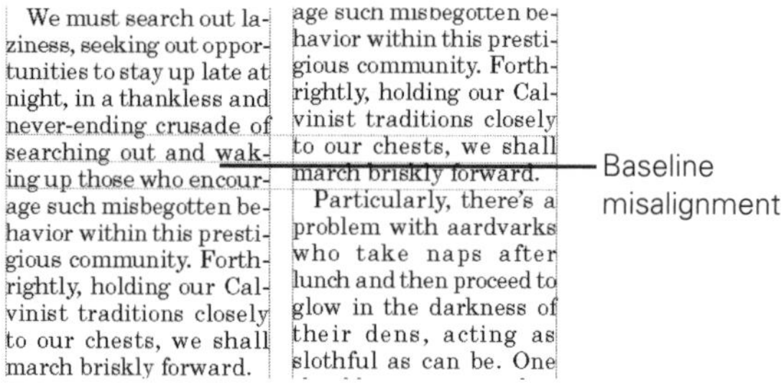

We must search out la-
ziness, seeking out opportunities to stay up late at
night, in a thankless and
never-ending crusade of
searching out and wak-
ing up those who encour-
age such misbegotten be-
havior within this prestigious community. Forth-
rightly, holding our Cal-
vinist traditions closely
to our chests, we shall
march briskly forward.

age such misbegotten be-
havior within this prestigious community. Forth-
rightly, holding our Cal-
vinist traditions closely
to our chests, we shall
march briskly forward.
    Particularly, there's a
problem with aardvarks
who take naps after
lunch and then proceed to
glow in the darkness of
their dens, acting as
slothful as can be. One

— Baseline misalignment

Fig. 13.27 ▲

Misaligned text-baselines in a multicolumn page.

Frankly, however, the world just doesn't line up really well on an everyday basis. Think of all the variables involved in lining up baselines across multiple text columns:

▼ Type size
▼ Leading
▼ Space before and after paragraphs
▼ Paragraph rules
▼ Inline graphics
▼ Body text size/leading

Set Up Automatic Baseline Alignment

One of the answers to wrestling all the variables into even baseline alignment is the Align to Grid command. It's buried deep behind the Rules button in the Paragraph Specifications dialog box, and it tells PageMaker to line up the baselines of your text on a sort of invisible grid. Any paragraph that has been assigned the Align to Grid attribute forces the next paragraph below it to align to this invisible baseline grid.

The invisible grid PageMaker uses for alignment is measured from the top of the text block. If the side-by-side text blocks of two columns aren't exactly lined up, then their baselines won't align either, even if you use the Align to Grid command.

Here's how to put the Align to Grid command to work.

Base Everything on Body-Copy Leading

First, you must decide on the leading for your body copy. In the examples used here, the body copy has been set 12/14.5 (12-point type on 14.5 points of leading). Your body copy leading becomes the basis for all your leading-grid decisions.

Turn on Align to Grid

Baselines of text as explained at the beginning of this section can be made to snap to an invisible grid. You do this with the Align to Grid command.

Let's just hit that explanation once more. Align to Grid doesn't align anything about the paragraph it's applied to. It actually adds space above the paragraph that follows it (below the paragraph marked for align to grid), shoving that following paragraph onto the grid.

This command has been buried three dialog boxes deep down the Paragraph Specifications dialog box. However, you can also find it on the right side of the Control palette when it's in Paragraph mode. Whichever way you choose to access the command, you almost always incorporate Align to Grid in a style. Because the objective is to align the body copy onto the grid, you usually use Align to Grid for any text that tends to fall off the grid, so the Align to Grid attribute will force the next paragraph (usually a body copy paragraph) back onto the grid. A paragraph style set up especially to hold inline graphic illustrations would be an ideal use of Align to Grid.

Turn on Align to Grid and type the amount of your body copy leading into the Align to Grid text-entry box. In our examples, it would be **14.5** because we have set body copy at 12/14.5.

Create a Custom Vertical Ruler

Next, in the Preferences dialog box shown in figure 13.28, create a custom ruler, using the measure of your body copy leading. For this example, use 14.5 points. The result, also shown in figure 13.28, is a vertical ruler marked off in major increments of 14.5 points. (Each number on the ruler marks off that many increments of 14.5 points from your zero point.) Within the major tick marks are smaller ticks, splitting your custom ruler increments into thirds. These measures are used to align the baselines of your text.

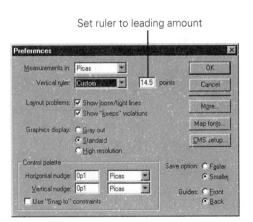

FIG. 13.28 ▲

Setting a custom vertical ruler and viewing the result.

By the way, if you ever need a compelling argument for using baseline leading (as discussed in Chapter 6, "Formatting Paragraphs"), you are looking at it in figure 13.28. With proportional leading, the baseline floats $2/3$ the way down in the slug instead of right at the bottom of it. In the old days, before we had baseline leading, it took a calculator and a lot of patience to develop a leading and baseline alignment scheme to align the floating baselines of the proportional leading method—figuring out multiples of $1/3$ a leading value like 13.2 or 14.7. In fact, that's the reason these custom ruler ticks are divided into thirds—because of the old proportional leading scheme from the days before we had baseline leading in PageMaker.

Set Snap to Rulers On (Usually)

The invisible grid is measured from the top of the text blocks. So it does no good to set up Align to Grid to make the baselines of adjacent columns line up unless you get the tops of the text blocks to line up.

You can do that by turning on Snap to Ruler in the Guides and Rulers menu. This step forces all your page objects to line up to the grid formed by the imaginary (and invisible) lines extending across the page from these major ruler ticks.

After you orchestrate all these settings—Align to Grid, Snap to Rulers, and the custom vertical ruler—your body-copy baselines will automatically line up on the increments of your custom vertical ruler. As you move graphics and text blocks, they too snap into place, automatically enforcing the structure of your layout design on a fine-grained level.

Many people refer to this process as *vertical justification* or *feathering*, but these terms are not accurate. It's better to call it *baseline alignment*. Feathering means adding leading evenly to all the lines of a column to get it to fill an entire column space—something that would actually throw off baseline alignment rather than achieve it. Feathering is justification in the vertical axis, not unlike justification of type to make it horizontally fill a line.

Establish a Leading Grid

Sometimes when you use the Align to Grid technique, you may run into a problem. If you have an out-of-synch headline (or an inline graphic) stacked in the middle of a vertical column of text, for example, PageMaker must work hard to make the following paragraphs fall onto the ruler grid. The result can be ungainly and unpredictable vertical spacing in your text, as you can see in figure 13.29.

The Align to Grid feature acts by inserting space before the next paragraph. The *Aardvarks* and *Running Dogs* headlines in the figure are not on the ruler grids and, therefore, the first body-copy paragraphs have also slipped off. The following paragraphs have been forced down to the grid, leaving ugly gaps in the text.

One possible solution is to apply Align to Grid only to paragraphs that are likely to fall out-of-synch with the body-copy baselines, such as headlines. That's what you see in figure 13.30. The headlines have been switched to Align to Grid, instead of using the attribute on the body copy, so space has been added after each headline and before the next paragraphs. The result isn't quite so bad, but notice that there's more space after the headlines than before them, making it look like they don't really belong to their body copy. Because both headlines actually have been set with zero spaces after them, there shouldn't really be any space added between the headlines and the body copy.

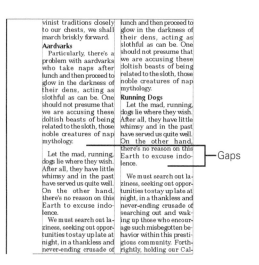

Fig. 13.29 ▲

Gaps in the text columns caused by Align to Grid's forced baseline adjustment.

Fig. 13.30 ▲

Bad headline spacing caused by Align to Grid.

The real solution? Add one more element to your layout grid system by designing a coordinated leading grid scheme for all the text in your publication.

The headlines have been set with 18-point leading; therefore they invariably throw the baseline alignment off by 3.5 points (18 points minus the 14.5 points in the grid equals 3.5 points). The problem only gets more complicated if you mix in some two-line heads because they would be off by twice that much (3.5 points twice, equals 7 points).

If you set the headline on a leading amount that's an exact multiple of the grid, everything falls into place, as you can see in figure 13.31. In this figure, the headlines have been reset to 14.5-point leading. Ugly spaces are eliminated, and the adjacent column text has perfectly aligned baselines.

> vinist traditions closely to our chests, we shall march briskly forward.
> **Aardvarks**
> Particularly, there's a problem with aardvarks who take naps after lunch and then proceed to glow in the darkness of their dens, acting as slothful as can be. One should not presume that we are accusing these doltish beasts of being related to the sloth, those noble creatures of nap mythology.
> Let the mad, running dogs lie where they wish. After all, they have little whimsy and in the past have served us quite well. On the other hand, there's no reason on this Earth to excuse indo-lence.
> We must search out la-ziness, seeking out oppor-tunities to stay up late at night, in a thankless and never-ending crusade of searching out and wak-
>
> glow in the darkness of their dens, acting as slothful as can be. One should not presume that we are accusing these doltish beasts of being related to the sloth, those noble creatures of nap mythology.
> **Running Dogs**
> Let the mad, running dogs lie where they wish. After all, they have little whimsy and in the past have served us quite well. On the other hand, there's no reason on this Earth to excuse indo-lence.
> We must search out la-ziness, seeking out oppor-tunities to stay up late at night, in a thankless and never-ending crusade of searching out and wak-ing up those who encour-age such misbegotten be-havior within this presti-gious community. Forth-rightly, holding our Cal-vinist traditions closely to our chests, we shall

Fɪɢ. 13.31 ▲

Headlines reset in multiples of the body-copy leading.

But what if you really want to have some space above these heads to open up the copy a bit? Just keep in mind that the Align to Grid feature bases its adjustments on the paragraph slug. Anything in your odd paragraph (the headline or the inline graphic element) that adds up to a mul-tiple will work. In figure 13.32, the space above has been added—exactly 14.5 points.

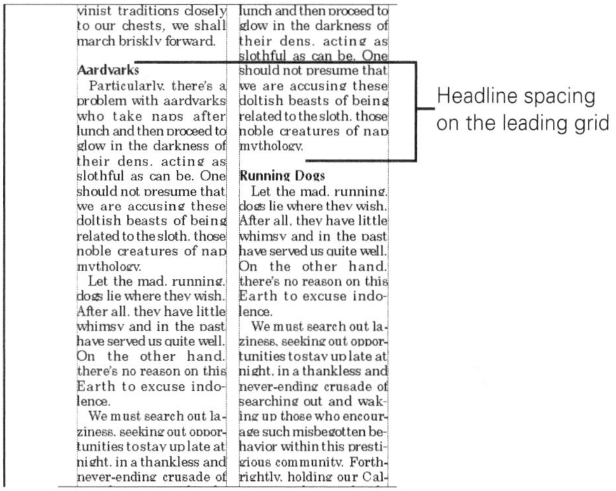

Headline spacing
on the leading grid

FIG. 13.32 ▲

Even with space above, headlines still fall on the leading grid because the mathematical relationships are preserved.

Anything that adds to the paragraph slug influences its capability to fit onto the grid. A paragraph rule can have a big effect, for example. After you've experimented and adjusted all your headline elements into styles that fit onto the leading grid, you will have a completely automated baseline alignment system.

So you may be asking yourself, "Why bother with Align to Grid when I'm going to adjust all the headline leading to fit on the grid anyway?" There are two main reasons why. If you are using inline graphics, it's extremely unlikely that the size of the graphics will be an exact multiple of your leading grid. Also, Align to Grid causes all objects on the page to line up automatically in some fashion to one another. This subtle alignment adds a professional sheen to your page.

Balance Columns

Some designers like to line up all the column bottoms in a spread, attempting to make the text in each column exactly the same height. Achieving this balance can be challenging, to say the least. So, PageMaker provides the Balance Columns Plug-in, available from the Utilities menu. Have a look at the Balance Columns dialog box in figure 13.33.

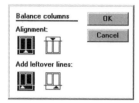

FIG. 13.33 ▲

The Balance Columns Plug-in dialog box.

Select with the Pointer tool—not the Text tool—the columns you want to balance. To align the bottoms or the tops of the columns you've selected, click one of the alignment icons in the Balance Columns dialog box. You usually align column bottoms.

If you want the excess lines between the columns you have selected to remain in the left-most column, click the bottom left icon. Click on the bottom right icon if you want the excess space on the right.

When you click OK, the Plug-in looks at each of your selected columns and averages the lengths. Then the Addition tries its best to make each column that length. It doesn't feather the column length by adjusting leading; it simply tries to even the number of lines in that column. You'll need to fine-tune the results, but this Addition makes a good start. All your paragraph control commands, such as widow and orphan control and Align to Grid, take priority over the efforts of Balance Columns.

Fitting Copy

Use this checklist to pull together all the tools you have for fitting text into your layout grid. It's sort of a mini-Tactics Recipe, providing you with a plan of attack for managing the copy-fitting task. Most of the items in this checklist are covered in Part II, "Working with Text." The idea is to link the layout grid concept with your PageMaker text tools.

Establish Horizontal Copy-Fitting Controls

These checklist items help determine how much copy will fit on each line of text in a column, and, therefore, how much text will fit in a given column-inch measure:

▼ *Coordinate type and column width.* Select type size and font with an eye for fitting all the text into your standard column. The type shouldn't be so big, for example, that it justifies or rags into ugly open spaces because you've chosen a narrow column width. You may need to experiment some to get the best results. Decide whether body copy will be justified or ragged.

▼ *Balance spacing and hyphenation with column width.* After you've chosen the type and column width, experiment with the letter and word spacing and hyphenation controls until you're satisfied with the "color" of your type. It should be even, with no rivers of space running through the columns caused by justification spacing, and with no ladders of hyphens down the right edge of the column.

Work Out the Automatic Vertical Copy Fit Parameters

After you've resolved the line-width issues, you can establish vertical spacing settings—the ones you'll lock into your body-copy styles:

▼ *Design leading grid.* Use the instructions in this chapter to design a leading grid, establishing the basic vertical spacing color of your text. Adjust the Align to Grid settings to eliminate holes and gaps in the vertical flow of your text.

▼ *Control widows and orphans.* Decide how sensitive you want to be about widows and orphans, and, thus, how paragraphs will break to the adjacent column or page. Will you tolerate a single line at the bottom or the top of a column? Set the controls for your body copy style.

Tune Each Page Manually

After PageMaker has fit the copy into your columns, it's time to put the rest of your tools to work to individually tune each page.

▼ *Apply Balance Columns Addition.* Use the Balance Columns Addition described in this chapter to tune column alignment across the top and bottom of the page.

▼ *Slide windowshades.* If you aren't happy with the Balance Column Addition results, try tweaking the column length by dragging the windowshade handle down or up to see how the paragraphs are breaking with your previously designed automatic settings. On a case-by-case basis, you may want to turn off some of these controls or adjust them slightly.

▼ *Tweak graphics.* It's often possible to adjust a column length by cropping or slightly resizing a graphic in the column. Be careful not to throw your graphics out of whack when resizing them. Use Magic Stretch and the Shift key constraint techniques to preserve graphics integrity.

▼ *Edit copy.* If it's permitted, light copy editing may often help you fit copy (in the most literal sense) into your columns.

Where to Go from Here

▶ You will have a hard time implementing a fine-grained layout grid unless you have a solid understanding of leading and styles. For those concepts, see Part II, "Working with Text."

▶ An automated leading and layout grid really pays off when placing text. Part II has more on the subject in Chapter 8, "Pouring Text into PageMaker."

▶ You'll get most of your power from the layout grid when you are positioning your page elements—which is why you should check out Chapter 14, "Precisely Positioning Graphics and Text."

▶ When you are putting together a long document format (reports, books, and so on), you will really appreciate the layout grid automation, especially the Guide Manager and multiple master pages, described in this chapter. For many more details on all aspects of multipage documents, have a look at Chapter 17, "Building Many Pages."

Chapter 14

Precisely Positioning Graphics and Text

This chapter on positioning graphics and text includes:

Using Undo and Revert to back your way out of positioning experiments.
▼

Displaying magnification to achieve PageMaker accuracy.
▼

Employing PageMaker tools to get precision readouts on the position and size of page elements.
▼

Using constraint options for snapping objects into precise placement.
▼

Achieving ultra-precise positioning with the Control palette.
▼

Skewing, flipping and rotating objects.
▼

Aligning and distributing objects on your pages.

PAGEMAKER HAS AMAZING potential as a precision layout tool and a lot of flexibility in how you can perform the basic layout task of putting text and graphics together on a page.

In this chapter, you will find our primary coverage of the Control Palette's object positioning power, as well as PageMaker 6.0's new grouping, alignment, distribution, masking and locking functions. ▶ ▶ ▶

Undoing and Reverting

Most designers use a sort of organized confusion to get to their end result. They try this. They try that. Tweak font spacing. Add a paragraph rule. Flip a graphic. Pull out a rectangle. Mess with line and fill. It's a process of experimentation.

Traditional mechanical paste-up artists use a special wax stick-'em so that they can pull up their page elements if they don't get them down just right, and repaste them in the right location. They sometimes still use those tools, even in the computer age, because it's a tried and true method of hands-on experimentation.

In PageMaker, you have similar tools—tools you explore in this chapter. Instead of paste-up wax, you have Undo and Revert. Instead of T-squares, you have ruler guides. You even have magnifying power, similar to the special magnifiers you see in graphic arts studios. Thank heavens, all these tools are much more powerful than old-fashioned paste-up wax, but they all drive at the same idea—experimentation leading to a final design.

Undo

Use the Undo command under the Edit menu to take back a move that didn't quite work. This command will take your publication back to the way it looked just before the last action you performed.

Unlike many graphics programs, PageMaker provides only one layer of Undo. That means, to do any good, you must use the Undo command immediately before making any additional moves. You can only undo the last move you made—no matter how tiny that move might have been.

There's a plus side to this limitation. Since there's only one level of Undo, you can use the Undo command to flip back and forth between two ideas during your experimentation process. Just use the keyboard shortcut, Ctrl+Z, to toggle between the two approaches so you can compare them and reflect on which one you want to keep.

Revert

Sometimes you need something more powerful than Undo. For one thing, the Undo command isn't available for all moves. You can't undo style definition and style application, for example. Also, you may not realize that you don't like a move until several steps down the road, and by then you've lost the opportunity to use PageMaker's single level of Undo.

For these situations, you need the Revert command, located under the File menu. This command will return your publication to the way it looked the last time you saved it. Rather than call it Revert, they might just as well have called this command the "close the current publication without saving it and reopen the one we saved awhile ago" command. But that wouldn't fit on the menu line.

Mini-Revert

If you don't want to do anything so drastic as the full Revert command, there's a middle ground. PageMaker saves a temporary copy of the latest version of your publication every time you navigate to a new page. (PageMaker does a mini-save much more often than that, but that's the main one. It also saves, for example, every time you print something.)

If you hold down the Ctrl Shift key while choosing the Revert command, you'll switch to the version of your publication as it existed before the last mini-save. make sure, though, to hold down the Shift key before clicking on the File menu. The Mini-Revert command doesn't show up on any menu; you just need to know that it's there. And now you do.

Backing Up as a Safety Net

If you want the ultimate insurance for backing out of your layout experiments, do frequent Save As command backups. You'll build yourself a safety net by saving your publication under a new name every quarter hour or so, or whenever you've made a major move. The Revert and Mini-Revert commands are nothing more than convenient ways to access an automatically generated backup copy of your document, but you can provide yourself with even more power to revert to an old version by saving copies of your publication as you build it.

Displaying Your Pages at Optimum Accuracy

When you increase the screen magnification in PageMaker, you increase your measurement accuracy. The rulers provide many more fine-grained tick marks at 400% or 800% custom magnification view than in Actual Size or Fit in Window view. Much of the time, you'll want to work in one of the wide views so you can get an overall sense of your design; but when you want maximum precision, crank up the magnification. The greater the magnification, the more accurate you'll be when positioning objects on the page.

Understand that PageMaker itself isn't more accurate at high magnification levels. It's just that the increased detail gives you a more accurate look at your publication when you are positioning an object. In any view, the Snap To constraints for positioning will still be accurate to within 1/1440 inches—and that's just as true in Entire Pasteboard view as it is in 400% view.

Toggling Magnification

Figure 14.1 shows the <u>V</u>iew submenu from the <u>L</u>ayout menu. Table 14.1 shows how you can get to the various magnification strengths using keyboard shortcuts and mouse actions.

Fig. 14.1 ▶

The <u>V</u>iew menu, showing Page-Maker's magnifying power.

What you see when you blow up the view of your page depends on what you select (if anything) or where you click just before you change magnification:

▶ If you have an object selected and you use the <u>V</u>iew menu, the selected object will appear centered in your window view.

▶ If you use the <u>V</u>iew menu without selecting an object, the page will appear centered on-screen.

▶ Most of the combination keyboard-and-click moves will center the new view on the spot where you clicked.

TABLE 14.1 Accessing Screen Magnification Levels

Magnification View	Keyboard Shortcut	Screen Click
Increase Magnification		Ctrl+spacebar+click. One step (magnifying glass cursor with plus sign).
Decrease Magnification		Ctrl+Alt+spacebar then click. One step (magnifying glass cursor with minus sign). The order is critical.

IV

Creating Page Layouts

Magnification View	Keyboard Shortcut	Screen Click
Custom view		Using the magnifying glass icon (Ctrl+spacebar), click and drag a selection marquee around the area you want to view at higher magnification. When you release the mouse button, that area will be blown up to fill your screen (upper limit 800% magnification).
Entire Pasteboard		(Entire PageMaker world)

Fit in Window (shows the complete publication and some surrounding Pasteboard)	Ctrl+0	Ctrl+Alt+click toggles between this view and 100% view.
		    Shift+click on page icon (Can be used going to new page).
		    Alt+double-click Zoom tool.

50%	Ctrl+5	

Actual Size or 100%	Ctrl+1	Toggle between 200% and 100% with Ctrl+Alt+Shift+ click or click of right mouse button.
		    Go to 100% from any magnification with Ctrl+Alt+click.
		    After the first use, Ctrl+Alt+click actions toggle between 100% and Fit in Window.
		    Double-click Zoom tool.

200%	Ctrl+2	Toggle between 200% and 100% with Ctrl+Alt+Shift+ click or Shift+right-click.
All to Same View		Alt+(View menu selection).

Managing Screen Resolution and Screen Redraw Time

While you're experimenting with your layout, or when you are knocking down pages for one of those rapid-fire multipage production jobs, give some thought to your screen display habits. You might save yourself a ton of time by cutting the time you spend watching the screen redraw.

Interruptible Screen Redraw

PageMaker has enough smarts to interrupt its screen redraw process if you go right to work on your next move. Just go back to work without waiting for every screen pixel to fill in.

You don't need to press any special keys. It's there all the time. Believe it or not, interruptible screen redraw has been part of PageMaker since Version 5.0. And it will cut your page tuning time in half—maybe more.

Unfortunately, we all have a tendency to sit there and watch the screen finish drawing before moving ahead. It's tough to get used to the idea that you don't need to wait for the redraw, but give it a try.

Use Lower Graphics Resolution

In Preferences, you can set graphics resolution. You can set graphics to Gray Out, Normal, or High Resolution. High-resolution graphics take the longest time for a screen redraw; a gray box representing a graphic redraws instantaneously.

For those moments when you need to see a graphic at its best resolution (TIFF graphics only), select it, and then hold down the Ctrl and Shift keys while forcing a redraw. Actually, you just need to press Ctrl+Shift before the graphic begins redrawing. It isn't absolutely necessary to hold it down while you are forcing the redraw.

To force a redraw without losing your view, you have a few options that will keep your work area centered:

▶ For the first time, PageMaker has an explicit screen redraw command—Ctrl+Shift+F12, new to Version 6.0.

▶ Use the key command for your current view magnification. If you are in Actual Size, press Ctrl+1 (to redraw at 100%) and press the Shift key as the screen starts to redraw.

▶ Toggle guides on and off with the Ctrl+J shortcut.

This temporary high resolution display trick doesn't work for EPS graphics because they are viewed on-screen with their embedded screen representations, and they are always at their best possible screen resolution, as poor as that may sometimes be.

The high resolution redraw procedure only works when you have graphics resolution set to Normal in Preferences. If you have it set to gray boxes, you only get gray boxes. And if you have it set to High, well, it's already being displayed at high resolution.

Positioning by Eye and Snap Guides

Most people develop their designs by fiddling around with the way things look on the page, using the Pointer tool to select objects and slide them to new spots. Creating a great page design almost always requires some of this eyeball positioning.

There's a whole class of moves that will help you doodle more precisely than you could by mere eyeball alone, and those are the tools we'll cover in this section. Even during experimentation, you can achieve impressive precision using the rulers, guides, the Snap To settings, and the Control palette. Old timers will note that this is the way we did all the layout work—before we got such newfangled tools and commands as the Guide Manager, Alignment and Distribution, and Grouping. Actually, for the first eight years of PageMaker, we didn't even have the Control palette.

Getting a Readout

You can always get a readout of where you are in PageMaker. The rulers tell you and so does the Control palette.

Ruler Readout

As you line up a block of text or a graphic, keep an eye on the short dotted lines, moving marks on both the horizontal and vertical rulers. These are the pointer tracking marks you see in figure 14.2. (If you are in Snap To Ruler constraint mode, the tracking markers jump from tick mark to tick mark.) If nothing has been selected, you get one ruler indicator for each axis, showing you the real-time position of your pointer. If you select an object, you see two tracking marks in each axis—horizontal and vertical—indicating the outer edges of the object. Often, you can accurately place an object on your page by using the ruler readout, without taking the time to pull out special ruler guides.

FIG. 14.2 ▶

Using the pointer tracking marks on your rulers for a position readout.

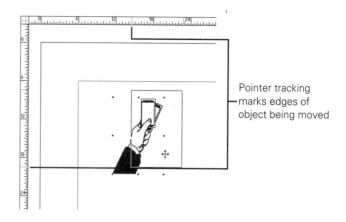

Pointer tracking marks edges of object being moved

Control Palette Readout

The Control palette's cursor-position indicator, the X and Y coordinates shown in figure 14.3, give you another way to get a constant precision readout on the object you are moving. The coordinates show the position of the Proxy point chosen for the object that has been selected. The *Proxy* is that square object on the left end of the palette, and the indicator dots at the center, sides, and corners are *Proxy points*. If you choose each of the Proxy points in turn, you will get X and Y coordinates for the corners, sides, and center of a selected object.

There's much more detailed information on all the object-positioning power of the Control palette in the section "Getting Ultra-Precise with the Control Palette," later in this chapter.

FIG. 14.3 ▶

A Control palette readout.

Position of moving object

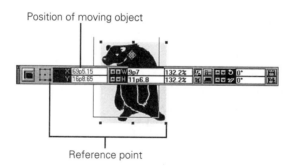

Reference point

Constraining Moves with the Shift Key

It can be tough to line up an object in two dimensions. You can ease the task by making the move one dimension at a time using the Shift constraint technique.

Locate the object correctly on one axis, then hold down the Shift key and slide along the other axis. When you hold down the Shift key like this, you lock movement as if you had mounted the object on a rail. You choose the rail with your first movement, even a tiny one.

The pointer will turn from a four-arrow cursor to a double-arrow cursor (see fig. 14.4), indicating that you've locked the object in place on one axis. The Shift constraint works strictly along vertical and horizontal lines—no diagonal moves.

Fig. 14.4 ▶

Shift constraint in use to lock an object onto one axis.

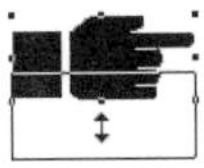

This Shift constraint move works well when you need a quick and rough alignment of two objects while you are doodling. Position the first object where you want it to end up. Then select the second object and drag it right over on top of the first one, so it precisely matches up (for example, align the top edge or the left edge). Now, while you still have object number two selected, hold down the Shift key and slide it horizontally or vertically to its final position, depending on which direction you are headed.

Of course, PageMaker 6.0's new alignment command was made for this kind of thing, but we're doodling, right?

Snapping To Guides

The Snap To Guides command (on the Guides and Rulers submenu of the Layout menu) can be used to precisely position text and graphics. Pull down a guide, make sure Snap To Guides has been turned on, and then slide each object near the guide until the guide's "magnet" effect snaps the object into position.

There's more information on guides, master guides, ruler guides, column guides, and margin guides in Chapter 13, "Designing a Master Page Grid."

Snap To Guides is especially helpful when you need to replicate standardized positioning on many pages or for many objects. Pull out a ruler guide on a master page or on a page where you will need to line up multiple objects. (You may want to use the Guide Manager to set the guide in place because you can type in a precise position.) Then, with Snap To Guides turned on, slide the objects into place. Simple as that.

To get high-precision eyeball placement, use an obvious technique that few people actually seem to remember when they are in the middle of a fast-paced project. After setting an approximate position, go to extremely high magnification using the custom magnifying glass (Ctrl+spacebar) to drag out an area to examine. Use the resulting extremely fine-grained tick marks on the rulers for high-precision positioning. Keep in mind that Snap To Rulers (on the Guides and Rulers submenu of the Layout menu) operates on guides as well as objects and text baselines.

Figures 14.5 and 14.6 show examples of high magnification placement techniques using Snap To Rulers and Snap To Guides.

FIG. 14.5 ▶

First establish the position of your ruler guide at high magnification.

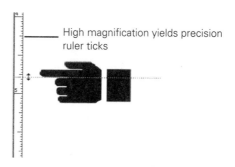

High magnification yields precision ruler ticks

FIG. 14.6 ▶

Then zoom out to a wider view to pull the object to the ruler guide. The PageMaker Snap To constraints and ruler tick marks operate to within 1/1440 inches accuracy.

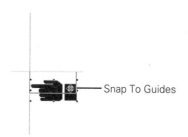

Snap To Guides

TIP ▶ Be Consistent In Handling Flipping Lines and the Pixel-Edge Effect

When using Snap To Guides on a line, remember that the guides operate on the edges of the pixels on your screen, and the line is measured from one of its edges, not its center. You get a flipping effect as the line tries to decide which side of the guide it should use for positioning. The key is to remain consistent in how you swing your lines up to the guides. That way you'll always get the same side of the flip effect. Always bring your line up to the guide from below, for example (or the top, whichever suits you, just so you always do it the same way).

Figure 14.7 shows three lines riding on a ruler guide. The thick lines make this pixel-edge effect easier to see.

In the figure, the first line has flipped below the guide, and the second above it. The third line didn't snap to the guide at all. As a sailor might say, its active edge, the edge with the handles, is in the lee, with the body of the thick line between the guide and the active edge.

Fig. 14.7 ▶

Lines are measured on one edge, not down the center, when being positioned on a guide.

Handles

Sensitive edge away from guide

Pixel edge

Original   Flipped

Positioning Tiny Objects

If you want to position a very tiny object by eye, it can be difficult to see what you're doing. Sometimes, on really small items, the arrow head of the pointer will even cover the object, especially in the lower magnification views. You have two ways to solve this problem. One is the tag team move, and the other is custom magnification.

Making a Tag Team Move

Check figure 14.8 to see how this technique works. Draw a PageMaker object near the small object, preferably on the opposite side of the guide you'll be targeting for your Snap To move. Now select both objects, either with Shift+click or by using the Pointer tool to draw a selection marquee around both objects (the method shown). After you have both of the objects selected, click on the large object and use it to maneuver the smaller one next to your guide.

Fig. 14.8 ▶

A tag team move, used to position a very small object.

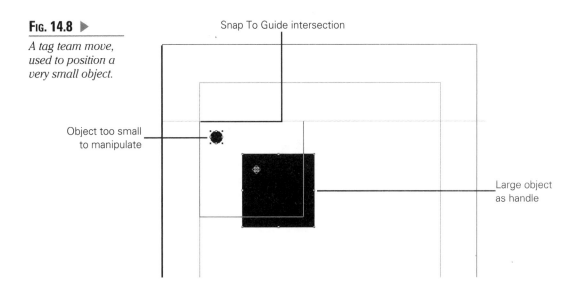

Snap To Guide intersection

Object too small to manipulate

Large object as handle

Applying Custom Magnification

Another way to deal with small objects is to simply take a closer look. Use Ctrl+spacebar to turn the pointer arrow into a magnifying glass. Click and drag a custom high-magnification area that includes your small object and the target location. When you release the mouse button, your screen will leap into a high magnification; you'll be able to select the small object and slide it next to a guide or use the readout techniques to achieve your positioning objective. (Once selected at high magnification, you can also use the arrow keys or the Control palette.)

Nudging with the Arrow Keys

In addition to sliding an object into position on your page with the pointer arrow, you can use the arrow keys to nudge the object into place. Just select the object and tap away in whichever direction you choose. If you press the Ctrl key while using the arrow keys, you will multiply the nudge amounts by ten because you'll be in Power Nudge mode. You can set the nudge amounts in Preferences.

Getting Ultra-Precise with the Control Palette

So much for doodling and the old reliable positioning methods. For final layout, and even sometimes for doodling, there's nothing that beats flying your Control palette.

With the Control palette there's no guessing, because the Control palette text entry boxes continuously provide you with exact coordinates and other kinds of precision feedback. With the Control palette, there's no such thing as "close enough."

There are two basic modes for the Control palette: Text mode and Object mode. The mode you're in depends on what you've selected before you go to the Control palette—type or object.

All the basics of accessing, navigating, and setting up the Control palette have been covered extensively, along with the Text mode and its two submodes for type and paragraph formatting, in Chapter 5, "Typing In Your Type;" Chapter 6, "Formatting Paragraphs;" and Chapter 7, "Designing a Text Style System." A map of the Control palette in all its modes has been included in the back of the book. And the keyboard shortcuts for flying the Control palette have been included in Appendix C.

In figure 14.9, you see how the Control palette looks with an object (text block or a graphic) selected.

Fig. 14.9 ▶

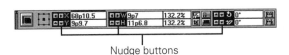

*The Control palette
as it looks when
you select an
object—a TIFF in
this case.*

IV

Creating Page Layouts

In a way, the Control palette works like the Toolbox. You select an object, and then choose the kind of work you want to do by selecting an area of the palette that fits your task (rotating, resizing, moving, and so on).

Taking Action with Nudge Buttons and Text-Entry Boxes

There are two basic ways to implement an action in the Control palette—the nudge button method or the direct-entry technique. (In Object mode, the Control palette does not provide the kind of pull-down lists you use in Text mode for selecting fonts or paragraph styles.)

When you are fine-tuning an object's position or size and want the visual feedback of evaluating your move as you go along, use the nudge button method. Click on the nudge buttons you see in figure 14.10; each tiny move takes effect immediately, yielding instant feedback for evaluation of an effect.

Fig. 14.10 ▶

*Nudge buttons in
the Control palette.*

Nudge buttons

Your Control palette nudge buttons work just like the keyboard arrow keys. The movement increments of both the nudge buttons and the arrow keys can be amplified by holding down the Ctrl key. This method yields results ten times the size of a regular nudge, so if you have the nudge amount set for 1/100 inch in Preferences, holding down the Ctrl key gives you nudge amounts of $^1/_{10}$ inch. In Preferences, you can set different nudge sensitivity for the horizontal or vertical axis. You can also turn on the Snap To constraints so your nudge moves will be magnetized to the ruler grid or any of the guides.

For those times when you know exactly where you want to end up, or if you are a keyboard person instead of a mouse person, use the direct-entry method. Type the amount directly into the text-entry box. Depending on the function, you might be entering a linear measurement, a percentage, or degrees of rotation and skewing.

Once you have typed in your measurement, the way you apply your move depends on where you want to go from there:

▶ Pressing Enter applies the move and returns to layout.

▶ Pressing Shift+Enter or clicking on the Apply button applies the move and stays in Control palette.

When working with linear measure direct-entry boxes, you have a choice of measuring systems, no matter what you set up as your standard measurement system in Preferences. To temporarily override the measurement system, you have two choices. Flip through the measurement systems with the key chord Shift+F12, which is a great way to see how picas and inches relate to one another. Or, use table 14.2 to look up the code for an alternate measure, typing it as directed. You can use these codes in any of PageMaker's dialog boxes.

TABLE 14.2   Temporary Override Codes for Measurements

To Get This Measure	Type This Letter	To Look Like This
Inches	**i** following the number	11.5i = 11 1/2 inches
Millimeters	**m** following the number	40m = 40 millimeters
Picas and points	**p** following the pica and before the point	16p6 = 16 picas and 6 points 0p14 = 14 points = 1p2
Ciceros	**c** following the number	17c = 17 ciceros

TIP ▷ **Use the Control Palette as an Object Positioning Calculator**

You can type mathematical calculations into the direct-entry boxes. Try this tip if you find yourself saying, "I wonder how this would look if a slid it over to the right by 3 picas?" Or maybe, "What if this rectangle was only half as wide?" Tab to the box, press the right-arrow key once to get a blinking insertion point following the entry (or click in the box), and type a math operator along with a number, as you see in figure 14.11. You can add, subtract, multiply, and divide. For multiplication, use an asterisk; for division, use a slash.

FIG. 14.11 ▶

Doing math in the Control palette direct-entry boxes.

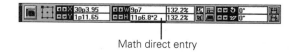

Math direct entry

Understanding the Apply Button

Besides putting your direct-entry actions into effect, the Apply button tells you what kind of object or tool you've chosen, as you can see from all the different kinds of Apply buttons shown in table 14.3. If you haven't selected an object, the Apply button shows the currently selected tool from the Toolbox. If you do have an object selected, you see pretty much the same icons you see when you import graphics or text with the Place command. Two exceptions—the text icon doesn't change to the Autoflow icon, and if you have several kinds of items selected, there's a special combination icon.

TABLE **14.3**   Various Apply Button Icons

Button	Type	Button	Type
	TIFF		Rectangle
	EPS		Oval
	Text Block		Line
	Multiple Objects		Dragging Ruler Guide
	Group		

Selecting a Reference Point with the Proxy

Before you can make a move with the Control palette, you must give PageMaker a reference point. When you tell the Control palette to move an object 6 picas to the right, PageMaker needs to know where to begin measuring the move—upper-left corner, center, bottom edge, and so on.

In figure 14.12, you see the Proxy, the section of the Control palette that you use to designate the reference point. You can tell which reference point has been chosen. It's the point that's been turned into a box in the upper-left corner.

Fig. 14.12 ▶

*Action reference
points are chosen
by Proxy.*

Reference (anointed) __
point

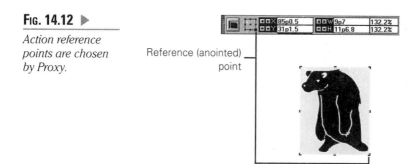

There are actually four ways to choose an object reference point using the
Proxy:

▶ Using the mouse, you can click on one of the points around the edge of the
Proxy or at its center.

▶ Again using the mouse, click on the corresponding handle of your selected
object. When you use this method, you can't select the center point, and
you'll need to reactivate the palette by clicking on it or by using the keyboard shortcut Ctrl+`(grave).

▶ Use the arrow keys, assuming you have selected the Proxy area of the palette by tabbing to it or with a mouse click.

▶ Again with the Proxy selected, use the numeric keypad with Num Lock on.
The "points" around the rim of the numeric keypad correspond to the corners and sides of the Proxy, and the 5 key activates the center reference
point.

Your reference point selection is "sticky." Until you change it again, the Proxy
will use the same reference point each time you select a new object.

Setting the Proxy Action Mode

The Proxy can be a Locked or Sliding reference for object moves. You switch between these two Proxy modes by clicking on the active reference point, or by
simply pressing the spacebar when the Proxy is active:

▶ In Locked mode, the Proxy reference point has been locked into its relationship with the other side and corner points. Thus, when you type in a
move in the Control palette, the entire object moves around or in relationship to the anointed (and locked) Proxy point.

In Locked mode, your Control palette moves are *measured from* the reference point.

▶ In Sliding mode, the Proxy point has been unlocked from its relationship to the other points on the object. Thus, when you type in a move on the Control palette, the Proxy point moves, and has the effect of resizing the object. For this reason, it's sometimes referred to as Resize mode.

In Sliding mode, your Control palette moves are *applied to* the reference point.

Figure 14.13 shows the Proxy in Sliding mode.

Fig. 14.13 ▶

*The Proxy in
Sliding mode
(double-arrow
reference point).*

Sliding mode
reference point

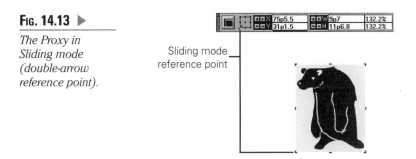

There's an exception to this behavior if you anoint the center Proxy point, explained in detail in the upcoming section "Understanding the Center Proxy Point."

Take a look at the next couple of figures to see the difference between Locked and Sliding mode for your Proxy reference point.

Figure 14.14 shows how a Locked mode move forces the entire object to move from its original position. Because the selected reference point has been locked into its relationship with the other reference points—the move is *measured from* the reference point—the entire object moves when you move the Proxy.

In figure 14.15, you can see how the Proxy point works in Sliding mode, where the chosen reference point switches to a double arrow. The reference point has been unlocked and actions in the Control palette move the anointed reference point in relation to the other Proxy points for your object. When you change the X and Y coordinates, the object will be stretched or shrunk as if you had grabbed that handle of the object and moved it.

FIG. 14.14 ▶

A box moved 12 picas to the right in Locked mode. For this move, the anointed reference point was the upper-left corner of the Proxy. As you can see from the guides, the box had been at the coordinates of 9 picas (X) and 9 picas (Y). After the move, the X coordinate became 21 picas.

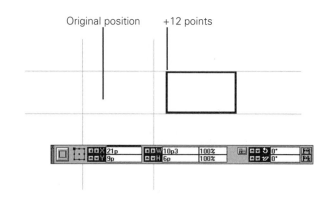

FIG. 14.15 ▶

A box stretched 4 points because the Proxy reference point was in Sliding mode. The anointed reference point was the upper-right corner of the Proxy, so the command to move the X coordinate by 4 points forced that corner to the right by that amount. The move was applied to the reference point.

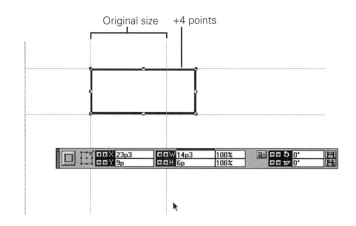

Understanding the Center Proxy Point

With the center Proxy point anointed, there's no difference in the action between Locked and Sliding mode. For example, Resizing applies in equal measure across the axis of the move. You can designate the center point as Locked or Sliding, but the action will be the same no matter the mode. Also, you get a different indicator for the anointed Proxy point—an intuitive four-way arrow.

So, (as in fig. 14.16), if you expand the size of an object with the center Proxy point anointed, you bump the width of the object down equally on both sides.

Fig. 14.16 ▶

The box expands equally all around with the center Proxy point chosen. With the center point selected, 2 picas were added on each side by selecting the center Proxy point and adding 4 picas to both the width and the height.

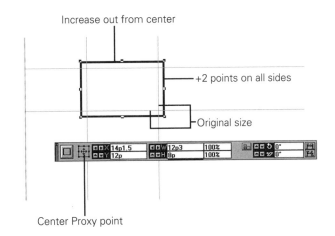

Increase out from center

+2 points on all sides

Original size

Center Proxy point

Moving with Multiple Objects Selected

If you select two or more objects, most of the Control palette goes away. All you'll have left are the Position section and the Rotating and Reflecting buttons (see fig. 14.17).

Fig. 14.17 ▶

The Control palette with two objects selected.

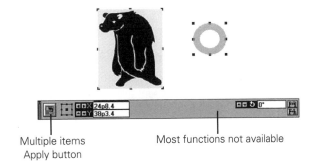

Multiple items
Apply button

Most functions not available

TIP ▶ **Use Alignment to Center Objects**

Up until PageMaker 6.0, there were endless tricks for centering objects, often based on the Control palette. For example, a lot of people used the Control palette with a center proxy setting to one-by-one stack multiple objects on the same center point. Forget all that and use the new Alignment command.

By the way, it always seems like you ought to be able to center multiple objects by selecting all of them, then making a single center point move with the Control palette. Sorry, it doesn't work. That merely moves the objects to a new location based on a center point calculated by PageMaker and based on the apparent center point of the entire collection.

Moving an Object with the X and Y Coordinates

In figure 14.18, you see how the Control palette looks with an object (text block or a graphic) selected. The figure also shows the Control palette features.

Fig. 14.18 ▶

The Control palette with an object selected.

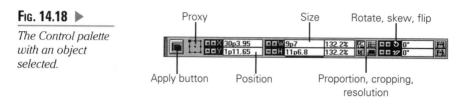

Proxy   Size   Rotate, skew, flip

Apply button   Position   Proportion, cropping, resolution

Using the nudge buttons or the direct-entry boxes for the Position options (the X and Y boxes shown in fig. 14.18), you can command the active Proxy reference point to a new coordinate spot on your page. You describe the spot with its X- and Y-axis coordinates, measured from the zero point.

If the Proxy is in Locked mode, the whole object will be moved, with the reference point placed exactly on your new coordinate entry.

If the Proxy is in Sliding mode, the object will change shape and size as the palette forces the reference point to the new X- and Y-coordinates (bear in mind the center Proxy point exception for Sliding mode).

TIP ▶ **Ruler Settings Make a Difference on Control Palette**

You probably have figured out that measurement system settings in Preferences determine the measurement system used in the Control palette, as they do throughout PageMaker. Here are a couple of nuances. If you set your vertical ruler for a different measurement system, the vertical coordinates in the Control palette—the Y and H coordinates—will display in that measurement system and the horizontal coordinates will express position using the main measurement system as you've set it in Preferences. Also, don't forget that on the Control palette, you can cycle through different measurement systems with the Shift+F12 keyboard shortcut.

Reviewing Scaling and Cropping Basics

To understand how the Control palette works on the size of an object, let's first quickly review the difference between cropping and scaling:

▶ *Cropping* cuts a part of the object away. It's only available for imported graphic objects—as opposed to PageMaker-created objects such as a text box or an object drawn with PageMaker's Line, Oval, Rectangle or Polygon tools.

▶ *Scaling* retains all of a graphic but changes its size and possibly its shape. You can scale any object in PageMaker—text block, imported graphic, or PageMaker-drawn object.

When scaling any object, you have the option of doing so proportionally, retaining its shape but changing its size. You also may have the option of using Magic Stretch from the Control palette, but only if you are working on bitmapped, black-and-white imported objects.

Remember, the Control palette activities in this section are available as mouse moves directly in your layout. Check out the section "Basic Moving and Sizing of a Drawn Object" in Chapter 10, or the section "Sizing and Cropping Graphics" in Chapter 11.

Sizing an Object with Scaling and Cropping

Figure 14.18 gives you a basic map for the Control palette version of all these sizing and cropping moves.

First, if you have selected an imported graphic object—as opposed to a text box or a PageMaker-drawn object—you will need to decide whether you want to crop it. If you do, click on the button that looks like the Cropping tool, and the rest of the options will drop off the Control palette. If you have chosen anything but an imported graphic, the cropping option won't be available.

If you will not be cropping, you will be scaling your object, so you need to choose the double-box button right above the cropping button (again, as shown in fig. 14.18).

You can scale any object, be it a text block, an imported graphic, or a PageMaker-drawn item. Your scaling options depend on the nature of the item. You make your choices using the two buttons just to the right of the cropping and scaling buttons:

▶ The Proportional Sizing button, located just to the right of the double-box scaling button, will determine the shape of your object. If Proportional Sizing is turned on, your object will retain its shape as it existed immediately prior to your move.

▶ You also have access in the Control palette to Magic Stretch for bitmapped black-and-white objects. To use Magic Stretch from the Control palette, click on the Printer Resolution Scaling button. (When working in the layout, you get Magic Stretch by Ctrl+dragging on the handle of the bitmap.)

> **TIP ▶ You Can Proportionally Size PageMaker-Drawn Objects**
>
> With the Control palette, you can retain the shape of a PageMaker-drawn object as you scale it. Remember that in Layout view the Shift+drag handle move constrains the object—snaps a rectangle into a square, an oval into a circle, and so on. On the Control palette, even with a PageMaker-drawn object, you can just click on the Proportional Scaling button.

After you have made your optional decisions about scaling and cropping, you can use the Sizing option (refer back to fig. 14.18). This option enables you to change the width and height of an object (or the length of a line, which is a one-dimensional object in PageMaker's object world). You perform that scaling operation with the W or H text boxes or their associated nudge buttons. Simply type in the values you want or use the nudge buttons, keeping in mind the effects of the Proxy point choices discussed earlier in this chapter.

If you are scaling an object, as opposed to cropping it, you have a third option—you can enter the size as a percentage. Your percentage will be computed in relation to the last completed scaling move you made. If you deselect an object after scaling it and then select it again, the Control palette will adopt that new object size as the new 100 percent scale figure.

Skewing, Flipping, and Rotating Graphics and Text

There's only one place in PageMaker 6.0 to perform flipping and skewing, and it's the Control palette. You can use both the Control palette and the Rotating tool to perform rotation.

The accuracy and nudge increments are the same for skewing and rotation: 1/10 a degree for nudge and 1 degree for power nudge. You can get even better accuracy (1/100 a degree) by typing your moves into the direct-entry boxes.

Figure 14.19 shows the right side of the Control palette. This end contains the palette's Rotating, Skewing, and Flipping controls.

Skewing

Another word for skewing is "leaning." When you *skew* an object, it's as if you climbed onto your page and shoved one corner of the selected object to the right or left, making the object appear to lean to one side.

FIG. 14.19

Skewing in Locked (box Proxy reference point) mode.

Anointed proxy point remains fixed

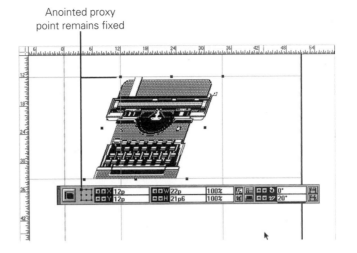

Figure 14.19 shows an object skewed with the upper-left corner Proxy reference point in Locked mode. Figure 14.20 shows the same move with the upper-left corner in Sliding (double arrow) mode.

▶ When you are skewing an object in Locked mode, the Proxy reference point will stay fixed, like an anchor point, and the rest of the object uses that point as a reference for how it leans (refer to fig. 14.19). The move is *measured from* the reference point.

▶ On the other hand, when skewing an object with the Proxy reference point in Sliding mode, the anointed Proxy point moves or leans while the rest of the object remains fixed (see fig. 14.20). The move is *applied to* the reference point.

Both figures have been skewed by 20 degrees. Negative numbers skew to the left, and positive numbers skew to the right.

Flipping

You can flip or reflect (as in a mirror) an object along its horizontal or vertical axis. The letter F, for *flip*, graphically represents effects of each of the Control palette's Reflect buttons.

In the following examples, notice how the anointed Proxy point (in double-arrow Sliding mode) has swapped its location and how the box has moved in relation to the ruler guides marking its original location. Figure 14.21 shows the horizontal flip.

FIG. **14.20** ▶

Skewing in Sliding (double arrow) mode.

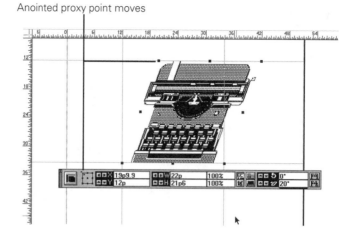

Anointed proxy point moves

FIG. **14.21** ▶

A horizontal flip.

Original position

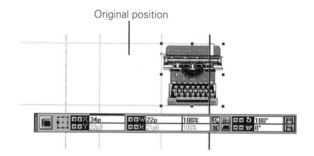

Likewise, figure 14.22 demonstrates the results of a vertical flip.

FIG. **14.22** ▶

A vertical flip.

Original position

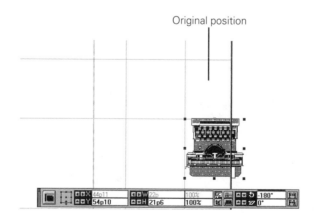

Rotating

With the Rotation option, you can rotate objects in finer increments than you can with the Flip buttons. The Control palette offers the greatest precision, while the Rotation tool is more visual and intuitive.

Rotating with the Control Palette

In the Control palette, the nudge buttons work in 1/10 degree increments, and one-degree increments in power nudge. You can get even greater accuracy by typing in your rotation moves, achieving an accuracy of 1/100 of a degree.

TIP ▶ Use Negative Numbers to Rotate Clockwise

Negative numbers typed into the Control palette's direct-entry box rotate the selected object clockwise, and positive numbers rotate the object counterclockwise. This may seem counter-intuitive—it does to me—but here's why it works this way. The answer is PostScript. Naturally, you can't rotate something without having a reference point, some zero point on an imaginary clock face. Culturally, most of us automatically assume that the zero point sits at 12 o'clock. Not true for PageMaker, which uses PostScript to "draw" pages. In PostScript, object rotation is measured from the horizontal axis—3 o'clock instead of 12 o'clock. You can test this yourself. If you use the Rotation tool and pull out a horizontal lever to make your rotation move, it will be at zero degrees, going positive if you rotate the lever up (counterclockwise). Or, should I say counter-intuitive?

If you want just a touch more in the way of arcane knowledge, it may interest you to know that FreeHand, Illustrator, and QuarkXPress all rotate objects in the same manner. They all use—are you ready for this—the four-quadrant Cartesian Plane model. That makes sense, when you think about it. It's the way we draw graphs along the X- and Y-axis, with the upper-right quadrant being positive on both axes and the lower-right coordinate being negative in the vertical and positive in the horizontal. It's also often used for map coordinates.

In figures 14.23 and 14.24, you can see how the rotation works differently, depending on whether your Proxy reference point is in Locked or Sliding mode. In the regular Locked mode (box reference point), the object rotates around the anointed point. In Sliding mode (double- or four-arrow reference point), the anointed point rotates. If you anoint the center point, you get the same rotation action in either Locked or Sliding mode. Notice that as you rotate an object, the Control palette Proxy follows along and spins as you perform the rotation move.

Fig. 14.23 ▶

Rotating an object in Locked mode (box Proxy reference point).

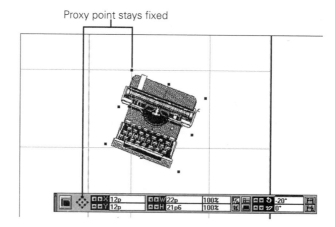

Proxy point stays fixed

Fig. 14.24 ▶

Rotating an object in Sliding mode (double-arrow Proxy reference point).

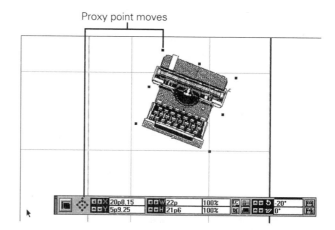

Proxy point moves

Rotating with the Rotation Tool

Instead of typing in your rotation or using the nudge buttons, you can grab the Rotating tool at the lower-left corner of the Toolbox and perform ad hoc rotation moves.

Figure 14.25 shows how this method works. Select the Rotation tool first, and then click it somewhere near the object you want to rotate. This gives you a fulcrum point. That's the crosshair pointer in the figure. Then draw out a lever by dragging your pointer away from the object you've selected. The lever is the line you see in the illustration, and you use it to rotate your object. The longer you make this lever, the more gradual your rotation move and the finer the control. Notice that the Control palette provides a readout of your angle of rotation.

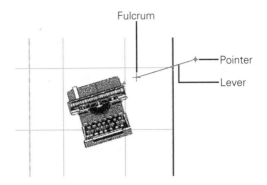

Fig. 14.25 ▶

Ad hoc rotation with the Rotating tool.

Like most PageMaker moves, there's a constraint mode for rotation. Often, you want to rotate an object around its center. Instead of setting the Proxy reference point, you have a keyboard shortcut to help out. Hold down the Ctrl key as you use the Rotation tool, as you see in figure 14.26. Notice that the fulcrum point is dead square on the center of the object being rotated.

Fig. 14.26 ▶

Doing a centered rotation using the Ctrl key and the Rotation tool.

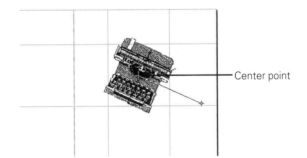

Editing Skewed, Flipped, or Rotated Text

Nothing could be simpler than editing text that's been skewed, flipped, or rotated. Simply click the text with the Text tool and edit. You can perform all your text-formatting and copy-editing functions on your transformed text. You can edit it right in Layout view, or you can triple-click into Story Editor—your choice. (There's none of that business you see in some programs where you must unrotate your text block before editing.)

Grouping Objects

PageMaker 6.0 finally has real grouping. It's a quick keyboard command away, and you don't have to go up to the Utilities menu and call on an Addition (now called Plug-ins) to use it.

Making a Group

To make a group, just select your objects with Shift+click, or draw a Pointer tool marquee around them, and then press Ctrl+G for Group. Or you can use the Group command from the Arrange menu. You can Ungroup from the menu or by pressing Ctrl+U. The keyboard shortcuts are so easy, I'm sure they will become second nature to you and you'll never look at the menu grouping commands again.

To see a before and after view of a grouping operation, check out figure 14.27.

FIG. 14.27 ▶

Three objects, selected and ready to be grouped on the left. On the right, the same set of objects has been grouped and rotated as a unit.

Understanding Group Idiosyncrasies

The PageMaker Group command has a few ins and outs, mostly having to do with the way it interacts with other aspects of the program:

▶ You can edit individual members of a group without ungrouping them. To work with objects, select them with Ctrl+click. To edit or format text, use the Text tool directly on the text object without ungrouping.

▶ Many times you will want to combine the Group command with the new Mask command, to lock together the relationships of the objects. To do that, hold down the Shift key while selecting the Element menu, and you will get a revised menu item called Mask and Group. You get the reversing command, Unmask and Ungroup, the same way.

▶ Ungroup does it all the way. In many graphics programs, the group and ungroup function works in stages. You might, for example, group the two hands in figure 14.27 and then add the bear to the group. In many programs, this would cause the items to be *nested*, and the ungrouping process would reverse these stages, requiring several steps to get everything completely ungrouped. However, in PageMaker, when you ungroup, you ungroup everything all at once.

▶ You can make a group of one. For example, if you need to wrap some text around a text block, group the text block to be wrapped. PageMaker will treat it as a graphic and allow you to set text wrap boundaries around it.

▶ If you have an individual text block as a group with text wrap (such as a pull quote) and then group it to text around it, it loses the wrap. You have to set the wrap for the full new group which won't allow you to wrap between the grouped text and grouped pull quote.

▶ Grouped text acts normally. Any grouped text, whether a one-item group or grouped with other objects, acts just like regular text. Unlike many graphic programs, the Group command does not lock the text at a certain type size or typeface. Therefore, you can't stretch it out of shape just because it has been grouped. In fact, the size handles on the grouped text block act just like the sizing handles on a regular text block.

▶ Unfortunately, groups can't be used as inline graphics. There could have been many tricks built on this possibility, but it just doesn't work.

▶ When you save a PageMaker 6.0 file as a Version 5.0 file, the groups will ungroup in the process. Grouping isn't supported in PageMaker 5.0.

▶ By the same token, when bringing PageMaker 5.0 files up to PageMaker 6.0, convert the groups. The best procedure is to ungroup before conversion and regroup once in Version 6.0.

▶ Creating a group brings that group all the way to the front in the stacking order. The objects within the group retain their relative stacking order but all move to the top of the stack. When ungrouped, they will be in front of everything else.

▶ You can proportionally scale a group, with all objects inside the group retaining their shape. Hold down the Shift key during the move or use the proportional option when making a sizing move within the Control palette.

▶ However, unlike the old PSGroupIt Addition, if you distort a group and then ungroup, the formerly grouped objects retain their distorted appearance.

▶ You can make a group containing an object that has been locked, but when you give the Group command, PageMaker will give you a choice of either unlocking the object or locking the entire group.

Aligning and Distributing Objects

In the last edition, there were pages of tips and tricks for working around the fact that PageMaker did not offer any actual distribution or alignment tools. Not any more. Real distribution and alignment has arrived in Version 6.0. You access these functions through the Arrange menu's Align Objects command, which yields the dialog box shown in figure 14.28.

Fig. 14.28 ▶

The Align Objects dialog box, demonstrating both the alignment and distribution options.

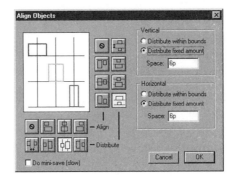

PageMaker will align or distribute any object, no matter what its type. You can center a text block on a box, line up the left edges of a collection of imported TIFFs, distribute lines on a grid exactly 1/4 inches apart, or align a grouped illustration and caption with a body copy text block. These are just examples, of course, and I'm sure you will use the Align Objects command dozens of times in a work session, in dozens of different ways.

Getting the Basics of Aligning and Distributing

Here are the essential basic facts about the effects of the alignment and distribution actions in the Align Objects command:

▶ You must select two or more objects or the Align Objects command will be grayed out and unavailable.

▶ Use the Ctrl+4 keyboard shortcut to call up the Align Objects dialog box.

▶ You can mix or match any combination of horizontal or vertical alignment or distribution. In other words, you could distribute along the vertical axis while aligning along the horizontal one.

▶ You can align or distribute objects based on their centers, or their top, bottom, left, or right edges.

▶ The choices available in the Vertical and Horizontal specifications boxes will change depending on your choices of icons.

▶ The Preview box in the upper-left corner of the dialog box displays the effects of your alignment and distribution choices as you make them.

▶ The Align Objects dialog box is "sticky," meaning it remembers the choices you made the last time you used the command. It remembers your choices even between work sessions. In PageMaker parlance, you set a Program default every time you change the Align Objects dialog box.

▶ If you only want to align or distribute along only one axis, choose the icon for No Alignment in the Axis where you want no action.

▶ The Snap To Guides and Snap To Rulers settings have no effect on alignment and distribution moves made with Align Objects.

Getting the Ins and Outs of Alignment

In addition to the basics already noted, when performing alignment, keep these points in mind:

▶ Edge alignment aligns everything to the object that is farthest out in the alignment direction and that object does not move from its spot. Right alignment lines objects up on the object that is farthest to the right. Bottom alignment lines everything up on the object that's lowest on the page.

▶ When centering items, Object Alignment brings all the selected objects in towards the center to line up on the center-most object, which does not move.

Making the Most of the Distribution Options

Here are more details on the specific effects of the Distribution function:

▶ If you choose Distribute Within Bounds, PageMaker will spread the selected objects evenly between the outermost objects in the selection. The outermost objects will not move. This means Distribution Within Bounds has no effect if you have chosen just two objects.

▶ Notice that the Distribute options include an icon to put an equal amount of space *between* objects, in addition to the options for distribution based on common edges or centers. It's the one that shows facing object edges with a double-arrowed line.

▶ You can enter a negative number in the Distribute Fixed Amount Space box if you want objects to overlap.

TIP▶ Undoing an Alignment or Distribution

Before performing an alignment or distribution, click on the Do Mini-Save option in the Align Objects dialog box. This gives you the ability to undo your alignment or distribution move. PageMaker's regular Undo command has no affect, but the check box tells PageMaker to perform a mini-save before carrying out the command. (It's the same mini-save procedure the program does automatically when you go to a new page or print your publication.) That means you can do a mini-revert by pressing Shift while choosing Revert from the File menu.

Pasting for Placement

Several variations on the standard Copy and Paste commands can be used in PageMaker for special purposes such as page-to-page precision placement and creating multiple copies of an object.

Pasting Multiples

If you are distributing or aligning several copies of the same object, consider using the Multiple Paste command in the Edit menu instead of the Align Objects command. Copy the object, and then access the Multiple Paste dialog box in figure 14.29.

Fɪɢ. 14.29 ▶

The Multiple Paste
dialog box.

Tell PageMaker how many copies you need of the item you have stored on the Clipboard. Enter into the offset axis the horizontal or vertical spacing you need for your objects. If you want the copies vertically or horizontally aligned, enter a zero in the offset box for that axis. Figure 14.30 shows four objects located exactly the same distance apart, with their tops exactly aligned—a move performed with Multiple Paste. Depending on the exact circumstances of your project, this can be a lot faster than copying an object and then using the Align Objects command to do the distribution—a two-step procedure.

Negative numbers in the offset boxes paste copies to the left or up from the original object. Positive numbers paste the copies to the right or down from the original object.

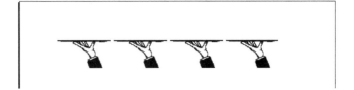

FIG. 14.30 ▷

Objects copied multiple times and aligned with the Multiple Paste command.

You may have a series of Multiple Paste moves to perform, all with the same offset and number of copy settings. If so, hold down the Shift key when choosing Multiple Paste. PageMaker will execute the command without showing you the dialog box and with the same settings you used the last time you used Multiple Paste.

Keep in mind the awful truth that Multiple Paste won't respond to the Undo command. Save right before making the move so you can revert back if the move doesn't work like you wanted it to.

TIP▷ Use Multiple Paste on Text

You can use Multiple Paste for type as well as objects. Copy to the Clipboard the text or inline graphics you want to duplicate and click a text insertion point where you want to insert the multiple duplicates; the Multiple Paste command will paste the number of copies you request at the insertion point. This could be great for repetitive text such as the lines on a form created by underlined tabs or paragraph rules. Just copy the entire paragraph, including the paragraph marker. The dialog box drops the offset boxes when you have text in the Clipboard, as opposed to graphic objects.

Power Paste Precision

Use the Power Paste trick to move objects between two pages, pasting them into the exact same location on the new page as they occupied on the old one.

Here's how it works. Do a normal Copy command and go to the page where you want to perform the Paste operation. Then use the Shift+Ctrl+P keyboard command instead of the regular Paste command. You can also hold down the Alt key and select Paste to do a Power Paste.

Many newer PageMaker users are so used to this between-page copying trick that they don't know that Power Paste is actually duplicating your last paste-and-move operation. When this command first appeared in PageMaker it was commonly used to paste objects repeatedly onto a page, each one with the same offset. In fact, this was PageMaker's forerunner of today's Multiple Paste command, and for a long time it was a key workaround for distribution operations, before we had Plug-ins or a command for that purpose. It works as it does between two pages because you Paste without moving the objects on the page.

To distribute objects using Power Paste, you first must Copy an object to the Clipboard. Next, Power Paste it once, and click and drag the pasted object to a new target location with the desired offset from the original spot. Now Power Paste once again, and a third object will be pasted in place at exactly the same offset from the last Paste location. Each time you Power Paste, you will put a new copy onto the page at that same offset. A new Copy operation will reset Power Paste.

Locking Graphics to Text as Inline Graphics

It's happened to you. The layout is finally complete with all the logos, scans, and drop shadow boxes carefully tuned to the text. But the phone rings and yes, you knew it. The client (or the boss, or the editor) wants to pull a couple of paragraphs out of the first few pages of the report (or brochure, or book, whatever you are working on). Naturally, all the text blocks are threaded, and when you delete the paragraphs, the whole mess of text slides up in the document, misaligning every single graphic.

If you place your graphics as inline graphics, you'll never worry about this again. As introduced in Chapter 11, "Placing Images," an inline graphic is placed or pasted into text with an insertion point blinking in your text. Therefore, the inline graphic becomes both a graphic and a special sort of "character" on the line of text.

There are several mechanical issues for precision placement of inline graphics. They are Autoleading, Align To Grid, and adjusting the baseline.

Keeping an Inline Graphic on the Leading Grid

Illustrations placed in the flow of text (such as screen shots for computer documentation or chart illustrations for a report) are perfect candidates for inline graphic placement. These kinds of documents are heavily edited and revised; the flexibility provided by inline graphics placement will save many long nights of redo labor. However, popping an inline graphic into the middle of text can be pretty disruptive to a page of aligned baselines (see "Tactics Recipe: Automating Your Layout Grid" in Chapter 13, "Designing a Master Page Grid").

The answer to this problem is to place the graphic in its own paragraph and turn on the Align To Grid function in the paragraph. Create a style for the purpose (I usually call mine "picture"). This will naturally force the following paragraph down to align with the leading grid.

Don't do this, however, if you have a caption paragraph right below the inline graphic paragraph, because it will push the caption down away from its picture. In that case, use the Align To Grid command on the caption style instead of applying it to your special inline graphic paragraph.

It's too bad that PageMaker 6.0 won't allow you to use grouped objects as inline graphics. It would be great to be able to group an illustration and its caption and use the two items together as an inline graphic.

Making Space for the Inline Graphic

Inline graphics will almost always be bigger than the leading for their text paragraphs. That means an inline graphic will slop over into the text paragraphs above and below it, as in figure 14.31.

FIG. 14.31 ▶

An inline graphic without benefit of Autoleading.

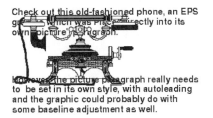

Check out this old-fashioned phone, an EPS graphic which was placed directly into its own picture paragraph.

However, the picture paragraph really needs to be set in its own style, with autoleading and the graphic could probably do with some baseline adjustment as well.

It may occur to you simply to assign sufficient fixed leading to an illustration that it would allow plenty of room and prevent what you see in the illustration. Problem is, inlines tend to vary in height, so it's tough to set up a style that will make consistent space above and below all the illustrations. Enough leading for one graphic might be too much or too little for another. This situation could result in brain damage when you are trying to automate the placement of several hundred pages that are subject to revision.

What's the solution? Ironically, even though you probably should use fixed leading in virtually every other layout situation, you want to use Autoleading. You need to set up a special style for your inline graphic style paragraphs that sets Autoleading (or apply Autoleading to each individual graphic if it is inserted in a paragraph along with some text). In either case—paragraph style or individual inline graphic item—use the Paragraph Spacing option, and set Autoleading at 100%. Add your paragraph Space Above and Space Below settings, using some exact multiple of the body copy amount in your leading grid. As you can see in figure 14.32, it works. By the way, the paragraph holding the graphic has also been centered, thus automatically centering the object with a high degree of precision between the two column edges.

Why does this work? Because PageMaker calculates the "Autoleading" of a paragraph based on the height of the tallest character in a line. In this case, the inline graphic acts like a "character."

FIG. 14.32 ▶

Autoleading makes space for an inline graphic.

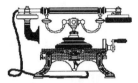

Check out this old-fashioned phone, an EPS graphic which was Placeddirectly into its own "picture" paragraph.

However, the picture paragraph really needs to be set in its own style, with autoleading and the graphic could probably do with some baseline adjustment as well.

If you use this Autoleading trick, you can use the Align To Grid command to keep your inline graphic on the leading grid without pushing the caption down too far.

Controlling an Inline Graphic's Text Slop

Sometimes you may want an inline graphic to slop into text. For example, slop can be a great tool for locking a screen or a text box in place behind a pull quote.

The trick is to control the slop by adjusting the baseline of the graphic, in effect turning it into a superscript or subscript character.

Mostly you'll want to do this by eye, as shown in figure 14.33. Using the Pointer tool, select the inline as a graphic, and drag it up or down against the baseline until it lines up where you want it. You'll get a double-arrow "elevator" pointer.

FIG. 14.33 ▶

Manually adjusting the baseline of an inline graphic.

Baseline "elevator" pointer

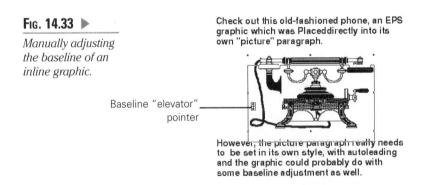

Check out this old-fashioned phone, an EPS graphic which was Placeddirectly into its own "picture" paragraph.

However, the picture paragraph really needs to be set in its own style, with autoleading and the graphic could probably do with some baseline adjustment as well.

Alternatively, select the inline as a graphic, and use the Control palette. Using the nudge buttons or the direct-entry boxes for the baseline adjustment option, you can precisely locate the inline graphic's baseline and do it the same way every time for as many inline graphics as you like.

Sometimes inline graphics are repetitive elements, such as EPS graphics used as headline visuals or companion column icons. When you have one of the elements set up just right, you can copy and paste it into all your other locations. The baseline adjustment survives the Copy and Paste operation just fine. In fact, in the next chapter, there's in-depth detail on setting up these kinds of companion column inline graphics.

Locking Graphics to the Page

PageMaker 6.0 has a new Lock Position command. It's simple to apply. Simply select an object and apply the Lock Position command in the Arrange menu, or use the Ctrl+L keyboard shortcut. To Unlock, use the menu command. There's no keyboard shortcut.

You can tell when an object has been locked because it will have gray handles. And in the Control palette many of the action items will be grayed out if you have selected a locked object.

Here are the specific effects of the Lock Position command:

▶ It nails an object to a particular spot on a page. It does not lock one object to another, or lock an object to a particular spot in some text. It is, literally, a lock position command.

▶ Even though an item has been locked, you can change it quite a bit, so long as you don't try to change its position on the page. You can change its color or fill but not its angle if it has been rotated or skewed, and you can't change its position or its size.

▶ Locking an inline graphic does not lock it to the page. It locks the items that affect the position of the graphic within the text block—size, baseline shift, and rotation for example.

▶ A locked text block can still be edited and even though you can't raise and lower its windowshade with the Pointer tool you can watch the windowshade go up and down if you delete or add text.

▶ You can lock an object on a master page.

▶ You can put a Text Wrap around a locked object.

▶ You can select multiple items and apply the Lock Position command to all of them at once, but that will not Group them.

Masking

You can use any PageMaker-drawn shape—oval, rectangle, or polygon—to mask any other object. The masked object could be a PageMaker text block or another drawn object, or an imported graphic. Have a look at figure 14.34 to see basic mask operation where a PageMaker circle has been used to frame an imported graphic. In fact, it helps to understand masking if you think of it as a variation on the Cropping tool.

Fig. 14.34 ▶

Making a circle mask.

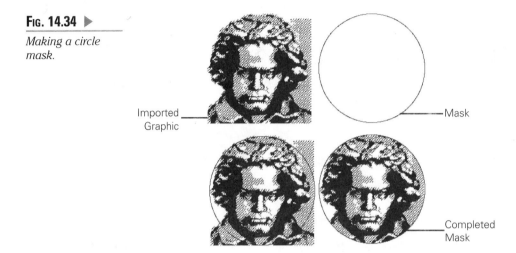

Imported Graphic

Mask

Completed Mask

In figure 14.35, you can check out some other effects of the Masking command.

In the top pair of figures, three objects have been combined in a mask. When you combine more than one PageMaker-drawn object, one of them will dominate the masking operation. The "winner" of the masking contest will always be the one closest to the top of the stacking order. In this case, the square is closest to the top of the stack so you get a square frame around the combination of the imported graphic and the circle.

In the middle of figure 14.35, the objects being masked have been slid around just as you would use the grabber hand to move an item that has been cropped. It's quite possible to lose an object by accidentally making it invisible—dragging it completely out of its mask area. Only the part inside the masking object will be visible, and if you take it completely outside the masking object, you won't be able to see it.

At the bottom of figure 14.35, you can see what happens when a masking object has a fill. Masking objects, put at the rear of a mask, show through any transparent areas of the object being masked.

Fig. 14.35 ▷

*Variations on a
masking theme.*

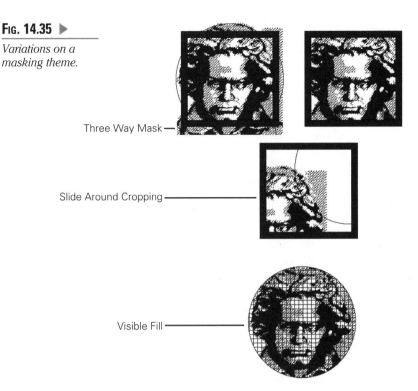

Three Way Mask —

Slide Around Cropping ————

Visible Fill ————————

It will be a rare mask operation where you do not want to also group the objects together. Hold down the Shift key before pulling down the Element menu, then select Mask so you can do both simultaneously. You can also simultaneously Unmask and Ungroup by using the Shift key modifier when pulling down the Element menu. Unfortunately, you can't combine the Shift key trick with the Mask keyboard shortcut of Ctrl+6.

Where to Go from Here

▷ If the inline graphics stuff got your heart beating pitter-patter, you'll love the next chapter, "Creating Special Effects."

▷ Also in Chapter 15, there's lots on how to put alignment, distribution, grouping, locking, and masking to work.

▷ Some of the techniques in this chapter do require background. There's tons of stuff that will be helpful in Chapters 12 and 13, "Setting Up a New Publication" and "Designing a Master Page Grid," and in Chapter 10, "Drawing with PageMaker."

Chapter 15

Creating Special Effects

This chapter on creating special effects covers these special techniques:

Hanging graphic objects, punctuation, and headlines outside the main body text.

▼

Formatting and embellishing headlines of all sorts (including kickers and decks) by using graphics and rules.

▼

Setting type for special needs such as fractions, and initial capitals—including dropped, raised, and hanging caps.

▼

Wrapping text around graphic objects and using PageMaker's text wrap feature to shape blocks of text.

▼

Molding type and turning letters into art.

▼

Working with boxes, backgrounds, and screens, and using Group and Mask to frame art and text material.

THE SPECIAL EFFECTS in this chapter use standard PageMaker facilities to create the finishing touches for your pages. In that respect, many of the concepts in this chapter aren't really special at all. That's the point—to show how you can combine PageMaker commands into visually exciting layouts that set off the information you are trying to convey in a more effective way. So, use the concepts in this chapter as starting points for your own exploration.

We'll start with techniques for manipulating text on the page and work our way into graphics tools, including the new grouping and masking commands. ▶ ▶ ▶

All the moves you'll see depend on your ability to use some plain old, basic PageMaker tools and techniques. If you aren't up on any of them, refer to the "Where to Go from Here" section at the end of this chapter for a cross-reference list of background chapters.

Hanging Type and Graphics

Hanging, in this case, has nothing to do with capital punishment. It has everything to do with positioning type and graphics to the left of your main column of text. For example, you may want a headline to run in a companion column or a Zapf Dingbat bullet to stick out to the left of a paragraph. Companion colums are discussed later in this chapter in "Companion Column Graphics," but the bullet point style hanging indent will be focused on first.

Hanging Multidigit Numbers

Your basic hanging indent uses one left tab to set the first line of the paragraph at the bottom split indent marker. That's fine as long as you are simply using bullets or single-digit numbering. However, if you must keep multidigit numbers lined up, you need to add a decimal tab to your arrangement. Figure 15.1 shows how a decimal tab works and how to arrange the Indents and Tabs ruler.

FIG. 15.1 ▶

Aligning multidigit numbers by adding a decimal tab in your hanging indent.

Decimal tab

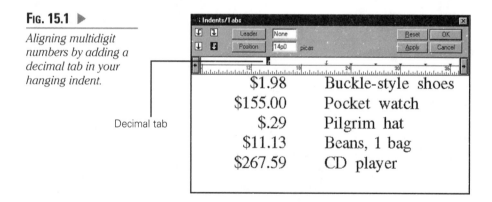

Companion Column Graphics

You don't need to limit yourself to Zapf Dingbats and numbers when you do a hanging indent. Hang a graphic out to the left of your main body of text by inserting it as an inline graphic in an artificial companion column. The column is "artificial" because no PageMaker column guides have been set for the space to the left of main body text. Instead, the column effect is achieved with a very wide hanging indent. Figure 15.2 shows the effect.

IV

Creating Page Layouts

Fig. 15.2 ▶

Hanging an inline graphic in an artificial companion column.

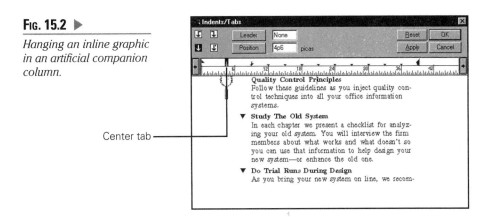

Center tab ──

You can use this narrow companion column space to give visual cues to the reader scanning through a book or a newsletter. In this instance, a graphic icon indicates the location of a helpful checklist. This effect of hanging an inline graphic works beautifully for technical documentation where the publication gets updated and edited frequently because you don't need to worry about re-adjusting all your companion column graphics when the copy shifts. Inserting the graphic inline means it is locked in position relative to the text.

After you create your main column (probably equal to the margin guides), set up a hanging indent arrangement as wide as your companion column space by using a split indent marker. Then set two tabs. The usual left tab goes at the location of the bottom split indent marker to bring the first line of text into alignment with the rest of the body copy. The second tab, a center tab, goes out in the mathematical center of the companion column space.

You usually need to adjust the baseline of the inline graphic so it will be vertically aligned with its associated paragraph of text. After you select the graphic with the Pointer tool, you can make that baseline adjustment by dragging the graphic up or down until it looks right (Baseline-Offset), or you can select the graphic as text with the Text tool and use the Control palette nudge buttons or text-entry box to set a baseline adjustment (Baseline-Shift), just like you normally do with text. Keep in mind that you must select something in addition to the inline graphic (a space or a tab, for example) in order to be able to set Baseline-Shift.

TIP ▶ Use the Find Command to Automate Inline Graphic Baseline Adjustments

Performing this baseline adjustment repeatedly for an entire lengthy document could bog you down pretty badly. You want to automate a process like this to make it less tedious and to ensure that the effect is consistent every time it shows up in your document. Try using a search and replace technique. First, code all your inline graphic locations with a unique combination of characters. Then, select the graphic with the Text tool and copy it, with its baseline properly adjusted, to the Clipboard. Finally, use the Find Again command repeatedly to find each coded location and insert your graphic from the Clipboard. It will come in with baseline adjustment intact.

For this trick to work completely, you must select the inline with the Text tool. If you select the inline graphic with the Pointer tool before you copy to the Clipboard, you will lose the Baseline-Shift adjustment for the copied inline graphic, and it will paste back into text with Autoleading, although the Baseline-Offset will be preserved. If you copy the inline as Text, highlighting it with the Text tool, both kinds of baseline adjustment will be retained. (As I've just indicated, there are two kinds of baseline adjustment for inline graphics. There's Baseline-Shift, the same kind you use on text. And there's Baseline-Offset, the kind only available for inline graphics, where you use the Pointer tool to drag an inline up or down against its baseline.)

Hanging Punctuation

For high-visibility type, such as display headlines in advertisements, your typesetting will look more professional if you hang punctuation outside the main edges of your text. Leaving punctuation to fall into its normal position makes your headline look odd, as if justified or forced-left type hasn't come all the way over to the column edge.

Figure 15.3 gives a before and after example for hanging quotation marks. In this example, kerning has been used to thrust the opening quote out to the left of the main text.

Fɪɢ. 15.3 ▶

Using an invisible space and kerning to hang punctuation.

"Aardvarks, in an air and sea assault, this afternoon began an invasion of the Arctic," usually chilly informed sources report from our listening post in the North.

Kerning——**"Aardvarks, in an air and sea assault, this afternoon began an invasion of the Arctic," usually chilly informed sources report from our listening post in the North.**

To create this effect, you can't simply kern outside the margin guides in PageMaker. The program won't allow it unless you give it somethign to kern against.

Type an em space in front of the quote (Ctrl+Shift+H). This em space provides an invisible character for you to kern against. Kerning then must be used to reduce the space between two characters. To achieve a hanging punctuation effect like the opening quotes in figure 15.3, click an insertion point between the em space and the quotation mark. Use Ctrl+Shift+– (keypad minus) to kern the quotes out to the left of the indent (the artificial margin), up to a limit of one em (the width of the inserted invisible character).

You can kern closing quotes (like those on the second line of the example in fig. 15.3). Type an em space after the closing quote. Then press the left arrow key once to get between the quote mark and the space, and then kern by pressing Ctrl+Shift+– (keypad minus) to trim down the space between the quote and the em space until finally the quote hangs outside the main text. In addition, the illustration shows some kerning for the space between the comma and the close quote to tighten them up a bit.

This example of hung punctuation has been exaggerated a bit to illustrate the concept. When hung punctuation is performed well by an expert typographer with an excellent eye, the effect is more subtle. Usually the punctuation hangs partly out beyond the edge of the type measure, not all the way. Aim for an optically pleasing look, nothing too extreme that calls attention to itself. That would be just as bad or worse than not bothering to hang the punctuation.

Simultaneous Forced Left and Forced Right

Sometimes you may need to achieve split justification or simultaneous forced left and forced right alignment of type. Old-time typesetting machine operators sometimes call this *insert* or *distribute space*. PageMaker doesn't have a specific feature for this kind of situation, but you can achieve a similar effect with a little bit of extra work. It involves a curious property of tabs and their interaction with margins and text alignment. Basically, this whole trick depends on the fact that the last tab in a paragraph assumes that paragraph's alignment.

Figure 15.4 shows a pretty common situation that involves a page footer with a publication title and a page number.

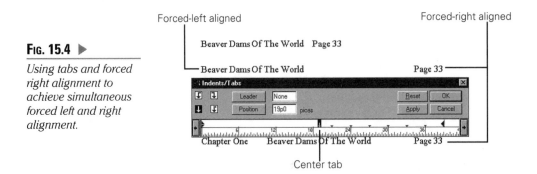

FIG. 15.4 ▶

Using tabs and forced right alignment to achieve simultaneous forced left and right alignment.

The illustration shows three versions of the same footer in the various stages of constructing the effect.

In the top version, the paragraph is aligned forced left, and the tab between the two items merely pushes the page number text over to the right a bit.

In the middle version, the paragraph has forced right alignment, and magically, the presence of the tab shoves the page number all the way over to the right margin (as if it had a right tab set on the right margin). No tab stop is set.

In the bottom version—below the Indents/Tabs dialog box—a center tab is set in the middle of the line, and the page number still thrusts over to the right margin. The center tab, however, keeps its text centered in the page footer margin.

Casting Headlines

Headlines introduce, organize, highlight, and visually frame your communication. You always hope your headlines have impact—that they jump off the page with enough visual interest to motivate the reader to read more. To that end, check out the following headline special effects.

Cross-Column Headlines

You can visually frame your text and add punch to your page if you spread a headline across several columns of text. You can accomplish this procedure in two basic ways, and which one you use depends on personal working style. You will also want to take into account the chances that your page layout will be edited or revised after you construct the multicolumn spread.

Figure 15.5 shows the first method. This method consists of composing two text blocks, one for the headline and the other for the text, and positioning them as you see fit on the page. The headline and body copy text blocks are not threaded together.

Fig. 15.5 ▶

Creating a cross-column headline.

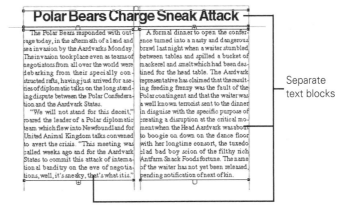

Separate
text blocks

The second method ends up looking exactly the same on the page, but it threads together your headline and text material so that they are all together in the Story Editor for easy editing access.

To use this method, you initially place your text across the two (or three, or whatever) text columns, as you see in figure 15.5. Everything will be in one wide column, headline and body copy. Now raise the bottom windowshade until just the headline shows. Pull down a guideline to match the windowshade bottom of the cross-column headline. Load your text icon by clicking the arrow windowshade tab of the headline text block and finish by placing the remaining body text into your narrower story columns.

TIP ▶ Column and Page Break Features Hold Threaded Headlines to Their Own Block

Use Paragraph Specifications to assign the Column Break Before attribute to the first paragraph in the story text. This trick locks the first paragraph into its own text block; then you don't need to worry about all your story text threading up into the cross-column headline text block if your story is edited, changing the story length above the headline block.

The same Column or Page break concept applies to the headline if you have threaded together your headline blocks with other headlines or body copy. Assign the Page Break Before or Column Break Before attributes to the headline. That locks the head at the top of a page or column.

DESIGN NOTE
Type for Headlines, Kickers, and Decks

All these terms—headlines, kickers, and decks—are left over from the days when some hard-boiled crime reporter would grab a candlestick phone and yell, "Get me rewrite!"

A headline is still, well, a headline. A *kicker* runs above a headline, providing a tantalizing tidbit from the story. Kickers are sometimes called *teasers*. A *deck* (sometimes called a *subdeck*) follows and augments the main headline.

For these three types of heads, you want to select type that clearly demonstrates your priorities to the reader. Compared to body text, all headline material is heavier and is often quite different in shape. The main head is biggest and heaviest. The kicker and deck come down a notch from the main head.

Figure 15.6 shows one common approach to selecting type for heads and body copy—sans serif for heads and serif for body copy. In this case, Optima Bold is used for the heads, and Palatino is used for the text. This design approach buys into the contemporary wisdom that serif fonts should be used for body copy because they are considered to be more readable in smaller point sizes. The serifs give the eye the clues it needs to sort out the letters.

FIG. 15.6 ▶

Using decks and kickers.

Kicker———

Deck———

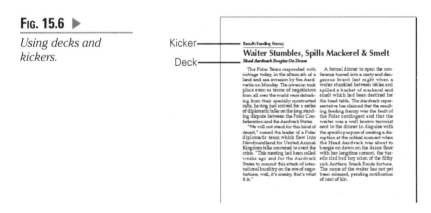

Cut-In Headlines

Figure 15.7 illustrates *cut-in heads*, also called *run-in heads*. They usually lead off a paragraph with bold type, although it can be any kind of type you choose. The techniques that follow are the same no matter what text formatting you apply.

Fig. 15.7 ▶

Example of cut-in headlines.

Cut-in headline ──────

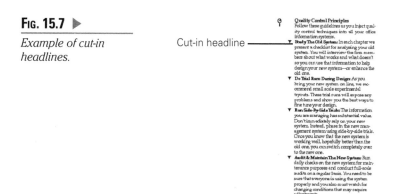

Cut-in heads, like these, would be much easier if PageMaker offered character-level styles. Unfortunately, PageMaker stops short and permits only paragraph-level styles. Alternatively, if you are an avid devotee of tedium, you could format cut-ins by going through your entire publication and manually formatting the first several words of each paragraph with bold (or italic, or whatever) wherever you want the cut-in headline effect. That's if you like tedium.

In the absence of character styles and in an attempt to eliminate tedium from your life, I offer two approaches to building cut-in heads. Both methods use the Change command in the Story Editor:

▶ Choose the indirect method (losing style coding) if you want to retain maximum existing formatting but are willing to lose all paragraph style assignments.

▶ Choose the direct method (retaining style coding) if you want to retain a paragraph style assignment in case of future formatting adjustments, but are willing to make some adjustments to compensate for some lost local formatting (such as hanging indents).

The starting point for both techniques is a setup where you have separate headline paragraphs. You then use the Change command to meld—to run in—the headlines into the paragraphs that follow them.

Indirect Cut-In Head Method (Losing Style Coding)

For the indirect cut-in head technique, you use a multistep search and replace system, working with a token you have embedded in the text to mark the points where the headline paragraphs should be joined to their body text.

Your cut-in heads must be in separate paragraphs and have their own style. Call it something like **CutInTemp**. Be certain that you style the cut-in head text exactly the way you want it, including type and paragraph attributes. This process converts the style attributes into local formatting so you won't be able to easily make changes after you put this cut-in head trick into motion. Use Find and Change on all occurrences of the CutInTemp style and replace the paragraph markers in those paragraphs with your token:

1. In the Find What box, type **^p**, PageMaker's carriage return metacharacter symbol that marks the end of a paragraph.

2. Set the Para attribute to seek out the CutInTemp style (or whatever style you assigned to the paragraphs with the cut-in head text in them).

3. In the Change To box, type **^p** again plus some unique set of characters— your token tag. Try something like **]*[**. This tag must be unique in your document and must not be duplicated anywhere else.

4. Set the Change To box to No style. Do the Find and Change operation, and the result is something like figure 15.8.

Fig. 15.8 ▶

Intermediate step in creating cut-in head- lines.

Search and replace tokens

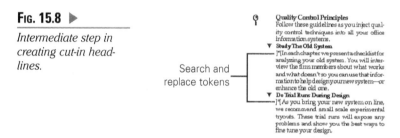

5. Alt+click on the Type and Para attribute buttons to clean out all the at- tribute information. Now enter **^p]*[** in the Find What box and type a space in the Change To box.

6. Run the Change again. This removes the token and pulls the two kinds of paragraphs together into one, with a space separating them.

Take note that these paragraphs have lost their paragraph style assignments. They are officially No style although they retained their formatting.

Direct Cut-In Head Method (Retaining Style Coding)

This faster technique requires two search and replace passes through the text, but you don't need to bother with the token tag method. Also, the CutInTemp paragraphs take on the paragraph style of the paragraphs that follow them. Be- cause some paragraph style information remains intact, this method gives you the most flexibility for making further changes.

Here's how to do it:

1. Type **^p** in both the Find What and Change To boxes. Use the Para attribute button and find the CutInTemp style attribute and change to No Style. (This step will convert the soon-to-be cut-in head paragraph to local formatting, such as bold or italic or whatever you've chosen for the CutInTemp style.) Run this first search and replace pass on the text.

2. For your second search and replace pass, type **^p** in the Find What box and type some punctuation and space (such as a colon or an em dash plus a space). Click on the Para attribute button and find No Style and change to the paragraph style of your body paragraph. In this example, the style might be CutInBody. Run the search and replace pass.

The result will look about the same as the one you get with the indirect method. However, the paragraphs have been assigned the CutInBody style and the cut-in heads are formatted with local formatting. They also lose their hanging indents. No problem—just tweak the CutInBody style to include a hanging indent.

TIP ▶ Weird Colors for Pseudo Character Styles

Despite the absence of character styles in PageMaker, there is one way that you can get some of that functionality by way of the enhanced Find/Change command in Version 6.0.

Take this cut-in head special effect example. You can now search and replace in the Change command for colored type. Go through your document and format each cut-in head location with an odd color, one you wouldn't otherwise use anywhere in the document. Now search and replace the color, adding to the color any special text formatting you may wish. Ultimately, before shipping your publication to the service bureau for imaging, you'll want to replace all the weird color pseudo character style formatting with black. (Or, instead of a weird color, just give the text a color of 100 percent tint of its "real" color, which in most cases will be black.) You can use the Change command to do that as well. However, during the construction of your document you'll have the ability to make global changes in the cut-in head "character style" locations identified by the weird color. You can even name the color "cut-in head" or some other name that identifies the purpose of the formatting.

Dave Saunders, one of the participants in the Learning from the Pros section at the end of this book, was the first person I know of to spot this neat trick, in a conversation on the CompuServe Adobe Applications Forum.

Companion Column Headlines

Hanging heads in a companion column out to the side of the main body copy has always been a pain in PageMaker. The program doesn't offer a side-by-side paragraph attribute. You also don't have a join or locking capability, which would allow you to put headline text in its own text block but permanently associate the headline block with its body copy. If PageMaker did have these features, companion column heads would be a heck of a lot easier to create.

With a little effort, however, you can create companion column headlines in PageMaker. The following sections explain how.

Tedious Multiple Text Block Method

The most straightforward and best known way to create companion column heads is to create many tiny stories, one for each individual headline, and place each headline carefully in position on the page in the companion column area out to the side of your body copy. However, this method has severe disadvantages. If the length of the text changes even by a single line anywhere above the headline point in the document, all the body copy text slides up or down and the companion heads are thrown out of alignment. Also, when placing the headline text, it takes a lot of extra work to line up all the heads consistently with their body copy, a big problem if you are putting together many pages of a report or book.

If you want to use this traditional method of multiple text blocks, you could use some techniques to make it easier on yourself:

▶ Use a technique similar to the cross-column headline technique. Instead of creating all those individual companion column headline stories, place the text as one story and break it into text blocks, placing each headline in its own block as you work your way through the publication.

▶ A good leading grid plan helps as you line up the heads, perhaps also using Snap to Rulers.

▶ Use the Column and Page Break tip from the cross-column headlines technique section to help keep the headlines from sliding into the body copy.

This technique has one advantage: you can edit your text easily in Story Editor, because all your text, including headlines, is strung together in one story. It's also easier to create a single story that includes the heads during the writing stages of creating the publication. However, the multiple text block method works well only if you can be absolutely positive that you won't need to edit text after you carefully position a couple hundred companion heads in your book. And if you believe that, I've got these penny stocks left over from the Wyoming oil boom in the Sixties.

Extended Hanging Indent Method

Here's another method that works best if you can be absolutely certain about the condition of your text. In this case, it works well if you can be utterly positive that all your heads will be only one line (a few words) long.

Try treating the companion heads as if they were extended bullets. Mimic the approach described a few pages back for hanging multidigit numbers by setting up a special hanging indent paragraph style.

Instead of making the first tab a decimal tab, make it a right tab, so the heads hang out to the left of the body copy as they do in figure 15.9. Technically, there's only one PageMaker column being created, not two; but the spacing between the first and second tab determines your *alley*, the traditional term for the space between two columns.

It is possible, although not recommended, to use this technique even though you have multiline companion heads. Use a new line character (Shift+Enter) at the end of the first body paragraph line and tab over to start the second line of the companion head. This has the disadvantage of looking unelegant because it creates large gaps above the body paragraphs in the main text column.

FIG. 15.9 ▶

Using a hanging indent to create short companion column heads.

Multiple Sources	Get prices from more than one supplier. Even if you don't instigate a bidding process, talking to more than one vendor will help you get educated about all the details you need to be considering.
Compare Apples & Apples	As soon as you can, lock the specifications for your purchase. That way each vendor is bidding on the same thing and you can easily compare their efforts. If there is a need for some variability, consider having the bids worked up with options that can easily be added or subtracted.
Speak With References	Don't make the mistake of ignoring the vendor's references. You may be surprised at the insight you'll get by asking the question, "If you were buying from this person again, what advice would you give me to make the project go even better than it did for you."
Check Word Of Mouth	Ask around the office and at the courthouse about experiences of others. Who would they recommend? Have they had experience with the vendors you are considering?
Demonstration & Tryout	You wouldn't buy a car without taking it for a test drive. And you shouldn't buy office equipment without a demonstration and tryout either.

Text as a Hanging Inline Graphic

Another way to create companion heads is to convert their text into graphics. Then lock each headline graphic into place as an inline graphic using the mutlitab hanging indent technique covered at the beginning of this chapter, as shown in figure 15.10.

Text converted into a graphic and placed in a double-tabbed hanging indent.

Rules to aid baseline realignment

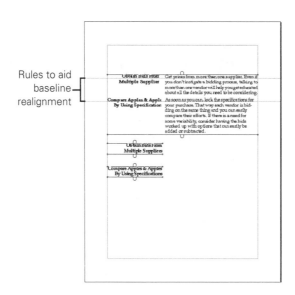

The best way to convert your headline text into graphics is through a PostScript drawing program like FreeHand or Illustrator. You have two different drawing program tactics you can use:

▶ Simply type the head directly into the drawing program, export it as an EPS, and place it as an inline graphic in the text.

▶ From inside PageMaker, copy the headline and paste it into the drawing program. From there you can export as an EPS and place the head as an inline graphic back into PageMaker.

With both of these techniques, you have the advantage of being able to use the Edit Original command to get your drawing program to edit your companion heads. You can also keep a copy of the original PageMaker text on the Pasteboard so you can get back to it if you need to.

Use normal inline graphic techniques to make any needed leading or baseline adjustments to your headline text graphic so that it lines up with the first line of your body copy.

Stacked Opposing Indents with a Headline Rule

A less complicated method of creating companion heads is to simply type them in your publication and accept that they will ride a line or two above your body text. You can do that by creating two opposing indent styles, one for your companion heads and one for your body copy. The companion heads that result from this method always rest above their body copy, as shown in figure 15.11.

The companion head has an extreme right indent, and the body copy has a matching left indent. For example, suppose you have a 36-pica-wide live area on the page and you want a 12-pica companion column with a 2-pica alley between the body and the companion head. You would set the headline paragraph style to have a right indent of 24 picas, leaving the headline column a 12-pica horizontal space. Then set the body copy to have a left indent of 14 picas (2 picas more than the width of the companion column) so that the body copy gets 22 picas plus a 2-pica alley. No tabs are needed.

Fig. 15.11 ▶

Stacked opposing indent companion headline and body copy.

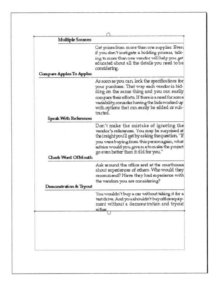

As with the example for the extended bullet technique, the heads are right-aligned. The difference is that you don't use a right tab this time. Because the head resides in its own paragraph, you can define the paragraph style to be forced right.

Style the text as you want. In this example, a bottom paragraph rule on the head visually ties together the companion head and its body text. The section on decorating headlines talks about asymmetrical headline rules.

Remember to set the paragraph style to Keep With a couple of lines (in Paragraph Specifications) so that your heads don't get separated from their body paragraphs at page breaks.

Baseline Adjustment for Aligned Companion Heads

Now that PageMaker 6.0 engineers have pretty much worked out the screen re-draw problem that has plagued the program from its early days, this may be the best technique of all for setting companion heads.

If you'd like to align your companion heads with their body text paragraph, you may use the stacked opposing indents companion head technique, combining it with a major baseline adjustment to the headline text. You set this up by creating a special style definition for the companion head, adjusting the baseline to a negative number that drops the companion head paragraph way below its normal point, aligning it with its following body copy paragraph (see fig. 15.12).

To get the right amount of baseline shift, select the entire companion head paragraph and experiment with the baseline adjustment box of the Control palette until you have the headline position adjusted just right. (The baseline adjustment should be roughly the same amount as your companion head leading.) Then assign that adjustment number to your style for single-line subscripted companion heads by using the Options dialog box from within the Edit Styles dialog box.

The illustration shows how the slug for the headline paragraph remains above the body paragraph. The text slides down, but the carriage return doesn't. This headline technique has the major advantage of keeping all your text together in an editable form. However, for convenient editing, use the Story Editor; otherwise, you'll have a lot of trouble selecting the text.

FIG. 15.12 ▶

A subscript aligned companion head.

Baseline adjustment ⎯⎯⎯⎯⎯⎯⎯⎯⎯

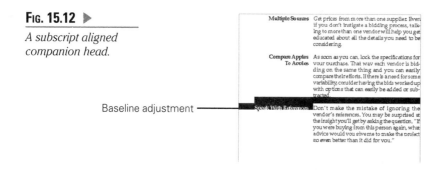

Trigger a Redraw When Text Disappears

If your text disappears or breaks into fragments on the screen, you are having a screen redraw problem. This difficulty still arises even though PageMaker has fixed the redraw problem for the most part. Just force a redraw so you can see your text properly again. Use the forced redraw command, Crtrl+Shift+F12, or press Crtrl+J twice (toggling guides view). The screen redraw difficulty comes from the fact that PageMaker redraws the screen one slug at a time.

You must work out some other more knotty problems if you decide to use this subscript companion head technique.

For one thing, if a head falls at the top of a column, the full size of the companion head paragraph slug pushes the body paragraph well below the top of the column.

Normally, you wouldn't need to worry about this because PageMaker automatically makes special adjustments for top-of-column paragraphs, but in this case the companion head's baseline adjustment merely drops the text down and the carriage return stays above the body paragraph retaining all its leading strength.

To solve this problem, you need to build a special style to apply to any companion head that falls at the top of a column. Set the companion heads in a special top of column style (try a style name of "CompHd Top") with 1/10 of a point leading and make sure you only have one line heads at the top of a column. (PageMaker permits zero leading, but that makes the type completely disappear on-screen. One-tenth of a point is the smallest leading you can set and still see what you are doing.)

If you build multiline heads, you will have inconsistent spacing between your companion heads and the body paragraph above them. Some will have double the space and some will have triple the space. That means you need to build special styles to accomodate these multiline heads.

The solution is similar to the one for top of columns. Build two styles for two-line companion heads and set the heads in two separate paragraphs. The first line of the head (say, "CompHd 1/2") has 1/10 of a point leading, and the second one (maybe "CompHd 2/2") has regular leading. Adjust the baselines so they are spaced properly, and you'll have the problem licked.

Figure 15.13 shows the final result—companion heads locked into place with their associated body paragraphs with even spacing all around.

FIG. 15.13 ▶

Styles for top of column and multiline heads solve the spacing problems.

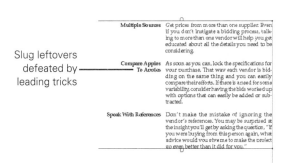

Slug leftovers defeated by leading tricks

The multiline head solution only works for two-line heads. It doesn't work for three-line heads, because at least two lines superimpose themselves due to the thin leading. The only answer is to avoid triple-line heads. Either rewrite the head or expand the width of your companion column if the three-line head temptation keeps coming up. In any case, heads are supposed to set up a story, not tell it, so you may want to limit yourself to two-line heads anyway.

One last note: you could drive yourself right around the bend using this deep baseline adjustment companion head trick in a publication where you have the Align to Grid and Snap to Rulers options activated. It's not impossible at all and it's a great technique—well worth the effort—so don't get the wrong idea. The point is you don't want to do it very often. If you decide to simultaneously use the baseline alignment and companion head techniques, experiment until you've got the two of them working well together and then write down all the settings and save the document as a template. Believe me, you won't ever want to do it from scratch again.

Decorating Headlines

By using paragraph rules and inline graphics, you can create some pretty flashy headlines and automate the process to boot. The following sections provide some examples and give specific directions for each technique.

Paragraph Rules

Stretch the edges of PageMaker's headline potential by combining rules and the custom line feature. Figure 15.14 shows two versions of the same headline technique, superimposing a wide and narrow rule and taking advantage of the fact that type always overprints rules in PageMaker. Remember that concept. Paragraph rules are always on the back layer.

You can put this kind of headline format into a style. Then you can apply this flashy effect to headlines all day with a quick click of the mouse.

Both headlines have been set as centered paragraphs. You can see, of course, the 4-point lines that stick out at the sides. What's not obvious is the fact that the 4-point line in both cases is not two lines. It's one line that runs right across the center of the head from edge to edge of the column.

There's actually a second 36-point custom rule set to just barely cover the width of the text, and it also hides the middle portion of the 4-point rule. Because rules go to the rear layers, the text rides over both rules so that it can be seen.

FIG. 15.14 ▶

Superimposing wide and narrow rules.

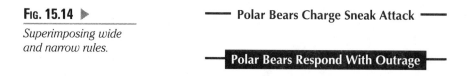

The 4-point line is set above the baseline by using the Paragraph Rule Options dialog box to adjust spacing until it is centered vertically on the height of the type.

The 36-point custom line is set to Text width and a minus indent, so the line actually sticks out 1 pica on either side of the text. It too has been centered vertically on the type.

The top example has the wide custom rule set to the color of the paper so that the wide rule knocks out the thin rule and gives the effect of two lines drawn on either side of the headline.

The bottom example has the type set to the color of the paper and the rule set to black so the type reverses against the wide rule.

Figure 15.15 shows the kind of headline rules often used for pull quotes.

Fig. 15.15 ▷

A pull quote type headline rule setup.

"We will not stand for this kind of deceit. It's sneaky, that's what it is."

This pull quote consists of three paragraphs—the pull quote body paragraph, the upper ruled paragraph, and the lower ruled paragraph. The upper ruled paragraph contains no text but has been set with an 8-point rule against a 2-point rule, with baselines adjusted so that the thicker line rides on the top edge of the thinner one. The bottom superimposed rule paragraph is simply the reverse of the top one. Both ruled paragraphs have indents set with the thick line getting a bigger indent than the thinner one.

Figure 15.16 shows how you can set asymmetrical headline rules.

Fig. 15.16 ▷

Asymmetrical headline rules and opposing indent heads.

Polar Bear

The largest carnivore on land, they are denizens of the arctic regions. Penguins, living at the South Pole, are utterly safe from polar bears as a rule. However, the ringed seals, bearded seals, harp seals and hooded seals are an entirely different story. Lately polar bears have also been a mite ticked off at the aardvarks.

Aardvark

One of the primitive ungulates. Often thought of as an ant-eater, but really a nocturnal mammal that much prefers clawing into a nice juicy termite mound. After a frenzy of digging, the aardvark inserts its long mouth and nose and uses its sticky tongue to dine on the scrambling bugs.

In the top headline, the single paragraph rule has been set on the headline paragraph. Even though it extends way out to the right of the headline, the rule is actually set for width of text. The secret of achieving this asymmetrical effect is the rule indent setting.

There are several combinations of settings that could accomplish this effect, but in this case, here's how it's done. Define a style setting the paragraph rule for width of text, not width of column. The rule will then ride all the way to the outer edge of the left-aligned headline. Then set the right end of the rule for a minus amount of indent. This makes the rule stick out beyond the edge of the headline text by a fixed amount, 4 inches in this instance.

You need to give enough negative indent to take the right end of the line all the way over to the right side of the column. You can do this fixed indent setup because each of the heads occupies a fixed width in the single column of text. That's why you can safely thrust the long side of the rule out by a fixed amount rather than use the width of column setting.

The bottom example in figure 15.16 is a twist on this asymmetrical headline rule technique, except there are two rules. This example uses a thick custom rule below the headline paragraph set to width of column but with enough indent on the right to bring it in out of the way of the headline text. The 1 point rule above is set width of text with a negative indent to thrust it out to the left to meet the thick rule.

Inline Graphics

You can plant about any picture or effect you want in a headline as an inline graphic. Try using scans of weird materials and cropping them to work as a background for the headline, as the final section of this chapter describes. Think about setting off chapter breaks with a simple graphic you sketch out yourself in a drawing program, as shown in figure 15.17.

Fig. 15.17 ▶

A simple inline graphic enhancement to a headline.

Place the inline graphic into its own paragraph above the headline, and adjust the baseline of the graphic so that it slides down under the headline text as a backdrop. You might use such a technique for every chapter break in a book.

TIP ▶ **Replicate Inline Headline Embellishments with Find Again and Clipboard**

Unfortunately, you can't set the baseline adjustment for the inline graphic headline decoration in a style. You must select the graphic as a graphic, as opposed to text, and PageMaker doesn't support graphic styles. Fortunately, however, the baseline adjustment will survive a trip through the Clipboard.

So, if you want to replicate your headline graphic setup many times in a publication, get one arranged just right. Select the entire paragraph containing the inline graphic and copy it to the Clipboard. Then search out all the special inline graphic paragraphs, using the Find command for the first one, followed by a series of Find Again search commands throughout your publication. As you find each graphic paragraph, switch from the Find dialog box to the Story and paste in the Clipboard paragraph replacement.

Setting Fractions

You can compose fractions—real fractions like a typographer would create—using an expert edition of a font, if the font manufacturer makes one. Figure 15.18 shows some fractions set in the Adobe Garamond Expert set, for example.

Fig. 15.18 ▶
_____

*A fraction typeset with
an expert set.*

$$1/3$$

$$1/2$$

$$1/23$$

$$23/100$$

Using an expert set, you simply select the numbers that are already in numerator and denominator form, inserting the special fraction slash mark between them.

If you don't want to use an expert set (perhaps you are using a font family that doesn't include an expert set option), you can set fractions through a combination of superscript and subscript. This procedure requires a fair number of steps, but it's otherwise straightforward (and there's a script that can do all the work for you in Chapter 28, "Automating PageMaker").

Figure 15.19 starts out with the pug-ugly non-typographical way of typing a fraction. The second fraction in the illustration is typed with the real fraction slash character, (Alt+0164, on the numeric keypad formatted in the Symbol font), as opposed to the slash in the lower-left corner of your keyboard with the question mark character. This real fraction slash has less space around it, so the fraction numbers can nestle together better.

Fig. 15.19 ▶

Setting a fraction using subscript and superscript.

$$1/255$$

$$1/255$$

$$\frac{1}{255}$$

Highlight the entire fraction and use the Type Specs Options dialog box to set the size and baseline relationships of your subscript and superscript attributes. You'll experiment to get the best results with your particular font. As a starting guideline, try setting super/subscript size to 58 percent. The numerator should be above the baseline by about 33 percent. The denominator sits on the baseline, so set it at 0 percent.

Format the numerator as superscript (Ctrl+Shift+\) and the denominator as subscript (Ctrl+\). The much-improved end result is the bottom fraction example in figure 15.19. Instead of using the subscript and superscript technique, you can set the point size and baseline shift attributes manually, using Type Specs or the Control palette.

TIP ▶   Setting the Inch and Foot Symbols

Desktop publishers pride themselves on using the real typographers' quotes, the curly ones, for the apostrophe, and single quote, and double quote characters. You can, and should, set this as an automatic option in the Preferences Other dialog box. But what do you do when you want to set an inch or a foot marker? You can go to Preferences and turn off the option just while inserting the characters, although that could be a bit of a pain.

Better yet, use the real inch and foot marks shown in figure 15.20. The first set of marks are the curly quotes. The second set are the typewriter style quote marks and they don't work for either the typographer quotes or the real inch and foot marks, which you see in the third set of marks. You can set them by formatting your text in a special font. The Symbol font that comes with Windows or Adobe's Universal Pi have a number of these kinds of symbols, including the real inch and foot marks.

Fig. 15.20 ▷
_____

*Setting the true inch
and foot marks.*

Wrapping and Molding Text

I saved the powerful Text Wrap command for this chapter instead of including it in one of the earlier chapters on PageMaker basics because it's a special effect all by itself. This section first covers the basics of the command, and then gets into using the command to customize text wrap to shape text around irregularly shaped graphics. It also covers using text wrap to mold the text itself into special shapes.

Using the Text Wrap Command

Check figure 15.21 to see how a graphic can push text out from around itself when its text wrap attribute has been switched on.

The graphic is selected, and dotted lines run around its perimeter, marking the no trespassing zone where text is not permitted. This zone is the *text wrap boundary*. It always starts as a box, but you can adjust it by adding more handles, which you then drag to new text wrap boundary points. You can create dozens of these handles to customize the boundary so that text snuggles in around the irregular edges of a graphic.

Figure 15.22 helps explain how you use the Text Wrap command. Select your graphic with the Pointer tool and use the Element menu to access the Text Wrap dialog box.

The top three icons in the dialog box describe what kind of text wrap is in effect for the graphic you have selected:

▷ The icon on the left turns off text wrap, allowing text to flow over the top of the graphic. This icon is chosen by default (unless you change it by setting a mini-default) when you first choose the Text Wrap command.

FIG. 15.21 ▶

*A graphic with text
wrap turned on.*

Result: Feeding Frenzy

Waiter Stumbles, Spills Mackerel & Smelt
Head Aardvark Boogies On Down

The Polar Bears responded with outrage today, in the aftermath of a land and sea invasion by the Aardvarks on Monday. The invasion took place as teams of negotiators from all over the world were debarking from their specially constructed rafts, having just arrived for a series of diplomatic talks on the long standing dispute between the Polar Confederation and the Aardvark States.

Raft arriving at conference with delegates. (Photo by NormKerr, Kodak PCD)

"We will not stand for this kind of deceit," roared the leader of a Polar diplomatic team which flew into Newfoundland for United Animal

Kingdom talks convened to avert the crisis. "This meeting had been called weeks ago and for the Aardvark States to commit this attack of international banditry on the eve of negotiations, well, it's sneaky, that's what it is."

A formal dinner to open the conference turned into a nasty brawl last night when a waiter stumbled between tables and spilled a bucket of mackerel and smelt which had been destined for the head table. The Aardvark representative has claimed that the resulting feeding frenzy was the fault of the Polar contingent and that the waiter was a well known terrorist sent to the dinner in disguise with the specific purpose of creating a disruption at the critical moment when the Head Aardvark was about to boogie on down on the dance floor with her longtime consort, the tuxedo clad bad boy scion of the filthy rich Antfarm Snack Foods fortune. The name of the waiter has not been released, pending notification of next of kin.

FIG. 15.22 ▶

*The Text Wrap
dialog box.*

▶ The middle icon sets a box boundary for the text no trespassing zone. All the corners of the box are 90-degree angles. You can convert a customized text wrap back to a box text wrap by clicking this icon.

▶ The icon on the right is an indicator rather than an option. It becomes active when you change the text wrap boundary to something other than a box.

The Text Flow icons in the center of the dialog box determine how text wraps around the graphic:

▶ The icon on the left won't let any text below the graphic on the page, forcing a column or page break.

▶ The middle icon causes text to leap over the graphic, leaving the sides of the graphic blank.

▶ The icon on the right tells text wrap to surround the graphic with text on all four sides, assuming the graphic hasn't been shoved against a margin guide.

At the bottom of the Text Wrap dialog box, you can set the amount of standoff between your graphic and text when you have the box text style wrap icon selected. The numbers you enter in these boxes describe the amount of standoff for the dotted line text wrap boundary from each side of the graphic's rectangular boundary. The standard numbers in the boxes for Standoff in Picas is 1 pica when you first begin setting a text wrap. Keep in mind that even irregular graphics are still contained within rectangles, as far as PageMaker is concerned, unless you customize the shape of the text wrap boundary.

TIP ▶	**TIFF Graphics Can Now Be Non-Rectangles**

In the past, one problem with TIFF graphic imports has always been PageMaker's— and every other graphics program's—insistence on viewing them as opaque rectangles. They may have looked transparent around the edges, but they weren't, even if you built a customized text wrap shape to allow text to come in around the edges and follow the outline of your graphic subject.

PageMaker 6.0 now understands and obeys the Clipping Path feature of the latest versions of Photoshop. You don't need to save it as an EPS to get the clipping path to work.

By the way, one of the tried and true methods of getting around this opaque rectangle problem was to use the Paste Inside maneuver in FreeHand and save the graphic as an EPS. It seemed that when PageMaker 6.0 first came out, it had lost the capability to print TIFFs that are embedded in EPS files. Well, it's not so. You can hold down the Shift key when you use the Place command and get a special import preferences dialog box. Turn off OPI Comments, and everything will be fine.

Customizing Your Text Wrap

Figure 15.23 shows the stages of customizing a text wrap boundary so that it fits around a graphic and the text flows into the new irregular outline.

Fig. 15.23 ▶

Customizing a text wrap.

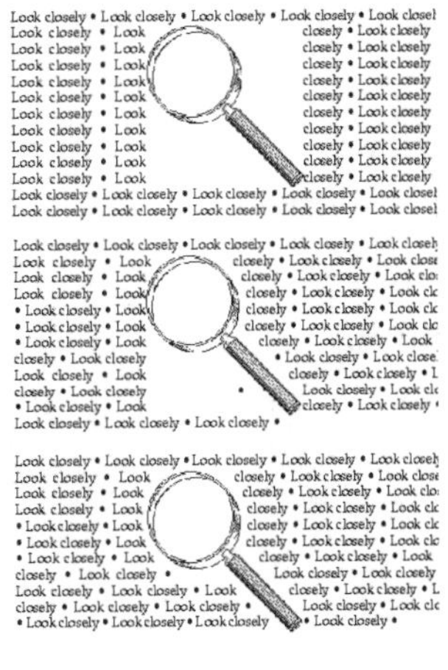

You need to know the following four basic moves to customize the text wrap boundary around your graphic:

▶ Click a text wrap boundary with the Pointer tool (without dragging) to create a new text wrap point. It will be a tiny diamond.

▶ Delete a diamond by a click-and-drag move, dropping the diamond directly over another diamond.

▶ If you click and drag a boundary line, instead of creating a new diamond you drag that entire side to a new location, determined by where you drop it by releasing the mouse button.

▶ You can click and drag any existing text wrap boundary point diamond.

TIP ▶ Use the Ctrl Key to Grab Handles When Text Wrap Interferes

Text wrap diamonds are entirely separate from the handles on the graphic object itself. If you ever set the text wrap box at zero standoff all the way around, you make these handles and diamonds coincide. That can make it tough to grab the object's sizing handles because the text wrap boundary has priority over the Pointer tool. No problem—just hold down the Ctrl key while clicking, and you'll get the object and its handles instead of the text wrap boundary or its diamonds.

TIP ▶ Hold Down the Spacebar to Prevent Rewrap While Positioning

Even with PageMaker's great interruptible screen draw feature, it's pretty boring to wait for the text to reflow around your graphic as you are customizing the text wrap boundary. Hold down the spacebar while you make your adjustments to put the text reflow on temporary hold. Also, to save redraw time, you can do the rough adjustments to the text wrap on the Pasteboard with no text placed around the graphic. Then, when you've got the boundary just about right, slide the text wrapped graphic into place on the text.

Molding Text into Shapes with Text Wrap

Use an invisible object with text wrap turned on to mold text. Figure 15.24 shows an example of setting angled text margins.

If you want to create this effect:

1. Draw a box and set Line and Fill to None.
2. Set Text Wrap to flow around with zero standoff.
3. Rotate the box using the Rotate tool or the Control palette.
4. Copy the box and paste it on the opposite side of the page.

Fɪɢ. 15.24 ▷

*Angled text margins
using text wrap.*

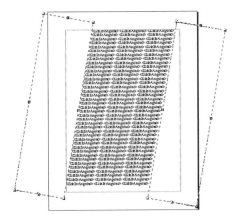

Line up the two boxes using a ruler guide and slide the text into the mold.

You might think that you could use a line instead of a box to perform this angle margin molding task. However, you can't set text wrap on a line. The minimum number of points for a text wrap is three, a triangle, which is difficult to manipulate for this kind of work. A box generally works out better.

You also might be wondering why you can't simply rotate text to get diagonal margins. You could do that, using the Skew command to straighten the text back to the vertical. The lines of text would still read at an angle, however, instead of reading straight across horizontally.

You can also use customized text wrap boundaries to force text into angles and other weird shapes. Make a sawtooth edge, a triangle, even an arc! Remember that all graphics are boxes to PageMaker (even a circle), so you can't just draw a circle to get a circular wrap boundary. You need to customize the boundary to get the effect.

TIP ▷ Text Wrap Boundary on Master Page Applies to All Pages

This works especially well now that we have multiple master pages in PageMaker Version 6.0. Placing a no line and no fill box with text wrap on a master page sets a text wrap boundary for all the pages assigned that master page. You can use this master page text wrap trick to do the following:

▶ Set angle margins on all your pages, as described earlier.

▶ Reserve space for a companion column as you pour text onto your pages (if you aren't using the indented paragraph techniques for hanging items into a synthetic companion column already described in this chapter).

▶ Reserve the lower half of all your pages for illustration placement with a text wrap boundary box across the bottom of a master page.

TIP ▶ **It's Easier Than Ever to Put Captions Inside an Illustration's Custom Text Wrap**

Especially in long form documents, it's usually best to use inline graphics techniques for illustrations. However, in newsletters and magazines, you may do a lot of independent graphic placement. In those situations, you don't want the text wrap to push the caption out away from its illustration, so just put the caption inside the text wrap boundaries. This used to be quite a delicate operation, but the good news about Version 6.0 is that when you group the graphic and the caption, the text in the caption becomes immune to the Text Wrap effect. Perform the grouping operation first, before setting the Text Wrap attribute, or it will push away the caption text before you get a chance to implement the Group command.

Text Inside a Shape

The Text Wrap command also can shape text inside its boundaries, but you must turn the wrap boundary inside out to work this special effect. Basically, you work this text shaping magic by swapping two opposite corners. You must also extend a tiny limb of the text wrap boundary out to cover the upper-left handle of the text block. The example in figure 15.25 was created in just this way.

For this illustration, I used the Zapf Dingbat heart character at about 400 points to act as a pattern. Because it's actually text, I put it on a master page where it could be seen for pattern purposes but would not be affected by the text wrap.

Slide the text to be wrapped over the pattern. In this case, a text block has been filled with the word hearts, alternated with normal sized heart dingbats, created in the text block with the Multiple Paste command.

To get the text wrap going, make a box with a thin line and draw it around the pattern. Eventually you'll turn off the line, but for now you want to be able to see the box so you can work with it. The text wrap should be of the flow-around type. Make sure the box sits outside the text block at first.

Fɪɢ. 15.25 ▶

*The beginning setup
for creating text within
a shape.*

Box to create
boundary

Text wrap boundary

Text block

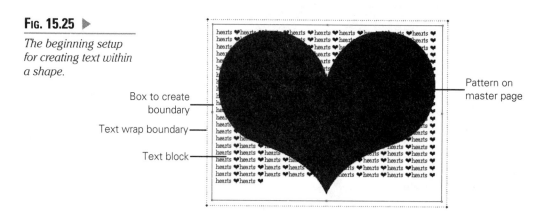

Pattern on
master page

Swap the lower-right and upper-left corners, as shown in figure 15.26. You could just as easily swap the other pair of opposite corners instead.

Fig. 15.26 ▶

Swapping opposite corners.

Original
upper-left
corner

Now start clicking diamonds and dragging them into the edges of your pattern, gradually forming a crude heart shape with all the diamonds. It might remind you of those connect-the-dot coloring books you had when you were a kid. In figure 15.27, the pattern heart on the master page has been switched to an outline style to make it easier to see what's going on.

Fig. 15.27 ▶

Pulling the boundary to the pattern.

Hook for upper-
left corner of
text block

Wrap boundary

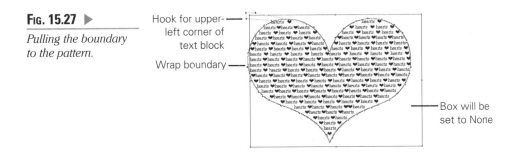

Box will be
set to None

Notice that a small hook of the wrap boundary has been left in the upper-left corner to hold the upper-left corner handle of the text block. Figure 15.28 shows the completed shaping job with the box set to a line of None and the heart pattern deleted from the master page.

Fig. 15.28 ▶

A heart-shaped text block.

Cutting In Initial Caps

Initial caps are a tradition going back to hand-penned books of centuries ago, when monks would create miniature works of art by "illuminating" the first capital letter on a page. It's considerably easier to do nowadays in PageMaker, although not as pretty as the Book of Kells in Dublin (even by a long shot).

There are three basic types of initial caps: the raised cap, the hanging cap, and the drop cap. In each case, you can also box the initial capital letter.

Raised Cap

Nothing could be simpler than making a raised cap. Simply increase the point size, as you see in figure 15.29.

Fig. 15.29 ▶

A raised initial cap.

Springing high in May, corn reaches for the warmth. Stalks of green, topped by blonde tassels of silken fertility, greet the golden sun. As the day grows, the workers' blue coveralls imprint the green-gold scheme. Then it's iced tea and fried chicken in the field for the hands and family at midday. And paced afternoon work turns the time drowsy until supper and a descending, waning globe of rusty, old metal against ragged spikes of leaf. At dusk, children romp through the rows, playing tag with the green flashing fireflies in sight of the folks on the screened veranda.

Always use fixed leading when creating raised caps.

You also need to consider how the raised cap might push the spacing out of whack with the paragraph above it. Generally, however, you use a raised initial cap at some logical break like the top of a page or column or perhaps with a pull quote or headline, so paragraph spacing ordinarily won't be a major problem.

Hanging Cap

To create a hanging cap, use the hanging punctuation effect from earlier in this chapter. In figure 15.30, the S has been kerned out over the indented main body type by putting an em space in front of it and then kerning the distance between the space and the capital S.

FIG. 15.30 ▷

FIG. 15.30 ▷

A hanging cap and a dropped hanging cap.

Springing high in May, corn reaches for the warmth. Stalks of green, topped by blonde tassels of silken fertility, greet the golden sun. As the day grows, the workers' blue coveralls imprint the green-gold scheme. Then it's iced tea and fried chicken in the field for the hands and family at midday. And paced afternoon work turns the time drowsy until supper and a descending, waning globe of rusty, old metal against ragged spikes of leaf. At dusk, children romp through the rows, playing tag with the green flashing fireflies in sight of the folks on the screened veranda.

Springing high in May, corn reaches for the warmth. Stalks of green, topped by blonde tassels of silken fertility, greet the golden sun. As the day grows, the workers' blue coveralls imprint the green-gold scheme. Then it's iced tea and fried chicken in the field for the hands and family at midday. And paced afternoon work turns the time drowsy until supper and a descending, waning globe of rusty, old metal against ragged spikes of leaf. At dusk, children romp through the rows, playing tag with the green flashing fireflies in sight of the folks on the screened veranda.

In the same figure, you can see a dropped hanging cap, created by adjusting the baseline of the initial cap. You can accomplish this baseline adjustment most easily in the Control palette.

Drop Cap

A drop cap "drops" into the text, as in figure 15.31. There must be two dozen ways you can make a drop, but three stand out. Which one you use depends on what you need to accomplish and the source of your initial cap:

▶ If you are using a font for your drop cap and you don't need to make the surrounding text fit into the drop cap's shape, use the Drop Caps Plug-in.

▶ If you are using a graphic for your drop cap, use the text wrap technique.

▶ If you are using a graphic as a drop cap but really need inline graphic locking power, try the hybrid method. Use this method if, for example, you are worried that future editing of the publication will throw independent graphics (including your drop cap) out of alignment.

FIG. 15.31 ▷

The results of the Drop Caps Plug-in, in this case using a special font for the initial cap.

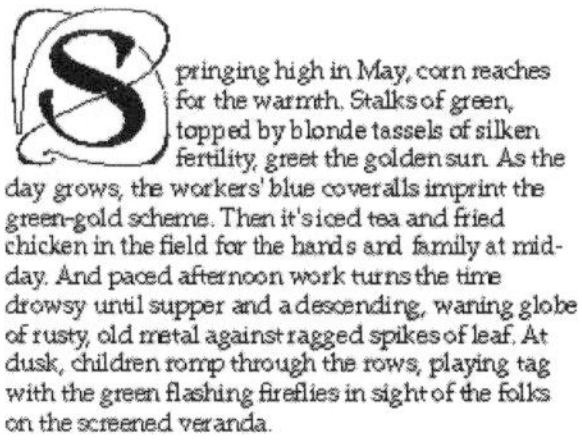

Springing high in May, corn reaches for the warmth. Stalks of green, topped by blonde tassels of silken fertility, greet the golden sun. As the day grows, the workers' blue coveralls imprint the green-gold scheme. Then it's iced tea and fried chicken in the field for the hands and family at midday. And paced afternoon work turns the time drowsy until supper and a descending, waning globe of rusty, old metal against ragged spikes of leaf. At dusk, children romp through the rows, playing tag with the green flashing fireflies in sight of the folks on the screened veranda.

The Drop Caps Plug-in

Select the first letter in the paragraph and use the Utilities menu to call up the Drop Cap dialog box. Notice that you can automatically move to the previous and next paragraphs, which makes this feature suitable for volume production work. This Plug-in also has Remove and Apply buttons, a major tedium reduction breakthrough.

After you specify how deep you want the drop cap to go (how many lines high the cap will be), the Plug-in takes care of the rest. Figure 15.31 shows the results. The example may look like a graphic, but the letter "S" has been set in one of the many available specialized initial cap fonts. In this case, I used a shareware font from the DTP Forum called KonanurKaps.

If you use one of these special initial cap fonts, be sure to set the first character in the paragraph in the font before using the Plug-in. Also, because the Plug-in uses forced linebreaks, it does not perform hyphenation, and you may need to manually go back into the text and add hyphens if you aren't happy with the way the text breaks.

The Drop Caps Plug-in automates a number of steps. I've listed them here so you'll have the background information if you need to do manual tweaking on the drop cap. The Drop Caps Plug-in automates the following drudgery:

▶ Increasing the character's point size by a multiple of the line leading. If you specify four lines high, the Drop Caps Plug-in makes the character roughly four times the leading height.

▶ Adjusting the baseline of the cap to drop it down into the text by the same amount as its new point size.

▶ Setting a tab just to the right of the newly enlarged drop cap character.

▶ Inserting hard line breaks (Shift+Enter new line characters) for each line of drop and then tabbing over to the new tab point. (Remember that hard breaks will break words in the middle withouth inserting hyphens. Go back over the text to see if you need to manually add hyphens.)

By using this list, you can do all or part of the job yourself if you want to make any adaptations. For example, you may find the tab has been set too tightly or loosely to the drop cap and can make an adjustment in the Indents/Tabs ruler. This list also helps if you need to use the hybrid technique for creating graphic-based drop caps.

The Drop Cap as a Text Wrap Graphic

Many people advise against using this technique because it's bush league. The independent graphic won't be linked to the text, and copy editing may cause the drop cap to fall out of alignment. But it has its uses, and it is really easy to do.

This method is suitable for clip art capitals or ones that you draw yourself and import into PageMaker. Or you can make a text block of a single letter and group it. In any of these cases, once you have the capital acting like a graphic instead of like text, you are ready to go to work by applying a Text Wrap.

Slide the graphic over your text. Size it and position it, and then set a text wrap around it, probably with a small standoff amount. Finish by clicking diamonds and sliding them up to the contours of the graphics cap. Figure 15.32 shows the result of this method.

FIG. 15.32 ▶

A graphic object drop cap set into place using text wrap.

Custom wrap boundary

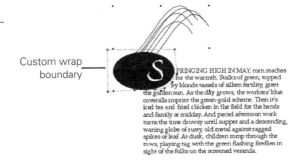

PRINGING HIGH IN MAY, corn reaches for the warmth. Stalks of green, topped by blonde tassels of silken fertility, greet the golden sun. As the day grows, the workers' blue coveralls imprint the green-gold scheme. Then it's iced tea and fried chicken in the field for the hands and family at midday. And paced afternoon work turns the time drowsy until supper and a descending, waning globe of rusty, old metal against ragged spikes of leaf. At dusk, children romp through the rows, playing tag with the green flashing fireflies in sight of the folks on the screened veranda.

The Plug-in and Inline Graphic Hybrid

If you are going to use a graphic as an initial capital, this method is the best. It locks your initial cap into place so you don't need to worry about edit changes throwing your cap and your text out of alignment.

By first using the Drop Cap Plug-in, you save yourself a little bit of work, and then you just have to fine-tune the placement of the cap by adjusting the tab settings. The result looks like figure 15.33.

FIG. 15.33 ▶

A hybrid Plug-in and inline graphic drop cap.

PRINGING high in May, corn reaches for the warmth. Stalks of green, topped by blonde tassels of silken fertility, greet the golden sun. As the day grows, the workers' blue coveralls imprint the green-gold scheme. Then it's iced tea and fried chicken in the field for the hands and family at midday. And paced afternoon work turns the time drowsy until supper and a descending, waning globe of rusty, old metal against ragged spikes of leaf. At dusk, children romp through the rows, playing tag with the green flashing fireflies in sight of the folks on the screened veranda.

Here's how to use the Drop Cap Plug-in:

1. Estimate how big a drop cap you want. Slide your graphic over the text and count how many lines you want it to descend into the text. In this example, the line count is eight.

2. Move the graphic out of the way, highlight the first letter in the paragraph, and apply the Drop Cap Plug-in, using your estimated line count.

3. After the Plug-in finishes, use the Pointer tool to select the graphic cap and copy or cut it to the Clipboard. Then use the Text tool to select the type drop cap created by the Plug-in.

4. Next, apply the usual inline graphic method. Paste in the graphic cap, re-placing the type initial. Select the graphic as text and set its leading to the normal leading for the paragraph. Make any needed baseline adjustments.

5. Now, fine tune. In this example, the graphic was wider than the type cap, so considerable kerning was applied, using the hanging punctuation tech-nique from earlier in the chapter. Also, a couple of lines broke even then, so new line characters had to be removed from the bad line break loca-tions and re-inserted in new locations, which meant replacing tab charac-ters as well until the whole thing was aligned. Not too bad. It took a couple of minutes.

Oh, by the way, the graphic drop cap in figure 15.33 was composed in FreeHand, using a clip art sunburst and the letter S. After applying the Convert to Paths command to the capital letter in FreeHand, turning it into a PostScript graphic object, the combination was grouped and exported as an EPS for use as an inline graphic.

Twisting and Mangling Type

Type can be art, as proven by the molded text heart in the "Text Inside a Shape" section. PageMaker's rotation and skewing, and the direct-entry precision of the Control palette make it easy to have fun communicating with type.

Spinning and Skewing Type

All the type in figure 15.34 was manipulated with the Control palette, using the rotation and skewing functions.

The top item was simply rotated 25 degrees. Note that you can edit type that's been rotated by simply moving the Text tool over the type. The Text tool even tilts for you when you are over the rotated text so that you can tell where to click the insertion point.

In the second item, the text block has been skewed 25 degrees to match the amount of rotation so that the type stands up straight (more or less), even though it's been rotated. After you experiment and get your kicks by spinning your type all over the place, you'll find that skewing it to an upright position helps readability.

FIG. 15.34 ▶

Type manipulated with rotation and skewing.

A heavy custom rule and reverse type in the third sample shows that you can apply all the text and paragraph formatting attributes to manipulated text.

More skewing has been applied to the type in the fourth example, augmented by a 150 percent width setting and an even wider rule, as background for the reverse type.

Advertising has used skewing for years to make things look fast, as if they were leaning into the wind. The bottom example enhances this appearance of speed by adding a couple of thin double rules to the paragraph formatting. The rules have asymmetrical indent settings so that the tails of the speed lines don't all match up, further augmenting the visual sensation of leaning and speed.

Playing with Baselines and Kerning

Everything you see in figure 15.35 has been created using baseline adjustment and kerning.

The earthquake example looks about like one feels—as you'd know if you lived here on the left coast. If you don't live here, you don't want to know.

Every other letter has a baseline adjustment of 1 pica, alternating plus and minus settings using the Control palette. It's set in big type, an important point because most type effects look best when they are created bigger than life.

Fig. 15.35 ▶

*Examples of the effects
you can create with
baseline adjustment
and kerning.*

E_{arthq}u_{ake}

V_{ictor}_y

S_{hhhhhhhhhh}

`Victory` combines baseline adjustment and kerning. It can be tough to select text that's been heavily kerned so the letters were first adjusted for baseline. Then, using the kerning keyboard shortcuts, the `V` and `i` were kerned together. Then the `y` was kerned underneath the `r`.

The bottom example is also an example of kerning combined with baseline adjustment. This one started with an adjustment of the type sizes so that they looked right together. Then the letters were nudged into alignment using baseline and kerning adjustments.

Stacking Up Drop Shadows

The shadow styled type at the top of figure 15.36 looks pretty simplistic and ordinary. You can get a much more elegant look using this technique.

Fig. 15.36 ▶

*An improved drop
shadow effect.*

Earthquake

Earthquake

Earthquake

Make sure your copy is final before setting this text effect. You'll go nuts if you have to go back through all the stacked type created for this effect to make a correction.

When you are ready and the text has been sized, kerned, and baseline adjusted, copy and paste your text twice. Use the Type Specs dialog box to color the copies in two different tints of gray.

Now stack up all three copies and use the Control palette or nudge them with the arrow keys to slide them into position, very slightly offset from each other. You need to use PageMaker 6.0's new Send Forward and Send Backward commands as well to get them on just the right layer. The idea is to get a sandwich effect of these gradations of gray, with the rear copy of the word slightly down and to the right of the next layer up. Work at a high magnification for precision and then decrease the magnification so that you can evaluate the effect. Shadow copy can be troubling to the eye, so make sure you haven't gone so far as to reduce readability.

When you are finished positioning the sandwiched text, group it all together so the pieces don't accidentally get knocked out of position while you work on the rest of the page.

Building Boxes, Backgrounds, and Screens

PageMaker possesses special talents for mixing type and graphics on the page. You can put a screen or a box behind type, or frame type with a border. For all their simplicity of execution, the techniques of boxes, backgrounds, and screens provide high impact emphasis for sidebars, pull quotes, and other communication elements that deserve special reader focus.

Using Keyline and Other Boxing Methods

It's incredibly simple to drop a box (or a circle) behind or around some type. Just draw the object, size it, and define the line and fill. Then adjust the position of the box to fit properly around the type.

It can be even simpler than that, though, if you use the Keyline Plug-in that comes with PageMaker.

Boxing and Screening with the Keyline Plug-in

The Keyline Plug-in (on the Utilities menu, under PageMaker Plug-ins) draws a box around any object you choose and then applies Group to stick all the boxed elements together.

The word *object* in that sentence is important. Keyline will not draw a box around selected text inside a text block, only around the text block itself (or any other object you like, as far as that goes).

After selecting your object and choosing the Keyline Plug-in, the dialog box shown in figure 15.37 appears. Tell the Plug-in how much of a standoff you'd like and whether you want the box sent to the back layer or brought to the front layer, and click the OK button.

FIG. 15.37 ▶

The Keyline opening dialog box.

You get something like the arrangement in figure 15.38.

FIG. 15.38 ▶

A boxed paragraph.

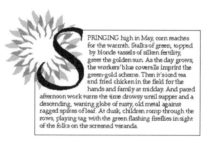

Use the Attributes button in the Keyline dialog box to reach the familiar Fill and Line dialog box. You can then set up any of PageMaker's custom lines and various fills and colors right when you draw the box. Or you can make modifications after the box is in place, as shown in figure 15.39.

You will probably want to set a standoff for the keyline with the Extends *xx* Points setting. Also, if you want a fill or color, use the Send Keyline Behind Object setting or it will cover the text block.

Don't forget to check the box for Send Keyline Behind Object, or the filled box will cover the type instead of emphasizing it.

Either way, the Keyline Plug-in is a fast, easy way to throw a screen behind some text, and it's great for highlighting sidebars or pull quotes.

Fig. 15.39 ▷

*A more dressed-up
boxed paragraph.*

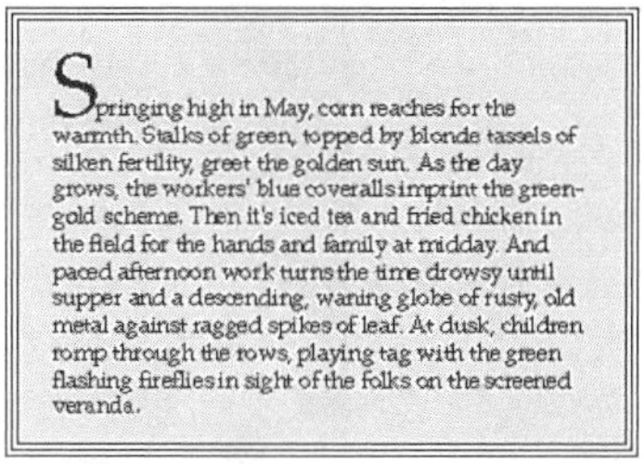

> S pringing high in May, corn reaches for the warmth. Stalks of green, topped by blonde tassels of silken fertility, greet the golden sun. As the day grows, the workers' blue coveralls imprint the green-gold scheme. Then it's iced tea and fried chicken in the field for the hands and family at midday. And paced afternoon work turns the time drowsy until supper and a descending, waning globe of rusty, old metal against ragged spikes of leaf. At dusk, children romp through the rows, playing tag with the green flashing fireflies in sight of the folks on the screened veranda.

Because Keyline draws symmetrical objects, you can use it to draw bull's-eyes or stacked squares, like the ones in figure 15.40. You can enter positive or negative numbers as standoff settings to cascade the sizes of the stacked objects and manipulate the layers so the larger objects are to the rear and the smaller ones are at the front. And, as of Version 6.0, the whole thing is grouped when you finish.

Fig. 15.40 ▷

*A square bull's-eye,
created (and automatically centered) with
the Keyline Plug-in.*

TIP ▷   Convert Text Boxes (and Other Highlight Graphics) to Inline

All these box and screen effects have the same problem if you are working on a project that may shift during the final editing and approval process. Boxes (and any other graphic objects), placed as independent graphics, are not locked into synchronization with the text; therefore, text editing can destroy your carefully arranged page layouts. So, if the copy might be changing, save yourself a lot of trouble by converting the effect into an inline graphic, thus locking the text and the graphic together. Put the box in its own paragraph right above the highlighted paragraph with zero leading so it won't throw off the leading grid, and drag the baseline down under your highlighted paragraph. Of course, sometimes this approach isn't practical. For example, most newsletters have too many small text blocks to make the inline graphic technique worthwhile. Also, you can't use grouped objects as inline graphics.

Making Fancier Boxes with Third-Party Products

Figure 15.41 shows a fancy clip-art box set into place manually, although it could just as easily be an inline graphic.

FIG. 15.41 ▶

A fancy clip art box.

One snazzy approach to fancy boxes is Fræmz, a third-party Plug-in you can purchase. You first draw a simple box wherever you want it. You then use the Fræmz Plug-in to specify the fancy frame you'd like. Fræmz uses the box you drew as the guide to build a fancy box like the one shown in figure 15.42.

FIG. 15.42 ▶

A finished fræmz fancy box.

Creating Vertical Rules

You know that PageMaker can't do vertical paragraph rules, only horizontal ones, right? Traditionally, if you needed a vertical rule in text, you would just have to draw it in as an independent graphic object and stand back for a lot of repositioning headaches if you needed to edit. (Tables always seem to need editing after layout, of course.)

You can use inline graphics techniques to create a vertical rule that will be locked to your text. It's not as good as PageMaker's paragraph rules or Microsoft Word's vertical line tab feature, but it is one heck of a lot better than doing all that reediting when the copy slips during the final stages of production. The vertical rule in figure 15.43 was set up using this technique.

FIG. 15.43 ▶

Line locked by inline graphic status.

Ye Olde Shopping List

$1.98	Buckle-style shoes
$155.00	Pocket watch
$.29	Pilgrim hat
$11.13	Beans, 1 bag
$267.59	CD player

Line locked as an inline graphic

After you set up the tab, positioning the vertical rule as an inline graphic in the first row of your columnar data, size your vertical rule to match the height of your list or headline by using the Pointer tool to grab the line handles and slide them to the right length. Hold down the Shift key to constrain this move, to prevent getting a slanted line. Of course, you don't need to limit yourself. You can have a slanted line if you want—no problem.

You may decide to incorporate vertical rules into a headline format (companion or sidebar introduction lines, for example). If you do so and your headlines vary in their number of lines, set up standard arrangements with vertical rules for every headline height you are likely to need. Store these headline and vertical rule combinations on the Pasteboard or in a library, and they'll be ready to use as needed.

Inserting Screens and Other Backgrounds

Don't hesitate to get a little crazy putting type over backgrounds. There's lots of clip art, and you can scan almost anything and import it for use as a background image. It all becomes even easier with Version 6.0 because you have Mask and Group commands to pull the pieces together.

Try scanning (or photographing and then scanning) marble, concrete, bricks, wood, crumpled paper, paper spatter with ink from a toothbrush, fur, bristle brush—anything with texture. Pull out bits of pictures and manipulate them in PhotoShop or some other image editing program. Check out figures 15.45 through 15.47 for some examples.

The Harbor Dredging Update illustration (see fig. 15.44) comes from a photograph, which was lightened in Adobe Photoshop and cropped to get the vertical format shot. A box was drawn to frame the entire effect and the type was set over the shot, with bold applied to the initial caps and italic for the rest of the letters. (The photo comes from the Kodak Photo CD sampler and was shot by photographer Alan Fink.)

Fig. 15.44 ▶

Combining a touched up and cropped photograph and type.

The Western Barns masthead (see fig. 15.45) was created using a picture of the side of an old woodshed, which was scanned and then heavily doctored in PhotoShop to emphasize the grain and lighten it enough to be suitable for a background. The type is Cottonwood, an Adobe display font.

Fig. 15.45 ▶

An old wooden shed used as a headline background.

The stylized marble for the Marble Work brochure logo (see fig. 15.46) comes from a clip art package, Artbeats, which specializes in creating EPS file format backgrounds. They draw them in FreeHand! In this case, a light gray line was drawn around the cropped background image to define and emphasize the image.

Fig. 15.46 ▶

Background EPS clip art for a logo.

Design Note
Use Heavy Type When Setting Against Backgrounds

These last few illustrations work as particularly good examples of how important it is to use heavy type when superimposing text over a background. Thin lines tend to wash out pretty badly in the confusion of image information from the background. In fact, for the Western Barns effect, the Cottonwood type was brought into FreeHand, converted to paths, and given a heavier line stroke to thicken it up enough to stand out against the wood grain.

Taking Full Advantage of Masking and Grouping

The new Mask and Group commands have tremendous potential for allowing you to whip up complex combinations of art. Here's a little gallery (see figs 15.47 through 15.50) that shows some of the possibilities.

The box in figure 15.47 was set up as a regular rounded corner box. Then another square corner box was placed over it and they were superimposed so one masked the other. That's why you can have what appears to be a PageMaker box with both rounded and square corners. This effect was actually created with a script from Chapter 28, "Automating PageMaker," kindly provided by CompuServe Adobe Applications Forum colleague Ray Robertson.

FIG. 15.47 ▶

Masking can give you asymmetrically round cornered boxes.

Ray Robertson also provided a script for this effect, shown in figure 15.48, otherwise it would have been tedious beyond words. Ray's scripts are all on the CD-ROM that came with your copy of this book. This effect builds a bulls-eye out of ovals, each one stepping up 5 percent in tint value of the original red color of the oval. The whole slew of ovals are then grouped.

FIG. 15.48 ▶

More than a dozen ovals have been overlapped to create this gradient fill in 5 percent increments.

Fig. 15.49 ▶

A sort of porthole on a text block, using the Mask command.

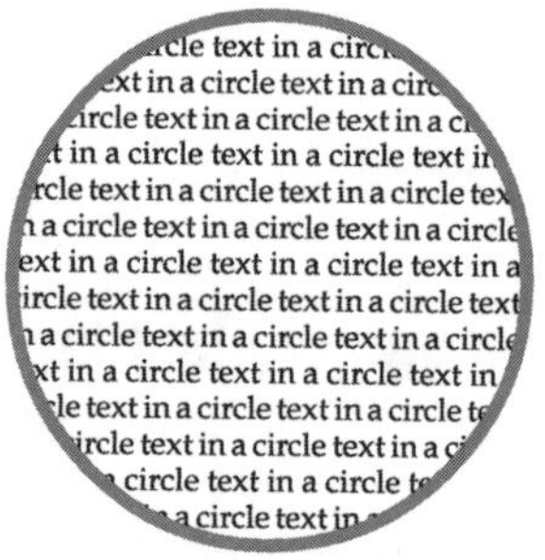

You don't need this effect every day, but when you do, you really need it. Masking makes it easy.

Fig. 15.50 ▶

The easy way, using the Mask command, to set type on two contrasting bands of color.

2 Horizontal Colors

It isn't too terribly difficult to make horizontal, two-toned text by lining up different color boxes and some type. But it sure is a lot easier to do it this way. Set one box of color down over the other one and mask them together. Then adjust the masked box until you've got the split just right. Alignment is easy this way.

Star Pig has been placed over a star, which is masking a texture of Granite. Most importantly, the pig is a transparent TIFF. It has a clipping path and was imported directly out of PhotoShop. Up until PageMaker 6.0, you always had to go through FreeHand to accomplish this effect of cutting the outline around the graphic. It's easy this way. (The pig comes drum-scanned and clipping path pre-cut from the PhotoDisc Object Series. It is one of ten high resolution Object Series graphics included on the CD-ROM that came with this book.)

FIG. 15.51 ▶

This Star Pig rests on a masked star burst.

Where to Go from Here

This chapter has shown you how to mix a number of basic techniques to produce special effects. If you need to go back and review some of the basic techniques, use the following list to help you find them in this book:

▶ Controlling type with the Control Palette. "Using the Control Palette to Set Type" in Chapter 5.

▶ Attaining object precision with the Control Palette. "Getting Ultra-Precise with the Control Palette" in Chapter 14.

▶ Stacking objects. "Key Concept: Understanding Layers and the Colors None and Paper" in Chapter 10.

▶ Grouping and masking objects. Chapter 14, "Precisely Positioning Graphics and Text."

▶ Custom lines and paragraph rules. "Setting Off Paragraphs with Spacing and Rules" in Chapter 6, and "Drawing Lines and Shapes" in Chapter 10.

▶ Styling paragraphs. Chapter 7, "Designing a Text Style System."

▶ Importing graphics and the Edit Original Command. Chapter 11, "Placing Images," and Chapter 30, "Linking and Other File Connections."

▶ Spacing lines with leading. "Spacing Lines with Leading" in Chapter 5, and "Choosing Your Leading Method" in Chapter 6.

▶ Reversing out type. "Selecting Type Attributes" in Chapter 5; "Key Concept: Understanding Layers and the Colors None and Paper" in Chapter 10; and "Placing Inline Graphics" in Chapter 11.

▶ Locking objects as inline graphics. "Precisely Aligning Inline Graphics" in Chapter 14.

▶ Alignment and distribution. "Distributing and Aligning Objects" in Chapter 14.

▶ Kerning type. "Adjusting Letter Space Using Kerning, Tracking, and Width" in Chapter 5.

▶ Shifting baselines. "Setting Subscripts, Superscripts, and Baseline Shifts" in Chapter 5.

Chapter 16

This chapter on formatting forms, tables, and databases covers the following:

Putting the new power of the PageMaker Table Editor to work.

▼

Understanding data basics, fields, and records.

▼

Managing the data publishing process, a tactics recipe to help you put all the pieces together in the right order.

▼

Making your word processor or spreadsheet part of your data publishing system.

▼

Using special formatting effects for your data tables and forms, including check boxes, shaded rules, horizontal lines, vertical rules, and graphics.

▼

Automating your data publishing process, including management of multipage tables.

Formatting Forms, Tables, and Databases

GOOD NEWS. THERE'S a strong new table editor for PageMaker called Adobe Table—a much needed replacement for the previous troubled table production program. This new tool will help in putting together well-formatted tables of information, one of the most common layout challenges encountered by PageMaker users.

In the meantime, the new add-on does have its limitations, and this chapter contains workarounds for those situations. ▶ ▶ ▶

Building Tables into Your PageMaker System

You have two main techniques to choose from when bringing a table into PageMaker. Let's spend a moment laying out the options so you can plan ahead.

Believe it or not, much of your strategy on how to manage a table layout situation boils down to whether or not your table will fit on a single page:

▶ If you can fit your table on one page, you can use Adobe Table and take advantage of its rich features to format your data. Choose between one of two methods of bringing your table graphic into PageMaker.

You can manage the Adobe Table connection using Object Linking and Embedding (OLE). This technique has the advantage of making a nearly seamless connection between PageMaker and Adobe Table. To use the OLE technique you must have enough RAM to have both programs open at once.

Or, you can use Adobe Table as a completely separate program and get your table on the page by importing it as an external file using the PageMaker Place command, and setting up a standard PageMaker link. In this case, you will want to ask Table Editor to export the table as WMF (Windows Meta File) or EMF (Enhanced Meta File), especially if your final output will be to a PostScript laser printer or imagesetter. In this scenario you only need to have one of the two programs open at a time.

The background on all these graphics linking techniques, PageMaker links and OLE, have been covered in Chapter 30, "Linking and Other File Connections."

▶ If your table will span more than one page, you have little alternative as to how to lay out your table. Bring it in as text, not as a graphic, and do your formatting in PageMaker. PageMaker doesn't have any efficient way to make a page break in the middle of a graphic such as an EPS file or an OLE object. Fortunately, PageMaker's powers of typography are robust, and this approach proves to be a good option.

For text-based table layout you will use the normal methods of importing text. This chapter explains some of the special ways you can use paragraph styles and other techniques to format the table in the most attractive—and most efficient—way possible.

You can, if you wish, use Adobe Table to organize your data and export the material as text, but you may prefer to use a database or spreadsheet program, or your word processor, for the job. Their features for sorting, search and replace operations, and other data management features will be superior to the Table Editor.

Later on in this chapter, I'll cover all the text table tactics. The next few sections cover what to do in the one page table situation, when you use Adobe Table and the graphic format option.

Managing an OLE Table

An OLE object exists only inside your PageMaker file. Unless you explicitly decide to make one, there's no other copy of your OLE table except within PageMaker.

Starting a New OLE Table

To begin a new table using the OLE technique, you start in PageMaker, not in Adobe Table. Also, since you will have both programs open at once, you will need to have enough RAM to hold them both.

Navigate to the page where you'll want the table to appear. Select the Insert Object command from the Edit menu.

Depending on your particular lineup of applications, you will probably see in this dialog box (see fig. 16.1) that quite a few programs besides PageMaker and Adobe Table support the OLE approach to cross-program productivity.

FIG. 16.1 ▶

Selecting Insert Object from the Edit menu.

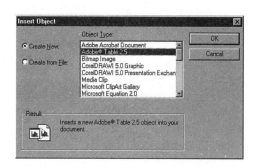

Select the Adobe Table option and click OK; this will start Adobe Table.

Opening an Existing OLE Table

To access an OLE table you have already created, navigate to its location in PageMaker and double-click it. Or you can select it and use the Edit menu command, Edit Adobe Table Object.

Updating, Closing, and Saving Your OLE Table

Updating happens like magic with an OLE table. The link is so intimate between Adobe Table and PageMaker through OLE that every change you make in your table will be echoed in your publication in real time.

If you select the Close command from Adobe Table's File menu, the program will remain open.

If you Exit & Return (there's no plain Quit command in this OLE situation), Adobe Table will be shut down, and the table embedded in your PageMaker publication will be automatically updated and saved—saved inside your publication, that is, and not as a separate document.

TIP ▶ Save a Backup Copy of Your Table

Use the Save Copy As command in the Adobe Table File menu to make a backup copy if you are using the OLE embedding technique to build your PageMaker tables. If, somehow, the link gets broken between your PageMaker publication and Adobe Table, you will have no way to edit the table. At least if you do a Save As you will have a way to recover your work.

Managing Your Table as a Standalone Graphic

When managing your table as a standalone graphic, you use Adobe Table as a utility program, and the link with PageMaker isn't as intimate as the OLE connection. You open Table Editor directly, not from inside PageMaker. You can choose to have PageMaker open or not, as you wish.

Opening the Adobe Table Program

You open Adobe Table just like any other program. If you open the program directly you will come into the Table Setup screen for beginning a new table. If you open Adobe Table by opening an existing associated table you will be taken directly to it, without the Table Setup dialog box.

Exporting and Saving a Standalone Graphic Table

Assuming you are going to insert the table in your PageMaker publication, you must Export your table using that command, located in the File menu.

You have two options: EMF (enhanced metafile) and WMF, a format only used on PCs and not usable under ordinary circumstances on a Mac.

After you have exported your table you will save it using the normal Save or Save As commands in the File menu. Note that, unlike an OLE table, when you have directly opened Adobe Table you do have a regular Exit command.

Importing an Adobe Table as a Standalone Graphic

From within PageMaker, use the Place command, just as you would import any other graphic.

> **TIP ▶ Place Tables and Charts as Inline Graphics**
>
> Keep in mind the inline graphic techniques in Chapter 11, "Placing Images." It's a rare informational graphic that doesn't have text associated with it; the inline graphic method will lock the graphic and its text together during any re-editing of your publication. This works especially well if you need to have a caption associated with your table. Certainly it will help you keep the table in place in its proper order in the text.
>
> You can use the inline graphic method on an OLE table, too. You'll need to create the table first, then Cut it with the Pointer tool selected, then switch to the Text tool and click the target location and paste it into position in the text.

Updating a Standalone Adobe Table Graphic

You have two choices for updating a standalone table graphic.

You can double-click, and PageMaker will ask you what program you want to open the Table with. You will have to find the Table Editor on your system, and then it will start, but without any table. You then have to use the File, Open command to open the table you want. Then export it again, and replace the current one. Unlike an OLE table, your changes will not be incorporated into your publication in real time. Instead, the publication's version of the graphic will be updated whenever you Save the updated table. Note that this approach requires you to have both the native Adobe Table file as well as the exported graphic file available.

Or, you can open the table directly, make your changes within Adobe Table, and re-Export it. Then go to PageMaker and update the publication's copy of the exported graphic through a standard Link update operation as described in Chapter 30, "Linking and Other File Connections."

Working with Other Table Editor Files

You can open older Aldus tables from Windows PageMaker 5.0's Table Editor.

If the table was created in a previous version of Adobe Table, one that came with Persuasion for example, you can't use Adobe Table 2.5 to work with it.

Table Editor files, created with the old utility that came with some earlier versions of PageMaker, can be opened with some loss of formatting in Adobe Table 2.5.

Making Page Breaks for Long Graphic Tables

If you have multi-page tables, you probably should use the text-based table methods in this chapter instead of graphic table techniques. But if you decide to go ahead with the graphic technique, PageMaker can't automatically break a graphic object, including a long table graphic, across pages. You have the following options:

▶ *You can presize the graphic to your layout.* This means you attempt to break the tables into page-size graphics in the word processor or spreadsheet program, guessing at how the breaks will go in the layout. However, that gives you virtually no options for copy fitting. What happens if you need another row of the chart to appear on page 13 instead of page 14? You'll be back in your originating program, doing a cumbersome edit.

▶ *You can try cropping the graphic to your layout holes.* Alternatively, paste the entire graphic multiple times, once for each page. Then use the Cropping tool in PageMaker to limit the amount of the graphic that shows on each page—in effect breaking it into page-sized pieces.

This technique has a major disadvantage because it increases your file size in a major way and means a much longer print time. PostScript devices do all the imaging for the full size of each object, whether it's been cropped or not, and then uses that full size as the basis for the cropping instruction. That means your table will be downloaded once for each page and then cropped inside the imagesetter or printer. All that extra processing activity takes a lot of time.

▶ *You can combine the two methods.* As an alternative, you could do both of the preceding methods. Working in the originating program, break the graphic into pieces that are somewhat over a page, overlapping the breaks in the graphic so the first and last several rows are duplicated in adjacent sections. Then use the Cropping tool in PageMaker for fine-tuning the graphics to the correct length.

Constructing an Adobe Table

The steps in constructing an Adobe Table begin with basic setup, followed by entering data, composing type, setting borders on rows and columns, and fine-tuning cell size.

Setting Up the Table

No matter how you do it, as an OLE object or as an independent graphic, or even as plain text, you will begin a brand new Adobe Table with the Table Setup dialog box shown in figure 16.2. You will also get this dialog box if you choose the New (Ctrl+N) or Table Setup (Ctrl+F) commands from within Adobe Table.

Fig. 16.2 ▶

The screen that begins all new tables in the Table Editor, the Table Setup dialog box.

Combination determines initial setting of column width and row height

Border every cell

Individually format table frame sides

Border all cells except table frame

Space between text in rows and columns

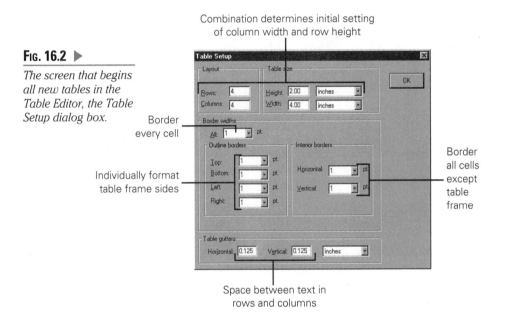

If you aren't sure how many rows or columns you will need, just click OK and go to work directly on your table layout. Keep in mind that you can change all the items you see in this dialog box during the table construction or updating process.

You might also want to compare the items in the dialog box to the features noted on the Adobe Table road map shown in figure 16.3.

If you've ever used a spreadsheet or the Table Editor in a word processor this all works as you'd expect. Here are some basic notes before moving on:

▶ In the Table Setup dialog box, your choice of overall size coupled with the number of rows and columns determines the width and height of the cells.

▶ Adobe Table will create a table 40 × 40 inches, with up to 100 rows and 100 columns.

▶ *Gutters* refers to the space between text in rows or columns.

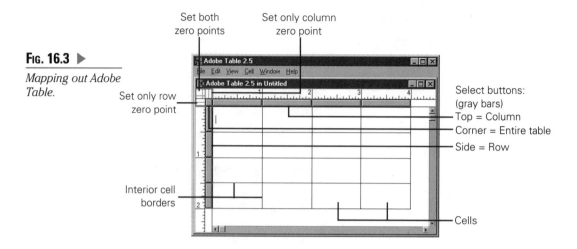

Fig. 16.3 ▶

Mapping out Adobe Table.

▶ When you are in one of the Adobe Table palettes it's easy to check the results of your adjustments as you go along. Just use the Apply button.

Entering Data

To get data into your cells, type it in. It's that simple.

Although most times you will manually type in your table information, you do have one alternative. You can import text from a plain text file (as opposed to a word processor's native file format). Use the File menu's Import Text command and let Adobe Table know whether the text will be tab- or comma-delimited. That means tab characters or commas have been used in the plain text file to separate each item or field of information in each row.

Navigating and Selecting Cells

For data entry you'll need to navigate from cell to cell, and table 16.1 spells out your options.

TABLE 16.1   Adobe Table Data Entry Navigation

Action	Key Command	Note
Character Right	right arrow	Cell Right if last character in cell
Character Left	left arrow	Cell Left if first character in cell
Cell Right	Tab	Adds row if Lower-Right Corner

Action	Key Command	Note
Cell Left	Shift+Tab	
Character/Cell Above	up arrow	
Character/Cell Below	down arrow	
Upper Left Corner	Home	
Lower Right Corner	End	
	Enter	New paragraph within cell(does not "enter" data)
	Ctrl+. (period)	Tab within cell (does not navigate to cell)

To format text and set borders you will need to select individual cells; the text within cells, rows, and columns; or sometimes the entire table.

Select an individual cell, which allows you to type in data or set a border around its sides:

▶ You can simply click on a cell.

▶ Navigate to a cell using any of the keyboard moves in table 16.1.

To select text within a cell so you can format it:

▶ Double-click a word.

▶ Shift+arrow key to select part of the text within a cell.

▶ To get all the text within a cell, click the gutter space, use the Select All command on the Edit menu, or the keyboard shortcut Ctrl+A.

To select multiple cells:

▶ Click and drag to select a range of cells.

▶ Begin a selection by holding the Shift key, then triple-click in the first cell. Keep holding the Shift key and click in the opposite corner of the block of cells you want to select.

▶ Select noncontiguous cells by clicking them while holding down the Ctrl key.

▶ Use the gray selection bars along the top and left side of the table. Select columns or rows by clicking individual gray bars. Select the entire table by clicking the corner.

Shaping, Sizing, Adding, and Deleting Cells

As you add data you may need to add rows or columns, or take them away. And once you have your text entered, you will need to make gross adjustments in the way the cells fit together, as well as in the width and height of cells so your data will fit properly. Chances are you'll fine-tune these things as you move through the design process as well.

Adding Rows and Columns

As you enter data and run out of room the editor will automatically add rows as you tab past the lower-right corner of the table.

Any time you add rows or columns, the new cells will pick up the formatting assigned to their neighbors.

In addition, you can add rows or columns by navigating to the location and using the menu commands of Insert Below or Insert Above for rows and Insert Before or Insert After for columns in the Cell menu.

The number of added rows or columns will be the same number as you have selected when you issued the command. If you have eight rows highlighted, then eight rows will be inserted.

It's also possible to insert rows or columns using Table Setup. Columns will grow the table to the right. Rows will increase the size of the table at the bottom.

Deleting Rows and Columns

Cut rows and columns with the Cell menu command Delete. Only contiguous selection is allowed for deletion. Any row or column in which you have a cell selected will be removed from the table. The Delete command will change between rows/columns according to what you have selected in the table.

Grouping Cells

For title rows or captions, you may want to shape a group of cells into a single cell. Simply select the cells you want to combine and use the Group command in the Cell menu (Ctrl+G). Figure 16.4 shows a before and after Group operation.

Ungroup cells with the Ungroup command, also on the Cell menu (Ctrl+U).

FIG. 16.4 ▶

*Combining cells
with the Group
command.*

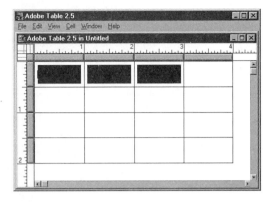

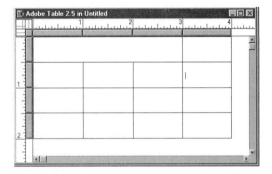

Adjusting Row Height and Column Width

The most common way to adjust row height is to type in enough text so that it wraps and takes up more than one line. That forces the cell and the rest of the row to expand to fit in all the text.

You have four ways to manually adjust the size of cells. All of them adjust entire rows or columns, or the entire table. (If you want to change the size of an individual cell you expand a cell by Grouping it with adjacent cells.)

One simple and hands-on way to adjust the height or width of a row or column is to click and drag its gutter. This allows you to adjust width by eye to fit the text. You must click the boundary between any of the gray column or row selection boxes to get the double-arrow sizing cursor you see in figure 16.5.

Take note that you have the option of retaining the current size of the table. During a normal click-and-drag resizing move, all the other columns or rows will keep their size. Thus, as you slide the columns or row boundaries, the overall size of the table changes. However, if you hold down the Shift key while you make the adjustment, the size of the adjacent columns or rows will be reduced or increased to compensate for the move, thus maintaining the size of the table.

FIG. 16.5 ▶

*Using a click and
drag move to shift
the boundary of a
column.*

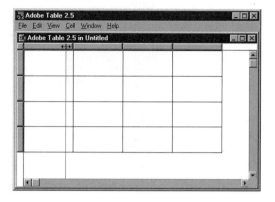

You can also adjust row or column size with the Row/Columns Size command
in the Cell menu. Navigate to any cell in the row and column you want to adjust
and call the dialog box. Type in your desired width and click OK. This one's nice
because you can change either row or column measurements. Also, you can select more than one row or column.

If you would like to get visual feedback on your sizing moves, use the Table palette, which you call up from the Window menu (Ctrl+8). Either use the nudge
buttons you see in figure 16.6, or type in your desired row height or column
width. Press Enter or Tab to the next field in the palette to see your move take
effect. If you are using the nudge buttons, you can hold down the Ctrl key and
release to magnify the amount of each nudge by ten times.

FIG. 16.6 ▶

*Sizing rows or
columns with the
Table palette.*

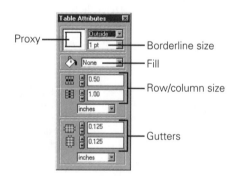

Finally, you can set row and column size for the entire table. Open Table Setup
(Ctrl+F) and turn on the Set Table Size check box. You will get a warning dialog
box stating that your changes can have unexpected results on cell layout. Type
in the new height and width. The reduction or addition to the old table size measurement will be distributed through the table's rows (height) and columns
(width). If the table had equally sized rows or columns, they will be maintained

as equal. If they were different sizes before the Table Setup adjustment, they will still be a different size after the move, but Adobe Table will remove or add an equal amount to their sizes. If you want visual feedback for your Table Setup move, click the Apply button without clicking OK. You can still cancel the move after using the Apply button, as long as you don't click OK.

Indirectly, you affect the size of columns and rows with another setting. You can adjust gutters, the space between text entered in cells. The gutter adjustments don't seem to affect the entire table; they just make the active areas in each cell smaller while maintaining the overall table size and dimensions. Settings for gutter width are available in the Table palette and in Table setup.

Setting Table Type

There's lots of familiar PageMaker typography power in Adobe Table to tune up your table's text. Figure 16.7 shows the Type palette. You can also use the Type and Paragraph Specs dialog box.

Decimal

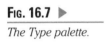

Fig. 16.7 ▶

The Type palette.

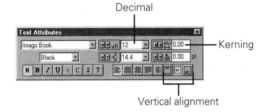

Kerning

Vertical alignment

These two tools look somewhat like their counterparts in PageMaker, except they combine type and paragraph functions into one location—palette or dialog box. In PageMaker those functions are kept separate in dialog boxes and in the Control palette.

The concepts behind the items shown in these two interfaces have been covered in talking about PageMaker itself—kerning, leading, typeface, type size, paragraph alignment, subscript and superscript, and so on.

There are two significant exceptions, because this is a table editor, after all:

▶ Adobe Table does alignment in two directions. In addition to horizontal alignment for paragraphs, there's vertical alignment. The setting will push text to the center of a row (the usual), to the top of a row, and to the bottom of a row.

▶ There is decimal style alignment in addition to the usual paragraph alignments of center, left, right, and justified.

Adobe Table does not have a real tab function. After all, it has columns. So, to line up decimals in your columns of numbers, select the columns and give them decimal alignment. Then type a tab in front of the text in each decimal-aligned cell, using Ctrl+. (period).

To adjust the position of the tab stop, turn on Show Tab Markers in the View menu. You can also see the tab characters, if you turn on Show ¶, also in the View menu. Click and drag the tab marker located in the gray column selection button to add more space for numbers to the left of the decimal point.

Setting Borders and Fills

To add lines and fills to your tables, you have two tools—the Table Setup dialog box or the Table palette. Here are some basic notes that refer to both the dialog box and the palette:

▶ You can choose the width of your border line from a pop-up menu. Or, you can choose None. Or, you can type in any value of point width, up to 9.28 points.

▶ In dialog boxes and menus, you will see a variety of terms for the location of borders:

All means every border in the table, including the frame around the outside and all the interior cell borders.

Inside or *Interior* means all the cell borders, excluding any of the outside edges of the table.

Horizontal refers to the tops and bottoms of rows.

Vertical means the sides of columns.

Outline or *Outside* refers to the border that frames the edges of the table.

Setting Up Table-Wide Borders

The Table Setup dialog box lets you establish borders for every cell, for the edges of the table, and for all the interior lines of the table.

You can do this table-wide border formatting when you first begin a new table, or later on as you are designing the table layout. However, if you have already established a table and opened the Table Setup, the dialog box has two features that you do not see in the version that appears when you first start up a new table:

▶ The Apply button lets you see the results of your work as you go, without closing the dialog box. In addition, if you don't like what you see, you can click the Cancel button and abandon your changes.

▶ If you have some cells with no borders at all, you can preserve that condition even though Table Setup generally works on the entire table at once. Click the check box to Maintain Zero Width Borders.

Setting Cell-Specific Borders and Fills

Use the Table palette to set borders and fills for selected cells. You can use the palette for a single cell, a rectangular selection of cells, or a discontinuous selection of cells.

After you make your selection, use the palette to tell Adobe Table which edges of your selection should get border lines. There are two methods:

▶ Choose from a list using the pop-up menu located next to the proxy.

▶ Use the proxy itself. Conceptually, it resembles the proxy in PageMaker's Control palette. Click lines on or off to tell Adobe Table where you want border lines placed. Note that the proxy box changes depending on the cells you have selected.

If you select a single cell, the proxy represents the edges of the cell.

If you select two or more adjacent cells, a rectangle, you can assign borders to the internal boundaries of the selection as well as to the outside edge of the entire selection.

If you make a discontinuous selection the proxy will only allow you to assign lines to cell boundaries, not to the outside edge of the selection.

Choose a percentage of black fill for your selection of cells by choosing from the pop-up menu, or type in a fill percentage in one percentage point increments. Solid means 100 percent black. Paper means the table will knock out all ink underneath it so the paper will show through. The setting of None means your table will be transparent.

You can reverse out type in selected cells by applying a fill (something dark, probably at least 80 percent or above for best readability) and setting type with the color white using the Type and Paragraph Specs dialog box or the Text palette.

Other than the color white in these two dialog boxes, Adobe Table does not offer color.

TIP ▶   **To Get Color In Your Table, Get None**

If you need color in your table, Adobe Table Version 2.5 won't give it to you. However, you can assign the fill setting of None, either to the entire table or to selected portions of it. None, in this case, means transparent. Then, when you bring the table back into

 **Continued**

PageMaker you can apply color by putting a colored PageMaker rectangle or other drawn object behind it:

▼ Try using the Keyline Plug-in, which automatically groups the resulting box to its target object. That way you can manipulate the newly "colored" table as one unit.

▼ If you want rows (or columns) to be colored in an alternating bar scheme, use the Keyline trick and simply designate alternating rows with fills of None (color will show through in PageMaker) and Paper (color will be blocked).

▼ Try using the same tricks, except instead of using a colored box use a graphic such as a textured background or a picture. You'll want to soften the background image by screening it back so it doesn't interfere with the readability of the type in your table.

Establishing Table Preferences

Adobe Table has program and publication defaults, just like PageMaker, as described in Chapter 3, "Personalizing PageMaker Preferences." Establish program defaults by setting the program's menus and palettes with no table document open. Publication defaults are established by your most recent formatting actions on cells, rows, and columns.

The Preferences command in the File menu also helps customize your table operations. In figure 16.8, you can see that it is possible to set standard percentages for subscripts, superscripts, and autoleading. You can also establish whether you usually will be importing text in tab or comma-delimited form, and choose which dictionary you want.

Fig. 16.8 ▶

Establishing Adobe Table preferences.

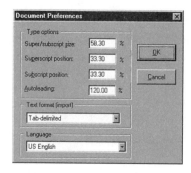

Importing Databases and Spreadsheets

Even though Adobe Table goes a long way towards helping PageMaker help you set table, there are some situations where you should use other techniques:

▶ You may have special formatting and typesetting needs.

▶ Your tables may be too long to fit on one page so they can't be handled as OLE objects.

▶ You may have so many tables to set that it would be easier to handle them as standardized batches of type in PageMaker instead of having to work one-by-one in an add-on program. In PageMaker you have tools such as paragraph styles and multiple master pages. In addition you could put scripting and the new tagging language to work.

There are two major steps to the process of working with raw table data in PageMaker. You must first import the data, and then you must format it. The "Importing Data" section focuses on getting the data into PageMaker. The section "Formatting Data Tables and Forms" tackles the formatting part of the job. A third section, "Precoding and Automating Data Formatting," describes ways to make the sometimes tedious task of constructing data tables go easier.

KEY CONCEPT:
The Nature of PageMaker Database and Spreadsheet Info

When PageMaker imports data it generally brings it in as tabbed paragraphs. For every record, there's a separate paragraph. And every tab marks out a field of information in that record. In other words, PageMaker data is usually *tab delimited*.

You can best understand this concept by thinking of the data as a matrix. The horizontal rows of information are called *records* and the vertical columns are called *fields*. Taken together, the rows and columns make up a database of information.

This matrix of records and fields works much the same way as a telephone book. If you want to find the phone number for John Smith who lives on Jicama

Street, you begin with the last name column where you search out the Smiths. Each Smith is a record. Then you scan over to the right to the first names and scan further until you find John. Each item in the record is a field. Then you move over to the right again to another field, to the one John Smith who lives on Jicama Street. You use three fields to refine your search through the telephone number database.

Happily, PageMaker gives you tools for applying styles and local formatting to each record and field, a topic covered in the section "Formatting Tools for Data Tables and Forms."

TACTICS RECIPE:
Setting Up Tables and Forms

The following plan can help you organize your thoughts the next time some table, database publishing, or forms project just sits there like an intimidating lump next to your keyboard:

▼ *Begin with the most complex table.* Study the table, form, or database material that will be the most complex. How many columns will you need? What family of type will you use? Where can you utilize rules, bars, and shading to help organize the information? In what order should the material be presented? Should it be chronological, alphabetical, by size?

▼ *Experiment in PageMaker with the most complex table as a model.* After you identify your most complex table formatting challenge and you've given some preliminary thought to planning out your approach, jump right into experimentation. Play around with this toughest design problem until it works just right on the page. Select type, tabs, rules, and the rest of the elements of the design and try them out, refining your original vision as you go. Try to base the design on some sort of grid so your information has an intrinsic visual logic.

▼ *Use your completed complex design as a publication-wide model style.* When you have a design, double-check to make sure that you can apply those size elements throughout your publication by visualizing other tables set with your new format.

▼ *Design your automation method.* After your model has been developed, plan out the combination of automation tools you will use, based on suggestions in this chapter, and the work flow steps that will work best for you in the long run, and then invest the time up front in building your system so the rest of the work can be handled more or less automatically as you place your data and format it. Think about styles, precoding, word processor or spreadsheet table building, format conversion, and the use of an add-on database publishing filter.

▼ *Construct or refine the data.* After you know how you'll be working on it, get your data into shape. Using a word processor, spreadsheet, or database, apply your system of styles to the data. If certain fields will be combined in PageMaker (first and last name, city with state and zip code), combine them before you import them, when it's generally easier to manipulate data. Apply any precoding, or add style tags in the fields of the appropriate records.

▼ *Place and lay out the table.* Import your data into PageMaker and make any adjustments. Use the Search and Replace tools on your precoding, for example. For the simpler tables—the ones that aren't as complicated as your complex model—you need to make adjustments to reduce the number of columns, while retaining the overall look of your publication's table style.

Importing Data

With that background out of the way, using the Place command to bring your data into PageMaker works pretty much like any other text importing operation. However, there are some nuances, explained in this section.

Raw Databases

Like plankton, plain ASCII raw data leads a primitive existence. It's the simplest of the data forms, low on the food chain of producing PageMaker pages—but in many cases essential to life as we know it.

Whenever you attempt to place plain text data in PageMaker, you get the Plain Text Filter dialog box shown in figure 16.9.

Fig. 16.9 ▶

Using the Page-Maker Plain Text Filter dialog box.

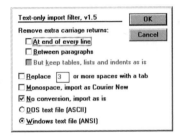

If you open a plain text data file in the Story Editor, you get something that looks like figure 16.10.

When you use the plain text filter on data, if it has already been broken up into fields by tabs, you will generally want to bring the text into PageMaker in its most unadorned fashion, by checking No Conversion, Import As Is. However, the other options may be of considerable help if you need to do some massaging of the file to clean it up as it comes into PageMaker.

Formatting this mess of tab-filled paragraphs may look daunting, but it isn't as hard as it may seem. You find out how to do it in the later section "Formatting Data Tables and Forms."

Fig. 16.10 ▶

*A Story Editor
view of a raw
data file placed
in PageMaker.*

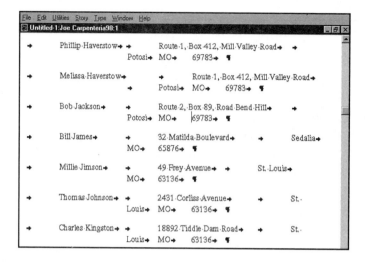

Spreadsheets and Databases

Many of the data files you will meet in your PageMaker travels will need to be converted into plain text for best results in bringing them in PageMaker. For that you would probably use the built in file export facilities of the application program used to compile the data file.

However, specialized Place filters have been built for several common spreadsheets and databases. As with word processor formats, the availability of data filters and their specific features change as often as the programs are updated, which is pretty darn often. To keep abreast of these developments, stay in touch with the usual sources for information on updates—online services, the Adobe Web site, Adobe magazine, consumer magazines, and so on.

Microsoft Excel is a good example for our discussion of application-specific data files because its filter has about the most robust capabilities of any of them. To import Excel, use the Place command just like importing any other text. Page-Maker automatically detects that you are attempting to bring in an Excel spreadsheet. In figure 16.11, you can see the resulting dialog box.

Choosing a Piece of Your Data

If you want, you can import the entire spreadsheet. However, it's likely that you will want to designate just a portion of your data for inclusion in your PageMaker publication. Pop-up lists search inside the spreadsheet and provide you with a choice of the spreadsheets inside the file, as well as any named ranges. You can also type in a range of specific cells, simply writing over the listing in the Cell Range box. You type out the upper-left and lower-right corner coordinates, separated by a colon (as in A4:H10). But the optimum way to manage the intake of spreadsheet data is to plan your spreadsheet for importation, organizing your sheets and designating named ranges for easy selection from these pop-ups.

FIG. 16.11 ▶

The Excel Import Filter dialog box.

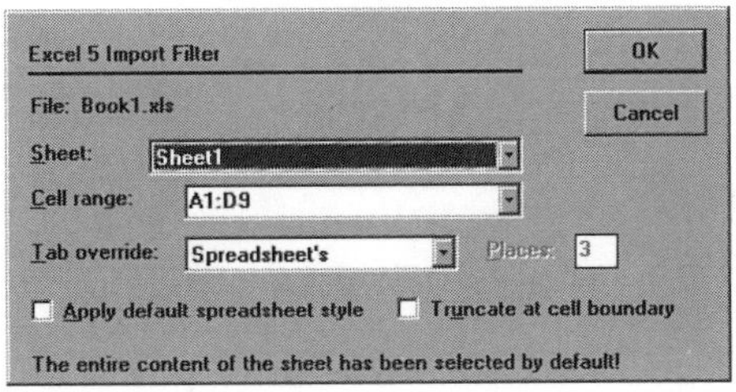

Excel 5 Import Filter   OK
File: Book1.xls   Cancel
Sheet: Sheet1
Cell range: A1:D9
Tab override: Spreadsheet's   Places: 3
☐ Apply default spreadsheet style   ☐ Truncate at cell boundary
The entire content of the sheet has been selected by default!

Formatting Data Before Importing

With a little advance work you can take several steps to use the import filter to format your data, potentially saving yourself quite a lot of manual work.

Your data import filter, as with the Excel filter shown in figure 16.11, may allow you to force the type of tabs used to align the data in each field of the imported records. This feature actually controls the type of tab PageMaker places in the paragraph formatting as it imports the data. The alignment option works only if there's a Number formatting style assigned in Excel.

In most cases, you will want to accept the default, the spreadsheet's existing alignment. You can choose to adopt whatever alignment has been previously designated in the spreadsheet, or you can force all fields to have left, center, right, or decimal alignment. If you opt for decimal tabs, you may also define your level of numeric precision—the number of places you want to the right of the decimal. For dollars and cents data, you will likely want two decimal places, for example.

The PageMaker data filters will not accept more than 40 fields, or spreadsheet columns, of data per record. As the data comes in, tab stops are set for each column of data based on the width of the spreadsheet columns.

You should almost always choose the check box Apply Default Spreadsheet Style to the imported records. Every paragraph, or record, of data will be assigned a style—XLS in the case of Excel data. Then you can edit that style to establish your choice of typesetting attributes for your data.

Finally, the Truncate at Cell Boundary check box throws out any characters that extend out beyond the edges of a cell as the spreadsheet is imported into PageMaker. You might use this option if you have a lot of verbiage in a memo field and simply want to import the first few words of the information.

Importing Word Processor Tables

PageMaker offers several alternatives for importing tables constructed using your word processor's built-in table editor. The number of available PageMaker word processing filters is even more plentiful than for databases and spreadsheets.

The filter for Microsoft Word Version 6.0, shown in figure 16.12, makes the point pretty well, about the constantly evolving nature of PageMaker filters.

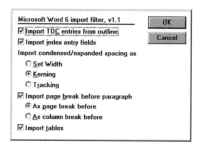

Notice that the filter has settings so you can import a table. But that doesn't mean you get a table nicely formatted with borders and such, like the ones created in Adobe Table. The text comes into PageMaker as a text file, retaining local formatting, including paragraph styles.

The point is, until this filter was available, to import Word tables you had to provide PageMaker with a special code in the Word file. In fact, you still have to do that if you want to import older Word files. The code requires placing a paragraph just above the table, containing the single capital letter "T" and formatted as hidden text.

Formatting Data Tables and Forms

Whichever method you use to import text into PageMaker (Word, ASCII tab delimited, Excel, megaphone, semaphore), you will want to make it look nice. You can use any of the type and paragraph formatting tools in the book to spruce up your tables, but you will probably make special use of the tools listed in this section. Rules, tabs, check boxes, and style sheets seem to come up over and over when you organize and present data in tables and forms.

TIP ▶ Planning Table Formatting Through Experimentation

Clearly, if you plan the ultimate look of the table before you bring the data into PageMaker, your job of formatting a table of data will be a lot easier. As suggested in the Tactics Recipe at the head of this chapter, experimentation can be a big help. It's tough to know all the ins and outs in advance, before going into the actual layout phase of a project.

What's the secret? Planned play. Pick out the most complex table you'll face in a project and isolate it. Import that table into PageMaker and plan out your rules and tabs and styles. When you know where you want line breaks and the local formatting for various fields, you can then implement the styling in your word processor and bring the table data into PageMaker in a halfway complete state, ready for your fine-tuning.

Cleaning Up Data

When your data finally arrives in PageMaker, you generally need to do some clean up. For that, use the Find and Change command techniques in Chapter 9. (You could also put to work one of the batch search and replace tools mentioned in Chapter 28, for use in connection with PageMaker's tagging language.)

For example, in figure 16.13, a Word table was imported, but tabs were included at the head and tail of each row of the Word table. In the figure, they are being removed using Find and Change. Notice that this search for the tabs and the carriage return between them (^t^p^t) includes the style sheet attribute for the row, otherwise, the removal of the carriage return would convert the paragraphs to No Style.

FIG. 16.13 ▶

Cleaning out leading and trailing tab characters using search and replace.

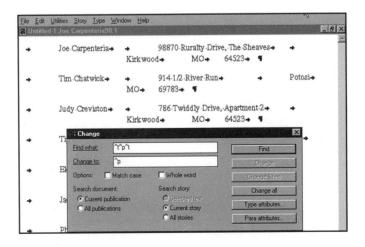

Setting Tabbed Columns and Hanging Indents

Once you have your data cleaned up, free of excess tabs and spaces and so on, you can begin the process of experimenting with the layout. One good way to start is to highlight the first record and a page full of records to go with it (see fig. 16.14). Then call up the Indent/Tab dialog box (Ctrl+I) and experiment with the tab positions until the formatting breaks just right, using the Apply button to check effects as you go.

When you have the columns just right, along with any hanging indent you need, adopt the experiment with a click on the OK button. The tabs will be adopted throughout the selected text. You can then use the properly tabbed record or records as the basis for a new paragraph style, or you can redefine the style already in place (see Chapter 7, "Designing a Text Style System").

Fig. 16.14 ▶

Experimenting with the tabs spacing for a table.

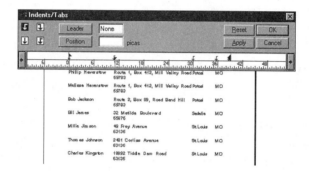

You can see that a large hanging indent has been used to set off the names in the data in figure 16.14. If you format records or table entries that need to be several lines deep, you use this hanging indent technique a great deal. The key to the trick is to format the data with a new line character where you need the data to break down to the next line.

A hanging indent is especially helpful when you must lay out a table with text descriptions. To help automate that kind of layout, be sure to put the multi-line field out in the right-most column, as in figure 16.15, putting the first line at the column edge and indenting all subsequent lines to the pseudo-column formed by the left edge of the text description.

If you lay out financial reports (for example, business presentations, corporate annual reports, SEC filings), you are going to love this next bit. As you see in figure 16.16, the PageMaker decimal tab understands the parentheses used to indicate minus numbers in financial tables. In days of old when doing fine typography on a table, you had to go through a table and kern the negative numbers (or add special space to the positive ones) so the column of numbers would line up regardless of the presence of the parentheses.

FIG. 16.15 ▷

A hanging indent used to format multiline table entries.

Animal	Area	Behavior
Dusky Dolphin	South Circumpolar	Populist. Enjoys large crowds and cavorting. Votes independent.
Ruffed Lemur	Madagascar	A loner who specializes in twins, ironically. Little known otherwise and often appears in the undecided column in voting polls. Did not return phone calls for this study.
Celebes Wild Pig	Sulawesi Island	Known for prominent facial warts. Highly vocal at rallies. Engages in rhythmic grunting called the courtship chant, especially during romantic, moonlit tropical forest evenings. Favored Bullmoose ticket during last recorded voting.
Capybara	South America	Largest rodent in the world. Leaders in the animal rights movement since the 16th century when Venezuelans began ranching them, after missionaries listed Capybara as okay for eating during Lent.

FIG. 16.16 ▷

Smart decimal tabs in PageMaker automatically line up negative numbers surrounded by parentheses.

Capital Investment	$1,000,001.01
Short Term Investment	599,999.02
Capital Gains	(425,499.99)
Quarterly Profit	(6.95)

> **TIP ▷ Use Column and Ruler Guides to Help Estimate Tab Locations**
>
> When you first begin to set tabs for a table, pull out some ruler guides or use the Guide Manager to set up a grid of temporary ruler and column guides. Define the same number of guides as you'll be setting columns of data. This kind of grid helps you to see how much space you need and gives you a visual guide for the initial placement of tabs. The upcoming section about formatting forms shows an example of creating a matrix to organize fill-in blanks by setting five columns with a zero pica alley between them. For this tip, you don't use the column guides to pour text, just as a handy way to split a page up into even columns to help you visually line up the information.

Emphasizing Data with Paragraph Rules

To emphasize data elements, use the paragraph rule facility. To accomplish this styling, you can use some of the headline special effects from Chapter 15, "Creating Special Effects."

In figure 16.17, a style was created with a horizontal rule in 80 percent gray, and the names were set in bold and reversed type so they knocked out against the rule. The rule has a large right indent to bring it in so that it just covers the name field.

FIG. 16.17 ▶

An indented column width rule is used to emphasize the name field of each record.

Joe Carpenteria	98870 Ruralty Drive, The Sheaves
	Kirkwood MO 64523
Tim Chatwick	914 1/2 River Run
	Potosi MO 69783
Judy Creviston	786 Twiddly Drive, Apartment 2
	Kirkwood MO 64523
Tipper Gill	2 Bonnie Lane
	Sedalia MO 65876
Eleanor Hakes	56873 Lankersham Drive, Apartment 3
	Kirkwood MO 64523
Jack Harwood	9245 1/2 Hatfield Place
	Kirkwood MO 64523
Phillip Haverstow	Route 1, Box 412, Mill Valley Road
	Potosi MO 69783
Melissa Haverstow	Route 1, Box 412, Mill Valley Road
	Potosi MO 69783
Bob Jackson	Route 2, Box 89, Road Bend Hill
	Potosi MO 69783
Bill James	32 Matilda Boulevard
	Sedalia MO 65876
Millie Jimson	49 Frey Avenue
	St. Louis MO 63136
Thomas Johnson	2431 Corliss Avenue
	St. Louis MO 63136
Charles Kingston	18892 Tiddle Dam Road
	St. Louis MO 63136
George MacDuff	RFD #2
	Sedalia MO 65876
Mary Parton	Route 3
	Sedalia MO 65876

In figure 16.18, the same technique was used to produce numbered square dingbats for each record. The technique was augmented by use of the Bullets And Numbering Addition and the placement of new decimal tabs at the head of each record. The rule has been reset to 20 percent gray.

FIG. 16.18 ▶

Numbered dingbats for your data, using right indented gray paragraph rules.

1.	Joe Carpenteria	98870 Ruralty Drive, The Sheaves
		Kirkwood MO 64523
2.	Tim Chatwick	914 1/2 River Run
		Potosi MO 69783
3.	Judy Creviston	786 Twiddly Drive, Apartment 2
		Kirkwood MO 64523
4.	Tipper Gill	2 Bonnie Lane
		Sedalia MO 65876
5.	Eleanor Hakes	56873 Lankersham Drive, Apartment 312
		Kirkwood MO 64523
6.	Jack Harwood	9245 1/2 Hatfield Place
		Kirkwood MO 64523
7.	Phillip Haverstow	Route 1, Box 412, Mill Valley Road
		Potosi MO 69783
8.	Melissa Haverstow	Route 1, Box 412, Mill Valley Road
		Potosi MO 69783
9.	Bob Jackson	Route 2, Box 89, Road Bend Hill
		Potosi MO 69783
10.	Bill James	32 Matilda Boulevard
		Sedalia MO 65876
11.	Millie Jimson	49 Frey Avenue
		St. Louis MO 63136
12.	Thomas Johnson	2431 Corliss Avenue
		St. Louis MO 63136
13.	Charles Kingston	18892 Tiddle Dam Road
		St. Louis MO 63136
14.	George MacDuff	RFD #2
		Sedalia MO 65876
15.	Mary Parton	Route 3
		Sedalia MO 65876
16.	Henry Perquitz	9968 Elm Avenue
		St. Louis MO 63136

Laying in Vertical Rules

Often you need vertical lines in table gutters, to separate data and to help lead the eye down a sort of visual alley of information. The obvious thing to do is to simply draw vertical lines where you need them when you lay out tables.

That would be tedious, wouldn't it? Besides, tables often must survive two harsh environmental factors. First, tables are data and therefore subject to frequent edits and updates, which potentially means lots of repositioning of lines if they are set as independent graphics. Also, tables tend to be deadline-driven, mass-production challenges, involving documents that have been jammed full of data (for example, corporate annual reports, business plans, technical documentation), so you generally want techniques that will help automate your work.

In figure 16.19, you see a vertical rule in a data table. It was placed as an inline graphic in the first paragraph of the record run, not drawn in as an independent graphic. Use the inline graphic technique in Chapter 15, "Creating Special Effects," adjusting the line's baseline and length to fit the table's dimensions. To position it horizontally, set a tab for its location in the first paragraph, the one used to anchor the line to the text block.

Fig. 16.19 ▶

A vertical rule, set as an inline graphic and positioned with a tab stop.

Joe Carpenteria	98870 Ruralty Drive, The Sheaves Kirkwood MO 64523
Tim Chatwick	914 1/2 River Run Potosi MO 69783
Judy Creviston	786 Twiddly Drive, Apartment 2 Kirkwood MO 64523
Tipper Gill	2 Bonnie Lane Sedalia MO 65876
Eleanor Hakes	56873 Lankersham Drive, Apartment Kirkwood MO 64523
Jack Harwood	9245 1/2 Hatfield Place Kirkwood MO 64523
Phillip Haverstow	Route 1, Box 412, Mill Valley Road Potosi MO 69783
Melissa Haverstow	Route 1, Box 412, Mill Valley Road Potosi MO 69783
Bob Jackson	Route 2, Box 89, Road Bend Hill Potosi MO 69783
Bill James	32 Matilda Boulevard Sedalia MO 65876
Millie Jimson	49 Frey Avenue St. Louis MO 63136
Thomas Johnson	2431 Corliss Avenue St. Louis MO 63136
Charles Kingston	18892 Tiddle Dam Road St. Louis MO 63136
George MacDuff	RFD #2 Sedalia MO 65876
Mary Parton	Route 3 Sedalia MO 65876
Henry Perquitz	9988 Elm Avenue St. Louis MO 63136

Inline graphics controlled by tab stops in a style are wonderfully consistent when you set many tables. In addition, as graphic elements, these graphics fall to a back layer in relationship to the text in which they've been embedded. That means you can use the before and after rules of the paragraphs containing your records.

Have a look at figure 16.20, to see how you can pull off some elegant formatting and save hours of intricate layout work, by combining an inline graphic vertical rule with paragraph rules. The top paragraph rule has been augmented by an indent and a gray tint to set off the name field in the data record. The bottom rule then breaks the vertical inline graphic rule alongside each record, automatically cutting it up into variable depths to match the height of each paragraph, no matter how many lines you include in each record.

Fig. 16.20 ▶

A grayed rule emphasis, combined with a reverse rule that knocks out the vertical inline graphic between records.

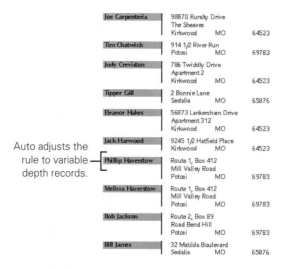

Auto adjusts the rule to variable depth records.

TIP ▶ Multiple Masters Aid Table Layout

Of course, if you opt to simply draw in your vertical rules with the Line tool, don't overlook the work-saving possibilities of master pages. Now that PageMaker has multiple master pages, you could draw vertical column borders on a master page, and use that page only when you are setting a table. This might be especially helpful if you are setting page after page of data that remains consistent in positioning, such as telephone or personnel directories.

Precoding Data Tables for Maximum Efficiency

If multipage tables are part of your layout life, you need to get precoded. The more you can do to precode your data, the easier it will be to format the data when you bring it into PageMaker. Done right, in fact, most of the formatting will already be done when the data arrives on the page.

Prestyling Your Data

Several of the PageMaker import filters will bring data into PageMaker with enough formatting to serve many of your layout needs.

Microsoft Word tables come through the filter with paragraph styles and field-by-field formatting intact. It's easy to do mass formatting in Word tables because you can select an entire column and assign it a particular type style, type face, or whatever. And paragraph styles can easily be assigned to word processor tables.

Spreadsheet records are automatically assigned a style by the PageMaker filter as they are imported:

▶ Once the paragraph styled data has been imported, edit the styles to suit your format. The illustration with a hanging indent and a rule could be entirely formatted in a style.

▶ Format particular fields with unusual type formatting that can be searched and replaced for special formatting in PageMaker. Don't forget to check on the Retain Format setting in the Place command dialog box.

Figure 16.21 shows a Word table imported into PageMaker. The fields formatted with unusual typefaces could be formatted using search and replace techniques on their "weird" typeface attributes and replacing those attributes with the desired formatting.

FIG. 16.21 ▶

A Word table in PageMaker, with formatting intact and ready for search and replace on "weird" field-by-field text style precoding.

Coding Paragraph Styles In Plain Text

If your data will be plain text, you can still bring it into PageMaker with paragraph styling in place. Use the style tags import feature described in Chapter 8, "Pouring Text into PageMaker."

Remember, the key to the style tags import technique is to check the Read Tags setting in the Place Command dialog box. Here are three ways to put style tags into your inbound data:

▶ If all your records should have the same style, this is your solution. Put a style tag at the head of the first paragraph. When PageMaker finds a style tag in its inbound text, it applies that style to every subsequent paragraph until it hits a new style code. You don't need to style every record.

▶ If you want different styles for different records, you'll need to insert them at the head of each paragraph. This might be used in a situation where you want alternating bars of screened color to make it easier to discern the different rows of data. In the application being used to compile the data, add a new first column and code the style tags into that first column.

▶ You can insert record-by-record style tags even if you don't have the originating application. Try doing a search and replace for the paragraph markers in the text, replacing each paragraph marker with a new one, plus the style tag for the following paragraph.

Supercharging Table Coding with Tagging

PageMaker's new tagging language, covered in Chapter 28, "Automating PageMaker," could be used to do major typographic management of tables. Fundamentally, the technique would be similar to the one just described. However, instead of adding a single column to the left-hand side of the table, in your spreadsheet or word processor, put a column between each field. Think of these new columns as the coding fields. Then in each coding field copy the proper tagging language codes to format the next field over to the right. Virtually all of PageMaker's formatting power will be at your fingertips.

TIP ▶ PageMaker Will Automatically Write Your Data Table Tagging Language Codes!

Begin your tagging coding by importing just a dozen records or so of data. Experiment with the formatting until you have it just right, including colors, paragraph rules, typeface, and style—every conceivable formatting option. Then export that small piece as tagging language. Open this tagging language fragment up and copy the codes into your database, spreadsheet, or word processor table. In other words, let PageMaker write your tagging language code for you.

Creating Lines and Check Boxes on Forms

PageMaker does a good job when you need to compose precision forms such as order blanks and employment applications or even data entry sheets for the Twin Cities Lonely Heart Dating Service.

At one time or another all the text formatting and special effects techniques come into play when creating forms. However, two special forms layout issues are universal—fill-in blanks and check boxes.

TIP ▶ Use Fixed Leading and Tabs to Lay Out Forms

Here's the universal law of forms. Find a way to use locked down positioning techniques, which generally means using fixed leading and tabs. Forms are highly structured and full of objects that the eye can line up on. That's why forms look hideous if the line spacing stutters down the page and the blanks jollywog every which way. Apply some kind of grid to the form so things line up with a sense of logic. Unless the form is extremely basic, any other layout will drive your reader crazy.

Setting Check boxes

For check boxes, use Zapf Dingbats. It comes with virtually every PostScript laser printer. Use the bullets and hanging indent technique to set consistent spacing (see Chapter 6, "Formatting Paragraphs"). Look at figure 16.22 to see how tabs can be used to line up check boxes in a form.

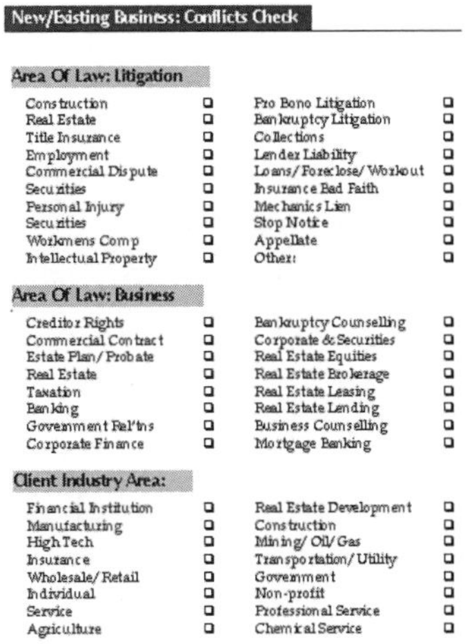

New/Existing Business: Conflicts Check

Area Of Law: Litigation

Construction	❑	Pro Bono Litigation	❑
Real Estate	❑	Bankruptcy Litigation	❑
Title Insurance	❑	Collections	❑
Employment	❑	Lender Liability	❑
Commercial Dispute	❑	Loans/Foreclose/Workout	❑
Securities	❑	Insurance Bad Faith	❑
Personal Injury	❑	Mechanics Lien	❑
Securities	❑	Stop Notice	❑
Workmens Comp	❑	Appellate	❑
Intellectual Property	❑	Other:	❑

Area Of Law: Business

Creditor Rights	❑	Bankruptcy Counselling	❑
Commercial Contract	❑	Corporate & Securities	❑
Estate Plan/Probate	❑	Real Estate Equities	❑
Real Estate	❑	Real Estate Brokerage	❑
Taxation	❑	Real Estate Leasing	❑
Banking	❑	Real Estate Lending	❑
Government Rel'tns	❑	Business Counselling	❑
Corporate Finance	❑	Mortgage Banking	❑

Client Industry Area:

Financial Institution	❑	Real Estate Development	❑
Manufacturing	❑	Construction	❑
High Tech	❑	Mining/Oil/Gas	❑
Insurance	❑	Transportation/Utility	❑
Wholesale/Retail	❑	Government	❑
Individual	❑	Non-profit	❑
Service	❑	Professional Service	❑
Agriculture	❑	Chemical Service	❑

FIG. 16.22 ▶

Tab-aligned check boxes using Zapf Dingbats formatting.

Setting Fill-In Blanks

For almost every form project, you are best off using the underline or leader tab technique described here. This technique is much faster and more flexible and precise than the usual techniques of endlessly tap-tap-tapping underline characters or sketching lines with the Line tool.

Paragraph rules are one alternative, although a limited alternative. Blanks almost always have text labels in front of them, and it's tough to juxtapose opposition-indented paragraph rules so you get a line that consistently spaces out from your label. Also, it's impossible to have multiple blanks on the same line because a paragraph rule is an all or nothing proposition. If you need multiple blanks on a line, you'll end up setting half a dozen independent text blocks for a simple business reply card, not to mention the valuable time you'll spend trying to get them all perfectly aligned.

Don't draw forms with the Line tool, and don't use the uppercase hyphen "underline" character, either. If you draw lines or use the underline character, you can't automate the creation of lines using paragraph styles. Not only that, the lines or hyphens are more difficult to edit than the leader method, and drawn lines are hard to line up with one another. Plus, assuming you are setting with proportional spaced type, the underline characters have an unsettling tendency to space out from one another into a dotted line effect.

Fill-In Blanks from Tab Leader

Look at figure 16.23 to see how a complex form can be set with tabs and lined up using (in this case) a five column guide grid set with a zero pica alley between columns.

All these lines were set using tabs. The labels have a tab in front of them with a right-aligned tab to shove them over to align on the grid. The next tab stop has been set with the underline character chosen from the Leader list in the Indents/Tabs dialog box. Double lines are set with two pairs of right-aligned tabs and leader tabs. Styles have been assigned to all the various types of lines, so it was easy to replicate the tab alignments when the proper tab setup was found for a given set of fill-in blank requirements.

Fill-In Blanks from Formatting the Tab Character

Keep in mind that the tabs take on the character formatting of the preceding character. Each of the blanks in this last illustration could have been set by inserting a thin space in front of the tab (Shift+Ctrl+T) and giving that space the underline type style. Then you would get an automatic underline for the distance covered between tab marks, instead of using the tab leader method.

FIG. 16.23 ▶

A form set with tabs and indents, organized using the five-column grid shown on the right.

Five-column grid for
visual organization

This technique's real power comes in if you want to set an unusual fill-in blank, something other than a simple line. For example, you could achieve a very delicate fill-in blank by setting a thin space in front of the tab and formatting the thin space with some special formatting. For example, you could use a dotted leader and format the thin space with a small point size to shrink the size of the dots. You could also format the thin space with a color or a gray tint.

TIP ▶ **Code Table Styles to Bottom of Dialog Box**

When you create style sheets for your tables and forms, you invent many special-purpose styles that you might use on just a few pages of your publication. Those few pages of special-purpose styles can create a closet full of clutter in your Style palette. Name these kinds of special-purpose styles so that they fall to the bottom of the palette; then they won't get mixed in with your more commonly used layout styles. Put the letter "z" in front of them, for example.

TIP ▶ **Database Publishing Tool**

Keep an eye on the news. As this book goes to press, at least one software manufacturer is rumored to be preparing a special tool for managing data in the PageMaker desktop publishing environment. It remains unclear whether Adobe will upgrade

continues

TIP ▶	Continued

InfoPublisher, the database formatting engine that it markets. (Over on the Macintosh side, DataShaper, the main database publishing software, became an orphan when its distributor went under.) Also, maybe something will come of the Adobe and Frame merger, as the new entity cross-pollinates FrameMaker and PageMaker. FrameMaker has good built-in table design capabilities.

Where to Go from Here

▶ In some ways, this chapter may have tantalized you a bit about the possibilities of special type effects. When formatting tables, you can put to work many of the special effects in Chapter 15, "Creating Special Effects," to give stodgy old tables of data some snap, especially when you use the headline and paragraph rule stuff.

▶ If you are producing tables or publishing databases, it's likely that you are producing long form documents. You can find much more about reports, books, technical documentation, business plans, and so on in Chapter 17, "Building Many Pages."

▶ Organizing information sometimes requires every tool in the book. And sometimes the tools are fun! Explore the use of color. Tinted bars, colored rules, screens behind tables—all these things can help the eye follow your data and at the same time give your reader a small tingle of eyeball delight.

Chapter 17

Building Many Pages

This chapter helps you organize the process of building a big publication by telling you all about:

Using the Book command, which is the foundation of PageMaker's large document building power.

▼

Navigating through all those pages quickly, as well as inserting, removing, and sorting them.

▼

Automating the generation of a table of contents.

▼

Putting together an index, using PageMaker's world-class indexing tools.

▼

Constructing special features for a book such as running headers and footers, unnumbered covers, and independently numbered front and back matter (prefaces and appendixes, for example).

STACKING UP A REPORT or a book—dozens or hundreds of pages—takes a special kind of organization. Just to name one example, the text of a book contains chapters and chapters of detail, so you need to generate tables of contents and indexes and illustration lists that make it possible for your readers to climb inside that book and find what they need to know. So, organizing a book full of information requires you to be organized in your work. Fortunately, PageMaker has an array of book-building tools to help you accomplish the task in an ultra-organized fashion. ▶ ▶ ▶

Building a Book List

Any long form document probably ought to be broken up into smaller pieces. Call them chapters for convenience, but the central concepts covered here work whether you call them chapters, sections, parts, front matter, appendixes, tables of contents, or indexes. By breaking your document into these smaller pieces, you:

▶ Gain the advantages of PageMaker's automated book-building command

▶ Allow specialized page numbering using chapter prefixes or different numbering styles for front matter, tables of contents, appendixes, and indexes

▶ Minimize the risk of problems at the service bureau or print shop, since you will have broken your job down into more manageable pieces

Using the Book Command

PageMaker's multiple document management features have been built on the foundation provided by the Book command. When you select this command from the File menu, a dialog box like the one in figure 17.1 appears.

FIG. 17.1 ▶

Assemble multiple files into one big publication with this Book command dialog box.

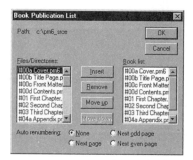

Composing the Book List

The side-by-side scrolling lists of files in this dialog box help you build a list of the files (the chapters, you might say) that you want to include in your publication (your book). Basically, you select each file you want to include in the book from the list on the left. Then you either double-click the file or use the Insert button to add that file to the Book List on the right side. As you'd expect, the Remove button deletes items from the list.

The order of the book list, on the right side, determines the order of your table of contents and the page numbering of your index items. One of the most common mistakes anyone makes with the Book List is to get the chapters out of order. The Move Up and Move Down buttons allow you to shuffle the order of the items on the list.

Renumbering Pages Automatically

Another common error involves settings in the Auto Renumbering section of the Book dialog box. If these are set wrong, you'll be wondering why PageMaker mysteriously inserted a bunch of blank pages and why your page numbers have shifted around.

The following list describes the Auto Renumbering radio buttons:

▶ *None.* This button turns off Auto Renumbering. PageMaker uses the page numbers as they exist in the publications in your book list. No new pages will be added to your book.

▶ *Next Page.* This button gives consecutive page numbers to all the files in your book list. If the first chapter ends on page 29, the second chapter is automatically numbered beginning with page 30. No new pages will be added to your book.

▶ *Next Odd Page.* This button and the Next Page button are the most common ones. With this button, PageMaker forces the first page in each new file to be a right-hand page and gives it an odd page number. If the first chapter ends on page 29, for example, PageMaker inserts a new page 30 in the chapter one file and moves on to begin chapter two with page 31. The new page 30 is blank except for the master page material but that inserted page forces the second chapter to begin on an odd number.

▶ *Next Even Page.* This radio button works just like the Next Odd Page button, except it makes the first page of the next file in a book list an even numbered page (a left-hand page), adding a fresh page at the end of the previous file if necessary.

By the way, Auto Renumbering only affects pages that have the PageMaker page number symbol on them (either directly or by way of the master pages). Ordinarily, the page number symbol is inserted in a footer or header text block on a master page (see the "Adding Standard Master Page Elements" section of Chapter 13 for details).

TIP ▶ Copy Book List to All Pubs

Ordinarily you pick one section of your book as the repository of your book list. However, it can be very useful to copy the list to all the publications contained in that list. That will enable you to access the entire book index from any of the book chapters. It also makes it possible for you to print your book list publication from any file in the list.

To copy your book list to all publications, hold down the Ctrl key as you select the Book command in the file where you've created your book list. PageMaker immediately copies that book list to every file in the book list you are opening. This copy operation is a onetime deal. You'll have to repeat it if you later change your mind about what ought to be in the book list, because no live update connection is established.

Organizing Your Book Files

On a multichapter project, with all those files floating around, you better have a good way to organize your file names. Ideally, the file naming system will automatically organize your files into their proper order, making it easier for you to make sure your book list is also in the proper order, and also making it easier for whomever must assemble the book at your service bureau and at the printer and bindery.

Try numbering the files like this, assuming you take advantage of that Windows 95 capability to have more than 8+3 file names:

> #00a Cover
>
> #00b Title Page
>
> #00c Front Matter
>
> #00d Contents
>
> #01 First Chapter
>
> #02 Second Chapter
>
> #03 Third Chapter
>
> #04a Appendix
>
> #04b Index

With this alphanumeric system, your files list in proper order in any alphabetical dialog box (such as the one for the Book command). At the same time, with the text characters you suggest the contents of each file, so you aren't relying on numbers alone. The pound sign (#) at the front of each file name assures that the files list together, organizing themselves into a group even in a cluttered dialog box. The use of double-digit numbers (placing zeroes before single-digit chapter numbers) ensures proper alphabetical sorting. If you leave the zero off the single-digit chapters, for example, chapter number 10 would list after number 1 and before number 2, because your computer sorts from left to right, one character at a time.

DESIGN NOTE
Templates Are a Fast Track Solution

Using templates can get your basic book structure on the screen fast, so you can get down to the fine points of design right away. A few long form document templates— such as a template for a technical manual—are included in your PageMaker package. Instructions for using them are provided in the "Opening Templates" section of Chapter 12. The hypothetical book used for examples in this chapter was produced with a template designed by Chuck Green for his DesignKit template product (a nicely orga-nized set of more than 50 simple but elegant templates). The potential time savings offered by templates are tremendous. This particular template, for example, produced a complete book structure in less than half an hour—including style sheet, basic lay-out grid, table of contents, title page, index, and page numbering footers.

Organizing Chapters with Prefix Style Numbering

Technical documentation and other highly structured long form documents of-ten use prefix style chapter numbering. The pages in the third chapter, for ex-ample, might be numbered 3.1, 3.2, 3.3, 3.4, and so on. And an appendix might be numbered with a letter prefix—A.1, A.2, A.3.

This prefix numbering has a major advantage when it comes time to revise the document (which happens all too often, as any tech writer will tell you). Each chapter starts with page one, with a chapter prefix in front, so each stands alone.

Therefore, using chapter prefix numbering means a change in midbook won't trigger a massive shift in page numbering that runs like a string of dominoes fall-ing through the entire book. Consecutive numbering of all the pages in a book, on the other hand, would mean re-outputting every single page past the revision point. For example, if you cut page number 19 in a book numbered from 1 to 200, you would have to re-output more than 180 pages just because their page numbering shifted. That's a lot more expensive than merely redoing a single chapter. Given the cost of service bureau output, prefix style chapter pagination can save you a very large amount of money.

You must work in two locations to implement prefix style numbering. First, you click the Numbers button in the Document Setup dialog box. You get the Page Numbering dialog box you see in figure 17.2. Type in your prefix and, of course, select the style of numbering you want to use.

FIG. 17.2 ▶

Creating chapter-level prefix style numbering.

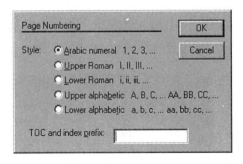

The Page Numbering dialog box only sets up prefix numbering for the table of contents and index. You must also change the page numbering on the pages of the chapter. Do that by typing the prefix before the page number in the header or footer story block on the master page (see fig. 17.3).

FIG. 17.3 ▶

Prefix numbering in headers and footers.

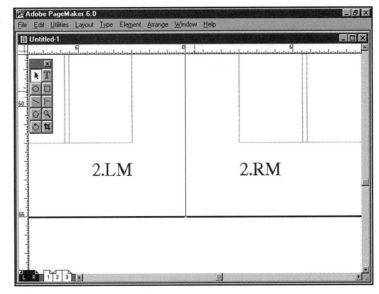

Manipulating and Navigating Pages

One challenge of a big publication is managing the sheer volume of pages. In this section, you find out how to add and remove pages and how to quickly navigate from page to page—even if you have to contend with a gigantic stack of them.

Inserting Pages

You can add pages to your publication in four ways. Autoflow adds pages to your publication automatically as it pours text into columns (see Chapter 8, "Pouring Text into PageMaker," for details). Tack as many extra pages as you like onto the end of your publication by using the Page Setup command (see Chapter 12, "Setting Up a New Publication," for more on this function). Add a single page with a new keyboard shortcut (Ctrl+Shift+'). Finally, add pages with the Insert Pages command (see fig. 17.4).

Fig. 17.4 ▶

*The Insert Pages
command.*

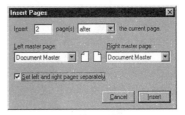

Your fresh pages are blank (except for any master page items). The pages will be formatted with the Document Master master page, unless you order otherwise in the pop-up lists provided in this dialog box. Notice that figure 17.4 has been set up to set the left- and right-pages separately, so you can apply different master pages to left- and right-side pages.

You can use the pop-up list to add pages before or after the current pages, or in between the two pages of the current spread. If you have Facing Pages checked in Page Setup, PageMaker offers to add two pages at a time. If you insert pages in the middle of threaded stories, the stories stay threaded but straddle over the inserted pages.

Watch out if you have set up Facing Pages in Page Setup. If you add an odd number of pages when you are working in Facing Pages mode, even numbered pages are shifted to odd numbered pages and vice versa. The result can be some pretty dramatic jumbling of graphics and text blocks on your pages. Chapter 12 has a detailed explanation of what you can expect in the section "Changing Page Setup (Beware!)."

Removing Pages

The Remove Pages dialog box, shown in figure 17.5, works in a very straight-ahead fashion. Just enter the numbers for the pages you want to remove; the program gives you a double-check warning box to confirm your decision before actually taking the action.

Fig. 17.5 ▶

Removing pages.

Any threaded story blocks on removed pages are gone forever, but the thread remains unbroken for the remaining story blocks located before and after the deleted pages.

TIP ▶ **PageMaker Now Has More Powerful Undo Command**

PageMaker 6.0 has a much more robust Undo feature! It includes the ability to Undo insertion and removal of pages. You can also Undo application of master pages. Don't forget that you also have, along with this new Undo power, the Remove Transformation command which has been moved to the Arrange menu from the Element menu where it was located in Version 5.0. Remove Transformation will, in one move, undo all rotation, skewing, and flipping. The only exception is a PageMaker drawn line.

TIP ▶ **Turn Layout Pages by Toggling Story Editor**

As you are chewing your way through a cluster of pages, editing in Layout view, you might wish that the pages would automatically turn for you when you got to the end of a page (or the second page in a spread). PageMaker 6.0 doesn't do this for you, but you can trick it into doing almost the same thing. When you get to the last text on the page, press the right-arrow key once. The cursor disappears from view. Press Ctrl+E to pop into Story Editor view, but before the screen has a chance to redraw, press Ctrl+E again to go right back to Layout view. Your cursor appears at the first text on the next page, ready to go. The trick to making this effective is to hit the keys so quickly that PageMaker's interruptible screen redraw has a chance to work its magic.

Sorting Pages

The Sort Pages Plug-in can get you into more trouble than it's worth. But when the deadline is nigh and the cold chill of the deadline witching hour is creeping up your spine, the Sort Pages command (in the Layout menu) may be worth the risk! We'll explore the dark side of Sort Pages in a bit; first let's have a look at how it works. Figure 17.6 shows how the Sort Pages dialog box looks on-screen.

FIG. 17.6 ▶

Use this Sort Pages main dialog box to get a quick overview of your publication as you reorder your pages.

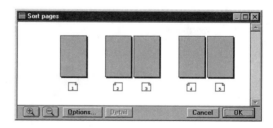

Simply select a page and drag it to a new position. A special pointer that looks like a stack of pages appears; the black bar you see in the illustration indicates where your selection will be dropped into place if you release the mouse button. You can select multiple pages by using Shift+click.

Select a single page of a two-page spread by holding down the Ctrl key as you click it. If you want to insert a selection of pages between two pages of a spread, hold down the Ctrl key before you click and drag your selection.

To get a wider view, you can stretch the window from any edge or corner. Get a better thumbnail look at any selected pages—with greeked text and graphics representations instead of gray boxes—by first clicking a page to select it and then clicking the Detail button.

If you click the Options button to access the Options dialog box (see fig. 17.7), you can see all the pages in Detail mode by clicking the Show Detailed Thumbnails check box in the Options dialog box. PageMaker remembers whatever you do in the Options dialog box, making your check box settings into defaults. If you turn on Show Detailed Thumbnails, you see that view the next time you open Sort Pages.

FIG. 17.7 ▶

*The Sort Pages
Options.*

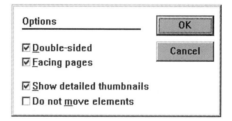

Be sure to save your file before sorting pages so you can use the Revert command to undo your move if necessary.

One potential bad effect of the Sort Pages Plug-in is similar to the problem that often arises with the Insert and Remove Pages commands. If you drop a single page into an existing spread, you shift the left page to a right page and the right page to a left page. That's not even considering the fact that the pages you are sorting into these new positions have their own left- and right-page attributes. This ripple effect can cause all kinds of drastic shifting of graphics and text objects on your pages. For details on the possible effects of converting left pages into right pages and vice versa, see Chapter 12.

The Double-Sided and Facing Pages check boxes perform exactly the same functions as the check boxes of the same name in the Page Setup dialog box under the File menu. As explained in Chapter 12, you should change these attributes only after careful planning and after making a backup.

If you must change the Double-Sided and Facing Pages settings, Sort Pages offers some potential mitigation. When you make the left/right page switch, the principle bad effect arises from PageMaker's attempts to keep objects aligned properly on the pages that get swapped between right and left. You may want to try using the Do Not Move Elements check box to freeze page objects into their pre-sort positions in relation to the left and right margins. A lot depends on how you laid out your pages, and every case is different. You can experiment with a backup of your particular layout to see how this might help or hinder your efforts. Again, you should also save your file immediately before sorting pages so you can use the Revert command to recover from unexpected results.

Constructing Tables of Contents

The Create TOC command on the Utilities menu does just what its name implies. But its function would be better described by a name like "Post Processing for Compiling Table of Contents Coded Paragraphs." The Create TOC command only takes a snapshot of your table of contents decisions; if you change them in any way, you must run the command again to update your table of contents.

To help understand this point, keep in mind that the process of creating a table of contents requires three steps:

1. First, you must define the paragraphs in your body text that are to be included in the table of contents.

   Simply mark the desired paragraphs for inclusion in the TOC by checking the appropriate box in the Paragraph Specifications dialog box. Usually you include this in a paragraph style definition for the items to be included in the TOC. For example, chapter heads and subheads are almost always chosen for inclusion.

2. Use the Create TOC command to process your publication (or your book list). This command creates a new story for your publication, compiling all the text entries that have been defined for inclusion in the TOC and assigning them special TOC style names and definitions.

3. Place the compiled TOC story and make any adjustments needed in the styles that format the TOC paragraphs.

Defining TOC Entries

Figure 17.8 shows the check box you use in the Paragraph Specifications command to tag a paragraph so it will be included in your TOC.

Fig. 17.8 ▶

The Paragraph
Specifications
box, showing the
Include in TOC
check box.

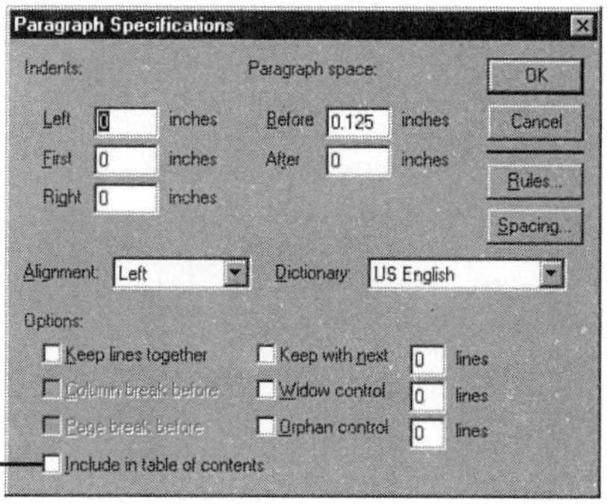

When selected, includes
paragraph text in TOC

In general, you will want to set up your table of contents scheme in your style sheet. You might, for example, designate your first-, second-, and third-level headlines for inclusion in the TOC. You also might add any special book features that you would like to appear in the table of contents—sidebars, tips, illustration captions, chapter descriptions, and so on. In fact, you can use the Create TOC command to compile special purpose tables of contents (create illustration lists by styling picture caption and figure number paragraphs for compilation).

TIP ▶ Nonprinting Items Can Make Special TOC Entries

PageMaker 6.0's new nonprinting item feature offers a nearly perfect solution for making a special table of contents entry. You see, PageMaker doesn't have any non-printing style for type; it offers no analog to the "hidden" style found in Microsoft Word and other word processors. Index entries are inherently invisible, but not table of contents items. However, you can set up invisible table of contents entries by putting them in their own text block and designating them as nonprinting in the Element menu. To keep the special entry item out of the way you can turn off the display of nonprinting items or you can hang the text block off the edge of a page. As long as some part of the text block rests on the live page area, the rest of it can hang out onto the Pasteboard, and PageMaker will see it and consider it during table of contents compilation. This is only a nearly perfect solution, however, because the tag text can't be locked to the main body text and will remain at its original page location even though the body text may shift by several pages during editing. In turn, this problem can blindside you by making your table of contents entry fall off by a page number or two.

Compiling the TOC Entries

After you have done all your page layout and stabilized your page breaks, it's time to use the Create Table of Contents command on the Utilities menu (see fig. 17.9).

Fig. 17.9 ▶

*Compiling your
table of contents.*

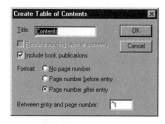

Before clicking OK in this dialog box, however, you need to take care of some business.

If you like, you can place a title at the beginning of your table of contents story. You can put any title you like in this space. The title you enter is assigned an automatic PageMaker style of TOC Title. If a TOC has already been created, you can check the box to replace it.

You can also check the box to include book publications if your publication will be composed of multiple files. This setting is the key to creating book-level tables of contents and chapter-level TOCs. The section later in this chapter called "Composing Chapter-Level Tables of Contents or Specialty Lists" spells out the possibilities.

You can choose to put page number references before or after each entry, or you can choose not to list page numbers at all.

And finally, you can make an important choice regarding the format of your TOC entries. PageMaker automatically inserts a tab between the entry and the page number unless you change the default choice. Up to seven standard or special characters can be placed in the Between Entry and Page Number box. In many cases, you might use this entry box to insert a thin space prior to the tab character so you can format the space (and thus the dot leader) for the tab. The use of thin spaces to format dot leader is covered in a tip in Chapter 6, in the section "Applying Tab Stops and Indents."

Placing and Tuning the TOC

When you finally click OK and run the Create Table of Contents command, PageMaker churns away, showing a progress thermometer bar and flashing page numbers underneath the bar. When the TOC is finished, you get a loaded text placement icon containing the table of contents story.

But wait! There's an awkward moment here. Where do you put the contents text? You have two alternatives. Put the TOC in its own publication, or include the TOC inside your document.

TOC outside the Publication

You can put the TOC in its own publication, as illustrated in this chapter, making it part of the publication book list. This way you can assign that file to use the customary small Roman numeral page numbers on your TOC pages. PageMaker will not let you restart page numbering or change numbering styles in midfile so you need to use a book list to accomplish that kind of formatting.

TOC inside the Publication

On the other hand, you can include the TOC right in your publication. This works just fine when you are dealing with publications such as long form business reports or academic papers that don't have formal chapter breaks. The problem with this approach is simple: if you add a couple of pages at the beginning of the publication to hold the TOC, you will throw off the page numbering for the rest of the document.

To get around this problem, you can add enough pages at the front of the publication to hold your TOC. Then run the TOC again, replacing the existing TOC, to automatically pick up the shifted page numbers.

Alternatively, you might tack the TOC on the end of your publication where it won't affect the numbering for the front part of the project. This can work out just fine, despite the extra work, because it doesn't matter how the pages come out of the Lino or the laser printer. You can stack them up any way you want. On the other hand, this method can create confusion at deadline time, and it could be especially confusing for anyone else who has to come after you to make edits.

Adjusting TOC Styles

PageMaker's TOC feature attempts to automatically format your contents page by assigning some standard paragraph styles to the entries in the contents list. PageMaker composes these styles by adapting your existing styles, assuming you have used styles to identify the text you wish to include in the TOC. The program does two things to the style. It adds the initials TOC in front of the base style name, and it adds a right alignment tab at the right margin of the TOC story.

It's a rare day when these TOC styles are suitable for your table of contents. Because they usually have been based on your book headlines, the TOC styles at first will contain all sorts of styling not appropriate to your TOC—paragraph rules, all caps styling, tab settings, and so on. You need to go through each TOC style and edit it to your liking using the techniques provided in Chapter 7, "Designing a Text Style System."

Here's the one caution to keep in mind as you edit TOC styles. You can make any style change you like, but you must not change the standard name of the style. If you do change the name of a TOC style, PageMaker will generate a brand-new TOC style to take the old one's place when you run the Create TOC command again and you will lose your TOC style tuning work.

Cleaning Up the TOC Story

Next, scan the table of contents story in Story Editor, looking for weird characters. One common cleanup problem will be the new line characters you inserted into headlines to make them break properly. You may also need to clean out dingbats, and maybe even graphics icons. Use Find and Change to clean out those and other undesirable characters.

By the way, the TOC can also be a great secondary proofing tool. I often pick up misspelled headlines or other errors at this point, such as forgetting to assign the TOC attribute to items you wanted to include in the list.

Finally, remove any unwanted contents entries, either by manual editing or with Find and Change. This often comes up as an issue when enough items have been coded to make a detailed table of contents to lead off each chapter but you don't want to include all that clutter when constructing your main book-level table of contents.

When you are done, you have created a clean and uncluttered table of contents like the one shown in figure 17.10.

Fig. 17.10 ▶

The finished TOC.

Composing Chapter-Level Tables of Contents or Specialty Lists

Nothing says that you must limit yourself to one table of contents—the one up at the front of your book. You might want to create a detailed table of contents for each of your chapters. Or you might want to use the TOC feature to compile a list of illustrations or special tips you have incorporated in the manuscript.

▶ Begin, of course, by defining the items to be included. Be as fine-grained as you like. Whereas your main book TOC might be limited to the first two headline levels, you might want to add subsidiary contents tables for all sorts of additional heading levels, sidebar heads, and illustration captions.

▶ Now, create and place as many table of contents stories as you need for your lists. Place each one where it is needed in your book. The main TOC and an illustration list might be at the front of the book, and chapter-level TOCs at the beginning of each chapter. If you are running several book-level tables, such as illustration or tip lists, you will have several TOCs that all look alike. At the chapter level, run a TOC for each individual file, re-membering to uncheck the Include Book Publications check box in the Create TOC dialog box for your chapter sub-TOCs.

▶ Finally, use the techniques we've just discussed to clean up your special-ized lists. Because PageMaker doesn't provide a way to select only the TOC paragraphs you want for each list, you will end up with many unwanted entries in your tables. Your main table of contents, for example, is likely to be filled with dozens (even hundreds) of unwanted subheads and illustra-tions. And your illustration list is likely to include all sorts of main heads that don't belong there. But these problems are easy to fix, because TOC coding works on the paragraph level and you have used styles to automate the process (haven't you?). Simply use the Find and Change command in each list, searching for the unwanted styles and leaving the Change To box empty, ripping out all the unwanted entries.

Coding Indexes

PageMaker's indexing tools are the best in the business. Here's why:

▶ You get three levels of indexing.

▶ A database list-type front end makes it easy to edit entries in one conve-nient location, even in a large publication.

▶ "See also" cross-reference entries are a snap. You designate the cross-reference and PageMaker automatically keeps track of it.

▶ You can index across a multifile publication using the Book command.

Some people get a little freaked by the power and complexity of PageMaker's in-dexing tools, but it's worth your time to learn how to use them. To help you sort it all out, this section provides a Key Concept explanation of indexing fundamentals and terminology, a Tactics Recipe covering the basic steps of indexing a publication, and a detailed description of the way each indexing task is performed using PageMaker's indexing tools.

KEY CONCEPT:
Understanding Indexes and Index Entry Types

Before getting started, you must decide whether you want a simple word list index, or a real index that includes multiple levels and cross linkages between entries.

A simple word list is called a *concordance*, in book editor talk. One dictionary defines a concordance as "an alphabetical index of the principal words of a book."

A truly useful index, however, delves further into the nature of the book. It is more conceptual than a simple word list. One definition calls an index, "Something serving to point out; a sign, token, or indication." A real index offers an "alphabetical listing of names, places, and topics along with the numbers of the pages on which they are mentioned or discussed."

What's the difference between these two index types? One difference is obvious. It takes a lot of work by you, the indexer, to put together a real index. But from the reader's point of view, a true index provides many more ways to access the information in a book. The rigorous indexer attempts to think the way the reader will be thinking when attempting to find some bit of data. Theoretically, an index might even include all the possible misspellings of an important topic! Certainly it includes cross-references and cites important themes of discussion whether or not they actually appear as words in the text.

A book on mammals which offers only a concordance might include references in its index for every species named in the text. But a mere concordance might omit useful references to endangered species or habitats or even quotes from poems that mention the animals. And that means the reader relying on the concordance for help might miss all that information.

Your choice—concordance or true index—determines the amount of work you must do. The computer can help you, but not even a powerful program like PageMaker can do the thinking for you, and there's no painless way to create either type of index. If you decide to take the high road, you are signing on for a considerable amount of thoughtful detail work. A true index organizes a book's information into a context of many layers of entries, such as the ones shown in figure 17.11. Many topic entries and cross references appear for each page location, providing all sorts of gateways that the reader can use to access the details buried within the mass of each chapter's prose.

First level ——— Automated litigation support   5.32 - 5.68 ——— Page range
         See also Litigation support
         Abstracted information   5.34
Second level ——— As electronic filing system   5.47
         Budget   5.40
             Include all factors   5.40
Third level ——— Merge with overall   5.40
         Budget checklist   5.43
         Coding
             See Coding
             See herein Automated litigation support: Taxonomy
         Deciding to use   5.32
             See also herein Automated litigation support: Budget checklist
         Full text   5.35
             Advantages   5.35
             Disadvantages   5.36
         Guidelines for using   5.33
         Implementation phases   5.43
         In-house advantages   5.37
         Outside vendor vs. in-house   5.37
         Phasing in   5.47
         Proposal checklist   5.41
         Proposal to client   5.40
         Tactics, using ALS   5.66
         Taxonomy   5.77
         Vendor hiring checklist   5.38

FIG. 17.11 ▲

A sampler of index entry types.

TACTICS RECIPE:
Composing a Book Index: A Tactics Recipe

Use the following steps to organize your thinking as you start your index. Ideally you should use these steps at an early stage of the book's creation—perhaps even in collaboration with the writer (who might even be you!).

Plan Your Index Strategy

Everyone has his or her own working style. You can choose the post-manuscript indexing method, the index-as-you-go method, or some combination of the two.

Many experts prefer to defer the indexing job until the last stages of book production, believing that the end result will be a purer listing of topics based on a stable manuscript. You might say that this plan offers the benefits of hindsight and fresh eyes.

Others, particularly writers who must index their own work, prefer to code index entries as they go (in the word processor, generally, rather than in PageMaker). They believe that this plan saves them a lot of work at the end of the project. They ask "Why not do it while we're here?"

The best solution might be a combination of both practices. Many rough index entries can be coded as the writer works on the manuscript. Be aware, however, that much of this early work will require massive editing (or complete trashing) later in the process. Writers usually don't have a an overall, holistic, conceptual view of their manuscript, especially when the manuscript hasn't even been written yet.

continues

TACTICS RECIPE:
Continued

Create a Master Topic List

Don't even consider making a single index entry until you have drawn up a master topic list. The more consistent you are in coding your index points, the more coherent your index will be. A master topic list also maximizes PageMaker's primary indexing advantage—the fact that it will automatically compile your index, bringing all the related page references together under one common heading. If you use inconsistent headings you will miss out on this power.

So, even if you are using the index-as-you-go method, start with a rough list that you can refer to as you make entries. One of the biggest index editing jobs of all is editing all the inconsistent entries caused by the evolution of the writer's thinking during the creation of the manuscript. The master topic list helps save you that work by providing a foundation for indexing consistency. Also, if you decide to change a topic at a later date, you can do it easily because the old entries were consistently coded based on the master list and therefore will be easier to find and change.

If you decide to do your indexing in PageMaker, create a master topic list in your word processor and then import it electronically. The index entries will be incorporated into PageMaker's entry list and you will be able to code your index by choosing from among the master list entries with a click of the mouse (another helpful way of ensuring index entry consistency). See the section "Importing a Master Topic List" for more details.

Code Your Entries

Marking your entries might be the simplest (and most tedious) part of the indexing task. In PageMaker you simply highlight a location and use a keyboard shortcut to list that point in the index database. You can create simple entries, multilevel entries, page ranges and several types of cross-references. More information on creating each of the many kinds of index entries is provided in a series of sections in this chapter, including "Doing a Basic Index Entry (Existing Topic)" and "Making a Cross-Reference Entry."

Review and Refine the Index

There's no such thing as a perfect index—especially the first time around. PageMaker enables you to easily edit your index electronically in order to clear up inconsistencies and gaps in your index conceptualization (not to mention spelling problems!).

TIP ▶ Build a Word List with Sonar

If you are indexing a completed manuscript, consider using the Sonar Bookends Plug-in. This Plug-in can help you build a master topic list by compiling a concordance of the words in your document based on their frequency of appearance. You can then massage this text file in your word processor, selecting only the topic words that make sense for your index, to create a master topic list for importation into PageMaker.

Sonar Bookends also provides page number locations and word substitution capability, so you could use it to automate concordance index creation. It does not provide the depth of coverage of an index which has been hand-tailored using PageMaker's indexing power, but it might be suitable for your project, especially if you are producing a concordance index.

Create and Place the Index

Once you have coded your index entries and locations, this one's the easy part. The Create Index command, like the Create Table of Contents command, represents the easiest part of a complex process. This command searches the text, compiles the index entries, organizes them into proper list order, styles them, and then loads a text placement icon with the index story. Finally, of course, you must place the story where it belongs in your publication. This process works very much like generating a table of contents.

Refine and Style the Index

Print out the index for this stage. It's hard to do a great job of editing an index on-screen. I find that mistakes I missed during electronic editing leap off the page when I get the index on paper. In addition to content editing, you will almost certainly want to refine the automatic index styles created by PageMaker when it compiles the index (using a process like the one used earlier in this chapter to establish a table of contents style sheet). These automatic styles all begin with the word *Index* rather than *TOC*.

Importing a Master Topic List

The fastest way to get a master topic list going in PageMaker is to import it from your word processing software. Using Microsoft Word (or any other word processor whose index entries are accepted by PageMaker), make a list of your topics and format them as index entries.

You can, as already mentioned, use Sonar Bookends to search out every unique word in the manuscript. This search will yield a text file suitable for placing as an index story in PageMaker after you add the index coding. Ideally, however, this file would merely be a thought starter for the index topics list. Go through the Sonar word list in your word processor and eliminate all but the key topic words before formatting them as index entries and importing the file as a PageMaker master topic list.

Of course, many writers want to work ahead. They do a lot of preliminary indexing during the writing process, and the manuscript's word processor coding comes into PageMaker automatically when the text is placed. Problem is, working piecemeal during the writing process often leads to inconsistencies that cause extra work for the person editing the index. If possible, supply the author with at least a minimal master topic list before the writing process begins, perhaps basing it on the outline for the publication.

> **TIP ▶ Beware of Page Ranges When Importing Index Entries from a Word Processor**
>
> When you are using the code-as-you-go method of indexing, your word processor document index entries can be translated into PageMaker entries when you Place the text. But there is one significant limitation to this process, because any page range index coding in the word process—Microsoft Word for example—appears as two entries in PageMaker, one each for the first and last page in the range. You should avoid making page range entries in your word processor, because you will find yourself searching out and deleting all the second index markers and recoding the first markers with PageMaker's page range information.

Coding Your Index Entries

After you have sketched out your master topic list, you're ready to go through the manuscript and mark all the page references for each topic.

Do your indexing in Story view. Even though the indexing tools work just fine in Layout view, there's no advantage to working on the page during indexing. The Story Editor route, on the other hand, offers you some significant advantages. With it, you are able to move faster and to see your index markers as you enter them (see fig. 17.12). The index markers don't take up any space on the page, of course, so you don't need to worry about your indexing work causing changes in line breaks or having any other effects on your meticulously designed pages.

FIG. 17.12 ▶

Using the Story view for indexing.

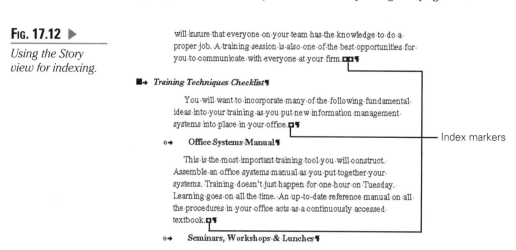

You can search for index entries using the Find and Change commands, and you can use a nice set of quick access keyboard commands as you work through a tall stack of book pages. Table 17.1 provides a quick reference chart of these shortcuts, which are discussed further in the next few pages. (The Appendix contains a master reference for these and all the other PageMaker keyboard shortcuts.)

TABLE 17.1   Indexing Keyboard Shortcuts

Function	Keyboard Shortcut	Notes
Add entry	Ctrl+;	The Add Index Entry dialog box appears.
Instant entry	Ctrl+Shift+;	The selected text becomes an index entry; the Add Index Entry dialog box does not appear.
Search	^;	Enter these characters in the Find box to search out index entry locations in Story view.
Name entry	Ctrl+Shift+Z	Enters the selected text—a person's name—so that it is listed last name first. Insert nonbreaking spaces to lock middle names and titles into correct positions.
Show current pub	Ctrl+"Show index"	Shows the index for the current publication only, excluding all the other publications in the book list and enabling the Capitalize button in the Show Index dialog box.
Remove entries	Alt+Add x-ref	Deletes all the recent entries (those made since you last clicked OK or Accept) from the Add Index Entry dialog box.
Restore entries	Alt+"Remove"	Reverses Alt+Add x-ref (as long as you haven't clicked OK or Accept yet).
Delete all	Ctrl+Shift+"Remove"	Deletes all entries of any kind.
Delete page referenced entries	Ctrl+Alt+"Remove"	Deletes all page references.
Delete cross-references	Ctrl+Shift+ "Remove"	Deletes all cross-references.

continues

IV

Creating Page Layouts

TABLE 17.1 Continued

Function	Keyboard Shortcut	Notes
Copy to empty boxes	Ctrl+OK	After you've filled in your main topics, use this shortcut in the Select Topic dialog box. Any remaining empty boxes in the Add Entry box will be filled with the corresponding topics from the Select Z Topic dialog box.
Inspect entry	Select marker+Ctrl+;	Select the index entry marker in Story view and then use this shortcut to view it. It's the same short cut you use to add an entry.

Doing a Basic Index Entry (Existing Topic)

Remember that there are two parts to every index entry: the topic (ideally chosen from your master topic list for consistency) and the location reference. Start with the location reference by clicking an insertion point in the text where you want to make a page reference. PageMaker represents your chosen location with one of those black diamond index markers you can see in Story view.

Now use the keyboard shortcut Ctrl+; (semicolon) or choose the Index Entry command from the Utilities menu to open the Add Index Entry dialog box (see fig. 17.13).

FIG. 17.13 ▶

Adding an entry in the Add Index Entry dialog box.

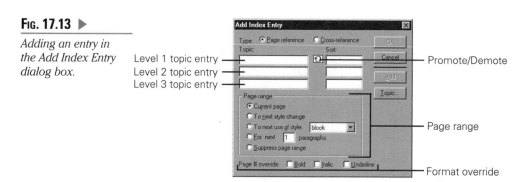

Notice that in the figure the Page Reference radio button has been selected automatically (a later section of this chapter explains how to make cross-reference entries by clicking the Cross-Reference button).

At this point, PageMaker knows where you want to locate the new index marker but still needs a topic to reference. You need to fill in the topic blanks. Although you can type in an ad lib topic of your own choosing here, it's important to work from your existing topic list as much as possible (for the sake of consistency). To do so, simply click the Topic button to open the Select Topic dialog box shown in figure 17.14.

Fig. 17.14 ▶

Selecting a topic from your master topic list.

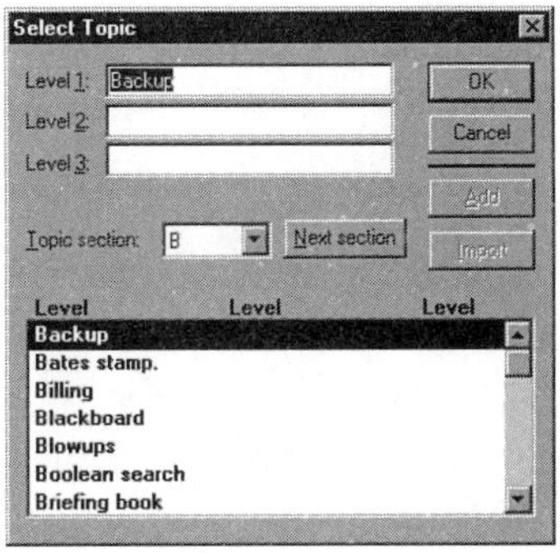

This dialog box does not list any page numbers; it simply provides a selection list of topics. Assuming you have created a master topic list as suggested earlier in "Importing a Master Topic List" (or precoded your index entries in your word processor before placing the story), you can now choose topics from that list in this dialog box. The listings are grouped alphabetically into sections. You can move to a new section by using the Topic Section pull-down list or the Next Section button.

If you are working on a publication composed of several files in a book list, be sure to use the Import button. That button tells PageMaker to look at every publication in the current file's book list and display all the index topics and entries for all the book list files in the topic selection dialog box. This step is important, because your topic lists will be inconsistent among your various book chapters if you don't synchronize them by using the Import button.

After selecting your topic, click the OK button. You are returned to the Add Index Entry dialog box with the level boxes all filled in.

Referencing Page Ranges

You might want to designate a page range by using the buttons in the Add Index Entry dialog box (refer to fig. 17.13).

In most cases, you simply want to make a single page reference to the current page so that you can usually stick with the default page range setting. If you want to extend the selection so that the entry refers to more than one page, however, use one of these other Page Range option radio buttons:

▶ *Current Page.* As you might expect, you get a single page number reference, tied to the insertion point you clicked in the text before calling the Index Entry command.

▶ *To Next Style Change.* Use this option to extend the reference until the next change in paragraph styles. This button helps a lot in situations that naturally breed style changes—for example, if you are referencing a sidebar that's formatted in a special style which then returns to body text style. Likewise, use this button if you are coding a topic that has been styled for body text and continues to the next subhead.

Remember that PageMaker uses your settings to calculate page references for you automatically, so multiple page references are compiled only if the parameters extend over one or more page breaks.

▶ *To Next Use of Style.* This radio button specifies the end of a reference that will be based on the next occurrence of a particular style. If you are making a reference at the beginning of a major headline section and the reference should carry the topic through that entire section, use this option and select the next major headline break paragraph style from the pull-down list.

▶ *For Next # Paragraphs.* If you know that the index topic runs for a certain number of paragraphs, this button lets you enter a number, such as 16. PageMaker would use that entry to spike the ending page reference for the index entry 16 paragraphs later.

▶ *Suppress Page Range.* In some cases, you might want to insert an index entry without a page number reference. Use this button when you are first marking up a publication and you are not yet sure about your eventual page range reference.

Assigning Special Text Formatting

You can assign special text formatting to the page number of a particular entry by using the Page # Override check boxes shown earlier in figure 17.13. How would you use this feature? Well, you might italicize the page number for all entries that contain illustrations. Or, you could use bold type to emphasize the main index entries for a topic.

Now here's the tricky part: the Page # Override check boxes are toggles, and they interact with any existing formatting, including paragraph styles. If you have used italic styling for any of your index paragraph styles, checking Italic for Page # Override will toggle off the already existing italic formatting for that entry's page number, giving you regular Roman type instead of italic.

Think of it this way: these check boxes have the same effect as if you applied the italic command (or bold or underline) to selected text using the Text tool. If the text is already italicized, then the command turns italic off.

One last thing about the Page # Override check boxes: they are smart and they remember your override decisions. When you click one of these check boxes, it stays clicked until you click it back off. In the meantime, until you turn off the check box, all your entries will be getting that Page # Override formatting. You could end up with dozens of unintended italic (or bold or underline) page numbers if you forget to turn off a check box. On the other hand, if you want to italicize a bunch of consecutive entries, you don't have to bother about constantly clicking on the override check box because it will stay clicked from entry to entry.

Customizing Index Entry Sorting

PageMaker uses strict ASCII sorting when compiling your index, sorting from left to right through each letter or digit of an entry. Spaces, symbols, and punctuation come first, followed by the alphabet.

When sorting numbers, PageMaker lists 1, 100, and 1000 together before proceeding to 2, 20, and 2,000,000. It sorts from left to right, one digit at a time, unconcerned about the magnitude of the multidigit number being indexed. And the name St. John, for example, appears in the index closer to entries for street, store and state than to an entry for Saint Joseph (where you might like it to be).

You can solve this problem, however, using the Sort boxes located just to the right of the Topic boxes in the Add Index Entry dialog box (see fig. 17.15). There's no global override for index sorting order and you can't set the sorting order for a topic. It must be done at the individual entry level, so you must make one of these Sort box adjustments for every entry you want to be specially sorted in your index.

Your Sort box entry tells PageMaker to ignore the spelling of the actual topic entry and to sort the entry as if it were actually spelled a different way—as if it were the word you have entered in the Sort box.

*Customizing
PageMaker's index
sorting order.*

The illustration shows an entry for the number 20, but tells PageMaker to sort it in
the index so that it falls into proper order with three-digit numbers. In other
words, this entry sorts with the other two-digit numbers because it has a leading
zero in the Sort box. Without the Sort box special instructions, this topic entry
would be sorted to the same location as 2, 200, and 2,000 because PageMaker
uses left-to-right ASCII sorting.

As to the St. John and Saint Joseph sorting problem, you would simply type out
the full sort name—**Saint John**—in the Sort box next to the entry for *St. John*.
That entry would then sort properly next to Saint Joseph in the compiled index.

Coding Multiple Entries at One Location

Use the Add button in the Add Index Entry dialog box to place more than one
entry at a single location, without troubling to go back to your text to click a new
insertion point. When you click the Add button, you get a new Add Index Entry
dialog box and must go through all the normal steps for setting a new index entry. A new index marker appears in Story view for each click of the Add button.

The previous entry information carries over so that you can reuse part of it if you
like. To save you from accidentally making duplicate entries, however, the Add
button becomes grayed and unavailable until you change the previous entry.

TIP ▶ **Copy Only the Topic Levels You Want**

You can have PageMaker automatically help you fill out your Topic boxes, using this
keyboard shortcut.

Normally a choice in the Select Topic dialog box completely wipes out any topics you
may have entered in the Add Index Entry dialog box. That is, you get a complete
wipeout when you Select Topic.

If, however, you hold down the Ctrl key as you click on the OK button, only the empty
Topic boxes will be filled in by Select Topic and the ones that are occupied will be
preserved.

Here's how you might use this trick. You double-clicked a word and want to make it an index entry, so you use the Ctrl+; (semicolon) keyboard shortcut. The Add Index Entry dialog box comes up with the selected word in the first Topic box. However, you know that this word ought to be a third-level topic and that an existing topic should be selected for the first and second levels. Use the Promote/Demote button to demote the selected word to the third level. Now, click on the Topic button and select any topic that has the first- and second-level items you need. Use the Ctrl+OK shortcut.

Back in the Add Index Entry dialog box, your new third-level topic has been left in place (not overwritten by your Topic entry) and the first- and second-level topics have been automatically filled in for you from your topic selection. If you had simply clicked OK in the Topic Selection dialog box, without using the Ctrl key, your fresh topic would have been completely wiped out.

Promoting Topics and Overlapping Topics

You are sure to want more than one index entry per location when you are dealing with overlapping topics. The Promote/Demote button, the one with the curvy arrow symbol between the Topic and Sort boxes, makes quick work of helping you compose these entries. By *overlapping topics*, I mean the kind of situation in which there are many different index gateways to a specific concept. For example, if you were indexing your cookbook, *Pasta for a Colorful Life*, you would naturally end up with a lot of interlinking entries for the different kinds of pasta.

Say you've just completed an entry for *Pasta: Macaroni: Green*, for example. Given the title of the book, you know somebody will want to access kinds of pasta by color. Click the Promote/Demote button. Each time you click it, this button rotates the topics on all three index levels like a carousel. The third-level topic moves to the top and the top-level topic slides down one. Your entry for *Pasta: Macaroni: Green* would rotate to *Green: Pasta: Macaroni*. Eccolo! You have a new index entry for the reader who might think to look under *Green* rather than *Pasta* or *Macaroni*.

Adding a New Topic from Text

You can make ad-hoc index entries by highlighting some text and choosing the Index entry command (or pressing Ctrl+;). You get an Add Index Entry dialog box that's already filled in.

If you simply clicked the Add button at this point, you would simultaneously make a new topic for the index and create a page reference entry at the location of the highlighted text. Before taking this step, however, you might want to tune the entry a bit by adding some second- or third-level topics, adjusting sort order, establishing a page range, or creating some special page number formatting using the overrides—all operations just described in the earlier section, "Doing a Basic Index Entry (Existing Topic)."

If you know you won't need to tune an ad-hoc entry, there's an even faster way to do this, bypassing the dialog box step. Simply highlight your text and press Ctrl+Shift+; and the Add Index Entry dialog box doesn't even appear. The index entry is made immediately using the defaults that are in place when you hit the key chord.

TIP ▶ Don't Worry About Initial Caps, Just Use the Capitalize Button

When you are tuning ad-hoc entries, don't worry about capitalizing their first letters (if that's the style you are using for your index). PageMaker's Show Index command offers a powerful automatic capitalization feature that is covered in the upcoming "Editing Your Index Electronically" section.

Making a Cross-Reference Entry

Cross-reference index entries don't have page numbers. Instead, they link two related topics with words such as *See also*. Under the index topic *pasta*, for example, you might find cross-references to *durum semolina flour*, *sauce*, and *linguini*. And each one of those subcategories relating to pasta would certainly have a cross-reference back to the main topic.

When you click the Cross-Reference button, the Add Index Entry dialog box looks slightly different than it does when you click the Page Reference button (see fig. 17.16).

FIG. 17.16 ▶

Adding a cross-reference entry.

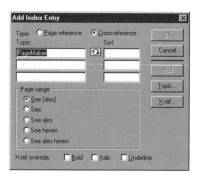

Many of the important dialog box features remain the same regardless of which type of entry you are creating—page or cross-reference. There's nothing different about the Promote/Demote button, the Topic and Sort boxes, or the Topic button. The X-Ref Override check boxes work just like the Page # Override check boxes, except the override formatting applies to the cross-reference entry rather than the page numbers.

By the way, the X-Ref button appears to function exactly like the select Topic button, opening a dialog box that looks and acts exactly the same (including Add and Import buttons). They look identical but they aren't. The Topic button gives you a dialog box with your existing Topic entry, if any, already filled in. The X-Ref box is blank so you can select a new topic for the cross-reference.

The cross-reference version of the Index Entry dialog has one major difference compared to the page reference version. Have a look right in the center of the box in figure 17.16—the buttons that set up your *See also* language. Figure 17.17 shows an example index fragment, showing the result you get from each button.

Fig. 17.17 ▶

An index fragment showing all the types of cross reference entries.

Cross references ─

Automated litigation support   5.32 - 5.68
    See also Litigation support
Abstracted information   5.34
As electronic filing system   5.47
Budget   5.40
        Include all factors   5.40
        Merge with overall   5.40
Budget checklist   5.43
Coding
        See Coding
        See herein Automated litigation support: Taxonomy
    Deciding to use   5.32
        See also herein Automated litigation support: Budget checklist
Full text   5.35
        Advantages   5.35
        Disadvantages   5.36
Guidelines for using   5.33
Implementation phases   5.43
In-house advantages   5.37
Outside vendor vs. in-house   5.37
Phasing in   5.47
Proposal checklist   5.41
Proposal to client   5.40
Tactics, using ALS   5.66
Taxonomy   5.77
Vendor hiring checklist   5.38

The following list explains each button's function:

▶ *See [Also]*. This button—the smart version of the feature—puts PageMaker in charge of choosing between *See* and *See also*, making it the best choice for most occasions. It's so good, in fact, that most people use this option exclusively and don't bother with the other options.

When the cross-reference coincides with some other entries, and those entries have page numbers, PageMaker gives you a *See also* cross-reference. In other words, there are two places to look for information—the location of the cross-reference entry and the location the cross-reference is pointing to. Therefore, the reader should also see the other location. You might think of this as a two-way cross-reference, where you would have a *See also* cross-reference for both index locations.

When the cross-reference stands alone at its topic level and is not associated with any other page number type entries, there's only one location to find the information. Instead of *See also*, PageMaker issues the more terse directive to simply *See* the other location. This type of cross-reference runs one way, pointing away from its location to another spot where you concentrate a set of complete index pointers.

Notice, in the illustration, PageMaker only looks at one topic level in deciding between *See* and *See also*. Even though there are plenty of page references in the "Automated litigation support" entry, there aren't any page references under the "Coding" topic, so PageMaker uses the *See* type cross-reference.

▶ *See.* Use this button if, for some reason, you want to bypass PageMaker smarts for cross-referencing and lock in an order for a simple, one-way style *See* cross-reference.

▶ *See Also.* Use this button if you are sure that the current topic will have some page number references and therefore want to lock in this type of two-way cross-reference.

▶ *See Herein* and *See Also Herein.* These two options work exactly like the *See* and *See also* cross-references, except you use them to refer to another location within a single level-one index entry topic. Use these cross-reference types to make sure the reader doesn't miss important information in an extensive topic area. In your scholarly work on pasta, for example, the level-one entry for *pasta* might run a page or more, including such subtopics as the various pasta shapes and sauces.

Indexing Every Occurrence of a Word

When you want to be sure that every occurrence of a word has been indexed, PageMaker makes the job easy using the Change command. With the help of figure 17.18, this section explains how to do this.

FIG. 17.18 ▶

Using the Change command to index every occurrence of a word or phrase.

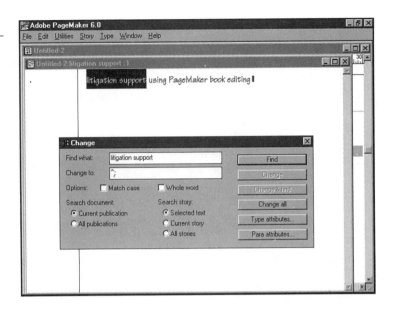

Enter the word or phrase to be indexed—*litigation support* in the example—in the Find What box. You only have to put "^;" in the Change To box, not the entire word/phrase (as shown in fig. 17.18). The word/phrase only has to be in the Find box. Typing in the word/phrase leaves you an opportunity to misspell something. These two initial characters represent the metacharacter or special character code for an index marker in PageMaker, which is how this particular search and replace setup finds every incidence of your word or phrase and indexes it.

Now you might be thinking, "What if my weird word appears in clusters, like maybe five times close together. Aren't I likely to get five index entries referring to the same page?" Nope, you don't need to worry. PageMaker eliminates duplicate references on the same page when it compiles the index. Even if you generate a veritable swarm of index markers, the practical effect will be one entry per page. Make a note of any searches you do, however, so you can check them during the edit and refine phase. You might want to tune some of these search and replace references, perhaps turning them into page range references or editing out adjacent page markers.

Indexing Names

PageMaker makes it easy to properly sort indexed names. If you highlight *John Doe* and use a special keyboard combination, your entry appears in the index as *Doe, John* so that it can be sorted in last name order.

The key combination to use is Ctrl+Shift+Z. This key chord has the same instant index entry effect as Ctrl+Shift+; except it converts the entry into name sort order.

However, there's one caveat to keep in mind when indexing names: PageMaker, without your help, has trouble making a last name sort out of any name that has more than two words in it. If you want to index a name such as *John Edwin Doe* so it lists under *Doe*, for example, you must insert a nonbreaking space (Ctrl+Shift+H) between *John* and *Edwin* so that PageMaker treats the first and middle names as a single word.

Yes, this technique affects page breaks. Even though I said earlier in this chapter that you should always do indexing in Story view, here's the one time where that advice breaks down. If you are doing name indexing using Ctrl+Shift+Z, and you are working with names longer than two words where you use nonbreaking spaces, you must check your line breaks as you index. You have two choices. You can work in Layout view so you can get instant feedback on the effects of your work, or you can work in Story Editor and flip over to Layout (Ctrl+E) to check line break effects whenever you make a complicated name entry.

TIP ▶ **Automatically Index All Occurrences of a Name**

If you are writing the definitive work on George Washington and want to index all occurrences of his name automatically, use the Change command. But instead of putting the index marker character ^; (caret+semi-colon) in front of the word in the Change To box, use the metacharacter ^z (caret+Z).

Editing Your Index Electronically

In the old days, before PageMaker gave us these powerful indexing tools, you would have spent a lot of time running your index, printing it out, marking up the hard copy, and scanning through the body copy to make corrections. Nowadays, with PageMaker's help, you can call an index up on-screen and edit entries with a quick double-click of the mouse. You will still want to do an editing pass on paper, but make a first pass electronically for maximum efficiency.

Using the Show Index Command

Choose the Show Index command from the Utilities menu to open the dialog box shown in figure 17.19.

It looks a bit like the bottom of the Select Topic dialog box, doesn't it? Except here you are actually seeing each page-reference and cross-reference for each of the topics.

When you execute the Show Index command, PageMaker does everything that it does when you use the Create Index command, short of loading a text placement icon with an index story for you to Place in your publication. Instead of the text placement icon, you get this electronic list of your index entries.

FIG. 17.19 ▶

*Using Show Index to
edit your index.*

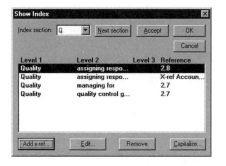

It helps to think of this as a database screen, because that's essentially what it is. It's a list of the entry information attached to each one of the diamond-shaped index markers embedded in your publication's text, plus the page number where that specific marker is located.

There's a lot to love about PageMaker's indexing power, but this database style index editing facility could really rouse an indexer's deepest passions. It's way out ahead of any of the other major layout and word processing programs. Instead of being forced to work all through your publication on dozens of scattered index markers, you can do all your index editing in this one convenient location—even if you are publishing a multifile book.

Use this Show Index screen to comb through your index for flaws, before committing it to the pages of your publication. Fix inconsistent entries (maybe you kept switching between two accepted spellings for an entry, for example, or alternated between the singular and plural versions of a word).

DESIGN NOTE
Consolidate Entries and Cross-References

If you have twenty subtopics under a single entry, there's no reason to duplicate those subtopics under a similar topic. Use a cross-reference instead. Your primary entry for *pasta*, for example, might include *spaghetti* as a level-two topic. If fifteen recipes appear as level-three entries under *spaghetti*, consider changing the level-two *spaghetti* entry to a *See* cross-reference. Then index *spaghetti* as a level-one topic with the recipes as level twos. You could use the *See* cross-reference button or you could let PageMaker automate the reference by using the *See [also]* button.

Editing an Index Entry

Unlike a word processor, in PageMaker you don't have to go through your document editing each of the entries one-by-one. You can edit every index marker in your publication by remote control right from this dialog box by clicking the Edit button or simply double-clicking the entry. Depending on the type of entry you choose (page-reference or cross-reference), you open a dialog box similar to the Add dialog boxes discussed in the last few sections. The only difference is the word *Edit* instead of *Add* in the upper-left-hand corner. Everything else looks and works the same—page ranges, various reference options, and type style override check boxes.

Adding Cross-References

Because indexers commonly want to add cross-references to existing entries, the Show Index dialog box has the Add X-Ref button for that purpose. Pressing it opens the Add Cross-Reference dialog box (rather than the Edit Cross-Reference box).

Saving Work as You Go

You will love using the Accept button, because it saves you lots of time. In a big book with a bunch of chapters, it can take quite a while to compile all the index entries for the Show Index box every time you open it. Yet if you click OK you will be dumped out of this dialog box and will need to compile the entire index again to get back to it. The Accept button saves you from that grief by adopting each step of your work as you go along—without having to close and reopen the dialog box. This button works like the Apply button in the Indent/Tabs dialog box.

Deleting One or More Entries

You can remove an individual entry by clicking the Remove button. If you want to remove all index entries of any kind, press the Ctrl+Alt+Shift+Remove key combination. Remove all page references with Ctrl+Alt+Remove, and remove cross-references with Ctrl+Shift+Remove.

If you want to remove only the entries you have made since you last clicked OK or Accept, hold down the Alt key while clicking the Add X-Ref button. You can reverse your decision (as long as you do it before you click Accept or OK again) by using Alt+Remove.

Understanding Entry Locations

You might see some odd-looking two-letter codes next to or instead of the page numbers in the Show Index dialog box. Here's what they'd mean:

▶ PB tells you that the reference is in text that appears on the Pasteboard rather than a page.

▶ LM or RM means that the index marker somehow got onto one of the master pages, left or right.

▶ OV indicates that an index entry has been orphaned in some unset text (or overset text, as the typographers sometimes say), in a text block with a solid triangle at the bottom windowshade.

▶ UN tells you that the index marker is in some unplaced text in the Story Editor.

▶ ? means that the page reference may have changed since the Show Index box was compiled.

▶ A page number in parentheses means the index marker was created with the page range suppressed.

Capitalizing Index Entries

PageMaker can handle the capitalization of all your index entries for you automatically. Just click the Capitalize button in the Show Index dialog box to open the box shown in figure 17.20. You can then choose to capitalize only the current topic, all your level-one entries (the usual form), or all entries.

FIG. 17.20 ▶

The Capitalize dialog box.

Beware of one major catch when using automatic capitalization. The Capitalize button only works for the current publication; it is turned off automatically when you have a book list in place. But you don't need to change your book list. Instead, simply hold down the Ctrl key when you select the Show Index command. Doing so temporarily opens just the index entries for your current publication so that you can make use of PageMaker's capitalization magic without messing about with your book list. After you've set your capitalization preferences, you can close and reopen the Show Index dialog box to conduct further editing on the entire book list.

TIP ▶ Use Search Again to Review Your Index in Context

Unfortunately, as terrific as the Show Index feature is for getting a lot of indexing work done in a hurry, you get no sense of context when you use the Show Index database to edit your index electronically. That index entry referring to page 98, for example, might or might not be perfectly appropriate and accurate for the text that appears on that page. For topflight index editing the only way to be absolutely sure is to go to page 98 and read your body copy, opening up the index marker to see what it says in context.

Use the Search Again command for this contextual index editing. In Story Editor, at the top of a story, open up the Find box (using the new version 6.0 key command Ctrl+F if you like). In the Find What box enter **[^];** (caret+semicolon). Click Find and

PageMaker highlights the first index marker. Click the Story Editor text to switch it forward without closing the Find dialog box. With the marker highlighted, you can use the Ctrl+; (semicolon) keyboard shortcut to quickly open up the marker so that you can see the entry and simultaneously read the text where it's located. To find the next index marker location, use Find Next by pressing Ctrl+G. Use this technique repeatedly to move through your text and you'll be able to conduct a fine-grained, contextual edit of your index.

Creating, Placing, and Styling Your Index

Now for the easiest part of making an index in PageMaker—actually turning all these index markers into a story you can place in your book. You can accomplish this step with the Create Index command on the Utilities menu; it works very much like the Create Table of Contents command. Create Index searches through your text, including all your book publications if you like, and compiles the topics and page locations into a list.

Keep in mind that Create Index works by post-processing and isn't dynamically linked. In other words, if you edit your index markers the index story is not automatically updated. You must run the Create Index command again after each index editing session (just as you would with the Create Table of Contents command).

Creating Your Index

The Create Index dialog box is simple to use (see fig. 17.21). Simply make a few obvious choices and then click the OK button, unless you want to spend some time tinkering with the formatting of your index. More on that intriguing Format button in a moment.

Fig. 17.21 ▶

The Create index dialog box.

You may automatically include a title in your index story by typing one into the Title entry box. Logically enough, it will be formatted with the Index Title style. Again, this works just like the Create TOC command.

If you have previously run the Create Index command, and have an index placed in your publication, you probably would like to replace the old one. If so, check the Replace Existing Index box.

You almost certainly want to check the Include Book Publications check box.

CAUTION

Do not check the Remove Unreferenced Topics dialog box unless you are *irrevocably and unequivocally certain* that you are at the final stage of making your index.

Sure, it's a great way to weed out orphaned topics. But if you are still at the draft stage you need to know about topics that have been left empty (that have no page numbers or cross-references associated with them). Or, maybe you just forgot to assign an index marker to a perfectly good item. In any case, doing an index run with this option checked deletes empty topics forever.

Take note that entries with Suppress Page Range checked in the Add Index Entry dialog box have been locked and won't be removed by this option; therefore they are reliable place holders. That's why this option makes a special kind of sense in this case. As you scan through your empty entries, weeding them out, you may want to edit the keepers so that their Suppress Page Range option is checked, protecting them from the Remove Unreferenced Topics process.

Formatting Your Index

Okay, time for that Format button. Click it and the Index Format dialog box shown in figure 17.22 appears.

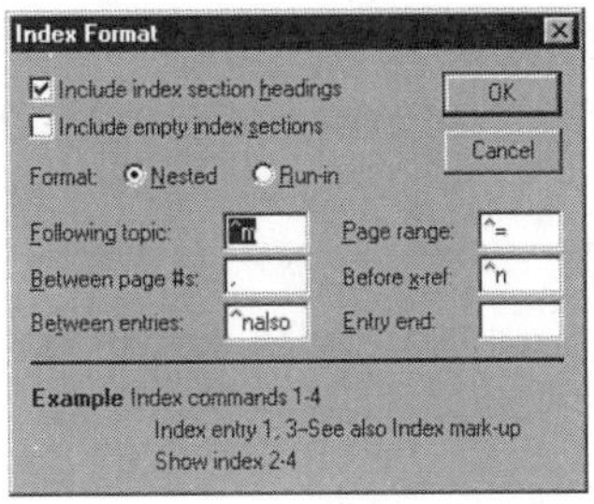

FIG. 17.22 ▶

The Index Format dialog box.

This fairly complex dialog box has been set up by default to handle most situations and you'll usually leave it just the way it is. Here's how to use it, however, for those times when you do need to customize the way your index section is formatted.

By default the index section headings are the letters of the alphabet, formatted with emphasis and space above and below to clearly break your index information into digestible pieces. Entries that begin with numbers, punctuation, or other special characters appear first in the index under a special Symbols section (unless you used the Sort entry boxes in the Add Index Entry dialog box to change their sort order).

In most cases, section headings are left out for any letters of the alphabet that have no index entries (such as Z or X, unless it's a biology text). You can override the default and include these headings by checking the Include Empty Index Sections check box.

A common formatting decision involves the choice of Nested or Run-in indexing styles. The Nested style is indented and allocates a separate paragraph to each entry. The Run-in style is also indented but runs together the entries for each level in a single paragraph, usually wrapping the entries within their column. Click each radio button to see the difference these two options make, as shown in the Example section at the bottom of the dialog box.

The remaining six entry boxes in the Index Format dialog box offer a great deal of formatting power. Whenever the Create Index command encounters one of the six situations listed here, PageMaker inserts one of these characters, which you can change to suit your taste. Using the various special characters (new line, nonbreaking space, ellipsis, carriage return, em space, en space, and so on) you can use these boxes to make your index sing your own special tune. Here's what each of the boxes does:

▶ *Following Topic.* The topic is the subject of the entry; whatever you enter in this box is inserted between each topic and its first page number reference at all three possible topic levels. In the example shown in figure 17.22 the ^m metacharacter places an em space in that spot. (You can get a list of all these metacharacters in Appendix C.)

▶ *Page Range.* Some folks place a hyphen between page numbers to indicate a page range. But because you're a typesetting pro, you want to use an en dash. The ^= metacharacter shown in the figure does just that.

▶ *Between Page #s.* In most indexes, the page numbers relevant to a topic appear in a list. The figure shows the use of a comma, which works well to separate page references. You might also try colons or semicolons. If you are working in a narrow column, it's a good idea to put a nonbreaking en space after the comma. Or if you are working with a large enough typeface, you might choose to separate page numbers with no punctuation and a regular space.

▶ *Before X-Ref.* Cross-reference entries (See, See also, and so on) generally ought to ride on their own line and shouldn't be mixed in with page numbers. The default for this box is a new line character (^n), which drops whatever follows down to the next line.

▶ *Between Entries.* The example shown in the figure represents a run-in style index; it has been formatted to insert the word *also* between the entries at a particular topic level. Check out the way the Example box picks up and displays the en dash and the word *also*. Great stuff!

▶ *Entry End.* An entry is any item that has a cross reference or a page number after it. The default entry is to leave this box empty, because PageMaker inserts a paragraph return automatically after each entry in the index.

Placing and Styling the Index

When you finally click OK in the Create Index dialog box, PageMaker goes through the same compilation gyrations that it did when you used the Show Index command or the Create Table of Contents command. After it finishes its work, you get a loaded text pointer and you can place your index story. Or, if you had previously generated an index and chose the Replace Existing Index option, the index will be updated automatically.

As with a table of contents, it's usually best to build the index as a separate docu-ment that can be included in the book list for a large book. Fortunately, you don't need to worry too much about making room for the index or interfering with your page numbering (unlike the table of contents) because the index al-most always appears as the last section of the book.

PageMaker potentially creates five automatic and standard styles for the index. I say potentially because it doesn't create a style that isn't actually used in the in-dex. Each style begins with the word `Index`; one is created for the title, the sec-tions, and each topic level (Index 1, Index 2, and Index 3). As long as you don't change the names of these styles, you can edit them into any format you want, just as you can work with the TOC paragraph styles. You probably want the en-tries, for example, to appear in a small point size (like 9 or 10) of the same font as your body copy.

Managing Book Special Effects

This section offers some finishing touch tweaks that can help you make your book-length document look more professional.

Making Running Headers and Footers

Running headers and footers are the entries at the top or bottom of pages that tell the reader at a glance the specific contents of the page. Dictionaries, ency-clopedias, catalogs, phone directories, classified ads— these types of publica-tions have traditionally been bone-wearying, tedious endeavors. The running heads had to be constructed by hand, and any change in the text triggered a whole new editing cycle.

Well, not anymore. PageMaker version 6.0 has significantly advanced the power-ful running header and footers function, introduced for the first time in version 5.0. There's an all new, easy-to-use, visual interface. In addition, the new version of this Plug-in works faster and smoother and offers user-friendly customization of running header/footer content.

Here are the fundamentals of how PageMaker's revamped Running Headers/ Footers Plug-in works:

▶ It processes your document after the layout has been finalized. It's a post-processor and you must rerun it to pick up changes if content changes. In that sense it performs its duties just like PageMaker's Create Index or Create TOC commands.

▶ It processes paragraphs pulling words from paragraphs based on a search definition that you construct, and looking in paragraphs tagged with your choice of a paragraph style. (Since you specify the style you'll need to plan ahead when you design your stylesheet to make this all work to your maximum advantage.)

▶ The Plug-in, for all its power, can only handle one story at a time. It will not construct running headers or footers for an entire book list.

▶ As you set up your running header or footer, it may seem as if the header or footer is being set up on a master page. It's not. The Plug-in generates text blocks on each page where the chosen story is present, no matter what master page has been assigned to that page.

▶ Those text blocks are editable on a page-by-page basis if you wish to perform fine-tuning, although your editing work will be wiped out if you rerun the Plug-in to update the header and footer entries.

▶ As a running header/footer should, any given entry will continue from page to page until the Plug-in runs into a new hit on its defined content and search style parameters.

You must select a text block within the target story with the Pointer tool before running the Plug-in. Figure 17.23 shows the Running Headers & Footers main dialog box.

Positioning Your Headers/Footers

Start by getting text blocks positioned in the preview box of the dialog box. These text blocks will be the containers for the information in your running headers and footers.

1. Once the Plug-in dialog box is open, select the grid you will use to position the running header or footer text block. Select from the pop-up menus at the top of the preview box area. You can choose any master page or a specific regular page. When you select regular page the page number boxes become active and editable.

FIG. 17.23 ▶

The Running Headers/ Footers Plug-in.

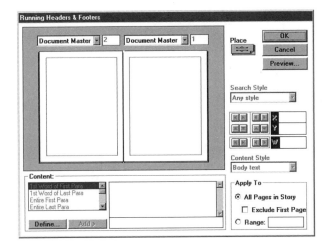

2. Use the Place button to drag a running header or footer text block out onto the preview area pages.

3. Use the X, Y, and W Position & Width boxes and the nudge buttons to position the running header/footer text block. The row of buttons on the left, with lines across the arrowheads, snap that parameter to a guide or the edge of the page.

4. If you need more than one header/footer, repeat the process until you have text blocks to meet your needs.

TIP ▶ Don't Forget to Design Space for Your Header/Footer

As powerful as this Running Headers & Footers Plug-in is, it does not move other page elements. It merely adds the header or footer to the page. That means you must design your page to leave space for the insert of the header or footer text block.

Setting Search and Formatting Parameters

Next, tell PageMaker what paragraph styles should be used for the running header/footer operation.

1. Select a Search Style. Often this will be a headline style. It might also be the style used for the listings in a directory. Or you can select Any Style to get the broadest possible search.

2. Select a Content Style. Generally you will want to set up special paragraph styles for this purpose.

3. Tell PageMaker which pages should get each of your headers and footers in the Apply To section. You can exclude the first page, as you would want to do if you were composing headers and footer for a chapter with a major chapter break. You can also list a page range in the provided text box.

Defining Header/Footer Content

Define the information that will be placed in each of the text blocks. Repeat this process until you have defined content for each of the running header/footer text blocks.

   4. Select a target text blocks by clicking it.

   5. In the Content section, select one of the predefined items. For example, you might want the running header on the left page of a text book to contain the "Entire First Para" of your chosen Search Style (which in this case would be one of your headline styles).

   6. When you click the Add button (or double-click the chosen item) the selection will be copied into the right-hand scrolling list.

   7. Add any static text you want to go with the extracted content. For example, maybe you would want to precede your content with the chapter number or title.

Defining Custom Content

You may want to create your own specialized content definition, or to prevent the standard content items from picking up certain words. For that:

   1. Click the Define button, and you will get the dialog box in figure 17.24.

Fig. 17.24 ▶

The custom selector dialog box for the Running Header & Footer Plug-in.

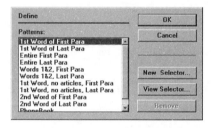

   2. Choose a Selector from the list. You can base your custom content definition on one of PageMaker's prebuilt definitions, or you can edit a Selector you had previously defined. You are only allowed to edit a Selector that you have created, so there's no way you can wreck the built-in Selector definitions.

      Usually it's easiest to choose an existing Selector and click the New Selector button. You will get the Edit Selector dialog box in figure 17.25.

   3. Name your new selector.

   4. Choose your defining terms. You can extract characters, words, lines (or sentences in a pull-down list), and paragraphs—all from items in your chosen story that match the Search Style you chose in the main Running Header & Footer dialog box.

Take special note that the character and word definitions allow you to exclude or limit content to certain letters or words that you can type into the available text entry box. You could exclude numbers, or foreign language items, or titles, or almost anything you like.

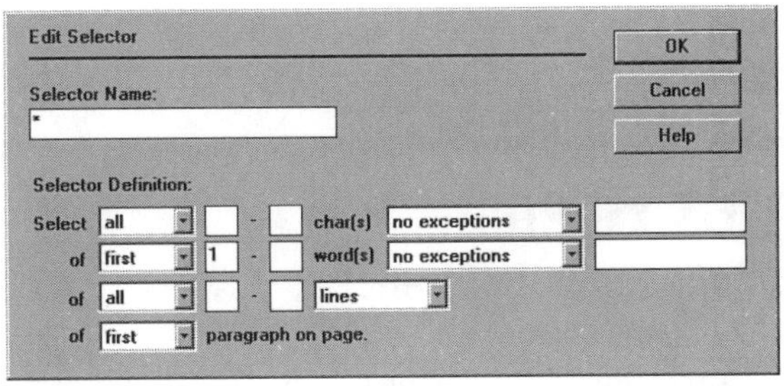

FIG. 17.25 ▶

The Edit Selector dialog box, based on the pre-built Selector "1st Word of First Para."

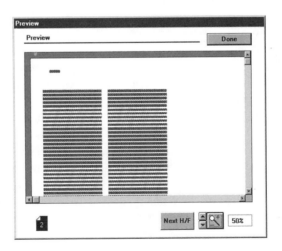

Previewing and Creating Running Headers & Footers

When you've got all this done, the rest seems a bit anticlimactic.

Click the Preview button to see your results, as in figure 17.26.

FIG. 17.26 ▶

Previewing your header/footer results.

In addition to choosing pages using the page icons at the bottom of the dialog box, you can flip from one header and footer to the next using the Next H/F button. And you can set magnification using the magnifying glass and its associated arrowhead buttons.

When you finally click OK in the main Running Headers & Footers dialog box, you will get a thermometer progress bar and be taken back to the location where you originally selected a text block for the target story.

You can run the Plug-in again at any time to update the entries.

Removing Headers or Footers

To remove headers or footers open up the Plug-in after clicking the target story. Then click and drag the header/footer text blocks off the preview box pages. They will turn into a No symbol and will be gone when you let go of the mouse button.

TACTICS RECIPE:
Coding Page Cross-References

A page cross-reference is where the text covering a subject on one page refers to some additional information on another page (for example, *for more information, see page 101*). Books tend to use a lot of these references; it would have been nice to have such a feature in producing this book, in fact.

Some word processors, particularly in the DOS world, automatically update these links between two pages, and the feature is sometimes called dynamic page cross-referencing. It saves all the work of going through every cross-reference in a book and matching it up with its companion page. But PageMaker doesn't support dynamic cross-referencing. You must do it by hand, which is not fun.

This tactics recipe offers a technique that reduces, but doesn't completely remove, the pain of creating page cross-references. It uses the indexing tools to automatically compile lists of the cross-references. Using these lists you can easily flip through your publication and type in the page numbers for the references. Really, you are simply using the index as an easily updateable database to manage the locations of all your page references.

Beware that you'll be generating a number of temporary index items, and at the end of the process you'll need to be absolutely certain you remove those items from the index. It would be horribly embarrassing if your book went to press with all those strange entries accidentally left in the index.

With that in mind, use the following steps to construct your semiautomatic page cross-referencing system:

▼ *Create and use a standard page reference and placeholder.* Always do your page references the same way and include a searchable and unique placeholder—something along the lines of (*See page [*]*). Follow this format rigidly, because that's the only way you will be able to find all of your references in the text using the Find command.

▼ *Back up your document in final nonreferenced stage.* When you are in the final edit stage, and the page breaks are unlikely to change, make a copy of your publication in case you need to do this job over again for some reason. Once you replace your searchable page reference placeholders with the real page locations you will have a devil of a time finding them again.

▼ *Use Story Editor and Find Again to locate references.* Get into Story Editor and search for your page number reference points. For the first reference, use the Find command. For the rest, use Find Next (Ctrl+G). Use the same technique as the one described in this chapter's earlier tip, "Use Search Again to Review Your Index in Context"; you need to see the context in order to make a proper page reference.

▼ *Code your references for compilation in a temporary index.* At each location, press the Index Entry keyboard shortcut (Ctrl+;). The Add Index Entry dialog box appears with the special page place holder characters highlighted in the first-level entry box. Type in a standard first-level index topic of your choice—perhaps something like Seek to indicate that these locations are seeking their referenced pages. In the second-level entry box, type a number that will sort properly in PageMaker—maybe a three-digit number with leading zeros. This number helps you match up the reference with the page being referenced. In the third-level entry box, type a word or two to remind yourself of the context for this reference.

▼ *Compile the page reference list using create index.* When you have coded every Seek location, compile and print the index. You now have a list (compliments of PageMaker's indexing tools) of all the locations where you typed (See page [*]), complete with a unique number, a context phrase, and a page number location.

▼ *Use the list as a guide to code the referenced locations.* Now go through the text, finding the correct locations for each page reference to be made. Code an index entry at each spot, using a first-level topic—such as *Locate*—that will be easy to find in the index. In the second-level entry box, type the number corresponding to the one for this page reference in your Seek list. You don't need any context entry here.

▼ *Create your master cross-reference list using create index.* When you complete that pass, compile the index again and print it out. Cut out the Seek and Locate lists, or cut and paste them into your word processor or spreadsheet side by side. The important thing is to line them up so that each entry in one list corresponds to the entry in the other list.

▼ *Use the list to enter your reference page numbers in text.* Now go through the book again with the Find command, searching for your unique page reference placeholder. Replace each placeholder with the appropriate page number, using the double list you have generated as a reference.

▼ *Be sure to remove the lists from the index!* When you're done, don't forget to delete the Seek and Locate lists from your real index.

TACTICS RECIPE
Setting Footnotes

PageMaker does not provide a footnoting feature, despite its impressive indexing and table of contents power. The best way to generate your footnotes is to compile them in a word processor such as Microsoft Word. PageMaker's Word import filter (see Chapter 8, "Pouring Text into PageMaker") leaves all the footnote numbers (in superscript) in place and collects all your page-level footnotes into endnotes at the end of the story. If you bring your Word text into PageMaker in chapter-size bites, you can create chapter-level endnotes with little discomfort.

What if you want page-level footnotes rather than endnotes? There's no good solution for this one, but here's a recipe you can try.

▼ *Use a master page graphic to create a footnote preserve.* Before you place your main body copy, lock a non-printing box at the bottom of the master pages that apply to your body copy where you will want footnotes. Set a Text wrap command for it. This step creates a dead area at the bottom of the page where you will be able to place your footnotes.

▼ *Place text.* Place your main body copy. Notice that the footnote preserve graphic fends it out of your intended footnote area.

▼ *Pasteboard the endnotes.* After the story has been placed, use the Text tool to cut and paste your endnotes onto the Pasteboard as a new story. You will pull your page notes out of this text.

▼ *Choose between two options for breaking out notes.* You have two choices for cutting endnotes.

You can cut the endnotes into chunks and float them on each page where they belong. Or you can run the endnotes as one continuous threaded story, forcing page breaks where needed. Try both and see which works best for you. (Or just use chapter endnotes and be done with it!)

Option One—Many Text Blocks. Remove your Text Wrap graphic from the master page and then work your way through each text page, cutting chunks out of the footnote story and placing them at the bottom of the correct page. This requires you to play with the text breaks until the footnote numbers and the depth of the page have been worked out properly.

Option Two—One Threaded Text Block and Page Breaks. After the main story has been placed, remove the Text Wrap box for footnotes from the master page(s).

Create a new one that covers the main text. Make sure the Text Wrap extends well outside the main body copy live area or you'll make a mess of the line breaks and have text shooting out all over the place trying to avoid the Text Wrap boundary.

Roll up the bottom windowshade of the footnote story until no text is showing and click the solid triangle to load the endnotes into a text placement icon.

Now go to the first page with foot-notes and place the story, aided by the Text Wrap barrier that's protecting the main text. After all the footnote text has been placed, go back through the pages and tune them. You can force page breaks when a footnote belongs on the next page by formatting it with Page Break Before from the Paragraph Specifications box.

This technique resembles the one used to create Multicolumn Heads (see Chapter 15, "Creating Special Effects").

TACTICS RECIPE
Creating Bleeder Tabs

Bleeder tabs are an excellent visual tool for getting a grip on a complex book (liter-ally!). Bleeder tabs are the bars of ink that step down along the edges of pages from one section or chapter to the next. The first chapter gets the top bleeder tab, the second chapter gets one slightly lower, and so on down the line.

Why are they called bleeder tabs? Be-cause they are a poor person's version of those die cut tabs you find in loose-leaf binders and some bound books. And be-cause they are created by bleeding the block of ink off the edge of the page, past the crop marks. The printer then trims the page, leaving ink right to the edge of the paper. The final result is a series of strips along the page edges that show you ex-actly where each chapter begins and ends.

To make your own bleeder tabs, fol-low these steps:

▼ *Consult with your printer.* You must consult with your printer before do-ing bleeder tabs. The success of this process depends on how much the ink spreads on the edges of the paper you have chosen, what press will be used, the size of the paper, how many pages are being printed in a signa-ture, and so on.

Describe what you plan to do and ask the printer how much bleed you need to allow outside the crop marks. The printer is likely to want at least 1/4 inch, and there's probably no such thing as too much. To repeat: you *must* consult with your printer before designing your bleeder tabs.

▼ *Compose your master page template.* Design a master page template that contains all of the bleeder tabs. Don't drive yourself crazy by following your first impulse and trying to place the tab in each chapter. Create a master page with all the tabs and save the document as a template.

In addition to setting up the tab index bleeder bars, you are likely to want to spin some type to label each tab. Remember that you should put the bleeder tabs only on the right-hand pages if you are working with facing pages.

▼ *Create your tab index.* You can use your master page template to create a *tab index page* (see fig. 17.27). It's the only other page besides your master template that contains all the bleeder tabs. It should probably be placed right in front of your table of contents, because it's the master reference to all the tabs in the book—the visual guide to your tab system.

In addition to the bars and their label text, spell out the names of the chapters across the page. You might want to add some directions on how to use the tabs, but they are common enough (and easy enough to use) that they don't require much explanation.

▼ *Set up the rest of your chapter files.* Open your master template and save a copy of it as a publication. Make any additions or other modifications you need to make it conform to your chapter text design. After you have a basic chapter publication set up, with all the styles and master page elements defined, save it and click Quit.

Now copy the document as many times as needed (one for each chapter in your publication), naming each chapter as you go to fit your file organization scheme.

▼ *Delete the unwanted tabs for each chapter.* Finally, open each chapter in turn and delete the tabs you don't need for that chapter. In the example shown in figure 17.27, you would delete *Planning* and *Promotion* in the *Background* chapter.

You now have a set of chapters all set up with perfectly aligned bleeder tabs in place on their master pages.

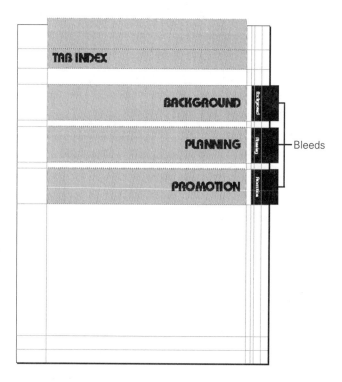

Fig. 17.27 ▲

The bleeder tab index page.

Where to Go from Here

▶ Try out some of the special effects described in Chapter 15, "Creating Special Effects," to spice up the look of your book.

▶ Many information-packed books require tables and charts. To get started on building them, have a look at Chapter 16, "Formatting Forms, Tables, and Databases."

▶ If the budget allows, make your long form document colorful! The next three chapters cover the subject.

▶ If you aren't doing color, you are ready to head for the final step of getting your document onto paper—the printing press. All of the chapters in Part VI, "Publishing," will help you out.

IV

Creating Page Layouts

PART V

Making Pages Colorful

18 ▲ Creating Colors

19 ▲ Applying Colors

20 ▲ Meeting Color Challenges

Chapter 18

Creating Colors

This chapter on defining PageMaker colors covers these topics:

Working around the fact that the color on your computer never perfectly matches the color on the printed page—even with PageMaker's new color management capability.

▼

Understanding the two kinds of color used in printing: spot color and process color.

▼

Planning the color system for your projects, choosing between a color-matching system (spot color) and process color or, perhaps, using both.

▼

Understanding and using a new form of process color, Pantone Hexachrome colors; and high-fidelity color ink.

▼

Using the Define Color command to make colors available for use on the PageMaker Colors palette.

▼

Adopting a standard color library to make colors consistent between publications.

THESE NEXT THREE CHAPTERS on color are out of order with the rest of the book…or are they?

Why the ambivalence? You really can't do color without understanding what happens on the printing press. On the other hand, you can't work with your service bureau and printer unless you understand the methods regarding color.

As you read these chapters on colors in Page-Maker, keep in mind that they need the backup of the chapters in Part VI, "Publishing."

This chapter covers the first step of working with color in PageMaker—defining your colors. You must define your colors before you can apply them to objects on your pages. To define and apply color, you do need to understand some basics about the science of color. ▶ ▶ ▶

✂ KEY CONCEPT:
Your Screen Doesn't Match the Printing Press

Yep, plain and simple, WYSIWYG does not exist when you arrive in the world of digital color. Sure, the type is shaped correctly and the line breaks are accurate. The problem is the color. Call up a picture of a dewy pink rose on any dozen computers and you are apt to get a dozen subtly different shades of pink. And the color you get on paper from a printing press won't match any of them.

What about standard color-matching systems, such as Pantone? Those colors are the same every time, aren't they? Well, sure, unless someone screws up when mixing the ink. But even though you get consistent colors on the printing press, your printed PMS color still won't match your computer screen.

Well, you say, I will be okay if I use a calibrated color system, right? Uhhh, yes, up to a point. Color management helps

and PageMaker's new implementation of color management has many professionals feeling as confident and excited about color accuracy as they have been for a long time. But these color-management systems still aren't perfect.

No matter how much color management systems improve, no calibration system will ever conquer one central difficulty: The way your computer produces color on the video screen and the way a printing press produces color on a page simply do not compare. Have a look at figure 18.1 here and in the color section. The computer screen shoots light at you by making phosphor glow inside a glass tube—projected light. A printing press puts ink on paper so you only see it from light that bounces off the paper—reflected light.

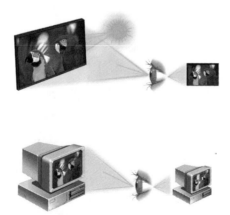

FIG. 18.1 ▲

Reflected light (top) and projected light (bottom) reach the eye in completely different ways, resulting in major differences in how we see the "same" color.

Aside from the core technological differences between computers and printing presses, a few other variables get in the way of seeing accurate color on-screen:

▼ Computer monitors build up colors from red, blue, and green (RGB), whereas printing presses build colors out of inks (some premixed, some blends of ink dots).

▼ Both the printing press and the computer can use any one of a dozen or so methods of describing colors— called color spaces. The translations between those systems result in more surprises and compromises than anyone really would like to admit.

▼ Printing press results will be inconsistent due to batch variations in the "same" ink colors and variations in the way plates are burned by different press operators.

▼ Phosphor varies from one computer screen to the other, resulting in inconsistent color representations.

▼ For that matter, as it ages a computer monitor screen sprays a varying number of electrons at the phosphor, resulting in brightness and contrast inconsistencies from monitor to monitor, even if they are plugged into the same computer and even if they are made at the same factory using the same batch of phosphor.

▼ Paper makes a major difference in the color of your final printed product, absorbing more or less ink (depending on the weather and storage conditions) and adding its own underlying tint to the color mix.

▼ The systems that provide color proofs—as good as they are—aren't perfect. So when the service bureau pulls a proof, you can't rely on it to match perfectly with the final printed page.

▼ You may not even be publishing on paper. If you are using PageMaker to create a slide or overhead presentation, other factors can create variations in color. Fundamental differences are triggered when you shine light through transparent material. For slides, many other variables are introduced by the operator of the film recorder and the slide developing process. And for overheads, the range of color printer options—from an inexpensive inkjet to a dye sublimation printer that costs as much as a Yugo—introduces yet more variables.

▼ And to top it all off, your brain constantly makes judgments, so you see colors differently depending on all sorts of environmental factors, such as the amount and type of overhead lights and the color of the walls in your design studio.

The point of all this? Don't trust the color you see on your monitor because it only resembles the colors on those standard ink swatches or the photograph of your dewy pink rose.

How can you work around this problem? Simply keep in mind that you can't pick or edit colors based purely on what you see on the computer screen. Be constantly aware of the challenge you face in translating color from the computer screen to some other medium.

Actually, the one partial solution to the challenge of getting the color you want in your final printed product is experience—either yours or the experience of your service bureau or print shop manager.

V

Making Pages Colorful

If you have an in-house, million-dollar imagesetter system and a six-tower litho press (another bunch of commas and zeros in the budget) and can do experimental color runs to your heart's content, you can learn pretty quickly what works and what doesn't—especially if you have an experienced hand to be your mentor.

Unfortunately, those tools aren't part of the average desktop publishing setup. And throwing out 10,000 muddy looking four-color brochures is expensive—especially if you have to eat the cost yourself because your client rejected the job.

If you don't have color experience and an unlimited budget for experimentation, you need to call on the expertise of others who have that kind of experience. That's why I made such a big deal at the beginning of this chapter, and at other points in this book, about the need to take into account the full publishing process. Collaborate early and often with the other people on your color production team— the print shop, the service bureau that provides your prepress services, and the photographer who shoots the photographs for your publication. Those folks' eyes have already been trained by years of expensive mistakes.

Working with Spot Color

When you use a rubber stamp or pick up a brush to paint the trim of your house, you are using spot color. In printing, *spot color* means you are smearing a solid swatch of ink onto the printed page. In a sense, when you print an all black-ink publication you are printing with spot color—the color of black ink in that case.

Usually, though, when someone says, "I just did a spot color job," they mean they have run a job on a printing press using black ink plus one or more additional spot colors. The spot colors are premixed ink, concocted by the printer or by the print shop's supplier, almost always using one of the standardized color-matching systems. That's how you pick your color—by selecting from standard color swatches.

Spot Color Means Accurate Color

Because you are working with premixed inks, within its limitations spot color pretty much solves the challenge of achieving accurate color.

You still can't see the color accurately on your computer, but you can see what you will get. You buy a book of color swatches just like the paint chips you get at the paint store. For the PMS swatch book for example, the Pantone company mixed up all those standard colors of ink under scientifically controlled circumstances and laid it down on paper so you can experience the color and specify it with a notation on the mechanicals you send to the printer.

Of course there are still some variables. Your paper choice will influence the results from the press, and your perception of the colors skews because of the ambient light as you examine the color swatch (fluorescent, sunshine, incandescent, RayBan or rose-colored sunglasses, and so forth). However, by and large, spot color means accurate color.

You *could* create a spot color in PageMaker without using one of the standard color matching systems. You *could* "mix" up a color on your computer screen and designate it as a spot color. But don't do it. You have no guarantee that any print shop in the country could come up with whatever color you design, and (as we have already discussed) your computer monitor probably doesn't accurately represent the color to you anyway.

Spot Color Overlays and Press Plates

When you work with spot color you generally use two or three inks, although you could have many more. The printer makes up a plate for black ink, a plate for your second color, and another for your third, then prints your pages by running the paper over all those plates. You can have as many inks as your printer can handle on the press during a single run. The print shop can even run the paper through more than once to add still more colors (at some point, however, it makes more sense to use process color, a discussion coming up in the next section).

In order to create these plates—one for each color you are specifying for the job (including black)—you need to make up paper or film *overlays*. As you can see in figure 18.2, each overlay mimics the printing press plate by isolating every little bit of its particular assigned color onto a single sheet of paper or film that the printer can use to photographically expose a plate.

FIG. 18.2 ▶

The work flow for creating spot color, from color-matching system swatches, to computer layout, to imagesetter output and then finally on the press.

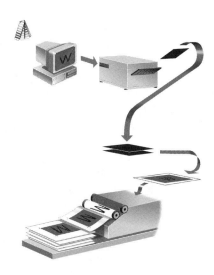

Why are these spot color mechanicals called overlays? Because that was the term traditionally used when a graphic artist pasted up a project for the printer. The type was pasted down on a stiff board and each spot color was represented by an acetate overlay mounted in layers over the top—overlays, in other words.

We now paste up our pages electronically, in the computer, instead of using an X-acto knife, T-square, Rubylith, acetate, and poster board or foam-core. Page-Maker can produce these spot color overlays for you and we explain how in Chapter 21, "Producing Mechanicals." You use PageMaker's Separations feature to produce overlays; it's in the Print command's Colors dialog box.

Working with Process Color

Think of process color printing as a major eyeball scam job. It might seem that the four CMYK colors—cyan, magenta, yellow, and black—are mixing on the page to create new colors. But that's not quite so. Each color is getting its own set of dots on the paper, generated by the screening process. It's your eye that is mixing the color, or maybe I should say it's your brain that mixes all those tiny dots when they arrive via the optic nerve from your eye.

You get the dots by turning your publication into four halftones, one for each color. Understanding about halftones is important, and you can get more detail on the concept and how it relates to resolution and line screens by checking Chapter 23, "Working with the Print Shop," in the Key Concept section "Understanding Halftones and Screens." Everything about black and white halftones and line screens and resolution applies to process color, except it's all four times more important because four screens make up your process color publication. (That is, four colors unless you are using one of the new high fidelity color methods, such as the six-color Pantone color system called Hexachrome.)

Understanding Traditional Process Color

At some point, if your full-color publication job is heading for a printing press, you must convert it to CMYK four-color process color.

In desktop publishing you separate your color work electronically by using a software program that breaks an image down into four separations—four layers of color that together compose a full-color image.

Fig. 18.3 ▶

(See color section.)

Before computers, this separation of color into four component parts was done photographically in a print shop darkroom. The process is called *separating* and the resulting screens are called *separations*. You can see how they all add up in figure 18.3, in the color section of the book. From left to right in the figure, you see: the original picture, the four negative films, the impressions from each in the CMYK colors, and how they combine to produce a final image.

Separating the image into the four CMYK colors of cyan, magenta, yellow, and black is just one part of the job. Those layers of color must be turned into half-tones called *screens*, and the screens must be turned at an angle to one another so they don't just stack up, one dot on top of the other. Why? Because that's how we pull off the four-color process scam. The famous four process colors aren't mixed on the press; they're mixed in your brain. At some level your brain conveniently ignores the fact that the page is as dotty as measles, and it blends the adjacent dots into a perceived color. Look at figure 18.4 to see how the dots mingle.

FIG. 18.4 ▶

The eye perceives the dots of different colors all together, not as individual dots, and "mixes" the color.

Keep in mind that cyan, magenta, and yellow can be mixed together to create almost any color you like, but they aren't actually mixed together except in your brain. Black is used in addition to the CMY trio because it allows purer blacks, since the CMY inks are never perfectly pure and therefore can never create a perfect black. Also, using three colors to get the single black color builds up a lot of ink on the paper. It's simpler to just use black. The percentage (size and number of dots) of each of the four colors on a scale of zero to 100 percent determines the apparent color on your printed page. Ideally, these dots all cluster together in a sort of rosette pattern.

Considering High-Fidelity Color

One of its prime movers, Mills Davis, has tried to explain the significance of high-fidelity color through comparisons. It is, he says, like stereo compared to mono, or cappucino compared to espresso. As a colleague from the Desktop Publishing forum on CompuServe put it:

```
"Adobe has again put a cutting edge technology into the hands of
regular computer users. Giving them the basic tools they need to
create high-fidelity color seps right from their desktop scanner
or Photo CD image and output to six-color film. That's impres-
sive!"
```

That's Jim Dornbos, who owns Dornbos Press in Saginaw, Michigan. He was in on the pre-release testing and trial for PageMaker 6.0.

The point is, high-fidelity color attempts to extend the range of traditional four-color process color systems. It does so by adding extra color plates to the printing process:

▶ Pantone's Hexachrome color matching system, which is included with PageMaker 6.0, adds two extra colors—green and orange.

▶ Big-Gamut CMYK adds additional "bump" plates of the standard cyan, magenta, and yellow process inks.

▶ CMYK + Special adds as many as four spot additional colors to the basic four CMYK inks, integrating them into the regular four-color process.

Most often, instead of traditional angle screens, with regular patterns, your service bureau and print shop will use stochastic screening. That means random dots instead of a woof and warp weave of dots.

Stochastic screening probably shouldn't be described as a screen at all, even though everybody does use the term that way. It is correct, however, to describe it as a halftone. The traditional screening methods—going all the way back to when printers sandwiched a finely engraved glass "screen" with a film to screen a photograph—produce a very regular pattern of dots in a grid pattern. That's the major difference: stochastic halftones have random dots. They aren't at any particular angle or in any particular pattern. The stochastic approach helps uncomplicate things when you have more than four inks going on the paper. It gets nearly impossible to calculate all the angles so that many ink colors can fit together without creating a puddle of muddy ink on the sheet of paper.

Even with all this well-deserved enthusiasm, the biggest thing to know about high-fidelity color is this: it's still new. Only a few vendors know much about it yet—mostly the ones who have been participating in the research to make it possible. Approach it with caution, with a loose deadline, and a willingness to learn a lot before you get optimum results.

Deciding Between Spot and Process Color

Up to a point, you choose between spot color and process color because of money. Basically, you want to use the minimum number of color plates on the press because the price goes up with every additional ink color (additional printing press plates). That means that if you have any more than three colors, you will probably want to use process color techniques. Why? Because as long as you have that many press plates in play, you might as well go to process colors using process colors (which require only four plates). When you are paying for four colors, you might as well use process color instead of spot color and have the freedom to design with as many colors as you like.

That's over-simplified, of course, because in some circumstances you need the accuracy of spot color's pre-mixed inks. However, the basic idea holds true—the more inks you use, the more complicated the job on the press and the more money you spend.

Sometimes, despite the expense issues, you have no choice in methods. You have to use process color to reproduce a color photograph, for example, because spot color simply can't do it. Conversely, for some jobs you absolutely must use spot colors. For those jobs you use standard inks from one of the color-matching systems. The Pantone Matching System (PMS) has become ubiquitous since its invention back in the early 1960s, but other systems for achieving standard color do exist. Some other spot color-matching systems are Dainippon (or DIC) and TOYO. Also, some color-matching systems bridge the gap between premixed inks and process color printing, since these process color matching systems are mixed from process colors.

When might a spot color-matching system be essential? Well, you need inks from one of the color matching systems to create certain unusual ink effects, such as fluorescent yellow, pearlescent blue, or metal-flake tangerine.

Also, companies or brands sometimes are very picky about their signature colors, and you have to specify that color from a color-matching system. This lesson can be bitterly learned—just ask about one job we did for a pharmaceutical manufacturer. (Better yet, don't ask.) The videotape package had color photographs and so was run with four colors. The client rejected it because the signature color of the brand name didn't exactly match the Pantone swatch. The job had to be rerun with a fifth color, a spot color specified with a PMS number.

So you can (and sometimes must) run a spot color and process color on the same job. You hear stories of eight-color jobs, where four-color process photos are combined on a page with several spot colors. These jobs aren't common, because they're so expensive. A job like that may even require multiple passes through the printing presses, which in turn means considerable amounts of expensive labor, press time, and wasted stock and ink to get the paper in registration during the second pass through the press.

In general, six colors (including any varnish coating) is the break-point of combining process and spot colors. Many large commercial printers have six-tower presses that can run that many colors in a single pass. Of course, you won't find that kind of expensive press at your local quick printer, but most of them can handle spot color jobs. And that brings us full-circle to our original point: the more colors, the more money.

Converting Between Color Systems

In PageMaker, "converting" colors between various color libraries and methods of describing color is dangerously and deceptively easy. Click on a radio button in the Color Editing dialog box and PageMaker seems to easily make the switch. I said "seems" to.

Your color computer monitor paints images on the screen using three colors and has three cables going into it—red, green, and blue—for RGB. In fact, many of the high-end, large-screen monitors literally have three cables going into them, one for each color. These RGB colors are often referred to as the primary colors, and you may have been taught in school that all color is made up of various combinations of these three colors. If you add equal proportions of all three primary colors, you get white. (Notice the word "add." For that reason, scientists call the RGB color model an *additive* color system).

But unless yours was a truly exceptional science class, your science teacher perpetrated a cruel hoax on you and may have scarred you for life as far as printing technology goes. This experiment only told half the story of how colors are made—the additive half. The experiment left out the important "subtractive" primaries.

Look at figure 18.5 to see how you get white on the press. You can see the RGB color definition dialog box from PageMaker, adding up 100 percent of each color to get white. At the bottom, you see the CMYK color process method of getting white, by subtracting colors until there is zero percent of each of the four inks (assuming you are printing to white paper, of course).

You can see, looking at these two PageMaker dialog boxes for editing colors, that RGB and CMYK color systems arrive at "white" through two different routes.

The CMYK colors are *subtractive* primaries because you see them by reflected light. This sounds too weird to believe, but light shines back from the paper minus some colors that have been absorbed, or subtracted, by that particular mix of the translucent CMYK inks. The inks absorb light rather than project it. So now you know the answer to the great mystery of why we use the odd colors of cyan, magenta, and yellow. Cyan, magenta, and yellow are opposites to the RGB colors. Cyan is a mix of green and blue. It absorbs (subtracts) red and reflects the remaining RGB colors from the original light source.

The rub really comes in when you try to convert colors at the outer limits of a color system's capability. Even with book-learning you need experience (or help from someone with experience) to predict how well or how poorly a particular image will translate from one color system to another.

Fig. 18.5 ▶

Achieving white color on the press.

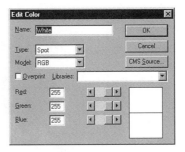

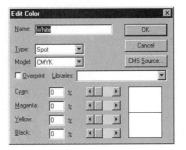

What you learn by experience is the gamut—the outer range limits for any given color setup. The range of colors you can see is the gamut of your personal color ability. The CMYK process has several gamuts, depending on variables such as paper and the printing press. In many color editing programs, such as Adobe Photoshop, you can set a gamut alarm to alert you when you exceed the gamut of colors that a particular color system can produce.

What trips the gamut alarm? Have a look at figure 18.6. The lines show the gamut for three different color systems, one of them being your eye. As you can see, your eye can discern colors that your computer monitor can't project, and the printing press can reproduce colors that your computer monitor can't manage. This situation explains a lot about the difficulties of getting accurate color.

Fig. 18.6 ▶

A graph of three color gamuts—your eye, your RGB color computer monitor, and a CMYK printing press.

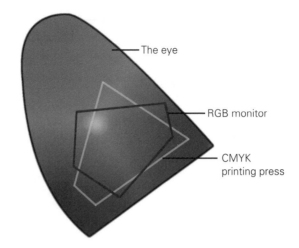

The eye

RGB monitor

CMYK printing press

In some production situations, there are some color-matching systems that make this whole color system conversion a lot easier. These systems specify spot color inks to be mixed out of the four standard process colors of cyan, magenta, yellow, and black. TRUMATCH, FOCOLTONE, or the Pantone Process matching systems all work this way, and if your commercial printer supports them, you can work in process colors and somewhat more accurately specify spot colors.

Color management systems help, too. The use of color management in PageMaker has been covered in Chapter 20, "Meeting Color Challenges." The primary function of a CMS is to make adjustments for the fact that desktop publishing involves several transformations between different color setups—from RGB scanner, to CMYK process color conversion as displayed on an RGB computer monitor, to actually putting ink on paper.

It's not easy to make all these transformations accurately. Just take a look at the color black. You might think that all black is equal. It's not true. Black created with process colors will not be as black as pure black ink. And neither one of those will look as rich as a black with some of the process colors mixed into it.

Fig. 18.7 ▶

(See color section.)

If you look carefully, you can see this effect in figure 18.7 in the color section of the book. On the left, the first black has been composed by mixing 100 percent of the three subtractive primaries: cyan, magenta, and yellow. The middle black is pure black ink. And the black swatch on the right has been mixed with 100 percent black ink and a touch of each of the CMY colors. The right hand black, in other words, is what some designers call "rich black." You might say it has been sweetened with the addition of these other colors.

You may notice that the middle black, the one made up of CMY only with solid black ink, has a sort of brownish, gunky look. This happens because no ink is pure, even the standard process colors of cyan, magenta, and yellow. So CMYK—with the addition of black ink—really is an artificial kind of color system that doesn't occur anywhere in nature except on the printing press. The addition of pure black artificially compensates for a fundamental problem with the technology of printing process color.

The addition of all those inks also adds up to a potential problem called over-inking. It may have occurred to you that 100 percent of CMY adds up to 300 percent, and adding another 100 percent of black would reach to 400 percent ink coverage. That's a lot of ink to be in one spot on a piece of paper. Commercial printers generally try to avoid ink coverage of more than 250 to 320 percent, depending on the ability of the press to handle the problem. To compensate for the technical problem of ink buildup caused by the artificial CMYK color system, prepress experts use something called *GCR*, for *gray component replacement*. This and many other technical issues relating to color and the printing press—including color management systems and trapping to compensate for mis-registration of colors on the printing press—are summed up in Chapter 20, "Meeting Color Challenges."

Defining Colors in PageMaker

You define colors in PageMaker by adding them to your Colors palette, ready for application to objects and text on your page. To define colors, you use the Define Colors command, located under the Elements menu. The Define Colors dialog box is the access point for adding, editing, copying, or removing colors on the PageMaker Color palette.

The scrolling list in the Edit Color dialog box shows all the colors in your Colors palette. By choosing any one of them on the list you can see what they look like (at least on your particular video monitor) in the color swatch next to Color at the top of the dialog box.

The [*None*], [*Paper*], [*Registration*], and [*Black*] colors (those in brackets) are always on your Colors palette. Here's what they mean:

▶ [*None*] means removing any color added in PageMaker and returning the object to what you might call its natural color. If you import an EPS file, you can assign it a PageMaker color that will override the colors contained within the EPS. This color of [*None*] removes all PageMaker assigned colors. It works the same way as the setting in the Print command to preserve EPS colors (for PostScript printers only), except it applies to any imported file to which PageMaker colors have been assigned, including TIFFs.

▶ [Paper] means no ink, or *knockout* (later in this chapter we talk more about using knockouts). PageMaker applies no ink to any area or object to which you assign the color [Paper], including any point where a Paper-colored object overlaps an object of another color. If you are printing to colored paper, you may want to edit the definition of the Paper color in that publication so you get a monitor display that more closely resembles your actual finished page. Just be sure to keep in mind that paper means no ink.

▶ Use the color [Registration] to put production notes and custom trim cross hairs on your publications. Anything assigned the color [Registration] prints on every spot-color overlay or process-color separation. That's because it has been specially defined as 100 percent each of CMY and as a spot color, so it will be separated to every overlay or plate. You cannot edit the [Registration] color.

▶ You can't edit the color [Black], either. From Layout view, the fastest way to get to the Edit Color dialog box is to Ctrl+click the bracketed [Black] item in the Colors palette. You can also use the same shortcut on any of the other bracketed colors.

TIP ▶ **Make a Registration-Colored Tag for Notes**

Make notes on your overlays and separations by making up a tag colored with the color [Registration]. Create and format a text block that overlaps the page, but don't let any of the actual text fall onto the page. This trick fools PageMaker into "printing" the text, rather than regarding it as a Pasteboard item. If you color the text with the [Registration] color, it prints on every color film. Also, you can rotate the text so it runs along a long edge of the page to help the text of the note fit within the paper size.

Adding/Editing a Color on Your Colors Palette

Clicking on either the <u>N</u>ew or the <u>E</u>dit buttons gives you the Edit Color dialog box, shown in figure 18.8. You use this dialog box to define colors on your Colors palette.

FIG. 18.8 ▶

The heart of PageMaker's color definition facility, the Edit Color dialog box.

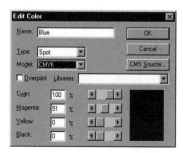

Using the Slider Bars and Color Evaluator Square

Using the slider bars, you can create a nearly infinite number of colors, which you can evaluate by observing the changes in the large, colored squares in the lower-right corner of the dialog box (keep in mind the limitations of the computer's attempts to show you what you get from the printing press). The square on the top changes as you modify the color in the edit box. The lower one shows the color you started with. If you are editing an existing color or creating a new one, the second square lets you evaluate your changes as compared to the old color.

TIP ▶ Use the Edit Color Dialog Box as a Color Picker

If you're bewildered by the hundreds of colors in the PageMaker color-matching system libraries (more on that in a bit), you can narrow down the choices pretty quickly. Tune the slider bars in the Edit Color dialog box to approximate the color you want. Then, pull out your color libraries from the Libraries pull-down list and select a color-matching system. PageMaker will do its best to automatically take you to a swatch that matches the values you set with the slider bars with one of the predefined colors within that color system.

TIP ▶ Set Color Management Preferences Early

For best results, set your color management system options when you first open up your publication. You can access your CMS Source from this Edit Color dialog box, but your best bet for consistency is to set your CMS in the Preferences command when first building your document. Then all your colors will be defined using the same color management parameters.

If you have a situation where you need some different settings—as when TIFFs are coming in from different scanners—you can make adjustments as needed. But all your PageMaker colors should be defined using the same monitor setup.

Selecting the Type of Color

Your first to-do item when creating a new color or editing an existing one is to select your type of color—spot, process, or a tint percentage of one or the other. For more on the difference between spot and process colors, look at the early part of this chapter in the sections "Working with Spot Color" and "Working with Process Color." Keep the following information in mind when selecting a type of color:

▶ Remember that using a spot color means you will be isolating everything assigned that color to a single color overlay. You aren't actually picking a color at all when you create a spot color. You merely are isolating all those spot color items to a single overlay, so the printer can burn a plate to apply a premixed ink.

▶ Using process color means that you will be creating color separations in CMYK.

▶ You can only create a tint after you have defined a base color. The tint will be a percentage of that base color. The "Defining Tints" section later in this chapter gives more detail on this special operation.

Make your color type selection with a clear idea of where you are heading in the design process. Use spot color if you are working with one of the spot color-matching systems, for example. If you know you will be working with a process color-based matching system and not with standard premixed inks, click on the Process Color radio button.

TIP ▶   Edit Spot Colors to Match Your Swatches

Given the limitations of working with color on a computer, your chosen spot color as it appears on your monitor may not match the appearance of your standard color swatch. If you are absolutely positive that you won't ever need to convert your spot color to a process color at some point, feel free to adjust your color to match the swatch. If you keep the color as a spot color, you won't affect the finished color of your printed piece because that color is determined by the printer's premixed ink, not by its representation on your screen. It may aid your design work to have a good match between the swatch and its on-screen representation. Remember this, however, if you ever make a conversion to CMYK color from spot color, the percentages will be all screwed up and you are guaranteed poor results from your separations.

Selecting the Color Model

Select a color model next, while keeping in mind the pitfalls we discussed earlier in this chapter. Theoretically, each system can describe a color accurately, but uses a different technique to do so. In practice, you need to carefully match your color model to the end result. For example, if you have chosen process for your type of color, right from the beginning you should define your colors using the CMYK color model. The Edit Color dialog box offers the following Model options:

▶ RGB gives you three slider bars for red, green, and blue, each one running from zero to 100 percent. (For more on RGB, refer to the opening sections of this chapter.)

▶ *HLS* stands for *hue*, *lightness*, and *saturation*, as you see in the slider bars shown in figure 18.9. We talk more about this model in just a moment.

▶ CMYK has four slider bars for each of the process colors, cyan, magenta, yellow, and black. (This chapter's sections "Working with Process Color," "Deciding Between Spot and Process Color," and "Converting Between Color Systems" help provide insight into using the CMYK color model.)

Fig. 18.9 ▶

*The slider bars for
the HLS color
space.*

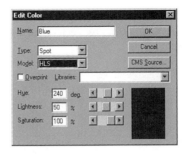

In the HLS color model the *H* stands for hue. Hue is, well, it's the color of the color. Hue is measured in degrees as a radial on a circle of color. A color's *hue* is the position of a particular HLS color on the visible color spectrum that evolves from red through orange, yellow, green, blue, and peaks out at violet.

As for *L*, that's *lightness* (or *luminance*). Sometimes people think of lightness as the gray value of an HLS color or a way of describing how much white there is in a color. In fact, lightness is the amount of light you see reflected or projected from the colored object.

S is for *saturation* and refers to the amount of pigment in an HLS color, the intensity or purity of the color.

HLS, HSB, and HSV color systems are all close cousins to one another. They share the *H* for hue and *S* for saturation component, and the *L*, *B*, and *V* all refer to the same component of lightness, brightness, or value.

HLS tends to come up when you take in material from professional digital artists. Many of these folks like HLS because it more closely resembles the way they work when they draw or paint something—compared to RGB or CMYK. Printers must continue to work in CMYK, however, because they can't very well get accurate color on the press without using that artificial color space. Meanwhile, those who work in television and other aspects of what we might call the "projected arts" will stick with their technology of RGB.

The advent of more reliable color management systems, not just in PageMaker but in all the various graphic arts software, should make it easier to make more accurate translation between all these color systems. That would aid collaboration among all these color-system bound creative types as the borders between the computer, the printed page, and the TV screen get increasingly fuzzy.

Selecting a Color from a Library

PageMaker includes a number of color libraries full of thousands of pre-defined colors, including a complete selection of the Pantone systems, the leading color-matching standard in the United States, perhaps in the world. These libraries are by far the easiest and most accurate way to define a new color onto the PageMaker Colors palette. Figure 18.10 shows the list of libraries you can choose from in PageMaker.

Fig. 18.10 ▶

A list of PageMaker's color libraries.

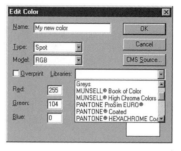

Notice that the new Pantone Hexachrome libraries have been included in PageMaker 6.0, as discussed earlier. Instead of a color model of CMYK, RGB, or HLS, the Edit Color dialog box lists the color model Multiple Ink. Also, the type of color is described as High Fidelity, instead of Spot, Process, or Tint.

In addition to proprietary color specification systems, PageMaker offers you custom libraries of crayon colors and grays. (The Crayon library, by the way, was based on the 64-pack Crayola color system. You know, the one you used when you were five years old and had trouble staying within the lines?)

There are five commercial ink standard color-matching systems ready for your use in PageMaker, not counting the foreign variations on the basic system from Pantone. Table 18.1 lists these systems and tells how each one gets built on the press.

TABLE 18.1   Proprietary Color-Matching Systems Built into PageMaker

System	Colors	Method	Notes
DIC (Dainippon)	1,280	Spot	Classified by category (gay and brilliant, quiet and dark, plus basics, grays and metallics).
FOCOLTONE	763	Process	Classified by quantity of one of the four process colors.
MUNSELL	Depends on system	Spot	Matching system based on the hue, value, and chroma (saturation) model.

System	Colors	Method	Notes
Pantone(r)	Depends on system	Spot or Process	The predominant color system in the United States, available in swatches to match various paper coatings. Also available in EURO form to match the European variations on the system, and a Process color version so you can compose standard swatch colors from CMYK inks.
TOYOpc	1,050	Spot	Colors classified by the HSV color model, hue, and saturation.
TRUMATCH	2,093	Process	Technically, a process color since it requires four color printing, but it can be called as a color match.

When you select a library from the menu, you get a scrollable window of color swatches like the one in figure 18.11. You click on the one you want and press OK to bring the color into the Edit Color dialog box. Another click on OK makes the decision final and inserts the color into your Colors palette so it will be available for your use during layout.

Fig. 18.11 ▶

One of the many color swatch lists reached from PageMaker's Libraries menu.

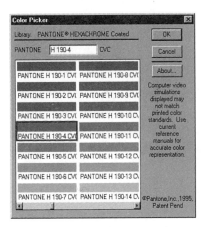

TIP ▶ Select Multiple Colors with Ctrl+Click or Click+Drag

You don't need to close your Library dialog box after each color swatch selection. You can make multiple swatch selections and define many new PageMaker palette colors at once. Just hold down the Ctrl key as you select colors or click and drag to select multiple swatches and load them into your Colors palette. The multiple layers of dialog boxes for the Define Colors command can get pretty cumbersome, so don't forget that Shift+click works here as it does elsewhere in PageMaker. Use Shift+click on the close box to close the current dialog and all its parent dialog boxes.

TIP ▶ Defining a Non-PageMaker Color-Matching Swatch

What if these libraries don't include your favorite color matching system, "Hues-R-Us?" And what if the screen doesn't match your color swatch? Simple, if you're working in spot color. Do the best you can to approximate the color on-screen, giving it a type of Spot color. The on-screen appearance has nothing to do with the color that will be printed since the ink determines the color. However, you should use the name and number from your color system matching swatch when you name the newly defined color in PageMaker. That will cause the ink name to be printed on that color's overlay if you check the Markings options in the Print command's Options dialog box. This overlay and plate labeling will help prevent a mistake in inking the press.

Naming Your Color

When you choose a color from one of the libraries, that color's name is automatically entered into the text box in the Edit Color and Define Color dialog boxes. When you or your service bureau prints out overlays for spot color, the color name is listed along with other printer's marks on its appropriate layer of film. As a rule, if you have selected a color from one of the color-matching systems (such as Pantone, TOYO, TRUMATCH, and so on), leave that name as it is to get the benefit of this built-in mistake prevention.

You can also name a color to remind you of the color's purpose. You might name some particular red you use for a corporate logo, for example, with the name of the company—"Widget Red," or something like that. If the logo is a PMS call, you can retain that as part of the name as a way to avoid confusion at the printer. Call it "Widget Red (PMS 186)."

Defining Tints

You must define a color before you can define a tint, because a tint can only exist as a percentage of a base color.

It is totally cool that PageMaker 6.0 will now allow you to assign tints to objects on an ad hoc basis, without first defining them here in the color dialog boxes. However, if you will be using a lot of a particular tint, you will still probably want to work most of the time with a defined tint. It saves time and improves consistency to be able to simply click on the color and tint you want from the Colors palette.

You define a tint this way. First, select your already defined base color. Select it in the Define Colors dialog box and then click on the New button.

Choose the Tint color type from the pop-up menu in the Edit Color dialog box. The dialog box transforms into what you see in figure 18.12. Set the percentage level of your tint by using the slider bar or by typing the percentage into the text entry box. The color evaluation square in the lower right corner splits in half, and the upper half shows you the effect of your adjustments. When you finish, click OK and the color appears in your Colors palette with a percentage sign in front of it to indicate that it's a tint.

Fig. 18.12 ▶

The tint specification version of the Edit Color dialog box.

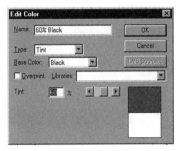

Most printing presses aren't capable of reproducing tints in all the fine gradations you could define in PageMaker dialog boxes. Check with your printer to be sure, but generally you should work in tint percentage increments of 5 percent.

When naming tints, include the percentage and the base color in the name. That will make it easier to know at a glance what the base color is and how much lighter the tint is from the base. This technique also helps when you need to sort out the possible effects of deleting a base color. If you remove a base color, its dependent tint is converted to black.

Specifying Overprint and Knockout

Using a check box in the Edit Color dialog box, you can define a color to always overprint. To really understand the significance of overprint, you need to understand the concept of a knockout.

Knockout means that the color on the top layer wins and all other colors behind it are blocked from printing. All colors (all objects) in PageMaker work as knockouts unless you take specific action to make them overprint. Knockouts prevent two colors from mixing on the page to create some unexpected or unwanted third color. Well, actually, there is one exception. Unless you are using the trapping facilities and change the settings, black text below 24 points always overprints.

Sometimes, however, you want to overprint. A common example of such a situation is using black type over a lighter color background. Rather than have the type knock out the lighter background (which may lead to press registration problems that leave unprofessional-looking white lines around the type), you simply have it print over the underlying color. You don't have to worry about an unwanted third color, because black can overcome most color mixing problems.

These concepts of knockout and overprint are critical to the process of manually trapping objects on PageMaker pages, a subject that's covered in considerable detail in Chapter 20, "Meeting Color Challenges." For more on PageMaker layers, see the Key Concept "Understanding Layers and the Colors None and Paper" in Chapter 10, "Drawing with PageMaker."

TIP ▶ Use 100 Percent Tint to Get Overprint Colors

If you need to overprint some objects but knock out others, you can designate the item to overprint in the Fill and Line dialog box. Or, if you want to have an overprint version ready at a click in the Colors palette, you can define two versions of the same color—one to knockout and the other to overprint. However, this won't work if you follow your first impulse and create two different color names. The dual definitions will generate two overlays (plates on the press) instead of one, causing extra expense and complication for the job. The solution is to use an important fact about tints and their base colors. They print on the same overlay. However, you can set the base color and the tint so one overprints and the other doesn't. Do this by defining a 100 percent tint of your base color, setting the base color to knockout and the 100 percent tint to overprint.

Making Color Definitions Consistent Within and Between Publications

Almost any service bureau operator can tell you horror stories of projects that came in with, for example, 20 different definitions on the Colors palette for the same color of deep violet. Naturally, the client wants all the violets to look the same, even though each had a slightly different value on the slider bar, and the variations in their names will cause PageMaker to look at each of the colors as a different ink and therefore trigger the production of 20 different spot color overlays.

This sort of thing happens mainly for two reasons:

▶ Imported objects come in with colors defined in other programs.

▶ Different people working on different aspects of the same publication used different color definitions. This section may help you avoid those pitfalls so you can avoid a starring role in your service bureau operator's nightmare.

Merging Colors

In PageMaker, you can permanently remove a color from the Colors palette and at the same time globally replace every occurrence of that color with a new color definition. The concept is similar to the way you replace or merge paragraph styles, although the process doesn't work in quite the same way. In Define Colors, define the color that will survive the merger of the color definitions. Then select the color you want to replace and click on Edit. In that color's name box, type the name of the new color, the one you want to end up as the surviving color in the merger. Make sure that both the new and old color names are spelled exactly the same and click OK. You get a warning dialog box, asking to confirm that you indeed want to replace the old color with the new one. Click OK and you're done.

Removing Colors

Removing colors from your Colors palette is an even simpler process. Select the color and click on the Remove button. If the color has been used anywhere in the publication, even as the base color of a tint, PageMaker gives you a warning dialog box asking for confirmation and letting you know that it will turn all the occurrences of that color (including the related tints) to black.

One excellent new PageMaker 6.0 feature is the Remove Unused feature. It's common to build up a clutter of unused colors if you are importing EPS graphics from a variety of sources. They often contain artifacts of the editing or design process. Other than the clutter, that might be okay if it wasn't for the fact that each of these artifacts will trigger the creation of a new color plate. Click Remove Unused to get rid of them.

TIP ▶ Reduce Clutter by Deleting Unused Standard Colors

Chances are pretty remote that you need those standard RGB and CMYK colors that come set up in PageMaker when you first get it. Delete them first by using Remove Unused. In fact, you can set a mini-default so they don't come up in a new publication, using the methods described in Chapter 3, "Personalizing PageMaker Preferences."

Copying Colors Between Publications

You can copy Colors palettes between publications just like you can copy paragraph style sheets. Simply go to the Define Colors dialog box and click the Copy button. You get a standard Open File dialog box. Select the publication you want and click OK, or just double-click on the publication title. Unfortunately, you can't pick and choose which individual colors you copy from the publication. The Define Colors Copy button is an all or nothing proposition.

Adopting Colors from Imported or Clipboarded Objects

You can copy colors between PageMaker publications and other software applications in another way, by adopting them. Many graphics objects come into your current PageMaker publication with their own colors attached.

After these adopted colors arrive in the Colors palette, you can use them just like a color defined right in your current PageMaker publication. This technique can help a lot in your efforts to achieve consistency between your drawing program and PageMaker. (The evil flip side of this feature is the one we've already discussed. This is the way a lot of those artifact colors get into your publication.)

Spot colors come into PageMaker from EPS graphics files very cleanly, and you can even edit them after importation. Named process colors can be imported and will be marked with the EPS icon in the palette.

PageMaker 6.0 has a new capability to control how these imported EPS colors come into your publication. When Placing an EPS, hold down the Shift key. You'll get an EPS import filter dialog box similar to the Smart ASCII filter or the enhanced dialog for the Microsoft Word filter. In this dialog box (see fig. 18.13) you can control how process and spot colors are added to your palette, and whether spot colors are converted to process colors when imported.

Fig. 18.13 ▶

Holding down the Shift key when placing an EPS gets you this maximum control dialog box.

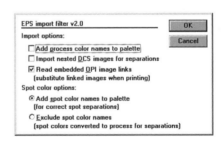

During the early release days of PageMaker 6.0, it was discovered that FreeHand 5.0 and the new PageMaker had fallen out of synch when it comes to file importation. If you have TIFF graphic files embedded in your FreeHand EPS, use Shift+Place and turn off the Read Embedded OPI Image Links check box. That'll solve the problem of embedded TIFFs not printing, even though they were visible on-screen.

PageMaker objects pasted or drag-and-dropped through the Clipboard bring their colors with them as well. You can use this technique to copy individual colors between publications. Assign the color to some quickly drawn box or circle as a temporary holder for the adopted color. Cut and paste it into your target publication and the color will be adopted by the target publications Colors palette. Then delete your "color carrier" graphic.

Using Color Templates and Mini-Defaults

Sometimes you develop colors that you use every time you open a new publication, maybe a set of gray percentages. For those colors, consider setting up a mini-default for your Colors palette (described in Chapter 3, "Personalizing Page-Maker Preferences"). Set up the Colors palette with no publication open, defining your standard set of colors and those colors will be there every time you open a new document.

You could also create templates for each of your common color publication situations and define the colors you use in each one. You might have a set of templates for each of your major clients (or in-house corporate departments).

Installing and Making Your Own Color Libraries

Want an elegant solution for making color consistent? For workgroups or for your most common color situations (frequent clients, monthly newsletter, and so on) you can set up your very own color library.

Define the colors you want in your library by selecting from PageMaker's Library dialog box, or by creating your own spot colors. (You can't store a tint in a library.)

After you have your color set all worked out, use the Create Color Library Plug-in. The dialog box is shown in figure 18.14.

FIG. 18.14 ▶

The Create Color Library Addition dialog box.

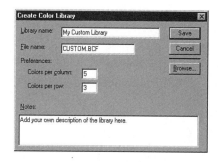

Name your custom library with the name you'd like to see in the Library Name pull-down list in the Define Colors command. Specify how many rows and columns you need (although it can't be bigger than 10×10), and add any notes you want to keep about the library. These notes are displayed when you click on the About button in the Library dialog box when you select your custom library.

Finally, click on Save or Save As, and save your library with a name of your choice as long as you do two vital things:

1. You must store this color library file in the COLOR folder, which you'll find in PM6/RSRC/USENGLSH.

2. The name must end with a period and the three letters BCF. If you forget about the BCF extension, the Plug-in will add it for you.

Where to Go from Here

▶ With all that color theory and info on defining colors, applying them may be anticlimactic because it's so easy to do. However, that's the subject of the next chapter, "Applying Colors."

▶ Two major color issues will require your skill—and your cooperation with your service bureau and printer. To get details on PageMaker's new color management and trapping capabilities see Chapter 20, "Meeting Color Challengers."

▶ Prepress—that's the name for the step between defining and applying colors and inking up a press. Your prepress service bureau can help you out a lot. For more on how, see Chapter 22 on "Proofing Your Publication."

▶ If you want to deal with color, you have to deal with your printer. You really must know how the publication will end up on the press before you can design a color publication. All of Part VI, "Publishing," will help, but especially Chapter 23, "Working with the Print Shop."

Chapter 19

Applying Colors

This chapter on applying colors tells you about:

Using the Colors palette, which is your access point for the colors you created in the <u>D</u>efine Colors dialog box.

▼

Fast-track color editing by using a mouse click in the Colors palette.

▼

Coloring PageMaker objects by using the Colors palette express buttons or the Fill <u>a</u>nd Line command from the menu.

▼

Applying color to and restoring the original colors of imported graphics.

PAGEMAKER'S COLORS PALETTE makes it easy to apply colors—much easier than understanding all the theory and technology of color printing presses. Of course, it's *so* incredibly easy that you must use some care and moderation because you could color your way into a murky mess of muddy ink and garish colors. That's why you need to get the whole picture. Be sure to spend some time with the background information in Chapter 18, "Creating Colors," and Chapter 20, "Meeting Color Challenges." ▶ ▶ ▶

Exploring the Colors Palette

Take a saunter around the Colors palette, using figure 19.1 as your map. You can summon this dialog box from the <u>W</u>indows menu, or you can use the keyboard shortcut, Ctrl+K.

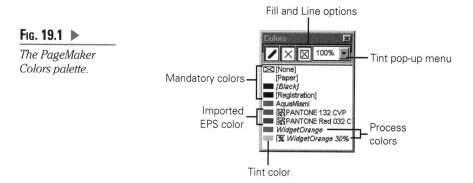

The PageMaker Colors palette.

Fill and Line options

Tint pop-up menu

Mandatory colors

Imported EPS color

Process colors

Tint color

Colors List

The scrolling list of colors in the Colors palette works just as you might expect: you select whatever you want to color, and then click on the color of your choice. In the Colors palette, colors are listed alphabetically using the names you established in the <u>D</u>efine Colors menu command, along with square color sample swatches to provide an on-screen representation of the colors.

Note that the Colors palette has much more visual information than the <u>D</u>efine Colors command. The <u>D</u>efine Colors command has no handy color samples and none of the specialized information about the origin or type of color. You can tell a great deal about the colors in the palette by the way they are listed. The following list decodes that information for you:

▶ *Italicized Colors.* Any color named in italics is a *process color*. No italic formatting means that the color has been defined as a *spot color*. You learn more about the difference between the two kinds of colors in Chapter 18, "Creating Colors."

▶ *EPS Symbol.* Colors with the PostScript logo in front have come into Page-Maker from an outside source, riding in with an imported EPS file. For more about the nuances of how this works, see the section "Adopting Colors from Imported or Clipboarded Objects" in Chapter 18.

▶ *Percent Sign.* The percent sign symbol means that color has been created as a tint of a base color. To learn more about creating tints, see the "Defining Tints" section in Chapter 18, "Creating Colors."

Instead of defining a new color just to get a tint, Version 6.0 gives you the option of assigning tints to objects on an ad hoc basis. (Of course, if you'll be needing to use that tint several times, it's probably faster to define a tint color so you can easily assign it from the palette.) Object level tints will not be listed in the Color palette.

TIP ▷ Design Color Names as Memory Aids

When you define colors to include in your Colors palette, use some of the naming tricks you see here. In the palette in figure 19.1, for example, it's easy to see at a glance that the imported colors were from PANTONE color-matching swatches. And you wouldn't need to go to the Edit Color dialog box to find out the amount of the tint defined for WidgetOrange, because the name has been defined to include the percentage. You can tell at a glance that it is a 30 percent tint.

TIP ▷ Use Braces Rather Than Parentheses or Brackets In Color Names

If you attempt to include parenthetical information in the name of a color as a memory aid, you get a message from PageMaker that says `Invalid character(s) in color name`, and the parentheses are not permitted. The same goes for square brackets. PostScript makes extensive use of parentheses and square brackets, so PageMaker reserves their use to avoid inadvertent errors. However, the curly brackets (*braces*, as they're properly called) are legal.

Coloring with Line, Fill, and Both

You have fast access to most of the functions contained in the dialog boxes for the Fill, Line, and Fill and Line commands right from the Colors palette. When working with PageMaker drawn objects, specify whether your color application will be applied as a fill for the object, only to the line portion of the object, or to both, by clicking on one of the three buttons in the upper-left corner of the palette.

The [None], [Paper], [Black], and [Registration] "Colors"

These standard color definitions—None, Paper, Black, and Registration—are in every Colors palette, permanently built into the PageMaker software:

▶ *[None]*. Removes all colors applied within PageMaker from an object. If you apply [None] to an EPS, for example, the original colors defined in creating the EPS before it was imported into PageMaker will be used when it is separated.

▶ *[Paper]*. Also a non-color; controls the way an object behaves when two items overlap. Anything colored [paper] will knock out everything else in the layers underneath it.

> ▶ *[Registration]*. Applied to an object; makes it print on every separation layer and is used for crop marks, notes to identify your film, registration targets, and so on.

> ▶ *[Black]*. Always print 100 percent on the black plate.

TIP ▶ Quick Edit Colors with Ctrl+Click

To get to the Edit Colors dialog box in a hurry, simply press Ctrl and click on the name of a color you want to adjust.

TIP ▶ Express Creation of New Colors

To instantly create a new color, press Ctrl and click on one of the four built-in colors by pressing Ctrl and clicking on [None], [Paper], [Black], or [Registration]. You get the same thing you would get if you first opened Define Colors and then clicked on the New button. The Edit Color dialog box will be filled in with a color specification based on the color selected prior to your Ctrl+click move, but the Name box in the dialog box will be blank.

Coloring Text

Applying a color to your text couldn't be simpler. You have three alternatives:

> ▶ *Direct selection.* Simply highlight the text with the Text tool and click on your color in the Colors palette. You can use the pop-up menu on the palette to assign an object level tint in 5 percent increments.

> ▶ *Type specifications.* You can also choose color from the Type Specifications dialog box, shown in figure 19.2. You can use the pop-up Tint menu to select an object level tint in 5 percent increments, or you can type in your own number in the provided box, in increments of 1 percent.

FIG. 19.2 ▶

Picking a text color in Type Specifications.

Color pop-up menu

Tint pop-up menu

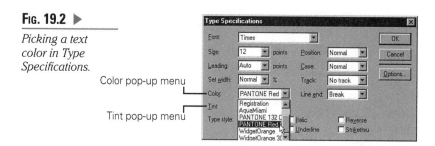

> ▶ *Paragraph styles.* Color entire paragraphs of type automatically by defining a special style. You can access the Type Specifications dialog box through

the <u>D</u>efine Styles command. Styles are the easiest way, for example, to easily assign colors to all your headlines.

DESIGN NOTE
Readability Issues When Coloring Text

Certain combinations of color are not good ideas for type. Problems arise primarily when you put colored text on a colored background, but even coloring type for placement on white paper has its considerations.

FIG. 19.3 ▶
(See color section.)

In the color section of this book, in figure 19.3, you can see a few examples of good and bad use of color with type. Here are some guidelines for you to keep in mind when you design colored type:

▼ *Seek Contrasting Letters and Background.* Be sure that you work with high contrast colors, not colors that are similarly dark or light. To the eye, for example, red and black "read" as having about the same darkness, so avoid using them together.

▼ *Test Colors in Grayscale.* To test the contrast of two colors, switch your video display over to grayscale for a quick look. This technique won't work absolutely every time, but it helps to evaluate readability. If the combination of letter color and background color looks okay in grayscale, chances are that this combination will work fine in color.

▼ *Stroke Letters.* If your design requires you to run text against background using a low contrast combination of colors, consider *stroking* letters (outline them with a contrasting color) to improve their readability. For display type, you may want to set the letters in a drawing program such as Illustrator or FreeHand, which enables you to convert to paths and assign separate stroke and fill colors. Another option would be to set the type in a paint program like Photoshop where you could use edge filters and *anti-aliasing*—meaning you would not need to worry about the trapping problems that might be caused by color strokes.

▼ *Avoid Vibrating Color Juxtapositions.* To the eye, yellow and red are irritating together; they tend to make you feel as though someone's scraping a nail over a chalkboard. Other color combinations also "ring" on you; sometimes these combinations are so bad that they make your teeth feel itchy.

▼ *Be Cautious About Trapping Effects.* Be careful about putting colored letters on a colored background if they must be trapped by *choking* or *spreading* them. Eyes are very sensitive to distortions of type; both these trapping techniques cause the type to get fat and block up (spread) or to get too thin to read (choked serif or cursive type). More information on choking, spreading, and other trapping issues appears in Chapter 20, "Meeting Color Challenges."

continues

Design Note
Continued

▼ *Consider the Effects of Size and Serifs.* If you need to spread the type for trapping (making it generally fatter), serifs or other cursive aspects of the type hold
   up better if the type is a larger size. Larger type won't block up as badly, meaning the open spaces in the type won't fill up with ink (for instance, the center of
   the letter "O" or the holes in the letter "B"). As a general rule of thumb, serif
   type blocks up worse than sans serif type.

Coloring PageMaker-Drawn Objects

You have two main ways to assign color to a PageMaker-drawn object: the Colors palette and the Fill and Line menu, plus a few related tweaks you can manage with the Fill menu and the Line menu.

Colors Palette

Applying color to a PageMaker-drawn object—oval, rectangle, polygon—is just a
little more complex than assigning color to text. You can color the object's perimeter line, the fill area inside that line, or both.

Use the buttons in the upper-left corner of the Colors palette to specify how color
will be applied to your selected PageMaker object (see fig. 19.4).

Fig. 19.4 ▶

*Using the Line and
Fill options of the
Colors palette.*

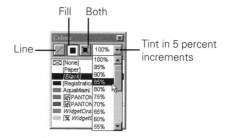

Fill and Line Dialog Box

The Fill and Line dialog box allows you more power over the fill and line attributes of a PageMaker object than you get by using the Colors palette (see
fig. 19.5). You can open it from the Element menu or via the keyboard shortcut,
Ctrl+F3.

Although it lacks many of the visual cues of the Colors palette—color swatches,
italics for process colors, EPS icons, tint icons—the Fill and Line dialog box gives

you simultaneous and independent color lists on both the fill and line halves of the dialog box, and you can make a more precise specification of tints by typing in the amount in 1 percent increments.

FIG. 19.5 ▶

Applying color by using the Fill And Line dialog box.

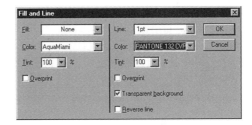

TIP ▶ **Avoid Very Light Tints or Small Tint Variations**

Consult with your printer beforehand so that you get good reproduction in these situations. Anything less than a 20 percent tint may be difficult to reproduce on a printing press, no matter how good the tint looks on your high resolution imagesetter film.

It's generally not a good idea to use a tint on a thin line. In either case, you may end up with faint color that looks more like dirt or a blemish than what you intended.

Keep in mind, also, that few printing presses can reproduce a difference of only 1 percent between tints. About 5 percent is the practical limit, which is why the pop-up tint menus in PageMaker are constructed in 5 percent increments.

TIP ▶ **Tints Are Cumulative**

Tints are always expressed as percentages of a base color—equivalent to the percentage of intensity of the color, as if it had been screened back using traditional print shop techniques. If you apply a defined tint color to a filled object and then apply an object level tint from the Fill menu or the Colors palette, you will be subtracting color twice. A 60 percent tint color with a 50 percent shade applied actually ends up as a 30 percent tint.

TIP ▶ **The PageMaker Fill Patterns Are Resolution Dependent**

The fill patterns available from the Fill drop-down list in the Fill and Fill and Line menus are not PostScript. They are actutally resolution-dependent graphics elements. If you plan to go to high-resolution imagesetter output, consult with your service bureau and consider having them test a couple of typical pages. When output on an imagesetter, PageMaker fills—imaged at high resolution—tighten up into very fine screens that will not convey the effect you see when you choose them from the menu.

Assigning Overprint Status

In both sides of the Fill and Line dialog box, you can click the Overprint check box. PageMaker objects and colors—by default—knock out all layers beneath them. Setting an object to overprint—or defining a color to overprint—overrides this default. *Overprint* means two overlapping objects can both print, thus mixing their inks on the paper. This option is extremely valuable, but you'll want to use it with some care because of the problems of inks mixing to create an unwanted color and the difficulty of building up too much ink on the page. You might want to consult with the print shop that will run your job to help evaluate the particular circumstances of your project.

TIP ▶ **Make Colored Lines Transparent**

Fig. 19.6 ▶

(See color section.)

Unless you are trying for some special effect, make colored lines transparent. The reason? If you don't, you really introduce a third color into your design—the underlying paper. As you can see from figure 19.6 in the color section of this book, the non-transparent dotted line gives you—as in this case—a red line on a green background with blotches of knockout between the dashes. In other words, you don't have a red line against a green background at all.

Coloring Imported Objects

There are only two kinds of imported graphic objects in the PageMaker color world: those that you can color, and those that come in with permanent and untouchable color. The difference? It's a moving experience.

Moving an Imported Object to an Overlay or Separation

PageMaker colors an imported graphic by moving it to the proper printing plate or plates. It doesn't modify anything in the guts of the colored object's file (or the guts of a black-and-white file, for that matter).

At print time, PageMaker merely substitutes its own directions for the color plate location, ignoring the ones built into the file. A black-and-white graphic could be sent to a spot color overlay, for example, rather than being put on the black layer. Likewise, all the process colors built into an EPS graphic might instead be sent to the black overlay and portrayed in their intrinsic levels of gray.

Some objects, however, simply can't be switched around like this at all, notably colored TIFF graphics and DCS files.

Keep in mind that a color assigned to an imported graphic applies to the entire object. You can't selectively color portions of a graphic.

Deciding Which Imported Graphics Can and Can't Be Colored

When considering color and an imported object, you have four issues to consider:

▶ What type of graphic is it?

▶ Does it have color already built into it?

▶ Will any color changes be visible on-screen?

▶ Can the object be colored in PageMaker?

Table 19.1 can help you sort out these questions. Look down the left column for the graphic format you are importing. Then select the row, depending on whether the graphic has color built into it. From there, you can answer the two questions concerning whether you can override any existing color in PageMaker and whether that coloring will be visible on-screen.

TABLE 19.1   A Decision Table for Coloring Imported Graphics

Type of Graphic	Can You Apply Color?	Applied Color Shows On-Screen?	Applied Color Prints?
Bitmap (B/W or grayscale)	Yes	Yes	Yes
Bitmap (RGB or CMYK)	No	No	No
EPS (Vector, B/W bitmaps)	Yes	No	Yes
EPS (Duotone, CMYK or RGB bitmap included)	Yes	No	No
DCS	Yes	No	No

Note: Bitmap formats include TIFF, PCX, BMP, GIF, and Scitex CT

Restoring Color

Version 6.0 has a new tool, especially for that situation when you need to annul an accidental assignment of color (say black on your fancy EPS multicolor graphic). Use the color of [None], which removes PageMaker's color assignments from the object and lets its true colors shine through. It replaces Version 5.0's Restore Color command.

V

Making Pages Colorful

> **TIP ▶ Importing Tag Along Colors Can Be a Bother**
>
> Do yourself a favor and remove all unused colors from the palette of your drawing program before you export the EPS file. You can end up with a PageMaker Colors palette that has about nine dozen colors in it, most of which are not used and just clutter the palette. It's easy to remove colors using your drawing program's color definition features. However, it isn't so easy to know which colors are used and which ones are superfluous. You may be able to tell by examining the object carefully.

> **TIP ▶ Use Remove Unused Colors to Eliminate Tag Along Colors**
>
> If you do have unused colors in your publication, decomplicate your life with a command that's new to Version 6.0. Go to the Define Colors dialog box and click on the button marked Re_m_ove Unused. If you have more than one unused color, you are given a choice between removing them all at once or one-by-one.

Where to Go from Here

▶ You really need to understand how color works to use it. Screen images have little to do with the reality of the printing press. For color theory, check out Chapter 18, "Creating Colors."

▶ Chapter 18 also has information on how to define colors so they appear in your Colors palette.

▶ Chapter 20, "Meeting Color Challenges," is where the ink really meets the paper. That's where you'll find coverage of PageMaker's two powerful new capabilities—color management system and trapping.

Chapter 20

Meeting Color Challenges

This chapter covers tactics and techniques for transforming an electronic page of color into paper:

Understanding and using PageMaker's color management system to help you optimize your computer for color accuracy.

▼

Items that require special attention (and collaboration with your printer and service bureau) when you design a color publication.

▼

The theory behind trapping colors together in order to compensate for inevitable imperfections in the registration of the printing press.

▼

A checklist for helping you decide when you might want to take care of simple trapping needs yourself and when you should ask your service bureau or printer to handle the work.

▼

Ways to design your publication to avoid the need for trapping.

THE COMPUTER SCREEN LIES. You can't depend on it to render color perfectly. That's why PageMaker 6.0 includes a color management system.

Printing presses are imperfect mechanical devices. You can overcome this with the most practical of the printer's arts—trapping. PageMaker now has built-in trapping, and you'll learn how to use it and when to let someone else handle it.

We'll also talk about collaborating. You need to work with the printer who knows how to get the most out of the printing press. And you need the help of the skilled service bureau operator. ▶ ▶ ▶

Collaborating with Your Printer and Service Bureau on Color

Here's where it starts. At the earliest possible stages of creating a color publication, bundle together your preliminary sketches and comps and set out for a talk with your printer and your service bureau. Don't consider doing a color publication unless you and your collaborators have given thought to the following:

▶ *Choosing a printing method.* Most jobs go on an offset lithography press, but will it be sheetfed or a web press? If you are doing point-of-purchase retail product displays or packaging, you may be designing a job that needs to go on a special press that can do flexography. Perhaps you are working on something that can be done best with the silk screening process. You may need to take into account the printing method when creating your design. These experts can point out those special considerations and save you time and money.

▶ *Deciding how many colors will be on-press.* Work out a color strategy. Should you specify color in CMYK so you can work with the four process colors (see the section "Deciding Between Spot and Process Color" in Chapter 18)? Or will you use black ink and a couple of spot colors? How many colors can the press handle? You may need to work out design (and cost) issues if the printing press requires multiple runs to achieve all the colors needed for your job.

▶ *Selecting a color matching system.* If you and your printer decide on spot color over process color, find out which color-matching systems the print shop supports. You will have wasted a lot of time and effort if you specify Hexachrome colors because you think Hexachrome high fidelity color is really hot and in vogue, and then find out the client's printer doesn't have the press to handle the job. The printer may recommend a particular color system as being best suited for your project. If you will be running both spot color and process color, a process color-based matching system may make sense and perhaps even save you a fifth plate on the press.

▶ *Choosing paper.* The absorbency and stability of the paper you print on determines some color printing parameters, such as how fine-grained a line screen you can use. Ask your printer if any alternative papers can get you the same effect but with improved quality (and, possibly, for less money).

▶ *Determining line screen for halftones.* You can't do process color without a line screen, and you can't do any prepress photo scanning (or have anyone do it for you) without planning the line screen frequency in advance. You also may need to confirm that standard screen angles will be okay so you can avoid moiré problems. The service bureau and printer may also have the capability of running stochastic screening.

Your choice of paper and the specific characteristics of the press (such as the equipment's age) have a major influence on your line screen frequency, and these issues are the domain of the print shop. Are you printing on newsprint or coated stock? How much ink will your job be putting down on the paper, and does the press have a heat-set oven to help dry ink as it goes through the press? All these issues help your printer decide how fine a line screen can hold on the press for your project.

▶ *Discussing ink issues.* Ask your printer if your project has any design considerations that may cause problems with dot gain or ink buildup. *Dot gain* is the spread of a halftone dot when ink soaks into the paper. Software can be used to provide dot gain compensation. *Ink buildup* happens when overlapping inks (usually in a process color situation) accumulate on the surface of the paper to such an extent that they can't dry fast enough. Based on your printer's advice, work with your service bureau on these issues. It has software that can compensate for these ink buildup problems.

▶ *Specifying mechanicals.* Your printer knows what's needed to get plates on the press. Will film or paper be best? If you ask the printer to use traditional methods to trap your publication's color elements, the printer probably will use paper. If you have halftones in your job, you should stick with film if possible. Specifying mechanicals is a point of collaboration and an important one. You need to pass these specifications on to your service bureau when you hand off your files.

▶ *Agreeing on responsibility for color proofs.* Whoever has responsibility for color accuracy probably should do the proofing on his or her own proofing system. If the service bureau has separated your job and trapped it for you, you need a proof at that point. On the other hand, the printer may not want to work without proofing on the print shop's own system as a point of reference.

▶ *Managing color image files.* High-end color photo scans are huge. Photo scans with a file size of 20M are normal, and high-resolution scans can climb up to 60M and more. Work with your service bureau on how to deal with this issue. The basic solution may be a low-resolution reference scan that can be linked back to your job after you finish your design and the publication is ready to be run on the imagesetter. The tactics for this linking vary a great deal, depending on the imagesetter system used by your service bureau, so you'll need to work with it on which option it offers (that is, OPI or APR).

Color correction and accuracy comes up in a big way when scanning photos. You need color proofs for any scanned photos. You also need to talk with the service bureau about who takes responsibility for the accuracy of color photos as well as the procedures to keep them accurate during the production process.

▶ *Agreeing on responsibility for trapping.* If your design has two or more colors touching, trapping will almost certainly be required unless your printer can guarantee perfect registration on the press (not likely, and potentially expensive). Up until the last few years, trapping was the responsibility of the printer, not the designer. These days, the issue isn't so clear, and PageMaker now offers built-in trapping that can handle many of the situations you will encounter. Even so, you'll need to get specifications from the printer so you know how to set up the trapping job.

Understanding Color Management

Your computer screen lies about color. Some systems tell smaller lies than others, but to one degree or another this basic premise holds true no matter how good your hardware and no matter how good your color management system. However, you can optimize your system so you get the most accurate color possible. And PageMaker includes a great tool for the purpose—the Kodak Precision Color Management System (CMS).

I don't make this point to discourage you from using color management. To the contrary, it's an important thing to do, and a big leap forward for PageMaker 6.0. However, it's critical that you stay aware of the limitations and that you don't automatically accept what you see on-screen as 100-percent accurate color.

This should not come as a big shock. After all, the printing press and your computer monitor are fundamentally different and couldn't possibly represent the "same" color in the same way. Your monitor combines three colors (red, green, and blue), whereas a process color printing job uses four (cyan, magenta, yellow, and black). And the press uses ink on a surface that reflects light to your eye, whereas a computer monitor uses a spray of electrons that shines directly into your eye.

For some fundamental background on this subject of color accuracy, check out the first few pages of Chapter 18, in the section "Key Concept: Your Screen Doesn't Match the Printing Press."

Ultimately, the only way you will really know what color your system produced is to go to the press check. You can also get a good idea of what your press check will look like if you get a high-quality color proof of your color separations, a must-do step for achieving accurate color.

The main point is that color depends on the device. We say that color publishing is device-dependent. Let's assume that you took a picture of a brick wall, and your camera captured the color pretty accurately. But now imagine the flow of your color work from that point forward and all the way out to the printing press and your final product:

▶ Your scanner may want to describe that red as a bluish-red.

▶ Your computer monitor may think red should be a deep red color with a touch of orange.

▶ Your composite proofing device, your Tektronix Phaser or whatever, may see the red as having a more brownish tone to it.

▶ This string of color imperfection deteriorates even further if, at any time during this process, you try to "correct" the color based on what you are seeing on your computer monitor or your composite proof printer.

▶ Finally, with all of these differences, who knows how the picture of the brick wall will actually turn out when you separate it and run it on the printing press?

Color management tries to smooth out all the differences by electronically adjusting color as you move from scanner to computer screen to printing press. In each case, the color management system translates the color for the appropriate device, "I know you tend to look at brick red and see bluish-red or brownish-red or whatever. Add a pinch of this and take away a pinch of that to compensate for your color error factors."

The CMS does not make these translations by going directly from one device to the other. In the background, it constantly is referring back to a sort of touchstone, a method of describing the color that is device-independent. It's the CIE color model (that stands for *Commission Internationale de l'Eclairage*, or in English, the International Committee on Illumination).

This business about CIE color is important to remember, because at various times in the process of saving color files, you have opportunities to cut yourself loose from device-dependent color descriptions and save your file as a "CIE Lab TIFF." One example would be when you import a Photo CD image directly into PageMaker.

One of the most important things you will do in working with color management is to specify for PageMaker the devices that are being used in the electronic publishing process. It needs this information so it can make the color translations between different devices. The color management system needs to be told:

▶ The source for the digitized color image files being used in the publication, usually a scanner

▶ The video monitor you are using to view the color images as you work

▶ The printing device you will be using for composite proofing of your color, often a desktop color printer

▶ The color characteristics of the printing press, the device that will use the process color separations you will be generating

When you make all these choices, you are selecting *device profiles*. These are files that electronically describe for the color management system the character-istics of the chosen device. In the case of PageMaker 6.0, you'll be using a dialog box to select from lists of Precision Transforms (PT), the device profile system used with the Kodak Precision Color Management System.

A number of these Precision Transforms come with PageMaker. If one of your devices isn't listed, you'll need to get a profile from the manufacturer, or you'll need to get the manufacturer's advice on which of the generic profiles would be best suited to emulate your device.

Color management can't be applied to all computer graphics files. Here's what the PageMaker color management system can manage:

▶ RGB bitmap images, such as TIFFs

▶ The screen image of CMYK TIFFs, because the screen displays RGB color

▶ Spot colors contained within EPS files

Here's what it can't manage:

▶ TIFFs contained within EPS files, because they are "protected" inside the EPS shell

▶ DCS files, because they have already been separated for commercial print-ing purposes

▶ WMF and PICT files, because their color is determined at print time by the system's printer driver

By the way, PageMaker 6.0 has been set up so you can use several different color management systems. It comes with the Kodak Precision Color Management Sys-tem, but you could decide to use another system if you wanted to. Each system will have its own idiosyncrasies of installation and use, but the basic principles of operation should be similar from system to system. Of course, most people will simply choose to use the Kodak system that comes with PageMaker.

Setting Up Color Management

The first color management task on your list is to determine what you expect from your color management system. Maybe there's no such thing as being too thin, too rich, or too color accurate, but there are some practical questions you can ask yourself to perhaps save some time and money:

▶ Are you working primarily in spot colors, perhaps specifying colors with a color matching system? Are you using color swatches, like Pantone books, to obtain color accuracy? Will you ask your computer monitor to simply give you some idea of what your decisions look like?

Like I said, there's no such thing as being too color accurate. But if this more results-based approach fits your needs for color accuracy, you can ease off on spending top dollar for your equipment and perhaps even save computer memory by simply turning off color management most of the time.

▶ Are you working in process colors, CMYK, or High Fidelity? Are you making major color decisions based on what you see on the screen, as opposed to standard color swatches? Will you be color-correcting photographs? Will you perhaps even be mixing custom colors?

If your work falls into this category, you will need to be ultra-methodical about your color management, get the best possible equipment, and set up your system in a distortion-free viewing environment. Nothing less will do.

There's a viewing environment discussion later in this chapter in the section "Optimizing Your Color Viewing Environment." Also, you'll want to get high-quality color proofs before committing to press. There's information on that in Chapter 22, "Proofing Your Publication."

Establishing Basic Color Management Settings

The heart of PageMaker's color management is the dialog box shown in figure 20.1. It hides in the Preference command, behind the CMS Setup button.

FIG. 20.1 ▶

The main Page-Maker color management dialog box.

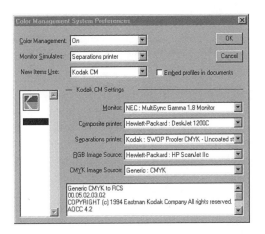

All the sophisticated color theory aside, hardly anything could be simpler than using this dialog box. Simply click through the pop-up lists to describe your system. Here are notes on some of the items you see:

▶ *Color Management.* If you don't actually need color management, turn it completely off using the pop-up list in the upper-left corner of the dialog box. It will save memory, and your publications will open faster because they won't need to take time to initialize CMS. If you see a dialog box as you open a publication that PageMaker is initializing CMS, you'll know what I mean. It takes awhile.

▶ *Monitor Simulates.* If you are trying to make color management decisions based on what you see on your monitor, have your monitor simulate your final output device. That might be the color profile for the device producing your separations for the printing press or the composite printer that will be used to print your overhead slides or handouts.

▶ *New Items Use.* If you designate a CMS, then the preferences in this dialog box will be applied whenever you define a new color or a graphic. If you set it to None, then you must choose CMS options for each item you want to color manage. You will almost always want to have this set to your CMS of choice, Kodak CM being the one that came with PageMaker.

▶ *Embed Profiles in Documents.* Because the whole point of having a color management system is to try to standardize your system's color view of the world, you will generally want to turn on this option so that when you take files to another system, all your color management systems will be brought right along.

▶ *Kodak CM Settings.* Sometimes you need to think through the color process to make decisions about these settings. For instance, suppose you make color corrections in Photoshop and output your files as CMYK TIFFs. You might think you should select some CMYK profile for the CMYK Image Source. But you would be wrong. Because you made the color correction decisions based on an RGB computer monitor, you should set your CMYK source for the RGB monitor you use with Photoshop.

Ad Hoc Color Management Settings

One of the really hot things about PageMaker's implementation of color management is its flexibility. For any object or color that can be managed, you can set a different source device and even a different color management system. Sometimes PageMaker handles this for you automatically, and other times you will need to make the settings yourself.

Let's say you are importing a scanned graphic. Here's how PageMaker looks at that file and decides how to apply your preferences:

▶ *KPCMS Source*. If the Kodak Precision Color Management System was used in producing the graphic, maybe by the program used to scan it, and that information is embedded in the file, PageMaker will read that information and automatically apply the CMS information.

▶ *Source Not Installed*. If the Precision Transform for the source used to create the scanned graphic is not installed on your machine, PageMaker will revert to whatever CMS you have designated in Preferences and will take its best shot at a PT that will work with the PT identification embedded in the file.

▶ *No Source Listed*. If the file doesn't have any embedded CMS identification, PageMaker will use the default CMS and the source you designated in Preferences (your RGB source preference if it is an RGB graphic or CMYK if it is a CMYK graphic).

But what if you want to take control instead of letting PageMaker decide by default? Well, you can. When you are importing the image, look for the CMS Source button. You can designate your own source Precision Transforms for each individual graphic object you import and for each new color you define. When you click the CMS Source button, you'll get the dialog box shown in figure 20.2.

FIG. 20.2 ▶

Defining ad hoc color management settings.

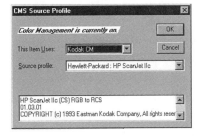

There's also a CMS Source button in the Define Colors dialog box and in the Photo CD Place dialog box. It's also listed as a menu item in the Image submenu of the Element menu.

You can also make ad hoc color management settings from the Print dialog box, where you get the same dialog box as the one reached via the Preferences command. However, be extremely cautious about changing the separations device setting at print time. Color management calculations made by your CMS as you design your publication are based on the destination device, so changing the device just before press time might throw off the accuracy of those calculations.

TIP ▶ **Calibrate Your Monitor**

Have you tweaked your color monitor? PageMaker comes with a nifty procedure to do a basic monitor calibration. Check out the Getting Started manual for instructions on using the Knoll Gamma control panel. You place some targets in a PageMaker file and look at them from a distance to determine whether you have the correct black-and-white points set on your monitor. You also set up gamma, usually for 1.8. Once you've done that, you are much better informed for picking a monitor from the CMS list.

If your monitor isn't listed, you can use your new calibration settings to make an educated guess about which profile to use if your monitor isn't specifically listed. Better yet, go to the PageMaker folder, Utilities folder, and use the Kodak Monitor Installer to create a custom profile that matches the calibration settings you just worked up.

There are devices you can buy that will help you perform extremely precise monitor calibration, but in the absence of that kind of help and budget, this procedure will go a long way towards helping you achieve better color rendering with your PageMaker system.

Optimizing Your Color Viewing Environment

This might surprise you, but the weakest part of your color management system may be the room you are sitting in right now. If you are in front of your computer, examine your environment, including your computer monitor, and see if your viewing environment may be distorting the accuracy of your color view:

▶ Work with a plain gray screen desktop, none of those fancy bozo backgrounds. They practically vibrate with distracting colors that zap any chance of your brain properly reading colors for the page you are setting up.

▶ The same goes for your work room. No distracting wallpaper. No wild colors. No extremes. Go for gray, and let the color happen on your monitor.

▶ Have the room lighting set to a moderate level. It shouldn't be much darker—or brighter—than the amount of light coming from your monitor.

▶ Windows and bright sunshiny days are great, but they play havoc with color accuracy. Sunlight in particular is a problem. Sunlight constantly changes color from sunrise to high noon to sunset.

Trapping

What a pain. This is progress? Science advances the art of desktop publishing, and you get stuck worrying about trapping.

Or do you? Is it really true that you ought to assume the responsibility? Perhaps it's less risky if you let the prepress service bureau or the print shop handle your trapping.

This section contains background information and decision-making tools to help you come to a solid business decision about who should do your trapping. Determining who does the trapping is just that—a business decision. You need to weigh any of your perceived savings in time and money and increased control over the final product against the risks of having to swallow hard and pick up the tab for an unacceptable job off the press.

KEY CONCEPT:
What Is Trapping and Why Do I Need It?

Basically, trapping exists because there's no such thing as a perfect printing press. As the paper screams past the plates at high speed (or even at low speed), it shifts around. It slips from side to side. It stretches. The paper changes dimensions as it soaks up wetting solution and ink. After all, a press is a mechanical device, and you can't expect anything made out of iron to roll all day without a little slop.

The Problem

A little slop might be okay when you are working with only one color. But slop is absolutely not okay if you are laying down multiple colors. The colors ought to align properly (*register* with one another). The chances are pretty strong, however, that anywhere two colors meet on the page, a little sliver of white paper will show through between them—unless you trap the point where those colors meet. Figure 20.3 shows two non-trapped abutting

colors, their misregistration exaggerated just to make the point.

You can see there are two problems caused by this misregistration. First, there's that sliver of pristine white paper showing through between the two brilliant cyan and magenta plates. Also, the misregistration has caused the creation of a third "accidental" color on the left side where the two ink colors overlap.

To trap the triangle and its background color together, one or the other of them must expand or shrink so they have a very slight overlap.

That's what *trapping* is, the intentional overlapping of two ink colors. It's a cover-up. As the crook said to the judge, "Sorry? Sure I'm sorry…that I got caught." Trapping doesn't make the press register correctly. It merely covers up the misregistration with a slap of ink—keeps you from getting caught, in other words.

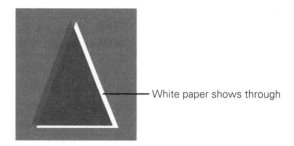

White paper shows through

Fig. 20.3 ▲

The dreaded little sliver of white is the reason you need trapping. (As with many of the black-and-white illustrations in this chapter, you can find this one duplicated in the color section of the book.)

Lately, trapping has somehow become the responsibility of the designer, not the printer. It wasn't always like this, that the designer had to fret about press registration problems. In times past, the printer and the stripping crew did the fretting. You generated your mechanicals, delivered them to the printer, and they came back looking great. The folks who worked on the light table with X-acto knives, masks, and Rubylith worried about registration problems. You may have learned to avoid certain design elements in order to make your printer's job easier, but you never had to seriously concern yourself about trapping.

Now we have the power to produce pages all stripped together electronically, ready to go to final film and be burned to plates. That means we can skip the expensive and time-consuming step of hand-stripping at the light table. When you put it like that—saving time on deadline and saving money on the budget—it really sounds great, doesn't it?

But as deadline approaches, reality sets in and maybe it doesn't sound so great any more. Now it's you who pops

the aspirin, and when it all looks like a mess on press, the client gives you one of those death stares that turns your stomach to ice. When you take on trapping responsibility, you have only yourself to blame if the job looks a mess. And it will be your bill to pay.

Fundamental Trap Construction

The easiest of all the trapping concepts to understand is the *choking* and *spreading* technique. You choke an object to make it smaller, and that's why chokes are sometimes called *shrinks* or *thinnies*. Spreads, also called *grips* or *fatties*, are the reverse. Figure 20.4 here and in the color section gives you the basic idea of a spread and a choke.

Ideally, you always trap using the lighter color. You spread (or choke) the color that is lightest in *neutral* density. Neutral density value is an indication of the intensity of a color, and it is the value that PageMaker uses when making decisions about which color to use for a trap.

Trapping creates its own problems because the two colors overlap. You get a line that adds the two colors where the

Understanding Color, Trapping, and Halftones

The first part of this special section gathers all the illustrations that have to do with color issues into one central location. So, you have a sort of booklet within a book on creating color on the printing press, trapping the color to mask misregistration problems, and the theory behind screening halftones to create grayscale images. Later in this section, there are examples of special effects, Web pages, and designs that feature "grunge" type.

The figure captions listed here correspond to the figure captions listed in the actual chapters of the book. You are also given page numbers so that you can easily refer to the text for more detailed discussion about these illustrations.

Making Color on the Press

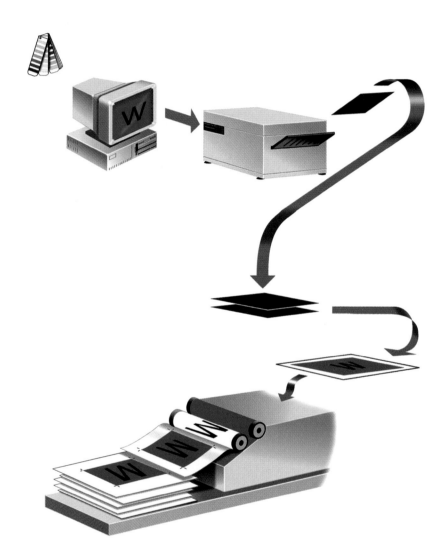

FIG. 18.2 (PAGE 495) ▲

This illustration shows the work flow for creating a spot color publication. You begin by picking spot color inks from color-matching system swatches. Then you lay out your project on the computer and send the pages to an imagesetter, separating the colors onto individual overlays. The overlays from the imagesetter are then used to expose the printing press plates. Finally, you have the press run, where your color-matching system inks are applied to their respective plates and printed on the paper you have chosen for the project.

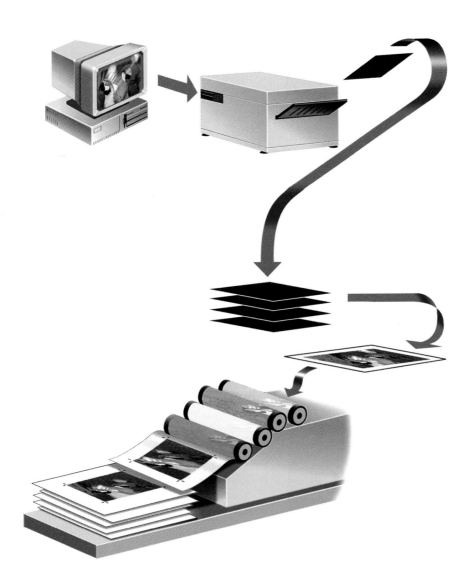

FIG. 4.5 (PAGE 77) ▲

The work flow for a four-color (process color) project in many ways resembles the spot color effort. Instead of picking inks from a swatch book, you design your color publication and then at output time the computer separates the color into the four standard colors: cyan, magenta, yellow, and black (CMYK). This electronically separated image then goes to the imagesetter where four pieces of film are output for each page. Each film carries the color information for its respective color, broken into levels of intensity represented by screened dots. Each film is then used to burn that particular ink plate for the printing press. When the four-color inks are combined on paper, thanks to the dots, the eye and brain are fooled into thinking there are thousands of colors and intensities of colors.

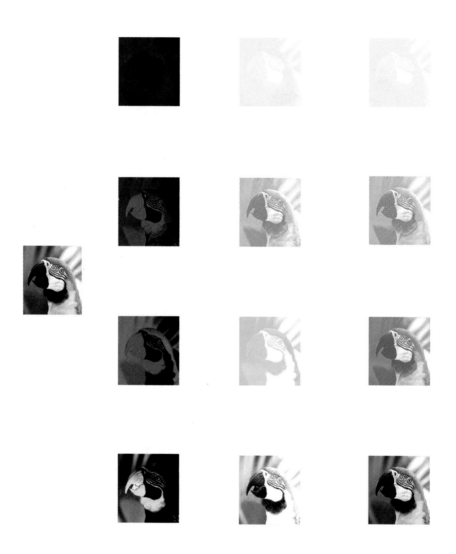

Fig. 18.3 (Page 496) ▲

Here's a closer look at how a full-color image gets broken down into the four CMYK process colors. From left to right, you see the original scanned image as it would appear on your computer monitor. In the next column, have a look at the four separated films. They look like black-and-white photographic negatives, except each one represents one of the four process ink colors. In the third column from the left, you see how those films look when associated with their colors and in positive, as if they were printing press plates coated with ink. On the right, the inks are added together, one by one, to create the finished full-color image in the lower-right corner.

Fig. 18.4 (Page 497) ▲

Separating the image is just one part of the process. Each of the CMYK colors must be broken down into dots—halftones called *screens*. Each screen runs at a different angle so that the dots don't simply print on top of each other in a mud of ink. The eye perceives the dots all together, and "mixes" the desired color in the brain.

Perceiving Color: What You See Is Not What You Get

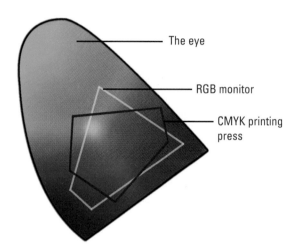

The eye

RGB monitor

CMYK printing press

◀ **Fig. 18.6 (Page 502)**

This illustration shows one of the fundamental difficulties you face in trying to get colors on the computer screen to match up with the colors you end up with on the printing press. It's the *color gamut*, or color range, of the three different color systems you use when creating a color image for the press—your eye, your RGB color computer monitor, and a CMYK printing press. It takes a great deal of experience to predict how well or how poorly a particular image will translate from one color system to another.

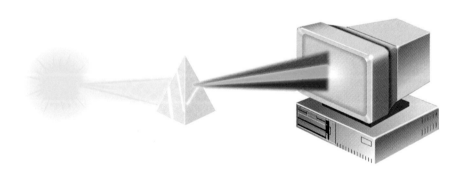

▲ **Fig. 18.5 (Page 501)**

Here's another inherent difference that makes it difficult to translate the color on your computer screen to the printing press. Most people think you add red, green, and blue to get white. However, that's only partly true when you are working with computerized color and a press. Your computer display is RGB, but the press is CMYK. In RGB, you add the three primary colors. With CMYK, the four process colors are subtracted to get white.

▲ Fig. 18.1 (Page 492)

Color also looks different, depending on how the light reaches your eye. In the top illustration, the eye perceives the color by reflected light. In the bottom illustration, the light has been projected into the eye directly from the computer screen.

Some Color Design Notes

▲ Fig. 18.7 (Page 502)

The "color" black can be more black than black, or it can be a sort of muddy, brownish black. It depends on how you make black on the press. On the left, the first black has been composed by mixing 100 percent of the three subtractive primaries—cyan, magenta, and yellow. The middle black is pure black ink. The black swatch on the right has been mixed with 100 percent black ink and a touch of each of the CMY colors. The right black, in other words, is a better black with the sweetening of the CMY colors. That's why some designers call it *rich black*.

Fig. 19.6 (Page 524) ▲

Unless you are trying for some special effect, make PageMaker's built-in dashed, dotted, and Scotch rule lines transparent when they lay over a colored background. The reason? If you don't, you really introduce a third color into your design—the underlying paper. The non-transparent dotted line here gives you a red line on a green background with blotches of knockout between the dashes.

FIG. 19.3 (PAGE 521) ▲

Here are some examples of good and bad use of color for type against a colored background. For best results, you should:

- Seek contrasting letters and background.

- Test colors for readability by viewing them in gray scale.

- Stroke letters with white or a knockout line if you must use low contrast colors.

- Avoid vibrating color juxtapositions such as yellow and red.

- Use larger type sizes so serifs won't get lost and openings won't block up with ink.

Understanding Trapping

◀ Fig. 20.3 (Page 538)

The dreaded little sliver of white is the reason you need trapping. This happens when two color plates don't quite register properly on the press. It's a mechanical device with a certain amount of slop in it, and the paper stretches and slides from side to side on the plates. You have the potential for this happening wherever two colors meet on the page, unless you trap them.

◀ Fig. 20.4 (Page 539)

Here are the two easiest trapping concepts to understand—the choking and spreading methods of overlapping the abutting ink colors. (The spread is on the top and the choke on the bottom.) You *choke* an object to make it smaller, which is why chokes are sometimes called *shrinks* or *thinnies*. *Spreads*, also called *grips* or *fatties*, are the reverse.

In the next three illustrations, you see the three basic methods of achieving a trap—the traditional darkroom technique, object-level trapping on the computer, and pixel-level raster trapping using a special software program.

◀ **FIG. 20.5 (PAGE 540)**

The traditional "light sandwich" photographic method is used by strippers to create a trap. The technician places a thin filling of clear material, such as plastic, between the original film and the contact film. This sandwich filling of clear plastic allows the light to spread out so that it creates an overlap on the receiving negative film. The amount of the trap can be varied by using different thicknesses of clear material and by altering the amount of light used for the exposure.

◀ **FIG. 20.6 (PAGE 540)**

For simple object-oriented trapping, you can spread and choke page element objects yourself. As you can see, do-it-yourself object trapping involves drawing a line around the object that needs to be trapped, which you can do in PageMaker's Fill And Line dialog box. Similar tools can be used for more complex shapes in your drawing program. This trapping technique is sometimes called *stroking*.

Designing Around Trapping Issues

◀ Fig. 20.7 (Page 544)

Share CMYK colors. As long as abutting process colors share a common process color, you don't need to trap them. The text gives information on calculating the colors you need. This technique depends on the fact that if the other colors slip on the page, the other process color inks fill in the gap and no dreaded white sliver of paper shows through.

◀ Fig. 20.8 (Page 544)

Frame a graphic with a border. If your design will allow it, consider running a frame around the edge of the item you are trapping. You thus cover any misregistration.

◀ Fig. 20.9 (Page 545)

Don't resize imported vector graphic objects. If you import a pre-trapped graphic and then resize it in PageMaker, you may need to redo the traps. Resizing changes the width of the choke and spreads stroking. An imported graphic must be trapped in its originating program before importing it into PageMaker. In this simulation, look at all the white spaces where complex shapes and colors could fall apart on the press.

◀ FIG. 20.10 (PAGE 545)

Avoid abutting blends. Overlapping gradations are impossible to trap using object trapping because you end up with a sharp line of a third trapping artifact color along the abutting edge. This example of two different-colored and abutting blends was trapped by cloning one of the blends and coloring it in a solid trapping color. The result is a dark trapping artifact line. Another approach is to trap the blends by the common color method, but that still gives you a solid line trapping artifact.

▲ FIG. 20.11 (PAGE 546)

Objects overlapping halftones. This shows one of the toughest trapping challenges—an object superimposed over a photograph. You simply have no way to stroke your object against the picture because all the colors are changing underneath the object, similar to the problems you have in trapping a gradation.

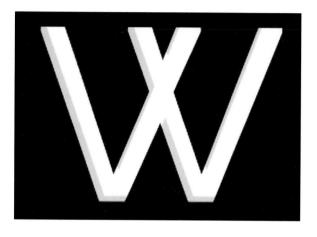

◀ **Fɪɢ. 20.12 (Pᴀɢᴇ 547)**

"Rich" black with reversed-out type. When creating a rich black, you can create a trapping problem when you reverse out the superimposed type. If the press misregisters, you get artifacts of cyan, magenta, or yellow hanging out into the no-ink area of the reversed letter.

▲ **Fɪɢ. 20.13 (Pᴀɢᴇ 547)**

Tandem chokes or spreads. Do-it-yourself object trapping works on an entire object. Trapping an object that crosses over more than one color or straddles a block of color is really difficult. Here you see some type superimposed over a couple of colors. The type has been stroked with one of the colors, with the result that the top half looks too thin and the bottom half looks too thick.

Understanding Halftones

This next group of illustrations helps explain why grayscale on a printing press has nothing to do with gray ink, but instead refers to a sort of pretend gray. It's achieved by screening ink into dots to make it look gray.

◀ **Fig. 23.2 (Page 633)**

Two squares of gray. The one on the top is a halftone gray, a "tint" of black. The one on the bottom is actually a Pantone shade of solid gray ink with no halftone screen to break it into dots.

◀ FIG. 23.3 (PAGE 633)

Gray ink won't give you a scale of gray values (unless it has been screened). This photo has been printed with gray ink, but it has no grayscale values. That's because it was scanned as line art, without halftoning.

◀ FIG. 23.4 (PAGE 633)

A halftone version of the same photo scan, with the gray ink broken up into spots. Ink on the press works a lot like the binary numbers that zip around inside your computer. Ink's either there or it isn't. It's only by breaking the image up into dots that you can produce a photograph on the printing press and have shades of gray in it.

300 dpi

2,400 dpi

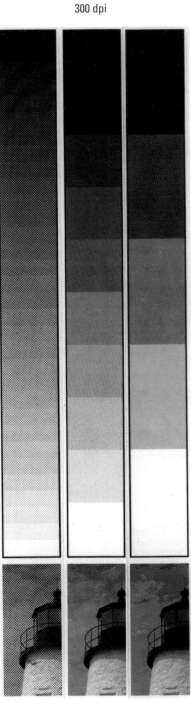

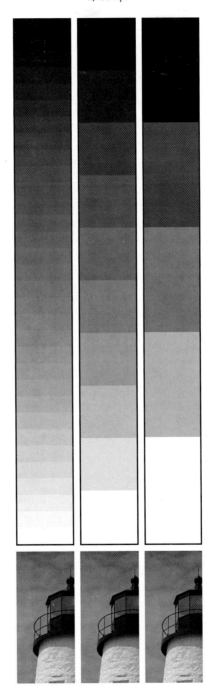

◀ **FIG. 21.13 (PAGE 588) AND 23.11 (PAGE 642)**

This series of halftones—at a variety of screen frequencies—shows the tradeoff between fine resolution, the potential grayscale levels, and the clogging caused by dot gain on the press.

55 lpi   90 lpi   150 lpi

55 lpi   90 lpi   150 lpi

◀ Fig. 23.5 (Page 634)

Before digital halftoning, the printer used a process camera. This conceptual diagram shows how the printer made halftones by putting a screen between the lens and the film. The screen is a piece of glass etched with criss-crossing lines.

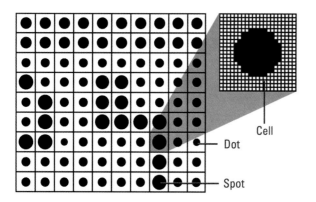

Cell

Dot

Spot

◀ Fig. 23.6 (Page 635)

Here's how an imagesetter performs the same function. It breaks the image up into dots, spots, and cells. Each of the spots in a digital halftone is made up of a bunch of imagesetter or laser dots. The spots are contained within a halftone cell, which is the square area bounded by the vertical and horizontal lines of the screen.

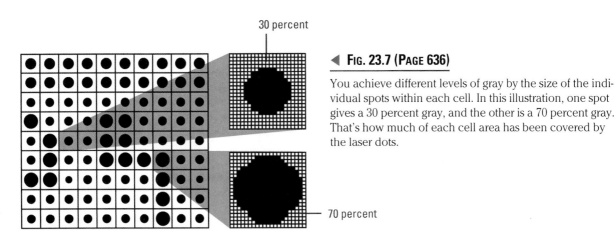

30 percent

◀ **FIG. 23.7 (PAGE 636)**

You achieve different levels of gray by the size of the individual spots within each cell. In this illustration, one spot gives a 30 percent gray, and the other is a 70 percent gray. That's how much of each cell area has been covered by the laser dots.

70 percent

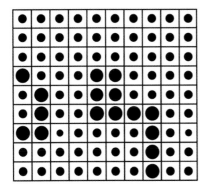

85 lines per inch

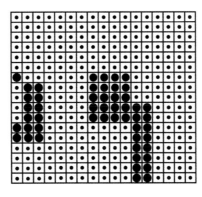

150 lines per inch

▲ **FIG. 23.8 (PAGE 637)**

The more laser dots you can cram into a halftone cell, the more different sizes of spots you can have. Therefore, more potential dot sizes would mean that you could have more levels of gray. You can see that the hypothetical magnified 85-lines-per-inch screen actually has the potential to reproduce more levels of gray, compared to the 150-lines-per-inch screen. The fine detail won't be as sharp with the coarser screen, but you'll get more levels of gray.

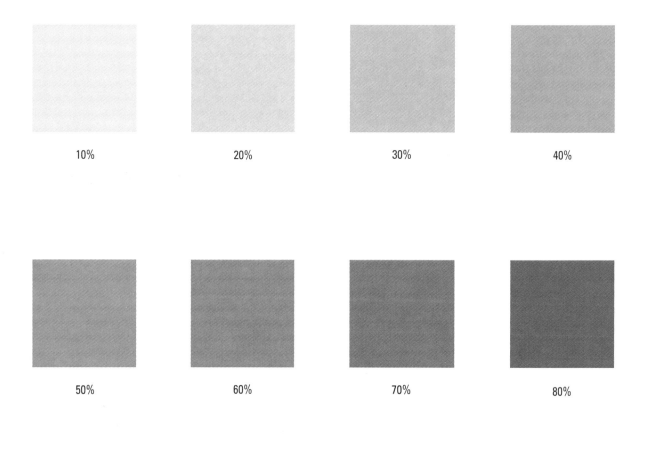

10%   20%   30%   40%

50%   60%   70%   80%

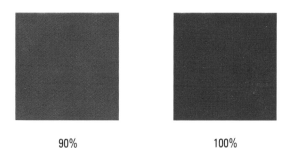

90%   100%

▲ **Fig. 23.9 (Page 638)**

A range of percentage tints of the same color. Screening (percentage tints) allows you to make many "colors" out of one when you do spot color. Mathematically, you break the color into dots and the size of the dots equates to the percentage of the screen.

▲ Fig. 23.10 (Page 640)

Process color screen angles keep dots from piling up on top of each other, so the eye and brain can "mix" the colors of each dot. However, when screen angles are off, you can get a bad moiré pattern. It's a sort of smeary wave effect that's enough to make you seasick. Think of it as the process color eyeball con job gone terribly wrong.

Grunge Type Design
(Carlos Segura, Learning from the Pros)

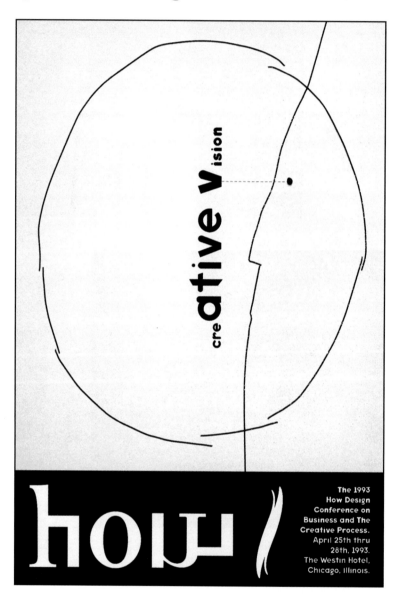

One of the promotional postcards from the HOW Conference. Along the bottom edge you can see the logo design that generated much of the controversy. On the right page is an example of using letters as design elements.

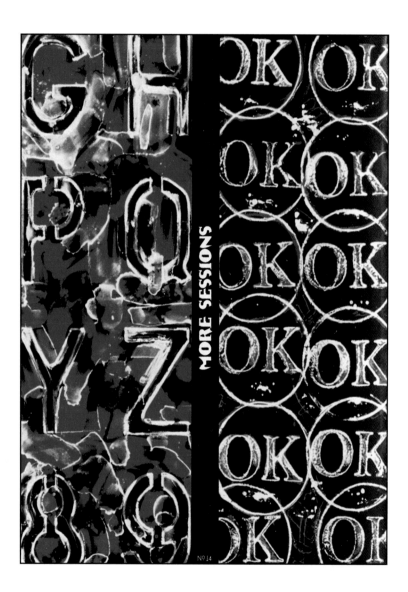

FIG. 32.2 (PAGE 798) ▲

"Hard-to-read" pages in Carlos Segura's experimental conference guide book. The typography may be outlandish,
but the layout is actually simple and easy to follow.

13
"Stress Busters"
Dr. John Jensen

14
"Inside the creative process"
Primo Angeli, Marshall Arisman, Lori Siebert

15
"Dealing for Dollars"
Patrick Fiorentino, Joel Fuller

16
"the secrets of pentagrams success"
Michael Bierut

HAVE DEADLINE PRESSURES, IMPOS-SIBLE CLIENTS AND DIFFICULT EMPLOYEES TIED YOUR STOMACH IN KNOTS? FOR YEARS, DR. JOHN JENSEN HAS BEEN SHOWING PEOPLE HOW TO COPE WITH STRESS—EVEN USE IT TO THEIR ADVANTAGE—THROUGH EFFECTIVE MANAGEMENT TECHNIQUES. IF YOU WANT TO LEARN HOW TO MAINTAIN CONTROL OF YOUR LIFE AND YOUR SANITY, THIS SESSION IS A MUST.

IF YOU'VE EVER WONDERED HOW THE NATION'S TOP ARTISTS GO ABOUT SOLVING DESIGN PROBLEMS, THEN THIS SESSION IS FOR YOU. WE'VE ASSIGNED A DIFFERENT HYPOTHETI-CAL PROJECT TO EACH PANELIST, THEN ASKED THEM TO PRESENT THE SOLUTION AND ALL THE INTRICACIES THAT WENT INTO REACHING THAT CONCLUSION, FROM BRAINSTORM-ING TO FINAL COMP.

TODAY'S ECONOMY IS AFFECTING THE BOTTOM LINE OF CLIENTS AND DESIGNERS ALIKE. JOIN PRINCIPAL JOEL FULLER AND BUSINESS MAN-AGER PATRICK FIORENTINO AS THEY SHARE HOW PINKHAUS DESIGN HAS MANAGED TO BEAT THE RECESSION WITH SOME INNOVATIVE BUSINESS DEALS THAT BENEFIT BOTH CLIENT AND DESIGNER, NOW AND FOR YEARS TO COME.

TAKE 19 CREATIVE GIANTS IN OFFICES AROUND THE WORLD, ADD SOME OF THE MOST DEMANDING (AND LUCRATIVE) CLIENTS THE DESIGN FIELD HAS TO OFFER, AND YOU HAVE THE MAKINGS OF PENTA-GRAM, A DESIGN FIRM THAT'S ACHIEVED NEAR-LEGENDARY STATUS IN ITS 21 YEARS. PARTNER MICHAEL BIERUT OFFERS AN ENTERTAINING AND PENETRATING LOOK AT WHAT MAKES PENTAGRAM TICK, FROM FINANCIAL ARRANGEMENTS TO THE CREATIVE PROCESS.

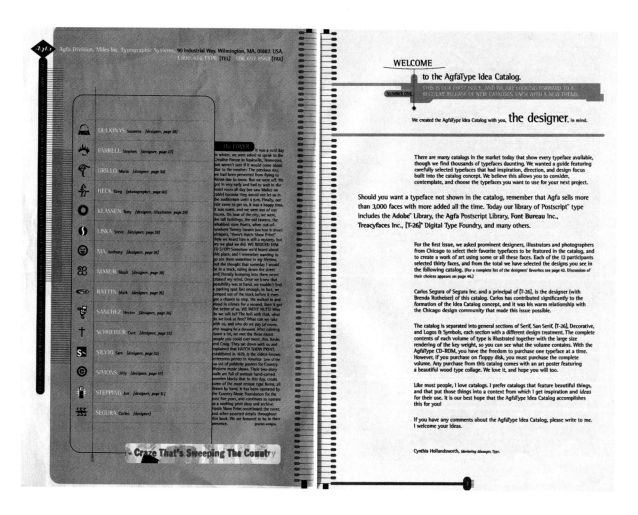

FIG. 32.3 (PAGE 799) ▲

The opening spread, table of contents and body copy,
from the AgfaType Idea Catalog. For a lively discussion of
the pros and cons of this design, see Chapter 32, "Setting
Grunge Type: Point and Counterpoint."

Designing for the Web
(Moe Rubenzahl, Learning from the Pros)

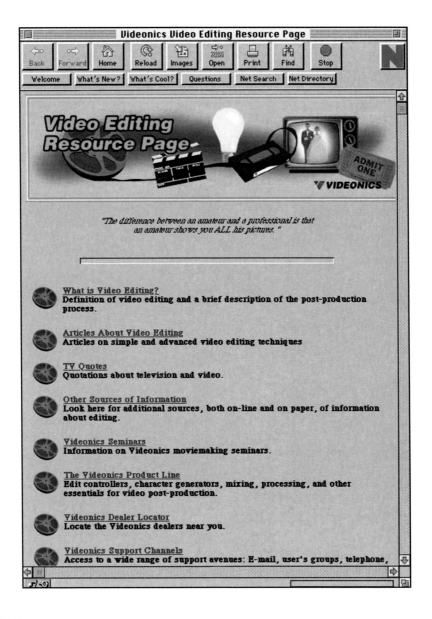

Fig. 33.1 (Page 808) ▲

The Videonics home page.

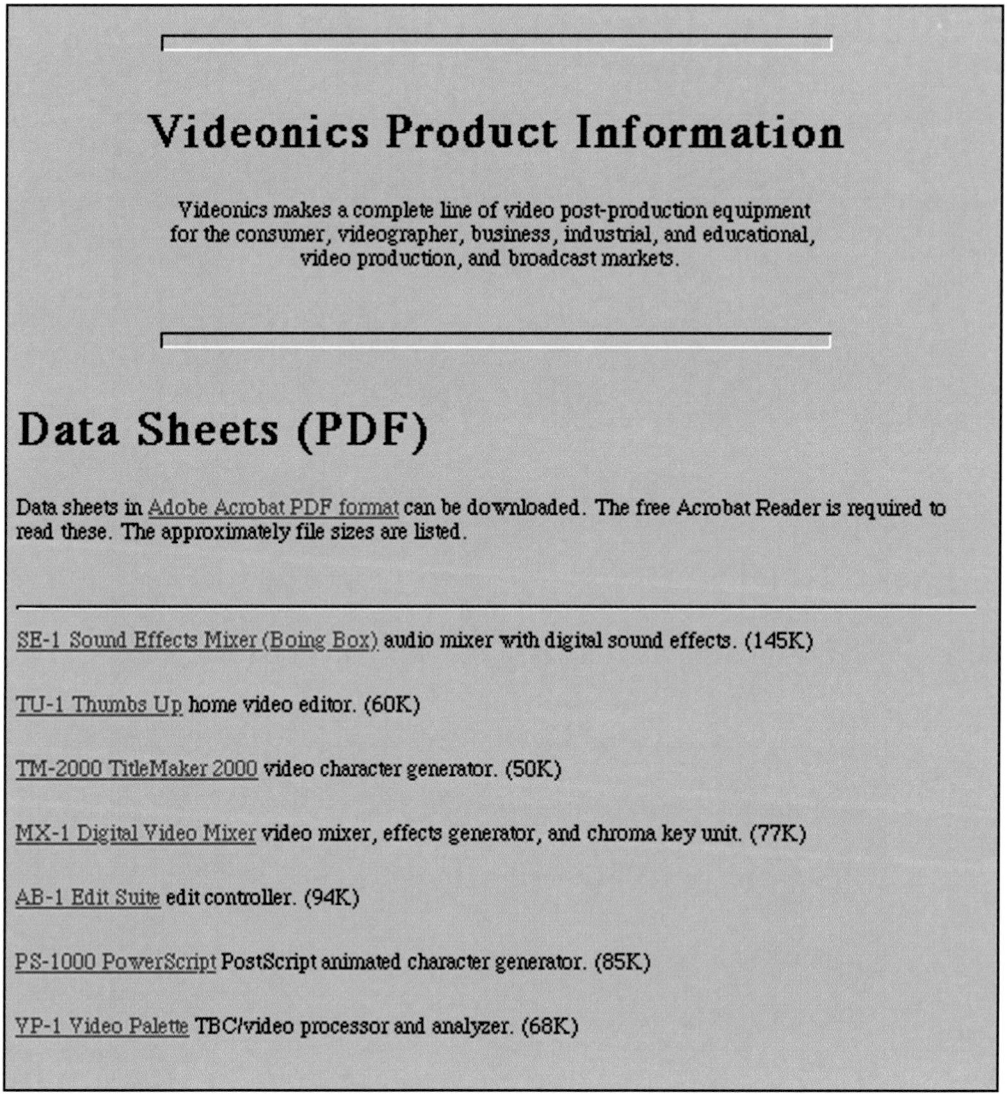

Videonics Product Information

Videonics makes a complete line of video post-production equipment
for the consumer, videographer, business, industrial, and educational,
video production, and broadcast markets.

Data Sheets (PDF)

Data sheets in Adobe Acrobat PDF format can be downloaded. The free Acrobat Reader is required to
read these. The approximately file sizes are listed.

SE-1 Sound Effects Mixer (Boing Box) audio mixer with digital sound effects. (145K)

TU-1 Thumbs Up home video editor. (60K)

TM-2000 TitleMaker 2000 video character generator. (50K)

MX-1 Digital Video Mixer video mixer, effects generator, and chroma key unit. (77K)

AB-1 Edit Suite edit controller. (94K)

PS-1000 PowerScript PostScript animated character generator. (85K)

VP-1 Video Palette TBC/video processor and analyzer. (68K)

FIG. 33.2 (PAGE 809) ▲

Don't just dump big files on your viewers. Give them the
option of downloading graphics files like PDFs, and tell
them what they are getting into by listing file sizes.

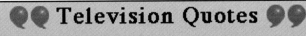

Television Quotes

A collection of quotes that pertain (loosely, in some cases) to television, the television industry, technology, or the creative process.

If you have more, please send them to webmaster@videonics.com. If you know the true source of one that is attributed to "unknown," please let me know. Corrections are also welcome.

As we add new quotes, they will appear at the top of the list so you'll be able to find what's new.

Note: Many of these quotations came from various quotation sources on the net.

"The difference between an amateur and a professional is that an amateur shows you ALL his pictures."
-- Unknown

"I never play the television. It's a curse, you know, television."
-- Peter Jennings

"Television is for appearing on, not looking at."
-- Noel Coward

"Inside every digital circuit, there's an analog signal screaming to get out."
-- Al Kovalick, Hewlett-Packard

"If I can't picture it, I can't understand it."
-- Albert Einstein

"Theater is life. Film is art. Television is furniture."
-- Unknown, reported by Murray Wilson

▲ **FIG. 33.3 (PAGE 810)**

Have fun and attract surfers to dig deeper into what you have to offer by adding extra information value to your Web site.

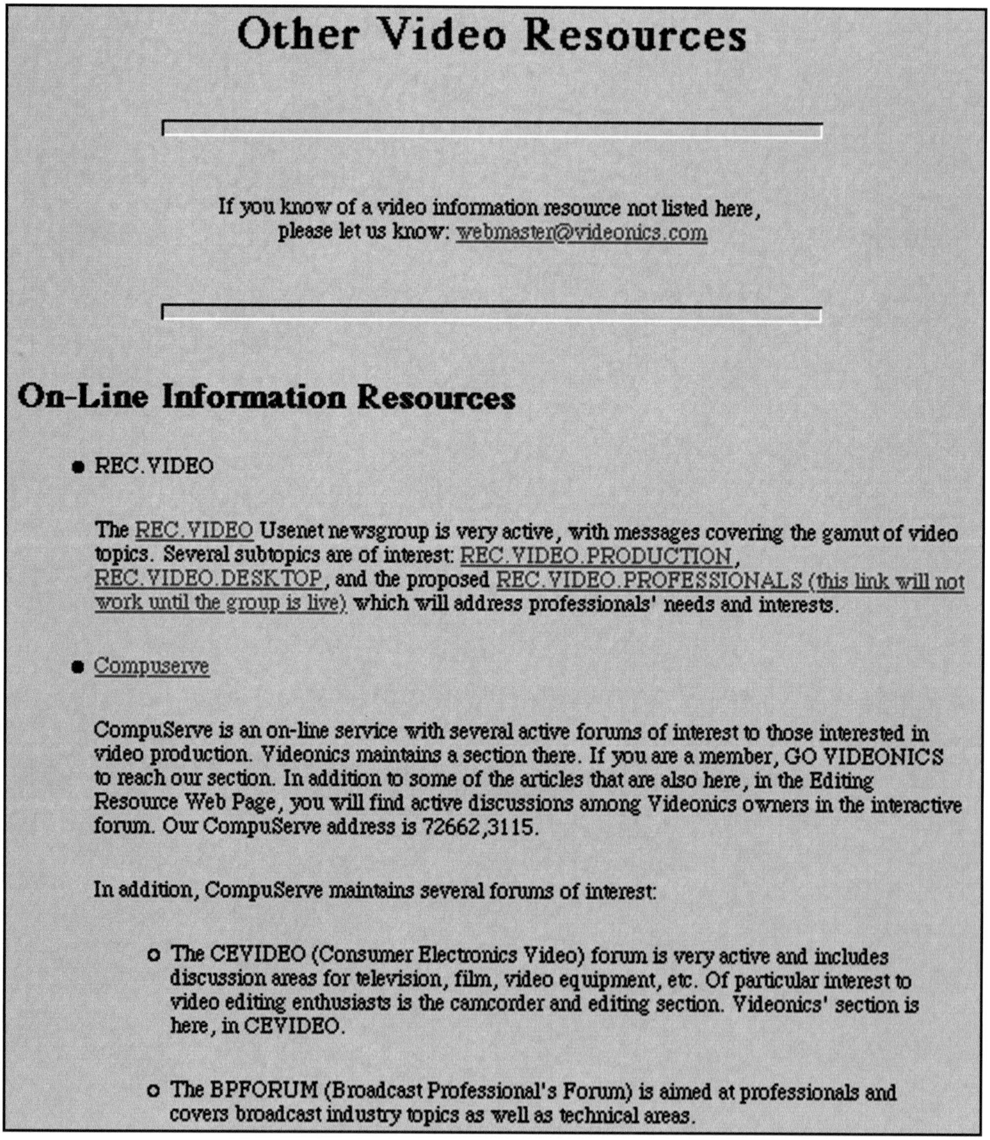

Other Video Resources

If you know of a video information resource not listed here, please let us know: webmaster@videonics.com

On-Line Information Resources

- REC.VIDEO

  The REC.VIDEO Usenet newsgroup is very active, with messages covering the gamut of video topics. Several subtopics are of interest: REC.VIDEO.PRODUCTION, REC.VIDEO.DESKTOP, and the proposed REC.VIDEO.PROFESSIONALS (this link will not work until the group is live) which will address professionals' needs and interests.

- Compuserve

  CompuServe is an on-line service with several active forums of interest to those interested in video production. Videonics maintains a section there. If you are a member, GO VIDEONICS to reach our section. In addition to some of the articles that are also here, in the Editing Resource Web Page, you will find active discussions among Videonics owners in the interactive forum. Our CompuServe address is 72662,3115.

  In addition, CompuServe maintains several forums of interest:

  - The CEVIDEO (Consumer Electronics Video) forum is very active and includes discussion areas for television, film, video equipment, etc. Of particular interest to video editing enthusiasts is the camcorder and editing section. Videonics' section is here, in CEVIDEO.

  - The BPFORUM (Broadcast Professional's Forum) is aimed at professionals and covers broadcast industry topics as well as technical areas.

FIG. 33.6 (PAGE 811) ▲

Invite return visits by establishing your site as a convenient route to more information.

Special Effects

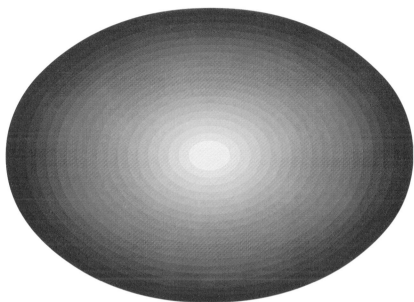

▲ **Fig. 15.48 (Page 402)**

More than a dozen ovals are overlapped to create this gradient fill in 5 percent increments. It has been produced using one of the scripts on the enclosed CD-ROM.

◀ **Fig. 15.49 (Page 402)**

A sort of porthole on a text block, using the Mask command. You don't need this effect every day, but when you do, you really need it. Masking makes it easy.

2 Horizontal Colors

FIG. 15.50 (PAGE 402) ▲

You can make horizontal, two-toned text by lining up different color boxes and some type. But the steps are much easier this way. Set one box of color down over the other one and mask them together. Then adjust the masked box until you have the split just right, as shown here.

FIG. 15.51 (PAGE 403) ▲

This Star Pig is placed over a star, which is masking a texture of granite. More importantly, the pig is a transparent TIFF; it has a clipping path and was imported directly out of Photoshop. Up until PageMaker 6.0, you had to go through FreeHand to accomplish this effect of cutting the outline around the graphic. This new method is easy. (The pig comes drum-scanned and the clipping path precut from the PhotoDisc Object Series. The pig is one of ten high-resolution Object Series graphics included at no charge on the CD-ROM that comes with this book.)

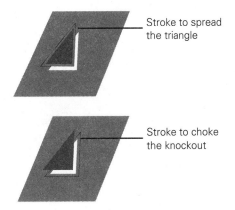

Stroke to spread
the triangle

Stroke to choke
the knockout

FIG. 20.4 ▲

The spread is on the top, and the choke is on the bottom.

inks overlap. The resulting artifact of the trapping process can be an unsightly dark line that looks worse than the dreaded sliver of white it covers up. However, by working only with the lighter colors, you minimize the effects of the dark line. As a rule of thumb, when the inks are laid down on paper, the dark color will dominate and win out over the overlapping light color.

Three Trapping Methods

How do we actually accomplish this spreading and choking? You have three techniques to choose from: the way it used to be done, mechanically on a light table; the object trapping method; and the high-end pixel edge trapping method sometimes called *raster trapping*. Those techniques are the subject of the next few sections.

The Way It Used to Be: Mechanical Trapping

To understand how all this trapping business works, it may help to have a look at the traditional, non-computer techniques used to create traps.

Printers used to create traps by using what you might call a "sandwich of light" to make a contact print from a film of the original image. Printers placed a thin filling of clear material, such as plastic, between the original film and the contact film (see fig. 20.5 here and in the color section). This sandwich filling of clear plastic allowed the light to spread out so it created an overlap (a spread type trap) on the receiving negative film. The amount of the trap could be varied by using different thicknesses of clear material and by altering the amount of light used for the exposure.

Fig. 20.5 ▷

The light sandwich method used by strippers to create a trap.

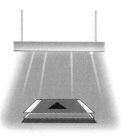

Some areas of a complex design might need different traps. To create varying traps on a page, the stripper photographically (not literally) carves up your mechanical into different zones with masks made of Rubylith and opaque material. Each zone is then exposed as needed, and the final trapped flat is then used to expose the lithographic plate.

This dependable technique has worked well for a long time. However, the technique takes time, which means money that you or your client must pay. Also, it goes against the grain to carefully paste up your pages electronically and then have a stripper use old-fashioned trapping techniques on them.

Object Trapping

PageMaker's built-in automatic trapping uses electronic object-level trapping methods.

As you can see here in figure 20.6 (and in the color section), object trapping involves drawing a line around the object that needs to be trapped. If you wanted to, you could perform this operation on simple objects using PageMaker's Fill and Line dialog box. This trapping technique is sometimes called *stroking*.

Fig. 20.6 ▷

An object stroked with a trapping line, a spread, drawn around the object being trapped.

Lighter color stroking object

Notice that the object knocks out the background, the normal behavior for a graphic object in any PostScript-based program, including PageMaker. The stroke line, however, has been set to overprint so it can overlap the background. Also, the lighter of the colors has been used for trapping.

The choice of the trapping color can be pretty mind-boggling. Thank heavens PageMaker automates this choice. If you are working with spot colors, you simply use the lighter of the two abutting colors. Process colors, however, can combine to make some really weird and garish third colors, called *trapping artifacts*. If you design yourself into a corner like that, get advice from your printer. Better yet, have someone else do the trapping unless you are experienced.

Raster Trapping

Raster or edge trapping beats one of the big problems with object trapping. Object trapping requires that you be able to access the object from within PageMaker. If it's an imported graphic, no desktop layout program—including PageMaker—can do any trapping on the areas inside that image. For trapping imported graphics, you would need to go back to the drawing or photo-retouching program used to create the graphic.

What to do? There's no better trapping available than raster edge trapping. If you have designed a job that PageMaker can't handle or if you are apprehensive about taking the trapping risk, you may need to send your job to a service bureau or printer that offers raster trapping. Several software packages for trapping are out there, and most of them have one thing in common—a purchase price of thousands of dollars. In the hands of a skilled operator, these systems can do excellent trapping work, but they aren't the kind of thing most of us are likely to install in our own studios.

A high-end trapping system goes into your completed PageMaker file, sorts it out right down to the pixel level, and automatically works out traps for everything on the page. That includes imported EPS graphics and depending on the system, virtually all the other "avoid-these-situations" trapping problems laid out in the next section. Raster trapping does a good trapping job quickly, no matter how convoluted those abutting color objects may be.

The two big names in raster trapping are Adobe's own TrapWise and Scitex FAF (Full Auto Frame). You don't need to care very much about what system is used, as long as your service bureau delivers a good looking job on time.

Deciding Whether to Do Your Own Trapping

Trapping isn't a mountain, and you don't need to climb it just because it's there. You may want to, but you don't necessarily need to.

V

Making Pages Colorful

Ask yourself these questions when deciding whether to do it yourself:

▶ *Money and time.* How much is your time worth, and how much will it cost to pay someone else to do the trapping? Although times are changing, trapping traditionally has been part of the printer's job.

▶ *Risk versus benefit.* Are you willing to risk it? When deciding, keep in mind that a success has many proud parents, but a failure is an orphan. If you take responsibility for the trapping and it comes out badly, you might be reaching into your bank account for some not-so-petty cash to pay for those 10,000 color catalogue sheets the client rejected.

▶ *Stripper or designer.* Do you really want to sit in front of the computer making trapping decisions? Or would you rather be designing another job?

▶ *Quality.* How good will the job be when you finish? Is the piece important or complex enough that it deserves high-end raster trapping? Do you have all the skills and experience needed to handle it?

▶ *Design to avoid trapping.* Is it possible to design around the need for trapping? If no colors touch one another, there's no need to trap. Or try overprinting, using one of the overprint techniques in the "Performing Simple Object Trapping" section. If you are working in process colors, design abutting objects to share one of the four process colors.

▶ *Job complexity.* Is doing the job yourself with object trapping techniques reasonable or even technically possible? PageMaker and your drawing program simply can't handle some things; the following section lists and discusses trapping situations you need to avoid.

Consider Running with No Trapping: Kiss Fit

Kiss fit means to run the job without trapping, allowing the abutting colors to "kiss" each other without overlapping. If you know your printer really well, you may very well be able to run the job just fine without trapping. If you don't know your printer really well and ask to print your color job kiss fit with no traps, the printer will give you a big belly laugh for a few minutes, then ask you to sign a waiver that any flaws in the job are your fault. Still, it's an option.

In fact, one of the newsletters listed in the "Getting More Help" section of Chapter 1, "Touring PageMaker," runs everything with absolutely no trapping. If you ever saw the 16-page *Before&After* newsletter, you would never guess that it's run kiss fit. It's full of tricky color, because that's the point. *Before&After* is a newsletter all about pulling off PageMaker design, primarily in color. For example, the newsletter's publishers run plenty of blends against blends, which are tough to do.

After seeing the note in *Before&After* that says everything's printed kiss fit, I thought it was worth a call to Publisher John McWade to ask, "Why do you do that, and how do you pull it off?" Here's his approach.

He says he prefers an occasional white line over having any bad traps, and that a publication looks cleaner if it can be run without traps. How does he get the printer to make the commitment? For one thing, *Before&After* is the most important job on his printer's client list. They do a very long make-ready run to get everything in good register, which wastes a lot of time and paper. But the printer regards the newsletter as a showpiece for his shop and believes it's worth the time and effort. Even more amazing, the print shop isn't a high-end shop. The shop does mostly one- and two-color work on uncoated stock. Their old press, built in 1968, has so much wear that it literally rattles during a run. (That's a manually adjusted press, by the way, not one of those laser-registered, computerized fountain jobs.)

One other thing—all the color in the newsletter gets specified as process color. As a result, abutting colors often share a common CMYK color component and that tends to minimize any misregistration because if two plates are not spot on, the other two plates will, by the law of averages, just naturally tend to cover for the errant pair (which just happens to be one of the trapping techniques covered in this chapter).

So some people do publish without trapping. It may not be something you want to insist on, but if you have a good collaboration with the printer, it's entirely possible that you will get good results.

Design Away the Need for Trapping

If your communications challenge permits, you can develop a design that does not require trapping, or at least avoid the worst of the trapping risks.

Overprinting Black

If you have black type to run over a colored background, just overprint it, assuming the type is large enough to read well. In PageMaker, black type up to 24 points in size will automatically overprint the background. Make sure you check with your print shop about the amount of ink being applied to the page. You could end up with too much.

Avoid obvious legibility and design problems such as putting black type on a midnight blue background. (The type would be unreadable.) Check contrast by having a look at the page design with your monitor set in grayscale mode.

Sharing CMYK Colors

As long as abutting process colors share a common process color, you don't need to trap them. For example, perhaps the adjacent objects contain at least 10 percent or 20 percent of cyan. (Check with your printer on the minimum amount of common color; 10 percent is a typical figure.) If the other colors slip on the page, the cyan ink fills in the gap, and you see no dreaded white sliver of paper showing through due to the misregistration. The sliver is cyan blue instead, but many designers and printers believe that's less noticeable than white.

This trick doesn't work with spot color mixed inks. However, process color-based spot color inks work just fine. Check with your printer.

Fig. 20.7 ▶

(See color section.)

Taken to its extreme, you could even overprint two process colors, as you might overprint black. You definitely need a swatch book if you want to try that one. The mixture of all those process colors could result in too much ink and an unsightly color to boot. Figure 20.7 shows how you can stack the two process colors to create a third color.

Frame the Untrappables

Consider running a stroke around the edge of an item that might otherwise be untrappable, such as a color photo. Simply put an intentionally visible frame around it. You need to decide whether you like the idea of doing this to your design, but it does (literally) cover any misregistration.

The setup has been illustrated in figure 20.8 here and in the color section. You simply use the Create Keyline Plug-in to run a box around the graphic, setting the amount of overlapping trap in the provided text box.

Fig. 20.8 ▶

"Framing" a graphic with a border as a means of trapping.

Design Away Trapping Nightmares

PageMaker's object trapping simply can't handle some things. You will struggle mightily—and probably be unhappy with the results—if you attempt to use PageMaker's built-in trapping in the following situations:

FIG. 20.9

(See color section.)

▶ *Imported and resized graphic objects.* This may be the most common and frustrating trapping dilemma of them all, because the whole point of having PageMaker is to perform this kind of electronic assembly of text and graphics. You have to trap imported graphics in their originating programs, unless you are using a raster trapping step on the whole file. Have a look at the simulation in figure 20.9 in the color section, and check out all the white spaces where all these complex shapes and colors could fall apart on the press.

Again, you must trap imported graphic objects in the programs that created them. You may want to reconsider doing your own trapping if your imported EPS graphics look as complex as the one in the figure. Trapping complex graphics takes time.

TIP ▶

Also, keep in mind that even after you have figured out a way to trap your imported graphic, you can't resize it unless you are willing to redo the trapping job. Resizing a trapped graphic changes the thickness of all the stroked lines and may ruin your traps.

Do an Electronic Stat Sheet of Pre-Trapped, Frequently Used Graphics

Some graphics get used over and over again. Logos are just one example. So, do the trapping once and save the items in a sort of electronic stat sheet. Compose a sheet of logos (or other frequently used graphic elements) in every size you might need. Trap them all, and then you easily can place these pre-trapped and pre-sized graphics in PageMaker without worrying about trapping.

▶ *Abutting blends.* If you design overlapping blends—anything that doesn't have a sharply defined edge—object trapping won't help you, as you can tell from the results in figure 20.10 here and in the color section.

FIG. 20.10 ▶

Overlapping gradations are impossible to trap using object trapping because you get a sharp line along the abutting edge.

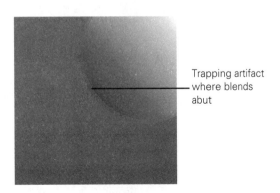

Trapping artifact where blends abut

This example of two different-colored and abutting blends was trapped by cloning one of the blends and coloring it in a solid trapping color. The result is a dark trapping artifact line. Another approach is to trap the blends by the common color method mentioned earlier in this section, but that still gives you a solid line trapping artifact. In both cases, the problem arises because the color of a blend gradates along its edge. The trapping color must track exactly with the colors of the blends, creating sort of a sliding trap.

You could also try to trap these gradated blends by simply stroking one of the blends with a line, but that would probably look worse than an untrapped white paper line, and it would defeat the design purpose of the abutting blends.

▶ *Objects overlapping halftones.* Figure 20.11 (shown here and in the color section) displays one of the toughest trapping challenges—an object superimposed over a photograph. You simply have no way to stroke your object against the picture, because all the colors are changing underneath the object, similar to the problems you have in trapping a gradation.

Fig. 20.11 ▶

The difficulty of trapping an object superimposed over a scanned photograph.

There's some good news in the midst of all these trapping design issues. PageMaker 6.0 can now handle trapping for several situations that used to be nightmares. These next two illustrations illustrate these two former nightmare trapping problems:

▶ *"Rich" black with reversed out type.* When doing process colors, it's common to add the CMY colors to the black to get a rich, solid black. People sometimes call this a *rich black*. If you reverse-out type against this black, it used to be that there was no good way to use manual object trapping to go into the CMY screens. If the press misregistered, you got artifacts of cyan, magenta, or yellow hanging out into the no-ink area of the reversed letter. Figure 20.12 here and in the color section illustrates the problem, now solved by PageMaker 6.0's automatic object trapping.

▶ *Tandem chokes or spreads.* Most object trapping works on an entire object. For that reason, trapping an object that crosses over more than one color or straddles a block of color is really difficult. PageMaker 6.0, however, can pick an object apart and work out traps for objects that cross several colors. Figure 20.13 here and in the color section shows some type superimposed over a few colors so that you can see the problem.

Fɪɢ. **20.12** ▶

Trapping failure in reversed-out type on a rich black.

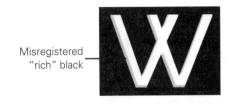

Misregistered "rich" black

Fɪɢ. **20.13** ▶

An example of the need to do tandem chokes or spreads, nearly impossible with object trapping techniques.

Letters look thinner

Bottom half outlined

Putting PageMaker's Automatic Object Trapping to Work

If you decide that PageMaker's built-in trapping can handle your design, it's time for the simplest part of the process. After all, it's automatic!

Getting Together the Technical Info

As a first order of business, it's collaboration time. You need to get some technical specifications in order to create your traps, and you'll need to get the info from your printer. You need, in fact, a fair amount of technical information so you can run the trapping controls in PageMaker—things like the neutral density values for inks, the black limit, when black should be over-printed, and so on.

You may see standard guidelines for these technical specifications, but it's just plain silly to trap without asking the printer what the trapping parameters are. Trapping is, after all, something you are doing to compensate for misregistration on the press, and it varies a great deal from press operation to press operation.

The most important item on your technical info list is the width of the traps you will want PageMaker to set for you. Your printer knows the looseness of the press, the line frequency of your screens, your paper, the position of your piece in the flat, and the dot gain. From that information your printer can determine the trapping amount. The amount of ink overlap will probably range from 0.18 to 2.2 points (0.0025 to 0.0308 inches), and there will be a different amount for black ink and all the other color inks.

Dot gain, by the way, is the way ink spreads on paper when printing a halftone. It soaks in and makes a bigger halftone dot (and widens the trap overlap).

V

Making Pages Colorful

TIP ▷ Take the Dialog to the Printer, Literally

One really good way to collect all this technical information is to take screen shots of the Trapping Options and Ink Setup dialog boxes to a meeting with your printer. Also take along proofs of your project. Ask the printer what values you should be typing into the dialog box, and if there are any areas of your design that will be trapping problems.

TIP ▷ Don't Do a Half Trap Job

Don't run PageMaker trapping if your design includes even one of the trapping nightmare situations illustrated in this chapter. Handing the printer films that have been trapped in some areas but not in others will make it impossible for the printer to complete the job. Trapping software like TrapWise and traditional printing darkroom techniques for trapping usually work over the entire area of a page. That creates sort of an all-or-nothing situation. Running trapping software over your existing PageMaker generated traps would give you double traps in some spots. That's not good.

Understanding How PageMaker Traps

Your publication will not actually be trapped until you output your separations. All the trapping settings can be changed at any time before you run your film.

One drawback of this flexibility is the fact that PageMaker can't preview traps for you because there's nothing to see in the actual PageMaker file. By contrast, high-end trapping systems allow the operator to examine each trap and make adjustments as needed. Until you go to color separations, PageMaker traps will not be visible. You can proof them using a laminate color proofing system as discussed in Chapter 22, "Proofing Your Publication." However, the traps will not show up on a composite color printer.

Here's how PageMaker tackles its automated object level trapping chores. First, it looks for all edges where two colors meet. It then decides which of the two adjacent colors is lighter (based on the neutral density values of the inks). As a general rule of thumb, the lighter colored object will be spread over the top of the darker value to make the trap. However, PageMaker sometimes mixes up a new color to construct a trap:

▶ If two adjacent process colors must be trapped (neither one being a spot color), PageMaker starts by selecting the lighter of the two colors. It then pulls a new color out of that lighter color, using the CMYK ink values that are more intense than the CMYK values found in the darker color.

▶ If the colors have equal or similar neutral densities, PageMaker runs a centerline trap. The program makes up a new color by combining elements of the two trapped colors, selecting the highest CMYK values from each, and then uses that new color to cover the join between the abutting colors.

Setting Trapping Parameters

Once you have the technical specifications and a basic grasp of how PageMaker trapping works, the rest is really simple. You merely fill in the blanks in the dialog boxes shown in figure 20.14.

FIG. 20.14 ▶

PageMaker's two trapping options dialog boxes.

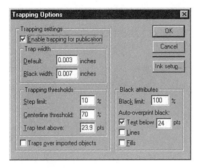
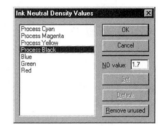

Here are some additional notes on how PageMaker trapping works to help you in filling out the dialog box:

▶ *Turn it on.* Don't forget to click in the Enable Trapping for Publication check box before you run your separations.

▶ *Two widths.* You need two trap width settings. One is only for black ink objects, and it is normally set for about twice the amount as the other setting, which is the trap width for all other colors except black.

▶ *Step limit tolerance.* The Step Limit setting defines when PageMaker should make a trap. If the colors vary by more than the amount entered in this box, the program will go to work and create a trap. The lower the step limit setting, the more PageMaker will trap.

▶ *Centerlines.* The Centerline Threshold setting determines when PageMaker goes to work with a centerline, as opposed to a full spread trap. A 100% setting would tell PageMaker not to do any centerline trapping, whereas a 0% setting would request that all traps be centerlines. If the Centerline Threshold is set at 70%, then PageMaker will switch to centerline when the lighter color is more than 70% of the darker color in neutral density.

▶ *Defining black.* The Black Limit setting defines what is considered to be black for trapping purposes. Sometimes blacks are screened back a bit, or designers use an enriched black with a little bit of CMY thrown in and a slight reduction in K. Under those circumstances, you can tell PageMaker trapping to consider as black any color that has, say, 95% black or more. You can also automatically set all black lines and fills and certain sizes of text to overprint, so they won't need to be trapped at all.

▶ *Trapping ignores overprints*. In fact, any color or object that has been set to overprint during layout will be ignored by PageMaker trapping. Overprinting means it won't knock out and therefore doesn't need a trap.

▶ *Opaque lines*. Color trapping does not work for opaque lines, meaning lines that do not have the transparent background setting checked in the Lines dialog box.

▶ *Text*. Don't set text trapping for type that's below 24 points unless you have a good reason and have talked to your printer about it. Trapping small type will unduly thicken the ascenders and descenders in proportion to the overall size of the letters and may plug up the openings in the letters as well.

▶ *Standard neutral density settings*. In general, don't mess with the Ink Setup settings for neutral density. They have been set to industry standards. In the U.S., the values used have been set by the Graphic Arts Technical Foundation, the same group that established the SWOP standards (Specifications for Web Offset Publications). If you have a special situation, metallic inks for example, consult your commercial printer regarding neutral density settings. A special instrument called a densitometer can be used to read the neutral density of a swatch of ink.

▶ *Imported objects*. Do not check the Traps Over Imported Objects box, except in extremely unusual circumstances. PageMaker can't trap imported objects, so it ignores them. But if you have stacked a PageMaker drawn object on top of a graphic and have another one behind it, PageMaker will try to trap the two drawn objects even though they don't meet.

Where to Go from Here

▶ A lot of the color theory you need to really understand this chapter is covered in Chapter 18, "Creating Colors."

▶ If you are doing color, you need to see Chapter 22, "Proofing Your Publication." You need high-quality proofs to evaluate process color accuracy.

▶ The first part of this chapter focused on collaborating with your printer and the special issues of putting color ink on paper. You have plenty more to coordinate, and you can find out about it in Chapter 23, "Working with the Print Shop."

PART VI

Publishing

21 ▲ Producing Mechanicals

22 ▲ Proofing Your Publication

23 ▲ Working with the Print Shop

24 ▲ Master Checklist for Desktop Publishing

Chapter 21

Producing Mechanicals

This chapter on producing mechanicals covers the following information:

Setting up the software to work with your printer.

▼

Customizing the printer description file.

▼

Printing laser mechanicals and proofs.

▼

Using PageMaker's Build Booklet feature to electronically strip together multiple pages on large print shop-sized flats for cost-efficient printing and binding.

▼

Batching up your laser print jobs.

▼

Deciding whether to send your prepress bureau a correctable, changeable PageMaker file or a locked down PostScript file.

▼

The logistics of assembling your materials and getting them to a prepress service bureau for output on a high-resolution imagesetter.

IT'S A RARE publishing project that doesn't require the creation of a master to be duplicated in the photocopying machine or film from the service bureau.

Mechanicals were sometimes referred to as *pasteups*, *artwork*, *keylines*, and *artboards*. Nowadays, your mechanicals are just as likely to be called Lino output, film, or *repro* (paper output from an imagesetter).

However you produce your mechanicals, this chapter pulls together all the parts of PageMaker used to do it, especially the richly featured suite of Print command dialog boxes. ▶ ▶ ▶

PostScript or Not?

One note about laser printers before we move into this chapter. You may notice a distinct bias here in favor of PostScript printers. The reason for that bias is that PostScript laser printers absolutely dominate the desktop publishing market. It's true, hundreds of thousands of inexpensive non-PostScript laser printers and color inkjets are out there, and they aren't PostScript. But non-PostScript devices don't give you all the typographical power of PageMaker because it has been designed with the PostScript standard in mind.

If you have a PCL-based printer (the Hewlett-Packard printer language, as opposed to PostScript), here's the situation in summary. Some of these points may or may not apply depending on which model of printer you have and whether you have the latest printer driver software. It's a complex situation with lots of variables:

▶ Some of the Print command features described in this chapter won't be available if you are working with a non-PostScript printer. You actually get two different dialog boxes in some parts of the Print command complex of dialogs—one with all the PostScript features and the other without.

▶ You may not get the best possible results when you output pages that use some of the PageMaker layout capabilities that depend on PostScript, such as rotation and skewing. It's likely that the quality won't be as good as can be expected on a PostScript printer.

▶ A special setting will be needed in order to print text reversed out against a black background—the print text as graphics setting.

▶ You should have it anyway, but if you have a PCL-based printer, you really must get Adobe Type Manager to get your PostScript type rendered well on your pages.

▶ EPS graphics will not print as high-quality resolution-independent vector graphics. Instead, the output will be from the low-resolution EPS preview image, which will in turn be imaged based on your current monitor resolution. (There are some partial solutions to this last point. Some drawing applications will let you specify a higher resolution for the EPS preview. Applications also sometimes let you specify WMF format for the preview instead of a TIFF, and WMF will sometimes print better.)

Selecting and Setting Up Your Printer Driver

You can't print a thing on your laser printer without a printer driver—the software that manages the electronic connection between your computer and your printer.

In addition, if you are working with a PostScript printer, the printer driver depends on a PostScript Printer Description file—a PPD—for its knowledge about the idiosyncrasies of your model of printer. The printer driver setup procedure, then, has several steps:

▶ Install the driver on your computer. (PageMaker will suggest updating your driver if its internal installation procedure determines that a newer one is available, but drivers are really a function of your operating system. The drivers are normally supplied by the printer manufacturer.)

▶ Choose your printer in the Windows Control Panel and do a quick setup operation.

▶ Customize your PPD to accommodate special features. Most people won't need this step.

▶ Tell PageMaker what printer and PPD (or model of printer) you are using in the Document Setup and the Print command dialogs. (Assuming that you are installing a PostScript printer.)

Making Your Setup Choices

I'm going to assume that you've got the latest printer driver installed on your hard drive and that your printer is set up and functioning with other Windows applications—especially since it's likely you've probably gone through the installation of Windows 95 which would have included this process.

Just make sure that you have selected your printer in the PRINTERS folder and set any Properties that seem vital. Actually, many of the Properties settings can also be controlled from within PageMaker so that part might not even be important.

If you are working with a PostScript printer, set TrueType fonts to be converted to PostScript. Go to the Properties settings for Printer and choose the Fonts tab. Select the radio button that says you want to Always Use TrueType Fonts. Then click the Send Fonts As button and in the Send TrueType Fonts As list box choose Outlines.

VI

Publishing

TIP ▶ Guarding Against Missing Fonts in EPS Graphics

One setup step that you can make elsewhere, outside your system printer settings, is to make sure the EPS Font Scanner is turned on. It's in the Utilities menu with the rest of the Plug-ins and should be turned on by default, but checking would be a good move. At print time, EPS Font Scanner will catch any calls for fonts inside EPS files in your publication; check to see that the correct fonts are installed in your system, and if they aren't, give you a warning.

Customizing Your Printer Setup

At a fundamental level, PageMaker manages its relationship with your PostScript printer based on the information contained in the Postscript Printer Description (PPD) file. Pretty much all PageMaker and your printer driver know about the specific features in your printer comes from the PPD. Your printer driver and PPD can't tell on the fly if you add printer options such as a hard drive for font storage, an extra paper tray, or more memory.

So, in this situation you need to make a custom PPD that will override and work in cooperation with the standard one. (This approach uses Update PPD from within PageMaker. There is also a stand-alone program called Update PPD that can be used outside PageMaker.)

Open the Update PPD Plug-in, reached via the Utilities menu. The Plug-in will automatically go out to look at your printer to determine it's general features and will come back showing a simple dialog box with a pull-down list in which you can select PPDs from any of your installed printers, as you see in figure 21.1.

Fig. 21.1 ▶

Updating and customizing your PPD.

Next, type in a new nickname for your Custom PPD, or simply accept the one that has already been suggested by the Update PPD program.

To adjust the memory setting in the PPD, if you have added some memory for example, click Edit VM (for virtual memory). Select the printer from the Select Printer list and click Print. The printer will print out a page with the actual printer memory on it. Use that information to type the new memory info in the New VM box.

PageMaker's knowledge of which fonts are resident in your printer (so they don't have to be downloaded at output time) comes from the PPD. To add or remove fonts, click the Add Fonts button and select your printer from the list. Add fonts by selecting them from the list on the left and then clicking Add. Remove fonts by selecting from the list on the right and clicking Remove.

Of course, you shouldn't put fonts on the PPD list if they haven't been installed. Usually you do that by adding the fonts to a hard drive attached to your printer. You can also put together special PPDs that list fonts you customarily download to the printer on an ad hoc basis for regular projects, but that's a bit dangerous if you forget the download. It'll cost you time and could waste expensive output media.

Click OK when you are done adjusting memory and font information.

The Save button in the main dialog will put your custom PPD on the hard disk in the RSRC\USENGLISH\PPD4 folder.

You're done customizing your own PPD. Hey! Don't forget to choose your custom PPD in the Print dialog box, now that you've created it.

TIP ▶ Performing Major Surgery on PPDs

If you are a PostScript programmer, you probably aren't even reading this. But just in case, the Advanced button in the main Update PPD dialog box gives you access to directly edit the PPD code.

For example, look for a reference to `*% Font Information`. That's the section of the PPD where all your fonts are listed, telling the printer driver what fonts are available on your printer. A note is there establishing the default font as Courier. That means, if a PostScript font isn't available, Courier will be substituted. Whenever you see the default font, something has gone wrong with your file—chances are high that you don't do much typesetting in a monospaced font like Courier. You might consider changing your default font to something even more obvious—something built into the printer—such as Zapf Dingbats, making it even easier to spot a problem on a proof.

Adobe has published a detailed technical note on modifications you can make to your PPD. You can get it from FaxYI, and at press time the number is (206) 628-5737. Ask for bulletin #100102.

TIP ▶ Vital Printing Issues During Document Setup

The Windows version of PageMaker relies heavily on knowing the printer characteristics as you compose a publication. That means you should have set some important parameters long before getting to this stage of producing mechanicals.

In the Document Setup dialog box, reached through the File menu, you must set the target printer resolution and the Compose to Printer information. If you change this at any time during the creation of your publication, you will need to check all your type and graphics to see that their positions and appearance have not shifted.

There's more information on these settings in Chapter 12, "Setting Up a New Publication."

VI

Publishing

Printing to a Laser Printer

Basic laser printing with PageMaker works about the same as it does with any other Windows application. What could be easier than Ctrl+P?

But there's nothing basic about the power of PageMaker when it comes to final production of your publication. You get a different version of the Print dialog box for each of the buttons you see running down the right side of the dialog box in figure 21.2.

Fig. 21.2 ▶

PageMaker's opening Print dialog box in Document mode.

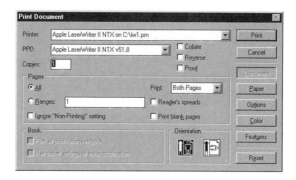

The Print dialog box opens initially in Document mode; the other versions of the Print dialog box are Paper, Options, Color, and Features. If you have a non-PostScript printer, the Paper dialog is replaced by Setup.

Notice the Reset button in the lower-right corner of the dialog box. The Reset button might better be named Revert because it returns the Print dialog box to the appearance it had when you first opened it, but the button does not reset the print functions to the program's default. You find it in all of the dialog box modes of the Print command.

Setting General Print Parameters in Document Mode

The form of the Print dialog box shown in figure 21.2 does most of the things that you expect from any program's Print command, with the following exceptions, nuances, and refinements:

▶ *Printer and PPD.* The printer you chose in Control Panel is indicated in the Printer line. In the Windows version of PageMaker (unlike the Macintosh version), you can change the printer driver here instead of in the system Control Panel.

What you see in the PPD box depends on whether you have allowed "nicknames" or not. The actual name of a PPD file follows the DOS naming convention of 8+3, something like "LWNTX518.PPD." The nickname for that

PPD would be just a touch more descriptive, "Apple LaserWrite II NTX v51.8." As we go to press, there's some question about how well PageMaker 6.0 can handle these PPD nicknames. The safe course may be to just stick with the regular DOS file names instead of using nicknames.

By the way, PageMaker 6.0 does not support the Windows 95 SPD (Simplified Printer Description) scheme. It uses strictly PPD files.

▶ *Number and order of copies.* In the Copies text entry box you tell PageMaker how many copies you want to make of your publication. You can print up to 32,000 copies, if you have a dump-truck size toner cartridge and don't mind using up enough wood fiber to paper all the mud huts of the world's third world countries. (Of course, not all printer drivers will allow you to print this many copies. This is what PageMaker will permit if the printer driver allows it.)

If you do more than one copy, PageMaker by default produces them all shuffled together. You get ten copies of page one, followed by ten of page two, and so on. Check Collate on, and you get the ten copies all collated. Collating takes longer, and the time you save in automatically collating a long publication may be wiped out by the amount of time you spend hovering over your laser printer inhaling ozone fumes.

Reverse order comes in handy if you want to check a passel of copy before you staple it. Have it come out in reverse order, and as you check each page, lay it down face up. When you finish, the stack is in the proper order. This also helps get pages stacked properly if you have one of the printers that normally output pages face up. Likewise, you may want to use Reverse Order if your printer has a straight paper path option for heavier paper or envelopes, where you open a back door and your paper comes out face up.

▶ *Proofing.* The Proof check box prints your page just as you see it on your screen, except the graphics that eat up all the computation time in your laser printer are replaced by plain boxes filled with an X.

This is especially useful as a troubleshooting tool. If you have a page that won't print, you can quickly narrow the likely problem down to fonts or graphics by checking the Proof check box. If your page now prints, look to your imported graphics for problems. If you page still will not print, it's time to take a closer look for problems with the fonts used in your publication.

▶ *Page selection.* Although in most situations you print all the pages of a publication, this feature lets you select a range of pages for printing. Click the Ranges radio button and type in a list of pages you want to print.

Follow each page or group of pages with a comma and indicate a series of pages with a hyphen, such as "1,3-5,8,7-20,3." When you hyphenate to get a series of pages, the lower numbered page must come first. Notice that you can repeat page numbers if you need more than one copy of those particular pages.

▶ *Reader's spreads.* We can finally print Reader's Spreads—one of the most applauded features of the new PageMaker. Reader's spreads put facing pages on the same sheet of paper. It makes it convenient—without using bits of tape to patch together sheets of paper—to evaluate the design of side-by-side pages. When you check this option, PageMaker automatically turns on the Reduce to Fit option in the Paper mode of the Print dialog, and you'll see that the layout has been changed to landscape orientation in the Fit preview box.

▶ *Print non-printing.* Ordinarily, the new ability to designate objects as Non-Printing would keep them from, well, printing. But you can check the Ignore "Non-Printing" Setting on, and they'll print after all. This works well when people have been adding notes and comments to a layout, and you want to get a printout with all the notes.

▶ *Print blanks.* Sometimes you insert blank pages in a document to make the right and left facing pages come out correctly. Clicking the check box to Print Blank Pages takes care of you in this situation; otherwise PageMaker tries to economize by skipping any page that's devoid of any marks.

When preparing a job for duplex printing or high-speed copying, having PageMaker print blank pages is crucial to keep the correct front sides imaging with the correct back sides. For imagesetter or color copy output, you'll probably want PageMaker to skip sending the blank pages. It will save money, but those high-end imagesetter or color jobs usually have a human being in the loop who can make sure pagination is correct.

▶ *Print both, even, odd.* You can choose to Print both pages in a spread or simply between printing odd and even pages, an especially useful feature if you need to laser print both sides of the paper (the perfect time to select Print Blanks, too!).

▶ *Orientation.* Orientation does the same thing it does in every other program. Use it to designate a horizontal (landscape) or vertical (portrait) orientation for your pages.

▶ *Book printing.* Book printing enables PageMaker to Print All Publications in Book at one time, and you turn it on here. The program uses the book list in the currently active document, so you must be printing from the document that contains the entire book list if you want to print all of the chapters.

When you book print, the Orientation set in the Print command of each publication is honored, no matter what you do with the Use Paper Settings of Each Publication check box.

If you are printing to a file (Options mode), the entire book is printed to the file.

If you are printing separations (Color mode), all inks are printed.

Your radio button choices are honored for the All or Ranges print settings of your active publication, and the Both, Even, and Odd settings in the active publication apply throughout the book list.

If you check the Use Paper Settings of Each Publication check box, you can go to each booked publication and set a different paper size and paper bin for each document in the book list.

Selecting Paper Size, Scaling, and Tiling

Use the Paper mode of the Print command, shown in figure 21.3, to manage the way your document fits on the printed page. (This fit includes size, scale, centering, and tiling.)

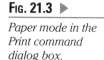

FIG. 21.3 ▶

Paper mode in the Print command dialog box.

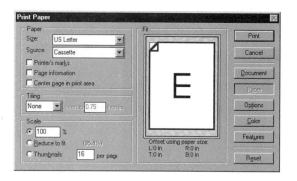

The following list explains each area of the Paper subdialog of the Print command:

▶ *Paper size and source.* Choose your Size from the pull-down list. (The PPD for your printer builds this list, as well as the Source information.) If your printer has more than one paper tray, you'll be able to choose from among them with the Source pop-up menu.

If your printer's PPD indicates that it supports custom paper sizes, you can choose Custom from the Source pull-down list and get a subsidiary dialog box for that purpose. Custom paper sizes are not something you generally need to worry about for laser printing, but it's very important to service bureaus who are trying to get the maximum number of your pages on a roll of material in an imagesetter.

▶ *Printer's marks and page information.* Figure 21.4 shows what these options look like.

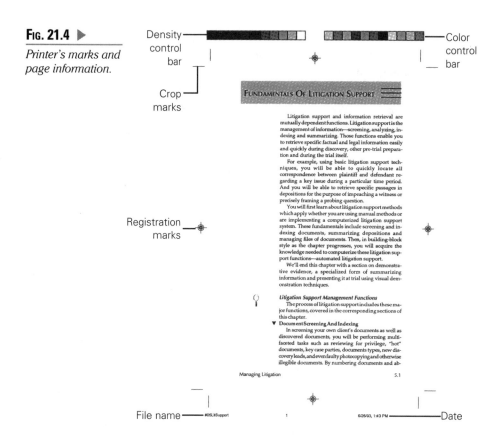

Fig. 21.4 ▶

Printer's marks and page information.

Density control bar

Color control bar

Crop marks

FUNDAMENTALS OF LITIGATION SUPPORT

Registration marks

File name ——— #05LitSupport   1   6/26/93, 1:43 PM ——————— Date

Printer's Marks include crop marks, registration marks, density, and color bars. If you choose printer's marks you will need an extra .75 inch of paper to fit everything on your document. That means, for example, that 7.75×9.25 inches is the largest page size that will print with printer's marks to a letter-size sheet.

Printers use crop marks to trim your printed pages out of the large paper normally used on a commercial printing press. The Color-control bar gives you a reference to check during a pressrun. Density or Calibration bars are used to gauge whether the ink and the imagesetter are running gray levels correctly. Registration marks are the target circles you see in the figure; the print shop lines them up to be sure that different colors of ink are all printing in the proper registration.

Turning on Page Information markings prints on each page the name of the file, page number, name of the spot or separation ink, and the date. It requires .5 inch of extra paper outside the regular size of your pages.

Selecting printer's marks and page information together requires .875 inches of extra paper.

▶ *Center page.* The Center Page In Print Area option centers your page in the normal page area used by your printer.

▶ *Fit.* If you have a PostScript printer, the page preview windows shown in figure 21.5 tell you how well your publication, its printer's marks, and page information will fit on your chosen paper size, based on the information contained in your PPD.

Fig. 21.5 ▶

Two views of your page fit.

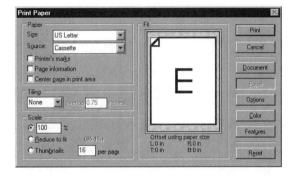

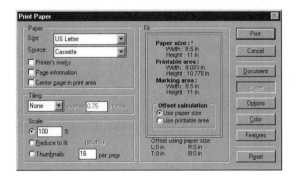

VI

Publishing

Switch between the two page fit views—graphic and numeric—by double-clicking the preview window.

If you exceed the possible print area, the offset numbers will be in red.

The preview shows black if you have chosen to print a negative, and the large E will read backwards if you have chosen to print a mirror image.

▶ *Tiling.* Choose from the Tiling list if you want to print a large page (up to 42 × 42 inches) on smaller pieces of paper. You can then paste up the smaller bits into a big one.

The Auto tile selection tells PageMaker to compute its own collection of tiles. Enter the amount of overlap you want to work with in the text entry box.

Manual tiling lets you take control of how the tiles get broken up. It just seems to work out that auto tiling will put a seam right through the center of a model's nose in your ad layout. The Manual tile option stays selected until you click it off. As long as it is on, PageMaker prints one tile for each time you click OK in the Print command, putting the upper-left hand corner of each tile at the location of the zero point. You adjust the location of the zero point each time before OK'ing again the Print operation, until you've captured the entire page.

There's a wonderful new improvement in tiling for PageMaker 6.0. It remembers whether you want portrait or landscape orientation as you print your tiles. Previous versions would forget you wanted landscape, and you had to remember to reset the orientation for every tile.

▶ *Scaling and reduce to fit.* Another way to print a large image on smaller paper is to scale the image to fit. You can enter any value from 5 percent to 1600 percent.

The easiest way to scale a publication to paper that's too small is to use the Reduce to Fit radio button. Checking this option gives you a terrific proofing tool, because it also allows you to include printer's marks if you are, say, trying to print an 8 1/2-by-11-inch publication page on paper of that same size.

▶ *Thumbnails.* You really can get a good feel for the overall design of a large format document by printing Thumbnails. Somehow looking at a dozen small sketches of pages all together on a single page helps you get an overview sense of how the pages are flowing. In the text box, enter the number of thumbnails you want PageMaker to print on each sheet of paper. You get something that looks like figure 21.6.

Fig. 21.6 ▶

*A thumbnail view
of a publication.*

Customizing Graphics Handling, Printing to Disk, and Overall Efficiency

Switching to the Op<u>t</u>ions mode of the <u>P</u>rint command takes you to functions for optimizing output efficiency for graphics, managing PostScript functions, and getting the most out of your printer's memory (see fig. 21.7).

▶ *Send image data and graphics quality.* The Normal setting in the <u>S</u>end Image Data pop-up menu will send bit-mapped graphics (TIFFs, for example) to the printer at maximum available resolution.

The Optimized setting downsamples graphic images (converts them to lower resolution) on the fly as they are printed. The setting works by sending only the information to the printer that will be needed to achieve best results with the line screen you have chosen in the <u>P</u>rint command's <u>C</u>olor dialog box mode. Bottom line, you can save a lot of time when printing because you don't need to send a scanned picture to the printer at a resolution suitable for a high-resolution imagesetter when you are merely printing proofs on a laser printer. The Optimized setting has been a bit controversial in the past because it is on by default. That means you must remember to switch it to <u>N</u>ormal when outputting to a high-resolution device.

VI

Publishing

Fig. 21.7 ▶

The Options dialog box for the Print command.

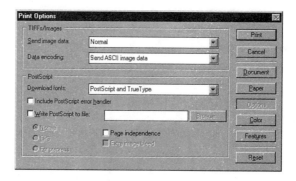

If you like the results (and most do), this option can be a great time-saver. But the biggest time-saver of all would be to scan the photograph at the proper resolution in the first place, and Chapter 23, "Working with the Print Shop," has more on that in the Key Concept section "Understanding Halftones and Screens."

When running proofs you can run the job faster if you use the Low TIFF Resolution mode. Instead of substituting a gray box (like the Proof check box in the Document mode), this option gives you all your graphics but sends to the printer a low-resolution version of any TIFF graphics.

Omit TIFF Files serves its major purpose when you are printing a file to disk, and your service bureau has done your scans. This option gives you an electronic placeholder in the file, where the service bureau's software can slip in the high-resolution scans.

TIP ▶ Maximize Available Memory for Graphics Printing

In Preferences, you can ramp up PageMaker's power to print large graphics when working with a PostScript printer. Go to the More Preferences dialog and the Memory Freed for Graphics setting and choose the Maximum setting. This setting allows PageMaker to temporarily remove fonts from printer memory to make room for graphics processing. It may slow overall print time, but it may make an otherwise unprintable job feasible.

▶ *Data encoding.* If you have TIFF files in your publication, setting Data Encoding to Send Binary Image Data may save you some time. The binary method, being smaller, transmits a TIFF image to the printer in a considerably shorter time, although the printer doesn't work any faster after it has the file. Most DOS/Windows stations are not set up to handle binary PostScript data sent to a printer, so the ASCII won't transmit binary data very well or even at all. The ASCII method is generally the safest choice.

▶ *Managing PostScript.* The PostScript section of the Options dialog box is the tool you use to print to disk. With these settings you can load your publication into a single, self-contained, and (hopefully) goof-proof file or group of files and have your service bureau run the job exactly as you intended. Unless, of course, you goof. You may also want to print to file so you can run the job on a PostScript laser printer elsewhere (perhaps at a computer rental shop), if you don't have one.

If any of these PostScript functions make your eyes glaze over like a couple of 4 a.m. doughnuts, a later section, "Packing Up Your Service Bureau Job," has more on the need or lack thereof for printing your publication to a disk.

▶ *Including downloadable fonts.* You may want to use the Download Fonts option in conjunction with the Page Independence button. If you have chosen to download PostScript and/or TrueType fonts, the fonts in your publication are embedded right in your file. Use this option when you have used fonts that the service bureau may not have (generally anything that's not an Adobe font). This option means your output file uses a lot of hard disk real estate which will make it more cumbersome to transport the file to the service bureau, but it may be absolutely essential to get good results. Again, work it out with your service bureau.

▶ *PostScript error checking.* If you check Include PostScript Error Handler, you include a section of PostScript language code that helps locate problems in a file that burps trying to go through an imagesetter or a laser printer. If you are going to a service bureau, don't check this option without checking with them. Most bureaus have their own PostScript management techniques, and this error handler might just get in the way. Also you might end up paying for a sheet of film that just has an error message on it.

▶ *Writing a PostScript file.* Once you check this box, several features of the dialog become active, and a suggested name is entered in the text box. You can click Browse to get a dialog box where you can tell PageMaker where to store the file on your hard disk. If you wish, it's okay to change the suggested file name in the Write PostScript to File text box.

If you click the Normal radio button, PageMaker names the file with your publication's file name followed by the extension PS to indicate PostScript. The file will be a continuous, multi-page, pure PostScript file.

If you click the EPS button, you get an EPS "picture" of each page, and each page-sized file is named with the first part of the file name, plus the page number, followed by the extension EPS. (Actually, you get a gray box on-screen because the file has no screen preview, but you will get a picture of the page when the EPS is run on a PostScript printer.) Use this setting if the document is to be post-processed by TrapWise or some other page-oriented prepress operation. TrapWise does automatic and highly sophisticated trapping of color files. You can also use EPS if you want to "take a picture" of a page and then load it into another program, such as FreeHand.

If you click For Prepress, the files are named with the file name and the extension SEP. Using this file, you can have your service bureau or the electronic prepress department of your commercial printer run your color separations for you, instead of running the separations out of PageMaker 6.0 yourself.

You also can make use of this setting when your document will be post-processed by one of the Adobe products such as PrePrint Pro or PressWise, or by another application that performs similar functions. PrePrint separates color files with more power and features than you get directly from PageMaker. PressWise is used by the service bureau to assemble your pages into a flat of pages for more efficient runs on the printing press. Your service bureau will tell you if this step is necessary. By the way, PageMaker 6.0 now will separate RGB TIFF files embedded in your publication, in addition to CMYK TIFFs, if you have color management turned on.

▶ *Page independence.* The Page Independence setting has to do with how PageMaker sends PostScript fonts to your printer. You rarely, if ever, check this setting when you are doing a paper printout. On the other hand, if you are printing to a file for prepress purposes, you may want to consider checking this one because it puts font information on each page. That could be a help if the pages will be imposed electronically, requiring the swapping around of pages to make up the printer's flats. To decide whether or not to use Page Independence, consult with your service bureau.

▶ *Extra image bleed.* Check the Extra Image Bleed option when you have a special situation that requires a graphic image to bleed off the page by an extra amount. By default, PageMaker allows a TIFF file to bleed over the edge of a page by 1/8 inch, but checking this option allows a bleed to extend as much as one inch beyond the edge of the electronic page in the print-to-disk file. This option is only available for two of the print-to-disk situations—when outputting EPS or For Separations files.

Selecting Features

If your printer has any special capabilities, they'll be hiding behind this button and available for your selection.

Among other things, the possibilities include duplex printing, the ability to print on both sides of the page. Duplex printing can get pretty confusing, but just keep in mind that your choices in the Orientation command (portrait or landscape) affect your choices for duplex. To keep track of the effects of your decisions just focus on whether the gutter for facing pages runs along the short or long edge of your paper. For example, if you choose portrait orientation and put the gutter on the short edges you will have a spread that opens like a tall legal tablet. If you choose a short edge gutter and landscape, you will have a horizontal book.

If you have a color printer, you are likely to get printer-specific features relating to the type of material you are printing on and any special color-enhancement technology the manufacturer has provided (something like the dialog shown in figure 21.8).

The main thing to understand is that the options you get here are determined by the printer manufacturer, and they are listed in the PPD file for your PostScript printer.

Non-PostScript Printer Differences

Mostly, the foregoing section has been written with the assumption that you are working with the most common printing platform in a desktop publishing situation—a PostScript laser printer. However, the Print command dialog boxes change somewhat if you choose a non-PostScript printer in the chooser.

For a non-PostScript printer, in the main Print command dialog you have a Setup button instead of the Paper button found for PostScript printers. The Setup button is the same one you would get by using the Windows printer setup program in the Control Panel.

If you click on the Features button when a non-PostScript printer has been selected, you will get a notice that you should select printer-specific features using the Setup button.

If you click on Setup, you'll get something that will vary from printer to printer but might look something like the dialog in figure 21.8. As you can see, the dialog takes several forms and offers a number of options, using the Windows 95 tabbed dialog format.

Fig. 21.8 ▶

Printer-specific features.

Comping and Imagesetting Color

If you are like most desktop publishers, your service bureau will be the major user of the Color mode of the Print command (see fig. 21.9). The service bureau, if you submit a PageMaker file for output on their imagesetter, uses this mode as part of the process of separating your publication into film or repro paper.

Before going to the service bureau, however, you will no doubt use this mode to print a laser printer output composite of your publication for approvals and for proofs.

Fig. 21.9 ▶

The Color mode of the Print command.

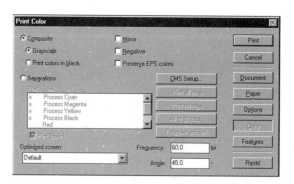

Also, if you send your color project to the service bureau by printing your publication to disk (using the Options dialog box), you need to do part of your setup for outputting the file in the Color dialog box.

All the Color dialog box options are discussed in the following list:

▶ *Composite.* Composite is the way you run almost everything to your laser or color printer. It gives you an assembled view of your publication, combining all the plates of color into a single image.

In Composite, you select the Grayscale button for almost every situation, including output to a laser printer or to a color printer.

The only time you click Print Colors in Black is when you are working on a spot color publication and want PageMaker to run the colors strictly at the gray percentages you have assigned. Any percentage tint, for example, is at that precise equivalent percentage of gray, regardless of the base color. Check with your service bureau or print shop before you use this particular option for material you are submitting to them.

▶ *Mirror and Negative.* Mirror and Negative are the options used to execute such arcane imagesetter film instructions as "right reading, emulsion down." A table is included here to help you figure out the effects of these settings and how they interact with one another.

The key to using the Mirror and Negative settings is to talk to your print shop. Ask the shop to specify what kind of imagesetter film they want in order to properly burn the printing press plates; then follow the print shop's directions. If you check Negative, the film image is reversed, like a black-and-white photographic negative.

Mirror flips the film as if you were holding it up to a mirror. Hence, the terms *right reading* and *wrong reading* mean just what they say. If a film is right reading, you can read it properly. A wrong reading film looks like a mirror image. When you change the Mirror settings, you change the way the film gets sandwiched together with the printing press plate (photo sensitive emulsion facing up or emulsion down).

To grasp the way this interaction works, use table 21.1 and read it from left to right like a decision matrix. For example, the print shop says it wants right reading film with emulsion up. You go to the first column and select right reading, then move over to the second column, where you pick the row containing "Up," for emulsion up. Now read over to the last column, and it tells you that you should set the Mirror check box to off.

TABLE 21.1   PageMaker Commands for Various Combinations of Emulsion

If the Print Shop Wants	and Emulsion Should Be	Then Set Mirror to
Right Reading (reverse off)	Up Down	Off On
Wrong Reading (reverse on)	Up Down	On Off

The most important thing to know about the Mirror and Negative check boxes, however, is to never consider using them unless you have consulted with the print shop and the service bureau.

A great deal of expensive imaged film gets wasted at the hands of DTPers. They make mistakes using these confusing settings when sending their files to a service bureau for output to an imagesetter. Service bureaus have in recent years taken control over this part of the job, because they often end up taking the blame for mistakes of this sort—even if it was really the client's error. If you have printed your publication to disk, as a PostScript file, the prepress output technician is likely to take over this aspect of the job and control these settings manually, right on the imagesetter. If you send the publication file to the service bureau as a PageMaker file, the prepress experts will go into this spot in the Print command and make sure the settings are as you have directed.

▶ *Preserve EPS Colors.* As you know from Chapter 18, PageMaker "adopts" the defined colors contained in an imported EPS graphic. Those adopted color definitions may be edited in PageMaker and used to color items that you create within PageMaker, helping you achieve consistent use of color in your publication. When it comes to print time, however, you may wish to maintain the integrity of the original color definition contained in the imported EPS graphic. Checking this box preserves the colors within the original graphic.

▶ *Separations.* You, or more likely your service bureau, use the Separations function to output mechanicals for color printing at your print shop. You also use Separations when you produce a print-to-disk file to send to your service bureau. However, your most common use of this option will probably be for running a laser writer proof to check the way your layers of color are falling in order to make sure that the right colors have been assigned to the correct objects.

An individual piece of paper or film gets imaged for each ink you choose in this area of the Color dialog box. You choose individual inks for printing by clicking the color in the pull-down list and checking the Print This Ink check box.

The column of buttons just to the right of the ink list contains two ultrahip new PageMaker features. They are good features in the first place, but it's even better that you can access them here at output time, in addition to their locations in the main part of the PageMaker program.

First, CMS Setup gives you complete access to Version 6.0's new color management capabilities, covered in Chapter 20, "Meeting Color Challenges."

The Remove Unused button allows you to get rid of colors that have been defined but remained unused in your publication. Service bureaus around the world are rejoicing over this feature. You should too, because it means you won't be paying for blank sheets of film. PageMaker will follow orders explicitly and turn out a sheet of film for each defined ink color, whether there's anything on that sheet or not. The Removed Unused button allows you to get rid of not only the colors but also the problem. It is covered in Chapter 18, "Creating Colors."

TIP ▶ Convert to Process in Define Colors, Not the Print Dialog Box

The All To Process option stands to get you in big time trouble if you are producing a publication where color accuracy is critical. As discussed in the section "Converting Between Color Systems" in Chapter 18, when you convert spot colors to process colors, you are putting the fate of your publication in the hands of PageMaker's color conversion algorithms. Often, your publication will turn out just fine. However, there's no such thing as a perfect conversion between color systems, and you must be careful to evaluate the resulting color accuracy with a healthy dose of cynicism.

Why would you use the All To Process button? It may be the fastest and most accurate means available to consolidate a long list of colors into four plates, the CMYK colors. Chances are that you'll be much better off using the techniques described in Chapters 19, "Applying Colors," and 20, "Meeting Color Challenges," to consolidate colors on a case-by-case basis in the Define Colors dialog boxes. In any case, never convert to process colors and then go to press without running a color proof to check the conversion results.

Also in this column of buttons, notice that the Print All Inks and Print No Inks buttons allow you to make some quick choices of ink layers. You might, for example, use the Print No Inks button to quickly deselect all the inks before selecting a single ink from the list.

▶ *Screens.* You must choose your screen frequency in collaboration with your print shop. Mostly, you probably shouldn't mess with screen settings unless there's some specific reason to do so and you've talked it over with your print shop operator.

Much depends on the paper and printing techniques that are used in your publication, and to make this determination, you begin at the end of the chain of steps in the publication process and work your way back. For that reason, all our discussions of halftones and resolution has been put in Chapter 23, "Working with the Print Shop."

As you know, screens are required to print photographs, gradations, blends, tints, screens, and anything else that requires you to put grayscale information on a laser printer, imagesetter, or printing press.

VI

Publishing

If you are trying for a special effect, you may have adjusted the screen frequency in the Image control dialog box, and in that case the Image control setting overrides whatever you do here—but only for the particular image you adjusted in Image control.

You have to decide on two issues: the screen frequency and the screen angle. The frequency of the line screen, the number of lines per inch, determines the resolution of detail achieved on the printing press.

Ordinarily, you simply choose your PPD in the Document Print command dialog box. The PPD contains a list of suggested screen settings, which show up here in the Print Color dialog box, and you choose whatever setting has been suggested by your print shop from the pull-down list. The process is that simple, unless you have some particularly challenging problem.

For black-and-white and spot color work, unless you are trying some special effect, the angle of the screen is always 45 degrees, and screens are only used by PageMaker when you have imported a halftone (grayscale) graphic. Many publications utilizing spot color don't use screens at all, unless you have asked for a tint setting at some point in the layout.

The screen angles in process color work have been standardized by tradition for many years, and it's a rare day when you want to change them. Change them only in consultation with your print shop. For example, if you have moiré patterns in your color proofs, you need to talk to the prepress professionals and your print shop about making screen angle adjustments. They know what to do. Also, if you are running five colors and the spot color has been assigned to a graphic, you need to know what screen angle to assign to the spot color.

The standard screen angles for the process colors are 105 degrees for cyan, 75 degrees for magenta, 90 degrees for yellow, and 45 degrees for black.

Optimizing Your Laser Printer Output Results

The tricks in this section help you get the most out of your laser printer—everything from richer blacks to higher resolution.

Poor Person's High-Resolution Output

Nothing beats a high-resolution imagesetter for getting typeset level quality. You can vastly improve the quality from your 300- or 600-dots-per-inch laser printer, however, by scaling up the output in the Document option of the Print command. Be sure to note exactly the amount of scaling you have done and then reduce the page to correct size when it's being reproduced (for example, tell the print shop, or use the zoom percentage on your photocopy machine).

You increase the dots per inch by the percentage of your scaling move and thereby make your final product crisper. Of course, you must be able to fit the entire page on the 8 1/2 × 11-inch letter-sized paper you are probably using. If you are working with a 6 × 9-inch final page size, you can scale it up by as much as 122 percent, depending on whether or not you need to leave room for printer's marks.

Adjust Toner Amount

Take a look at the fine print on your page. See if the openings on the letters are plugging up with toner. Try adjusting the toner for the finest possible rendering of your letters.

Rock It and Clean It

Every once in awhile, pull your laser cartridge and rock it back and forth, from side to side. The motion evenly distributes the toner inside the cartridge.

Also, use the tool provided with the laser printer to scrape along the corona wire inside the cartridge. Check your manufacturer's directions, but on most printers this wire is located behind a black plastic covered slot.

Clean the rest of the machine's insides while you are at it, again following the manufacturer's directions.

Fixative Spray

You get blacker blacks if you spray your laser pages with artists' fixative, available at art stores. Some people use hair spray. In any case, do it in a ventilated area.

Warm Up with All Black Pages

When you have an important job and you are using laser mechanicals for reproduction, "warm up" your laser printer by running some all-black pages through it. The first page will be sort of streaky, and you will never get a perfect black because of the nature of laser printers. However, the final black copy will have a denser black than the first one. Run ten or so. This trick works because the drum picks up laser toner thanks to static electricity generated within the unit. The all-black pages evenly build the static charge to maximum levels over the entire surface of the drum.

To make an all-black page just draw a box on the page and fill it with 100 percent black. This page also graphically demonstrates to you just how much of the edges of your page are unreachable for your laser printer because of memory limitations and the mechanical construction needed to grip and feed the paper.

VI

Publishing

Print to Rented 11" x 17" for Imposition and Bleeds

Speaking of usable, printable area, if you need to do bleeds off the edge of a page of 8 1/2 × 11-inch paper, you need a large format laser printer. If you don't own one, check the local computer rental shops where you can go in and pay for using a machine by the hour. After your project is all set, take it to the shop and run it on 11 × 17-inch paper. You get a full-size page and all your crop marks so the printer can trim the bleed edges. At least in large cities, these computer rental places are reproducing like guppies.

High-Resolution Laser Is Not the Same as Phototypesetter

"Great," you say, "I'll just run down to the computer rental place and run this on their 1,200 dpi laser printer. That's just as good as 1,240 dpi imagesetter output, isn't it?"

Nope. The dots per inch are comparable sure enough, and many fine publications use high-resolution laser printers for mechanicals that go to the print shop. But the two processes are different.

The photographic reproduction of a 1,200 dpi imagesetter will always be much better than the reproduction of a 1,200 dpi laser printer. A laser printer's toner fused into paper simply can't do the job as well as dots imaged onto photo sensitive paper or film in an imagesetter.

Use a high-resolution laser, sure. But don't fool yourself that it's just as good for a high-end project.

Also, laser printer mechanical workings aren't nearly as accurate as imagesetters. Some people run color separations from laser printers, but the results can be a major disappointment as well as a major headache to your printer who is trying to achieve registration.

Laser Photos on Copiers

The idea may seem a bit perverse, but a coarser line screen sometimes gives you better results if you are doing laser output for photocopying. Whether or not this fact holds true for your project depends a great deal on the photograph and on your photocopier, so you need to experiment. Try a 45-line screen, for example, and compare it to the results you get with your laser printer's standard 53 or 60 lines per inch.

Use Special Papers

Browse through office supply, art supply, and mail order catalogs for special laser papers. One outfit (Paper Direct) offers preprinted and scored brochures on card stock with multi-color blends and art on them, specially designed for running through a laser printer. This stock is great for small run stuff, and the final product looks almost like it came from a color press. Well, it did, actually. It went through the press before being sent to you, and you just added your black text over the top. The suppliers offer more than brochures, of course, that's just an example of the special papers available.

Also, use the high-contrast, pure white laser paper for laser writer mechanicals. The extra-white and smooth surface provides a superior foundation for the particles of laser toner and gives you better results on the press.

For color inkjets, even the really inexpensive ones, the results can be improved by an astonishing degree if you use special-purpose papers designed to hold the tiny dots sprayed onto the paper by the printhead.

Laser Shirts, Foil Embossing, and More

You can run special iron-on paper through your printer to do t-shirts, and you can emboss display heads with foil. The Flash, a laser printer specialist, has made a cottage industry out of supplying special laser cartridges with toner that heat-transfers to fabric. They also carry other weird stuff, like materials for making rubber stamps with a process that uses your laser printer. The foil embossing materials are available from a variety of sources.

Give the Landfill a Rest

C'mon, you know that those laser cartridges are reusable. No sense tossing them in the landfill. Even if you aren't one of the folks who buy refilled cartridges, other folks do. Besides, some office supply stores and refillers are paying for these cartridges. That's better than a sharp stick poked in your eye, isn't it?

Using Printer Styles

Printer Styles have now been fully incorporated into PageMaker. Behind the scenes the function is still a Plug-in, but it has now been given a menu position of its own, and you don't need to go to the Utilities menu to access the feature.

Another terrific grace note to the updated Printer Styles function is the ability to create style definitions on the fly. While in the Print dialog box, get it set just the way you want it and then hold down the Ctrl key. The text inside the Print button will switch to say Style, and you can click the button to define a new style based on the current Print command settings. Just name the style when the dialog box comes up, and that's all it takes.

You access the new Printer Styles command through the File menu.

Choose an existing printer style from the submenu, and the Print dialog box will open up, all set up as defined in the style. Click Print (or Save if you are printing to a file), and your job will be on its way—either to the printer or to a file, depending on what you specified in the style. You can go around the Print dialog box and straight to printing by holding down the Shift key while selecting a printer style.

A few attributes can't be defined in a style so you must set them before okaying your print job. For example, style definitions can't include a range of pages. Spot color ink frequency and angle settings are also not available.

To create a new style, either use the Ctrl+Print(Style) command or choose the Define submenu. The Define choice leads you to the Printer Styles main dialog box (see fig. 21.10).

Fig. 21.10 ▶

The main dialog box for Printer Styles.

Click New, and you'll be asked to name your new style. Then select it and click the Edit button to define the parameters of your new style using a group of dialog boxes that nearly duplicates the Print command suite of dialog boxes. To copy an existing style, set that style before beginning the definition of a new style.

Set all your options in the surrogate Print dialog boxes, and click the OK button when you are done. (OK replaces the Print button.)

The printer styles command saves your definitions in a file called PSTYLES.CNF. You can share these files among colleagues.

In addition to the New button, you have an Edit button to modify existing printer styles and a Remove button to delete a style.

Using the Build Booklet Plug-in

You'll love Build Booklet. It's based on the high-end (and very expensive) page imposition program from Adobe called PressWise, and it brings some of that power to your very own desktop.

In fact, Build Booklet will do something for you that PageMaker alone can't do. It'll make up a three or four panel spread, as you might compose for a brochure. It will also assemble the pages of a booklet—or a full-sized book—into the proper order for running on large press sheets instead of on the 8 1/2 × 11 sheets we normally use in laser printers and photocopiers.

Taking the Imposition Risk

One exciting, but scary, new feature of Build Booklet is the fact that it will work with PageMaker's Book printing feature.

But before you put Build Booklet to work on a really big project, ask yourself one big question. Do you really, really want to do your own imposition on that 300-page book? If you do the imposition on a publication, you take on a certain amount of risk—risk that the print shop normally assumes for you.

For example, if you are going to saddle stitch (or center staple) your book, how much creep should you apply? Creep happens because paper isn't so thin when you put together a number of sheets of it. Think about how a ream of 500 sheets is. So, in a book, each sheet folded together adds to the thickness of the middle fold, and that means the outside edges of the folded pages will creep out away from the center. If you make a bad creep adjustment, or no adjustment at all, the outer margins will be too narrow on the outermost pages. If you are going to assemble 20 pages or more, the creep problems are big enough that you should consider having your binding done by the printer. Certainly, you should consider breaking your publication down into smaller subassemblies called gathered signatures, which are then assembled into a perfect style binding designed to solve just this problem.

Then there's the page order. Actually, we should say the pages out-of-order. If you print two pages to a sheet and stack up 16 pages worth, you have a total of four sheets, printed front and back. But page 1 actually comes second, after page 16, and page 15 will be on the same sheet as page 2, on the back side of the sheet with pages 16 and 1. It can get pretty confusing—and that's an example of the simplest kind of binding—a single pair of pages on each side of a sheet. If you were doing more pages to a sheet, called multiple ups, you could hardly be blamed for getting a headache trying to figure it all out. Fortunately, Build Booklet has been created just for the purpose of helping you with this problem, but you definitely assume some risk. It's expensive to screw up.

VI

Publishing

So when should you use Build Booklet? It's great for multi-panel brochures and small booklets, and it can save you a lot of tedium and possibly some money if you use laser printer output for mechanicals. Just be sure to coordinate with your printer when you figure out your layout so you can be sure to take into account their needs for the printing press, the folding machine, and the trimming guillotine. Printers know this stuff cold and can tell you just what they need to see.

Don't even consider using Build Booklet without making a test of the way the pages come out of the laser printer. Dummy up the pages to see that the work is just right, and use the dummy to communicate with the printer about the way you want the pages to go together.

Getting Ready

In England, they sometimes call imposition by a different name. They say "planning." That's really an appropriate way to put it. Remember that you must plan ahead for imposition spreads. If your finished pages are 8 1/2 × 11 inches, there's no way you'll get two of them side by side on legal-size sheets.

It's terribly important that you start your booklet with an odd-numbered page. Build Booklet just assumes you will do so.

Double-check to be sure that you have plenty of hard drive space. Build Booklet does a great deal of disk work, because it builds an entirely new publication from your original, which will be left untouched.

Do your imposition last, after all your layout work has been completed. That includes indexing and running your table of contents one last time. Working on the Build Booklet spreads to correct typos will not make you happy.

Building a Booklet

You'll find Build Booklet under the Utilities menu in the PageMaker Plug-ins submenu, assuming you installed it with PageMaker. You'll get a dialog box like the one in figure 21.11.

First, select what kind of layout you want to use. You get a pull-down list, shown in figure 21.12.

A 2-up Saddle Stitch means two pages side by side, with the large sheet they are printed on, folded down the middle, and stapled or stitched. It's your regular old booklet arrangement, and when you stack up all the pages, two by two, you end up with them all in the correct order.

VI

Publishing

FIG. 21.11 ▶

The main Build Booklet dialog box.

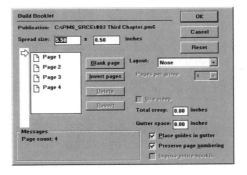

FIG. 21.12 ▶

Choosing your booklet layout.

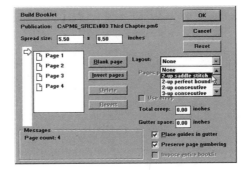

When you choose 2-up Perfect Bound, you are creating more than one sub-booklet, so the series of booklets can then be collated and bound into a bigger perfect-bound book, one solution for the creep problem. When you choose this option, the Pages Per Group (per subbooklet) text entry box is active. You tell the Build Booklet addition how many pages to cluster in each intermediate booklet, and then, when you stack them all up, the booklets are arranged so the page numbers are properly consecutive. You must consult with your printer and bindery when constructing a perfect-bound imposition plan. There are some important variables to consider, such as the size of sheet the press will take and thus how many pages should go in a group to best fit on that sheet.

The consecutive layout options (2-up Consecutive, 3-up Consecutive, and 4-up Consecutive) are side-by-side arrangements, as you'd see when you put together a multi-panel brochure.

When you pick a layout, check the upper-left corner of the Build Booklet dialog box for the spread size. If the indicated size won't fit on the paper you're using, you need to print to a bigger sheet of paper or go back and change the page size of your original publication.

If you chose one of the saddle or perfect-bound options, you can set your creep, after you get advice from the printer. If you are on your own (maybe you're running your pages in a photocopier), there's only one way to get the creep setting: Dummy up the job using the actual paper you'll specify for the work. Make sharp folds in the sheets, and fit them together just as you'll do when you assemble the book. Measure the difference between the edge of the outer page and the edge of the innermost page. That's your creep value.

Normally, you specify gutters by setting your inside margin in page setup with Facing Pages turned on. You can also add space here in Build Booklet by entering a measurement in the Gutter Space text entry box.

Placing a guide in the gutter means that you'll have a ruler guide running down the page between the pages that Build Booklet combines into single sheet layouts.

Preserve the page numbering by checking the Preserve Page Numbering check box, if you like. More on this in a minute.

Check the next box if you wish to impose the entire book list. This option will be grayed out and unavailable if no book list has been established for the publication that was active when you called up the Build Booklet Plug-in.

Ordinarily, if you needed to do some page re-ordering you would probably use the Sort Pages Plug-in. But Build Booklet lets you adjust page order at this point in the process if you like. Just select the page (or pages) by pressing the Alt key and using the stacked pages icon to drag the page to its new location. You can select multiple pages by using Shift+click to choose a series of adjacent pages and Ctrl+click to choose multiple noncontiguous pages.

You don't need to sort the pages, mind you. The Build Booklet Addition automates this process for you. Mostly, you'll sort pages so you can arrange the folds of a brochure or, more likely, so you can add blank pages where they need to go if you are working in the perfect-bound layout format, where you need to insert blank pages between groups of pages (signatures).

To insert a blank page, click the horizontal arrow pointer at the location you want the new page, and click the Blank Page option.

You can delete pages by selecting them and pressing the Delete button. Toggle between regular and reverse order with the Invert Pages button.

You can always take back all your changes with the Revert or Reset buttons.

When you have everything all set, click the OK button. PageMaker asks if you want to save the current publication, of course, and then builds a completely new publication with the pages arranged as you directed.

Build Booklet strips all the items off your master pages (master pages will be blank in the new publication) and puts them on the proper pages. For example, instead of auto page numbering, you will have hard-coded manual page numbers wherever the page marker occurred on your master pages.

TIP ▷ Turn Off Snap Settings Before Running Build Booklet

Leave S̲nap To Rulers and S̲nap To Guides turned off before running Build Booklet. When Build Booklet reassembles all your pages, it will be flying all the objects on those pages around in PageMaker. If the Snap settings are on, the objects may be sucked out of the positions they held on their original pages.

Preventing the Output Time Blues

In the days when you could buy a gallon of gas for a quarter, the designer really couldn't get in too much trouble—couldn't accidentally design an impossible-to-print page. For one thing, there were some limitations to what you could accomplish with physical pasteup technology. For another, the print shop and its staff of strippers translated the design to the press and acted as a last line of defense.

Now, you design things on your screen, an electronic form of pasteup, and can do things that the graphic artist of yore never even imagined. And you don't get the automatic benefit of a press person's advice, because you generate final film to give to the print shop. The result? Sometimes designers create absolutely unprintable files that just plain won't work in the laser printer or imagesetter, let alone the printing press.

The tips in this section help you avoid that fate. Not only will they make your job print faster, but these tricks may make all the difference in whether a publication containing large graphics images or especially complex designs will run through the laser printer or imagesetter at all.

Use Checklists and Consultations

Most service bureaus and print shops provide checklists you can use to make sure you have handled your files correctly. Even more important, as we have advised throughout this book, consult with your print shop and your service bureau when your publication is at the planning stage.

Buff That File

As you are doodling your way to a final design, you naturally do a lot of experimentation. The result often is a very rough file that looks terrific on the surface but prints slowly or not at all because it has been filled with electronic land mines that are bound to choke the imagesetter at the service bureau (or your

VI

Publishing

personal laser printer if you are producing laser mechanicals). Buff it down. Go through your electronic pasteup and polish the rough artifacts that will sandbag you at deadline time. It may seem like a bother, but it may save your deadline.

Here's why: when you manipulate an image in PageMaker, it hasn't been fundamentally changed. PageMaker has imported the unrotated, unsized, uncropped, and unskewed graphic as is; it then applies all your manipulations to a screen image of the graphic. The graphic still exists in it's original form, unchanged. At output time, PageMaker sends all the instructions for each page to the laser printer or imagesetter, ready for processing by your PostScript output device. In order to calculate your page image in its own computer, the PostScript printer must then swallow your entire graphic image before it can conduct any of the cropping, sizing, rotation, or any of the other transformations you have created within PageMaker. Thus, any image manipulation you do must actually be done twice, once in PageMaker and again inside the laser printer or imagesetter. This process takes a lot of time and could cause your job to abort when you are on deadline. At minimum, a job with manipulated images takes longer to print.

One step you can take is to proof your job on your PostScript laser printer before sending it to the service bureau. If your laser printer chokes on a file, it's giving you a good clue that you have a file complexity problem. It's true that an imagesetter has a more powerful computer, but in this case that doesn't mean the imagesetter will be able to pass a gallstone-sized file that a laser printer could not manage. The imagesetter has many more calculations to compute. The calculations required for a 2,400-dot-per-inch imagesetter to draw a page are geometrically higher than those required for a 300-dpi laser printer. Therefore, the imagesetter is performing a job with orders of magnitude more complex than the laser printer.

Also, go through and consolidate all the color definitions and use the Remove Unused Colors command. If yours is a two-color job, you should have only two colors listed in your Colors palette. See the section "Making Color Consistent Within and Between Publications" in Chapter 18, "Creating Colors," for more information.

Size and Crop Graphics Before Placing Them

Do as much sizing and cropping as possible before placing your graphics. One service bureau tells the story of a designer who needed to place elements from a page of electronic clip art. The clip art file contained a few dozen images. Instead of cutting the file into pieces and individually placing each fragment of art, the designer placed the entire file a couple of dozen times and cropped the large image each time. The result was a huge file that took forever to run through the imagesetter.

If you are going to reduce a scanned photo, do it before you place it. If you plan to take that 8×10-inch scan down to a 2×2-inch sized and cropped image, scan it at a lower resolution in the first place. When you reduce it, you end up with the final resolution you need anyway, and you will save tons of imagesetting time.

Remember, your bit-mapped images (scans and TIFFs) only need to be twice the resolution of your line screen frequency, and some people say that one-and-a-half times is just fine.

No White Boxes, Please

It seems like the most natural thing to do; simply place a white box over some graphic or text you want to eliminate from a page. But again, remember that the PostScript device actually computes all the objects on your page from the back layer forward. Even though you can't see what you hid behind the white box, the imagesetter or laser printer sees it and spends time computing the hidden image just so it can be covered over by the white box.

Yes, sometimes you can't avoid the dreaded white box trick. But try. In the old days before Version 6.0, the white box syndrome often came from trying to select only certain master page items for inclusion on a given page. Now we have multiple masters instead, so that'll help a lot.

One service bureau tells the tale of a client who did a monthly newsletter. Every month the thing ran through the imagesetter slower and slower. Finally, after some months, it just plain wouldn't print. Investigation revealed the problem. The designer had simply put white boxes over the previous month's edition and put a whole new publication on top of the old one. It was like unearthing an archeological find.

Complex Graphics Can Choke the Output Device

Nesting EPS files inside one another can create a boggling mess of computation for your laser printer or the imagesetter at the service bureau. Simplify if you possibly can.

If you have more than a dozen blends in a single page, you are probably asking for trouble.

If your placed graphic is causing problems at output time, try going back to the drawing program that was used to create the graphic and reduce the complexity of curves and masks. In the drawing program, see if you can reduce the number of points on the curve, or use the Flatness command (FreeHand calls it that) to reduce the complexity of an element.

Paste Inside Masks Can Be Problems

This one ranks right up there with nested EPS files. When you mask something (FreeHand calls it Paste Inside) you require the laser printer or imagesetter to compute all the objects and then meld them. This process takes time and can make a file blow up at output time. That warning doesn't mean you should never mask objects; it just means you may want to look for another method of achieving the same effect, and you should try to simplify the effect as much as possible. Do test your masking effects on your laser printer to see if they print okay before going to expensive time on an imagesetter.

By the way, the new version 6.0 Mask command, unlike the Crop tool effect, sends all data to the printer just like the EPS masking effect you get from your drawing program. It won't solve this issue of the difficulty to output complex masks.

Avoid Embedding Text in EPS Files

One form of nesting is including text in an EPS drawing. Sometimes the imagesetter or laser printer just can't see that font because it has been included in an EPS file, and you get an ugly Courier font substitution.

Of course, you often need to put text in an EPS file. So, instead of leaving the text in the form of an actual font, consider converting it to a graphic object. In FreeHand, this is the Convert To Paths command. This conversion has two benefits. First, you don't have to worry about the service bureau not having some unusual font you used. Convert To Paths makes the graphic into a font-independent image. Second, all the computation involved in whatever fancy manipulation you did on the font is done in advance, making the graphic simpler to print. This last bit doesn't hold true if there is a lot of text. It's not practical to convert a lot of small text (12 point for example), but it works really well to covert display size type (headline size).

One caveat about Convert To Paths, this may be counterproductive if you have a lot of text, or the text is set in a smaller type size. The process of converting to paths can sometimes thicken type and change its spacing. Also, converting a page full of body copy to paths will introduce an imagesetting choking amount of complexity to a page.

If it makes sense for your particular layout situation, consider setting the type in PageMaker over the top of the plain graphic. Text and graphic could then be welded together using the Group command. This has the advantage of being editable right in PageMaker, so you don't need to go out to your drawing program to make type changes.

Rotate Graphics Before Placement

It's great that PageMaker can rotate text and objects. However, you save printing time and reduce file complexity if you rotate objects outside PageMaker. Even though you have rotated a graphic in PageMaker, it is not rotated when it is first sent to the imagesetter. The out device takes in the entire object and then recomputes the rotation all over again as it composes the page in its own computer. As described earlier, the rotation actually must be done twice; that's simply the way PostScript works. The difference in printing time is particularly noticeable for TIFF files. In some cases where the file is very large, this rotation issue prevents the file from printing. Consider rotating TIFF files in your photo retouching program, such as Adobe Photoshop. This tip also applies for EPS files that contain TIFF files.

Avoid TrueType Fonts and WMFs (Imagesetter)

These two beasties are not PostScript file formats. The desktop publishing community is increasingly accepting of TrueType fonts, but most service bureaus give you the death stare when you use them.

Compute Blend Steps to Avoid Banding

When you create a blend in a drawing or painting program such as Illustrator or Photoshop, you are asking your printer to make a smooth transition from a starting percentage of gray (or a color) to an ending percentage. Because of the mechanical process of creating one of these gradations, however, blends are subject to an unsightly effect called *banding*. This effect varies from really bad to barely noticeable or even nonexistent, depending on variables that you must design for if you want to limit the problem. Those variables are the screen frequency you are using, the dots-per-inch resolution of your laser printer or imagesetter, the starting and ending percentages of the blend and the length of the blend. Because of these variables, your laser printer or imagesetter sometimes doesn't have enough levels of gray to work with in order to make a smooth blend.

Banding happens because the steps of gray in the blend become visible, as you can see in figure 21.13. In this illustration, all the blends are the same, except one of the variables that can cause banding has been varied. All these blends are from 20 percent to 90 percent of gray, but the screen frequency has been varied. The top gradated bar has been printed at a screen of 25 lines per inch. Each bar gets a progressively finer screen in 5 lpi intervals, continuing up to 55 lpi. Notice how the banding becomes more and more obvious as the screen frequency increases.

Fig. 21.13 ▶

A series of blends showing how banding—sometimes called stepping—varies with the screen frequency.

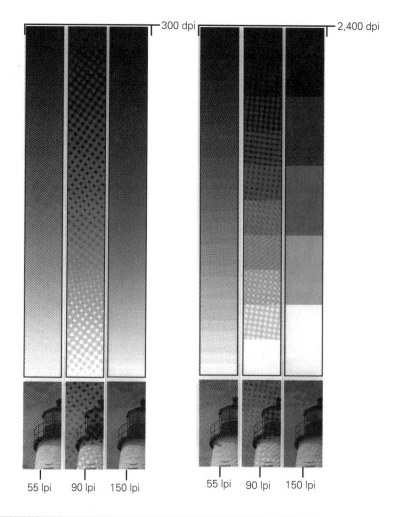

TIP ▶ No Spot-to-Spot Color Blends, Use CMYK

Don't create a blend from one spot color to another. Yes, the process looks like it works on the screen, but that's just proof of how electronic pasteup can fool you into creating impossible designs that turn out looking terrible on the printing press. The problem is that your monitor is displaying RGB color and doesn't give an accurate rendition of how some spot colors will appear when mixed as ink on paper. Unless you like mud, use with caution! You can't have a blend between two colors unless you mix them. Process colors, defined using CMYK, are designed to mix, and you can create reliable blends from one color to another in that color system.

Happily, both Illustrator and FreeHand automatically calculate a suggested number of steps for the blend you are trying to create; so banding has recently become a less common difficulty. By understanding banding, however, will help you avoid it completely.

Keep in mind also that banding in your laser proofs often won't be a problem by the time the file runs through a high-resolution imagesetter and is subjected to the printing press. On the other hand, if your final mechanicals are coming out of a 300- or 600-dpi laser printer, you really need to keep banding in mind. And, of course, you can't completely rule out the possibility of banding on an imagesetter.

You prevent banding by computing the optimum number of steps you need in the blend before you create it. To repeat the concept, banding is caused by the limited number of gray levels a PostScript device can achieve over a given distance for a given line-screen frequency. Because your line screen is preordained in collaboration with your print shop, your best bet is to see how many steps you can fit into a given space for that screen frequency, as in this formula:

Steps = $(DPI/LPI)^2$ multiplied by the Change Percentage

You can break this formula down into these steps:

1. Divide the printer resolution (dpi) by the line screen (lpi) and square the result. Hold that number.

2. Subtract the low tint percentage from the high tint percentage for the percentage of change, the range of the blend.

3. Multiply those two numbers, and you get the optimum number of steps to enter into the blend command in your drawing program.

To find out how wide your steps will be for a given blend width, use this formula:

Step Width = Distance divided by Number of Steps

The figures should all be in points. If your step width will be any wider than one point ($^1/_2$ point is better), you may perceive banding in your printout.

Rather not deal with all this nonartistic, overly technical math? Here's a rule of thumb. For every 10 percent of change in the blend percentages, allow 26 steps. You would need, then, 216 steps to cover a blend from 20 percent to 80 percent.

To double-check your blend for suitability, be alert for banding problems if your blend doesn't fit this formula:

Highest LPI = Imagesetter Resolution/16

Your lines-per-inch screen frequency should be no higher than the resolution of your output device divided by 16.

Strictly from the point of view of doing blends, if you are going to a 2,450-dot imagesetter, your screen frequency should be no higher than 150 to get good blend results.

VI

Publishing

Packaging Up Your Service Bureau Job

This section describes the logistics of assembling a service bureau imagesetter run. You should use this section hand-in-hand with the section "Preventing the Output Time Blues," a guide to things you can avoid in order to keep your file from turning out badly at the service bureau.

Deciding on a Tactic

You have a tactical decision to make before you begin getting your job together for the service bureau. Do you send the service bureau a PageMaker file, or do you print to disk and send a PostScript file?

This discussion is a little bit biased in favor of sending the native PageMaker file. The Macintosh edition of this book has a major bias towards native PageMaker files, but it is harder to make that strong a case on the Windows side of things.

The news is getting better and better all the time, however. A few years back, service bureaus were virtually all Macintosh-based, and it was nearly impossible to find a service bureau that had PC capabilities, or one that was Mac-based and willing to solve the cross-platform leap. Back then, a lot of PC-based PageMaker designers knew more about what it took to talk to an imagesetter from Windows than their service bureau "experts." Today, you should be able to find a PC-hip service bureau in your area. Still, veteran PC-based designers feel safer when sending in a PostScript file for imaging.

Consider the points in the following sections as you decide whether to send a native PageMaker file or a print-to-disk PostScript file.

Taking Responsibility

Your decision between these two options primarily revolves around responsibility. Who has the most responsibility for the final result? If you send a PostScript file, your service bureau will love you because you are taking them off the hook. You, on the other hand, will be completely on the hook for any wasted film, repro paper, and time on the system.

Being Tamper Proof Versus Being Rescued

If you send the native PageMaker file, the prepress techs at the service bureau who look at problem files every day may catch problems when they preflight the project before putting it into the production queue. They may even be willing to fix small problems for you. You are ultimately responsible, of course, for problems caused by your design, but most service bureaus take some initiative to see that your file will run properly. In other words, if you submit a native PageMaker file, you give the service bureau the chance to rescue you if it turns out to be a problem. They may charge something for their work, but it may save your deadline, and it is likely to be far less expensive than running a job that can't ultimately be used.

On the other hand, if you don't want anybody mucking about in your document, the print-to-disk method pretty much eliminates that worry for you. Also, there have been cases when a Mac-based service bureau ran a PC file from a Mac, knowing that the PageMaker files are cross-platform compatible. Problem is, the fonts aren't the same on the two platforms. Carefully placed fractions, a characteristic of PC fonts, get replaced with ligatures, common in Mac fonts. Such a disaster would not, of course, be your fault, but trying to settle the resulting dispute with the service bureau won't be easy or fun.

Dealing with Special Situations

In some situations, you may decide that you need to be tamper-proof. Perhaps you have done something special in the file, such as defining your own crop marks, or maybe you are nervous that the service bureau will screw up an unusual setting that you have implemented. Maybe you used an unusual font, and you want to be font independent. You may be worried about your carefully hyphenated copy reflowing on the page. In short, you could have a bunch of reasons for wanting to lock your files down.

TIP ▶ Submit Original Files Just in Case

If you do decide to submit print-to-disk PostScript files, give yourself a backup option in case there's a problem in running the file. Despite your best efforts, you may have forgotten a setting. It could happen. Include on your disk a copy of the original document, hidden away in a folder titled "SPARE" or some such name. If a problem occurs, you can simply tell the service bureau tech to go to the original publication file.

Negotiating Lower Rates with a Service Bureau

If the service bureau knows you and knows that you are going to submit a good file, the print-to-disk method might just save you some money. After all, dumping the file to the imagesetter, without worrying about finding fonts and such, is a lot easier for the prepress technicians. And you will bear the cost and risk if the file is bad. With this in mind, assuming the service bureau is confident of your track record in building printable documents, you just might be able to negotiate a lower rate.

Regardless of your tactical decision about a print-to-disk submission, do try to negotiate a discount on a big project. A 300-page book of straightforward files that the bureau can run overnight, without any hitches, is the kind of volume that can be seductive to the service bureau.

VI

Publishing

Prove that you have done a good proof. Show that the files have at least run okay on a laser printer, and if you use a more elaborate proofing method (such as LaserCheck), demonstrate how the service bureau can feel confident that your publication will run on the imagesetter without any problems. Time on the system costs money, and trouble-free files are more profitable than files that give "time out" errors and trigger a cycle of madness as the service bureau attempts to troubleshoot your file over and over again.

If you can, get the file in early and negotiate price with the service bureau on the basis of deadline. If the service bureau can run your 300-page book over a week's time, using it to fill in otherwise dead schedule holes, they may be inclined to give you a discount in return.

More and more print shops are offering service bureau-type prepress services. Many already have imagesetters, and many more are acquiring them, as a natural extension of their traditional roles of offering typesetting and stripping physical, pasteup-type mechanicals. You may be able to get a good deal by bringing your entire job to a full service operation. By packaging the entire job together, you represent a larger single piece of business and may be in a more attractive negotiating position. They won't give you prepress services at no charge—the equipment costs way too much money for that—but they may discount their prepress work as a means of capturing your printing business.

Specifying Your Service Bureau Run

The three top causes of bad imagesetter runs are poorly filled out disk submission forms, missing fonts, and poor proofing practices. Avoid those pitfalls and save yourself lots of time and money in the long run (even though the process of filling out forms isn't a tenth of as much fun as designing dynamite pages).

Figures 21.14, 21.15, and 21.16 include a number of service bureau forms, just to give you an idea of how they work.

The following list describes the submission form's elements. If you have decided to run a print-to-disk PostScript file, many of the items in this list are your responsibility, and you set them in the various dialog boxes for the Print command:

▶ *Contact info.* Don't just include the company name. Include the name of the person responsible for decision making on the publication and if possible include after-hours contact numbers as well. Time on the system is everything at a service bureau, and the ability to reach you at a moment's notice may keep your job from being bumped. Your deadline is at stake.

▶ *Time line.* The shorter the deadline, the more the job will cost you.

FIG. 21.14 ▶

The Disk Submission Form used by Holland Litho Service, Inc., in Holland, Michigan

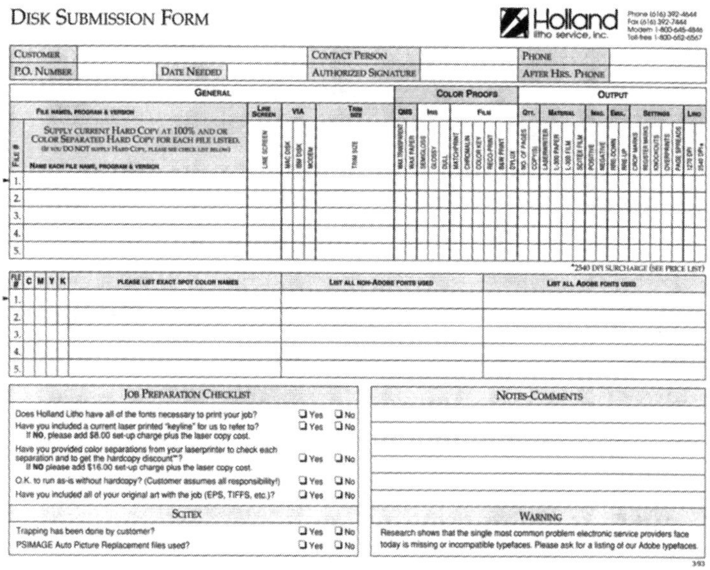

DISK SUBMISSION FORM

Holland litho service, inc.
Phone (616) 392-4644
Fax (616) 392-7444
Modem 1-800-645-4846
Toll-free 1-800-652-6567

CUSTOMER | CONTACT PERSON | PHONE
P.O. NUMBER | DATE NEEDED | AUTHORIZED SIGNATURE | AFTER HRS. PHONE

GENERAL | COLOR PROOFS | OUTPUT

FILE NAMES, PROGRAM & VERSION | LINE SCREEN | VIA | TRIM SIZE

SUPPLY CURRENT HARD COPY AT 100% AND OR COLOR SEPARATED HARD COPY FOR EACH FILE LISTED.
(IF YOU DO NOT SUPPLY HARD COPY, PLEASE SEE CHECK LIST BELOW)

NAME EACH FILE NAME, PROGRAM & VERSION

FILE # 1. 2. 3. 4. 5.

*2540 DPI SURCHARGE (SEE PRICE LIST)

FILE # | C | M | Y | K | PLEASE LIST EXACT SPOT COLOR NAMES | LIST ALL NON-ADOBE FONTS USED | LIST ALL ADOBE FONTS USED

1. 2. 3. 4. 5.

JOB PREPARATION CHECKLIST

Does Holland Litho have all of the fonts necessary to print your job? ❑ Yes ❑ No
Have you included a current laser printed "keyline" for us to refer to? ❑ Yes ❑ No
If **NO**, please add $8.00 set-up charge plus the laser copy cost.
Have you provided color separations from your laserprinter to check each separation and to get the hardcopy discount**? ❑ Yes ❑ No
If **NO** please add $16.00 set-up charge plus the laser copy cost.
O.K. to run as-is without hardcopy? (Customer assumes all responsibility!) ❑ Yes ❑ No
Have you included all of your original art with the job (EPS, TIFFS, etc.)? ❑ Yes ❑ No

SCITEX

Trapping has been done by customer? ❑ Yes ❑ No
PSIMAGE Auto Picture Replacement files used? ❑ Yes ❑ No

NOTES-COMMENTS

WARNING

Research shows that the single most common problem electronic service providers face today is missing or incompatible typefaces. Please ask for a listing of our Adobe typefaces.

3/93

FIG. 21.15 ▶

The Disk Submission Form used by Alan Litho in Los Angeles, California

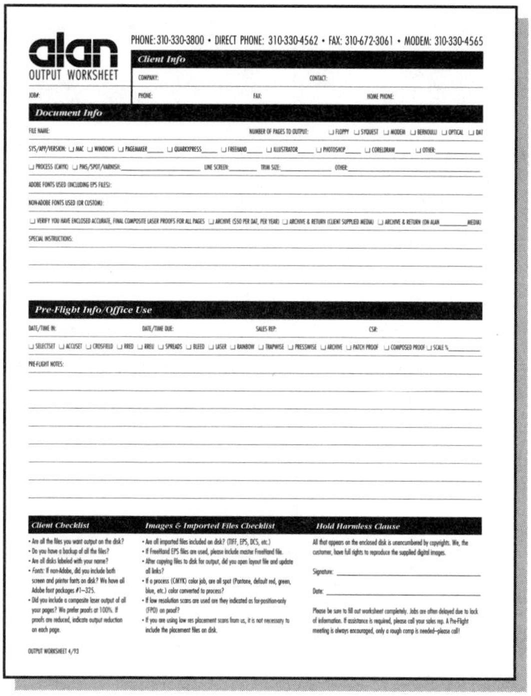

alan OUTPUT WORKSHEET

PHONE: 310-330-3800 • DIRECT PHONE: 310-330-4562 • FAX: 310-672-3061 • MODEM: 310-330-4565

Client Info

COMPANY: CONTACT:
JOB#: PHONE: FAX: HOME PHONE:

Document Info

FILE NAME: NUMBER OF PAGES TO OUTPUT: ❑ FLOPPY ❑ SYQUEST ❑ MODEM ❑ BERNOULLI ❑ OPTICAL ❑ DAT
SYS/APP/VERSION: ❑ MAC ❑ WINDOWS ❑ PAGEMAKER____ ❑ QUARKXPRESS____ ❑ FREEHAND____ ❑ ILLUSTRATOR____ ❑ PHOTOSHOP____ ❑ CORELDRAW____ ❑ OTHER:____
❑ PROCESS (CMYK) ❑ PMS/SPOT/VARNISH:____ LINE SCREEN:____ TRIM SIZE:____ OTHER:____
ADOBE FONTS USED (INCLUDING EPS FILES):
NON-ADOBE FONTS USED (OR CUSTOM):
❑ VERIFY YOU HAVE ENCLOSED ACCURATE, FINAL COMPOSITE LASER PROOFS FOR ALL PAGES ❑ ARCHIVE ($50 PER DAT, PER YEAR) ❑ ARCHIVE & RETURN (CLIENT SUPPLIED MEDIA) ❑ ARCHIVE & RETURN (ON ALAN____MEDIA)
SPECIAL INSTRUCTIONS:

Pre-Flight Info/Office Use

DATE/TIME IN: DATE/TIME DUE: SALES REP: CSR:
❑ SELECTSET ❑ ACCUSET ❑ CROSFIELD ❑ RRED ❑ RREU ❑ SPREADS ❑ BLEED ❑ LASER ❑ RAINBOW ❑ TRAPWISE ❑ PRESSWISE ❑ ARCHIVE ❑ PATCH PROOF ❑ COMPOSED PROOF ❑ SCALE %____
PRE-FLIGHT NOTES:

Client Checklist

- Are all the files you want output on the disk?
- Do you have a backup of all the files?
- Are all disks labeled with your name?
- *Fonts:* If non-Adobe, did you include both screen and printer fonts on disk? We have all Adobe font packages #1–325.
- Did you include a composite laser output of all your pages? We prefer proofs at 100%. If proofs are reduced, indicate output reduction on each page.

Images & Imported Files Checklist

- Are all imported files included on disk? (TIFF, EPS, DCS, etc.)
- If FreeHand EPS files are used, please include master FreeHand file.
- After copying files to disk for output, did you open layout file and update all links?
- If a process (CMYK) color job, are all spot (Pantone, default red, green, blue, etc.) color converted to process?
- If low resolution scans are used are they indicated as for-position-only (FPO) on proof?
- If you are using low res placement scans from us, it is not necessary to include the placement files on disk.

Hold Harmless Clause

All that appears on the enclosed disk is unencumbered by copyrights. We, the customer, have full rights to reproduce the supplied digital images.

Signature: ____

Date: ____

Please be sure to fill out worksheet completely. Jobs are often delayed due to lack of information. If assistance is required, please call your sales rep. A Pre-Flight meeting is always encouraged, only a rough comp is needed—please call!

OUTPUT WORKSHEET 4/93

VI Publishing

Fig. 21.16 ▶

A Disk Submission Form from Graphics Plus in Culver City, California

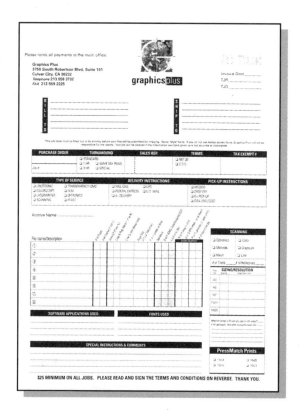

▶ *List and include all publication and linked files.* You have a great tool for this task, built into PageMaker. The Save As command will bundle all your files for you. Choose the Files Required For Remote Printing option. It automatically makes a copy of every file needed by a service bureau and puts the copy in whatever location you designate (usually a special folder you've set up). The one category of files that PageMaker won't grab for you is fonts. If you are sending fonts to the service bureau with your files, you need to gather them up by hand to make sure they're included.

The Save As command with the Files For Remote Printing option copies all needed linked files, as well as any special files that are needed (such as the file that contains the tracking information, an essential one if you have edited your tracks) so that your job will print as it should at the service bureau. The Save As command also has the advantage of consolidating your PageMaker file, just like the Save Smaller Preferences setting.

People hate to write the file names down on service bureau forms. One file isn't a big deal, but if you have a multi-chapter book to run, ask your service bureau to send along a screen capture of the folder where you have stored all the files, and then staple the resulting list to the disk submission form.

If you have had the service bureau do high-resolution drum scans for you, be sure you note that. This procedure usually indicates that you worked with low-resolution files for position purposes, and the service bureau has been storing the graphic images in its system. They need to know this so that they can link everything back up.

Make sure the service bureau can handle the files if you send along a Photo CD for your scans. If disk space permits, you may be better off providing your shots on disk rather than CD. In all probability, you have modified the pictures to some degree (cropping, rotation, color correction, and so on), so those Photo CD shots need to come to the service bureau on disk.

TIP ▶ Including Your Original Art as Well as EPS Files

You also may want to include original art. If you used a drawing program that exports non-editable EPS files (FreeHand comes to mind), include the original file in case there's a problem at output time. The service bureau techs may be able to help out with a quick fix if they have access to your files. Store the original art in a clearly named folder, out of the way, where it can't confuse anyone.

Be sure to pull any old files off your Syquest cartridge (or whatever you are using for removable mass storage to transport your files to the service bureau), so they can't be confused with the current files.

Do run a backup before sending your disk to the bureau; don't send your only copy.

TIP ▶ Include a Complete Backup if the Disk Has Room for It

If you have room on the disk, you can take another step to ensure success at deadline time. In a folder titled SPARE or something like that, run a compressed backup of everything (if you lack disk space, back up your publication files only).

The backup helps in two ways. First, if the file transfer has some defect, you already have a backup at the service bureau. Second, the backup can help solve any dispute about the way you set up the file.

One service bureau ran a job after opening it for inspection. Several hundred pages of film had to be thrown out when it was discovered that all the page numbers were in the same corner and the gutters were all along the same edge, not done left/right style. The pages, obviously, had been run single-sided instead of double-sided.

continues

VI

Publishing

TIP ▶ Continued

The service bureau claimed that their technician had run the file as received and that the fault was the designer's. The dispute over several thousand dollars of billing was resolved in favor of the designer, thanks to the StuffIt backup file that the designer included on the Syquest cartridge. The backup showed that the file was sent in as double-sided; this information was proven by the fact that the good file's last modified date was the day before the file was delivered to the service bureau. It turned out that an inexperienced operator didn't understand that turning off double-sided in the Page Setup dialog box would mess up the page layout and had been afraid to admit that he had made the switch while inspecting the file.

▶ *Programs.* List the programs used to create your publication, including the version numbers. If the technician needs to help you out, this information makes it easier.

▶ *Resolution.* Yes, you are going to hear the advice again: coordinate with the printer. Ask your print shop what screen frequency to use for your choice of paper and printing press.

▶ *Type of imagesetter.* Many service bureaus have more than one type of imagesetter. Be sure you understand the choices you are making. In general, you pay more for higher resolution (dpi) and precision, as well as the imagesetter's capability to render halftone dots (usually expressed as the capability to hold a certain line-screen frequency).

Imagesetters are either capstan or drum types. Capstan machines take a cartridge and wind the film or the repro paper between a couple of rollers, with a capstan (like a tape machine) providing the driving power. Drum machines work with fixed-length paper mounted on a drum, and they don't stretch or pull the paper. For that reason, the drum machines are considered to be more capable.

If you are doing a 133-line screen color job, or going to newsprint with an 85-line screen, you should have no trouble using a capstan-drive imagesetter. If you are headed into the 175-lines area or have demanding color needs, the service bureau will probably recommend one of the drum-drive imagesetters.

▶ *Film and paper specifications.* Ask your printer whether you should order emulsion up or down film, and whether the film should be right or wrong reading. The most common setting is emulsion down, right reading.

Also, ask your printer whether you should order negative or positive film or paper. Most printers prefer negative film and positive paper.

▶ *Printer's marks.* Specify the trim size of your publication and, in most cases, ask that printer's marks be turned on. If you created custom crop marks in conjunction with an imposed layout (special brochure format, small publication laid out as spreads, and so on), make sure the service bureau understands that they are to leave the automatic crop marks turned off.

▶ *Delivery method.* Help the service bureau find the file by letting them know that it is coming by modem, if that's the case. Is it on a floppy, a Syquest cartridge, or a less common disk format? Has the file been compressed to fit on the disk with PKZip or some other compression program?

▶ *Size and status of project.* Describe the number of pages. Specify the number of scans that must be done by the service bureau, how many of them are included, and how many will follow.

▶ *Colors.* If you are running process color, of course, specify that.

If you are using spot colors, list the names of the colors you have defined. One common problem with files submitted to service bureaus is multiple duplicating colors, all representing the same color, but with different names. This problem happens when people import graphics images and when many different folks work on the same publication. PageMaker 6.0 makes this problem a lot easier with its Remove Unused Colors command. Those features don't eliminate the problem, however, and that's why service bureaus want this information.

▶ *List and include your fonts.* Ask for your service bureau's list of supported fonts. You must provide fonts for your publication if your service bureau doesn't already own them. Generally, you'll need to provide any non-Adobe fonts. Most service bureaus guarantee results if you use strictly Adobe standard fonts, because they have purchased the Adobe font library collection in a special arrangement made available to them by Adobe.

The best approach—even if you think the service bureau has all the needed fonts, and even if they are all Adobe standard fonts—is to include your fonts on the disk when you submit the job. This last bit of advice becomes especially important if you have used Kern Edit to construct your own kern pairs in a custom version of a font.

When you list your fonts on the disk submission form, be sure to include the company name. Adobe's Helvetica may be quite different from someone else's, even though the fonts superficially resemble one another.

▶ *PostScript error checking.* If you are printing to disk, ask the service bureau if you should click the Include PostScript Error Handler check box in the

VI

Publishing

Options dialog box of the Print command. Chances are high that the service bureau already uses a more sophisticated error checker, such as the one from Systems Of Merritt, the Advanced PostScript Error Handler, or a diagnostic tool provided by the bureau's imagesetter manufacturer.

▶ *Send your laser proofs.* At a minimum, include a composite laser print of your publication.

For a color publication, include a separated laser proof as well. If you are running a long document, however, you may not want to send proofs for the entire job. In that case, you can pull some sample pages, and, if it's a spot color job, clearly mark them with directions on how the separation layers are supposed to work. The stack of laser paper may just go to waste in that situation, so check to be sure the service bureau wants the separated proof for a long document. It's hard to imagine most prepress techs making much use of four-color separations of a 300-page book. That's 1,200 pages!

▶ *Obtain proofs.* In addition to sending proofs along with the job, you must also specify to the service bureau what proofs you want to receive.

For a black-and-white publication or simple spot-color job, you may decide against running a service bureau proof and simply double-check that each page is separated okay. The printer will probably do a blue line for you when the project has been assembled.

If it's a process-color document or a complex spot-color job requiring trapping, get a color proof, and make your choice of proofing method. Certain types of proofing are better than others for evaluating trapping. Chapter 22, "Proofing Your Publication," describes proofing methods in detail.

▶ *Check output.* Be sure that basic kinds of things are okay on your output. See that the crop marks are there, that the separation or spot color layers are correct (with knockouts where they ought to be). How about traps? Are the bleeds correct? Do halftones and tints look okay, just with a visual inspection? Did any fonts go missing? You can tell right away if some Courier is slugged in where you were expecting something more elegant.

Someone with experienced eyes and some special tools also needs to do quality control on the imagesetter's film output. Technicians use an instrument called a *densitometer* to be sure the exposures are correct. Also, the film needs to be inspected for dust, photo processing stains from dirty chemicals, scratches, and other basic elements of quality.

TIP ▶ Use Plug-in to Help Specify Your Service Bureau Job

All this specification business to send something to the service bureau can get pretty tedious. Use the Pub Info Plug-in that comes with PageMaker to help out. It will list fonts, styles, and links. However, keep in mind that it lists any font referred to anywhere inside the publication, even if it is not actually used. It might, for example, list a font from an unused text paragraph style.

Using the Service Bureau for More PrePress Services

Think of service bureaus (or the prepress department of your print shop) as the electronic strippers of the universe. Most of them, at least to some degree, can perform all those traditional services we all took for granted back in the days when printers were printers and had nothing to do with laser beams. As always, be sure to coordinate all the prepress services listed here with the folks who run the presses—the print shop.

High-Resolution Photo Scans and Color Correction

It's one thing to run a scan of a black-and-white photo in the company newsletter, but it's quite another thing to use a desktop scanner for production of a really critical color photo. What's it worth for you to acquire years of experience in color correction? What's the cost if your product shot of the new mousetrap takes on an unattractive bilious pea green at press time, instead of its proper chartreuse? Resolving this question really boils down to making business decisions. At least talk to your service bureau about the possibilities and calculate the cost of the desktop color scanner, your time, and the results against the fees charged by the prepress house.

If you are going to commit to Photo CD for your scans, ask your service bureau if they perform that service. Many are joining the parade, knowing that the cheap scans are going to cut deeply into their photo drum-scanning business. An experienced service bureau color artist running a Photo CD imaging setup will get much more out of the system than your average high-volume quick photo outfit. Maybe each scan will cost you $3 instead of $1, but how many $3 pops can you buy for the cost of a desktop color scanner, and how much time will you save?

Trapping

For a complicated color job, think about having the service bureau do the trapping work for you. Time on a TrapWise or Scitex work station may be cheap compared to the time it would take you to do the job manually, especially since the TrapWise or Scitex system may produce better results in some situations. (Chapter 20, "Meeting Color Challenges," has more information on the general

VI

Publishing

subject of trapping and the powers and limitations of PageMaker 6.0's built-in trapping capabilities.) The main thing to remember is: Don't partially trap a job. Don't run PageMaker 6.0 trapping unless it can do the whole job. It's extremely difficult and sometimes impossible for a print shop to trap a piece that has already been partially trapped.

Separations

PageMaker 6.0 can directly produce color separations for almost every situation you face (now including RGB TIFFs). Those separation capabilities fall very short, however, of the high-end capability usually offered by a prepress house. They will have the tools to handle such technical issues as Under Color Removal and dot gain compensation.

Imposition

Imposition means setting up the pages of a publication so they come off the press ready to be folded and trimmed. Why have it done at the service bureau, especially since imposition is still traditionally done at the print shop? Well, having your film all imposed and ready for press saves time and steps. This question is one of those business-decision things where you need to look at the total cost of a project. Maybe your printer will give you a price break if you bring in imposed pages. On the other hand, the printer may be reluctant to let anybody outside the print shop do it. Check first on who should take responsibility for imposition.

Imposition can get pretty complex, much more complex than the simple capabilities of Build Booklet. Several imposition systems are in use by professionals. Adobe makes one, in fact, called PressWise. If you want to get a look at how complex imposing your own files can be, the new Build Booklet Addition has been based on PressWise.

Where to Go from Here

▶ Well, go to press, of course! Chapter 23 covers "Working with the Print Shop."

▶ One critical aspect of producing mechanicals is striving for color accuracy on press. Check "Meeting Color Challenges," Chapter 20, for more information on color management systems and trapping.

▶ Do run proofs all through your project, but especially before you head for the most expensive step of all, the press run. Chapter 22, "Proofing Your Publication," explains a range of proofing options.

▶ One major mistake people make, heading for the final stage of a job, is to forget something. Avoid that by using Chapter 24, "Master Checklist for Desktop Publishing."

▶ Linking and the other file assembling technology is of vital importance when you are packaging a service bureau job, so have a look at Chapter 30, "Linking and Other File Connections."

VI

Publishing

Chapter 22

Proofing Your Publication

This chapter covers these topics:

Ways you can check for typos and other copy problems.

▼

Proofing the layout of your project—the way the graphics and type go together on the page.

▼

Checking whether the project will print at the service bureau.

▼

Determining whether your publication will be color-accurate off the press.

▼

Methods of checking on your project while it's at the print shop.

SOME PEOPLE (clients, especially) just seem to go blank whenever they look at an easy-to-fix—and cheap—laser proof. It seems as though they can only mark up and rewrite copy on a blueline after the film has been run by the service bureau. Maybe people feel that changing type is about the easiest thing you can correct, and that's true enough, but the longer you wait the more it costs. Late in the game, it costs about the same to fix a typo as it does to fix a color graphic, because by then you've run the film—or even gone to press. ▶ ▶ ▶

Unfortunately, many desktop publishers—not you, of course—do extensive publication proofing about as often as they back up their hard disks. That's pretty much never.

Since a report in the last edition of this book, many service bureau operators have responded with agreement to this statement:

```
"One high-volume commercial printer with an in-house service
bureau reports that roughly half of its electronic prepress
jobs come in without proofs, even though the company charges
a setup fee for proofless documents (to pay for the necessity
of running the proofs themselves). They also don't guarantee
any job that comes in without laser proofs. That threat of
potential misfortune still doesn't work to encourage better
proofing habits."
```

Proofing needs to be a way of life, if you hope to get your job done correctly, on deadline, within budget—and approved by the client.

Checking Copy

Last-minute changing happens so often in the printing business that there's even a name for late copy changes, requested when the project already has arrived at the prepress bureau or the print shop. They are called *AAs*, for Author's Alterations.

These next few sections give you some down-to-earth and easy tips for fixing copy at the cheap and easy-to-fix stages early on in the process. Spelling checking software, professional proofers, indexing tools, sign offs—these can all be part of a system for top-notch, money-saving copy proofing.

Run the Spelling and Grammar Checkers

Use PageMaker's spelling checker, naturally, to check spelling. Also, the spelling in the copy should be checked before ever being placed on the page.

Also, consider running a grammar checker on the text, even if you are one of those folks who don't believe grammar checkers are smart enough yet to really fulfill their promise. Sometimes a grammar checker just gives you a new look at your copy and unearths something that you had overlooked. For instance, it helps find what I call the "too" words—words that sound alike but are spelled differently, as in too, two, and to. The wrong "too" word is likely to trigger the grammar checker. It won't even cause a spell checker program to raise an eyebrow.

If you've done quite a bit of copy editing in PageMaker and still want to run a grammar check (which isn't possible inside PageMaker), export the text and run the checker on the text file. Don't import the text back into PageMaker, because that would destroy any kerning, inline graphics placement, and other typographical and special effects work you've done. Just use the grammar checker on the exported text file as a means to spot problems and then make any changes on the PageMaker version of the text.

Spot Check with an Index and a Table of Contents

The indexing and table of contents tools can also give you a whole new view of your copy, possibly exposing mistakes you missed when proofing the text. A headline or a word on a page may look okay when it's cluttered in there with all that other copy, but when the item has been isolated onto a list, you are more likely to spot a problem.

Along this same line, if you are using the Sonar Bookends Plug-in to generate the initial index master topics list, put the tool to additional use as long as you've bought it. Sonar works by building lists of every unique word in a document and reports their page location. If you get all the similar words lined up in a list, an odd word stands out right away and acts as a flag so you can double check it in context.

Hire Professional Proofreaders

Consider hiring a professional proofreader or an editor. A few people on this planet love to find mistakes in copy—and are good enough to be right all the time. These professional nitpickers are worth whatever you have to pay them because they will save you money.

You'll want to keep in mind that proofreading charges depend on the nature of your need. Proofing always happens on the worst possible deadlines, and in that tension it's important to have a clear and specific agreement on what's to be accomplished and for what fee. Simple proofing for spelling errors and typos is less expensive and less time-consuming than a full-blown editing job, where your collaborator actually helps you do a rewrite.

Finding a professional can be tough, especially if you need the person on a project-by-project basis. Try hiring people who have worked the desk at the local newspaper, or legal secretaries who want to pick up some extra cash. Keyboarding services in larger cities often offer good proofreading work. Try putting a message up on one of the online services, such as the Desktop Publishing Forum of CompuServe. Your local service bureau may know of someone. Also try your

VI

Publishing

print shop, especially if they have a typesetting operation (desktop or otherwise), because some of the best proofers are people who have stared at type for the last couple of decades. They seem to be able to smell mistakes.

Use In-House Proofing Tricks

Never let the person who did the keyboarding do the proofing. They don't have fresh eyes—and fresh eyes are mandatory for proofreading.

If you must work alone, read the copy into a tape recorder. Let the whole thing sit for at least a few hours if you can and then come back to it. Proof the typeset copy as you listen to the original that was read into the tape recorder.

Have two people do proofing of critical non-prose material such as scientific data tables or financial information. One reads the original to the other person, who is checking each character in the typeset copy.

Get Formal Sign Offs

Almost every project has an approval cycle of some kind. Ultimately, the sign off will probably come from the person who's picking up the tab.

Make sure that everyone in the approval loop for your publication signs off formally. Do not accept a verbal approval. Ask the approver (that is, the client or boss) to read the material carefully, and (if it's true) warn the person signing off that the expense of copy changes to the approved proof will be high—and will come out of their budget.

Actually, making sure that the key approver signs off on the publication holds true for all proofs, not just copy proofs, and the further along you are in the project, the more important it is.

Laser Proofing

You already own (or have access to) an extremely cheap tool for getting sign off for the layout of your publication—your laser printer. These next sections describe your laser printer layout proofing tools.

Thumbnails

Running thumbnails gives you an overall feel for your multipage project of how it all flows together from a visual point of view. If your publication has been set up with facing pages, use PageMaker 6.0's new capability to print out reader's spreads so you can evaluate pages as they will look when finally assembled at the bindery.

Composites

They may not be in full color, but grayscale composites (using the Print command's Color dialog box mode) tell you a great deal about the basic design values of your pages, even if they are multicolor layouts. If text is unreadable because it doesn't have adequate contrast against a background, the problem will probably show up in grayscale laser proofs. Composite laser proofs are also an important client sign-off step before going to expensive image setting and color proofs.

The Proof Check Box

If you need to print out laser proof layouts for typesetting approval (that is, kerning, line breaks, hyphenation), save time and visual clutter by clicking on the Proof check box in the Print command's Document dialog box. PageMaker will then run placeholder boxes in the place of photos and other imported illustrations. That dramatically speeds up the printing time, especially for a complex design or a long publication.

Running Pre-Service Bureau Proofs

About the worst thing you can have happen at the service bureau is one of the dreaded PostScript error codes. It means your job won't run as-is through the imagesetter. Another terrible fate—which you also can prevent—is to send a print to disk file to the bureau with the wrong settings. Ever pay for 211 useless pages of positive film without crop marks? I guarantee, you won't like it.

At the very least, these kinds of troubles will cost you your deadline. Even worse, you can be out big bucks for bad film or wasted time on the service bureau's system (they call it overtime, no matter the hour of the day). It's best to search out and remedy this sort of thing early on, before taking your files to the service bureau. Take the following preventative proofing steps so that your publication will fly right through the imagesetter.

Listen to Your Laser Printer

One service bureau tells about the client who sent in a complex design for film output. After four hours of trying to get the job to run, the technician called the client to talk about the trouble. Asked whether he had run a laser proof (one didn't come with the job), the client replied, "Well, I tried to run one, but it wouldn't print on my laser printer. It ran for half an hour and gave me a PostScript error." The trouble at the imagesetter suddenly became very clear—the file was unprintable. If your file burps in the laser printer, fix it so it at least

VI

Publishing

will print completely and correctly there. It's a sure thing that if your publication won't print at the laser printer's relatively low resolution of 300 or 600 dpi, it almost certainly won't print at 2,450 dpi in the imagesetter.

Check for Problems On-Screen

Use the bulleted list in the section "Preventing the Output Time Blues" in Chapter 21, and scan your publication for these kinds of problems. Look for potential problems such as complex graphics, cropping masks, embedded fonts, nested EPS files, excess use of graphics rotated in PageMaker rather than a graphic application, and so on. Buff that file—in other words, now that the frenzy of design has passed and you are getting ready to send it off to the service bureau.

Don't rely on the screen to evaluate color—even with PageMaker 6.0's new color management system capabilities. For the best proofing of your color results, see "Proofing Color at the Service Bureau" later in this chapter.

Use a PostScript Error Checker

PageMaker has a PostScript error checker built right into it (see the Options dialog box of the Print command). During your proofing stages with the laser printer, you should definitely use the PageMaker error checker if you are having trouble printing a file. It may give you a clue as to what's wrong.

If you are running a print to disk file, check with the service bureau before including the PageMaker error checker. They may be using something more robust at their end, such as Systems of Merritt's Advanced PostScript Error Handler.

You may be working with a service bureau that will provide you with an error checker. To install it for use with PageMaker in place of the one that comes with the program, copy the error checker file to the USENGLISH folder in your PM6 folder. Change the name of the file to P6ERROR.PS.

Turn Your Laser Printer into an Imagesetter Proofer

Look at figure 22.1, keeping in mind that this page came out of a laser printer. LaserCheck is a special program that you download to your PostScript laser printer before you run your proof. The LaserCheck program then lives inside the memory of your laser printer, taking in whatever PostScript is being sent to it and formatting the information into a proof page like the one you see here.

FIG. 22.1 ▶

A LaserCheck proof page from a laser printer.

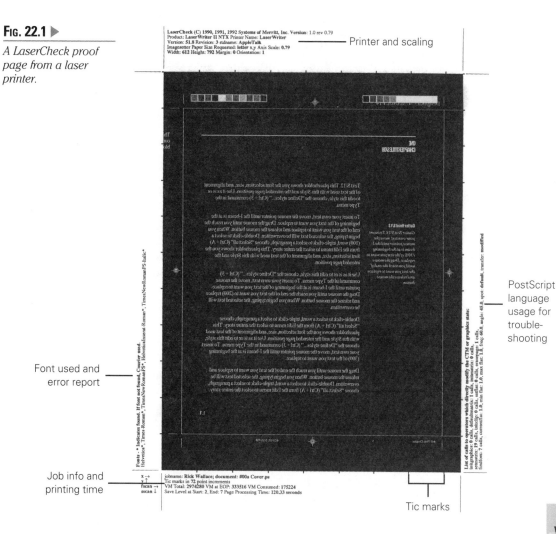

Printer and scaling

PostScript language usage for trouble-shooting

Font used and error report

Job info and printing time

Tic marks

Notice that it looks just like a reduced copy of the imagesetter film your service bureau would deliver, including the fact that it's reversed and negative. Of course, it has a lot of proofing information in the margins, including the status of your fonts and information on the PostScript code used to generate the image.

LaserCheck makes a lot of sense if you submit print to disk files to the service bureau, because you can't otherwise double-check your PostScript output on-screen or on a laser printer. It's about the only way you can actually proof the contents of your print to disk output. Granted, you can use LaserStatus or any of the other PostScript downloaders to send the file to the laser printer, but that wouldn't solve the problem of fitting your 8 1/2 × 11-inch page with crop marks and other printer's information onto a letter-sized page of printer paper. It also wouldn't help you troubleshoot any of your problem files.

VI

Publishing

LaserCheck, as you see, emulates the imagesetter by reducing the image down to the laser printer page and annotating it. By the way, if a PostScript error shuts down the job, rather than blow off the entire page, LaserCheck prints as much of the page as possible, stopping at the bad spot so that you can see right where it is.

As indicated in figure 22.1, you get a fonts list for each page, the job status, information on what PostScript calls were made (for troubleshooting assistance), and complete details on page orientation, size, and the name of the printer.

One real hot thing is the printing time noted at the bottom of the page. The printing time—which shows how long processing the page through your laser printer took—is the biggest worry at the service bureau. The people at the service bureau worry that your difficult-to-print page will tie up their equipment for hours when the file should have taken just a few minutes. Show the service bureau this proof, and you'll be positively demonstrating that the file will output with no problem; you might possibly be able to negotiate a better rate on that basis.

Proofing Color at the Service Bureau

Ultimately, you won't know what your piece will look like until it runs off the press. You can get a good idea, but no test can beat the color accuracy of the final printed product, and the ultimate test of your project is a proof that comes back from the printer. So, in addition to the color proofing techniques discussed in the following sections, read "Checking Your Publication at the Print Shop" later in the chapter.

Test Separations on a Laser

One color-proofing technique that doesn't cost a bundle is testing your separations on your laser printer. Run non-composite laser proofs to see that spot color objects and type are going to the correct layer. Of course, evaluate the grayscale composite for reality testing of your colors, just to see that objects which should be dark are dark, and so on.

Running separated proofs to the acetate overlays used on overhead projects can be useful. That way, you can see that everything is falling together properly. You can even invest in laser-printer cartridges of different colors and actually generate color overlay proofs. But registration probably will be terrible, so don't fool yourself that this is a legitimate color evaluation technique. A laser printer just can't achieve real precision. It's usually good enough to catch gross errors, however.

Inexpensive Color Printer Comps

Inexpensive color printers have been flooding the market. Everyone, for a few hundred dollars, can have color output. However, even with excellent color management systems, these printers can't possibly provide you with an accurate view of your color results on press.

Used with care, they can still play an extremely valuable role in the proofing process. Show color composites to your client. There will be no question that the coat on the model was supposed to be red. The client sign-off proves it. However, consider putting some kind of disclaimer on your sign-off block indicating that the color comp is only an estimate and that there may be considerable color variation when the project goes to press.

It doesn't cost much to produce these color comps, but they can be invaluable approval tools—as long as everyone understands that they don't represent 100 percent accurate color as it will appear on the printing press.

Set a Color Goal

To proof color, you need to set a goal. Do you need the color to be only pleasing to the eye, or must it precisely match the original subject? If you are producing a book full of art photos, for example, you might choose to go for art rather than accuracy. On the other hand, if you've got a standard product color—like for a brand of soda pop, for instance—the printed photos of that product better be an extremely close match. When you've got the goal defined as clearly as you can state it, get a sign-off from your client (or boss, whoever the approver might be, if it isn't you) and convey the goal in your conferences with the service bureau and the print shop.

Focus on the Memory Colors

Focus in on the so-called memory colors when evaluating color proofs of scanned photographs. Some colors just stick out in a person's mind instantly if they seem wrong. Those are the memory colors.

Flesh tones are especially important memory colors. You need to pay particular attention to flesh tones if you have different races in the same shot, because that visual environment will make color accuracy problems even more glaring. The flesh tone memory colors may be the most important ones of all. Crayola even provides a variety of flesh tones for different races in these more aware times (although the old so-called flesh color, the pinkish/salmon one, never looked quite right anyway, did it?).

VI

Publishing

There are other memory colors, too. Blue sky, oranges, apples, hamburgers, familiar brand-name products such as soft-drink cans—any objects that are really familiar also must look real and believable.

Evaluate Colors In Controlled Light

Actors have known about this for years, of course. The color of everything, including your skin, varies depending on the lighting. Your facial color is different if you're outside at dawn, under the incandescent lights in your dining room, or under fluorescent lighting at the office. If possible, evaluate proofs under standard lighting in a color evaluation booth. Most prepress service bureaus and print shops have such lighting or have rigged up the equivalent. The booths attempt to duplicate the color of daylight at midday.

Choose Between Composite and Laminate Proofs

You can break color proof sheets down into two types: composites and laminates (or separation-based). The choice between composite and laminate proofing methods will probably be a money issue, so you need to understand the benefit that might cause you to buy into a laminate proofing technique (the more expensive of the two).

Using Composites of Color Proofs

Composite proofs have become more and more common as color desktop publishing has grown. These proofs are generated digitally, straight out of the computer into a color desktop printer—usually a rather expensive one. Some people even refer to them as *digital proofs*.

Keep in mind that much of this discussion relates to the proofing of process colors. Your color proofing process may not need to be so rigorous if you are printing in spot colors, because they come from premixed ink.

On the other hand, even with premixed spot colors, you may need to worry about proofing your trapping, if any, and about checking for moiré patterns in screens. Because composite proof printers don't build color in layers, a composite proof always will look like your document has been built with a perfect abutting of colors and blends. The lack of color build, however, means that the proof can't show the problems caused by overlapping colors.

Three basic types of composite color printers are available:

▶ Color copiers, driven with special color controller boxes. You might see one of the Canon color laser copiers, for example, driven by EFI's Fiery unit or by ColorAge's ColorQ.

▶ Thermal dye sublimation printers, such as the 3M Rainbow, apply color to special glossy paper.

▶ High-end inkjet printers spray ink on the paper in microscopic dots, not unlike the inexpensive color printer that you may use for color comping. You'll hear names at your service bureau such as Iris and Stork Bedford.

Your service bureau will probably offer one, or maybe two, of these printer types on their price sheet.

Two of these printer types—the color copiers and the inkjets—can print to your actual paper, the stock you'll be using for your printed piece. The third requires special paper.

Using Laminate (Separation-Based) Color Proofs

The most expensive type of color proofing is the best. Building proofs from layers of colors, just like it would be done on the printing press, the laminate or separation-based color proofs will reveal any trapping or moiré flaws in your piece.

You can get overlay proofs where the color is built up from loose acetate sheets of each color, all bound together in register. If you are offered an overlay proof, it's likely to be a 3M Color Key or a DuPont Cromacheck.

The best proofs of all are the ones that are bonded together in a lamination. Your film is shot to the layers of proofing materials, processed, and registered. Then it's sealed together in one solid sheet. It doesn't get any better than this. Look for names like Cromalin (DuPont), Matchprint (3M), and ColorArt (Fuji).

Checking Your Publication at the Print Shop

After all this talk about not believing the color you see on your screen, you can believe the color results at one place—the actual run on the printing press.

But the press check isn't the only proofing service you can get from the print shop. The following sections explain other services you can get.

Swatches of Ink and Varnish

The term *proofs* doesn't strictly describe these two swatch techniques, but they help you predict results, and that's what a proof is supposed to do, isn't it? Both methods deliver color-accurate information from the inks you'll actually be using on the paper you will be specifying for your job. Use these two ink trial methods for spot colors, although the spot colors can be mixed from CMYK inks.

First, you can ask the print shop just to smear some ink on your chosen paper for any given project. By using a palette knife or a rubber roller, they'll apply the ink so that you can see how it works on your paper stock. You may sometimes hear this technique called a *draw down*, and you probably won't be charged for the sample unless the printer must special order the ink.

VI

Publishing

For day-to-day use in your designs, select your paper (or the papers you most commonly use for your projects) and run some swatches of your own rather than relying on commercial spot-color palette swatches. Make up a PageMaker document of the colors you need in various tints and run it through the service bureau imagesetter you commonly use. Then have your regular printer run it on the press. If you work with this printer quite a bit, they won't charge you an arm and a leg for this calibration work. You may even be able to get it on press as shared work, taking up spare space on a flat.

Make sure that you understand how varnish will affect your job. If you'll be using it, try out the varnish on some swatches to see how much it darkens the color.

Printer Inspection of Films

Nobody may be better qualified to inspect your imagesetter output than the person doing the printing. Even if the service bureau has checked the films, have the press people run another analysis with those experienced eyes that have been watching stuff come off the press for hundreds, maybe thousands, of print runs. The more eyes the better, and odds are high that your print shop folks have the best of all.

Blueline

The *blueline* is the place to verify that the print shop understood your trimming and folding instruction. It's also the only proof you'll get that indicates how fronts and backs go together—obvious for book jobs, not always so obvious for multifold brochures, or a postcard that might have a horizontal front and a vertical back.

A blueline is made pretty much the same way a blueprint is. Light-sensitive paper gets exposed to light in a one-to-one contact print with your actual stripped-together films—the flats about to be used to make up your printing press plates. It's the most intimate and close-to-the press method of proofing—outside the press check itself—and tells you whether the print shop has properly collated all the separations for your job. A blueline is, well, blue.

Dummy

If you are creating a multipage document, your print shop may provide you with an *imposed proof*—a dummied-up copy of how all the flats will be folded when they are printed to paper and then trimmed. The *dummy* shows you the spreads and how they will all fit together when bound.

If you need one, ask for it in your initial meeting—or at least let the printer know you'll want one if you award the job to them. They're usually used to testing how differing text and cover stock look together, and to gauge the thickness of the spine for book binding.

Press Check

Do a press check at least once sometime in your life, even if you aren't working on color critical publications. It's magic to see your design coming to fruition, and there's no better way to absorb into your gut the process of getting images onto paper from a printing press.

On the other hand, if you are one of those people who rejects the first two bottles of wine at a fancy restaurant, just to show you know your stuff, you may not enjoy the experience. It's certain the press crew won't enjoy it if you cop an attitude. Remember, the goal is a collaboration between designer and print shop.

When you arrive (on time, right?), you'll go to the press room, where the press will be ready to roll or close to it. When the crew hits the button, a lot of waste, called *make ready*, will result. Sheet after sheet of paper (if it's a sheet-fed press) or yards of paper (if it's a Web press) roll along as the printing crew adjusts everything.

When they are satisfied, they'll shut down the press and bring a sample to you before rolling the press again to finish the job. This is no time to discover a typo. That should have been done long ago. You are there to see that the colors are accurate and that no obvious defects exist in the work. If you are happy, you'll be asked to sign the proof, and the crew will use it as a standard for evaluating the rest of the pieces off the press for the rest of the run.

What do you look for at the press check? Ask a lot of questions and look—really look—at the piece as it comes off the press:

- ▶ Ask the crew to share their technical check with you. If you aren't familiar with some of their tools, you can't do better than ask them to explain what they are and how they work. The new knowledge will help you make the transition from computer screen to ink on paper on future projects.

  How did dot gain look on the star targets? These spoke wheel-like patterns look a little like a miniature TV test pattern.

  What did the densitometer show about how the inks are laying down on the page? Have them explain what they discovered as they examined the color and grayscale density bars.

  The press crew will already have done this, but take the extra care to double-check that all the registration marks are lined up.

▶ Go through the piece and check that colors are as you want them to be, suited to the accuracy goal that everyone agreed on. If there are critical items for color matching, such as product shots or color matching system swatches, make sure that they are there at the press check and use the standard light table to make a comparison. Don't work from memory.

▶ Look for physical defects caused by the printing process. Wrinkles, print through from the back side of the piece, impurities such as hair or dust sticking to the plate and printing on the piece, smudges, blotting from undried ink transferring between stacked sheets—these are the kinds of defects you need to look for.

The best approach to a press check is abject terror, moderated by pride and concentration. Be afraid you'll miss something. Focus all your energy on looking over the results of the effort you've put into the project, while remembering that a mistake now could waste all that work.

TIP ▶ **Bring Along Memory Aids for Color Checks at Press Check**

If color accuracy has major importance for the project, don't evaluate from memory. Bring along the original, or have the prepress people bring it to the proofing session. If you are matching a product shot, bring the product. Bring your spot color swatches for comparison as well. If you are matching a previous press run, bring along the signed press sheets.

Of course, this is no time to bring a new element into the picture. If you have memory aids, previous samples, or color swatches, you should show them to the printer early in the process, preferably at the original meeting. Also, the memory aids should be shown to the printer when the film and proofs are handed off. Ideally, the printer will get an extra copy to keep with the job.

Where to Go from Here

▶ Much of the proofing suggested in this chapter relies on your laser printer. You can't do that without the Print command, which is covered in Chapter 21, "Producing Mechanicals."

▶ Likewise, the process of getting a project into the service bureau has much to do with the proofing results you'll get from your prepress collaborators, and you'll find that background in Chapter 21 as well.

▶ Working with the printer involves more than doing a press check, and the collaboration begins when you begin, at the start of a project. Look at Chapter 23, "Working with the Print Shop."

▶ You cannot do a color proof without understanding the technology of color. For foundation information, see Part V, "Making Pages Colorful." The technology that makes process color work is explained in Chapter 23.

VI

Publishing

Working with the Print Shop

This chapter on working with the print shop covers the following information:

Running a preflight conference with your printer before you get to the electronic layout stage of your project.

▼

Creating final specifications for your print shop work and getting a bid.

▼

Specifying the paper for your job.

▼

Inspecting the final product.

▼

Understanding the concept of halftones and screens and why your print shop needs to tell you how best to set your line screen and compensate your photo scans for best results on the press.

BECAUSE THE PRINTER is at the end of the publication process, he or she can tell you how best to begin. Think of your publication process as a journey, a long drive with a deadline for your arrival, plus a budget limit on your transportation costs.

The printer helps you draw up a map—a plan to get you to your destination. The printer also gives free advice on alternate routes that may give you better quality, plus ways to avoid potholes and other road hazards. It's important to mention that the printer can make suggestions that can help you save money on fuel for the trip as well. ▶ ▶ ▶

Your commercial printer also brings to your collaboration a quantity and quality of experience that you can't possibly hope to match. In a week, your printer sees the number of jobs that you see in a couple of months or more—and that's being conservative. If you've done a hundred jobs, the printer has done a thousand. It's dead sure that those jobs have included a lot of mistakes by the people who designed them, which means that all those designers who made those expensive mistakes gave your printer a free education about what you should be avoiding and how to help you evade the same problems.

Furthermore, the ability to instantly design beauty on the computer screen has cut us adrift from the basic printing press technology that ultimately makes that beauty possible. But the commercial printer remains—a bastion of practical experience, able to translate your design from the high-tech world of computer chips into your low-tech destination, paper and ink on the printing press.

Running a Preflight Check

Ideally, at some point, you will hold a preflight meeting with your printer. In this utopian world, your preflight check happens before you begin to perform the electronic layout work for the job so that you can use the advice from the printer to do the job faster, cheaper, and with better quality. It can't always happen that way, of course, but that's the ideal timing for your initial meeting at the print shop.

There aren't any solid granite rules for this sort of collaboration and, obviously, there's a wide range of help that your printer can offer or that you may require. You need to make your own decision about how much of this section to use for any given job.

Some jobs are so simple that they don't need much collaboration, especially if you've been buying printing for years. And some jobs are so small that you really can't expect the printer to give you hours and hours of hand-holding—unless you are going to be a regular customer. On the other hand, some jobs are so complex that they demand that you collaborate with your printer very early on if you want to have a whisper of a chance to bring the job in on time and on budget. For that matter, even a single detail of what appears to be a straightforward piece of work can make a major difference in how you execute your early conceptual design.

Which Comes First: Preflight or Bidding?

At some point in this process, someone's bound to say, "How can you make all these preflight decisions with a printer when you haven't collected a single bid?" That's true. You don't know that you will work with that specific printer; another printer's press setup could change the approach you need to take.

Well, I confess a bias in favor of meeting with the printer earlier rather than later. That bias is implicit in the order of the topics in this chapter. Assume that you go into layout without a preflight, and, as a result, you go out to bid armed with a fully developed design. You may end up needing to do a redesign when the bids suggest cheaper ways to accomplish your goals. On the other hand, a good preflight session pretty much tells you whether you have started out with the right kind of print shop for your job. If the shop is not right, you'll know soon enough in that initial meeting. If the printer obviously isn't the right one, chalk up the time spent as education and move on to a second preflight with a more appropriate printer.

Putting aside my bias about when to meet with the printer—everyone has his or her own style of handling all these planning issues; in the end, you need to satisfy yourself. When it comes to collaborating with a printer, a standard way of working does not exist. Some things in life simply require muddling through.

If you do an early preflight, you'll need to reconfirm all of your decisions at bid time. If you wait to preflight with the winning bidder, you'll still need answers to all these questions, especially the ones that appear later in this chapter in the section "Developing Tactics."

Preparing for Your Preflight Meeting

Obviously, do some thinking, planning, and designing before you go meet with the folks at the print shop. Stay flexible, of course; or you won't take in all the suggestions you'll be getting. The degree of efficiency and focus in the meeting, however, will be in direct proportion to your ability to be clear about your needs and goals. At the minimum, you need to have made some preliminary decisions about each of the following categories:

▶ *Intents and purposes.* When people use the phrase, "For all intents and purposes," they are usually being practical. That's the essence of your preflight session. You must be able to spell out the intents and purposes—the practical aspects—of your publication. Who's the audience, and what is the goal?

▶ *Rough sketch, comp, mock-up.* You use this early version of your publication to convey the basic format of your publication.

Your rough sketch may be on the back of an envelope, but at least go into the preflight meeting with some idea of what your publication will look like. If there's something specific to get started on, collaboration works best. Sketch out the layout in rough blocks or thumbnails so you have a visual representation of all the other issues in this list.

If you can, mock up the job. For a brochure, fold a piece of paper the way you think the panels should go, and draw in the blocks of information. This can help both you and the printer get a good idea of what you need in the way of bindery services (sewing, folding, scoring, insertions, perforating, and so on).

TIP ▶ **Use Samples for Communication**

Samples are great tools. Collect them incessantly. There really isn't much that's new in the world of publication design. Samples can aid your communication in the preflight meeting if you can say things like, "I saved this gold-embossed piece I got in the mail the other day, because it has just the effect I want." Or perhaps, "Here's a pamphlet I picked up at the Eggplant Eater's Rights Rally the other day. I like this deckled-edge paper that they used."

▶ *Size of run and budget.* A process of negotiation is ahead of you, so you don't want to name the price that you are willing to pay. Maybe you'll be able to improve it. However, you can save both yourself and the printer lots of time by suggesting your rough expectations at the preflight session. If you ask to do four colors and 5,000 pieces for a one-sheet flyer, it's going to cost more than $1.98.

▶ *Quality.* Keep in mind your overall needs for quality. Again, this has a lot to do with how the piece will be used. If it's a sales presentation and the product costs several thousand dollars a pop, the quality will be different from a church newsletter done on a volunteer basis and funded out of the weekly collections.

▶ *Deadline.* How soon does the job need to be done, and how long before you can get your design firmed up? When does the printer need to get the job in order to deliver on time? What's the last possible day? What's the best day for best price and quality?

▶ *Ink and varnish.* How many inks do you think you will need? Have you planned to do process colors? Have you thought about how a couple of spot colors might do the job just as well? What color matching system do you prefer (as opposed to what the printer might actually support)?

▶ *Paper.* Because the way the piece is used has a lot to do with your paper requirements, bring along some paper swatches if you can. Do you need covers as well as paper for body text? Do you want a special finish on the paper? Do you need envelopes printed?

▶ *Special sensitivities and crazy ideas.* What are the touchy spots? Does a product shot need to be precisely matched for color? Does the client (or do you) have a phobia about some previous bad experience with a print job?

Most any creative task involves a fair amount of brainstorming. That's the fun part, and you will be well-served to let your printer have some of the fun, too. Go to the preflight session with whatever crazy ideas have spun off your imagination. Maybe the printer will find a way to pull off one of those ideas, maybe even within your budget.

Beginning the Collaboration

Armed with all your preparation, go to the meeting with your printer, bringing some goals clearly in mind and stating them right up front, as follows:

▶ *Electronic publishing experience.* Does the printer have experience working with desktop publishing output? There's no sense doing a publication in PageMaker and then taking it to someone who doesn't understand the first thing about digital art.

▶ *Reality testing.* You want a reality check. Ask the printer to look at what you are attempting, and to point out any problems that you are building for yourself. Print shops are in business to accomplish things for people, but they are, above all, temples of practicality—at least the good ones are. Printers know that clients tend to hold them responsible for problems, whether the problems are the fault of the printer or not. They have a vested interest in steering you through the tough spots, and they usually welcome this "reality check" question.

▶ *Quality.* Aside from suggestions about preventing problems, does the printer have any suggestions for improving quality (and how much will it cost)?

Keep in mind that printers are set up to deliver a range of quality, and that your job may not fall in their range. A quick printer may be great for running stationery or forms, but would be completely out of the question for running a four-color hard-bound book. Some of this has to do with the kind of press equipment a shop owns. It also has to do with the way the shop carved out its customer base. For example, there's no negative here about quick printers—it's just that quick printers usually build their business on small print runs, quick turnaround, and heavy volume from walk-in customer traffic.

> ▶ *Time.* Are there suggestions about scheduling? Would it help if the covers were delivered first so they can be embossed, foil stamped, varnished, and scored while the rest of the job goes through collation?

> ▶ *Money.* What suggestions does the printer have for saving on the budget? Maybe you have in mind a paper that only comes in a size that wouldn't be efficient when trimmed to the size of your publication. The printer may suggest a similar paper that would allow you to fit more pages on a sheet, making for big savings.

Developing Tactics

Here's the most vital aspect of your preflight session. Don't leave without developing a tactic for how you will work with the print shop. Aside from all the other pre-bidding brainstorming you see in this section, you need to resolve the following essential prepress and logistics issues:

> ▶ *Color matching and ink strategy.* If you are going to use spot colors, you must know what color matching setups your probable print shop supports. It's probably going to be Pantone, the most commonly used system in the United States.

> Will you want to use high-fidelity color? If so, be sure the printer supports it. Although the high-fidelity color system has been rapidly growing in popularity, it is by no means available everywhere. Pantone Hexachrome high-fidelity color libraries come with PageMaker.

> Whatever color matching setup you and the printer agree on, you'll need to decide on paper. The libraries and swatches differ, for example, between coated and uncoated paper stocks.

> Work with the printer on inking strategy. If you combine spot and process colors, for example, it may make a lot of sense to go with a process color-based color-matching system.

> Also, ask the printer to give some thought to the order in which the inks are laid down on the paper. That may help you make choices when you design reverses, knockouts, and overprinting.

> Aside from inking strategies, PageMaker 6.0 now has cutting edge color management capabilities. If the printer will be supplying prepress services, get an agreement on which color management system will be used. PageMaker comes with Kodak Precision Color Management System.

> ▶ *Line screen.* Given the paper you plan to use and the press that's probably going to be used, what's the optimum line screen? This frequency has a major impact on how you handle photo scans and blends, among other things.

Does the printer have any other advice on specifications for you or the prepress service bureau when scanning photos? Discuss issues such as compensating for dot gain; for color photos, you need to know about undercolor removal and gray component replacement.

For more about line screens, see the Key Concept section in this chapter.

TIP ▶ Have the Printer Strip in the Photos

Let's be practical. Just because you can scan pictures doesn't mean you must. Are you a designer, or would you rather spend your time working as a prepress technician? Consider having traditional printer functions performed by the printer. That way, you can concentrate on design, and the printer can concentrate on execution.

Here's an example. For years, designers have been leaving FPO (For Position Only) low resolution placeholders for the printer to fill, letting the printer strip the photos into mechanicals. This way, you don't need to worry about eating an expensive print job because you didn't get the scan corrected quite right for the press.

The cost is likely to be nominal or even nonexistent, especially for black and white photos. In many cases it's just considered part of the service. So, at least inquire about having your photos shot and stripped in by the printer. Use low-quality desktop scans to provide cropping and sizing directions to the print shop.

On the other hand, if you have some special image manipulation in mind—something beyond a simple photograph—you may need the design control you can achieve by using digital photo techniques.

▶ *Trapping.* Who will do the trapping, if any? Does the printer see any ways to slightly modify your design approach so the need for trapping can be eliminated?

▶ *Imposition.* In your preflight session, make sure that you get clear agreement on who will be responsible for imposition.

A service bureau can generate a large format film by using a program such as Adobe PressWise. Print shops that have created in-house electronic prepress operations are shutting down their stripping labs and doing imposition in the imagesetter. It's past the point of being the future. It's here, and it could save you considerable money. However, the shift in roles and functions in the work flow for imposition raise issues of coordination that make the proofing process even more critical. For example, who pays if the pages are set up in the wrong signatures, and the printer has to do extra work to collate and trim your publication?

VI

Publishing

For more on imposition, and to understand what you may be able to do yourself using PageMaker 6.0's Build Booklet addition, see Chapter 21, "Producing Mechanicals."

▶ *Specifications for mechanicals.* Given the number of other decisions you are making, what does the printer want to see in the way of mechanicals? Will high-resolution laser output be okay for this job? Or do you need imagesetter output? Should the imagesetter output be positive resin-coated paper or negative film? Fine line screens in the range of 133 and above almost demand films.

If you do films using a service bureau, what directions do you need to give the bureau? Will it be emulsion down or up, negative or positive, and right or wrong reading?

Will the printer work directly with the service bureau on other prepress issues such as trapping specifications, dot gain compensation, and imposition? Or maybe you will decide to have the print shop handle those and other prepress tasks in-house, which would make many of the coordination issues moot.

For all the details and nuances of getting your publication to the camera-ready art stage, check out Chapter 21, "Producing Mechanicals." This chapter covers the issues of creating your camera-ready art with a laser printer as well as with a service bureau's imagesetter.

▶ *Proofs.* At the preflight, get an agreement on proofing procedures. Will there be a press check? Will the print shop accept the service bureau's color proofs? The shop may want to do the proofs on their own system because they know how it relates to their presses.

TIP ▶ Going Digital Direct to the Press

In the last edition, we talked of something new that was about to wash through the printing industry. Well, direct-to-press and small-run color technologies have arrived. Many printers now offer a direct-to-press process of going right from the computer to the printing press plates, which are mounted on the press at the time!

Plan in advance and find the right printer, and you'll be able to simply take your Syquest or Zip cartridge to the printer (they'll burn the plates right from your PageMaker file). You can go from computer to printed page in less than half an hour. And that's full-bore process color, often at much lower prices than traditional work flow that requires more intermediate steps.

Bidding the Job

If you read through the preflight section, it must be clear that the process of collaborating with your printer won't be linear. There's a considerable blur factor between the tasks of planning your job and the tasks of getting a specification and locked down bid for the work. After all, you don't stop collaborating just because you completed your preflight. In fact, if the collaboration is going well, you'll probably change your publication a fair amount between the planning and the printing. It's often an evolutionary process.

Fig. 23.1 ▶

A bid specification and request form for you to customize to your own job needs.

Bid Request & Specification

Vitals
Job Name: _____
New Job ❑ Exact Repeat ❑ Repeat With Changes ❑ Previous Job Number: _____
Type Of Publication: _____
Date Requested: _____ Date Quote Due: _____ Job Deadline: _____
Contact Info: _____
_____
_____
_____

Printing
Size Of Run: _____
Number Of Pages: _____
Finish Size: _____
Body
Paper: _____
Inks/Varnish: _____
_____

Cover
Paper: _____
Inks/Varnish: _____
_____

Notes/Critical Elements/Quality: _____
_____
_____

PrePress
Service Bureau Specifications
Film ❑ Repro Paper ❑ Negative ❑ Positive ❑
Right Reading ❑ Wrong Reading ❑
UCR/GCR Coordination Required ❑
Trapping Coordination Required ❑
Imposition Coordination Required ❑
Print Shop PrePress:
Halftoning/Stripping: B&Ws:_____ Duotones: _____ Color: _____
Screens/Reverses/Solids/Bleeds: _____
Trapping Required: _____
Bindery
Sewing ❑ Stapling ❑ Gluing ❑ Comb ❑ Spiral ❑ Drilling ❑ Padding ❑ Carbonless ❑
Perfing ❑ Die Cutting ❑ Embossing ❑ Foil Stamping ❑ Folding ❑ Scoring ❑
Inserting ❑ Tipping ❑ Stuffing ❑
Fulfillment
Packing Instructions: _____
_____
Delivery Instructions: _____
_____

VI

Publishing

Developing a Bid Form

The bid form you see in figure 23.1 tries to cover the broad spectrum of desktop publishing. You could just photocopy this form and use it, but chances are you'll be better off if you work up a specific bid form for every project you do. Naturally, a newsletter job requires much the same kind of form as the last one you did, so you can recycle your bid forms in a word processor template. Whatever you do, use a standard form like this one to collect your bids, so all the print shops are bidding on the same job.

TIP ▶ Use a Bid Specification Request Even for Your Regular Printer

Many desktop publishers develop a steady relationship with one or two print shops that do all their work. That's good, because it enhances collaboration and improves your chances of getting good prices on severe deadlines—the print shop will work hard to keep your steady business. However, even in that situation, using a bid specification form will help you ensure that there's no question about what you want out of a job. Also, if you form a steady print shop relationship, it's a good idea to get a competitive bid every once in awhile just as a reality check on price and service.

TIP ▶ High and Low Bids are Warning Systems

If radical differences exist between the bids, think twice before settling on the low bidder. Use the high and low bidders as warning systems for problems that you may not have considered or as opportunities to economize. It's entirely possible, for example, that the high bidder noticed some vitally important problem that's implicit in your bid. The low bidder may have come up with a cost-saving technique that saves you a lot of money—or could result in a job that doesn't meet your quality expectations. Call the bidders, and ask for explanations of major price differences.

Specifying Paper

Selecting your paper may be the most important collaboration you have with your printer. To a great extent, it determines your line screen choice and certainly has a major impact on the price of your publication.

When you select paper, keep in mind all the factors that you thought through when you were getting ready for the preflight session with the printer. In fact, the best time to make a paper selection may be in that session. The printer can't recommend an optimum line screen for you without knowing what kind of paper you'll be using.

You will probably select your paper from a swatch booklet, sort of like picking a carpet or an upholstery fabric or a Pantone color. But selecting a paper turns out to be much more complicated than just picking what you like. It's the foundation of your printed piece, and it must physically and visually support the purposes of your publication.

Here's a 60-second quick start primer about specifying paper. Entire books have been written about choosing paper, but if you understand these fundamental characteristics, they can help you get more effective help from your printer in selecting a paper that will work best for your job:

- ▶ *Ink holdout.* The paper's holdout characteristics are the major element for determining dot gain. If the paper is a coated stock, the ink won't sink in nearly to the degree that ink spreads on newsprint.

- ▶ *Paper types.* The paper and printing industries break down paper types into some categories that are pretty standard. For each one of these four categories, there are probably at least a dozen subcategories, which vary a great deal from paper manufacturer to manufacturer.

  Bond is paper that you see used for stationery and in photocopying and laser printing. It is designed to provide a good writing surface for one-sided jobs.

  Regular book or *offset* has been formulated to run well through a printing press. *Coated book* has been coated with a substance that makes it slick. Because of that stable surface, coated book is the most common surface for color printing. It is designed with more opacity than bond papers to accommodate printing on both sides of the sheet.

  Among other characteristics, *cover stock* has a thickness suitable for covering a book or report, or for solid-feeling brochures.

  Specialty papers abound and defy enumeration here. Examples include adhesive coated stock, bristol board, and plastic coated, as well as the paper used for carbonless multipart forms.

- ▶ *Surfaces.* One paper manufacturer lists 30 different surfaces for paper, not including variations within each type of surface. Felt, for example, comes in a dozen different textures. Here are the major categories. Notice that there's some blurring of the types of papers and their surfaces.

  Wove paper is the most common kind of paper that you see. It's also called *smooth*, and it's most common in bond papers.

  Laid paper might be bond, or it might be uncoated book stock. It has a texture to it, often a surface that reminds you of fabric.

  Felt surface paper has, well, a hairy surface—as if it were felt. It has a nap to it.

VI

Publishing

Smooth, *book*, or *offset* has usually been smoothed with a machine process. The smoother the paper, the higher the quality. The smoothing process is called *calendaring*, which involves a sort of polishing operation using rollers.

Coated stock has been coated with a substance, usually a clay wash, and polished even more than smooth stock.

There are also lots of specialty surfaces such as linen, antique, parchment and vellum.

▶ *Color.* Obviously, paper can come in almost any imaginable color, and if it works for your design, that's one way to add another color to your publication without the expense of an additional ink (assuming that the paper doesn't cost more than the ink would). Also, when you select white paper, all white is not equal, so compare whites for brightness. Keep in mind that you can get paper designed to match the various color matching systems.

▶ *Weight and size.* There are several different and complicated systems for measuring the weight of paper, depending on the size of the paper as delivered to the printing plant. Unless you have intellectual curiosity about how paper weight is calculated, you may want to simply focus on how the paper's weight and size will affect your job.

Think carefully about how the piece will be used. You may need a thicker (heavier) paper to handle the task. On the other hand, if you must ship the paper to a trade show or put it into the mail, consider going with a lighter stock if the extra weight would throw you over budget for postage.

The delivered size of the paper has a huge impact on how your printer bids the job. Your favorite choice may not even come in a size that fits on the printer's press, or it may come in 8 1/2 × 11 sheets only and thus be impractical for most commercial presses. It's not a letter-sized world out there.

To handle this issue of weight and size, come to the preflight meeting with some paper samples you like, and ask the printer to suggest similar ones that can be obtained at a good price but are optimal for that shop's press. Don't hesitate to ask the printer to reality-check your choice, given the purpose of your piece. If you want the finished sheets to fit a certain envelope size, the printer may suggest a different approach from the one you had in mind, for example.

▶ *Opacity.* Place the paper you are considering down on top of a printed page. If you can read the page through the paper, you probably don't want to print on both sides of that paper stock. That's opacity. Your printer can advise you whether your job will work with the opacity of a certain paper.

▶ *Grain.* Paper has a grain, a predominant direction in which the paper fibers run. You don't much care what it is, but you do care that the printer thinks through how the paper will be folded and tells you that your paper choice has a grain suitable for your project. Grain running against the fold means crackly and uneven folds.

Arranging for Bindery Services

To a printer, *bindery* means just about anything that involves the physical construction of your publication.

In the regular run of things, your print shop handles all the binding tasks for your publication. Even quick print shops tend to have fairly sophisticated capabilities these days (or can hire them from outside), and any printer handling a book job for you will certainly have the skills to not only print it, but to bind it as well.

Here's the meaning of each of the terms mentioned in the sample bid form. A book binder sews, staples, and glues together the pages of a book. You can have *perfect bound books*, which are like paperbacks, or *case bound books*, which are like hard covers.

A lot of desktop published jobs end up being *comb* or *true spiral* bound. They may also be drilled for loose-leaf ring binders. Or you can have forms put into a tear-off pad, and sometimes you use carbonless paper so you can generate duplicates of the form.

Sometimes a printer must *perf*, or *perforate*, a pull-out or tear-off card. *Die cutting* can be used to shape labels or to create cutouts in covers. *Embossing* involves a special metal stamp that presses a shape into the paper. *Foil stamping* works a bit like embossing, except metal leaf gets pressed onto the paper.

Machines can do folding, and there are some cases where varnished or particularly heavy stock must also be scored with a special machine that creases the stock prior to folding. You can also have scored work shipped to you flat and then fold it as needed, something that's often done with presentation folders.

Inserting means slipping cards or pullouts into a magazine, usually the kind that fall out on the way into the house from the mailbox. *Tipping* works sort of like inserting, except the item gets glued in, which you may do for specially reproduced pictures in an art book. *Stuffing* means sticking the publication in an envelope or similar carrier.

VI

Publishing

Inspecting Your Finished Job

When you inspect your completed job, do pretty much everything you do at the press check session described in Chapter 22:

▶ Check to make sure that the color matches the press check sheet, if you did one. If you didn't, check the piece against the proofs.

▶ Pull some random samples from different points in the run. See that they are consistent with your proofs and with the other pieces in the run.

▶ Look for wrinkles, print through, hairs or dust, blotting between sheets, and smudging from the paper feed apparatus of the press.

▶ Also, inspect how the piece lines up. Whether the piece has color or not, there's an issue of registration and alignment. Rules in headers and footers should match on the front and back of pages, for example. Spreads should line up.

▶ Inspect that the job has been boxed or banded or shrink-wrapped as you requested, and attempt to estimate that you received your full quantity of product. Remember that most printing contracts allow for a percentage of overrun or underrun caused by the variables of the printing and binding process.

KEY CONCEPT:
Understanding Halftones and Screens

Why in the world would anybody put halftones here, in the section about printing presses? "Outrageous," you declaim in an offended tone. "We needed to know about this stuff back when we placed the graphic into PageMaker!" Or, "We needed to know about halftones even further back, when we were pulling graphics out of the scanner or off the Photo CD."

Excellent. Very perceptive of you. You absolutely do need to know about line screen way back there. And the place to find out is right here, where the folks with the aprons hang out in the press room. Handle this issue in your printer preflight:

Don't do a single scan or select even one photo from that CD without getting your printer's input about what line screen to use.

The line screen makes it possible to break up a sheet of ink into small dots, so it can make your eye think that it's seeing gray. You'll be well down the path of understanding halftones if you picture them as a bad case of gray measles—as in spots, dots, pixels, and cells—all of which will be explained shortly. To understand completely, however, you need to start with the fact that a printing press can't print shades of gray.

There's No Gray on the Printing Press

First, you need to keep in mind that there's no such thing as gray ink when it comes to reproducing a photograph. When someone says a photograph has 256 shades of gray—a grayscale image—there's no gray ink in that image at all. Sure, by screening black ink to make it look gray, you can have a pretend gray. You can also have an ink called gray, and it will give you a square of gray on the page, as you see in figure 23.2 in the color section of the book.

Fig. 23.2

(See color section.)

Gray ink, however, won't automatically give you a scale of gray values. That would be like trying to buy striped paint! In figure 23.3 (also in the color section), you see that gray paint does not make a grayscale. This figure has been scanned as line art, without halftoning. It's printed with gray ink, but it doesn't have any grayscale information in it.

Fig. 23.3

(See color section.)

Ink on the press works a lot like the binary numbers that zip around inside your computer. Ink's either there or it isn't. On or off. One or the other.

So what's the answer to this dilemma? How can you produce a photograph on the printing press and have shades of gray in it? Halftones, of course. We need spots.

In figure 23.4, the same photo has been given a case of the measles—big spots so that you can see them.

Fig. 23.4 ▲

A halftone version of the photo scan, with the ink broken up into spots.

VI

Publishing

continues

KEY CONCEPT:
Continued

Here we have the great halftone eyeball scam. Notice how your eye has been fooled into perceiving that there are shades of gray in the scanned photograph. However, no gray ink is on the page. It's pure black ink broken into dots—gray measles, in other words.

Before Digital Halftones There Were Process Cameras

Traditionally, before we had computers doing this work, halftone spots were all created by a screen. Literally, a screen gets shoved between the original photograph and the film or paper used to photographically create the plate for the printing press (see fig. 23.5). That screen breaks up the original image into halftone spots.

Image —

— Lens

— Halftone screen

— Film to make plate

FIG. 23.5 ▲

A conceptual diagram of how a printer's process camera works. The camera is set up to make halftones by putting a screen between the lens and the film.

In figure 23.5, the screen is the traditional piece of glass etched with crisscrossing lines. More commonly today the screening is accomplished by making a sandwich of the original photo negative, the screen and the film for making the plate. In that case, the screen is made up of vignetted dots instead of rules, but the result is the same.

You can still have a photograph traditionally screened, by the way. The world hasn't gone entirely digital yet. Like the debates between those who still love vinyl records and CD aficionados, some designers prefer the look of the rounder and softer dots created for a traditionally halftoned photograph. It just means doing mechanical pasteup or stripping instead of using desktop publishing to its fullest extent.

Why do they call them halftones? The idea comes from the concept of removing "half" the information from the original image—a halftone. It doesn't literally work this way, but that's the idea behind the term. The original photograph is called a *contone*, or continuous tone image.

Now It's PostScript Digital Screening

How does a laser printer or an imagesetter make a halftone? These machines don't have a process camera hidden inside them, right?

Figure 23.6 helps to explain. You can see that each of the dots in a digital halftone is made up of a bunch of imagesetter or laser spots. The dots are contained within a halftone cell, which is the square area bounded by the vertical and horizontal lines of the screen.

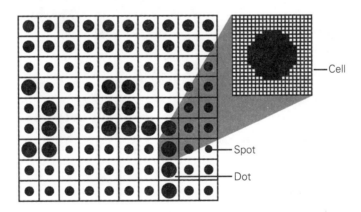

Fig. 23.6 ▲

Dots, spots, and cells, and how they all relate to one another.

All this dot and spot stuff gets confusing because people tend to blur the meaning between laser spot and halftone dot. In fact, there's no universal agreement on the use of these terms. Think of it in terms of a hierarchy:

▶ The screen divides the image into cells.

▶ These cells contain halftone dots.
▶ Dots are made up of spots. In a laser printer, the spots are microscopic bits of plastic toner which are fused under heat to the paper. In a photographic typesetter, the spots are the grains of photosensitive material on the positive resin paper or the negative film.

continues

VI

Publishing

KEY CONCEPT:
Continued

The number of spots per inch that an imagesetter can resolve (300 dpi laser printer, 2,450 dpi imagesetter, and so on) determines the capability of the machine to create fine gradations of perceived gray in a scanned photograph.

But how does the imagesetter or laser printer make the screen that breaks the image up into cells and dots in the first place? The screening capability is built into the PostScript language that lives inside most laser printers and image-setters. It's done mathematically instead of photographically.

You Get Gray from the Size of the Halftone Spot

Notice in figure 23.7 the comparison between two different halftone cells; one gives a 30 percent gray, and the other is a 70 percent gray.

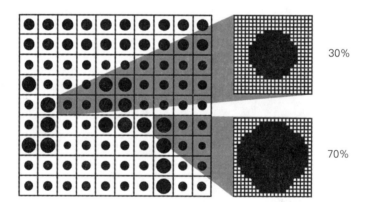

FIG. 23.7 ▲

Comparing two gray halftone dots.

What makes these halftone cells 30 and 70 percent? That's how much of their cell area has been covered by the laser spots. The size of the cells is the same, but it's the size of the dots that varies and thus provides different levels of gray.

It wouldn't matter whether your scanned image was 80 percent chartreuse or 20 percent brick red. Both those images would have the same number of cells and hence the same number of halftone dots. The size of the dots would be different, however. The 20 percent brick red would have a smaller spot than the 80 percent char-treuse.

More Grays from Fewer Cells

The smaller the laser spots, the more of them can be crammed into a halftone cell. The larger the potential number of spots in a dot, the more different sizes of spots you can have. More potential dot sizes mean that you can have more levels of gray.

Here's the problem. The old fashioned photographic method of making a halftone could give you an infinite number of halftone dot sizes, no matter which lines per inch screen grid you used. Not so with digital halftoning, because your output device has fixed resolution. You can't change it.

Remember, however, that the only way to get more gray levels is to find a way to jam more laser spots into a single halftone cell. This means that to get more levels of gray, you need to increase the size of the halftone cell, which means using a coarser halftone screen. So, the only way you can change the number of laser spots that can fit on a halftone dot is to make the cells bigger by using a lower halftone screen frequency.

In figure 23.8, you can see that the magnified 85-lines-per-inch screen actually has the potential to reproduce more levels of gray, compared to the 150-lines-per-inch screen. The fine detail won't be as sharp with the coarser screen, but you'll get more levels of gray.

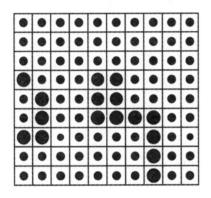

85 lines per inch

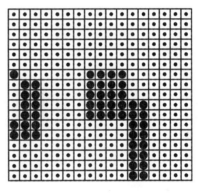

150 lines per inch

Fig. 23.8 ▲

Comparing the detail (resolution) and grayscale level's trade-off between coarse and fine-line screens.

Chapter 21 includes a discussion on banding that closely relates to this same issue—the frequency of the line screen and the number of steps in the grayscale.

Screening Color

This concept of screening or doing percentage tints helps you make many "colors" out of one when you do spot color.

By using the PageMaker Define Colors command or the fill side of the Fill and Line command, you can screen back the apparent intensity of a given color of ink. Mathematically, you break the color into dots, and the size of the dots equates to the percentage of the screen (see fig. 23.9 here and in the color section).

continues

VI

Publishing

KEY CONCEPT:
Continued

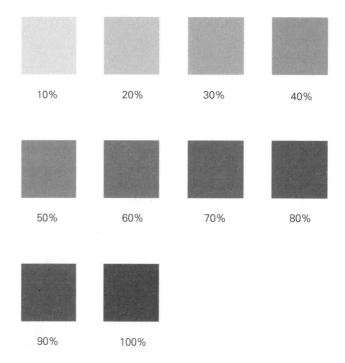

| 10% | 20% | 30% | 40% |

| 50% | 60% | 70% | 80% |

| 90% | 100% |

FIG. 23.9 ▲

A range of percentage tints of the same color.

Screen Angles and Process Color

The screens in all these illustrations have been at 45-degree angles. That's because making the dots run horizontally or vertically emphasizes their linearity and makes the lines stand out to the eye. The traditional angle for any black or spot color ink screen is 45 degrees, chosen years ago as the best angle for enhancing the great halftone screening deception.

Why do you care about the angle of the screens? Well, if you are like most PageMaker owners, you care most of all

because there's this screen angle entry box in the Print command's Color dialog box. It almost invites you to change screen angles. This screen angle issue ranks right near the top of all the questions asked by desktop publishers. "What screen angle am I supposed to use?" they say. "The darn thing's there as if I'm supposed to use it. Why else would they put it there if I'm not supposed to tweak it?"

Well, it's there so you can change it, alright, but don't. It's almost never done. The angles you see there have been standardized over the decades of printing halftones and color images with the printing press. Also, there's an optimal screen angle set into the PPD for the printer you select in the document dialog box.

Unless there's some really special reason for changing screen angles, and you are doing it in consultation with your print shop collaborators, don't mess with the screen angle setting. If you are running color, chances are good that you are going through a service bureau that will do the output anyway. You'll just be setting a booby trap for them. And even if you think there's a better angle for a certain color, it would almost certainly throw off the printing press crew. They would be booby trapped, just like the service bureau, expecting to see the standard angles rolling off the press.

This whole screen angle thing gets to be a major deal when you do process color work. There are two reasons why. First, you can't do process color without running the colors at all different angles; otherwise the dots would all pile up on one another in a sort of mush. The angles should allow the dots to stand alone so that your brain combines them, fulfilling

its role in the great process color con job. Of course, some dots inevitably land on top of each other, but the process color inks are translucent, so that's okay. However, a lot of experimentation has gone into the screen angles for the CMYK colors, and you should have a real good reason before you decide to mess with the standard angles. Ultimately, you want the angles to create a rosette pattern like the one at the top of figure 23.10. You might think of the rosette as being almost like a super spot, a major agglomeration of halftone spots that collectively create the impression of the final mixed process color.

At the bottom of the illustration, you see the second reason why angles are so important when you run process color on the press. If the angles are off, you get a moiré pattern. It's a sort of smeary wave effect. Think of it as the process color eyeball con job gone terribly wrong.

There's much more on the challenges of printing color in Chapter 20, "Meeting Color Challenges" and more on the creation of color in PageMaker in Chapter 18, "Creating Colors."

continues

VI

Publishing

KEY CONCEPT:
Continued

FIG. 23.10 ▲

Process color screen angles and a bad moiré pattern.

Choosing a Line Screen with Your Print Shop

Now, here's the point of why I'm giving all of this information on halftones. The print shop can only guarantee that halftone spots will remain distinct spots up to a certain point. After that point, you get dark mush instead of detailed grayscale. The finer the screen (the more lines per inch), the more critical this becomes. You need the printer to give you this recommended setting for the lines per inch of your screen.

Understanding the Effects of Dot Gain

The printer calculates this line screen mush point, for the most part, based on the anticipated dot gain. When the ink hits the paper from the press, the paper absorbs the thick, greasy ink as a sponge or a blotter soaks up a spill. You can imagine what happens to the tiny spaces between the dots of ink in a halftone. They are liable to clog up. That's why you can pretty well depend on a halftone to print darker than it looks like it would print from the service bureau's proof. Why? Because dot gain means you get bigger dots, and that means a higher percentage notch up in the grayscale.

To understand the effects of dot gain, look at figure 23.11. As the screens get tighter and tighter, the printing press eventually can't hold the dots anymore. This set of illustrations also shows the greater gray levels you get as you move to a coarser screen. Detail goes down, but the number of grays goes up.

What To Do with the Line Screen Information

When you have the printer's recommended line screen, you are armed with the data for two vital action steps: scanning resolution and output line screen setting.

When you scan a photograph, the dots-per-inch setting sets the intrinsic resolution of your digitized photograph. There's no sense collecting any more resolution in the scan than your line screen can deliver on the press. You just waste hard disk real estate. Even more importantly, you waste precious disk space with a file that's much larger than necessary.

Be really clear on one point—the photo hasn't been screened at this point (at least it shouldn't have been). We are talking here about the pixel resolution of the photo, and that's not the same as the halftone resolution.

Anyway, when you know your line screen, you know the resolution you need to use when you scan a photo or edit a previously scanned one. Most experts say it's a waste to scan at any more than twice the lines per inch of your halftone screen. If you work with 85 lpi on the press, scan at 170 dpi. If you will be at 133 lpi, scan at 266 dpi.

Fig. 23.11 ▶

A series of half-tones at a variety of line screens, showing the tradeoffs between resolution and dot gain on the press.

55 lpi   90 lpi   150 lpi   55 lpi   90 lpi   150 lpi

Some folks claim that scanning at double the line frequency still wastes time and disk space for no significant gain on the press. They recommend scanning at one and a half times the line screen. Check with your printer and your service bureau for more advice on the specific challenges of your piece, given the types of photos you are running and the issue of dot gain.

Now, for line screen setting. You need this recommendation from your printer so that you can tell your service bureau when they output your job what line screen setting to use, or so that you'll know the one you should use if you are doing your own output.

Setting the line screen should almost always be nearly the last thing you do before you output your job. Your line screen, by the way, should usually be set in the Print command's Color dialog box. It's rare when you set line screen using PageMaker's Image Control command. Use Image Control for special effects, or to solve specific problems in collaboration with your service bureau or printer.

Here's one nasty side effect of setting screens in Image Control. Commonly, a service bureau runs your job through the imagesetter in the most efficient way possible in an attempt to save film or repro paper. If you lock in a line screen for the photo in Image Control or Adobe PhotoShop or wherever you edited the graphic, and the service bureau runs pages horizontally instead of vertically on the film, the screen angle will be twisted around to face the wrong way.

Some Line Screen Guidelines

A given paper produces a given dot gain on a given press, and nobody can tell you what line screen to use for each press and paper combination better than the person who runs that press. However, table 23.1 shows some widely accepted guidelines that you can use in a pinch.

TABLE 23.1   Choosing a Line Screen for Given Paper and Press Conditions

Paper/Press	Lines Per Inch
Newsprint	65 to 85
Standard coated	85 to 133
Better press/high grade coated paper	133 to 175
Superior paper and press conditions	175 +

Compensate Scans for the Press

Because of dot gain, halftones tend to come off the printing press darker than they look on your computer monitor. Also, there's an issue of ink buildup when you work with multiple inks, as you do when building a process color piece.

Edit Contrast/Lightness

You can apply some dot gain compensation yourself. You'll probably want to limit do-it-yourself dot gain compensation to simple black and white and spot color tinted scans.

In general, you'll want to knock back contrast and increase lightness. Each can be adjusted by five to fifteen percent, depending on the line screen and the paper you are using (the two factors that most affect dot gain). You need more and more compensation as you work with finer line screens or more porous paper.

You can compensate for dot gain in PageMaker's Image Control command. Do bear in mind that Image Control edits may be lost or ignored if your job is run through a prepress processing program for trapping or separation (Adobe PrePrint Pro, for example), so you may want to favor the use of outboard and permanent editing in a retouching program like Adobe Photoshop.

Your print shop may have some very specific advice for these dot gain compensation adjustments, especially if they saw your photos or proofs of your scans, and especially if they regularly work with desktop publishers.

TIP ▶ **Calibrate Your Eyes**

It's a good idea to calibrate your expectations for halftone results by running some tests. It takes some time and money, but it's a great way to be more sure of your results. Scan some black-and-white photos in a range of lighting conditions and subjects. By using Photoshop or a similar retouching program, adjust the lightness and contrast in bands across the photo much the way Ansel Adams applied the zone exposure system to working in the darkroom (if you're familiar with that concept). Then the next time you run a job through the service bureau and printer, put these tests into the job. Ask your collaborators to fit the calibration tests in as they can, as a means of economizing. Have the tests run on a variety of papers, if possible.

If you can't see making a special project out of it, tag your standard set of banded scans into regular jobs as you get the chance—perhaps every time a different paper requirement comes through.

As you get the results, put them in a notebook, and you'll have a ready reference for what it takes to edit your scans in your particular environment. You will have calibrated your eyes.

Dot Gain Correction Software

It's quite possible that your prepress provider uses a program that can apply dot gain correction using your print shop's specifications to produce your films. This especially comes up when a color job is separated.

For color images, that's also true for multiple ink buildup (under color removal and gray component replacement).

Adjusting for Multiple Inks

Compensating for ink buildup on a color page can be quite a technical ordeal. It's necessary because process color inks pile up on top of each other and place so much ink onto the page that it exacerbates dot gain and makes drying difficult. The technical terms are *UCR* (under color removal) and *GCR* (gray component replacement). Either way, the print shop should advise you on this, perhaps communicating directly with the service bureau.

Where to Go from Here

▶ Chapter 21, "Producing Mechanicals," and Chapter 22, "Proofing Your Publication," give important information about taking your publication to the print shop.

▶ Almost all the information specific to creating color with PageMaker has been collected into Part V, "Making Pages Colorful." So if you are doing a color publication, you'll want to spend some time in Chapters 18, 19, and 20, in addition to reading the information here on halftones and the screens that create process color.

▶ In most desktop publishing cases, scans end up as digital halftones. That makes it pretty important to blend the halftone information in this chapter with the background in Chapter 11, "Placing Images."

▶ Big graphics are generally linked into PageMaker, instead of storing them twice on your hard disk (once alone and once in PageMaker). There's information on linking as well as the other technology for connecting programs in Chapter 30, "Linking and Other File Connections."

VI

Publishing

Chapter 24

Master Checklist for Desktop Publishing

This master checklist chapter includes the following information:

Planning your publication, from the initial step of defining the goal and audience to setting a budget and deadline.

▼

Executing your plan by perfecting all the page elements from text to graphics and then setting up the publication for placing on pages.

▼

Fine-tuning the layout of each page and then finalizing the table of contents and index.

▼

Handling prepress elements such as trapping, separating, and creating mechanicals for reproduction.

▼

Proofing the mechanicals and getting final approval before imposing the pages and going to press.

SOMETIMES IT SEEMS as if desktop publishing would be more logical if it ran in reverse—from printing press back to the first thumbnails, rather than the other way around. As much as possible, figure out where you want to end up—then think about the best way to get there.

This looking-ahead work approach runs through this entire book. That's why Chapter 4 appeared at the beginning of the book, linking this checklist across all the other chapters in between. ▶ ▶ ▶

> **TIP ▶ Use This Checklist as a Thought-Starter**
>
> Desktop publishing involves many kinds of publications and hundreds of variables of budget, technique, and deadline. So, many items in the following lists won't apply directly and precisely to your current job. Rather, in many instances, the items have been designed as reminders and brainstorming tools. Many of the items ask, "Did you think of this area of concern?" as opposed to the kind of detailed step-by-step approach that says, "Now do this, followed by that."

Planning

As you might expect, making a plan means starting with the goal. How can you make a plan to get where you want to go if you don't know the final destination?

Defining the Goal and Audience

Try to write down a description of the audience and the specific communication objective for the publication. Use the suggestions in the following sections to help you.

Audience

You can usually define the audience in terms of some common factors or characteristics. There are as many possible factors as there are people on this planet, so your options are broad, and your intent should be to narrow them down. For example, consider the demographics of your audience:

▶ Age

▶ Sex

▶ Family role (spouse, parent, sibling, child, and so on)

▶ Home location (for example, urban, rural, suburban)

▶ Geographic location (for example, Southwest, Northeast, foreign country)

▶ Income bracket

▶ Education level

Keep in mind that the Census Bureau doesn't have a lock on describing an audience. Think about what some marketing types call the "psychographic" or "sociological" profile of your target audience:

▶ Use of recreational time (for example, hobbies)

▶ Possessions (pets, cars, stereos, size of home, style of home decoration)

▶ Membership in organizations (fraternal order, bridge club, church, alumni group)

▶ Political (special interest groups or party affiliation)

Most of all, you must spend some time thinking about the reader's relationship to your publication and the topic:

▶ How is the reader involved in the topic? Is the reader reading it for work, for a hobby, or from a need to accomplish a certain goal?

▶ Where does the reader's knowledge of the topic begin? Is the user beginning, average, or advanced?

▶ Can you expect the reader to understand certain jargon and terms specific to the topic?

▶ How will the publication be used? Will the reader be using the material as a reference (book), a tutorial (syllabus or course outline), or the latest news (newsletter)?

Goal

Your publication—whether it's a magazine, newsletter, book, or brochure—has a purpose. After you define your audience, there's a good chance that the purpose will be crystallized in your mind. You might start with an idea about your objective, but it is almost always easier to state an objective in the context of the target audience.

Generally, your goal already exists in your head. You just need to turn those vague churnings of thought into a written goal statement, which a client, a boss, or you can sign off on before you move ahead with planning.

If you are doing a series of publications (an ad campaign or a newsletter), you will want to define a broad goal and then a specific goal for each element of the series. Of course, if you are creating a one-time piece (a brochure, for example) you only need to define the goal once.

Try these ways of focusing your thoughts:

▶ *What are you selling?* It may be toothpaste, a thesis, or a business plan; but whether you realize it or not, you are probably selling some thing or some idea.

▶ *What are you telling?* Even if you think you don't have a point of view that you are selling, you are at least trying to give someone some information.

▶ *What is the competition saying?* If you are in some competitive arena, such as retail point of purchase or advertising, your competition probably has a very good idea of what you are selling or telling. That's a good clue to center your thinking about your goal.

▶ *What have you already been saying?* Look through back issues or other previous publications for your target audience and ask yourself what they were trying to say. If you are doing an in-house newsletter for a company, that company's advertising campaign can give you clues for your goals in the newsletter, although you need to filter your ideas through the target audience.

▶ *What would you say?* Quite literally, say your message out loud. If possible, do it in the context of the delivery method for your piece. If it's a newsletter that will be delivered by mail, literally stand at the mailbox and talk to an imaginary member of your target audience. If it's a sales sheet handout, role play with yourself (and someone you feel comfortable around) on a pretend trade-show floor. Just say what you feel—that gives you a good start on focusing your thoughts about the goal.

Setting a Budget, Deadline, and Schedule

There's no magic to this. You need to have at least some idea, formally or informally, of when the publication must be ready and how much you can spend to produce it.

Budget

Unfortunately, unless you have an unlimited budget, there's no way you can let your creativity range freely on the execution of your project. Most of us have budget limits, so here are some questions to help you get to the bottom line:

▶ *What's the project worth?* What you spend may depend on what you will make. It makes sense to spend more per printed piece on a brochure to sell cars than it does to spend that same amount on a weekly supermarket flyer.

▶ *What are the client's expectations, and what will the market bear?* Sometimes it's true that the emotions of the client and the client's pocketbook dictate the budget. If the client is enthusiastic and wants to spend the money, you can go all out.

▶ *How many do you need of what?* One dominant budget factor has to be the number of copies you need. After that, a rough vision of the format of the publication should at least get you some ballpark budget information.

▶ *What's the minimum cost?* You might base the budget on the concept of minimums. (Can you say the word "cheap?")

▶ *What has the project cost in the past?* Don't overlook the track record—yours and those of the publication. If a newsletter has been published every week for a year, you can get a good idea of the cost of the next one. If you have been doing similar jobs for other folks, you probably have a good idea of the costs involved.

▶ *Should you come back to the budget?* So what if these guidelines say that you should have a budget before you develop the concept? You probably have some idea of where the budget stands, so maybe you should just take the gamble, move on to concept development, and come back to the budget. You can do a great budget after you finish a preliminary planning session with the printer, for example. You should certainly revise your preliminary budget after you meet with the printer.

▶ *Are time factors involved that affect the budget?* Consider the deadline and ask yourself if the project demands extra funds in order to be completed on time. Overtime can be expensive and rush orders at the service bureau cost plenty, but if the deadline is immutable, you may not have a choice.

Deadline and Schedule

Here's another one of those situations where you start from where you want to end up. The concert happens on the date the auditorium is booked, whether or not you think you can finish the playbill and program. If you are creating an annual report, there are often legally proscribed filing deadlines. What's the newsletter mailing date or the submission deadline for the advertisement?

Get out a calendar, maybe one of those desk planners. Sometimes print shops put out special calendar forms designed to help you plan print jobs. Begin with the last possible date you need the job, allow a bit of leeway, and count backwards, providing time for each of the functions in this chapter full of checklists. Only experience—yours or that of a collaborator—can help you fill in the blanks for how much time each element will take. Printing and bindery schedules are generally very reliable. The time to allow for writing the copy (accounting for writer's block), well, that's between you and your keyboard.

For each one of the following steps, plot the length of time for the task as well as the "by when" date—the deadline by which the task must be completed so that the next task can follow and be completed by its "by when" date:

▶ Allow time for approvals after each one of these steps—a variable that depends on your client relationship, assuming the client isn't just you.

▶ For each of the steps, plan who will be responsible. (In many cases, it will probably be you.) You want someone to coordinate the project, and you need to know the writer for the copy, the layout artist, and the production services you need (illustrator, proofreader, probable service bureau, probable print shop, and so on).

▶ Estimate the time it will take to sketch out and further develop the core creative concept.

▶ How long will it take to test the concept and refine it further after the testing? Be especially certain to allow time for conceptualizing the structure of the publication, including the text styles and the color scheme.

▶ A planning session with the print shop and service bureau won't take long, but allow time for it. It's a must.

▶ Leave plenty of time to perfect the text and graphic elements of the design, including time to write the copy and create the illustrations.

▶ Executing the layout steps will bring the design to fruition, so don't shirk on time needed for that. You need to set up the publication's geometry, place all the text and graphics, and then fine-tune and elaborate the layout with special effects and color.

▶ For a table of contents and index, leave extra time at the end of layout.

▶ Develop a sense of the time that it takes to do the prepress steps of trapping, separating, and then outputting the mechanicals. Whether you send material to the laser printer or an imagesetter, you need time to do this output step.

▶ Final proofing and approvals pay back the time investment in saved money and a better product, but these steps won't happen instantaneously. You will need an elapsed time estimate and a "by when" date for each of the proofing and approval stages.

▶ Manufacturing time varies, depending on whether you use a photocopier or a six tower web press. This time also depends on the way the publication will be folded and bound.

Developing Your Core Creative Concept

Developing your core creative concept means fleshing it out and bringing it to life with details. Development is the major sweat factor for the creative process. The rest of the effort to complete is the execution. Based on the target audience, design the way you'll accomplish the goals of your publication. Some of your core creative concept can be doodled out right in PageMaker. Use the following thought-starters to help you prime your creative pump:

▶ *Driving force and dominant design item.* In almost every design, some single element comes to the front. It's a good place to start. As you stare at the screen or cradle that sketch pad in your lap, mulling over how to tackle the design, ask yourself what that element might be. Maybe you can use some slogan or logo to focus the eye. How about a product shot? Or maybe you want to use the title of a report or the masthead of a newsletter.

▶ *Organizational structure.* Applying a structure to your concept primarily concerns the written part of a publication design, but it can also be useful when you organize a concept visually on the page.

Try an outline. Look at your subject matter using journalism's big five: who, what, when, where, and why. Apply some hierarchy of thought to the idea or ideas you are trying to convey.

You can also try the age old saw about expository writing: Tell 'em what you're going to tell 'em. Tell 'em. Tell 'em what you told 'em. To say it more formally: state a proposition, expand on it with factual detail and discussion, and end by summarizing the proposition in its supported and elaborated state.

▶ *Overall style*. You need to come up with an overall style that plays to your target audience and the purpose of the piece. When you hit this style, you can almost always sum it up in a single image or word. The word might be as vague as the word "formal" or "informal," but you'll be best served by words that evoke some sort of picture in your mind. Think about style names like deco, antique, garden, sand painting, English, French, Japanese, impressionist, metallic, furry animal, and so on. Your goal will be to find a kernel around which you can accrete a pearl inside that oyster-like brain of yours.

▶ *Graphics style*. You don't want to hop all over the map with your illustrations. Your publication will look most cohesive and purposeful if you select an approach to your illustrations and stick to it. Do you plan to use illustrations, and will they be realistic, line drawings, or abstract? Maybe you need photos to tell your story. Will you add charts and tables?

▶ *Writing style*. Get an idea of the way your target audience speaks, which will put you on the trail of the writing style for your publication. But keep in mind that lawyers speak with one style in court in front of a jury, and quite another when they hang out at the swimming pool. So if you target your brochure to market a high-end golf club to a special mailing list that reaches lawyers in their homes, you'll want to take that point into account.

▶ *Paper style*. Paper says a lot about the style of your publication. Stately royal blue covers that would work well for a business plan probably wouldn't be as appropriate for the covers of a fun-filled brochure selling cruises to the Bahamas.

▶ *Type style*. You don't sell colonial pine furniture with art deco type, and you don't usually sell computers with a country and western style theme—that is, unless you are Borland, which did it very successfully. Remember the program *Sidekick*? In that case, the name was the dominant element for the core concept; it dictated all the other design choices, including the western style type and the cartoon sidekick character.

VI

Publishing

Think about the type style in light of all the other conceptual creative factors. You will probably want to link your type style to the imagery evoked by your overall style and by your dominant design element.

▶ *Size and format.* It may seem obvious, but you do need to decide what kind of publication you are doing, and it needs to be suited to the audience and goals for the project. More than anything else, that means making the size and format suitable for the delivery method. If the publication is in the mail, for example, it may need to fit an envelope or at least conform to postal regulations. Brochures in "take one" pockets at counter point-of-purchase displays must fit the pockets.

So, will it be a newsletter, a brochure, a calling card, a book? What form will the publication take? How big will it be? How many pages? What will be the trim size, and how much of the page will be margins and how much will be "live" area?

▶ *Visual structure of a page.* Given all these other creative elements, can you conceptualize the column grid yet? How will graphics and text fit together? How will headlines (which sort of straddle the line between type and graphics) occupy their prominent position on the page?

Testing the Concept and Getting Preliminary Approvals

It goes without saying that your designs sell a million of those widgets and always have those subscribers hugging the mailbox (or the postal carrier) waiting for the arrival of your bimonthly newsletter on Peruvian corn cultivation. Of course, you're the world's most insightful and perceptive designer, but deep down inside, are you really sure? Here's how you can test your new concept:

▶ *Dummy it up.* Make a mock-up version of the publication. There's no other way to test your concept. Let's repeat that. In order to test your concept, you must create a prototype. Describing it won't work, even if you wave your arms a lot.

Also, the dummied up publication will help you crystallize your thinking and show you whether it will physically work. Did you ever hear about the designer who produced 50,000 resort promotion brochures for travel agents and specified an oversized job that would be different and stand out in the crowd? It was different all right, but nobody saw it because the brochure wouldn't fit in the distributor's standard display rack.

▶ *Use informal testing.* Imagine cold water, reality check, horse sense— think of all these good things about an informal test. Some people call it a "grandma survey." Try out the dummy publication on anyone you can find who might have a point of view, including consumers, sales people, and distributors.

For example, if you are thinking about informally testing a video sleeve design, try it out on some potential viewers of the genre. Don't just ask them how they like it. Give the product to them and watch to see whether they handle it. Do you think they would really pick it up off the shelf and rent it?

▶ *Use formal audience research*. If the project has enough importance and budget, maybe you should get some professional testing. The marketing pros test out product packaging ideas and concepts for new magazines by using focus groups and shopping mall intercepts.

▶ *Make adjustments*. Why test your concept? So you can change it, of course, and make it better. The feedback from all these people who see a mock-up will show you how to refine your approach. Be emotionally prepared to make adjustments, based on your research, to your great idea.

▶ *Build a consensus and get a sign off*. So, all this testing leads to one thing— consensus. In addition, you can get a formal sign-off on the mock-up, plus any written analysis you did based on the checklists up to this point.

Communications make—or break—a project. The better the job you do of bringing the client and everyone else on the team on board, the easier time you'll have from this point on. Those people who actually held a sketch of the end result in their hands and who experienced your mock-up concept are less likely to second-guess the refinements when you begin to execute the project. People like to own the things they are involved in, and your dummied up pub and your concept testing will help the folks you are trying to please, including you, achieve that feeling of ownership and involvement. Sometimes it's called "emotional buy-in."

Collaborating with the Printer and Service Bureau

At this point, you establish your prepress strategy and finalize your bid specifications. Precisely when you perform each of these steps in relation to your design process will vary, depending on your working style and your approach to getting the bid. Also, the print shop and service bureau issues get mingled together in real life (as opposed to checklist life), so think about your specific project needs when you apply this reminder list.

What to Bring to the Preliminary Meeting

Bring these items to the print shop or service bureau preliminary meeting:

▶ Purpose and audience for your publication

▶ Your rough sketch, comp, or mock-up

VI

Publishing

▶ Samples of other publications showing what you like

▶ Size of run and budget

▶ Quality expectations

▶ Deadline and schedule estimate

▶ Estimate of ink and varnish needs

▶ Thoughts on paper

▶ Special sensitivities regarding the project

▶ Crazy thoughts and brainstorms

Answers, Decisions, and Feedback for You to Get at the Preliminary Meeting

Before you do extensive layout work, you are best off resolving these production and prepress issues:

▶ Determine the method of reproduction (photocopy, sheet fed, web press, roto, screen printing, and so on).

▶ Finalize paper choice.

▶ Determine line screen frequency for scans.

▶ Identify items for service bureau prepress work and items that are less expensively or otherwise better handled with traditional prepress approaches at the print shop.

▶ Work out a trapping strategy (PageMaker internal, design to avoid the need, have service bureau do it). If you won't be doing the trapping, determine who will—the print shop or the service bureau. If you decide to use PageMaker trapping, be sure it can handle your specific design challenges.

▶ Discuss strategy for inks (process CMYK, number of spot colors, varnish).

▶ Coordinate implementation of a color management system or a color matching system such as one of the PANTONE libraries.

To get the most out of your collaboration with the printer and the service bureau, these additional points will help you:

▶ Reality-test your creative concepts and how you plan to execute them.

▶ Suggest ways to improve the quality of your piece.

▶ Determine ways to save money, perhaps by making acceptable adjustments to the design concept.

▶ Make suggestions regarding efficiency to cut down production and manufacturing time.

▶ Make recommendations for proofing (laser comps, composite color, laminate color, and so on).

▶ Discuss the probable approach for imposing the piece, based on the printer's particular press size and the probable size of the paper to be used.

▶ Determine whether it makes sense to submit imposed film, or whether the printer should strip together the flats.

▶ Discuss ideas for bindery (need for scoring, foil stamping or embossing, die cutting, loose-leaf, perfect bound, case bound, spiral, comb).

▶ Determine the best way to package the job for shipment and use.

The following issues have to do with your work with the service bureau in producing mechanicals:

▶ Will you need imagesetter output, or would laser printer output be just fine?

▶ If you need them, what are the specifications for imagesetter mechanicals (film or paper, right or wrong reading, negative or positive)?

▶ Do you need dot gain compensation on black-and-white halftones or on color scans?

▶ Do you need under color removal (UCR) and gray component replacement (GCR)?

▶ What strategy will you use for handling the large files produced by high resolution color scans?

▶ How will the service bureau manage your Photo CD scans, if you decide to take that approach?

▶ Should you print to PostScript or submit native PageMaker files?

Bidding

You will probably want to develop a bid and specifications form for the project. The form should cover these items:

▶ Contact information

▶ Indication of whether this is a new job, a repeat, or a repeat with changes

▶ Type of publication

▶ Dates (request date, quote due date, art ready date, date for completing the job)

▶ Size of run

▶ Number of pages in the piece

▶ Final trim size of the pages

▶ For text pages: paper, ink, and varnish

▶ For cover stock: paper, ink, and varnish

VI

Publishing

- ▶ Notes on critical issues in production and quality expectations
- ▶ Specifications for mechanicals to be provided by service bureau
- ▶ Specific needs for traditional prepress to be provided by print shop
- ▶ Bindery needs (sewing, stapling, gluing, comb, spiral, drilling, padding, carbonless, perfing, die cutting, embossing, foil stamping, folding, scoring, inserting, tipping, stuffing)
- ▶ Instructions for packing
- ▶ Shipping and delivery instructions

Making Up Your Pages

After all that planning, here's the execution phase, which puts to work all the PageMaker power described throughout this book.

Perfecting Your Elements

Before you actually place the elements into your layout, you need to perfect all the elements of your publication. In most cases, you will probably begin by forming a strategy for word processing.

Managing Your Text

How will you get those words created so they can then be put on pages? Of course, this question assumes that you actually took care of the writing, which may be the biggest challenge of all. As for the logistics of managing the text, consider these points:

- ▶ Choose a word processor, or perhaps use the PageMaker Story Editor.
- ▶ Plan ahead to make sure that there won't be any conversion problems when you import your text into PageMaker.
- ▶ If an outside writer is involved, find out whether that person's word processor allows for styles, or if you need to, plan for the use of style tags.
- ▶ If the files come from a Macintosh, you need to determine how to get them onto your PC and how to convert them to a format that's PageMaker readable.

Planning and Setting Up Your Style Sheet

You need to form a strategy for your style sheet arrangements and, preferably, set up the same style sheet names in both your word processor and PageMaker:

- ▶ First, remove from the Style palette the PageMaker default styles, which are unlikely to match your own needs.

▶ Name styles so that the most-used ones are at the top of the Style palette and ad-hoc special purpose styles are alphabetized at the bottom.

▶ Decide on your work style. Will you design the style sheet in advance, create it as you go, or will you use a combination of both methods?

▶ Create base definitions for the common denominator styles (body text, headlines, bullet indents) that share a common typeface.

▶ Define the rest of your styles to cascade from the base definitions, using the Based On style attribute.

▶ For easy reference while you're working, list your styles in writing, probably using one of the Plug-ins or third-party utilities provided for that purpose (for instance, PageMaker's Pub Info Plug-in).

Style Sheet Formatting Options

As you set up your styles, here are all the factors you may want to consider including in your style definitions, beginning with the ones in the Type Specifications dialog box:

▶ Typeface

▶ Size of type

▶ Leading

▶ Set automatic kerning

▶ Set tracking

▶ Set width

▶ Line break option

▶ Subscript, superscript, baseline shift

The paragraph level definition possibilities are contained in three commands: Paragraph Specifications, Hyphenation, and Indents/Tabs:

▶ Alignment

▶ Word and letter spacing for justified text

▶ Hyphenation

▶ Tabs

▶ Leaders

▶ Indents

▶ Keep together

▶ Widow and orphan control

VI

Publishing

- ▶ Page and column forced breaks
- ▶ Space before and after
- ▶ Rules
- ▶ Leading method

Cleaning Up Your Text

Before you can put your text into the publication, you need to do a good copy cleaning job:

- ▶ Decide which kinds of edits should be done in PageMaker, probably those that aren't feasible in your word processor because they involve some special PageMaker characteristic such as kerning.
- ▶ Run that spell checker again.
- ▶ Build a custom dictionary, or import it from your word processor.
- ▶ Translate word processor formats.
- ▶ Remove flaws.
- ▶ Code the text for importation if you have some special moves you need to make inside PageMaker.
- ▶ Apply mass formatting, using text processing utilities.
- ▶ If you've decided to hire an outside proofreader, work with that person and make scheduling and logistics arrangements.

Assembling Your Graphics

Produce your graphics. As with text material, keep a wary eye on how your graphics will ultimately be brought into PageMaker:

- ▶ Will you do tabletop scanning in black and white, or will you have high-resolution scans (corrected and proofed) at a service bureau?
- ▶ Will you rely on PageMaker-drawn objects?
- ▶ Will you create original illustrations, or hire outside illustration help?
- ▶ Gather your clip art.
- ▶ Scope out your sources for Photo CD processing.
- ▶ How will you generate graphs?
- ▶ Does your table formatting strategy involve clipboarding material into PageMaker as graphic images?
- ▶ Consider any graphics conversion issues. If you are working between Macs and DOS machines, for example, stick to TIFF and EPS files.

▶ You need to know if you'll be working in spot or process color so you can ultimately share color definitions among all your different graphics sources.

▶ Create custom color palettes to share among all those working on the project.

▶ Plan for sizing and manipulating (rotating, skewing, and so on) your images before you import them into PageMaker.

▶ Consider how the items will work as inline graphics, if that's your plan.

Setting Up Your Publication

This checklist boils down all the information for setting up your publication into a short list.

▶ Determine whether you will be working from a template or building your publication from scratch.

▶ Set up your Style, Color, and Library palettes, removing the default styles and colors.

▶ Plan your page numbering, including your numbering style (in Page setup).

▶ Plan your master pages and set up your Master Pages palette, including your design grid.

Setting the Master Page and Design Grid

Your master page design grids require the following:

▶ Set up your page geometry using Page setup (page size, margins, print on both sides, and facing pages).

▶ Plan your columns.

▶ Set up any ruler guides you want to have on every page.

▶ Set your zero point if you want it somewhere other than the default (upper-left corner of a single page and the common edge of facing pages).

▶ Set your vertical ruler measurement and leading grid.

Working with Books and Other Long Form Publications

Here are some special considerations for you to think through, if you are working on a long form document:

▶ Set up your chapter breakdowns, using the Book feature to pull together each chapter file.

VI

Publishing

▶ In your style sheet planning, provide for automatic generation of your table of contents.

▶ You'll probably want to produce an index.

▶ If you'll need page cross-referencing, you'll want to use the index-based technique.

▶ Footnotes need special handling.

▶ Consider whether you want to use bleeder tabs or some other visual indexing method.

▶ Along those same lines, your style sheet planning will have a lot to do with how you use the PageMaker addition for creating dictionary style running footers and headers.

Setting Preferences

Using the Preferences command, you'll probably want to consider setting preferences for all the following items, although your working style may differ from some of these specific recommendations:

▶ Set your measurement system to picas, unless you prefer one of the other systems, such as inches.

▶ Set the Preferences command to pinpoint layout problems by highlighting violations to your settings for spacing and line breaks.

▶ Most people work with graphics set to normal resolution. Keep in mind that you can always turn graphics on to high resolution using the redraw trick.

▶ To prevent accidentally grabbing guides as you work, set guides to the back.

▶ It's generally a good idea to keep file size down by setting the Smaller option, especially when you are working with very large documents.

▶ Set your personal preferences for Control palette nudge amounts and Snap To characteristics.

▶ Set Autoflow on or off, depending on your preference. I prefer it off, as being the most flexible setting for my work style. Autoflow must be turned off before using Build Booklet. Also, Autoflow could cause you to accidentally pour out a bunch of pages when you just wanted to set one text block. I use keyboard shortcuts to toggle Autoflow on when I need it.

▶ The internal image size defaults are pretty good, but with PageMaker's ability to store all graphics outside the publication, some people link all graphics, storing them outside PageMaker.

▶ Turn on typographer quotes unless you are setting type for a math or computer programming text, where you need the straight quotes.

▶ Set the greeking level, usually 4 pixels or below.

▶ Set your Story Editor preferences to show paragraph and other symbols and to display your text in a typeface and size of your choice.

▶ Work your way through all the menus, with nothing selected, setting your personal preferences for each item that's not grayed out. You'll probably want to particularly focus on the settings in the Type, Element, and Window menus.

Placing Text and Graphics

Using the Place command becomes pretty anti-climactic, if you've done all the advance planning. Here are some thoughts to guide you through:

▶ Depending on the nature of the piece, and your personal working style, you'll want to decide whether it's best to place text or graphics first.

▶ Do a couple of pages first to see how things are working; then make any adjustments to your styles and such before finishing up.

▶ You may want to adjust the mini-default for the Text Wrap command as you see how the layout gels during the first part of the Place process.

▶ As you bring inline graphics into the pages, you'll learn how the graphics and the text formatting work together, and you may need to make some style sheet adjustments.

▶ As you import graphics, you may want to compress any TIFFs to save disk space.

▶ In particular, you need to experiment as you bring in tables to be formatted using PageMaker's tabs and styles functions. Start with the toughest table and develop the basic form of your layout before you move on to the rest. If your tables will be limited to a single page, it may make sense to use the Table Editor.

▶ Keep the various positioning techniques at the front of your mind as you work.

▶ In most situations you will want to save disk space by linking graphics as much as possible, keeping the original outside of your publication.

VI

Publishing

Fine-Tuning, Producing Special Effects, and Coloring Your Pages

Next, you go through each page and fine-tune, putting into place any of your special effects and taking care of assigning element colors. It's a page-by-page tweak process where you check and adjust each of the following page elements:

- ▶ Hanging indents
- ▶ Headline treatments
- ▶ Fractions, formulas, weird type
- ▶ Text wrap
- ▶ Initial caps
- ▶ Rotate, skew
- ▶ Vertical rules
- ▶ Rules above and below
- ▶ Screens and drop shadows

In addition to checking those items, be sure to take care of the following tasks:

- ▶ Perform any kerning that's needed.
- ▶ Check picture captions for placement and line breaks.
- ▶ Adjust page breaks and column breaks.
- ▶ Look for ungainly line breaks.
- ▶ Be certain that all objects have their proper color assignments.

Generating Contents and Index

Implement the final stages of building your long form document by doing the following:

- ▶ Generate the master table of contents.
- ▶ Run the chapter level table of contents pages.
- ▶ Using the table of contents facilities, create any other specialized lists you'll need, such as tables of illustrations.
- ▶ Generate the index.

Publishing

You made all the decisions when you did your preliminary and bid specification work. Now it's time to implement those decisions.

Submitting Files to the Service Bureau

It may be a drag, but you need to fill out the service bureau work order form. It's the only way to be sure your job is done right. To complete the form, you need to be prepared with this information:

▶ Contact info (24 hours)

▶ Deadline

▶ A clear statement that indicates whether you are providing PostScript print to file data, or native PageMaker files

▶ A list of all files being transmitted

▶ A list of fonts

▶ A list of programs used to create your work

▶ Specific line screen setting

▶ Selection of the type of imagesetter

▶ Film or paper specifications (for example, negative or positive, right or wrong reading, emulsion up or down)

▶ Specific list of printer's marks

▶ Description of the number of pages

▶ A list of the number of high resolution scans to be performed

▶ Specific colors (and therefore, separations needed)

In addition to gathering all that data, check on these items:

▶ Check to see whether you should include PostScript error checking code if you are submitting PostScript files.

▶ Consider trapping issues, whether you should do it yourself, and, if not, provide any needed trapping directions.

▶ Request imposed film, if that's needed.

▶ Order proofs to be provided with output.

▶ Give delivery or pick up instructions.

Bundling Up Your Files for the Service Bureau

Herd up those files and organize them for minimal confusion. Here are some suggestions:

▶ Fine-tune your files, following the checklist provided in this section.

▶ Submit files with laser proofs (composites or LaserCheck).

▶ Use the PageMaker Save As command with Files For Remote Printing to gather your files.

▶ Include all files to be run as well as linked files and original art files (for example, original of EPS export graphic).

▶ Provide fonts not supported by service bureau.

▶ Include "spare" folder, backup.

Buffing Your Files for Optimum Laser or Imagesetter Output

Prevent problems at output time by buffing your files for the best possible output:

▶ Calculate your blend steps.

▶ Make sure that there are no spot color to spot color blends.

▶ Outlaw white boxes.

▶ You may want to re-Place some graphics, sizing and cropping them in their originating programs for faster output results.

▶ Likewise, rotate graphics before placement.

▶ Search out and see if you can eliminate nested EPS file problems.

▶ Adjust the flatness of complex clipping paths.

▶ Search for TrueType text that may choke the imagesetter.

▶ Likewise, look to see whether any non-EPS or non-TIFF graphics have snuck in and determine whether you need to replace them.

▶ Hairlines can disappear down to nothing in the imagesetter.

Proofing and Final Approvals

Here's a list of all your proofing options. Make sure that you get a written sign-off on any proofs for client approval; otherwise, you may end up paying for a botched job where there's no proof of your proofing.

Copy Proofing

Checking for typos, misspellings, and other problems with text is your first line of defense against errors in your publication. Use the following list to make sure you don't miss even one of your possible copy-proofing tools:

▶ Use the spell checker—more than once, even.

▶ Note that indexing and table of contents lists often reveal bad word usage and spelling problems.

▶ You may want to hire a professional proofreader—it may be worth the investment.

▶ Read into a tape recorder and listen back while scanning the printed copy, or have two people do the check with one reading and the other proofing. You can also, believe it or not, try reading backwards. Putting material out of context like that sometimes makes errors stand out better.

Pasteup Checking with a Laser Printer

Before spending money on expensive imagesetter film or color proofs, run laser proofs on the following items to be sure your layout works:

▶ Thumbnails

▶ FPO proofs with gray boxes using the Print command

▶ Composites

Proofing Prior to the Service Bureau

All of the preceding proofs will be next to worthless if you end up wasting a lot of money on mistake-ridden film at the service bureau. Perform the following proofing steps before going to the imagesetting stage:

▶ Laser printer reality check: the law is, if it won't go through the laser printer, it almost certainly won't run on the imagesetter. Naturally, to be an effective reality check, it must be a PostScript laser printer.

▶ Run a visual inspection of what you see on-screen, particularly in relation to the hot spots named in the earlier checklist, "Buffing Your Files for Optimum Laser or Imagesetter Output."

▶ Use a PostScript error checker (but be sure to turn it off before running PostScript files for your service bureau).

▶ Run a LaserCheck proof.

Color

Producing good quality color can be pretty intimidating, unless you have the security of good quality control steps like the ones in this list:

▶ Work toward a quality goal. (Do you want accuracy, or do you simply desire pleasing-to-the-eye color results?)

▶ Naturally, coordinate with your printer and service bureau on the use of PageMaker's color management system.

▶ Check color using a standard color evaluation booth.

▶ Test separations on a laser printer.

▶ Check memory colors, such as flesh, familiar objects, blue sky.

VI

Publishing

▶ Composite color proofs.

▶ Laminate (separation-based) proofs if you need to check trapping.

Print Shop Proofing

Until you've actually seen your publication come off the press, you have no way of being certain of what you'll get—especially for a color publication—no matter how much proofing you've done. In order to improve your chances of getting from the press what you designed on the computer, have your print shop help implement the following proofing tools and steps:

▶ Create your own swatch system.

▶ Ask for a draw down so you can see your ink on your paper.

▶ Have the printer inspect the mechanicals.

▶ Get and check blue line proofs.

▶ Ask for a print shop-created dummy of how the project will be imposed.

▶ Request a press check inspection.

Going to Press: Imposing, Folding, and Binding

Now the print shop runs the job based on your bid specifications, as revised during the long process of putting together the finished project. The last job you have is to inspect the results.

▶ Pull random samples through the job for inspection.

▶ Satisfy yourself that the random samples show consistent results, including consistent color matching.

▶ Look for wrinkles.

▶ Inspect to see whether there's print through—where the ink shows through from the other side of the paper.

▶ Look for foreign material, such as lint, hairs, or dust, stuck in the ink.

▶ See whether there's any blotting of ink from the front of one piece to the back of the next.

▶ Sometimes you find smudging from the paper feed mechanism.

▶ This is the first time you've seen your project since it's been through the bindery, so look for physical registration problems, across spreads for example.

▶ See that the packing instructions have been followed and satisfy yourself that you received the full count on your order.

Part VII

Supercharging PageMaker

25 ▲ Developing a System for Managing Your Type

26 ▲ Completing Your Own PageMaker System

27 ▲ Leaping Across Platforms

28 ▲ Automating PageMaker

Chapter 25

Developing a System for Managing Your Type

To help you build your personal type system, this chapter includes:

Understanding the basic nature of Windows type technology.

▼

Organizing your fonts, a Tactics Recipe.

▼

Background on the PANOSE font substitution technology—and what it can and can't do for you.

▼

Setting up PANOSE.

▼

Working with the real fonts that have rubber faces— Multiple Master PostScript fonts—flexible, yet not substitutes or simulations.

WITH ALL THE THOUSANDS of fonts out there, how do you manage to put together a coherent system of managing type? It's a pretty fundamental issue, since the majority of the work you do in PageMaker involves typography.

In this chapter, we discuss the various type management utilities and techniques you need to build a complete PageMaker type system. ▶ ▶ ▶

KEY CONCEPT:
Windows Type Technology and Adobe Type Manager

There are three kinds of fonts in the Windows world: Windows system fonts, PostScript fonts, and TrueType fonts.

System fonts are the ones used in dialog boxes and menus in Windows. They really don't have anything to do with desktop publishing at all.

TrueType fonts have become as common as dirt in the office environments where Windows rules over the Macintosh. They are a competing font technology to PostScript. They are fine for office work, where you never need to consider much more than getting output from the office laser printer.

However, for desktop publishing, where the object is to get the most out of PostScript-based programs such as PageMaker and devices such as high resolution imagesetters, the standard is PostScript. Actually, it would be more accurate to say that the standard is a combination of PostScript fonts and Adobe Type

Manager because you couldn't very well make the whole thing work in Windows without ATM.

Scalable Fonts

The key thing to know about PostScript type (and TrueType for that matter) is the fact that it is *scalable font technology*. You can make a single font file pretty much as small or as big as you like without hurting its quality.

Before Windows 3.x and Adobe Type Manager, we were burdened with bitmap fonts, one for each specific size you needed to use and one for each specific size clogging up your hard disk. They were pre-built out of a pattern of dots. If you tried to blow them up to larger sizes, they still had the same number of dots and would consequently acquire a bad case of the "jaggies." The result would be as you see in figure 25.1.

Jaggies

FIG. 25.1 ▲

A bitmapped font, blown up to show the jaggies.

Instead, for desktop publishing, we have scalable, outline fonts, written in the PostScript language. PostScript uses complex commands and mathematical equations to describe the curves of a letter,

instead of trying to compose the screen image from a collection of dots. That means you can tell PageMaker to use any size of type you want, from 10.2 points to 72.1 points and sizes above, below, and in-between. (You can actually choose any size between 4 to 650 point.) Whatever the size, the software and computer equipment will calculate the image for the letter on-the-fly and use the PostScript equations to paint the character out of as many dots as it takes to make it look smooth, as you see in figure 25.2.

Smooth

FIG. 25.2 ▲

A smooth font, drawn using a PostScript outline.

In the world of Windows, what makes this possible is Adobe Type Manager. Not only can we have these equation-based characters scaled in our imaging machines (PostScript laser printers, Linotronics and Agfa imagesetters, and so on), we can have that type on-screen as well.

ATM paints the type images on the computer screen, taking its instructions from the scalable PostScript outline fonts. (The technical term is *rasterize*.) Adobe, by the way, is the company that invented PostScript in the first place. The company is probably the leading source of fonts for desktop publishing because, if for no other reason, their basic 35 fonts have from the beginning been built into almost every PostScript laser printer on the market.

Putting PostScript Fonts to Work

PostScript outline fonts get to your printer for use during an output job in two basic ways:

▼ First, some fonts are already there, built right into the laser printer or loaded onto a special hard disk attached to the laser printer to expand its font storage capacity.

▼ As years of desktop publishing work roll by, however, you'll find yourself collecting many more fonts than those that came with your laser printer. That's the second way PostScript fonts get to the laser printer so it can do its work. These new outline fonts are downloaded to the laser printer as needed during a print job. For this reason, PostScript outline fonts are sometimes called *downloadable fonts*.

Making this downloading process happen, and making the fonts available for display on your computer screen and available for downloading to your printer, requires several steps:

▼ You must copy the font files to your hard drive.

▼ You need to let your system know that the fonts are there. For PostScript fonts, you do this through the ATM Control Panel's Add command.

▼ You need to let your PostScript printer know the fonts are available for downloading. When you go to the Add dialog box in ATM, there is an Autodownload For PostScript Printer button. Checking that will install the fonts so that they will download automatically.

All that being said, you can pretty much forget it. It's just as cumbersome as it sounds, and there's a much easier way to take care of all these details. It's called a *font manager*, and we'll talk more about the most common one, FontMinder, in just a bit.

Font Files

Here's a rundown of all the various kinds of font files you are likely to find on your hard drive and where they are likely to be stored.

System Fonts

The system font files we talked about are stored in the FONTS folder in the Windows 95 WINDOWS folder. They all end with the FON extension.

TrueType Fonts

TrueType fonts are also normally stored in the FONTS folder, and under the standard Windows 95 setup it's easy to install new ones. You just click and drag the font files to the FONTS folder. The TrueType files end with the extension TTF. Windows 3.x requires a second TrueType file, an auxiliary item called a FOT file which "points" to the TTF file so applications will know where it is located. Windows 95 has done away with the FOT file, although to maintain compatibility with older applications that still need to look for the FOT there's a special, hidden file called TTFCACHE. In any case, under the font manager approach we're about to discuss, you are

well-advised to store all your TrueType fonts in a folder of their own, bypassing the standard Windows 95 arrangement.

PostScript Fonts

PostScript fonts come in four components:

▼ *PFB (PostScript Font Binary) files* are the actual PostScript outlines used in your printer or in the imagesetter to produce letters on paper.

▼ *PFM (PostScript Font Metrics) files* have all the information on kerning pairs, character width, names for the applications menus, and other fundamental management information needed by PageMaker, Windows, and ATM to make the whole system work. If you don't have PFM, the font won't appear in any menus.

▼ *AFM (Adobe Font Metric) files* aren't actually used in Windows. AFM files are the files you see on both the Mac and the Windows side that provide the basic font information needed to install PFBs and PFMs on your computer system.

▼ *INF (Font Info)*, like the AFM file, exists only for installation. Combined with AFM, the installation process uses the INF data to build the PFM file.

The bottom line is, once your installation is complete, the PFB and PFM files are the only ones needed on an ongoing basis by your system. Keep your masters of course, but you can save disk space by deleting the AFM and INF files from your hard drive.

By the way, the words *font* and *typeface* tend to get used interchangeably in the desktop publishing world. Old-time metal type punchers know what these words used to mean but, unfortunately, the proper meanings have become totally corrupted since the desktop publishing revolution took hold.

A *font* is a given size and style of a set of characters. If you choose to set a headline in 24-point Palatino Italic, that's a

font. A *typeface* is a collection of fonts, all the sizes and all the styles. That means Palatino Italic in 14 point is in the same typeface family as Palatino Bold in 30 point.

However, in the computer world, these terms get mixed up because you use a single font file to make up many different weights within a typeface collection.

TACTICS RECIPE:
Organizing Your Fonts

Before we continue, I'll just mention Rik Bean. His dry British wit and calm grace have been well known to many on CompuServe's Adobe and DTP forums. And his special insights into managing Windows type technology, especially as it relates to Windows 95, have been a major aid in putting this chapter together.

If you ask a group of desktop publishers how they organize their fonts, you'd better stand back. Every single one will have a different plan. They will all be shouting that their way is the right way. And every one of them will be right—for their own publishing environment. So this will be an idiosyncratic approach to managing fonts.

Designing Your System for Safety and Accuracy

Before you get started on organizing your fonts, there's one really important point to make. Aside from just organizing all those hundreds of fonts you collect, the overriding concern must be safety—making sure that your printed output accurately

matches what you see on-screen. Okay, it's not life threatening or anything, but font problems can cost hundreds or even thousands of dollars if a job needs to be redone or you lose a client.

You could blow precious time as well. Even if you are simply printing to a laser printer, the last thing you need is a botched presentation for the visiting group of execs from corporate headquarters.

So, however you choose to modify the font organization advice presented here (and you will), at least hold on to one all-important credo—play a conservative font management game.

Font Organization Overview

The sections that follow contain more detail and discussion, but here's the bottom line right up front—a Tactics Recipe for organizing fonts.

Use a font manager:

▼ This will allow you to bypass all the pain of that cumbersome installation procedure.

▼ It also lets you minimize the number of fonts in your system at any given moment—especially important when you have hundreds of them.

▼ A font manager allows you to build packages of fonts so that you can acti-vate or de-activate whole lists of fonts used regularly on projects in just one step.

Because you'll be using a font manager, you will be able to set up a system of font folders of your own design. Don't keep all your fonts in the Windows FONTS folder and the ATM PSFONTS folder set.

▼ Most importantly, this multiple folder setup will improve system perfor-mance. Windows and DOS really slow down when a folder is jammed up with anything more than about 100 files.

▼ Backing up your fonts will be easier because they will be segregated into easy-to-manage groups in your hard drive structure.

▼ It will be easier to bundle up your files for sending publications to the service bureau.

Organizing Your Fonts on Your Hard Disk

One major advantage of using a font man-ager is the fact that it makes it easy to seg-regate and organize all your font files in locations on your hard disk that make sense to you.

Setting Up PostScript Font Folders

In the ordinary scheme of things, ATM will set up a C:\PSFONTS folder. Within that folder will be subfolders for the various kinds of PostScript font files.

Here's the problem. If you keep all your files in that one folder, you won't be able to find things very easily and you will probably degrade the performance of your system, perhaps severely. The more files in a folder, the longer it takes Windows to open and work inside that folder. Something like 100 files is the practical upper limit.

To solve that problem, try creating a set of folders that breaks down your font collection into groups. You might try the system used by Rik Bean:

C:\PSA (PFBs go here)

C:\PSA\PFM

C:\PSA\AFM

C:\PSA\FONTINFO

C:\PSB (PFBs go here)

C:\PSB\PFM

C:\PSB\AFM

C:\PSB\FONTINFO

C:\PSC (PFBs go here)

C:\PSC\PFM

C:\PSC\AFM

C:\PSC\FONTINFO

The point is, you have all these PS folders (PS for PostScript, right?), and then you break down your fonts into alphabeti-cal categories. If you have a smaller col-lection than Rik's (most of us do), you might consider grouping more than one initial together—PSA_F, PSAG_K, and so on. You could also make categories that suggest the nature of the type—PS_SER, PS_SANS, PS_DISP, PS_PI—for serif, sans serif, display, and pi. Don't forget that the longest path name permitted in ATM 3.x is 34 letters.

Rik, by the way, strongly suggests keeping his fonts and clip art on a separate hard drive. He has a policy of segregating data and applications data. One advantage is that he doesn't need to back up the fonts and clip art very often, because they don't change nearly as much as the data folders.

Setting Up a TrueType Font Folder

Windows 95 has an idiosyncrasy that will bedevil your use of a font manager. If you keep your TrueType fonts in the official FONTS folder, Windows 95 will foil your font manager moves. As soon as you open the FONTS folder in Explorer, Windows 95 has a "special feature" that automatically "reinstalls" the fonts.

The solution is to establish a special TrueType folder, C:\TTFONTS for example. Then use your font manager to copy your TrueType fonts to that folder and manage them from there.

One really important exception must be considered, however. Leave the Marlett font in the FONTS folder. Marlett is essential for the proper running of Windows 95, and it must stay in the FONTS folder.

Working with a Font Manager

To be fair, there are several font managers out there. QualiType produces FontHandler, for example. However, virtually every desktop publisher I know on the Windows side of things uses Ares FontMinder. Many of them have been using it since it was a freeware product, written by Dennis Harrington. Dennis is still taking care of the product, and is often on CompuServe to support those who have questions about using it.

Have a look at figure 25.3 to see the main dialog box for FontMinder 3 for Windows 95 and Windows 3.x.

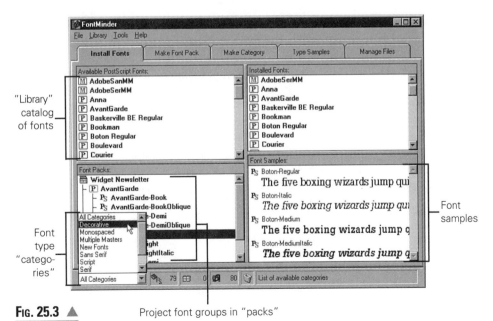

"Library" catalog of fonts

Font type "categories"

Project font groups in "packs"

Font samples

Fig. 25.3 ▲

Use FontMinder to catalog your fonts, organize them by type of font, view and print font samples, and bundle fonts into project-oriented packs for one-step loading and unloading.

For a busy desktop publishing situation, all these categorization and easy loading and unloading features should have obvious benefits. You can, in one location, manage your font library.

Maybe my favorite aspect of FontMinder is the capability to install fonts—all kinds of fonts, anywhere I want them. No need to drag and drop on a FONTS folder. No need to use ATM. You don't need ATM to install fonts, though; you just need ATM to use the fonts.

By clicking the Manage Files tab, you get a dialog box that will help you copy the files to your hard drive, using the font organization folder structure we've just described.

Then, as you see in figure 25.4, FontMinder will install the fonts in Windows and let your printers know their whereabouts.

Fig. 25.4 ▲

One-stop shop installation, using a font manager, for all kinds of fonts to all the necessary stops.

Getting the Font You Ordered

One problem you will encounter with some fonts is the issue of complex font family linking. You have to remember how your complex fonts "link" to the bold formatting menu in your applications (including PageMaker). In Windows, a font has four simple styles, usually called something like regular, bold, italic, and bold italic. It's simple enough until you get to some of the more complex font families.

For example, take Adobe's Bauhaus, which has bold, demi, heavy, light, and medium weights (it doesn't have any italic style). Bauhaus Light, formatted bold with the PageMaker menu, gives you Bauhaus Demi. Bauhaus Medium, formatted bold, gives you Bauhaus Bold. So you need to know what the effect will be when you apply bold to a member of one of these complex families.

A font manager can help there as well, as you see in figure 25.5.

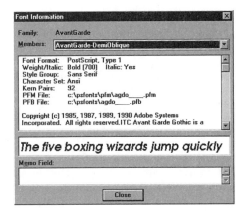

Fig. 25.5 ▲

FontMinder's Font Information dialog box, provides detailed information on the structure of a complex font family.

Managing PANOSE Font Substitution

Lots of folks would like to be able to share documents in a completely open manner—no worries about such things as whether everyone has the same software, computer platform, disk format, and fonts. Wouldn't it be great? Well, the new universal type technologies do make it possible to a certain degree and in carefully considered circumstances.

Lots of other folks empathize with these goals but love good typography when they see it. These are the people who understand that close enough just isn't good enough in typography. They know all too well that some of these substitute font methods make for letter hash and succotash on a well-tuned page. That's the "Oops!" part.

In a way, you are joining one of these two camps when you make a choice to use PANOSE font substitution. So is it an *oops*, or is it an *oh boy*? Let's cover some background.

Getting an Overview

The PANOSE font substitution technology, built into PageMaker, does not use fake fonts. It uses real PostScript fonts. (There's a technology on the Macintosh that does fake fonts, called SuperATM, and Acrobat Reader uses a form of it as well, even in Windows.)

PANOSE is not limited to PostScript fonts, though. It will work with TrueType (TT) fonts. Actually, there are probably more TT fonts with PANOSE information built in than PostScript.

PANOSE estimates the best possible real font to substitute for one that's missing from a PageMaker document you are opening up. It uses a best-guess basis, evaluating the relative weight and width of the incoming font and trying to match it with something you have installed in your system. Its primary aim is (at least) to match the line breaks in the incoming document.

This may sound great. It sort of sounds like you could reduce the number of fonts you keep around because PageMaker will use PANOSE to find a good substitute. You buy a few sets of fonts, and you never have to worry again about whether you have the right designer font or not? Sorry, think again—it doesn't quite work out that way.

PANOSE substitutions can hurt you when you least expect it. If you create one of these substitutions and you don't catch it when you are running your mechanicals at the laser printer or imagesetter, you will not get the real thing. Furthermore, because they are substitutions, any kerning and tracking you apply when they are in place is bogus and might mess you up royally when you put the real fonts into place.

The *oops*, therefore, can be summed up in a simple rule. Never use these substitutions or simulations when it comes time to do the real thing. Think of font substitution—PANOSE—as an editing tool, and that's all. It's not quality typography. It may let you get some work done if you don't have the correct fonts, but they aren't the real thing.

▶ *Corollary number one:* If you have done any editing of any kind with the fakes in the document, run a careful proof one last time with the real fonts in place before sending the job to the mechanical production stage. Pay particular attention to line and page breaks.

▶ *Corollary number two:* You might be thinking you can use font fakes during composition and then have the service bureau run the job with the real fonts, saving you the considerable expense of buying the real thing. Sorry. If you are doing any sort of kerning or other fine work on your type, including automatic kerning in justified type, don't rely on fake font methods. You stand a major chance of getting unexpected results.

Getting the PANOSE Greeting

Your first experience of PANOSE will probably come in the shape of a dialog box that appears when PageMaker tries to open a publication with missing fonts (see fig. 25.6).

Fig. 25.6 ▶

*The PANOSE Font
Matching Results
dialog box opens
when a publication
uses fonts that you
don't have in-
stalled.*

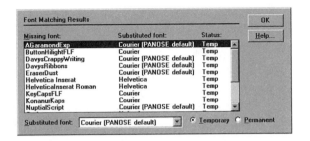

If PANOSE finds any improvements, they appear in the Substituted Font column. In some cases, or even all cases, the default font you have selected in Page-Maker's Preferences command will be suggested because PANOSE couldn't find any font to improve on it. A lot of the time, PANOSE will simply suggest using Courier.

You can accept the suggested font substitutions by clicking OK, or you can further tune the results to your taste by using the Substituted Font drop-down list at the base of the dialog box. That list enables you to select any of the missing fonts and manually impose font substitutions.

You can also record your font substitutions as Temporary or make them Permanent by clicking the appropriate radio buttons.

If you click the Permanent button, your entries are recorded in the Exceptions dialog box (opened within the Font Matching dialog box) and will be the suggested substitutes in all future situations where that font is missing, until you decide to change them. (PANOSE won't ever substitute a font without giving you a warning with this dialog box.)

TIP ▶ Missing Font Alert Tool

This PANOSE dialog box works as a great way to catch missing fonts. At print time, you can have PageMaker scan any EPS graphics in your publication to see that you have the proper fonts installed. Make sure the EPS Font Scanner Plug-in found in the Utilities menu has been turned on. It's on by default.

Setting PANOSE

Take a look at the Font Matching Preferences dialog box in figure 25.7. To reach this dialog box, choose Preferences from the File menu, then use the Map Fonts button in the Preferences dialog box.

Instead of using PANOSE to substitute for a missing font, you may actually get the best use out of it as a guard dog for missing type. Set up PANOSE a certain way, and it will alert you when opening a publication that contains fonts not presently loaded in your system. As long as PANOSE is on (Show Mapping Results), you will see in the PANOSE box if there are any missing fonts.

Fig. 25.7 ▶

The main control point for substitution of fonts.

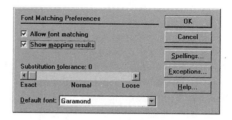

To train your type guard dog, turn on the Show Mapping Results check box in the Font Matching dialog box. The slider bar in the center of the Font Matching dialog box enables you to tell the system how close (exact) a substitution font has to be. You can set the substitution frequency on a scale running from Exact (0), allowing you to get the PANOSE default more often, through Normal (50), to Loose (100), enabling you to get the substitution font more often. Set this scale to Exact to make sure PANOSE lets you know about missing fonts.

Setting PANOSE Defaults

You can choose PANOSE's default font by using the pull-down list provided for that purpose.

TIP ▶ **Spot Font Substitutions More Easily**

Set the PANOSE default in Windows 95 to Marlett. Then the substitutions will be painfully obvious when you look through your document.

If you use the PANOSE alert dialog box to substitute fonts when you first open a publication, your entries are recorded in the dialog box reached through the Exceptions button. A list of your substitutions appears there, including notations as to whether they are temporary or permanent. You can also use the Exceptions dialog box to edit your substitution defaults.

Perhaps the coolest button of all in this dialog box is the Spellings button. It opens a dialog box that simplifies your efforts to swap PageMaker documents between Windows and Macintosh platforms by listing the fonts that translate from one to the other. The Macintosh font name appears on one side and the Windows font name appears on the other. Often the two versions of the font differ primarily in spelling, due to the filenaming standards of the DOS Windows computing platform. This spelling difference can cause major pains in cross platform sharing of PageMaker publications; the PANOSE font substitution Spellings feature solves it all very neatly. The dialog box comes set up with the most common fonts shared between the two platforms.

Recognizing Fake Font Signals

How can you know that you're working with a substitute or simulated font?

You can always tell when PANOSE has substituted a font. In figure 25.8, the bracketed entries indicate fonts that have been substituted by PANOSE.

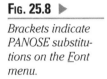

FIG. 25.8 ▶

Brackets indicate PANOSE substitutions on the Font menu.

Where to Go from Here

▶ This chapter goes hand-in-hand with the chapters on setting your type in Part II, "Working with Text."

▶ For help with making sure that you send everything off to the service bureau with your job, refer to Chapter 21, "Producing Mechanicals."

VII

Supercharging Pagemaker

Chapter 26

Completing Your Own PageMaker System

This chapter on building a PageMaker system includes the following information:

How to install and run Plug-ins.

▼

A quick review of the Plug-ins that you already own, since they came right inside your PageMaker box.

▼

Some recommended Plug-ins from outside developers, and how to find out about the dozens of others that are available.

▼

Recommended utilities for all the categories of work you do in PageMaker—managing text and graphics, converting files, and so on.

WITHOUT A DOUBT, PageMaker has come a long way from its original simple ways. It does plenty more than merely combine pictures and type on pages.

By far, the most powerful way for you to add to your system will be through the Plug-ins technology that allows you to literally plug functionality right into PageMaker. But you'll also want to consider stand-alone programs that help you get your pages onto the press. ▶ ▶ ▶

Managing Your Plug-ins

In this section, we cover the add-ons that work from within PageMaker—Plug-ins. There's information on installing new Plug-ins, as well as the PageMaker trick for listing all the Plug-ins you have already installed.

Installing Plug-ins

Depending on whether you bought your Plug-in from a third-party developer or got the Plug-in from Adobe, you'll need to use slightly different techniques for installing a new Plug-in.

To install most Plug-ins supplied by an independent developer, simply drag the Plug-in file to your Plug-ins folder. It's located within the RSRC folder, in the language folder that for those of us living in the United States will be called USENGLSH. A few Plug-in manufacturers have some additional steps, so read the directions to be on the safe side.

As for PageMaker-supplied Plug-ins, if you did a Custom install you might not have installed all the Plug-ins that came with the program. Or, you might need to install a new or updated Plug-in. In either of these cases, use the PageMaker installer facilities, because the Plug-ins are shipped to you in compressed form. Simply locate the Plug-in you want to install on one of the PageMaker disks, and double-click it to open the Installer, which walks you through the procedure.

Finding Out What You've Got

How do you know what Plug-ins you have installed? The quickest way is to pull out the Adobe Plug-ins submenu under the Utilities menu. If it's listed, you've installed it.

For more complete information, from within PageMaker hold down the Ctrl key and choose About PageMaker from the PageMaker Help menu. You get a scrolling list complete with version numbers. This method also gives detailed information about other aspects of your PageMaker setup.

Running Plug-ins

Running a Plug-in couldn't be simpler. Most of the time you'll first need to make a selection of an object in Layout view so the Plug-in will know where to focus its action—on the selected object or objects. Then simply click on the Utilities menu, pull out the PageMaker Plug-ins submenu, and choose the Plug-in you want.

Using the Plug-ins That Come with PageMaker

Most of the Plug-ins that come with PageMaker have already been covered in this book where they fit into the mainstream of putting PageMaker to work. Here's a sampling of what was scheduled to be included in the PageMaker 6.0 package as we go to press:

▶ *Add Cont'd Line.* This Plug-in automatically cuts the selected text block by one line and slips a tiny new text block at the base of the selected text block pointing to the next page in the story thread. You also can have the jump page line put at the head of a text block pointing back to the previous page. (See Chapter 17, "Building Many Pages.")

▶ *Balance Columns.* By jockeying the number of lines in each column of a multicolumn page, this Plug-in works to equalize the length of all columns of the same story on the page. (See Chapter 13, "Designing a Master Page Grid.")

▶ *Build Booklet.* If you need to compose multipanel brochures or small booklets, this Plug-in sorts out all the pages of your publication so that they properly impose when folded together and trimmed. (See Chapter 17, "Building Many Pages.")

▶ *Bullets and Numbering.* This Plug-in automatically numbers or adds your choice of dingbats to a series of paragraphs. (See Chapter 6, "Formatting Paragraphs.")

▶ *CleanSweep.* Use this Plug-in to convert batches of Version 5.0 publications to PageMaker 6.0 format.

▶ *Create Color Library.* After you develop the perfect palette for a project, share those choices of colors with everyone on the team by defining your own library of colors. (See Chapter 18, "Creating Colors.")

▶ *Drop Cap.* This Plug-in enables you to produce a giant-sized initial letter on a paragraph of your choice. (See Chapter 15, "Creating Special Effects.")

▶ *EPS Font Scanner.* You might never notice this little item, because it comes set to On when you install PageMaker. Unless, for some weird reason, you decide to turn it off, this Plug-in works in the background when you print and warns you if you try to print a publication containing an EPS that uses a font you do not have installed on your system. (Check Chapter 21, "Producing Mechanicals.")

▶ *Guide Manager.* A new one for PageMaker 6.0, this Plug-in allows you to automatically set up what's known as a Swiss grid—a pattern of guides and columns that you can use to provide your layout with underlying structure. (See Chapter 13, "Designing a Master Page Grid.")

VII

Supercharging PageMaker

▶ *HTML Author.* You use this Plug-in as the first step to converting your paper-based publication to a World Wide Web page, and there's nearly a full chapter devoted to its use. (See Chapter 29, "Publishing Electronically: The Web or Acrobat.")

▶ *Keyline.* This Plug-in draws a box around any object, using your choice of line and fill. It does a great job of keylining photo scans or creating special effects. (See Chapter 15, "Creating Special Effects.")

▶ *Open Template.* This Plug-in uses PageMaker's scripting language and the Plug-in's technology to build template files from Adobe-supplied scripts, with a resulting major savings of disk space. (See Chapter 1, "Touring PageMaker," and Chapter 12, "Setting Up a New Publication.")

▶ *Pub Info.* Use this Plug-in to get a report on all the fonts, paragraph styles, and linked graphics contained in your publication. It's a good tool for gathering information you'll need to submit with your files when you hand them off to a service bureau for imagesetting. (See Chapter 21, "Producing Mechanicals.")

▶ *Running Headers/Footers.* With this Plug-in, you can set up dictionary- or encyclopedia-style dynamic headings at the tops and bottoms of pages. It's considerably enhanced in this version of PageMaker. (See Chapter 17, "Building Many Pages.")

▶ *Update PPD.* This Plug-in automatically collects information about your printer (or imagesetter for mat matter). It then customizes your PPD (the link between PageMaker and your printer driver) to take advantage of any printer enhancements you've made. (See Chapter 21, "Producing Mechanicals.")

If this list of Plug-ins seems a bit shorter than the list of Additions that was included with PageMaker 5.0, that's because a number of the 5.0 Additions have now been built into PageMaker in one way or the other. The PS Group It Addition, for example, has been replaced by the new Group command in the new Arrange menu.

Adding Third-Party Plug-ins

A steadily maturing market has been growing for Plug-ins developed by independents—companies other than Adobe who see market potential for providing functions that PageMaker doesn't contain when it comes from the factory. In fact, so many of these Plug-ins are now on the market that it's tough to track them all.

Shopping for Plug-ins

The CD-ROM that came in your PageMaker package includes a catalog of many of the Plug-ins offered by independent developers. Check in the Plug-ins folder, in the folder full of "tryouts." The catalog is published by the Adobe Plug-in Source, a cooperative of developers of add-on products for Adobe products and an important resource for the small and hardy band of developers who produce these PageMaker add-ons. You can reach the cooperative at (800) 685-3547 in the U.S., or fax them at (800) 648-8512 or (206) 489-3446.

Also on the CD-ROM in the PageMaker package, you'll find demo versions and electronic brochures for a number of Plug-ins.

When you register your copy of PageMaker, you will no doubt be put on the mailing list for the Adobe Plug-in Source catalogs. You will also be put on the list to automatically receive *Adobe Magazine*, which is a good source of information on Plug-ins.

Basic Plug-in Recommendations

Here are some Plug-ins that, depending on your day-to-day workflow, might be real "must haves." I've tried to select them not just on the basis of my idiosyncratic needs, but also because they or their developers have received some sort of broad endorsement in the PageMaker community. There's no way to fit all the available Plug-ins into this space, and besides, I haven't used all of them. This is a selected group, not a comprehensive listing.

Plug-ins That Manipulate Objects

For years, people asked Adobe to put alignment tools into PageMaker. Two developers responded—Zephyr Designs and Extensis. Now, PageMaker has put the functions right into PageMaker, and you have to ask yourself what they'll do for an encore. Let's start with the answer to that question.

Zephyr Specs

Boyd Multerer of Zephyr Designs was pretty much the original breakthrough guy on Plug-ins. In fact, he did the programming for a number of the Plug-ins that are now built into PageMaker (Align and Distribute, Library palette, and several more, including the CleanSweep Plug-in).

His latest offering is Zephyr Specs. If you ever use the Library palette, you will find Zephyr Specs indispensable because it goes way beyond the capabilities of the Library palette. And if you ever need to copy styles one by one instead of a whole sheet at a time, you will love Zephyr Specs.

Zephyr Specs is a super sophisticated library palette. You can load a publication's definitions for color, column settings, sets of ruler guides, text styles, whole layouts, and collections of objects into a library file and then apply them to other publications at will. And you can apply them selectively, one color or one style at a time, redefining the specifications as you do so.

This allows you to create collections of much-used specifications and pass them around a workgroup. Or, if you work alone, simply save intricate sets of specifications so you don't have to build them twice.

Zephyr also offers SuperSnap, which acts like a steroids-crazed version of PageMaker's Snap to Guides and Snap to Rulers commands. SuperSnap will allow you to snap a selected object to any of what you might call "landmarks" on a page—guides, corners, margins, other objects. It works not just for placement, but also for sizing of objects.

MapSoft also makes a Plug-in that performs some of these same functions. It's called Style Groups.

Extensis PageTools

Extensis has swept into the PageMaker add-on market with such force that it seems like it would have been difficult to top their existing offering of ten Plug-ins for one pretty low price. Well, as we go to press they are working on Version 2.0. It's too early to know how the product will change, but the Macintosh Version 2.0 went from ten Plug-ins to 19.

The key identifying feature of PageTools is the PageBar. I have never found this to fit my personal style, but thousands of people would vote against me. The PageBar puts on your electronic worktable instant mouse click access to any of the PageTools Plug-ins and virtually any other PageMaker command item.

However, I'm not much of an icon bar person, so I've always found the most valuable part of PageTools to be its component parts. If the Macintosh Version 2.0 is any clue, and the products end up looking similar across the two platforms, maybe the most important new additions to PageTools Version 2.0 will be PageType and PageCaps.

PageType (as constructed for the Macintosh version) lets you assign collections of type attributes to selected text. It's not quite character level styles, but it is as close as you can come as we go to press. It makes it easy to assign a lot of formatting with one click of a mouse button. The only ingredient lacking is the ability to globally change your mind about what a character style definition should be, as you can with PageMaker's paragraph level style definitions.

PageCaps (again, as seen in the Macintosh version of PageTools 2.0) include the ability to change the case of text to, as they say in their brochure, "ALL CAPS, Title Caps, Sentence caps, lowercase, or RaNdOmCaPS." And you can create an exception list.

Because PageTools was bundled with PageMaker 5.0 for some months prior to the release of Version 6.0, it is likely that many users will already be familiar with its functions. Some have been rendered a bit redundant because the feature has been included in PageMaker Version 6.0. Some, like PageMover, have as much importance as they did when PageTools was first introduced. PageMover lets you select items and relocate or copy them to another page without leaving your currently active page. PageRulers lets you create floating rulers. PageColors allows you to change colors of PageMaker objects throughout your publication.

PageScaler resizes objects, even multiple selections, by a percentage value you enter. The types of objects that can be resized include text, graphics, and line widths. If you are one of the people who thinks PageMaker's Group command should resize text when the Group is resized, then you'll love PageScaler because it will resize a multiple object selection, even the text inside a text block.

ExecuTable

A new facility for creating tables may be the answer to many prayers. ExecuTable, from ExecuStaff Composition Services, works with PageMaker text blocks, rather than going out to a separate table editing program like Adobe Table.

This means it can set multipage tables. It works with just two dialog boxes and will set rules, and straddle heads across table columns, table titles, colors, and hanging indents. It even will do wrapping text within a "cell."

It has a singular drawback, however. It breaks the text block up into many small text blocks. They aren't threaded, so you can't edit them in Story Editor, and if you need to adjust the table, you need to erase all those text blocks and rerun the Plug-in on the original text. (You just keep the original text on the Pasteboard in case you need to edit.)

Arrows, Frames, and Stars

If you need lines with arrows, you need Shadetree Marketing's Arrowz Plug-in. You can set an arrow with a border, head and tail, selected thickness, and even a curve. That's right. You *can* have curved lines in PageMaker. Just set an arrow with no head or tail using Arrowz.

Shadetree also offers the Fraemz border generator and a Starz generator, which has a bit more flexibility than the Polygon tool in PageMaker 6.0.

Galley Oops! and Other Sundaes

Sundae software offers a collection of Plug-ins that many find useful. The one I find attractive is Galley Oops!. There's no substitute for a fine proofreading, but a run with Galley Oops! will find suspicious typography in selected PageMaker text, and it can search a whole publication if you like. It looks for things like excess spaces between words, and bad quote marks or em dashes.

The company also offers several grid managers for both ruler guides and lines, and a set of tools for adding crop marks and publication information to film.

Bar Codes

There must be a dozen companies producing various Plug-ins and stand-alone programs for producing those bar code symbols. Azalea and Synex both have relationships with the Adobe Plug-in Source and deserve a look from you if you need this capability. A lot will depend on which of the bar code methods you need—Code 39, UPC, EAN, POSTNET, MSI-Plessy, and so on.

Editing the Uneditable

There will inevitably come a moment when you simply must edit or otherwise manipulate a file. The file might be corrupted so badly that you can't open it, and you need to rescue the contents any way you can. Or you may need to work on an EPS file that, by definition, is encapsulated and therefore uneditable in the normal course of events. This section covers those parts of your PageMaker system that will break into those files no matter what.

Going Native for Editing

This may seem obvious, but you'd be surprised at how many people don't take this logical first step. First, before you try anything else, pull out one of your applications programs and try to open the file.

If it is a text file of any kind, it is likely that you'll be able to open it in some way with a word processor, even if it is filled with junk characters. If it is a graphic file, try to open it in Photoshop, FreeHand, or Illustrator.

Failing that first step, there are a variety of alternatives that may help out.

ArtSPREE and Transverter Pro

You usually think of EPS files as being bulletproof. You can't get into them to edit the contents. Well, TechPool makes two products that will let you edit the uneditable.

ArtSPREE is a Plug-in for manipulating EPS files from within PageMaker. It will let you make a color image gray, or turn it into line art. Most importantly it will let you *ghost* an image—make a fuzzed and dimmed shadow of an EPS object.

Transverter Pro will take a PostScript file and process it within your computer, just like your PostScript printer does it. The difference is, instead of paper output, you end up with an editable image. If you have an EPS file that has no preview because it came over from that "other" platform, place it into PageMaker, and run it through Transverter Pro. If you want to get some assurance that your PostScript output file is okay before you hand it off to the service bureau, run it through Transverter Pro and look at it right on-screen.

Text and Type Management Utilities

Aside from Plug-ins like Galley Oops! and PageType that work from within PageMaker, you may want to add to your system an array of extra tools for working with text.

Tagging Text

One of the hottest new features of PageMaker 6.0 is its ability to work with tagged text. To get the most out of the tagging language, you will want to work with some batch search and replace utilities. The CD-ROM that comes with this book includes the acknowledged leader on the PC platform for batch search and replace operations. It's Thomas Lundin's SNR (for search and replace).

Making Book Features

If you need to make indexes or citation lists, Sonar Bookends from Virginia Systems will compile a word list, or concordance, index from your publication. It won't build an actual PageMaker index, but it will give you a list of all the unique words in your publication along with their page numbers. You can set filters to omit common words to avoid jamming up your index with trivial material.

Proofing

One useful text proofing program, besides Galley Oops!, is DocuComp from MasterSoft. It will compare two word processor files for differences. This is handy if you ever need to make sure you've made all requested changes in a document or if you need to run a check on how text changed from edition to edition of a publication.

Converting Files

Even though PageMaker has all those filters for working with different sources of page elements, they don't cover everything.

On both sides of the platform pond, Macintosh and Windows, the name brand has pretty much become DataViz. There are other file translators out there, but DataViz seems to have pretty well dominated the market lately:

▶ MacLinkPlus includes the software to hook up a Mac and a PC and exchange files directly, translating them in the process.

▶ On the PC side, Conversions Plus lets your PC read Mac disks.

▶ For all of the above, DataViz supplies a suite of dozens of translation pairs for almost any imaginable combination of text format and some graphics formats as well.

Compression Tools

Shipping files back and forth usually means finding a way to bundle them together, or to shrink them down for faster and cheaper transmission via modem or to fit them on a disk.

There are two basic standards for file compression you are likely to encounter. There's PKZip and StuffIt:

▶ PKZip is a DOS utility for file compression. You can also find WinZip on most of the online services and on the CD-ROM with this book. It will let you run PKZip from Windows, including Windows 95. On the Macintosh side, your colleagues can unzip a file you send them by using ZipIt. Files that have been zipped, as you might guess, end with ZIP.

▶ StuffIt is a commercial product these days, although it didn't start out that way. The StuffIt standard is to identify the file with the letters SIT on the end. On the Windows side of things, there's StuffIt Expander that will decipher your colleagues' stuffed file. I've included it on the CD-ROM for your convenience. Actually, it does a lot more than StuffIt format. It will expand Zip (ZIP/EXE), Arj (ARJ/EXE), Arc (ARC), gzip (GZ), UUEncode (UUE), BinHex (HQX), and MacBinary (BIN).

Where to Go from Here

▶ This chapter focuses on paper publishing. The chapters on electronic publishing (Chapter 29, "Publishing Electronically: The Web or Acrobat" and Chapter 33, "Designing for the Web") have information on the additional tools you'll need for building World Wide Web pages.

▶ The use of a font manager has been covered in Chapter 25, "Developing a System for Managing Your Type."

▶ Generally, the Plug-ins that come with PageMaker have been covered on an individual basis where they would naturally come up. Alignment, for example, is covered in Chapter 14, "Precisely Positioning Graphics and Text."

▶ Contact information for third party add-ons has been listed in Appendix E, "Resource Guide."

Chapter 27

Leaping Across Platforms

This chapter on commuting between computers covers the following:

Making the leap by getting your files across the platform gap.
▼

Strategizing for graphics transfers.
▼

Translating text files into a usable form, either before or after they make the Macintosh/PC jump.
▼

Making PageMaker work between the two platforms, including details on links, graphics, and font issues.

IN THE BEGINNING, graphics people pretty much used Macintoshes. Not everyone was, but the vast majority of designers used a Macintosh when it came to desktop publishing. Boy, have things changed. It's a much more ecumenical world out there now.

PageMaker has had a Windows version for years now, waiting for the Windows platform to become more graphics capable—and it gradually has become such. But suddenly Windows 95 has flooded the world with new power.

PageMaker will remain a bi-platform graphics community for the foreseeable future. And leaping across platforms is what this chapter is all about. ▶ ▶ ▶

Getting the File Across the Gap

Before you can ever do anything with a publication or one of its graphic or text elements, you must get the file across the gap between its platform and your own. This isn't strictly a PageMaker issue, but it is a vital one for anyone who must deal with a cross-platform DTP environment. There are way too many variables for me to be able to cover every single possibility you may encounter, but we'll cover the most likely basics here.

Slipping a Disk

Things have really come a long way since the last edition of this book. For example, you can now put a cross-platform disk right into the floppy drive of either PageMaker computing platform. Macintosh has been able to read DOS disks for awhile through third-party extensions, but now that functionality has been built right in to System 7.5. More recently, it has become possible to read a Mac disk in a Windows machine as well.

Reading Mac Disks In a DOS/Windows Machine

I have to admit, it still feels a little weird to put a Mac disk in the floppy drive of a Windows machine, but I do it almost every day—even though Microsoft unfortunately didn't build the capability directly into Windows 95.

There's a whole raft of options to help you do this. MacSee is Paul Thomson's popular shareware program for reading Mac disks on a PC. There's also Mac-Ette and Mac-in-DOS. DataViz, the people who make MacLink and seem to dominate the file translation market, have a product called Conversions Plus that will allow a PC to format and read a Mac disk.

Reading DOS Disks In a Mac

There's no reason why you shouldn't be able to just hand your DOS disk to a Mac person and expect that person to use it without any trouble. Because PCs outnumber Mac machines, Macintosh users have had to develop a number of options for reading a DOS disk. If they say it won't work, just show them this list:

▶ This capability has been built right into Macintosh System 7.5.

▶ For Macintosh System 7.1 users, Apple File Exchange came with the Macintosh System software. Just start it up and then slip in the DOS disk, and choose the file as if it were a Macintosh floppy on your Desktop.

▶ Alternatively, again for System 7.1 users, they can use one of the System extensions that allow the DOS disk to appear right on the Desktop without going through the cumbersome Apple File Exchange step.

In this System extension category, I'm partial to Access PC from Insignia Software, the people that make the Windows and DOS emulator software, SoftPC, for the Mac folks.

This discussion has focused on floppies, but all these capabilities are available for the removable format drives such as Syquests, Zips, and Bernoullis.

Connecting Directly

Sometimes the fastest way to get a large file, or group of files, across the platform gap is a direct connection. There are a range of possibilities, running from a cable, to a phone line, to a network.

Connecting One-on-One

If you are using Conversions Plus for cross-platform disk reading, you know about DataViz. DataViz publishes MacLink, which includes a special cable to connect the serial ports of your Mac and a DOS machine so that the files can be transferred. DataViz has become the widely accepted standard bearer of file translations modules, and the DOS or Windows software allows you to simply take over a Macintosh and send and receive files from the Mac's hard disk.

Connecting via Telephone

Transmit the file by modem between the computers, either via a direct connection or by posting it through e-mail on an online network such as America Online, CompuServe, or the Internet.

TIP ▶ Watch Out for MacBinary

Any time you are going cross-platform by modem, you must be on guard against MacBinary. This adds a thin but troublesome 128-byte header to the transferred file. Your PC programs will probably choke when trying to read a MacBinary file. The solution is to have the Mac user turn off MacBinary in their communications software. Or, you can strip off the MacBinary header by using Stuffit Expander. Also, you may need to decompress the file, and you can find out all about that in the upcoming section "Decoding Cross-Platform Compressed Files."

Connecting More Permanently by Networking

This book is being written in parallel editions, one for the Macintosh and one for Windows 95. Talk about leaping platforms—we've done a lot of it on this project.

If you do platform leaping to a significant degree, connect the computers more intimately through a network. Basically, all the computers on the Net will then be capable to freely transfer files, regardless of whether they are Windows, DOS, or Mac machines.

You could go for Ethernet or one of those industrial-strength networks. These days, even smaller businesses are using such cross-platform solutions. If you are in that category, you don't need me to tell you how to make cross-platform connections.

Another option is to make the connection through the Apple operating system network solution. This is an inexpensive and easy-to-set-up connection solution that's available even if you are primarily a PC person. If you have a Mac, you already own AppleTalk. If you have a PC, you will need to invest:

▶ If you'd rather not get into the guts of the PC in your shop—installing a special card—make your LocalTalk connection through the parallel port of the PC.

Apexx offers an excellent solution for the hardware, and Miramar Systems does for the software. Based in Boise, Idaho, Apexx makes a miniature plug-in AppleTalk connector that takes up almost no room, plugs into the PC's parallel port, and has AppleTalk connectors on it to make connections to Apple printers and to Macintoshes.

With that you need software. Fortunately, Miramar Systems of Santa Barbara, California, makes Mac-Lan Connect. With this software, you literally see your Mac files and drives on the PC, and vice versa.

▶ For more speed, you may want to get an AppleTalk card installed in your PC. It'll shuffle data faster because it doesn't have to push the bits through the slower parallel port.

The name everyone mentions when you ask around about this option will be COPS—short for CoOperative Printing Solutions, based in Norcross, Georgia. They've been around for quite awhile, providing PostScript server solutions, and much of that experience has found its way into their AppleTalk network offering. The network adapter card they offer runs with their own software, COPSTalk.

Translating Foreign Page Element Files

Even after you manage to transfer a file across the platform gap, you still have to be able to work with the data. You will often need to read text and graphics files submitted as page elements from the opposite platform. Maybe you are working on PageMaker in Windows 95, but the Spokane office wrote the text in MacWrite—that sort of thing.

Stick to Platform Agile Graphics Formats

If you are using anything but EPS or TIFF, ask yourself if it is worth the trouble. Not only are these two formats robust and proven, they are relatively solid when going across platforms. True, there are some differences, but they are minor compared to the problems encountered with some of the alternatives.

EPS files generated on one platform may appear as gray boxes on the other because their preview files are not compatible across platforms (PICT for the Mac or WMF for Windows), but they print just fine. You can, in many graphics programs, save EPS files so they will be previewable on both platforms by saving them with TIFF previews. (A pure PostScript EPS file, one without any embedded platform-specific graphics, should print fine on either platform, although you may be missing a preview and see just a gray box on-screen.)

TIFF files generated on the Mac have a slightly different format than Windows TIFF files, but that is rarely a difficulty, especially when using PageMaker's TIFF filter, which is designed to accommodate the difference.

If you know you will be swapping with a Mac person, you should both avoid PC Paintbrush (PCX), WMF (Windows MetaFile), and PICT (Macintosh graphic) files. You can import all these formats on either platform, but that doesn't mean you should do it. Any service bureau will tell you horror stories about problems trying to spoon-feed these files through their imagesetters. It takes time, and that costs money. And in the end, it sometimes just doesn't work.

Photo CD files are a special case. They are fully cross-platform compatible. However, they can't be stored inside PageMaker so you will need to supply the Photo CD disk to the service bureau at output time. Or you can use the Save as Lab TIFF option when you import the image. There's more on Photo CD issues in Chapter 11, "Placing Images."

If you can't get the graphic element in EPS or TIFF from the get-go, you may need to translate it. Here are some options to check out:

▶ For bitmapped graphics, if you have Photoshop you've got it made. Open the graphic in Photoshop and save or export it as a TIFF. You even have the option of saving it as a Mac or PC flavor TIFF.

▶ For vector graphics, open the file in Illustrator, FreeHand, or CorelDRAW and save it as an EPS. Photoshop, Illustrator, and FreeHand have the advantage of being available on either platform.

▶ Also on the PC side, have a look at HiJaak for graphic file conversions.

▶ Techpool makes Transverter Pro, which does an excellent job of breaking into PostScript files and making them editable.

▶ You will find the shareware programs PaintShop Pro and VuePrint on the CD-ROM that's in the back of this book.

▶ On the Mac side, there are quite a number of graphics convertors that your fellow file traders can use to help out with the cross-platform exchange process.

  Thorsten Lemke has created the highly regarded Graphics Converter.

  Equilibrium makes the batch processor Debabelizer, especially terrific if you have a large number of files to translate.

Making Words Flow Across the Gap

Well, good news. This whole area has been getting easier and easier, probably because there's almost no such thing as a foreign word processor format anymore.

The major application developers have, on an increasing level, been making their products available simultaneously for both platforms just as a matter of increasing their market potential for the same dollar. The result? Almost any word processor you or your colleagues are working on is likely to have a Save As or Export command. And that's the gateway to saving the work in the format that will make it easy to cross the platform gap. That being said, here are some strategy notes:

▶ *Save in a PageMaker filter format.* This seems pretty obvious, but stay in tune with the filters available for PageMaker, and if possible get whomever is submitting the word processor file to do so in a format you can just read directly into PageMaker through the Place command.

▶ *Try an intermediate format.* If, for some wild reason, it isn't possible to save out of the word processor in a format that's directly readable by a PageMaker filter, find a half-way step.

  Rich Text Format (RTF) files are a good *lingua franca* for text because they will preserve most of the important local formatting someone has done, and—this is an important timesaver—RTF supports styles.

  You can pretty well depend on even the most obscure DOS programs being able to put out some form of ASCII file.

▶ *Translate.* Get one of the text file translation utilities. DataViz is the household name in this category with its Conversions Plus package or MacLink packages, including hundreds of DOS/Mac file translation filters.

Decoding Cross-Platform Compressed Files

Naturally, when you exchange files between computers, you commonly compress them to reduce their size. This saves transmission time if you link computers directly, and disk space if you swap floppies.

On the DOS side, the standard is PKZip. On the Mac side, the compression standard is StuffIt or Compact Pro.

If a Mac person gives you StuffIt files, you can decode them on the PC side, but as of this writing you can't generate a StuffIt file on the PC. Look on the online services for SITEX10.EXE, the file name for StuffIt Expander 1.0 for Windows.

You can send ZIP files to Mac people if they have the right program. StuffIt Deluxe has a built-in translator for ZIP-encoded files. You can also try out ZipIt, an excellent shareware program for the Mac that decompresses zipped files.

Making PageMaker Jump the Gap

Everything so far in this chapter has been about getting all your elements on the correct side of the gap, and translating those elements to PageMaker-readable form. Sooner or later you will run into a situation where your actual PageMaker file must make the platform leap. Here's a running start at it.

Setting Up PageMaker

You must take care of a couple of fundamental issues even before you transfer your PageMaker publication to its new home:

▶ Even though Windows 95 allows long file names, the fact is that files have historically been named in very different ways between the two platforms. As a result, if you are bringing a Mac publication into Windows, name it with a file extension of **PM6** (for a regular PageMaker publication) or **PT6** (for template). That way, Windows PageMaker will be able to "see" it.

▶ The file must be at the same major version level before you bring it over. You can't use Macintosh PageMaker 6.0 to open a PageMaker 5.0 file created in Windows.

Making Transfer Decisions

When you bring the PageMaker file over to the opposite platform, the program will detect that the inbound publication originated on the opposite platform and will ask a few questions right away.

You will see the dialog box shown in figure 27.1 if the inbound document contains fonts that have not been installed on the targeted machine.

FIG. 27.1 ▶

PageMaker making a font match.

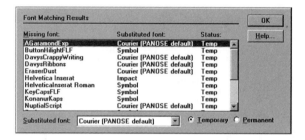

This is no different than the PANOSE font matching dialog box you get even when you haven't done a cross-platform file exchange, except in this case the problem may not be merely a failure to provide the needed fonts. It may be because of inherent differences between fonts on the Windows and Mac platforms:

▶ If you need to get the publication across just for editing purposes, and it will be heading back to the other platform, go ahead and substitute fonts.

▶ If you will be going to final output from the destination platform, you will need to make more permanent arrangements. There's more detail and strategy for handling font issues in the next section.

Also, PANOSE and other font substitution issues are covered in Chapter 25, "Developing a System for Managing Your Type."

Next, PageMaker gives you some Translation Options, as shown in figure 27.2.

FIG. 27.2 ▶

Selecting your gap-leaping Translation Options.

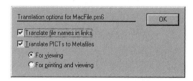

If you have files linked to the inbound PageMaker document, PageMaker will attempt to translate the filename path by trying to automatically link to files stored outside the publication. So these links can be made, you should have already transferred linked elements to the destination drive. If you are making a permanent transfer, be sure to check this option.

Metafiles (Windows-specific) and PICTs (Macintosh-specific) are commonly used as the preview portions of EPS files:

▶ If you want them translated so you can see previews while positioning EPS files included in the inbound publication, select the Translate PICTS to Metafiles option (or vice versa if you are going the other direction). Only check this option if you are making a permanent transfer.

▶ Notice that you can choose to translate for viewing only (EPS previews) or for printing as well (if you've used these non-PostScript formats as actual graphics in your publication).

▶ This PICT/Metafile translation only works on elements stored in the publication, not for externally linked files.

Understanding Linking Effects

Even though PageMaker will try, at your request in the Translation Options dialog box, to automatically handle the links in the inbound file, that isn't always a smooth process. Here are some notes on link issues:

▶ In general, my advice is, if you know a document will be transferred, stick with PageMaker's own Place and Link technology, and don't use Pub & Sub or OLE, especially in this situation, where you are complicating the work process by a cross-platform transfer.

▶ When Macintosh files cross to Windows, any Publish and Subscribe links will be broken. You will still have the information in the file, but you will no longer be able to edit it because this linking technology is Macintosh-specific.

▶ OLE links survive the transfer but only if there is a linked file. OLE objects that have been embedded will not be editable. Linked OLE objects will only be editable if the same application that created them exists on the destination platform.

TIP ▶ Tables May Be a Problem When Making the Platform Leap

As we go to press, the Adobe Table situation is in a bit of an uncertain state. This may have an impact on cross-platform transfers of PageMaker files. For one thing, if you are using Windows 3.x instead of Windows 95, you will have a completely different version of Adobe Table—Version 2.1 instead of Version 2.5. In addition, it appears that Windows users of Adobe Table will not have an option to save or read tables as EPS files, the format of choice for moving between platforms. It's not yet clear whether OLE embedded tables will translate between platforms.

You have two play-it-safe options. First, you can transfer the Table file and reimport it on the destination platform after resolving any cross-platform font issues. Second, don't use Table and set your tables using PageMaker text and paragraph styles.

There's more on this whole area of links in Chapter 30, "Linking and Other File Connections."

Jumping the Font Hurdle

Windows fonts and Macintosh fonts are different. That's true even if you use what seem to be the exact same Type 1 PostScript fonts from the same manufacturer. Here are the issues you'll need to consider:

▶ You will need to deal with the difference between the characters. The upper portion of the character set, the weird characters above 128 in a grid of the alphabet, are often assigned to different keys between the two platforms. On the PC side there are fractions, for example. On the Mac side there are no fractions, but there are ligatures.

One solution is to open the character set template supplied with PageMaker on both platforms. Assign the font in question, and run a print test set on both sides. That will provide you with a "program" for the font differences in the fonts used in your particular publications.

▶ Check every single page for unintended line breaks, unexpected widows and orphans, and overset text. Even the same manufacturer may work with different kerning pairs and other font metrics specifications between the two platforms. Plus, you may have had to substitute a font.

▶ To compound the problem, PCs use two different schemes for assigning characters within a font. ASCII is the standard on DOS machines. ANSI is the Windows standard. This will come up, particularly when you bring plain text files across the platform gap. When you are importing these plain text files you can tell the PageMaker filter which scheme to use.

TIP ▶ Double-Check Cross-Platform Issues When Going to a Service Bureau

Hear the one about $11,000 worth of worthless film? A colleague submitted a huge project to a service bureau. Because it was a Windows PageMaker file, they were told to run the files on a PC. Someone who didn't know any better ran the files out from a Macintosh. Fractions turned into ligatures, justified lines blew out like a Scrabble game in an earthquake, and all that film had to be thrown away at the service bureau's expense after what you might call a sincere heart-to-heart talk between the designer and the owner. Make sure your service bureau understands cross-platform issues and checks your proofs. Imagine if the project had gone to press.

Where to Go from Here

▶ There's lots more information on font issues in Chapter 25, "Developing a System for Managing Your Type."

▶ For information on linking and other file connections, check out Chapter 30.

▶ You can get details on Photo CD-specific issues in Chapter 11, "Placing Images."

Chapter 28

Automating PageMaker

This chapter on automating PageMaker includes:

An explanation of the difference between scripting and tagging and why you should use these powerful tools.

▼

Quick Script experiments so that you can see how PageMaker scripting works.

▼

A rundown of the scripts that come with PageMaker.

▼

How you can put to work the more than three dozen scripts included on the CD-ROM for this book.

▼

Things you can't do with a script in PageMaker.

▼

Generating a tagging file and why you'd want to.

▼

Fast and easy mass text formatting by using search and replace techniques on a tagging file.

▼

Some basic tagging language rules.

PAGEMAKER HAS TWO powerful facilities for saving you time. One of them is brand new for Version 6.0, and the other has been significantly enhanced. These powerful tools are *scripting*, a sort of macro programming language, and *tagging*, a language for describing the look of your PageMaker text.

The focus in this chapter is to get you to take the plunge into some easy experiments with scripting and tagging. Even if the whole concept of "writing a program" sends you into fits of collywobbles and the tagging language looks like Sanskrit to you—give these two automation tools a try. ▶ ▶ ▶

KEY CONCEPT:
Scripts and Tags Are Just Fancy To-Do Lists

Let's start with the idea of a script and then we'll move on to tagging.

Write One Script, Save Time Many Times

The magic power of scripting is the way it allows you to write a single script containing dozens of tasks. Once the script has been written, you never have to actually do those dozens of tasks again, at least not one-by-one. You simply double-click on the script in the Scripts palette, and the whole mess of jobs is performed automatically—automating PageMaker—while you go out for a cup of coffee.

When you write a script, you write out a sort of to-do list of orders for PageMaker. You can have a one-item list, or a list of hundreds of PageMaker commands. And these scripts can do almost everything in PageMaker except tie your shoe. (Yes, even PageMaker's scripts have their limitations, which we'll discuss in the upcoming section, "What PageMaker Scripts Can't Do.")

You could, for example, have a script that sets up a document from scratch, complete with default Print settings, paragraph styles, placeholders for text and graphics—everything. In fact, that's what you do when you open one of the template publications that come with PageMaker. Those templates are shipped as long scripts of PageMaker commands. (They are actually pretty good learning tools for how to set up various jobs in a

script, so they are templates in more ways than one.)

Obviously, it's easier to write and comprehend a short list than a long one. But what's even easier is to run a script that's ready to use, written for you without you having to do any programming. In this chapter, we'll spend a fair amount of time on some scripts that introduce you to the power of this tool, and then give you some of the basic information you need to modify those scripts for your own purposes or even write some of your own from scratch.

How Tagging is Different

In a way, tagging is a lot like a script. For one thing, a file of tag codes is nothing more than a to-do list of orders for PageMaker. There are some differences, however.

Tags do not implement menu commands; they describe the way text should be formatted. In this way they resemble other description languages that you may know about, such as Rich Text Format (Microsoft's RTF text format), and PostScript (Adobe's page description language).

Unlike a script, you would almost never sit down and write out a to-do list of tag codes. Generally what happens is you generate the codes from within PageMaker or maybe by using a third-party utility for this purpose.

For example, you might bring some text into PageMaker and discover that it really needs a lot of formatting work—tuning the width of em dashes, standard kerning combinations you always employ, setting up special formatting for certain combinations of words that shouldn't ever break at the ends of lines, and so on.

You could do some of this work with a series of passes through these publication using PageMaker's new and improved Find and Change commands. But there are some kinds of formatting you simply can't do that way, even with these enhanced commands. In any case, while you would not mind a repetitive search-and-replace process if you only had to do it once, it would certainly be tedious to have to do it over and over again, each time opening up a new text file. These kinds of standard formatting operations can and should be automated, and PageMaker's tagging language is just the ticket for doing up batches of work.

The heart of automating your tagging language processing system is in fact some kind of utility that can perform massive search-and-replace operations in big batches. We'll talk about some of the tools for accomplishing that work in the tagging section of this chapter.

What's In It for Me?

Automation performs repetitive actions for you, so you make a bit of an investment up front in order to receive major gains down the line. At some point, after repeated use, you'll be at break even on this invest-ment, and every time you perform some repetitive task you'll be saving large amounts of time. For a designer or production person, that's money in the bank. To summarize the benefits:

▼ *You save time.* A script or a search and replace batch does work as fast as a computer can do it, instead of as fast as you can do it. You aren't keying in many different items on the to-do list. You just hand the to-do list to the computer and tell it to get to work!
▼ *You prevent errors and guarantee consistency.* You can use a script or a batch operation to perform a series of tasks in a standard way—every single time you use it. You don't need to worry about forgetting one little item in a list.
▼ *You can reduce boredom.* If you have to perform the same move hundreds of times, or a lot of moves a half dozen times, scripts and tagging will help you minimize brain-dulling repetition.

With all these benefits, you'll be able to spend the time you save reading James Joyce's *Ulysses*, and you'll understand it. Strangers will call you and ask for advice. You won't be lonely on Saturday night. You'll finally be able to work out your relationship with your parents. And if you are a victim of male pattern baldness, even though scripting and tagging will not stimulate new hair growth, you won't mind.

Using the Scripts Palette

If there's one thing that will vaccinate you against that bubonic plague fear of scripting I mentioned earlier, this is it. Figure 28.1 shows PageMaker's new Scripts palette.

Fig. 28.1 ▶

Making scripting accessible—the new Scripts palette.

Running a Script

In previous versions of PageMaker, in order to run a script you had to go up to the Utilities menu and crank up a Plug-in (back then an Addition), and then take a few more steps beyond that just to have the convenience of running a script. Small wonder that people who were already a little nervous about programming a script would feel like maybe it wasn't worth the trouble.

Now, with the Scripts palette, you just double-click and go. That's it. No cumbersome menus. Just do it.

If you happen to be reading this in front of your computer, go ahead and try it out. One of the first things I did when I saw the Scripts palette was to look at what was there. One thing I found was the script you see highlighted in figure 28.2.

Fig. 28.2 ▶

Double-clicking to run a script.

This one removes all those useless default styles that PageMaker always puts in your Styles palette. Double-click on it, and in a nanosecond you save yourself, by actual count, the ten separate little steps it takes to remove each of those default styles by hand.

Managing Scripts in the Palette

The list of commands you get by clicking the arrowhead in the upper-right corner of the Scripts palette (refer to fig. 28.1) shows that you can do most of your script management in one convenient spot. In a lot of cases you won't even need to go outside PageMaker to use a text editor. You can create and edit scripts right from the palette.

The most important thing to understand about scripts is this: they are plain text files. They aren't PageMaker, Microsoft Word, or WordPerfect files. Of course, you can create plain text files in all of those programs, but you must consciously tend to it; otherwise your scripts just plain won't run.

Also, the structure you see in figure 28.2, with plus and minus signs and folders in a sort of outline view, should look familiar. It's like an outline of the material on your hard drive. Each indent is a nested folder, and you can use the arrows to shrink or expand your view of the outline.

All the scripts shown in the palette live inside the SCRIPTS folder. You subcategorize them by storing them inside subfolders. They show up in the palette under those subfolder organizational headings like the ones you see here: "LAYOUT," "COLOR," "PRINTING," and so on.

The SCRIPTS folder can be found inside the PLUG-INS folder, which is in your language folder (usually USENGLISH), which is inside the RSRC folder, in turn located inside the main PageMaker folder itself (usually PM6). Isn't it nice that you can just use the palette instead of burrowing through all those folders?

Here's what each of the items on that menu does:

▶ *Add Script.* Copy a script file from a floppy or another hard drive location to your SCRIPTS folder, or one of its categorizing subfolders.

TIP ▶ Drag and Drop Doesn't Work on Scripts Palette

The PageMaker manual says you can simply drag and drop files to the Scripts palette to add them. However, it appears that this is a feature that the engineers just couldn't get together in time for the release. (The manual also says you can edit a script in Trace mode, and that wasn't working either as this book was going to press.)

▶ *New Script.* Open a new text file right from within the palette and just start typing your script.

▶ *Remove Script.* This doesn't erase a script. It simply moves a script out of the palette by moving the file to a folder called SCRIPTSD.

▶ *Restore Script.* Moves a script back into the SCRIPTS folder from what you might call the disabled list.

▶ *Edit Script.* Open a script and make changes. Through this command you have a very simple plain text editor. You can also edit a script by holding down the Ctrl key and clicking on its name in the palette.

▶ *Trace Script.* Steps through each line of a script to help you figure out where it goes wrong. Programmers call this *debugging*. You can edit the script right in Trace mode, making it convenient to fix problems when you find them.

A 20-Second Solo Flight

In the last edition, this was a 60-second solo flight. Thanks to the palette, it's faster this time.

To change your PageMaker measurement system without benefit of a script, you must navigate to the Preferences menu and change two different pull-down lists. During this move, you often change not only the overall measurement system but also the one for the vertical rule. What a drag.

Here's how you can try out scripting and get some useful work done at the same time. Timers ready? Go!

1. Use the pull-out menu and the New Script command. You'll get a standard dialog for saving your script. Call it **inches**, and save it in the main SCRIPT folder.

2. Type the following words in the text box that comes up, leaving no space between *measure* and *units*:

   measureunits inches,inches

3. Click OK. Repeat steps 1 and 2, but instead name it picas and type:

   measureunits picas,picas

   At this point, you have stored two scripts in the palette. Now it's just a matter of putting them to work. The clock's ticking, so keep moving.

4. Look at the rulers and see which measurement system you are in, probably inches or picas. Whichever it is, double-click on the opposite script in the Scripts palette.

The ruler ripples to the new measurement system almost instantaneously, and you're done. Quick and easy, huh?

To change back to picas (or the other way around, if you started with inches), select the appropriate script and double-click.

Pushing the Script Envelope with Ray

But you've got an even bigger treat ahead of you. Meet scriptmeister Ray Robertson. Ray has put together a series of scripts for readers of this book, and you'll find them in a folder on the CD-ROM that comes with this book.

As I mention in his introduction in Chapter 34, this spot is where we are erecting a bronze plaque in Ray's honor. (He also participated as a member of an online panel of desktop publishing professionals in that Learning from the Pros chapter. You'll find out a bit more about Ray there.)

What do you say about a guy who misses family holidays so he can meticulously craft some scripts, just because he likes to help people? Well, you probably ought to say, "Thanks, Ray. Seeing as how you went to all that trouble, I'll give these scripts a spin, and please say hi to the wife for me."

Aside from helping out people who desperately need scripting solutions, Ray tells me he's proud of living in the small town of Cartersville, outside Atlanta, where you'll find him singing tenor in the church choir (and occasionally preaching). He also wanted me to especially mention his two children and that he is extremely grateful to his wife of 13 years, Marina, who doesn't mind him spending so much time "on the phone" with his friends online. You too will be grateful for Marina's understanding ways when you start using the scripts Ray wrote for you.

With a background as a computer typesetter, Ray began using a computer for publishing purposes in 1986, and in an effort to get the most out of his machines he has, among other things, delved deeply into PageMaker's native scripting language.

If you have questions about the scripts on the CD-ROM, or suggestions for improving them, Ray would love to hear from you. You can find him, usually, in the DTP Forum on CompuServe, and his user ID is **71155,3033**. You can always send me a message as well at **75036,3263**.

Trying Out the CD-ROM Scripts

It's time to take a look at your presents. Load Ray's scripts by copying them from the CD-ROM into the SCRIPTS folder on your hard drive, leaving them right inside their subcategory organizing folders. Here's what you'll have in your script palette:

▶ *Crops.* Select any PageMaker object, including a Group, and run this script to put crop marks around it. That means you can gang several small items onto the same PageMaker page and save film charges at the service bureau.

By the way, like all good programmers, Ray annotates his scripts with comments. If you ever wonder how one of them works, just select it and use the palette's Edit command to have a look, as in figure 28.3. All the items with double hyphens in front of them are *comments*, notes on the script's inner workings.

FIG. 28.3 ▶

Checking out the details in a script using the Scripts palette Edit command.

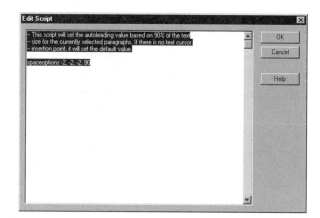

▶ *Find/Change.* If you are really hesitant about getting into tagging, these scripts do a number of things that people often use tags for. They will replace double hyphens with real em dashes, replace double spaces or double paragraph ends with single ones, and condense em dashes to 75 percent width (a preference expressed by a number of the pros in the DTP Forum).

In the next section, we'll talk about the Find/Change script writing engine Ray has provided, for automating even fancier Find/Change moves.

▶ *Graduated Screens.* You may think that PageMaker doesn't offer graduated screens, but you would be wrong. Ray has written a series of scripts that prove otherwise. They all work, in one way or the other, by drawing a series of PageMaker circles or boxes that graduate from No Fill to 100% fill in 5 percent increments, and then they are all grouped together. You can see an example of the results here, in figure 28.4, and in the color section.

These aren't really graduated screens in the sense of the screens produced in FreeHand or Illustrator, but they do a good job of demonstrating script capabilities for copying elements, resizing elements, changing tints, and grouping objects. Use caution about including these in files, because they are complex images that may take a long time to print.

Fig. 28.4 ▷

Graduated screens in PageMaker, including two fills—one with a dark center and the other a light center—plus a bevelled frame and a drop shadow.

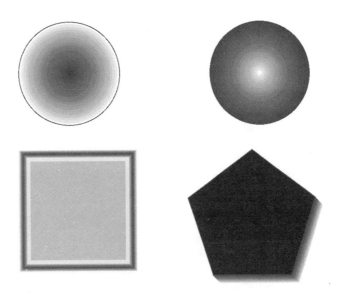

▶ *Guides to Object.* These handy scripts will put guides on an object, or delete all guides. In figure 28.5, you can see that Ray built a script for us that will even put guides on the center point of an object, horizontally or vertically.

Fig. 28.5 ▷

Center guides on an object from a script.

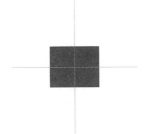

▶ *Measurement System.* Use these scripts to instantly switch your units of measure, Ray's more complete version of the script you typed out for the 20-second solo flight earlier in this chapter.

▶ *Place Text.* When you are laying lots of text onto a page, it can be a bit cumbersome to pick up the text gun icon from the bottom of a text block windowshade and then put it exactly at the top of the next column. Aside from that, your eye may not be quite as precise as PageMaker's column guides. This set of scripts will pick up the text of any text block you have selected and precisely place remaining text at the top of the next column, the first column of the next page, or the next page in precisely the same coordinates as the selected block.

▶ *Split Objects.* You probably thought you couldn't build shapes like the ones in figure 28.6. The Split Objects set of scripts can do it. By using the Mask and Group commands, the split into quarters script Ray created will build you a section of an oval (or a box) by simply dividing an oval or box into four equal parts.

Fɪɢ. 28.6 ▶

The Split Objects scripts can cut a box or oval into two or four pieces.

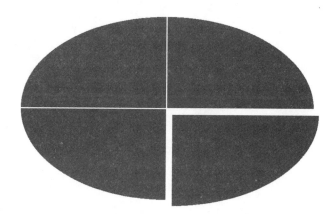

▶ *Straighten Rounded Corners.* In the same way, using Mask and Group, you can run scripts to mix rounded and straight corners on a box, like the one in figure 28.7. Draw a round cornered box, and these scripts will put square corners on whichever side of the box you wish.

▶ *Zeropoint of Object.* During layout, it is often helpful to be able to measure from a particular point on an object. It's easier to do that measuring if you can simply read from the ruler. To do that effectively, you need to drag the zeropoint of the ruler to the desired spot on the object. These scripts do it for you (and more precisely). Select the object and run the script of your choice to reset the zeropoint to the midpoint on any side, the center, or to any of the corners.

Fɪɢ. 28.7 ▷

*There's now a way,
using Ray's scripts,
to create a box with
a mix of rounded
and square corners.*

Supercharging Find/Change with Scripting

One of the most powerful new advances in PageMaker 6.0's scripting capabilities
has to be the new ability to script Find and Change runs, and to activate them
within the Layout view, in addition to the usual Story Editor mode.

Say you have a weekly newsletter where you always need to run a bunch of
cleanup Find/Change operations on text submitted by half dozen contributors.
You need to color some text. You need to assign a no break attribute to a two-
word name. Lots of cleanup has to be done, and it's always the same week after
week, taking up maybe an hour each time. Well, it can take just a couple of minutes a week from now on, complements of scriptmeister Ray.

You can have all the benefits of Find/Change scripting, without learning all the
fine points of writing a script. Look at the CD-ROM that came with this book, and
open the folder of scripts. The PageMaker template file you will find in the
SCRIPTS folder is a script writing engine.

Here's how to set it up, and, believe me, it takes longer to spell all this out than it
does to actually do it:

1. Install the scripts. Do that by copying them and the FIND/CHANGE TEM-
   PLATE folder to the SCRIPTS folder on your hard drive.

   If you had PageMaker running when you copied the scripts, it's always
   a good idea to use the Refresh command to allow PageMaker to, figura-
   tively speaking, clear its head about what scripts are in the palette. Access
   Refresh by clicking the right mouse button anywhere inside the Scripts
   palette.

2. Open the Find/Change Template file. It will open as an untitled new
   publication.

The use of a template file means you are working with a cc py and don't need to worry about messing up the original. In fact, after you use the template to write your scripts, don't bother saving the file, because the script will be safely stored away in the SCRIPTS folder so it can be used from your palette. You won't need this temporary PageMaker file.

Look around the two template pages and read through Ray's notes and tips. Notice that the template script at the top of page two contains every conceivable find and change parameter in scripting language.

Also, notice that almost every item in the Scripts palette is paired.

You run the Find version of a script to tell the script template what your target will be—what you want to Find.

You run the Change version of a script to specify your end result—how you want the target to Change.

3. After you have the lay of the land, pick the Find job you need to perform from the palette and double-click. You will be delivered to the script portion of the template. The part of the script that you need to modify to accomplish your Find/Change task will be highlighted.

4. Type in the desired value right over the top of the highlighted text. This is the only tough part. You may need to look up some instructions in Ray's notes on the page right below the template script. Or, you can open the Script Guide that came on your PageMaker CD-ROM.

5. Now repeat the script template modification procedure by double-clicking on the Change version of the script.

6. Repeat these last two steps until you've built up the script with as many Find and Change parameters as you need.

   Now you need to save the template script. Ray describes a couple of methods, but here's the one I recommend.

7. Click the Text tool in the text block with the template script and Select All.

8. Open a New Script box in the Scripts palette, and give your script a name. Store it in the SCRIPTS folder.

   The highlighted script text will already be automatically pasted into the New Script box.

9. Click on OK.

You just wrote a script!

From now until you disable it, that script will be in your palette whenever you need to perform that Find/Change operation.

Having our scripts and templates on one CD-ROM and the PageMaker Script Guide on another will make it pretty cumbersome to use them. The whole idea is to have scripts make your life easier, not more cumbersome, so copy all the script material to your hard drive. That way it'll be ready and standing by for your instant access.

Setting a Fraction

If you really want to get wild and crazy and write your own script from scratch, try this one.

The following script automates all the directions contained in the fraction-setting instructions from Chapter 15. It's a slightly modified version of the fraction script that shipped in past versions of PageMaker:

```
-- This script will change the format and the appearance of a
--    manually typed fraction. It substitutes nonbreaking fraction
--    slash for a standard slash, and then changes the numerator to
--    a superscript character and the denominator to a subscript
--    character.
-- To run the script, type a fraction like 2/3. Insert the text
--    cursor just to the right of the fraction (do not highlight the
--    fraction). Then use Run Script to run this, as a text file.
-- Select and reformat numerator by making it a superscript
--    character and adjusting the size and position.

    textselect -word

-- Sets the type options for small caps and super/subscript.
--    80=80% of type size for small caps size
--    58=58% of type size for super/subscript size
--    33=33% of type size above baseline
--    0=0% below the baseline for subscript
--    Adjust these to suit your particular typeface choice

    typeoptions 80,58,33,0

-- Set the denominator to subscript

    position subscript

    textcursor -char
```

```
-- Select regular slash (/)
-- Replace / with "real" fraction slash
-- Assumes that user has Symbol font installed
```

textselect +char

font "Symbol"

textenter "/"

```
-- press Alt, type 0164 on numeric keypad
-- Select and reformat numerator
-- Moves, typeoptions, position are as above
```

textcursor -char

textselect -word

typeoptions 80,58,33,0

position superscript

```
--Leave the cursor where you started, ready to resume typing.
```

textcursor +word

textcursor +word

```
-- Ensure next characters entered are normal position
```

position normal

Scripting Survival Guide

Now that you've had some time with scripting, and maybe feel like modifying scripts or writing your own, here's a survival guide. In this section I'll try to underline some of the most important basic information you need in order to put yourself in control of your own scripting power. For more detail, use this guide in conjunction with the complete Script Guide that came on the PageMaker CD-ROM.

It's easier to understand scripting if you think of it as a language, because that's what it is. It's a language of action, a language for describing your commands to PageMaker. For that reason, the language consists almost exclusively of verbs.

Grammar and Syntax

Like any language, PageMaker's scripting commands have grammar. There's a syntax of rules for composing a script, and without them PageMaker responds to your commands with a sort of lackadaisical "Huh?" Nothing will happen, or you'll get an error message because the program simply won't understand what you want. Continue reading for a quick overview of the most important syntax rules.

Understanding Parameters

The Army used to have a saying that was a favorite of drill sergeants when explaining the facts of military life to a raw recruit. "When I say jump," they yell, "You don't ask why, you ask how high!"

PageMaker is no different because it can't take action without being told how high to jump. A *command* is the verb that tells PageMaker what to do, and the *parameter* is the information that tells where, when, or how much to do it.

The Rotate command in a script has the "how high to jump" part tacked onto the end of the script command:

```
rotate center 25
```

These are parameters. In this case, the word `center` means to rotate around the center proxy point, as though you had clicked it in the Control palette. The number **25** means to rotate 25 degrees.

Many commands in the PageMaker scripting language require such parameters, and much of the grammar of using the language involves the way you make commands specific by using them.

Separating Parameters

If you spelled the Rotate command without any spaces, as so:

```
rotatecenter25
```

PageMaker would ignore you. The program can't sort out what you want, as though you yelled out your lunch counter order without any pauses, like this:

pastramionryewithmustardandpickle

Don't try that in PageMaker scripting, by the way. It's an undocumented command that gives your computer a Yiddish accent.

You can separate your command parameters with spaces, as you've probably already observed. You also can use commas, tabs, or parentheses.

Using Empty Parameters

Many times you really couldn't care less what a parameter does. You use the Preferences command, for example, to set most of the items behind the Options button in the Preferences dialog box. You can choose from a list of 13 possible parameters. To skip them, you can use the number `-2`, or eloquently spell out your sentiments with the empty parameter placeholder, `dontcare`, with no spaces and no apostrophe. Both the number `-2` and the weird word `dontcare` perform the same function, then, as empty parameters.

```
preferences -2, -2, -2, -2, -2, faster, true, dontcare,
dontcare, dontcare, dontcare, 1000, 1p, 1p
```

Some command parameters you can't skip. In the case of preferences, for example, the last three parameters for the size of the graphic image and the nudge amounts won't take a "skip this parameter" placeholder.

A Case of Spelling

All PageMaker commands are run together without any spaces:

```
measureunits

guidevert

pagemargins
```

Also, use upper- and lowercase characters in any way you like, because the scripting language is not case-sensitive. Many people use a mixture to make the command easier to read:

```
pageNumbers

printOptionsPS

styleBegin
```

Stringing Commands Together

If you want to do anything more than a single command—like a real script or program with several steps—you must separate each command. You can do that with a carriage return to put each command on its own line, in its own paragraph. Or you can type a semicolon after each command and its parameters, if you wanted to rotate and skew an object. You don't need two scripts—just put both commands in the same script, as the following examples show:

```
rotate center 10; skew center 10;
```

or

```
rotate center 10
skew center 10
```

Including Comments

If you create a script for a project and then return to it months later, you'll drive yourself crazy trying to figure out what in the world you were trying to accomplish with that particular command. To solve that problem, programmers have for years included *comments* in their work.

If you look at any of Ray Robertson's scripts from the CD-ROM, you'll see notes in there that tell you how to use them and that specify any idiosyncrasies you need to watch out for.

You can do the same by putting a couple of hyphens in front of any words you want PageMaker to ignore. Everything between the double hyphens and the next command break (carriage return or semicolon) is disregarded. That means your comments can be on lines of their own, or contained within a script command line.

Specifying Zero Point Page Positions

In the command `newstory -10, -10` in the script just quoted, the numbers are coordinates. Ever play the game Battleship, or create a spreadsheet? The row and column numbers and letters describe a location on the sheet, based on the intersections of horizontal and vertical lines. PageMaker works the same way, using a sort of invisible grid. What you need to keep in your head, however, is the starting point of the grid. In a spreadsheet, the grid always measures from the upper-left corner. It may seem like PageMaker ought to work the same way, but it doesn't.

Unless you specify otherwise, PageMaker almost always measures the grid from the zero point. (Chapter 13, "Designing a Master Page Grid," says more on the zero point.) If you just pop out a couple of x (row) and y (column) matrix points, as in the `newstory -10, -10` command, you'll get a location in relation to the zero point.

Specifying Relational Page Positions

If you like, you also can have your script specify a location in relation to some item on a page. You can specify locations in relation to columns, guides, and objects. A collection of what you may call *relationship words* can help you describe how a PageMaker script command should act in this relative way. If it wasn't clear before, I'll say it clearly once again. The word is *relative*. You can use the following words as parameters to specify relative positions:

▶ *Edges*
```
left
right
top
bottom
```

▶ *Columns, guides, and pages*
```
column
guide
rightpage -- Assumes this page if you don't specify leftpage
```

▶ *Left-to-right order*
```
column 1 left -- Left edge of first column from left
column 4 right -- Right edge of fourth column from left
```

▶ *Drawing order*

```
first left -- Left edge of first object (rearmost layer)
third right -- Third object from rear layer, right edge
guide 3 -- Third guide drawn on page
last left -- Left edge of object on top layer
```

Keep in mind that PageMaker numbers objects from back to front, in the same order it draws them on-screen. You can change the order by selecting an object and sending it to the front (or back).

Guides are numbered in the order they are drawn, and unlike columns, aren't numbered from left to right.

Also, you generally would want to specify an object's edge, or PageMaker won't have a proper relationship anchor. A guide has no dimensionality, so top, bottom, left, and right don't matter. All other objects, including lines, have edges.

The Last command has scripting cognoscenti very excited. It's not well documented in the scripting guide, but if you'd like to see how you can put it to work, Ray used it very effectively in the Crops on a Box script.

You can use all these relationship words to describe movement or points in relation to the target object:

```
select 3 -- First select the object, 3rd from back
delete   -- Then delete it
deletevert 2 -- Delete second vertical guide
```

You can even have intersections:

```
select first left, guide 2
        -- Select the object at the
        -- left edge of the first drawn object
        -- and the second drawn ruler guide
```

Overriding Measurements

Any coordinates you specify with just plain numbers assume the value of the measurement system you've set up in Preference. For this purpose, any special vertical ruler measurement is ignored. If you've set your measurement system to inches, the number 10 gives you 10 inches. If you've set picas, you get picas.

Because you can't be absolutely certain what measurement system might be in effect when a script runs, play it safe by always specifying the measurement system in the command, using the ad hoc measurement systems codes in Chapter 14, "Precisely Positioning Graphics and Text." The letter *i*, for example, gives you inches; the letter *p* before a number does points, whereas the letter *p* after a number connotes picas.

Text

Names of things (files, colors, styles) or actual text you want the script to "type" for you must be enclosed in quotation marks. It's generally good practice to use straight quotes, not the curly typographer quotes; although in most cases, the typographer quotes will work just fine. This can be particularly important when exchanging scripts between Mac and PC, given the unexpected shifts in character results you can get across the two platforms.

However, building a script to turn typographer quotes off by using the Preferences command is easy. You want the seventh of the 14 parameters the command will take:

```
preferences -2,-2,-2,-2,-2,-2,false,-2,-2,-2,-2, 1000, 1p, 1p
```

Turn curly quotes back on with

```
preferences -2,-2,-2,-2,-2,-2,true,-2,-2,-2,-2, 1000, 1p, 1p
```

Tips and Gotchas

To follow up on those grammar lessons, here are some quick traveler's phrases to help you get along until you become acclimated to this new foreign land of scripting.

Just the Text, Ma'am

Scripts must be in plain ASCII text. If it's not working and you don't see any obvious programming faults in your script, check that you didn't save it in your word processor format instead of plain text.

Restarting Redraw

A common script-writing technique is to use the command to turn off the screen redraw before sending commands, and then turn redraw back on at the end of the script. Scripts run faster that way because they don't have to wait for the screen to catch up. If your script has an error and stops before completion, however, it never turns redraw back on, and your screen will be frozen. So always keep the following script in your palette, just so you can unfreeze your screen when a script goes awry:

```
redraw on
```

Turning a Script Off

You can't. There's no way to stop a script in the middle of its execution. The Esc key doesn't work. Of course, if the script comes up against some error or other kind of problem it can't solve, it will come to a halt on its own. The point is that—assuming that the script doesn't have an error in it—there's no way for you to call an emergency halt to the execution of a good script once it's running.

Undoing the Damage

The Undo command doesn't work, either. Your only hope is the Revert command. So, always do a Save before executing a script. That way you can always recover from a mess.

Ray almost always puts a mini-save command at the head of his scripts. That way if you don't like the result of the script, you can do a mini-revert and get back to the way you were before the script was executed.

Thinking Through the Unexpected

If you could think the unexpected through, it wouldn't be unexpected anymore, would it? The number one candidate for a script resulting in the unexpected is the failure to take into account a variable. Do you absolutely, without fear of a resulting mess on your page, swear that your zero point is at the upper-left hand corner of the right-hand page? Also, don't send a command with x and y coordinates, unless you know the measurement systems. There's nothing like moving a block of text an inch to the right when you wanted to move it one pica.

The solution to the unexpected? Prevent it. Set the zero point, defaults, measurement system, and other preferences in your script so that you can be certain of what they are. At the very least, set the ones that have an effect on the way you take action on the publication. Most commonly, the preferences and zero point need to be locked down.

Checking Your Spelling

A regular spelling-checker dictionary won't do any good on your PageMaker script because the language isn't composed of real words. But you *can* check the spelling of the script commands. Follow the directions in Chapter 9, "Editing Copy with the Story Editor." Add the Script Spell List file to your dictionary and pull your script out onto the Pasteboard so you can run a spell check on it.

Tracing the Problem

Just like a high-end programming language, the PageMaker scripting command interface comes with a tracer. People tend to forget it's there, but it's right in the pull-out menu for the Scripts palette.

This function lets you walk through your script, one line at a time. It doesn't have all the bells and whistles of a real debugger, but it's enormously helpful in finding the bad line in a script. Click through the lines with the Step button and note your progress. The line that throws back an error message is the one that needs your attention.

Understanding Defaults and Mini-Defaults

You need to understand how the command language has a range of effects, from narrow and very specific to wide and quite general. When you run a script, you duplicate the moves you would make with your mouse and keyboard, and the pecking order for effects works exactly the same for scripts as it does for real-time use of PageMaker. If, for example, you run a script with no publication open, you'll likely be setting a default for all new publications, as described in Chapter 3, "Personalizing PageMaker Preferences."

What PageMaker Scripts Can't Do

Clearly, there's a ton of power you can have over your work process by learning just a little bit about scripting. However, there's plenty that you simply can't do with a PageMaker script.

You may have heard someone say that the PageMaker script language basically can do anything that you can do with a mouse and the keyboard. It's a way of giving PageMaker its due that you can dish out written orders to the graphical user interface. That's true, but it's only true up to a point. Here's a list of PageMaker commands that aren't available through scripting:

- ▶ *File menu.* None of the Microsoft Mail commands can be scripted.
- ▶ *Edit menu.* You can't script the Undo and Redo commands, and there's no Show Clipboard Script command.
- ▶ *Element menu.* The Image Control dialog box can't be accessed through scripting, nor can the Copy Colors command from the Define Colors dialog box.
- ▶ *Utilities menu.* You can index highlighted words or phrases with the Index Entry command if you use it in Autoindexing mode—as if you had highlighted an item and used the menu command or the Ctrl+; (semicolon) keyboard shortcut. However, none of the other indexing facilities are available through scripts.
- ▶ *Type menu.* This one hurts—you can't script the Copy Styles button in the Define Styles dialog box. The only way to script the dissemination of a style sheet is to define the styles in a script and then apply the script to each publication. Wouldn't being able to script a command to copy a bunch of styles automatically to many other files in a multichapter book be *great?*
- ▶ *Windows and palettes.* No script capability for moving or resizing windows or palettes is available.
- ▶ *Help.* You can't reach PageMaker's online help through scripting.

▶ *Import/export.* None of the import or export filter settings—the ones with dialog boxes like the ASCII or Microsoft Word or Excel filters—are reachable through a script command.

▶ *Interactivity.* Finally, PageMaker scripting has one huge failing for anyone who gets motivated to go beyond this macro or batch-type programming of making up to-do lists. It lacks the standard kinds of structures you'd find in a real programming language. The programmers miss them, and after you get more familiar with scripting, so will you. They are the elements that can make a program seem intelligent, where the software asks a question and then applies logic to react to the answer.

Taking the Next Step: Conversing with Your Computer

It's a fact: as powerful as PageMaker scripting can be, on its own it is really quite a limited language, a pale gray shadow of a rich, full-color programming language.

To sum it up very briefly, the problem is that you can't hold a conversation with PageMaker. You can order it around with the script command verbs, but you can't ask PageMaker any questions about its status or the status of objects on a page. And you can't build scripts that interact with the user by asking questions and acting upon responses to those questions. PageMaker scripts can't have dialog boxes.

Programmers call some of the missing things by technical names such as If-Then-Else logic loops, error checking, and concatenation. It doesn't matter what these terms mean, exactly. What counts is deciding whether you'd like to take the next step to PageMaker scripting power so that you can build these inherently more useful scripts.

Here's the good news. All these things and more are, in fact, possible—you just can't do them from within PageMaker alone. PageMaker's script language does have queries built into it, but the queries haven't been implemented for use inside the program itself. You need another program to act as a go-between to help you communicate interactively with PageMaker. You need the ability to have an *external script*.

Why would you invest your time in climbing this particular learning curve? You may want to consider the benefits of two-way powerful programming for PageMaker if you have a job you do over and over—with some variations. Perhaps the task requires some input along the way to take into account the details:

▶ Think about how much easier it would be to use the Find/Change script writing engine if it gave you a dialog box similar to PageMaker's own Change command, allowing you to point and click to build your script.

▶ A quick printer might love, for example, the idea of scripting a business card program but need interactivity to enter the name to go on the card.

▶ A corporation that produces quarterly reports of sales results might use an interactive script to combine the output of all the company's spreadsheet programs, generation of the graphs, and then the creation of the report document in PageMaker.

These ideas are just a glimpse at the power you can have to customize PageMaker to your own needs. They are just a possible next step.

Experts like Ray Robertson (and some other folks you could meet in the CompuServe DTP Forum where people like Phil Gaskill and Dave Saunders tend to hang out) make PageMaker do interactive pirouettes through external scripting.

To make external scripts for PageMaker for Windows, you need to get familiar with something called *DDE*, for *Dynamic Data Exchange*. (It's the equivalent to AppleScript and Apple Events on the Macintosh. In fact, DDE is available in Microsoft applications on the Macintosh platform, but PageMaker is not set up for DDE and can only work with external scripts in AppleScript.)

I promised that I wouldn't go technoid on you, so we aren't going to get too deeply into DDE. However, here's a leg up the learning curve if you decide you'd like to explore the possibilities of external scripts for PageMaker:

▶ To have a DDE conversation with PageMaker, you'll need an external program to send and receive commands and information. The external program you use for this conversation with PageMaker can be any of the applications that support DDE commands, such as Excel, Word, or Visual Basic. (It's a Microsoft technology.)

▶ The scripting guide on the PageMaker CD-ROM includes some script examples that may help you get started.

▶ If you use Microsoft Word or Excel as the DDE command center, perhaps because you probably already own them, you will write a macro and run it in order to hold the conversation with PageMaker.

▶ Include the necessary DDE commands in the macro, along with your PageMaker script. You don't use the Scripts palette to run external scripts.

▶ You can include queries in the script. There is a group of DDE commands that are designed to ask questions and massage the answers, which you can then incorporate into new commands.

▶ All DDE communications happen through channels. You open up channels and communicate through them. Each of these channels is also sometimes called a *DDE link*.

▶ Because you can build dialog boxes in Word, Excel, and Visual Basic, you can have custom dialog boxes for PageMaker using the DDE conversation technique. I don't want to overstate the case, but it's almost as if you were able to write your own Plug-ins.

KEY CONCEPT:
Tagging Your Text

PageMaker's new tagging language will be a lot simpler for you than scripting.

That's good, because if you are doing any kind of work where you shovel many files a day through your computer, or manage large book-sized files, you need to be a tagger—and I'm not talking about graffiti, either.

So, why will it be easier to work with tags compared to scripting? Because you don't actually write tags like you do when you sit down and type out a script. You get the computer to do it for you.

Have a look at what some tagged text looks like in figure 28.8. On the left you see some text in PageMaker. On the right, the same text has been exported from PageMaker using the tag filter.

Isn't it nice knowing that you won't have to type out reams of stuff like that? Who am I kidding? You'd never even be tempted. It's not exactly a language you'd choose for sitting down at the kitchen dinette set to tap out a chatty letter to Aunt Mabel, is it?

The tagging language, as you can see, consists of codes embedded in the text. There's a code for bold, italics, superscript, and on and on. Some codes set character level attributes, and others set paragraph attributes. In most cases, the codes come in pairs, with an on code and an off code. You'll find this concept easy to understand if you work in Show Codes view in WordPerfect or you were a WordStar user in the early days of desktop computing.

By the way, figure 28.8 is an ideal example of why you would want to bother learning about tagging. See all those key caps symbols? They are in a special font called PIXSymbols. In a book-length project (this happened to be a 25-page mini-manual), you could have hundreds of these little symbols. Each one might need some tweaking to fit in well with your body copy and to otherwise lay down well on the page—some special kerning, no-break formatting to keep a key combination from breaking at the end of a line, and so on.

Now how would you best deal with a situation like this—where you have hundreds of locations in a publication that require maybe a dozen formatting moves?

▼ You could go through the text by hand and specially format each of the hundreds of locations.
▼ You could try to do some of the work with Find/Change.

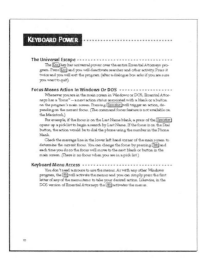

```
0)<CTRACK 127><CSSIZE 70><C+SIZE 58.3><C-POSITION 33.3><C+POSITION 33.3><P><CBASELINE
0><CNOBREAK 0><CLEADING 14><GGRID 0><GLEFT 18><GRIGHT 0><GFIRST -18><G+BEFORE
5><G+AFTER
0><GALIGNMENT "left"><GMETHOD "base"><G& "ENGLISH"><GPAIRS 4><G% 120><GKNEXT
0><GKWIDOW
2><GKORPHAN 2><GTABS(18 1 "")><GHYPHENATION 2 29 2><GWORDSPACE 85 100 125><GSPACE
0 0 0>><@form...line><FONT "Palatino"><CCOLOR "Black 50%"><SIZE 11><HORIZONTAL 100
><LETTERSPACE 0><CTRACK 127><CSSIZE 70><C+SIZE 58.3><C-POSITION 33.3><C+POSITION
33.3><P><CBASELINE 0><CNOBREAK 0><CLEADING 14><GGRID 0><GLEFT 51><GRIGHT 0><GFIRST
0><G+BEFORE 14><G+AFTER 0><GALIGNMENT "left"><GMETHOD "base"><G& "ENGLISH"><GPAIRS
4><G% 120><GKNEXT 0><GKWIDOW 2><GKORPHAN 2><GTABS(424 r ". ")><GHYPHENATION 2 29 2
><GWORDSPACE 85 100 125><GSPACE 0 0 0>><@heading 1>Keyboard Power
<@heading 2>The Universal Escape
<@body>The <FONT "PIXymbolsShadowkey"><SIZE 12.5><i>q<FONT "Palatino"><SIZE 11><P
> key has universal power over the entire Essential Attorneys program. Press <FONT
"PIXymbolsShadowkey"><SIZE 12.5><i>q<FONT "Palatino"><SIZE 11><P> and you will deactivate
searches and other activity. Press it twice and you will exit the program (after a dialogue box
asks if you are sure you want to quit).
<@heading 2>Focus Means Action in Windows Or DOS
<@body>Whenever you are in the main screen in Windows or DOS, Essential Attorneys has a
"focus"<HORIZONTAL
75> <\-> <HORIZONTAL 100>a next action status associated with a blank or a button on the
program's main screen. Pressing <FONT
"PIXymbolsShadowkey"><SIZE 12.5><i><FONT "Palatino"><SIZE 11><P> will trigger an action,
depending on the current focus. (The command focus feature is not available on the Macintosh.)
For example, if the focus is on the Last Name blank, a press of the <FONT
"PIXymbolsShadowkey
"><SIZE 12.5><i>z<FONT "Palatino"><SIZE 11><P> opens up a pick list to begin a search by Last
Name. If the focus is on the Dial button, the action would be to dial the phone using the
number in the Phone blank.
Check the message line in the lower left hand corner of the main screen to determine the
current focus. You can change the focus by pressing <FONT
"PIXymbolsShadowkey"><SIZE 12.5><i><FONT "Palatino"><SIZE 11><P> and each time you do so
the focus will move to the next blank or button in the main screen. (There is no focus when
you are in a pick list.)
<@heading 2>Keyboard Menu Access
<@body>You don't need a mouse to use the menus. As with any other Windows program, the
<FONT
"PIXymbolsShadowkey"><SIZE 12.5><i>a<FONT "Palatino"><SIZE 11><P> will activate the menus
and you can simply press the first letter of any of the menu items to take your desired action.
Likewise, in the DOS version of Essential Attorneys the <FONT
"PIXymbolsShadowkey"><SIZE 12.5><i>a <FONT "Palatino"><SIZE 11><P>activates the menus.
```

FIG. 28.8 ▲

What a PageMaker text block (on the left) looks like when converted into tagging language (on the right).

▼ Better yet, you could figure out the formatting you need in tagging language and make all those formatting moves in just a couple of minutes.

The time saved by going the tagging route would make this worthwhile for just the one project. But, taking our computer keys example, if you do a lot of computer books where this kind of formatting task came up all the time, the tagging tactic will reap weeks of personnel hours in saved time over the course of a year. You'd run every file you got through your tagging language procedure.

Aside from the specific keyboard character formatting situation I've just described, as desktop publishers every one of us probably comes up against standard formatting jobs every day of the week. Just think of all those files you get in for layout where somebody hit a double hyphen every time he wanted an em dash, double-spaced paragraphs by hitting Enter twice and tried to "help out" with the formatting by putting all sorts of ugly underlining formatting in the text. I could go on for a few dozen more examples I'm sure. Then you have the typographical niceties you'd like to apply to the text—things like fine-tuned punctuation marks such as em dashes, inserting specially formatted thin spaces before the tabs in tables with leader characters, plus a few dozen more examples.

The point is you could perform all these dozens of cleanup and formatting chores in a single pass through your document by converting it to tagging language. Here's how it might work.

TACTICS RECIPE:
Working Through the Tagging Process

Generally, the way you work with tagging is to perform your text formatting—or at least the majority of it—while the text is in raw form. Here's the basic work flow for a tagging project:

▼ *Design your moves.* You'll need to list everything you want to accomplish. These moves are, in essence, the type specs for any given project. Maybe you don't usually draw them up in such a formal way, but to get the most out of tagging you'll want to work out the design in advance. The point is to be efficient and produce large volumes of work in the shortest possible time.

You'll have certain formatting moves you make on every project. With projects you do regularly every week or month or so, you will quickly develop a standard list of moves required for that particular client or format. For new projects, you may find it easier to do some on-screen thinking, scratch padding, and experimentation in PageMaker to get layout and other design issues settled. You'll then use the Export command to generate sample sets of tags from the results of your doodling—instead of having to write tag codes from scratch.

▼ *Get tagged.* One way or the other you will need to get your text converted into tagging language. As I said earlier, the good news is you don't need to write the stuff yourself. You just have the computer do it for you. (See the upcoming "Getting Tagged" section.)

The most accessible way for you to get tagged is by using the built-in tagging facilities of PageMaker. You Place the text and then use the Export command under the File menu, selecting the Tagged Text file format. You could, of course, edit your tags into a text file in a word processor.

▼ *Design tagging moves.* Here's the learning curve part. You'll need to spend enough time with the tagging language to figure out how to implement your list of formatting moves. You might, for example, want to do a search for all the instances of an em dash and add some formatting codes before and after it. (See the "Tagging Survival Guide" section coming up.)

▼ *Test the process.* Before making a commitment of this many changes to a file that runs several hundred pages, test your moves on a small section of the file, saved to your hard drive under its own name.

▼ *Batch it.* When you have everything designed and tested out, go ahead and use a search-and-replace routine on your tagged text to make the changes. For this, you will want a search-and-replace utility that can process your text in batches. (See "Batching It," later in this chapter.)

Here's where you realize the power of tags, and it's the second bit of the learning curve. You really need to acquire and get comfortable with one of the plain text batch processors. These search-and-replace engines let you build up sets of dozens and even hundreds of little changes. Then you can process all those changes in a batch, applying changes to a file or even dozens of files in one fell swoop. Now that's automation!

▼ *Page it.* Place the batch massaged text file with all its changed codes into PageMaker.

Done right, virtually all your text formatting will be done. Text will be styled, and standard kerning and other formatting moves will be completed. You'll still want to examine each page so you can repair any glitches and fine-tune line breaks and page breaks, but all of the hard work will be done.

Getting Tagged

Your options here are fairly limited as we go to press. The number of options may grow, however, and I'll tell you why. QuarkXPress has had a tagging language for quite some time, a language that PageMaker Version 6.0 can read. This will make it relatively easy for developers who created products for the QuarkXPress tagging market to release products for PageMaker as well. Watch for developments in all the usual locations—Adobe Magazine, CompuServe DTP Forum (**GO DTP**) and Adobe Application forum (**GO ADOBEAPP**), and catalogs from the Adobe Plug-ins Source developers' cooperative.

For now, you must bring your text into PageMaker through the normal means, the Place command. Then use the Export command to send the text back out in Tagged Text format (see fig. 28.9)

Keep in mind that you don't need to lay out the text, just import it. PageMaker will convert the whole story to tags when you use the Export command, even if dozens or hundreds of pages have not yet been put on pages. That means you can use the Place command and simply lay out one page, or even Place the text within the Story Editor.

A variation on this approach would be to bring the material into PageMaker and do some of your formatting there, then export to tagging language for fine-tuning. This might be an especially good course if the text were produced in a word processor using paragraph styles, because you would then be retaining valuable existing formatting work.

Fig. 28.9 ▶

Getting tagged with PageMaker's own tagging language filters.

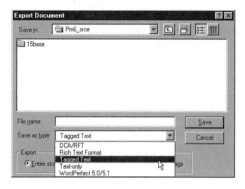

Tagging Survival Guide

Here are the basic ins and outs you'll need to know to climb the tagging learning curve. The most important element of the learning curve isn't here, however. It's the tagging language guide in Appendix D, a complete description of all the PageMaker tag codes.

Tagging Language Grammar

Like the scripting language, tagging has a grammar all its own, although it is not nearly so complicated as scripting. You need to know some basic words, how to structure a tag, and how to put in parameters.

Tag Alert

When you try to Place a tag file, PageMaker must be alerted that it is receiving tags. The very first thing in the file must be

```
<PMTags1.0 win>
```

TIP▶ **Watch Out for Tag Alert Documentation Error**

Ordinarily you won't need to worry about this because you'll have PageMaker generate your tagging code for you in most situations. However, in the early days of PageMaker 6.0, the PageMaker manual had an error in it, listing some of the elements of the tag alert out of order. It has been listed correctly here.

Less Than and More Than and Tag

All codes begin and end with the less than and more than signs. The code for type size is `<size 11>` to set the type 11 points.

On and Off Codes

Most tag codes come in pairs. Unlike the normal behavior of PageMaker, you don't select some text and designate it bold or italic. You turn on bold with a code in front of the text and then cancel it by putting the same code at the end of the text.

If you put a bold code in the middle of a story and fail to put the matching bold code into the text to cancel it, the entire rest of the story will be bold.

Unlike WordPerfect and some other word processors, the codes for turning attributes on or off are exactly the same.

Character, Paragraph, Special Characters

You could classify codes into three basic types.

Character codes are, as you might expect, embedded in text almost anywhere to assign character-level attributes to type—size, font, color, bold, italic, leading, baseline shift, and so on.

Paragraph codes are inserted at the beginning of paragraphs and describe paragraph attribute formatting—center, left align, tabs, leading method, paragraph styles, rule below, include in table of contents, and the like.

Special character codes don't get turned on or off. They simply insert a code— a thin space, an em dash, a non-breaking space, a page number marker, and so on. You can "type" any character into a tag file by inserting it with its ASCII three number code. For example, <\#169> in tagged text will insert the copyright © symbol.

Tag Tricks and Insight

You might think of the following as tagging language slang, the little ins and outs of communicating and communing with your text file through the tagging language.

Leave It—I Don't Care

You have a choice among several symbols that leave current settings in place. They are sort of like the `dontcare` item in the scripting language. This can be really useful when you have a tag code that has several parameters but you only want to change one.

The caret sign (^) symbolizes the current mathematical setting for whatever attribute you are working on. See the "Tags Have Your Number" section that follows.

A pair of parentheses or double quotes will just fill the spot in a list of parameters, in essence leaving the current default in effect.

A dollar sign ($) tells PageMaker to apply the attribute from the current style. For example, you might have put a code in place before some text, but then want to return to the old setting at the end of the text:

```
<size 36>Big Type<size$>
```

Tags Have Your Number

Unless you specify otherwise, any number you put in a tag code will be interpreted as a measurement in points. If you want inches, put a double-quote mark after the number. It's p for picas, c for ciceros, and m or mm for millimeter.

The PageMaker tagging filter does math, too. You can specify relative sizes with mathematical operators. Let's say you want some text in a paragraph to be twice as tall as any other text. You construct your tag code, and instead of specifying a specific size, you type a caret to indicate the current size and then do your arithmetic, in this case multiplying by 2:

```
<size ^*2>
```

Quote Me

When naming something—a font name or the name of a style, or a color—put quotes around it.

Hardcoding Slash

If you want to insert a character that's used in the tagging language but want it to be taken literally, not translated, you have to let PageMaker know that you want to be taken literally. Put a backslash in front of the at sign (@) character or the less than or greater than characters (< >):

```
\@
\<
```

Take My Graphic, Please!

You can use tags to bring inline graphics into PageMaker.

Let me say that again. You can use tags to bring graphics *into* PageMaker.

Unfortunately, the tagging filter won't export graphic references, but this is still a mighty powerful feature you'll want to explore if you are a big user of inline graphics.

You could use tags to publish a catalog style database containing pictures.

You could also use tags to do a mass insertion of icons in text. For example, use the trick in Chapter 15 where we hang icons in a fake companion column using a hanging indent paragraph style.

Make PageMaker Work for You: Macros

More than any other single tag code, the macro feature will harness the power of the tagging language for you. Learn to unlock this extremely easy bit of code, and you will have real power. Once you put it to work, you'll feel like you broke the four-minute mile and the land speed record all in one.

The PageMaker tagging language enables you to define in one spot a powerful collection of formatting moves that can be applied all at once and automatically by the tagging filter at import time. That means you can use PageMaker to write complicated tagging codes that you might not otherwise bother with yourself, and you can do it in a fraction of the time.

Let's say you have a complex bit of formatting set up in PageMaker's Layout view. For example, check figure 28.10. Much of this styling is normal headline paragraph-style code stuff to draw the dotted rule and format the head as Helvetica Inserat at 36 points. But that fancy dingbat doesn't exist in anybody's special pi type collection. It's a carefully kerned and baseline adjusted pair of Zapf Dingbats, with the square one being colored "paper."

FIG. 28.10 ▶

A fancy headline, with a fancy dingbat.

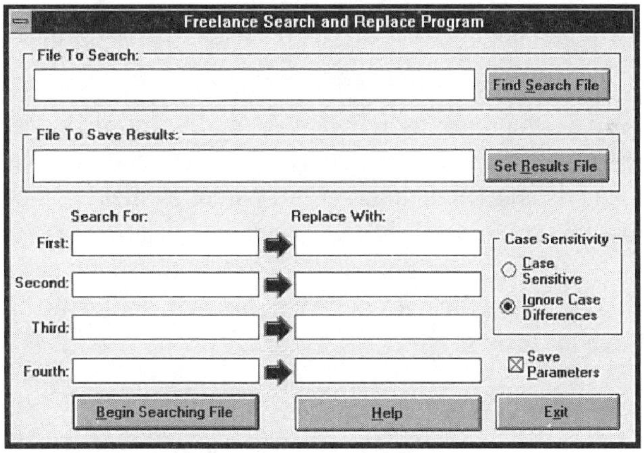

Cutting out all the normal tag codes, here's the fragment that creates the combination dingbat:

```
<FONT "Zapf Dingbats"><SIZE 44><LETTERSPACE -0.55><CBASELINE
-2>t<CCOLOR "Paper"><SIZE 14><LETTERSPACE 0><CBASELINE
14>n<FONT "Helvetica Inserat"><CCOLOR "Black"><SIZE
36><CBASELINE 0>Fancy Headline
```

Now, this is not a trivial bit of tagging. If you had to write it from scratch and import it several times to be sure you had everything correct for the effect you want, you'd pretty well go nuts.

So instead, format the prototype in PageMaker Layout view. Then select the text and export it as tags. You now have your code already written for you. In fact, that's how the code you see here got where it is—through Copy and Paste.

Now, in your target tagging file, insert a macro at the top of the file:

```
<#define_FD_="[insert all your stuff here]">
```

You could have any set of characters—an abbreviation really—defined. I just chose FD here. However, you must have underscore characters before and after the abbreviation, linking it with the `#define verb` and the equal sign.

Insert **FD** everywhere in your file where you need the special formatting, and you can even include text such as the characters to be formatted in this example as Zapf Dingbat. Then, without any further work on your part, that gazillion character set of tagging codes will automatically be inserted wherever you insert your defined macro abbreviation.

Batching It

You need a batch processing search and replace program to get the most out of tagging. You can do the job with a word processor's Search and Replace command, especially if it is just an occasional task you need to perform. But to really harness PageMaker's tagging automation, you need a batch text cleanup engine.

With a batch processor, you make a sort of shopping list of text search-and-replace operations you want to perform and then do one sweep through a text file to clean it up in quick order. You don't need confusing and time-consuming multiple passes of search and replace, because the program takes a list of chores and does them one right after the other in a single pass. You could list three steps (or 20 of them, or more) in one of the batch text processors to combine them into one move.

Generally, for working with tagged text, you would build a list of find and change pairs—each pair consisting of a target and an intended result. If you want every instance of a hyphenated company name to be formatted with No Break text attribute, your target would be the hyphenated name, and the intended result would be the company name with No Break tagging codes around it.

The power of batch search and replace comes from building up long lists of such chores so you can accomplish them all in a single pass.

As a rule, with a few exceptions, these batch processors tend to work only on ASCII text files. Of course that's just fine because tag files are raw text anyway.

Currently, the most popular program for batch code search and replace operations is Thomas Lundin SNR (for search and replace). It's included on the CD-ROM so you can try it out right away.

SNR has been used for quite some by Ventura and QuarkXPress tagging experts who all say it's really simple to use. I'm not sure I agree that it looks all that simple to use, but in fact it is easy once you get the hang of it. What makes it look a little daunting is the fact that you run it from the C:> prompt in DOS. You must make up batch files of commands that SNR then uses to "filter" your text files.

Now here's the good news. Tom says he's taking a look at making a Windows version of the program, and anybody who registers for the DOS version will be shipped the Windows version as soon as it's ready (he estimates it'll ship in the first quarter of 1996).

Tom will be happy to assist you in developing conversion routines for your tagging needs. You can leave him e-mail at **70523.262@compuserve.com**, and he will make every effort to help you out as time permits. If he sees a pattern developing in the type of problems that users need to have solved, he will gather the solutions into a FAQ-like upload to be placed in the DTP Forum.

If You Don't Want to Bother

So what if you are still totally freaked out by the prospect of writing a script or messing with the tagging language? Well, you still have plenty of ways to relieve tedium, save time, and be consistent. Here are some PageMaker automation tools that don't require scripting or tagging:

▶ You can copy colors and styles from one document to the other using the Copy button in the Define Styles and Define Colors dialog boxes.

▶ Using templates, you can set up systems of styles that you easily can retrieve without using `stylebegin` and `styleend` script commands.

▶ The Print Styles Addition lets you create a sort of printing style sheet to automate the process of setting up a print job. In fact, if you hold down the Ctrl key, in the Print command you can define a style from your current settings in just a single click.

Where to Go from Here

▶ One good way to understand scripting is to understand PageMaker. The script commands basically follow the menus, and most of the time the commands are even spelled like the menu commands.

▶ Imitation is the highest form of flattery. Another good way to learn about scripts is to just use the Edit menu item in the Scripts palette to open existing scripts and find useful bits of work.

▶ Likewise, use PageMaker to write your tagging codes for you. That's the best way to learn the right way to put together the tags you need for a particular job.

PART VIII

Riding the Cutting Edge

29 ▲ Publishing Electronically: The Web or Acrobat

30 ▲ Linking and Other File Connections

Chapter 29

This chapter on electronic publishing with PageMaker includes:

A Key Concept overview of the electronic publishing scene to give you some context for these new PageMaker tools.

▼

A suggested work flow for creating World Wide Web HTML language documents.

▼

Instructions for working with the HTML Author plug-in for creating World Wide Web documents.

▼

A survival guide of notes on how to avoid some common PageMaker to HTML translation pitfalls.

▼

Instructions for making an Acrobat document from within PageMaker.

Publishing Electronically: The Web or Acrobat

DON'T YOU JUST LOVE all these swinging, dangling, and connecting words? World Wide Web? Acrobat? They do give you a sense of what goes on though, the concept of easily swinging through an interlinking universe of information.

PageMaker now has the capability to produce two kinds of files for communicating your messages in the cutting edge environment of electronic publishing. ▶ ▶ ▶

Using a new command in the file menu—Create Adobe PDF—you can now convert your PageMaker paper-based publications into Acrobat PDF (Portable Document Format) electronic publications from inside PageMaker, instead of the former cumbersome method of printing to EPS and then using the Adobe Distiller program to convert to PDF.

The new HTML Author Plug-in will help at least start the process of converting your PageMaker publications into HTML documents that can be read on the World Wide Web. It's not as straightforward as the Acrobat conversion, mostly because of the inherent differences between paper-based and Web-targeted documents.

Take time to check out the interview with Webmaster Moe Rubenzahl in Chapter 33, "Designing for the Web." There's lots of valuable information on how to make sure people visiting your site will stay awhile and return in the future, and insights into the rationale for choosing between PDF and HTML files for use in your particular electronic publishing situation.

KEY CONCEPT:
Making Electronic Publishing Choices

Much of your decision-making about electronic publishing depends on how you will distribute your documents and how much control you wish to retain over how people see your valuable information.

Acrobat Rich

Odds are, you are looking at this chapter because you are contemplating a crawl out onto the World Wide Web, primarily a modem and telephone-based electronic publishing environment, although many access through high-speed networks. You've probably at least glanced at a Web page or two, perhaps through one of the browser facilities available via the commercial online services.

Most of what you have seen so far was probably done in HTML, the worldwide standard for laying out information on the World Wide Web—and only on the Web.

But Acrobat files offer an alternative and increasingly important and well-accepted form of electronic publishing.

You may actually need to find a way to turn your PageMaker documents into something that isn't quite so flexible as an HTML-based Web page. Perhaps you want to have more control—and have the option of displaying your information in a much richer graphic environment with a variety of typefaces and more vivid graphics. You'd like your documents to be easily distributed and viewed in a variety of electronic environments—such as CD-ROM, the Web, and for local output on a desktop printer.

If that describes your electronic publishing need, you might want to put your publications into one of the standard electronic document formats such as Acrobat, Envoy, or Common Ground. PageMaker has the capability to compose files in the Adobe Acrobat format, called *PDF files* (*Portable Document Format*).

Acrobat files certainly can be used on the World Wide Web, and Web browser manufacturers—notably Netscape—are quickly moving to build PDF file capabilities into their HTML-based software. However, it's important to keep in mind that PDF files are a bit on the large size.

Beleaguered Web surfers working through regular phone lines and modems tend to dislike being forced to endure the boredom of waiting through the download time. On the other hand, PDF files are terrific for CD-ROM distribution. The encyclopedia of Symbol and Pi fonts on the CD-ROM that came with this book was produced in Acrobat (see fig. 29.1) by type distributor Precision Type.

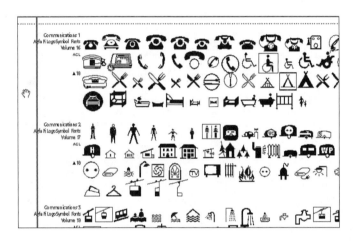

FIG. 29.1 ▲

A good example of a situation where it's critical to maintain the look of a document using the Acrobat file format.

As you can see, even all these weird fonts are portrayed on screen with excellent results. This really would be nearly impossible in the Web-preferred format of HTML. (You could convert each graphic into a GIF or JPEG file for viewing online, but that has its own set of problems.)

Even though PDF format is probably the best solution for this kind of situation where you need that kind of graphic-rich potential, these can be larger files than plain old HTML. As Moe Rubenzahl suggests in his interview in Chapter 33, if you put PDF files up on the Web, you'll want

to give the viewer a choice of whether to take the time to download the material and post the file sizes so they know what they are getting into.

HTML Web Language

Yes, you can use PageMaker to convert your documents into the *lingua franca* of the World Wide Web—*HTML, Hypertext Markup Language*. Adobe's name for its PDF files aside, HTML actually is the most literally portable electronic publishing format you could imagine. (Well, except for

ASCII text, but who would want to look at that for very long?) HTML is designed to be read on pretty much any computer in the world.

There's a trade-off, however. The HTML language doesn't specify a lot of the details that we desktop publishers are used to controlling—typeface, type size, width of page, colors, and so on. HTML must be like this, loose and vague, in order to adapt to all the different sized computer screens and viewer setups likely to

be used in the field. Also, the HTML format removes the need to transmit a lot of the modem-stuffing graphics information, so it makes telecommunications very efficient. Nonetheless, you lose much of the control of the look of your document if you go the HTML route. Figure 29.2 shows how the same page looks in two different Web browser setups. *Browsers* are the programs people use to read the HTML material they get through their phone and modem information pipelines.

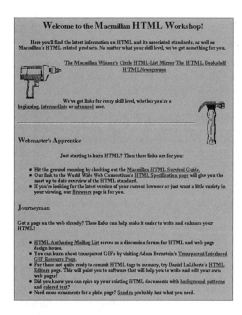
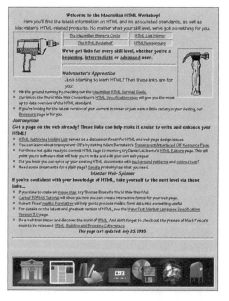

Fig. 29.2 ▲

Two views of the same Web page—a standard Netscape browser view on the left, and a personalized Mosaic browser view on the right.

You may think throwing in this illustration of the Macmillan Publishing World Wide Web location (**http://www.mcp.com**) is a shameless attempt at promoting the sale of my publisher's books—and you'd be right. However, there's another perfectly good reason to turn you on to this location.

There's no better place to learn how to become a Webmaster than on the World Wide Web itself. And this is the HTML Workshop page on the Macmillan Web site. It has excellent one-stop-shop links to many locations where you can learn all about the issues you encounter as you embark on your journey on the digital ocean of electronic publishing. Sorry, wrong metaphor—begin crawling out onto silken information threads of the electronic publishing web.

Looking to the Future

Electronic publishing has been changing so much and so fast that it is tough to predict the contours of the publishing landscape six months from now, let alone project out along the year or two this book will be on the shelves.

Literally, I have a stack of books several feet high on my desk right now that will be at least partially obsolete in short order. All of them deal with writing HTML or otherwise navigating the Web. Yet, a new version of Hypertext Markup Language (Version 3.0) has just started flowing out into the digital environment as press time approaches. It will radically enhance the power of this fundamental component of Web communications.

There's even something called *VRML* (*Virtual Reality Modeling Language*) that some folks are saying will replace the current standard HTML (**http:/vrml. wired.com/**).

For another thing, HTML and Acrobat formats have been coming together, thanks to the deal-making between Adobe and Netscape, the leading Web browser software manufacturer. The modem download time issue of PDF files won't go away, but Web users will find it much easier to access the two formats as Netscape makes it more and more feasible to combine the two formats in Web documents. (This move to merge PDF and HTML at some level or other is one of the primary reasons I lumped the two together in the same chapter. They are quickly becoming two sides of the same thing.)

By the way, the shortest book in that stack I mentioned is 250 pages long and one of them reaches nearly 1,000 pages. So, it's pretty clear that in a couple of short chapters we aren't going to be able to discuss every nuance of electronic publishing. I'll be putting the focus on tactics for using PageMaker to accomplish your electronic publishing goals.

VIII

Riding the Cutting Edge

TACTICS RECIPE:
Paper-Based to Web-Based Document Work Flow

You could certainly use PageMaker and the new HTML Author Plug-in as a primary authoring tool for creating Web pages. I think you'll agree after you get familiar with HTML Author that it isn't all that hard to do. The HTML language is so simple, in fact, that many people are writing Web pages in simple-minded word processors,

and there are plenty of special purpose Web-authoring tools out there. We have included a few of them on the CD-ROM packaged in this book. One that is just being released as we go to press is PageMill, and it shows promise of changing HTML editing forever with its drag-and-drop and WYSIWYG editing ease.

It's more likely, given the context of this chapter, that you are facing the more complicated challenge of "repurposing" existing paper-based documents so they can be used on the Web. Maybe you've got a library of documents to convert, or perhaps you are designing new material and want to try to make it fly in both distribution environments.

To accomplish your goal, you need to find a way to get from something that looks like the PageMaker document on the left in figure 29.3, to what's on the right—a Web-ready HTML document. In the center you see the HTML code that produces the one on the right.

FIG. 29.3 ▲

The goal: going from PageMaker to HTML. In the end, the Web-ready page will consist of some HTML language that looks like what you see in the center.

In the end, the Web-ready page will consist of some HTML language that looks like what you see on the far right.

There is a series of main parts to this job and that's how the work flow should go, especially if you want to use PageMaker's HTML Author Plug-in to do the work:

▶ *Consult with your Webmaster or Internet provider.* As I said, things are changing rapidly on the Web. First, before doing anything else, you really must collaborate with whoever administers the network aspects of your Web site. Your pages must conform to

that environment or they flat out won't function, or will otherwise embarrass you.

The issues range from the internal capabilities of the Web computer server, to the software your Webmaster supports. For example, will the server support lists, interactive forms, or image-mapped links? These terms may not mean much to you right now, but within a few weeks of getting set up on the Web, you will know and will want to use them. At the moment it's enough to know that you need to know about this sort of stuff.

One terribly important item: ask for precise instructions on how to set up your folder structure so it mimics the structure of the Web server site. If you don't understand this issue, don't walk away until you do. Make whoever it is sit down with you—buy 'em lunch if you have to—and talk you through this part of it. It's the secret to being able to build documents on your computer that will easily transport to the server, with all your internal links intact and ready to go. I can't cover it adequately here; there are too many variables, but you need to know about this.

▶ *Convert and re-link your graphics*. The graphics in your publication probably aren't right for the Web, and you'll need to convert them and re-import them into your document.

If you've followed my advice, the graphics in your paper-based document almost certainly will not be GIFs or JPEGs. The standard for paper-based publishing is EPS and TIFF.

Unfortunately the standard for the Web is GIF and JPEG. Fortunately, PageMaker's Place and Link technology eases the burden of accomplishing this task. We'll discuss that and some conversion strategies in the section "Converting and Re-Linking."

▶ *Make your layout web-like*. It's unlikely that your paper-based document has been structured even remotely like a Web page. You'll need to make adjustments before using HTML Author to get good results. Have a look at "A Web Layout Survival Guide," later on in this chapter.

A good paper-based layout has a certain visual complexity that en-

gages the reader. Many layouts have multiple columns. However, a Web page generally must be much simpler. For one thing, it runs inline from top to bottom—no columns.

Web documents link to other locations—your own documents, graphics within your documents, and other locations on the Web. You'll need to plan out how to break down your PageMaker document so it can take on this Weblike structure.

▶ *Run HTML Author Plug-in*. Converting the text in your document to HTML will be the easiest of all these tasks. It's HTML Author's main purpose in life. See "Running HTML Author" later on in this chapter.

Hopefully you've used paragraph styles throughout your document, because HTML is a style-based way of describing documents, and HTML Author provides good tools for this aspect of the conversion.

▶ *Test your Web stuff*. There's nothing worse than logging onto a Web site and having to sit through a 100K download of some graphics that could have been either a lot smaller, or could have been a user option.

You've got to test the look and speed of your Web page design through a normal system to see what real users will experience; otherwise, your page will be an instant first impression bad experience and all those surfers will head for a different and more friendly beach. Don't forget, too, to check that all the links are working correctly once your site has been constructed and installed on the Web.

VIII

Riding the Cutting Edge

Keep in mind that most folks are communicating through modems over phone lines. They aren't coming through ISBN high-speed data lines, and most of them aren't even coming online through dedicated networks like the ones that seem to be installed in virtually every newly constructed college dorm room these days.

Converting and Re-Linking

The fundamental challenge here doesn't need much explanation. You need to take your paper-oriented graphics, your EPSs and TIFFs, and get them converted over to GIFs and JPEGs.

The question is, do you do that conversion before or after you get your PageMaker text converted to HTML? I'm recommending that you do the conversion first. That way you'll get the most out of HTML Author Plug-in. It will help you build the links you need to your graphics, a less complicated process than trying to go back afterward and create the links.

After you do the file conversions, you'll need to re-place the graphics so the PageMaker links are back to the GIF and JPEG versions of the files. See Chapter 30, "Linking and Other File Connections," for complete details on Place and Link.

There must be a dozen or more file conversion tools out there on the commercial online services and on the Internet. Everybody has to face this file conversion issue, not just for working on Web graphics, but for many other aspects of publishing as well. Here are some notes to get you started:

▶ For an EPS file, consider opening the original file in its application program (FreeHand or Illustrator, probably) and snapping a screenshot in bitmap format of that high quality image. You can then easily convert the screenshot image to a GIF or JPEG using PhotoShop or one of the other conversion utilities.

▶ PhotoShop, in fact, is a great solution in itself if you own it. It's kind of expensive just to use for these conversions, but it certainly should be considered as a nearly essential tool in the kit of almost all desktop publishers. So, as long as you have it, why not?

▶ As Moe also suggests in his interview in Chapter 33, consider making your GIF transparent so it will look like a discrete object (instead of an object in a square) against whatever background your viewer chooses in the browser at the receiving end of your Web page.

For this purpose, you can use the Adobe GIF89A export module for Photo-shop, which is available at no charge from various online sources, including the Adobe Web site.

▶ I've included PaintShop Pro and VuePrint on the CD-ROM. They'll handle about any bitmap conversion you are likely to need.

▶ For converting PostScript files—including EPS files—to GIF or JPEG, consider purchasing Transverter Pro, a program developed by TechPool Software in Cleveland.

A Web Layout Survival Guide

Here are some notes that may help get you through some of the most common conceptual barriers people face as they crawl out onto the Web, especially when they are trying to ease their way over from the paper-based publishing world:

▶ *Use styles*. If you use styles extensively in PageMaker, you have virtually all the conceptual information you need to understand HTML. It is, more than anything else, a list of hierarchal styles—body copy, various levels of head-lines, and so on.

There are a few little glitches you may face in the translation from PageMaker styles to HTML styles. PageMaker (grimace) still doesn't have character level styles, which are a basic part of the HTML format. And HTML Author will only let you map one PageMaker style to each of the HTML styles. You might have two different kinds of headline styles to ac-commodate single and multiline heads, or two different styles for bullets. You either have to edit after conversion to deal with this problem, or you should consolidate styles while still in PageMaker, probably the best approach.

▶ *Early versions had character translation problems*. Early versions of HTML Author had some problems translating characters. Hyphenated words, for example, would be broken into two. Some non-HTML characters, such as bullets or em dashes, would be oddly translated, into line feeds for example.

▶ *HTML doesn't "do" columns*. Because you can't tell whether someone will view your Web page on a 9-inch Windows laptop or compact Macintosh, or a 21-inch two-page behemoth of a monitor, there's no way for HTML to allow you to work in columns. HTML Author will convert your columns to a single column structure as long as the stories are threaded, giving you notice of the problem in the error analysis when you first begin the process.

▶ *Cross-the-fold graphics don't work.* Because there are no pages in the sense of how we use them for a magazine or book, HTML doesn't even begin to comprehend the idea of a graphic object crossing the fold in a two-page spread. You'll need to edit those to one page or the other before converting to HTML.

▶ *Use long pages.* On the other hand, Web surfers are quite used to "pages" that are 6 inches wide and 30 or 40 inches long. On the Web, a page is a dynamic thing that people scroll through, so it's completely okay to think about making a "page" out of a PageMaker story that's three, five, or seven pages long. Do make sure you set up a table of contents with anchors to access the key points in this long "page" so your viewer doesn't need to scroll endless to get to their point of interest.

▶ *Don't use big graphics.* Sorry for the repetition, but now we're getting a bit more specific. Your entire Web page including all the graphics should be under 50K—even better if it's around 30K.

It helps to think of a Web site as a fast food location for brain stimulation. Which fast food site do you think will get more customers? The one that takes 10 minutes to serve up the food, or the one that plunks it onto the consumer's tray in 30 seconds or less? If anything, competition for consumers on the World Wide Web is far more intense than your average strip zoned district headed out of a small town in the Midwest. (There's some sort of analogy about drive-in windows in there somewhere, I'm sure, but you get the point.)

▶ *Do offer graphic download options.* At the top of the page, consider putting a line that gives the viewer an option to jump to a page with no graphics on it. Many people don't understand that they can set Auto Download Graphics off in their browser so you can do them a favor by offering the option onscreen.

At least for now, until some major change in technology bridges over this barrier, Acrobat files do not belong as an integral part of a Web page. Use the smaller GIF and JPEG formats.

In fact, do as Moe suggests in Chapter 33, where he shows us a page that has a list of available PDF graphics shown in tiny thumbnail form along with a file size advisory for each one.

▶ *Offer visual interest.* You don't need huge files to make your pages visually interesting. Think of yourself as a Mark Rothko or Frank Stella instead of Sam Francis—they did pretty well with just a few colors and have managed to interest a few people along the way. Interesting shapes and subjects don't take up nearly as much file space as colors.

▶ *Test all monitoring conditions.* Run tests with various browsers and monitors. Have a look at your Web pages on a grayscale monitor, a laptop (Windows and Mac both, maybe even an Amiga), and on a color monitor set to 16 colors instead of 256.

▶ *Test all browsing conditions.* Browsers are all over the map, and while it's true that Netscape seems to have a lock on the market, it certainly would be a mistake to leave out the 30 percent or so of the audience who don't use Netscape.

As we went to press, the HTML Author Plug-in used an underline style code that was standard for Mosaic and MacWeb browsers but not for Netscape. You need to stay abreast of changing browser feature sets and language extensions. Pretty much everybody can read HTML 1.0, more can do 2.0, and 3.0 is just coming in. (Of course, if you read this a year after we are on the shelf, it's likely we'll be talking about some other version, or possibly a completely different hypertext language.)

▶ *Tune your page in a more robust HTML Editor.* At least as we went to press Adobe appeared to be planning an update to the initial 1.0 version of HTML Author Plug-in. The section on translation issues with HTML was the single biggest section in the README advisory file that accompanied the initial release of PageMaker 6.0. So, HTML Author in its early form may be great as a first step, especially because it allows you to convert PageMaker documents from within the program. But HTML Author will become much more powerful as time goes on, and more powerful HTML editors are already available. Bottom line—use a more robust HTML editor than Version 1.0 of HTML Author to put the final polish on your Web page.

VIII

Riding the Cutting Edge

TIP ▶ Get DTP Info on the Web, Too!

In addition to learning about the Web on the Web, there are a number of sites that have been devoted to paper-based publishing, although because of their location they tend to have a cyber-view consciousness as well. Try these for a start:

▶ **http://www.adobe.com**—Adobe's World Wide Web stop for information on PageMaker and Acrobat.

▶ **http://the-tech.mit.edu/KPT/KPT.html**—The place to get info from Kai Krause, world famous guru of Photoshop filters.

▶ **http://www.mccannas.com/newtips.htm**—Photoshop information.

▶ **http://www.winternet.com/~jmg/GetInfo.html**—Newsletter on DTP Tips & Trips.

▶ **http://wwwiz.com**—Kare Gram newsletter by one of the regulars on the DTP Forum.

> ▶ **http://www.prepress.pps.com**—Site operated by PrePRESS Main Street.

> ▶ **http://www.yahoo.com/**—Of course, the ultimate way to find anything on the Web, the index called Yahoo!. As we go to press, Yahoo! listed 66 Desktop Publishing items **(http://www.yahoo.com/Computers_and_Internet/ Desktop_Publishing/)**, but when you clicked that connection you ended up with a list of hundreds of subentries.

The DTP Forum on CompuServe has, by way of cross-pollinating the electronic and paper publishing paradigms, a section on designing for online environments.

Running HTML Author

Although it's clear that many changes lie ahead for HTML Author and for the World Wide Web in general, the basic process of converting a PageMaker document to HTML won't change all that much in the near future. Let's walk through that process.

Before we start, here's a reminder. You need to know the structure of your Web site. Remember the advice in the work flow sections at the beginning of this chapter about having a conversation with the Webmaster? You can't work in HTML Author—setting up hypertext links to your several Web pages, your graphics, and other remote locations—without understanding how your Internet provider prefers to manage these details.

Getting a Problem Spotter Report

When you first open HTML Author, you will get a report on any translation problems (see fig. 29.4). The report will help you search out facets of your PageMaker publication that need your special attention to get them ready for the Web.

FIG. 29.4 ▶

Getting a to-do list of HTML clean-up issues for your PageMaker document.

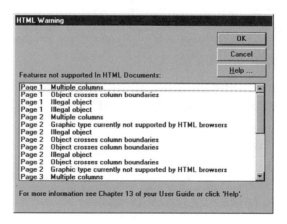

If this list is too long, you really should consider building your Web document from scratch in an HTML editor, instead of a conversion program. You can certainly export the text and re-use the graphics, but it may be easier to start fresh instead of attempting to restructure an existing complex document.

Establishing Content and Web Pagination

Let's assume you've taken some of the basic steps—had the Webmaster conversation, reset your publication into a single column structure, converted and re-linked your graphics to GIFs or JPEGs, and so on. Your document's in pretty good shape.

The first actual step you take with HTML Author Plug-in, after opening it up from the Utilities menu and getting the automatic problem report, is to establish the content of your Web pages. You do that by clicking on the Contents tab you see in figure 29.5.

VIII

Riding the Cutting Edge

Fig. 29.5 ▶

Breaking up your PageMaker publication into Web bites.

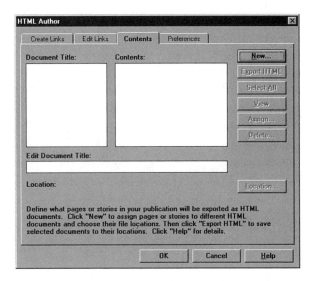

You click the New button to establish a title for a given Web page location. One basic content decision you'll need to make at this point is whether to organize your Web pages on the basis of PageMaker pages or PageMaker stories (see fig. 29.6).

FIG. 29.6 ▶

Each page gets a title, and you'll need to decide whether to build pages out of PageMaker stories or pages.

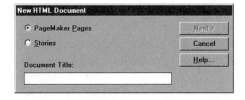

Some of your decision-making on this score will depend on the nature of the document, too. PageMaker's threading-based story structure methodology helps organize information no matter what pages it happens to reside on. For example, a newsletter or magazine that has several stories jumping across many pages probably would best be broken up by stories rather than pages. On the other hand, a catalog of single-page sales sheets would be perfect for a page-based Web conversion.

Personally, I prefer the story approach, largely because I'm a heavy user of inline graphics and my personal work style just fits that story-oriented approach. In addition, it seems to me to facilitate the creation of graphic anchors—graphics as hypertext link buttons.

As you establish each content element, you'll be asked to choose a folder where the exported HTML document should be stored. Ideally this will be the same location as your graphics files, and it will be named exactly like the location you'll be using on your Web server (per the discussion with the Webmaster).

Lining Up Your Styles

After organizing the content of your Web project, take care of paragraph style assignments. Everything in HTML depends on styles. That's what gives a Web page its structure, even though the person in Paducah may assign Helvetica Inserat to headlines and Tekton to body copy (shudder), while the Web surfer in Wichita has chosen Optima for heads and Lubalin Graph for body (oh my!). You can fairly well depend on headlines being bigger and bolder than the body copy, and you can bet that first-level headlines will be more prominent than fourth-level headlines.

You can either establish a style assignment conversion within HTML Author, or you can rename and reassign styles in the PageMaker document. Personally I prefer to use both, sort of a one-two punch at the style cross-over task.

First, use the Preferences dialog box you see in figure 29.7 to establish relationships between your styles and the standard HTML styles. Header 1 in your PageMaker document might become the HTML style H1, for example.

Then click OK to leave HTML Author. When you do so, the Author will add all the HTML standard styles to your Styles palette.

FIG. 29.7 ▶

Making style translation connections.

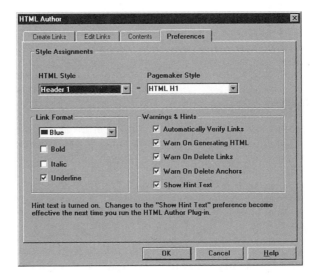

Now go through your document and pick off any areas that need to be edited or restyled, using the new HTML styles you see in figure 29.8 from the Styles palette.

FIG. 29.8 ▶

HTML Author automatically copies the HTML style set into your document.

It's important to keep in mind that any style changes you make in your PageMaker publication are not live-linked to the HTML version of the document. No changes are live. If you make changes in your source document, you'll need to re-export HTML.

VIII

Riding the Cutting Edge

TIP ▶ Modify Your Styles to Match Browser Defaults

It's easier to evaluate how your page will look when it is on the Web, as you are redesigning it, if you modify all the styles to match browser defaults. Check out Netscape to see what those are likely to be, because it is the most popular browser of the moment. For example, it usually comes supplied by providers with all the styles set to Times. You can do the same. Also, while in preferences, set your Link Format to match browser defaults—probably blue and underlined in this case.

Making Your Links

Now you make your links—last thing before exporting your document to final Web page HTML form. Saving this step until last reduces the chance you'll accidentally mess up a link during editing.

You can insert two kinds of hypertext links in your Web documents—URLs and anchored internal locations.

URLs are simply the addresses of documents on the Web that you want to point to, so your visitors can link from your location to other interesting sites. (We've listed several in this chapter already, as in **http://www.adobe.com**.) If you become known on the Net for having the best link list for your interest area (for example, bottom-feeding fish nutrition, watermelon hybrids, tie dying), you'll have many more visitors to your site. They'll come for the convenient links and, of course, stay for your sparkling page design.

Internal locations are spots within your document where you want the viewer to be able to make easy jumps. For example, you would probably set up one of your pages as a home page, and then have links on that page to all the other documents at your Web site:

▶ These links are established by creating an *anchor*, a location for the link to aim for. So, to make a link, you first must establish an anchor. Either highlight some existing text in the document, or design a location where you type in some directive text and highlight that.

▶ Open HTML Author and go to the Create Links tab (see fig. 29.9).

▶ Type in a name for the anchor in the Enter Anchor Label box.

▶ Use the Create pop-up menu to describe the link.

▶ Click Create to complete the link description process.

The link's anchor text in your PageMaker document will now be formatted as you chose in Preferences. If you didn't change the Preferences, it will be colored blue, as in most browser default settings.

Fig. 29.9 ▶

*Highlight a location
and establish it as
an anchor.*

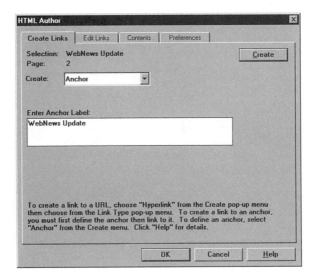

Review a list of your hypertext links and fine-tune them by using the Edit Links
tab. By the way, early release copies of the PageMaker documentation said you
could establish 500 of these hypertext links. In truth, the upper limit was 50 for
Version 1.0.

Inline graphics, because they are viewed as text by HTML Author, may be defined as anchors, and that's the way you get PageMaker and HTML Author to
make graphic buttons. That's another reason why using the Story mode and placing your graphics inline is a good idea when making a PageMaker conversion to
HTML. However, Version 1.0 of HTML Author could not link properly to an anchor on the first-last character in a paragraph, so you'll need to be careful to
avoid that situation until the Plug-in goes through another revision cycle.

Keep in mind that HTML won't be able to do you any good in bringing your
graphics over to HTML if you copy and paste graphics. You must place them.
HTML depends on PageMaker links to keep track of location of graphics.

One more thing before you anoint your page with the qualities of Webness. It's
about how you make links to Acrobat PDF files. The formula for editing your finished HTML file to include Acrobat graphic files is fully set down in Chapter 33,
in the interview with Moe Rubenzahl, who was kind enough to offer us a very
specific example.

Export to HTML

When you have everything arranged just right—all your text styled in HTML
styles, or at least marked for conversion in Preferences, and all your hypertext
links in place—return to the Contents tab in HTML Author (see fig. 29.10).

FIG. 29.10 ▶

The final step in using HTML Author, Export HTML.

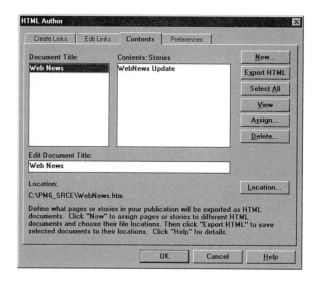

Click on the Export HTML button, and your PageMaker document will be turned into a Web page for you.

Here again, it will be critical to the success of your project that you export HTML to a folder that matches the internal structure of the Web server the publication will be living on. Talk to your personal Webmaster about this, or if you are the Webmaster, talk to the guru of your Web site about how to structure your files and folders.

Acrobat and PDF

Web pages and HTML are fairly easy to produce, but a PDF document is a piece of cake.

To create an Adobe Acrobat file out of a PageMaker file, you simply pull down the File menu and choose Create Adobe PDF. Click on the Create button in the dialog box you see in figure 29.11.

There are a few options in this dialog box and some nuances about workflow you should know about, but there's not much more than that to it.

Fig. 29.11 ▶

The opening dialog box for Create Adobe PDF.

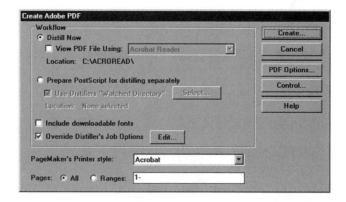

Font Issues

Maybe the biggest reason of all to even have PDF files has to do with fonts. How could you possibly share files with someone unless you had the same fonts?

The answer, if you play your cards right, is Acrobat PDF format, generated from right inside PageMaker. You have two choices:

▶ *Embed fonts.* You can actually include a copy of the fonts inside the Acrobat PDF document. If you include fonts, the file will be bigger, a particular issue for World Wide Web distribution but generally not a problem at all if you are distributing via CD-ROM. If you don't include fonts, Acrobat's approximation of the font may not please you. And don't even think about not including fonts if you are using Symbol or Pi fonts like the ones on the Precision Type font reference on the CD-ROM.

▶ *Local fake fonts.* Or, you can depend on the viewer's local copy of Acrobat to try to make up the fonts on-the-fly. This does a surprisingly good job as long as the font resembles one of the mainstream type designs.

Install and Manage Distiller

The Create Adobe PDF Plug-in, even though it resides on a main PageMaker menu, really is just a way for PageMaker to run Distiller by remote control. Distiller is the program that takes in the PostScript output of PageMaker (as if it was printing to a PostScript printer) and distills it into a PDF file.

You absolutely, positively, can't make a PDF file without Distiller. So you must install it. It comes free on the CD-ROM that comes in your PageMaker package. It's not a full copy of Distiller, but is rather Distiller PE, for personal edition. It will only work from within PageMaker 6.0 or on a file created by PageMaker 6.0's Create Adobe PDF menu item and by selecting Prepare PostScript for distilling separately.

Distill Now or Delay

You will need to decide whether to distill your PDF file out of PageMaker immediately or allow PageMaker to make up a PostScript file that can be distilled later. In either case, you will need to use the Create PDF menu item. (A full copy of Distiller would let you print to a PostScript file and run the distillation process outside of PageMaker. Distiller PE inserts special code in the Create PDF output file to enable it to work in Distiller.)

Why would you want to delay? Well, one major reason could be the amount of RAM you don't have. Many computer systems just don't have enough memory to handle both programs simultaneously. PageMaker takes at least 8M, and Distiller grabs another 8. If your system is a bit on the thick side, you could run through 20M in a hurry.

Another reason to delay is speed. If you have many files to distill, it will usually be faster for you to run a PostScript file and Distill later at your leisure.

Manage Distiller Options

Because Create Adobe PDF Plug-in has such intimate contact with Distiller, it can set some Distiller options from within PageMaker. Click the Override Distiller's Job Options check box, and you'll be able to set up Thumbnails, use LZW compression on text and graphics, store the file in raw ASCII text, and embed fonts.

In this same dialog box, you can also set preferences for working with graphics images.

You can also set preferences to methods used for graphics embedded in PDFs by Distiller. You can put graphics on a diet with downsampling, choose to compress graphics, and if your PDF will be seen mostly on-screen, you can convert images to RGB from CMYK.

Managing Automatic Hypertext Links

PageMaker will make all the cross references you need, in the PDF file. That means you can easily provide your reader with easy to navigate structure by putting to work the structure you've already developed for the document. Just set up a table of contents and an index prior to running the Create Adobe PDF command, and they'll be translated into your Acrobat file.

You can set up these links by clicking on the PDF Options button to reach the dialog box in figure 29.12.

FIG. 29.12 ▶

FIG. 29.12 ▶

Setting up hypertext links from within the Create Adobe PDF Plug-in.

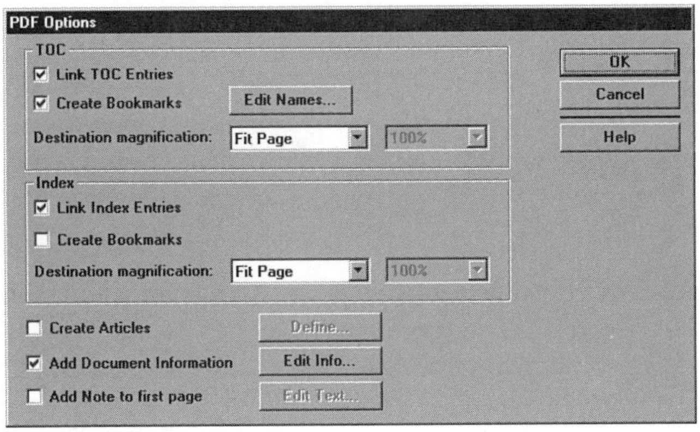

The TOC and Index portions of the PDF Options dialog box shown here work in exactly the same way.

The check boxes for Link TOC Entries and Create Bookmarks check boxes really perform the same function. They create hypertext links between the table of contents page and the locations referred to in the TOC. The difference is you can edit the anchoring bookmarks if you click on the Edit Names button next to the Create Bookmarks check box. You can also set up the standard magnification for pages where you link from a TOC entry.

As with HTML language, you can perform your PDF conversion on the basis of PageMaker stories instead of pages. Do it by clicking on the Create Articles check box.

Document information is text that appears in the Acrobat viewer's Document Info box.

And you can type out a note to appear on the first page of your PDF document. Just click on the Add Note to First Page check box.

Page Structuring

Bundle together booked publications by simply opening up the document that contains the book. You'll get an alert box like the one in figure 29.13.

VIII

Riding the Cutting Edge

FIG. 29.13 ▶

Choose Yes to wrap all your booked publications into one PDF document.

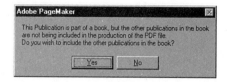

Keep in mind that you may need to fix your page numbering before going the PDF route. Acrobat numbers everything from 1 to whatever, with no special DTP niceties like small Roman numerals for the preface and table contents. Often, in PageMaker, there are much more complex page numbering schemes.

Also, you can't have Reader's Spreads set in the Print dialog boxes. That will break Acrobat. The safest thing to do is to use the Acrobat printer style. You can choose it from the opening dialog box of Create Adobe PDF.

Where to Go from Here

▶ Styles being such an essential part of the concept behind HTML, it would be a good idea to get to know how to use PageMaker's paragraph styles, and that's in Chapter 7, "Designing a Text Style System."

▶ Without Place and Link, HTML Author just plain wouldn't work. Find out more about links in Chapter 30, "Linking and Other File Connections."

▶ Check out the Learning from the pros section. Chapter 33, is an interview on designing for the Web with Webmaster Moe Rubenzahl.

▶ Some of Moe's (and other's) favorite Web page authoring tools have been included on the CD-ROM in the back of the book.

Chapter 30

Linking and Other File Connections

To help you evaluate the benefits of each kind of link, this chapter includes:

A discussion of why you might want to use a link in the first place.

▼

An overview of the two link alternatives and how they differ from each other.

▼

In-depth information concerning the Links technology that has been part of the PageMaker program since Version 4.0.

▼

Coverage of Microsoft's OLE and how to utilize it in PageMaker.

EACH TIME YOU import a text or graphic file into PageMaker (except when you simply use the Paste command), you form a link. A *link* is a software connection or relationship between source material and the original.

Linking has the power to save you disk space; it also enables you to update the linked material easily using the word processor or graphics program that created it. But is linking for you? And if it is, which kind should you use? ▶ ▶ ▶

Assessing the Link Strategies

For Windows users of PageMaker, there are two kinds of links you can forge between your original word processing or graphics file and PageMaker. One is the internal link you get automatically with PageMaker whenever you use the Place command. The other one is a part of Microsoft's vision for the future of the Windows operating system and is called *Object Linking and Embedding (OLE)*.

Before we go any further, I'll state my bias. It's a conservative—but reliable and safe—approach. I almost always favor using PageMaker's own Place/Link methods over the Microsoft OLE technique.

So, why does anyone use linking? Should you use linking for text or graphics or both? Why do you have to decide between these two methods? And after you decide to link, how does each choice work? This section answers all these questions, starting with the most important one: *why bother?*

Why Do We Link in the First Place?

When you get right down to it, there are really just three reasons to link. You do it because you want to economize on disk space, because you must update the contents of a publication frequently, or because you need to share your work with someone else.

Save Disk Space

You actually store a file twice when you simultaneously include it in your publication file *and* keep the original for future reuse and editing—once internally and once externally. On the other hand, when you link a file, you can set things up so its complete form only exists *outside* the publication and is merely represented visually in your publication for the purposes of WYSIWYG layout editing.

If you make a habit of storing 20 to 60M graphics files twice instead of just once, how much hard disk space will you have left? That's a primary reason why the folks who created PageMaker invented its linking interface; these huge graphic files are vital to desktop publishing, but there's only so much hard drive space available on most desktop publishing computers.

Likewise, if you use a small graphic file repeatedly (like the images used to highlight information and chapter breaks throughout this book), doesn't it make sense to store it once outside the publication and then apply it many times using a link? Otherwise, when you place a 250K graphic 200 times, you waste 50M of expensive hard disk space.

Updating Work

Many publications exist in a world of change. What do you do, for example, if you are publishing the documentation for a manufacturing process? Let's say that the process changes often as worker time and motion studies and new technology offer ways to improve speed and economy. You need an easy way to update the contents of such documentation. Linking enables you to set up your documentation using easily updatable modules and then do a good part of your editing in the originating applications (programs for drawing illustrations, drafting, spreadsheet charts, and so on).

Sharing with a Group

To take the documentation publication example a step further, imagine that this is a really big document and there's an entire team of people producing the publication: illustrators, writers, designers, engineers, and management. All these people have contributions to make, but they aren't all going to take turns sitting at one computer located at a spot in the building that's sure to be inconvenient for most of them! Nor would it be efficient for them to pass around a single copy of the publication.

They want to collaborate, and the only way that can happen is by being able to work simultaneously, feeding their efforts (editing comments, illustrations, charts, and so on) into the main publication document. Such collaboration is much easier when linking allows sharing of all these files in a modular fashion.

Linking Is Mostly for Graphics

Sure you can link text. In fact, it's just as easy to link a passage of text as it is to link a graphic. But when you think about the following three motivations for linking, they don't come down conclusively on the side of linking text:

▶ For collaborative projects—work group situations—linking text does seem to make sense on surface.

But there's one mammoth drawback to any sort of text updating using linking. Updating text through a link throws away such niceties as fine typography, complex indexing structures, and inline graphics—some of the very reasons you are using PageMaker in the first place. Now, to some extent this problem has been relieved by Version 6.0's new tagging language capability, but that does not completely wipe away this issue.

▶ Aside from the issues of preserving typography and other work, text does need updating, and links would help to do that. But PageMaker has excellent internal text editing capabilities, whereas its graphics editing capabilities are extremely limited.

VIII

Riding the Cutting Edge

▶ When it comes to saving space, text files aren't that big compared to graphics files.

An example might help to make this point. Imagine putting together some carefully crafted documentation, perhaps for the manufacturing process mentioned previously. Headlines have been kerned (autokerning, the Expert Kerning Addition, manual kerning). Illustrations have been placed carefully on pages in relation to the tuned text, and some graphics have been Placed as inline graphics. The index has been carefully coded into a three-level index with lots of cross referencing and page range entries. Lots more has been done, but just these factors alone make it clear that you would breathe fire if you lost all that work.

But if you went out to your word processor to do the editing, using the link to export and import the text, that's just what would happen. You would lose all those elements. No word processor can equal PageMaker's capabilities in typography, indexing, and melding graphics with text. If you update a link to the original word processor at this point in order to pick up someone's copy edits, you lose all the hours of meticulous labor that went into creating this PageMaker-specific excellence. And the whole point of linking is to save labor, not waste it.

For this reason, you will find that most of the linking information in this chapter pertains to the process of importing graphics rather than text. You can, of course, work successfully with linked text. But the major benefits of linking lie on the side of graphics work.

Why Two Choices?

Evolution. That's what has brought us to the point of juggling two competing linking technologies. At least that's the short answer. Here's some more detail.

More than a decade ago, when PageMaker first came out and we first began using computers for desktop publishing, we didn't need to worry too much about communicating with the rest of the world, did we? Now it's mix-and-match document time, and we need to work with the rest of the world.

In the old days, big graphics files didn't exist, either. It seems pretty obvious now, but no one strongly considered the idea that people who work with pictures would just naturally gravitate toward using bigger and bigger picture files—with color in them. Digital artwork takes up vast quantities of hard disk space.

But as the world changed, the computerized graphics environment evolved.

Necessity being the mother of invention, one of the firstborn from this evolution-ary crucible was the Links technology for PageMaker. Aldus, the original devel-oper of PageMaker since merged with Adobe, had no choice but to invent some sort of linking technology. The users needed to work with multi-megabyte graph-ics files—gonzo files—and that meant they needed to save disk space. So Aldus had to get Links out into the DTP community well before the rest of the comput-ing population needed and got more general solutions for linking—solutions that worked at the operating system level where linking really ought to happen.

But now those operating system linking solutions are here, and they are being adopted throughout the desktop computing community. In the DOS Windows camp, there's OLE. On the Apple side, there's Publish/Subscribe.

It's evolution.

Understanding the Differences

We aren't at the survival-of-the-fittest stage yet with these evolutionary (if not revolutionary) methods of linking files into your PageMaker publications. No one knows at this point which one will dominate the jungle in the next few years.

In the limited world of PageMaker, it is likely that the Place command Links will be the survivor. But there's a turbulent swirl of market activity involving the OLE technology. In fact, you can no longer run PageMaker unless OLE is installed.

Although each of these sections gives you some idea of how you make a link us-ing the two linking methods, you'll find the details on actually forging links in the section "Making and Managing Links" later on in this chapter.

Overall Linking Control

PageMaker has been providing its own linking system for quite some time now. So it's only natural that PageMaker engineers included control over Microsoft's OLE in the Link command's master control dialog box when OLE technology became available.

This single dialog box, with its related sub-dialog boxes and commands, enables you to control the way that items get updated using PageMaker Links and OLE (see fig. 30.1).

VIII

Riding the Cutting Edge

Fig. 30.1 ▶

The master control panel for managing all links in PageMaker: the Links dialog box.

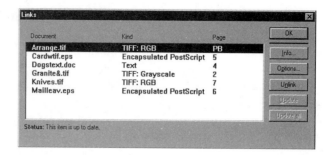

Universal Linking Truths

The following are some general operating truths which hold for all linked files, whether they are connected via PageMaker Links or Microsoft's OLE linking or even the Macintosh's Publish/Subscribe technique:

▶ You need some external application program to do any editing outside of PageMaker—usually the same program that originated the source file. Often you will need to be able to load both PageMaker and the editing program at the same time, putting a double load on your computer's RAM.

▶ You need the original source file in order to print your publication if you have chosen to save disk space by storing the file outside of PageMaker. OLE's embedding option, as opposed to an OLE link, is the one exception to this rule.

▶ You can update all the occurrences of the file throughout your publication by editing the source and renewing the link using the particular method's updating protocol. Again, the one exception is OLE embedding.

▶ All of the linking methods can be centrally managed for updating purposes, if you like, using PageMaker's Link command. The only exception, again, is OLE embedding.

PageMaker Place And Link

You create a PageMaker Link by using the Place command. The Link is forged every time you import a file (see fig. 30.2). The design philosophy is to track the original source file so that you can store it outside the document to save disk space and in case you want to go back to it for editing and updating.

Here's a run-down on some of the advantages of PageMaker Place command-based Links:

▶ When you create PageMaker Links using the Place command, you get all the benefits of the import filters—generally a robust means for retaining the formatting of inbound text and graphics—and you maintain your ability to edit the material.

FIG. 30.2 ▶

*PageMaker's Place
Document dialog
box.*

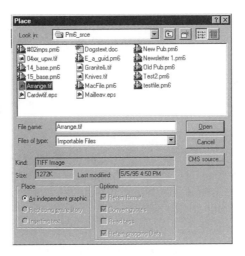

▶ However, if there's no filter for whatever you want to import, or if the originating program cannot export in a format that PageMaker can read, you can't have a Link. You must instead resort to other means to get the material into your publication.

Working from within the item's originating publication, you might save the item in a different format or use a third-party file conversion program. It's a rare program these days if it can't find a way to export a file suitable for a PageMaker filter, but they do exist and for those situations you might want to opt for OLE.

▶ Working with a PageMaker Link, you can make on-the-fly choices between storing a graphic internally in PageMaker or saving disk space by storing it outside and updating it with the Link.

▶ You can even have cross-platform connections by using a Link, connecting a Macintosh graphic to a Windows PageMaker file and vice versa. This would also be possible by using the Microsoft linking technology, OLE.

▶ By using Hotlink to make the connection, you get instant editing capability right from inside PageMaker, so you don't lose the connectivity you achieve via OLE.

Microsoft OLE

With OLE (Object Linking and Embedding), you can link, or you can embed. You decide between the two based on your starting point. OLE embedding begins inside PageMaker; OLE linking starts inside the originating application. The specifics of forging an OLE connection are included later in this chapter.

VIII

Riding the Cutting Edge

Following are the main characteristics of Microsoft OLE linking and embedding as compared to PageMaker's Place and Link facility:

▶ OLE might be an option if your originating application supports it but isn't supported in any way by the PageMaker Place command filter collection.

▶ OLE brings objects into PageMaker as graphic objects that can only be edited in their originating programs, even when they are nongraphic source material such as text (a data layout created in Adobe Table) or a spreadsheet.

▶ Because OLE works with a graphic representation of the object, your importation will be limited to one page of text. No page breaks are allowed in the middle of a table.

▶ OLE embedding only works by way of the Clipboard, so it's RAM-intensive, requiring you to have both PageMaker and the originating application open at the same time. You might run into difficulties, for example, if you attempt to bring a large graphic file into PageMaker by this method.

Making and Managing Links

After deciding which linking method to use for your PageMaker file importing challenge, you need to know how to create and manage that link. This section tells you how to do that.

Controlling Your Links

Use the Link command in the File menu to reach the link management master tool (see fig. 30.3). From this one central location, this tool tells you the status of any link in your publication, lets you update or break the link, and decides how the link should be managed from this point forward.

FIG. 30.3 ▶

Command central for managing your links.

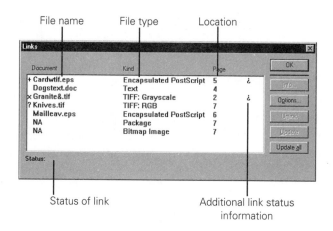

File name   File type   Location

Document	Kind	Page	
+ Cardwtif.eps	Encapsulated PostScript	5	¿
Dogstext.doc	Text	4	
x Granite&.tif	TIFF: Grayscale	2	¿
? Knives.tif	TIFF: RGB	7	
Mailleav.eps	Encapsulated PostScript	6	
NA	Package	7	
NA	Bitmap Image	7	

Status:

Status of link   Additional link status information

A variety of codes indicate the status and location of each link. Check table 30.1 for more detail on the meaning of these codes.

To view or set link options for one object:

1. In Layout view, select an object and choose Element > Link Options.

TIP ▷ Modify Link Settings

You can also modify a linked objects's link settings by choosing File, Links, selecting a file from the list, and then clicking Info or Options.

---

2. Specify options as follows:

   ▶ The Store Copy in Publication option determines whether an imported file is stored inside or outside the publication. (Text files are always stored in the publication, so you can edit the text).

   ▶ The Update Automatically option updates the copy of the file stored inside the publication when its original file is modified. This option is always on for externally stored objects.

   ▶ The Alert Before Updating option presents a dialog box notifying you when PageMaker is about to update a link, and asks you to approve the update.

3. Click OK.

TABLE 30.1   Symbols Used In the Links Dialog Box

Links Symbol	Definition
Page Location Codes	
UN	Some or all of the linked material is in a story that has not been placed, so its page location is ambiguous.
LM, RM	The linked object is on one of the master pages, left or right.
PB	The linked item is on the Pasteboard.
OV	The linked item has been stranded in some text that hasn't been poured onto a page yet (OV means overset).
>	Document contains a link established in Macintosh PageMaker that is not supported in Windows PageMaker.
Link Status Codes	
NA	No link to an external file. Item either pasted in using the Clipboard or embedded using OLE.

TABLE 30.1 Continued

Links Symbol	Definition
(circle with slash)	Link broken to an EPS graphic that contains links to one or more Open Prepress Interface images, but PageMaker can't locate the images.
?	The link has been broken. PageMaker cannot locate the linked file.
+	External file has been modified since last update. It will be updated the next time you click the Update or Update All button or the next time you open the publication.
– (hyphen)	External file has been modified, and you have instructed against automatic updating.
!	You have edited an external file in two locations—both inside and outside PageMaker. If you trigger an update, the external file changes will overwrite the internal changes.
X	Object linked to an external file that has been modified.
¿	An image will most likely not be printed at high resolution (missing linked file, filter or OLE file not available, cross-platform translation).

If you select one of the linked objects and then click the Info button in the upper-right corner of the Links dialog box (the Info button is grayed unless you select something), the Link Info dialog box appears (see fig. 30.4).

FIG. 30.4 ▶

Getting information on a specific linked item.

This dialog box provides you with a complete description of the file's location and enables you to relink or completely replace the item with a new or updated file. To do so, just select the new file and click the Link button or press Enter.

Retain Cropping Feature

The Retain Cropping Data check box that you see in figure 30.4 can save your life. In past years before Version 5.0, PageMaker would relink your new file without paying any attention to the careful cropping you had done. If the overall size of the incoming file had been changed, the result looked a lot like a fun-house mirror. Leaving Retain Cropping Data deselected may lead to the fun-house mirror problem. You have a fighting chance to get a good-looking image if you click it. It won't, however, help much if you have changed the proportions or the size of the incoming file.

Back in the Links dialog box (moving one button to the right), the Options button opens a dialog box like the one shown in figure 30.5.

Fig. 30.5 ▶

The Default version of the Link Options dialog box.

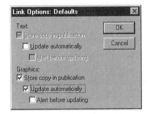

The Link Options Defaults dialog box shown in the figure appears if you click the Options button without selecting an object in the Links dialog box. This feature is terrific because it lets you establish your standard way of handling text and graphics link updates. It's especially terrific if you are working on a project where you'll be flying—importing a lot of objects. Setting the default here means you won't have to worry about the setting each time you bring in a new item.

If you selected an object in the Links dialog box before clicking Options, the same dialog box appears but is cut in half. You'll see the text half if you selected a text object and the graphics half if you had selected a graphic object.

The most important part of the Link Options dialog box concerns your updating options. You can choose to have PageMaker update the linked object automatically each time you open the publication. If you are nervous about this kind of automatic modification of your internal linked material, check the Alert Before Updating check box to have PageMaker provide a fail-safe dialog box for update control.

VIII

Riding the Cutting Edge

You also can enter the Link Info and Link Option dialog boxes by selecting a linked item in Layout view and then choosing one of these options from the Element menu. These individual item menu commands take you to exactly the same dialog boxes you get through the Info and Option buttons in the master links information dialog box.

The Unlink button breaks an existing link. This can be a great advantage if you want to be absolutely sure that someone in your work group doesn't inadvertently update a file that you want to preserve in its present stage.

At the far right end of the Links dialog box are two buttons for updating links. You can update an individual item by selecting it and then clicking the Update button. Or you can simply click Update All and conduct a sweep of all the linked objects shown.

> **TIP ▶ Helping PageMaker Find (or Not Find) Linked Files**
>
> It's easy to accidentally break links when you reorganize the way your files reside in folders on your hard disk or take in a file from someone else who (naturally) had organized their disk in a different manner. The next time you open your publication, you might be told that PageMaker cannot find files that have been rearranged.
>
> PageMaker will help you relink everything if you give it a few hints. When you relink a single file in a group of files, PageMaker adds that folder to its "search" list for links and will relink all the other items in that folder automatically. If you want to prevent this automatic relinking to the items contained in the new folder, hold down the Ctrl key as you click OK, or press Enter.

Editing Originals

This feature might be the best reason of all for using links—the ability to easily and quickly open up a linked object for editing in its originating application. When you finish editing, save the original file and Quit the application. You end up back in PageMaker with the linked object updated by your editing session, assuming you've set your link options to allow updating. It takes longer to describe it than to do it.

To do it, simply select a linked item and use the Edit Original command located at the bottom of the Edit menu in PageMaker.

If you select an OLE object, the menu reads a bit differently. Instead of Edit Original it says Edit followed by the type of file to be edited (Edit Excel Chart Object, for example).

An alternative to dragging out the Edit menu is to Alt+double-click the linked object, and PageMaker sends you out to the original file that created the object so you can do your editing. In the case of an OLE embedded object, you can simply double-click, and the Alt key won't be needed.

If you want to edit the linked object in an application other than the one that created it, hold down Shift+Alt as you double-click the object or choose Edit Original. This will open a Choose Editor dialog box. The box that appears is a standard open file dialog box which enables you to choose to use FreeHand, for example, to edit an Illustrator graphic. The Choose Editor dialog box contains a status panel that tells you, among other things, whether you can edit the chosen document using the program you have highlighted in the list box. Choose Editor is only available for objects which use Place command-based links; it does not work for OLE objects.

TIP ▷ Use Edit Original Shortcut System

The Choose Editor dialog box takes you to the folder where PageMaker 6.0 lives. At that point, you might be tempted just to use the dialog box from there to find the application. But you can make it easier for yourself. Make Windows 95 shortcuts for the programs that you frequently use for editing material in PageMaker. Just right-click the mouse on a program file and you'll get a list of commands, including one for creating a shortcut. After creating your shortcuts, move them into the PageMaker folder for easy access without having to search through multiple folders for the application you need.

TIP ▷ Keyboard Direct Access to Edit Original

For direct access, just double-click the linked graphic if it's an OLE object. Or use Alt+double-click if it's some other form of linked item. In each case, you get the same effect as if you had chosen Edit Original from the Edit menu. If you need to use the Choose Editor dialog box, use Shift+Alt+double-click (but remember that Choose Editor doesn't work for OLE objects).

Making a PageMaker Link

Of the three alternatives, the PageMaker Links technique gives you the most flexibility and control. That's why it is so obviously favored in this chapter. Standard PageMaker Links are created by way of the Place command.

To summarize one aspect of Links flexibility, you can edit a PageMaker Links object in the following ways:

> ▶ If you are dealing with imported text, you would probably edit the text right in PageMaker. You can choose to edit in the original program, but you lose formatting and inline graphics in that case.

▶ You can use the Edit Original command (or Alt+double-click) to return to the originating application for editing purposes. When you save and quit, you trigger an automatic update.

▶ You can always open the linked object directly in its original application, do your editing, and Quit. When you return to PageMaker, trigger an update of the link or a relink, and you have completed your edit.

Linking and Embedding with OLE

You have two ways to use OLE in PageMaker:

▶ You can *OLE link* an object, meaning there is an intermediate file that is the source of a link between PageMaker and the application that originated the object.

▶ You can *OLE embed* an object, meaning it has no intermediate file and exists only in PageMaker, although there is a software link directly between PageMaker and the application that originated the object.

Here's one practical difference between linking and embedding. Because OLE linking works with an intermediary file, that file can be edited and, with a single update move, the file can be used to simultaneously update all occurrences of that object within a PageMaker document. In this sense, an OLE linked object works just like PageMaker's Place command. However, an OLE embedded object does not have this intermediate file and, therefore, can only update one location in your PageMaker publication.

OLE Linking

To OLE link an item into PageMaker, you have two approaches to choose from. Either one of them establishes the OLE connection through a file saved out of the originating application:

▶ You can Paste Special from the Clipboard, after creating, saving, and then copying the material in its originating application. Using this technique, if you wanted to use OLE to link an Excel chart into PageMaker, for example, you would start out in Excel by constructing the chart, saving it, and copying the chart to the Clipboard. Then open PageMaker and use the Paste Special command.

When you use the Paste Special command, you may have a choice of formats, depending on the capabilities of the application that created the object that you are OLE linking.

▶ You can use the Insert Object command and in the resulting dialog box (see fig. 30.6), choose Create From File and click the Link check box.

To use this method, you would first create the Excel chart and save it. Then you would use the Insert Object command and click Create From File and Link and select the Excel chart file.

The Result box in the Insert Object dialog box (refer to fig. 30.6) will read:

```
Inserts a picture of the file contents into your document.
The picture will be linked to the file so that changes to
the file will be reflected in your document.
```

FIG. 30.6 ▶

The Insert Object dialog box set up for an OLE linked file.

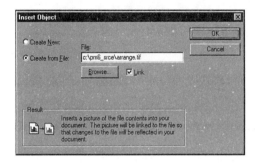

OLE Embedding

As with OLE linking, you can use two methods to create an OLE embedded object, but you work exclusively through the Insert Object command. Paste Special can't embed OLE objects.

Perhaps the most important thing to understand about OLE embedded objects is the fact that they don't exist outside PageMaker. Even if you base the embedded object on an existing file, all you have in PageMaker is a picture of the material in the file. That picture—not the file—is the sole basis for the link between PageMaker and the originating application. You don't have a master linked file that can be changed and updated. You can, however, use Edit Original to update embedded objects, and you can double-click to open up the object in the originating application:

▶ Probably the most common way you will create an embedded OLE object is to use Insert Object from within PageMaker and choose Create New from the Insert Object dialog box. This literally creates a new object that exists only within PageMaker.

▶ Alternatively, you can embed an OLE object based on an existing file. Just choose Create From File in the Insert Object dialog box, but do not click the Link check box.

Remember, even though you have embedded an object from a file, once you have completed the OLE link, the file doesn't count anymore. Changing the file won't update the embedded OLE object inside PageMaker.

VIII

Riding the Cutting Edge

After you are done and quit the application, you are bounced back to PageMaker where you can position your OLE embedded object on the page. If you were to do a Link Info command on the resulting object, you would see that it isn't linked to a file location.

There's related material on OLE embedding in Chapter 16, "Formatting Forms, Tables, and Databases," in the section on Adobe Table.

Where to Go from Here

▶ Use Chapter 8, "Pouring Text into PageMaker," and Chapter 11, "Placing Images," to bone up on the nuts and bolts of PageMaker's Place command.

▶ For more information on preventing broken links and for double-checking the condition of your linked files, review Chapter 21, "Producing Mechanicals."

▶ Broken links pose one of the biggest problems people have with linking (aside from just being confused by all the options). The most common way to break a link is by moving your publication files to your service bureau. Refer to Chapter 24, "Master Checklist for Desktop Publishing," for help on this one.

PART IX

Learning from the Pros

31 ▲ Thinking On-screen

32 ▲ Setting Grunge Type: Point and Counterpoint

33 ▲ Designing for the Web

34 ▲ Putting PageMaker 6.0 to Work

Chapter 31

Larry Miller,
Daddy Desktop,
Atlanta, Georgia

Thinking On-screen

LARRY SAYS, "LIKE ALL good art directors, I started out reading comic books, writing stories and drawing them. I think many art directors and graphic designers began by falling in love with comics. You get involved with heroes, and dream up fantasies. Nowadays, I believe rap music will create a lot of serious musicians because—like comics—it's easy to get started with."

As for formal training, Larry studied at Brooklyn Museum School and at Cooper Union, the free public college in New York City, before spending fifteen years in ad agencies and design firms in the Big Apple. He founded a firm there,

which he ran for eight years; it was an agency for freelance artists and writers of the design and advertising community.

Then Atlanta beckoned. He says, "Atlanta does not have black snow banks, which destroy street aesthetics. It also is warm and clean. But it lacks sidewalks and has only one museum."

In addition to his design firm of Plato Picasso Midas Miller, Inc., Larry has started another Atlanta firm. Daddy Desktop is a consulting firm for desktop publishers where the client does the execution but can buy designing advice brainpower by the hour.

How did the computer epiphany happen for Larry Miller? "Saul Ash, a direct response marketing expert from the Bay Area, had been badgering me for two years about computers, and I wouldn't hear of it. Finally, one day in 1986, he got me—under duress—to go to a demonstration. My mouth fell open. Two weeks later I was an owner and addict."

The most important thing a designer can do is not to make things look good, but to figure out what the job really is.

The following conversation describes a process of design with two points of view combined. First, it takes you through one approach to using PageMaker, where the designer just jumps onto the computer and starts thinking. As you will see, Larry advocates plain old pen-and-ink thumbnailing as part of the design process. Nevertheless, Larry tackled electronic thumbnailing as an exercise based on revising a project he had previously done for MTV, to show some of the potential of thinking on-screen. Second, you get some gratis Daddy Desktop time (well, except for the price of the book), because Larry treats the project pretty much as he would if he was providing a consultation.

Q. **What are we going to work on?**

This is a situation where I redefined the design problem. The most important thing a designer can do is not just make things look good, but to figure out what the job really is. I thought that might be a useful base for our exercise in thinking on the PageMaker screen.

This is a bimonthly piece for MTV. They had been thinking about a newsletter or brochure of eight pages to promote their new record releases. It occurred to me that the same size press sheet used for the brochure—25 × 38 inches—would make a good poster. Why not run a poster and send it in the mail like a brochure, folded so it works as both a newsletter and a poster?

Q. **The first thing we have is a simple black square (see fig. 31.1). That's how you started, with this grid and a square?**

I knew I wanted something active and energetic to get that MTV style. But I didn't want it to be helter-skelter. The grid gives everything a sense of order even though there may be a sensation in the final design of the elements jumping all over. The piece must convey information, and that requires an underlying structure. You can work intuitively, but first create order.

In previous versions of PageMaker, I divided the space into eight PageMaker

FIG. 31.1 ▷

Beginning with a simple grid and a square.

columns and had to calculate the spacing to split the columns into squares. In PageMaker 6.0, I can use the Guide Manager and pop a grid onto the page without doing any calculations at all. PageMaker will figure it out for me.

Then I drew a box the size of one square. Using PageMaker's Line and Fill utility, I gave the box a white line and a black fill. The white line visually separates one box from the next.

Next, a couple of pretty logical moves, extending the box into a row of boxes (see figs. 31.2 and 31.3).

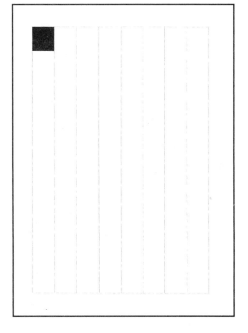

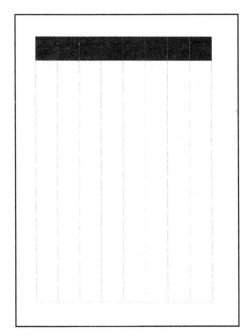

FIG. 31.2 ▲

Creating the building blocks by multiplying the box into a row of single boxes…

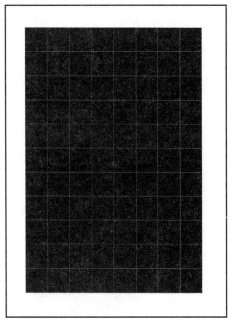

FIG. 31.3 ▲

…then multiplying the row of boxes to fill the page.

The grid gives everything a sense of order, even though there may be a sensation in the final design of the elements jumping all over.

I made a copy of the box and used Multiple Paste to paste seven copies, horizontally offset 1.308 inches, the width of the box.

Then I used Select All to copy the first row of boxes and multiple-pasted it ten times with horizontal offset of 0 and vertical offset of 1.378 inches, the depth of the box, almost a square.

PageMaker's Multiple Paste command, you can see, makes all this possible. Otherwise, the process would be so slow that I'd be more busy with mechanics than design and wouldn't be getting the

benefit of sketching on the screen like this.

This gave me a page of boxes that are all the same size and all touching precisely and accurately. I used to have to rule such elements with a Rapidograph, or cut them from Rubylith. One mistake killed an afternoon. This is easier on the eyes and head.

PageMaker's Multiple Paste command, you can see, makes all this possible.

Q **Looking at this, it seems like the first thing you did after building all these boxes was to get rid of some of them (see figs. 31.4 and 31.5). It feels like you are designing, at this point, by removing design.**

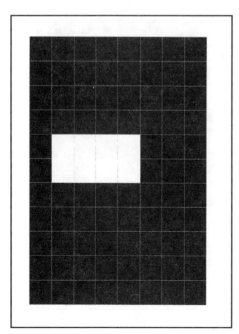

Fig. 31.4 ▲

Seeking a fulcrum point for the design…

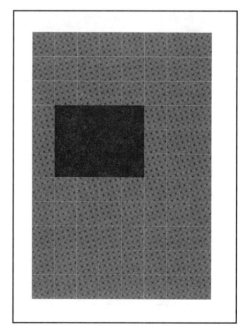

Fig. 31.5 ▲

…and trying to stay off-balance.

Design by subtraction—an interesting idea, Rick. One thing about this business: you never stop learning, and you never should. Anyway, yes, experimentally, I delete eight boxes, leaving a space for the calendar month.

I see that my goal now is to make that box proportionally larger, while still observing the grid system I've set up to create a sense of order—before I *violate* that order.

I see a substantive difference between a free-form page and one with a grid that is selectively violated. In jazz, you remain aware of the underlying melody. With this approach, you remain aware of the underlying grid. A larger box will allow one element to serve as a fulcrum for all other page elements to spin off from—to serve as a focus, a hub, a gravitational center, better than it does on the original.

So, I made that central box one row taller, adding that depth above. Had I added it below, the unit would have been centered, which I did not want. I was seeking an off-balance approach to balance— dynamic balance, dynamic symmetry, as some call it.

> *...still observing the grid system I've set up to create a sense of order—before I* violate *that order.*

Fig. 31.6 ▲

Hitting the sketch pad stage and adding some type.

might if you were using a pen and tracing paper.

I set the type, pushing it as tight as possible. Perhaps the leading is too tight, but we'll use this for a while and refine details later. Using PageMaker's new Align command, I precisely align the text blocks with the panel.

I also turned off the guides at this point (Ctrl+J). They were showing through the white type and distracting me.

Q It's tough to see because of all the boxes, but you've added something (see fig. 31.7).
Right. I changed the tints and unreversed the type because I want to experiment with a drop shadow. I copied the box,

Q Now there's some type showing up (see fig. 31.6). Would you say you are at the sketch pad stage here? It seems like this all happens in a very fluid manner.
Yes, definitely. PageMaker works as a sketch pad for exercising a design concept as long as you keep moving. If you treat it that way, like a sketch pad, PageMaker moves at least as fast as you

made the copy solid, and pasted it; now you see it in its default offset position. (I may later move it for a more dramatic shadow.)

Fig. 31.7 ▲

Working toward a drop shadow.

Using PageMaker's new Align command, I precisely align the text blocks with the panel.

Things got pretty confusing here because of the layers. I got it straightened out pretty easily, though, thanks to Version 6.0's capability to move objects one layer at a time. The pasted black box was in front. If I sent it to the back like in the old days, it would have been lost behind all the other little boxes—invisible. I moved the `April`

heading and the box it was in to the front. Now the layers are correct.

I also made the text flush left, which may or may not turn out to be a good thing. We'll see.

You have to stay alert about things like layers, or you get bogged down in mechanical details. Work quickly so your intuitive part comes through, even though it's being guided by the grid. But don't worry about being pure: make useful notes about layers on a notepad.

Q What's the little box all about, the one that flits around inside your main box (see fig. 31.8)?

I need to bring in another element, the word "Europe," and I think it's going to end up as a boxed item.

Dreaded indecision hits me here, while trying to explore positions for the Europe box.

I had to reduce type by 1 point and reposition slightly— all made easier by the Control palette. (I remembered that in the Control palette, you don't need to retype or remember a long measurement. You can just type a plus or minus sign and the increment. Easy. Feels good, too.)

Work quickly so your intuitive factor comes through, even though it's being guided by the grid. Otherwise, it won't be a sketch pad anymore.

In the Control palette, you don't need to retype or remember a long measurement. You can just type a plus or minus sign and the increment. Easy. Feels good, too.

FIG. 31.8 ▲

Thinking ahead to new elements.

These three elements together will begin to control the flow of the rest of the elements. Well, maybe they will.

Q. Larry, you said "dreaded indecision." If we weren't doing this interview, what would you be doing about indecision? Get up and do some push-ups? Raid the refrigerator?

Yes, any of the above. I have a chinning bar I just like to hang from. Get away from the project a bit. You can come back without the emotional investment and start where you left off or even from a completely fresh point of view. You'll know better what to do after letting the idea gestate overnight.

Q. So, let's say we're picking back up on the next day. What's the first thought in your head?

Never mind Europe for now. Keep moving.

Q. And instead, you go right to the main block, the dominant visual element on the page (see fig. 31.9).

To make the main panel more dominant, I play with the Rotation tool. The trick is to rotate several objects at once and not rotate extraneous items. So I carefully select the related elements, then use the Group command before rotating. In this case, the little Europe square rotates with the type and the main box with its drop shadow.

FIG. 31.9 ▲

Rotating elements in a search for emphasis.

To make the main panel more dominant, I play with the Rotation tool.

This leaves a hole among the blocks of the grid, but that's no problem, really. Good designers are a little like good jazz musicians; you use the unexpected to challenge yourself. We'll see how this sits for a bit.

I then use the Skew command in the Control palette to tilt the type backward so that the vertical strokes are parallel to the sides of the page.

How is it so far? Do you like the sketch pad approach for this project?

You're right to say "for this project." Every piece needs a different application of all the tools you have. We should talk a bit about using traditional marker-thumbnails.

Anyway, to answer your question, yes. PageMaker works as an electronic sketch pad for this project. Except there's one thing—if I were doing pen and ink thumbnails, I'd be able to get an overview of how things are changing, sort of like the time lapse photography feel. In PageMaker, you don't get that so easily, so I use the slide show trick.

Not many know about this. Get all the pages at the same view. Hold down the Alt key and select a view—in this case the Fit In Window view. That forces all the pages in the document to the same sized view. Then you can use the Slide Show command to quickly browse through all the thumbnails, by holding down the Shift key while selecting the Go To Page command.

Every piece needs a different application of all the tools you have.

Okay, you've had a global look. Anything come to the forefront (see fig. 31.10)?

When I rotated the type, I made it flush left, but it still didn't appear to align properly. Pay strict attention, especially with large type, to the difference between mechanical alignment and optical alignment. Even when elements are perfectly aligned by PageMaker, they still may not look right, and you usually need to do some kerning. The trick I use in this case is Ctrl+Shift+H (which

Pay strict attention, especially with large type, to the difference between mechanical alignment and optical alignment. You usually need to do some kerning.

Fig. 31.10 ▲

Almost ready for design complexity.

moves the type forward with a non-breaking space character), then I bring the type back to the correct spot using Ctrl+Shift+Backspace kerning until it looks right. Generally, a few proofs are needed to adjust it, because type on-screen is still not representative to the *nth* degree of the printed result.

I un-rotated the single-unit `Europe` box and moved it down. It needs a drop shadow (I think). Now we can start to place large pictorial elements—photos of the recording artists.

🔳 Wow, that's a big change (see fig. 31.11)! You okay? Didn't strain yourself?

Ha, it's nothin'. Now we can really see the beginnings of a finished piece. And I'm just a bit concerned.

Fig. 31.11 ▲

Rushing toward maturity.

The structure is where I want it, but the job still looks piecemeal and patchy. A lot of new-wave design lacks structure, by intent. I prefer structure and controlled visual relationships.

This next bit is where the talent part comes in. When talent fails, that's where tenacity comes in. And when tenacity fails, that's where it pays to put it away again for a few hours or days. Then come back and take a fresh look and maybe make some bold decisions.

For now, my goal on the next version is to make some large units, which may contain type or pictures or both. I see no reason not to make the type smaller, even much smaller, and set type more open—lighter—to achieve light typographical "color," permitting more dramatic elements to dominate by contrast with the lighter elements. Here goes…

🔳 Okay, we'll stand back and watch (see figs. 31.12 and 31.13).

There, I think things are now reasonably well blocked in. Clearly, this piece needs just a limited number of hotspots—bold or dynamic areas. Units of type and their headlines can be more reticent, laid back, quiet. When they are all in position, maybe a few areas of emphasis can be added.

The top unit is colored Paper, to hide the vertical grids behind it. I copied a grid unit and rotated it 45 degrees, but it was

> *When talent fails, that's where tenacity comes in. And when tenacity fails, that's where it pays to put it away again for a few hours or days.*

not precisely square, and this asymmetry became noticeable and disturbing when rotated, so I adjusted the proportions. (I cheated.)

Let's see. What's missing? Using the Rules command in the Paragraphs dialog box, I put an 8-point rule above the top unit of type, providing a starting point for the page.

I move the "The Clash" unit down, adjust alignment and letterspacing on the main "April" unit, make some boxes lighter, and do a variety of other weight and position adjustments. I am now satisfied that I can begin to set all the actual type and drop in the MTV logo. It'll go pretty smoothly from here.

Q. To wrap up, you said you want to talk about thumbnails done by hand with pen or marker.

Right. I print this out so I can work on it. There are two choices. To get a doodling surface from this electronic sketch, I can use the Print command's Reduce To Fit option. Or I can tile the piece so I have a poster-sized surface to work with.

If I were working for you, as Daddy Desktop, I'd prefer to tile it up into a nice big piece and start doodling, and let you have that to work on for a while, with the idea that you could come back for more refinement later on in the execution phase. Actually, this sort of project is atypical, because Daddy Desktop projects tend to be newsletters, small ads, or brochures, and not heavily designed posters. Clients tend to be non-designers. You know: editors, marketing people, entrepreneurs.

Fig. 31.12 ▲

Just about finished with the computer sketching…

Fig. 31.13 ▶

…and the doodling begins.

To get a doodling surface from this electronic sketch, I can use the Print command's Reduce To Fit option.

They often have a feel for design and enjoy museums and fine movies. But while we all know a little about each other's job, that doesn't make us truly effective in each other's discipline. They love a low-key pro looking over their shoulder and providing useful tips and improvements.

Q So, we see where the doodles led you here (see fig. 31.14). Why doodle at all? Why not just do what we see here right on the computer without going to hand work?

The computer sketch was still too patchy. Some designers can do all their thinking on the computer; some can do little—creating only on paper and executing on the computer; and some do both. In this case, I followed my impulse to go to paper. I came back to the computer again after that idea development process.

I learned early on to trust my hands. Yes, one thinks; one cogitates; one reasons; one syllogizes; but more often than not, your hand knows better.

Q So, what else would you do here, in this particular example?

I try to create dynamic lines that take you from here to there. Note the word LIVE in the lower left which works well. As I was drawing it, I used triangular crossbars on the capital "E", as in Novel Gothic. That's stuff you can't really do well on the computer, and doodling on paper helps.

Fig. 31.14

The exercised-to-maturity layout concept.

Clearly, "The Clash" panel was interfering with the element I wanted to dominate and control the page, so I made a note to move it down, as well as other notes.

While I would like to fantasize about the paperless office, I do use paper, and I like to sketch.

After you let your fingers talk, you review the sketching intellectually. That's a good point to close on, really. It's important to be self-critical.

In a phrase I use often, "I trust my fingers," which often know better than my conscious mind what I should do.

Chapter 32

**Carlos Segura,
[T-26], Inc.
and Segura, Inc.,
Chicago, Illinois**

Setting Grunge Type: Point and Counterpoint

CARLOS SEGURA STARTED [T-26], a new digital type foundry, in 1993. (His design firm, Segura, Inc., opened its doors in early 1991.) [T-26] has quickly gained a worldwide reputation for experimentation.

"There's no denying that some of the stuff we're doing is extremely controversial. But to my surprise we have been welcomed with open arms in every country. People send faxes and letters and call us to say they've been looking for this; that 'We've been wanting to play. We've been wanting to experiment,'" Carlos says.

For Carlos, the break-out into his own design business followed a dozen years of working in ad agencies—all the big ones. He says, "I was extremely frustrated. There were a lot of limitations, and I discovered I was more a designer than an art director. One day I just quit. I couldn't do it anymore.

"Also, I wanted to do print rather than TV. I don't know how many times someone said to me, 'If you don't put together a reel, you'll never amount to anything.' But I didn't like TV. Too

many people were involved. And I don't think I draw worth a damn. I'd literally get sick every time I had to do a storyboard."

Carlos says of [T-26], "I was looking for a new way to express myself—be more experimental. The one link between all my work has always been typography. I decided to see how far I could push typography. I would dedicate this new foundry to experimenting with type."

Along that line, Carlos takes a different view of how typography relates to the creative world. "We make a hero of the designer. We name the designer on all references to the font in direct mail and advertising. We pay 50 percent royalties to designers.

"We make an effort to give a full-page display to every font. Instead of using standard font sample sentences, we hired a poet to create specimen copy. Each quarter we run an icon font project called AIDing™, with proceeds going to an AIDS benefit organization. Each keystroke in the font goes to a different designer who responded to an international call for entries."

Joe Treacy, Treacyfaces, Inc., West Haven, Connecticut

As a counterpoint to experimental Carlos, we invited font craftsman Joe Treacy to participate in this discussion.

None of this is to say that Joe is not experimental or creative—or that Carlos is not a craftsman. It's just that at Joe's foundry the typefaces generally speak to a somewhat different market. As you'll see from the interview, both these individuals care a lot more about making type work well for its intended audience than they do about any labels we might put on them.

The first thing I ever heard about Joe's work is that he builds type that has many thousands of built-in kerning pairs. That's impressive—a sign of care and quality, because many of the fonts in the large foundry libraries contain less than 100 pairs, if any at all.

Joe will tell you that "people tend to fixate on the kerning thing, but it is just a subset of what we do at Treacyfaces. We create and offer new and different designs, but they tend to fall into a more widely usable vein."

So when I was trying to think of how to energize a back-and-forth discussion about grunge type, I just naturally thought of Joe. It would be fun to match him up with someone who has been accused of intentionally setting type so that it would be virtually unreadable.

Joe began his career right out of high school in Norfolk, Virginia, as an apprentice in a small design studio. From 1973 on, Joe worked as an art director and creative director in various ad agencies and design studios.

He incorporated Treacyfaces in 1984, and took the full-time plunge into working for himself in 1988, when Treacyfaces began selling fonts. In 1994, the foundry absorbed the venerable Headliners International, guaranteeing a good home for some of the most-used headline fonts of the last 35 years. In addition to designing typefaces for sale, he licenses the work of other designers for sale through his foundry. He also spends considerable time creating custom faces and corporate logotypes for ad agency art directors and corporate creative shops who need something special. (For example, when you see an ad for a Chevrolet Geo or truck, chances are high that you are looking at a font specially fine-tuned by Joe.)

Note: Both Carlos and Joe have been kind enough to make some special offers to SE Using PageMaker *readers. You'll find information in the back of the book and on the CD-ROM. Also on the CD, you will find electronic references for the entire [T-26] and Treacyfaces libraries. A comprehensive catalog of virtually every known pi and symbol font has also been included on the CD-ROM, compliments of Precision Type, a well-known type distributor who carries the [T-26] and Treacyfaces libraries. Precision Type has also made an offer of free and discounted fonts, and there's information in the back of the book and on the CD-ROM.*

Q Carlos, you sent me a lot of material from that _HOW_ conference in Chicago a few years ago. I've seen it before in the trades, I think. It was a turning point, wasn't it? And pretty controversial at the time (see fig. 32.1)?

Carlos: If ever you would have an audience where you could push design, it ought to have been at this conference. But I was asked to come and be in a room of 100 people and defend what I had done.

When I got there, I just couldn't believe what I was hearing. One woman called me a communist!

In fact, I almost didn't go. Knowing how I am, I thought I was going to lose my temper. But in the end, it was a wonderful experience. I actually believe I changed some minds, helped them understand that this experimentation is an opportunity to show many ways of thinking, a way to address target marketplaces in a targeted way.

Joe: How do you feel about the *HOW* logo you designed, like that comment about being a communist? Was it meant as a "Russian" design?

Carlos: No. *HOW* magazine wanted me to put their logo all over the place. But I was trying to get them to separate the conference and the magazine. They are two different things. The magazine addresses a more limited audience than the

> *When I got there I just couldn't believe what I was hearing. One woman called me a communist!*

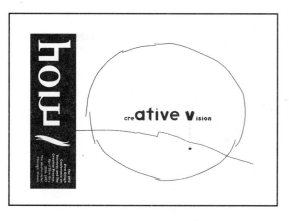

FIG. 32.1 ▲

One of the promotional postcards (front and back view) from the HOW conference. Along the left edge, you can see the logo design that generated much of the controversy.

design conference, which is a bigger umbrella.

Joe: So there was no "Stalinesque" meaning. It was just a matter of combining some letter forms and finding the result to be striking?

Carlos: Yes. And the reason that was proper for the conference was because I was trying to somehow express that the conference is about many different things put together—new things that you've never seen before and old things seen in a new way. By the way, this was the beginning of the first font I did, which I later called Neo. It was really the birth of [T-26].

Joe: I remember at the time reading a lot of letters to the editor about the program design. People said they couldn't read it, that they had no idea where conference sessions were (see fig. 32.2). As I'm looking through this booklet, I don't see anything abnormal or hard to read. The most outlandish thing is maybe the typography. But it's a simple and easy-to-follow layout. The relative use of sizes and different weights of type help the eye find its way through the information.

Carlos: You know what I said to that meeting? If no one in this room could read it, how did you all get here? They could read it. That conference was proof. They expected 500 attendees. They got 1,020. That was the biggest response to date.

That campaign has won every single award I've ever entered, and it has been published by almost every trade magazine in our industry.

You know what I said to that meeting? If no one in this room could read it, how did you all get here?

Q **Sounds like the people at that conference really didn't understand what you are trying to accomplish. What do you say when people ask you to explain some piece of design? They seem to get a bit huffy about it.**

Carlos: Sometimes when people ask me to explain what I've done, I have a hard time. It just comes from within. I expect people to respond to it negatively and positively. That's the sign of a good piece. I don't want everybody to like what I do, because then I'm not doing my job.

But it's much like looking at MTV back when it first came on the air. People said, "Wow that's great!" Now it's just something on Channel 33. We get used to things, and they get less intrusive as time goes by. Now, just two years later, the *HOW* conference materials wouldn't be as unique. The typography is pretty conservative compared to stuff coming out now.

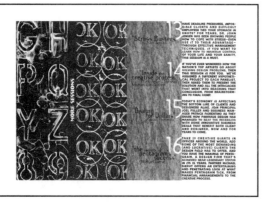

FIG. 32.2 ▲

A "hard to read" page in Carlos Segura's experimental conference guide book.

Q **You use the words "creative vi-sion" in a number of locations. Or should I say "creATIVE Vision?" How did you decide to make the "ATIVE V" letters bigger? Any particular reason?**

Carlos: Those letters are strictly a design element. It has nothing to do with readability or message. They are that way, really, just because I felt like it—because I was in a position of power to do it.

The type on the back of the cards is a different story. I wanted each postcard to be different, with different typography. The reader wouldn't assume that he or she was getting the same postcard over and over. Each one is on a different subject—last chance to register, first chance to register, directions, judges, and so on.

Q **Surprisingly, so far you guys seem to pretty much agree on philosophy! Let's find a page or two of type and get to some specifics. How about this AgfaType Idea Catalog you designed, Carlos (see fig. 32.3)?**

Carlos: In this type catalog, the concept was to show that all of us have a different way of seeing things. The commercial message was that Agfa has a font to address every individual designer's way of seeing things. Every spread has an experimental typographical expression.

In a lot of situations, design comes down to a judgment call. These pages enhance design elements throughout the book—the ovals down the spine, the way type is set throughout the book—dividing up different kinds of information.

Joe: Let's talk about that. Why hack up the body copy into chunks like that?

Carlos: I do that a lot, actually. This kind of layout gives the reader the ability to read chunks they are interested in reading first, without having to follow a

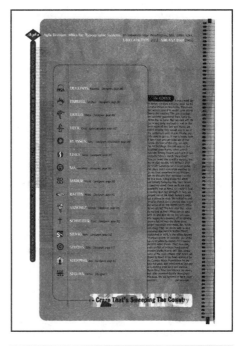

FIG. 32.3 ▲

The opening spread, table of contents, and body copy, from the AgfaType Idea Catalog.

structured order. At least for me it comes from the fact that I'm not a very big reader. In particular, I don't like to read continuous passages, and I like areas that give me stop and go. I find it to be pleasing communication-wise but also visually. You can even do it as in this somewhat conservative case. All these elements are very readable. It allows the typography to act as design element.

> *Why hack up the body copy into chunks like that?*

Joe: Carlos is perfect to promote type to the type-using community, just for that reason. He believes in type. Although I have to say, I happen to hate this text typeface. It's Rotis.

Carlos: This is the beautiful thing, Joe. I love this typeface, and this couldn't be a more perfect example of what we've talked about today. One guy can hate it, and the other love it.

Joe: The overall texture of this face is good. But look at the phrase you've blown up, the words `the designer` at the top of the right-hand page.

There's a disturbing difference in stress and attitude between the `d` and the `e` in `designer`. The `d` has a very vertical sort of orientation in this size. In fact, the `d` and the `s-i-g-n-r` are all vertically stressed. But the `e` has a horizontal stress. The finishing stroke of the `e` comes down and looks like it finishes on the baseline instead of coming back up. The way the swell works in the thick area of the `e` gives me an uncomfortable feeling. I just don't personally find it to be drawn well.

Carlos: I love this. It's why experimentation is good. Your view helps me see things that I don't see. That comment you just made taught me something,

exposed me to things that I will now combine with things I like about the face.

Joe: I notice you have a way of bringing forward textures you enjoy, throwing them out on the page and recombining them until they work together. These very fine rules marching down the edge of the pages remind me of the demarcations on Schaedler precision rules, whose design I really like. So when I saw your use of this in this layout, I sort of warmed up to the page immediately because it gave me something I liked.

> *Your view helps me see things that I don't see. That comment you just made taught me something....*

The emotional packets on the page are appealing.

But why did you crash the body copy against the rounded rectangle on the contents page?

Carlos: I put it on the edge because I wanted it to have a visual reference that it was talking about the page before it, the cover. These design decisions may not be visible to anyone but me, but there was a reason for doing it. That's what I was thinking about when I put it there. Of course, I just happen to like the way it looks; that's part of the designer's duty to decide how things look good, and that's why clients pick a particular designer.

Joe: I would definitely think twice about doing it myself, especially with a rule this thick. But I have to say from a textbook design perspective that Carlos did exactly the right thing by contrasting the thickness of rule with the weight of

> *I would definitely think twice about doing it myself, especially with a rule this thick.*

the type. It's not a repeat of the hairline comb. It's jarring, but interestingly enough, I believe it doesn't interfere with legibility. Carlos, by doing this kind of work, shatters a preconception and shows this can work perfectly well, as long as you're not dealing with an excess of copy.

Why did you decide to put the explanation of the icons off to the side like that? Here's this important information that would help someone use the book, and you've put it in all caps, spun it 90 degrees, and reversed it out of the black bar up the left side of the page.

Carlos: Making it off-kilter makes you look at it. It is visually linked to the Agfa logo, which is what the book is all about. And the hairlines connect the logo and the contents of the book together.

Is it your opinion that the way the icon explanation is treated makes it less important?

Making it off-kilter makes you look at it.

Joe: I can't help but answer by saying I would never obscure information like that. It seems central to why all these icons are there. Here it's treated as kind of an aside.

It's really odd. I find things interesting, texturally, on this page, but this style of graphic design is not my style. I can't really relate to all of it.

Carlos: All the reasons you list are the reasons why I say it works, making it more communicative and more visible than if I had just left the icon explanation as an intro paragraph to the icons. It's a difference in technique, I guess.

Joe: Wouldn't it be nice if it was more immediately related? It seems to me you want people to start with the main

text and then get some inkling of the personality of the designers from the icons. If I was asked to solve what to do with that copy line, I might bind it to the main rectangle's left edge, near the bottom. Make it flush right, and bind it to the rectangle the way the body copy binds itself to the rectangle on the other side.

Carlos: I just did a project for a radio station, Q101. The client literally forced me to put some type in the gutter because he wanted it hidden—wanted readers to look for it—so it would become an interactive experience even though it was a printed piece. It was to promote a Red Hot Chili Peppers concert in Italy, and there was a list of 18 tracks with one additional bonus track. The client forced me to put the bonus track information in the gutter, so listeners would search for it and that would underscore that the CD contained a bonus track.

...he wanted it hidden—wanted readers to look for it—so it would become an interactive experience...

Q Is that what this grunge type thing is about—that somebody is young, or listens to rock and roll, or watches MTV?

Carlos: Well some of the audience have watched MTV all their lives. We are all molded different ways. You don't think the way I do. I don't think the way young people do. My father doesn't think like any of us. But I'm 38, so this isn't just about being young.

And it isn't whether one typeface is legible or not, or deciding whether it is right or wrong. The more important thing

If you were to set Raygun Magazine *like* Time *magazine, it would die in a month.*

to me is to use the proper typeface for the proper job. If you were to set *Raygun Magazine* like *Time* magazine, it would die in a month. The same is true of *Time*.

Joe: Our ages are pretty close. I'm 40. This has nothing to do with readability or legibility. We really need to step back from that issue a bit and ask whether the mood of a typeface really suits the needs or objectives of the ad or promotional piece.

Carlos: I do tend to see things toward the younger side. We have to be willing to recognize that they do see differently. This alternative audience doesn't always start at the top of a story. If you put type in a gutter, they'll find it, if that's what they're interested in.

One of the best questions I was ever asked was from a student in a group that visited my office. One woman said, "This work is great. It's groundbreaking. You are a trendsetter. Where do these things come from? How do you do it when you are so old?"

So, it's not how old you are. It's how you feel about things. I know a lot of teenagers who have blinders on. In my first meeting with a client, I scare them as much as I can. I tell them, "You must be willing to accept that you may have to buy something you don't really like. You may have the money, but you are not the target audience."

▌Q **What do we call this way of looking at things, then? I used grunge type for the chapter title, but is that right?**

Carlos: Well, you have to call it something. I guess grunge is okay. It's the grass roots street term.

Joe: It also plays well by relating to alternative concepts in fashion design.

Carlos: The words *alternative* type might be more accurate, but that's another one of those buzz words of the '90s.

Joe: And there's quite a lot of design work using some of these techniques that's not that grungy.

Carlos: *Garage type* is another phrase.

Maybe what we are dealing with is really a market segment. We started addressing a market that every other foundry dismissed or didn't realize was there. Since then, every other foundry has jumped on the bandwagon. Even Adobe has its Wild Type collection.

Carlos: Take the typeface Lomba, by Luiz DaLomba (see fig. 32.4). You know, Monotype can't keep it in stock, but we can't seem to sell it at all. And Monotype charges $100 more than we do for the same face. We took it, with some hesitation, because we were trying to expand the vision of even the experimental designers we primarily sell to. They just

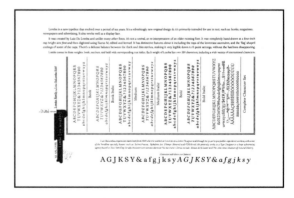

Fig. 32.4 ▲

A new "classic" style typeface from [T-26].

won't buy it. That's not what our target wants. They want experimental.

Joe: Judging from the overall attitude of the typefaces in your catalog, Carlos, I'd say the experimental or alternative designers want to work with typefaces that are emotional (see fig. 32.5). The faces are not built around the classical models. They may have internal balance, but more than anything, these typefaces have a point of view—a mindset all their own.

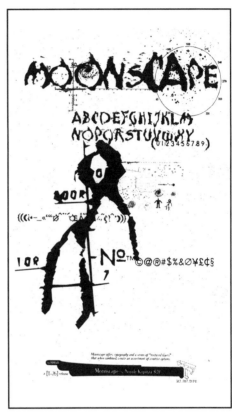

FIG. 32.5 ▲

Some examples of the experimental fonts offered by [T-26].

Carlos: Unfortunately, people are using these kinds of fonts as a design solution instead of a typography solution. So often I'll get a call, "I have this project that's due tomorrow. Send me the fonts by modem." I always think, "Don't you think you are leaving this to the last minute? Do you really think this is going to solve your design problem?"

These faces have so much character and personality that they literally change the meaning of the design. Changing the face will completely change the message because these faces carry a design element.

Joe: This movement came along at a convenient time for a lot of art directors. They've been getting progressively lazier for a long time. That's one reason the U.S. has lagged behind the rest of the world in quality of output—why in many corners of the design world you don't hear people saying the U.S. is on the cutting edge.

> *These faces have so much character and personality they literally change the meaning of the design.*

The ability to pull from a brand-new palette of extremely emotional typefaces was a way to be fresh. But it often forces them into a layout they have no business being in. That is, however, why alternative type has helped the whole arena of typography. It has given a lot of people a kick in the pants.

As with all display faces—especially such emphatic display faces—you can make wrong decisions extremely quickly, and with some of these deadlines, you're spending a lot of money very quickly. They demand real thought and consideration. They may look haphazard, but they aren't always.

Carlos: Back to the issue of legibility, our society has more awareness of typography than ever before. When somebody talks about legibility issues, I always ask them to look at a book from the 16th century and see if they can read it. It's really hard to do. Typesetting conventions—and technology—were completely different back then. And if ever there was a time when type should have been legible, that was it. Books were rare, and most people who could read could barely do so.

There are situations where a designer is thought to be creating unreadable work. But one or two years in the future, it becomes more acceptable. Look at the titling sequences happening on MTV. Now you see that stuff every day on NBC and CBS. It has a way of trickling down so the average consumer is aware of different type treatments.

Joe: While I'm agreeing with you to some extent, not everything has to be a textbook or a primer—we do have to be conscious of legibility.

Q. **The proliferation of typefaces of all sorts has been extraordinary. Where do all these hundreds—thousands—of faces come from? Carlos and Joe, you both have royalty arrangements with designers, of course. And you design your own faces as well. But all these faces couldn't be original designs.**

Joe: I've been speaking out about one aspect of this lately. A lot of these experimental faces have been sampled. They are actually based on another font or have bits and pieces of other fonts very obviously collaged together, and the original artist or foundry is not being credited as part of the creative source.

Carlos: I share your concern, and that's one issue I'm most torn about. We've stopped taking new sampled fonts completely, and our contract requires the designer to state that the design is original by them.

I'd like to add that we see these experimentation exercises as collage. They just happen to be typographical collages.

Fig. 32.6 ▲

A "collage" typeface, Entropy.

> *We see these experimentation exercises as collage. They just happen to be typographical collages.*

One example is the typeface Entropy by Stephen Farrell (see fig. 32.6). Entropy, in my opinion, doesn't compete with the original typeface or take away from it. I actually don't know what the original face was. It would be a problem if you couldn't tell the difference between this face and the face that provided original. But in this case, it is so drastically different it is almost like a rebirth of something.

Joe: I think one of the biggest problems currently undermining the type industry are the cheap knock-offs. That's a bigger issue than what you might call "sampling," analogous to audio sampling in popular music, or collage usage. It's easier now to electronically copy a face. A lot of companies are just knocking off typefaces, stuffing 300 of these poorly made fonts on a CD, and selling them for $19.95.

Carlos: It's too bad. Students and others just getting their first computer buy all these fonts, and it will be a long time before they buy any well-constructed fonts. But that's what it will take for them to really understand that these things aren't very good at all. There's a danger that good quality typography just won't get through to a lot of people.

Chapter 33

Moe Rubenzahl,
Videonics,
Campbell, California

Designing for the Web

I first met Moe in the DTP Forum on CompuServe. From that online experience, he has branched out. I still talk to him all the time in the DTP Forum and the Adobe forums, and he still does a lot of publishing on paper. But now he's a Webmaster—a guru of online-Webness—and he administers a World Wide Web site and designs the pages himself.

The site is the Videonics World Wide Web page (**http://www.videonics.com/**). Moe is marketing director at the company, which makes video editing and post-production equipment that enables camcorder owners and videographers to edit raw video footage. It's a fast-growing company, with an expanding product line and $31.5 million in worldwide sales (1994).

Moe has a BS and an MS in Electrical Engineering, but says he's always done a lot of drawing and writing as a natural adjunct of being an engineer and just seemed to gravitate toward high-tech marketing.

This entire interview was conducted online, over the course of several dozen e-mail messages. Final edits were made by electronically exchanging files.

Q. Well, first, I think we ought to visit your Web page (see fig. 33.1). As we look it over, here's your first question. Videonics has a pretty substantial investment in paper-based documentation. Why does the company also use the World Wide Web, and does this replace paper?

Our Web page supports our paper-based publishing—it will rarely replace brochures, ads, and such.

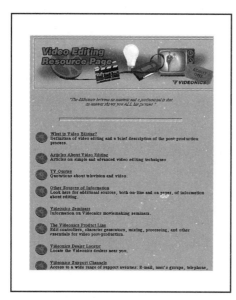

Fig. 33.1 ▲

The Videonics home page.

The most important advantage of the Web is that it's immediate. It is amazingly easy to keep the Web information up-to-date—it takes literally just a minute to update the Web pages. With the right tools, we can place new documents on the Web in very short order.

Another advantage is the quality of information we can deliver. We have used e-mail and CompuServe for years, but that information was largely text-based. The Web makes graphics easy to deliver and supports links—the ability of the customer to get the desired information with just a click.

Finally, the quantity of information we can deliver at almost no cost is a real boon. When we mail a customer a brochure, postage and printing costs limit what we can send. The Web page includes the information in our brochures and much, much more. We have articles on editing, a video glossary, full spec sheets, application notes, and a great deal more. And because the Web is interactive, the customers decide how much information they will receive, spending as much or as little time as they like.

Q. Sounds like it's an educational vehicle as well as a sales vehicle.

Video editing and post-production is still quite a new industry, and we find that customer education is an essential part of the business. Customers at all levels are very hungry for knowledge. The more they know, the better for us, so we jumped at the chance to provide this much information at such low cost.

Q **We hear about all these people surfing the Net, but I wonder how many times a good site withers on the vine because it has not been designed for optimum viewing by the average Web explorer—or, more likely, dabbler. Tell us about some of the design challenges.**

There are tons of interesting issues to consider: GIF versus JPEG, modem speeds, HTMLing existing documents versus creating new ones, and keeping HTMLs up-to-date when existing docs change.

Take modem speed, for example. Many Web authors have access to the Net via fast dedicated lines—ISDN or T-1. But most Web viewers are using modems. Not only that, they may be using slow-speed modems. As a Web page designer, I have to pay attention to all recipients, balancing the big flash of eye-catching graphics against the possible burden found by modem users.

Wise Web authors test their pages using a modem connection to see if they've designed too many big graphics and large pages. If you are marketing high-end gear to very Net-savvy customers, you may be able to assume your customers are all connected by high-speed links, but modem testing is smart for other audiences.

It is fair to assume a 14.4 or 28.8k modem, I think.

The most important thing is to minimize the use of large graphics. Use them where they make sense. When they do make sense, try not to concentrate them on one page.

> *Wise Web authors test their pages using a modem connection to see if they haven't designed too many big graphics and large pages.*

Use the height and width parameters so a browser can write all the text around the graphics and fill in the graphics later. That way, the customer can read while the graphic is coming in.

In the case of big graphics, provide a page that lists the available graphics, letting the users download only the ones they want. I provide file sizes on-screen so the users know in advance how much they are requesting (see fig. 33.2).

Fig. 33.2 *(See color section.)*

Q **What was that about height and width parameters?**

You can specify the size of a graphic in the HTML that defines the page. For instance, this line

```
<IMG WIDTH=410 HEIGHT=23
SRC="banner.gif">
```

tells the browser that the graphic is 410 pixels wide and 23 high, so the browser can leave room and start displaying text immediately, then fill in the graphic later. Not all browsers support this parameter, but those that don't will ignore the extra parameters.

By the way, this is a good moment to add that there are many options for HTML, and you should learn which ones are supported by which browsers. PageMaker's HTML Author Plug-in is quite conservative and uses HTML that is pretty universal. I use some extended HTML code, but try to stick to commands that are commonly supported.

▐Q **The logistical barriers—modem speed and the size of graphics—are pretty clear. Now, what about content? How do you get a surfer to visit your particular Web beach for a while?**

I think the best advice I can give is to provide value. Many Web pages merely list products and specs, information about the company, and the like. Some people will be interested in that kind of information, but they are likely to be customers who were on their way to you anyway.

It's much better to create a page that educates the customer. Customers appreciate the value. For instance, we sell video editing and production equipment. Our page defines editing, has how-to articles, a video glossary, and more. It makes our page a must-see for someone who is interested in making videos.

We also have fun things (see fig. 33.3), such as a page of television quotes ("The difference between an amateur and a professional is that the amateur shows you all his pictures").

Fig. 33.3 *(See color section.)*

And of course, we have product info (see fig. 33.4), but we don't stop there. We complete the sales cycle with an automated dealer location page, ways to reach us for technical support, information on our seminars, warranty information, and more.

Another thing we do is keep it changing—I try to add or change something every week or two (see fig. 33.5). All this value makes our page something to visit time and time again.

It's an Internet tradition to offer added value by linking to other related locations (see fig. 33.6). Visitors will learn that you are an easy gateway to more information about their own topics.

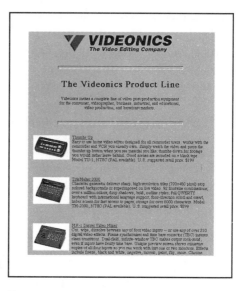

Fig. 33.4 ▲

The product page—important, but maybe not the best draw for attracting potential new customers.

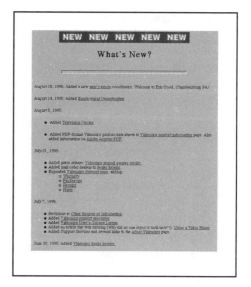

Fig. 33.5 ▲

By regularly freshening the site and promoting the newness to the visitor, you'll encourage return visits.

FIG. 33.6 *(See color section.)*

It's also important to promote the site. The obvious first step is to promote it on the Net by having the site linked in all the indexing services, such as Yahoo and Lycos. We include our Web address on business cards, in ads and newsletters, and in product literature. We encourage present and prospective customers to use the Web for support and information. We even use it internally. When a customer wants a dealer name, I don't use the dealer list—I fire up the Web browser and check our own page!

Much better is to create a page that educates the customer. Customers appreciate the value.

Q So how will you use PageMaker 6.0 to help manage this site?

We should draw a distinction between two Web publishing tasks: the creation of new Web pages and placing existing documents on the Web. Right now, I am using PageMaker only for the latter—for "repurposing" existing PageMaker documents, to get them onto the Web quickly.

Others see the HTML Author Plug-in as a way to make PageMaker into a Web authoring tool. As the plug-in matures from Release 1.0, the one that shipped initially with PageMaker 6.0, I think that will be more and more practical, making PageMaker a tool for creating Web pages from scratch.

Q I think I see where you're headed. There are really two formats Page-Maker users can utilize to approach the Web.

Yes. PageMaker 6.0 provides two new facilities to help make existing PageMaker documents ready for the Web. It is important to understand the difference. Most Web pages are HTML, a format that displays very quickly, but that gives the designer relatively little control of formatting and appearance. This is an unusual situation for designers who are used to having full control. It's a little like e-mail in that the sender controls what is said, but has no idea what font, size, or margins will be seen by the reader.

The second way to place a PageMaker document on the Web is via Acrobat. The advantage of this method is that you truly preserve the look—the designer has full control, and the reader sees the document almost exactly as it looked as a Page-Maker document. The disadvantage is speed—an Acrobat document takes a lot longer for the reader to download.

So Web authors can use HTML for efficiency and Acrobat for appearance control.

Q How do you decide which work path to take—whether to go the Acrobat or HTML route?

As Marshall McLuhan said, the medium is the message. I think the content needs to be adapted to this new medium in most cases—which means redesigning documents using HTML. Web surfing lends itself to looking through vast amounts of information very quickly, stopping to read in detail only when the

A good Web document is concise, with smallish graphics and links to larger graphics, detailed sections, or other information.

right information has been found. A good Web document is concise, with smallish graphics and links to larger graphics, detailed sections, or other information. Existing documents can be the basis, but most of the time, a redesign is in order.

Sometimes I use an existing document rather than Web-izing the information. One reason is that often there is no time to do it any other way! I published all our product data sheets in just a couple of hours by outputting them from PageMaker 6.0 as Acrobat PDFs. I placed the resulting files on a page for people to download and read or print using the Acrobat Reader. I can make HTML versions later, but I know that will take hours to do well. In the meantime, the information is available.

The second reason I leave documents as they are and put them out in PDF format is that they many times are tightly formatted and communicate well as standalone documents. The data sheets are a good example again. Everything is there—product pictures, features, specs, and more. Even after I make HTML versions, I will leave the PDFs there and provide links to either the HTML or the PDF, as customers desire. Customers who want a quick look at the product can grab the HTML. If they decide they want more detail, one click will download the PDF, which they can print. In this case, the Web becomes a delivery medium, and customers end up with the same thing they would have received by mail.

With the Acrobat document, I have control over the presentation, and I get to present a richer-looking document online.

With HTML, the document is more portable and not nearly so modem-intensive if done right, but the presentation varies depending on the whims of viewers who have customized their browsers to their taste.

Q Would you give us a look at how you use PageMaker 6.0's new tools for creating these formats: HTML Author and direct PDF output?

The HTML Author Plug-in helps the designer convert PageMaker documents to HTML. It's very convenient and does a pretty good job of exporting page elements to a new file that is ready for editing using an HTML editing tool. Release 1.0 of the plug-in works pretty well—it nicely exports all the text and adds tags to add the required paragraph return tags, identify headings, and such. It's not perfect, though. I use this to start the job; then I use an HTML editing tool to adjust the results before placing them online. As Adobe continues along this path, I imagine HTML Author will become a very good tool to do most or all of the job right inside PageMaker.

For Acrobat format, I used Adobe Distiller in the past. It is a miraculous solution, but required that I first print as a PostScript file, then run Distiller on that file. With PageMaker 6.0, the intermediate steps are gone. I just invoke the direct PDF output plug-in, and I'm finished. It's a considerable productivity advantage.

Q Because Acrobat documents are not yet directly supported by Web browsers, how do you set up links to them?

This is pretty simple. On the Web site, provide a folder or directory and place the PDF files there. Provide a link to that file. Here is the HTML code I use:

```
===

<H1>Data Sheets (PDF)</H1><P>

Data sheets in <A HREF="About-
Acrobat.html">Adobe Acrobat
PDF format</A> can be down-
loaded. The free Acrobat
Reader is required to read
these. The approximate file
sizes are listed.<P>

<HR>

<A HREF="DS-PDF/SE-1.pdf">SE-1
Sound Effects Mixer (Boing
Box)</A> audio mixer with
digital sound effects.
(145K)<P>

<A HREF="DS-PDF/TU-1.pdf">TU-1
Thumbs Up</A> home video
editor. (60K)<P>

<A HREF="DS-PDF/TM-
2000.pdf">TM-2000 TitleMaker
2000</A> video character
generator. (50K)<P>

<A HREF="DS-PDF/MX-1 data
sheet.pdf">MX-1 Digital Video
Mixer</A> video mixer, effects
generator, and chroma key
unit. (77K)<P>

<A HREF="DS-PDF/AB-1.pdf">AB-1
Edit Suite</A> edit control-
ler. (94K)<P>

<A HREF="DS-PDF/PS-
1000.pdf">PS-1000
PowerScript</A> PostScript
animated character generator.
(85K)<P>

<A HREF="DS-PDF/VP-1.pdf">VP-1
Video Palette</A> TBC/video
processor and analyzer.
(68K)<P>

<HR>

<H1>Photos of Products </H1>

Click on small pictures to see
a large photo of the product:
```

```
<P>

<hr size=8 width=70%><P>

<body>

<a href="Graphics/products/TU-
1-500.jpeg"><IMG hspace=7
SRC="Graphics/products/TU-1-
100.jpeg">

Thumbs Up (30K)</a><P><BR>

((((...etc. Pics of other
products follow.))))
```

▽ Link to About-Acrobat page. I have a page that describes Acrobat. It, in turn, links to the Adobe home page to allow download of Acrobat Reader.

▽ File sizes.way people know what kind of wait is coming.

▽ Following PDFs, I have small product photos. Users can click on those to see full-size photos. Fun with JPEG, you know. Eventually, I will also have HTML versions for those who wish to read online.

When the user clicks on these links, the appropriate file downloads, and the user can then open it with the Acrobat Reader. A user can configure the browser to open it immediately, as well. In future browsers, Acrobat Reader will be fully integrated, so PDF will become an even better method—although it has the disadvantage that the files tend to be much bigger than GIFs or JPEGs.

Q You were saying that you tend to do some additional work on a page after your initial processing run-in PageMaker and HTML Author. What kind of things need to be done?

Because PageMaker is so much richer than HTML, the HTML Author Plug-in must

> *The problem is that PageMaker files generally contain EPS and TIFF graphics. But the Web requires GIF and JPEG.*

make some assumptions about formatting. This usually requires some general tidying afterwards. In addition, I always need to do some work with the graphics.

The problem is that PageMaker files generally contain EPS and TIFF graphics. Those are standard for desktop publishing on paper. But the Web requires GIF and JPEG. So you must convert the graphics outside PageMaker.

If you have the original graphics handy, Photoshop is probably the tool of choice. Adobe's ScreenReady may end up being the ultimate tool as it would image the PostScript for you, turning it into one of the bitmapped graphic formats you need for display on the Web.

Believe it or not though, the main toolkit I use right now is a combination of Distiller, Reader, and FlashIt (my screen capture program of choice). One good way to get PageMaker graphics to the Web is to distill the PageMaker file. Then open it in Reader. Then capture a screen shot of the graphic as PICT. Use Clip2GIF or Transparency to make the file into a GIF. Or, use Photoshop to go to JPEG. Kludge? You bet. But it works, and it's quite fast.

Q. **What other tools do Web construction meisters need to have handy, assuming they are like you and are focused around PageMaker 6.0 in one way or another?**

Here are the tools I use constantly. Note that I work on a Macintosh, and there are roughly comparable tools available for Windows and UNIX.

Clip-2-GIF is one of these tools, and, to a somewhat lesser extent, GraphicConverter. For making GIFs transparent, there's Transparency and also a new shareware Photoshop filter called PhotoGIF that sounds wonderful. Adobe has made a GIFF89 Plug-in available online at no charge, and it also performs this function.

Adobe's PageMill, just being released as this book is going to press, is very cool. PageMill is a WYSIWYG editor. You never see HTML code. Instead, you see the page pretty much as it would look in a browser. To bold something, you highlight it and press a key or use the menu. You can bring in graphics directly, and PageMill converts certain types to GIF for you, also letting you set transparency. To establish a link, you highlight the location and select the link from a list. HTML Web Weaver is another serviceable HTML editor. It is by no means perfect, but until PageMill, I used it any time I was post-processing a Page-Maker-generated HTML file.

SiteMill maintains links. If you change a file name, SiteMill tracks where that file is used and changes the HTML in all files that refer to it. You can reorganize your folders, and all the links will be updated automatically. RTFtoHTML does a good job of generating HTML from any word processor or desktop publishing program that can export text files in Rich Text Format.

And of course, there's PageMaker's HTML Author Plug-in.

These tools are rapidly changing, and designers would be wise to prowl the Web for the latest. Almost all my tools right now are shareware or freeware, but several commercial products such as Adobe PageMill and SiteMill are arriving, and I am adopting them as they become available.

Q You mentioned using the program Transparency as one of your tools. Why do we want GIFs to be transparent? What's the application?

Transparency in a GIF means that one color is designated as transparent, and all pixels of that color are rendered transparent. The background shows through anywhere the original graphic used that precise color.

Have a look at the film-can icons on my home page, and you'll see. The film cans look like discrete objects, instead of looking like film cans that have been placed on the page in little boxes. A round button should look round rather than like a round button on a square tile.

The alternative would be to place the button on a field that is the same color as the background—but a browser user may change the background color. Also, backgrounds can be patterns, and irregular objects would not look right without transparency.

Q Let's go back to the GIF and JPEG graphics issue. If all these EPS and TIFF graphics need to be converted, which is the best format between the two? How do you choose?

This is a common question for Web authors, and even pretty experienced ones don't know all the trade-offs.

The two are useful for different things. I use GIF most of the time. All browsers support GIF graphics, but most also support JPEG.

GIFs can be interlaced. They can be assigned a transparency. They are supported by all browsers. GIF compression is lossless (no artifacts or fringes).

Use GIFs for non-continuous tone graphics or those with 256 colors. Its lossless compression will make the resulting graphic sharper and more accurate, with no fringes or other artifacts. Use GIFs for small graphics, especially icons. Use GIFs where transparency is needed.

JPEG images can support a higher bit depth (24-bit, while GIFs are restricted to 8-bit). This means better quality for continuous tone graphics, especially photos. JPEGs tend to be much smaller. You can control degree of compression and thus control the trade-off between size and quality.

In general, use JPEGs for continuous tone images (for example, photos or graphics that use widely graduated color sweeps). Its support for 24-bit color means these color ranges will be accurately portrayed; whereas GIFs, with their 8-bit restriction, would have to be dithered. Large photos are almost certainly better as JPEGs.

To see a GIF versus JPEG example, check out **http://www.acxes.com/hm/photo.html**. (Giving credit where credit is due, bits of what I've just said comes compliments of Chris Stone, whom you can reach at **cjstone@cmu.edu**.)

Putting PageMaker 6.0 to Work

Online Professional Panel

WHAT ARE THE TEN most valuable new features for designers working in PageMaker 6.0?

This one seemingly simple question grew like Jack's beanstalk into a discussion of work methods to achieve maximum efficiency and effectiveness from PageMaker 6.0's enhancements. In fact, it quickly grew into a chapter all of its own—one that was written entirely online by the participants in a unique round-table—and discusses far more than ten features.

All the members of this special on-line professional panel are daily participants in the DTP forum (**GO DTPFORUM**) and the official Adobe Applications forum (**GO ADOBEAPP**) on CompuServe. In fact, that's where I first met them! You will find an expression of my gratitude in the front pages of this book, for they contributed to far more than this chapter by many weeks of support and exploration. They are true collaborators, one and all.

▶ *Kathleen Tinkel*, a long-time graphic designer, has used PageMaker since Version 1.2. She now spends most of her time writing about graphic design and computers for computer, prepress/publishing, and graphic arts magazines (*MacUser*, *MacWeek*, *Publish*, *Adobe Magazine*, and *Step-by-Step Graphics* and the companion *Electronic Design* newsletter). She's also a sysop on the DTP forums on CompuServe—the virtual saloon on the frontier in this business.

▶ *Phil Gaskill* is a New York freelancer focusing on textbook production. He has produced books for many major book publishers. Prior to moving to New York, and prior to the Aldus/Adobe merger, he worked at Aldus for four years, first in technical support and then as a technical writer, finishing as the PageMaker engineering writer. He has been published in several magazines, including *Aldus/Adobe Magazine* and *MacUser*. He was the technical editor of *Real World PageMaker 5*; and he was the coauthor of *QuarkXPress Tips and Tricks*, 2nd edition. He is a sysop on the Adobe CompuServe forums, where he contributes often on one of his favorite subjects—fine typography.

▶ *Jim Dornbos* is president of Dorbos Press, Inc., a commercial printing company located in Saginaw, Michigan. DPI serves quality-oriented business customers with hardware and software consulting, typesetting production, hi-res imagesetter output with stochastic screening capabilities, color copier prints and transparencies, sheet-fed offset printing, and a complete letterpress department for specialities such as embossing, die-cutting, and foil stamping. Jim has been involved in the printing industry for the past 20 years and has been working with computers for the past ten years. After hours, you may find Jim flying the skies of Aries' Air Warrior, a multiplayer flight combat game available on the Internet. Look for Rocket on your 6!

▶ *Dave Saunders* has been using computers since the mid-60s, starting as a programmer for a UK air defense company. He came to New Jersey in the mid-70s as an operating system programmer. He transitioned to product management and marketing of software, and from there to product marketing. Here he first encountered the Mac (when it was still called Lisa). In 1990, he started his own desktop publishing company, with PageMaker at the center of his operations. Working with his wife, a proofreader and indexer, under the name PDS Associates, he now focuses on production of technical textbooks for book packagers, and various marketing collateral and newsletters for local clients.

▶ *Ray Robertson* says he's a proud resident of the small town of Cartersville,

Georgia. He is systems manager for Type Solutions, Inc., a graphic design firm in Atlanta that still provides traditional typography in addition to DTP training and service bureau work. With a background as a computer typesetter, Ray began working on a Mac Plus in 1986, and was appalled at the lack of keyboard shortcuts. That's why he's one of the ranking experts on QuicKeys, a Macintosh shortcut utility, and has delved deeply into PageMaker's native scripting language. He's the real star in the chapter that contains most of the scripting information—Chapter 28, "Automating PageMaker." That's also where I've dedicated a small bronze plaque on which you will find him more fully described—with thanks for his invaluable help.

In addition to the participants directly quoted here in this chapter, these people also contributed to the discussion:

▶ *Moe Rubenzahl* frequently tuned in to the discussion in the weeks of development of the book, and of PageMaker 6.0. His special knowledge of graphic arts as they relate to the Internet has been explored in Chapter 33, "Designing for the Web."

▶ *J.B. Whitwell* managed admission to the online discussion circle and pitched in where she could, given her wider duties as a volunteer administrator of the Adobe Forum on CompuServe. Anybody who has ever asked for help in the DTP Forum or Adobe Applications Forum has known J.B.'s gentle and authoritative helping hand.

▶ *John Cornicello* participated daily in this round table as Adobe's online coordinator and Wizop of the Adobe forums on CompuServe. John didn't just chip in when appropriate to give a poke or nudge to this chapter. He has put his stamp on this entire book as tech editor and general all-around guardian of quality assurance.

Q **No area of PageMaker has seen as much change as its capabilities to organize objects on pages. Layout power was a primary point of discussion during the weeks of preparation for the release of PageMaker 6.0.**

Dave: Grouping is nice, as is masking. Grouping a graphic with its caption facilitates moving them around together.

Phil: Yes to Group, and to Lock as well. Lock keeps things from accidentally getting moved. Say you're laboriously building a table manually, with rules and stuff. You might want to lock that all in place, either while you're still working on building it, or at least afterward so it doesn't get bumped while you (or someone else) is doing other paging or editing.

Kathleen: Alignment and distribution, finally. Bizarrely missing for all these years, the Alignment function now lets us center something on a page or in a column, align objects on edges or centers, and do all those other things that designers must do but have been forced to do by fakery and workaround until now.

Phil: And I agree. With Align/Distribute, we can now tell PageMaker, "Align these two objects along their left edges," or "Center this text on this graphic," or "Separate these six objects by exactly 1p7.4." It's a very powerful feature.

Jim: Masking is really a hot one for us. We've been doing a weekly real estate publication and for several of the ads they want round-cornered photos. After screwing around with a couple of workarounds to accomplish that, we moved the publication to PageMaker 6.0—and those ads have been a breeze ever since.

> *Bizarrely missing for all these years, the alignment function now lets us center something on a page or in a column, align objects on edges or centers...*

Ray: I have no doubt masking should be the number one item in a PageMaker 6.0 Top Ten. At first, I thought masking was just a workaround for handling frames and pictures like Quark, and fell short of the mark in some ways. Now, I realize that in other ways it is much, much more than what I can do in XPress.

For example, we can mask text. Maybe we don't do this every day, but the ability to show half a type character as a design element is very nice. In the past, I could not have done this in Page-Maker or Quark, unless I had no background and could use a white box. I would have to resort to one of the drawing programs with the Paste Inside feature. Now this can be done right in PageMaker. Not only that, but I can mask duplicate lines of type, show the top half of the type in one color, and the bottom half in another color. The type can even be trapped (something that could not have been done with an external EPS graphic).

> *I have no doubt masking should be the number one item in a PageMaker 6.0 Top Ten.*

Also, say I want to show a circle cut out of a bunch of type as a design element. Do I do a weird runaround or something? No, now I can just simply mask the type in a circle and get the same design effect.

Masking multiple objects: one frequent quandary of Quark users is, "Why can't we import two graphics into the same picture box?" With masking in PageMaker, we can now put as many objects as we want into the same frame, maybe with some fully included and others cut off at the edges. Not only that, but I can mask all types of graphics and text, all within one mask.

Using it as Paste Inside: ever have to fiddle with a table in PageMaker? I'm sure people will still have to do this, even with the Adobe Table available. Making sure all rules are aligned at top and stretched to fit the bottom exactly (and the same for left and right) is a difficult, tedious task. Now, all I have to do is draw all rules to an extreme depth or width, and then mask them within the surrounding box. Wow!

I can also do simple maps within PageMaker now. A 20-degree rule can be correctly cut off at the edge of the border by masking it. In extreme cases, I could even make some rules look curved by putting a section of a large circle within the mask. Two rules can be made to look joined perfectly at a mitered corner, because in fact they are part of a masked corner from a rectangle.

Weird shapes: we could go absolutely crazy creating weird elements with masking, maybe to the point of driving service bureaus crazy if the files won't RIP out! Try creating a starburst polygon and then masking it with a circle. Try masking the intersection of two overlapping circles with another circle. Neat!

Phil: Multiple master pages will be a major help. Think of a book, where the first page of each chapter has a different layout than the other pages. Also, the end stuff in a chapter might be different, too, if there are notes or references or the like. Multiple master pages allows you to have a master page for each scenario you'll encounter.

Weird shapes: We could go absolutely crazy creating weird elements with masking…

Kathleen: Adobe's manuals do seem to imply that this would be of use only in very complex documents, but in fact they seem teasingly useful to me for all sorts of things. For example, I like to use bars of gray or color as edge guides for different sections in a book. Before I had to create a new document for each section even if it had only a few pages (or add the color strip on each spread by hand). Now I can use master pages to apply the bars.

I will often cheat in the centerfold of a newspaper by using the whole page (no inner gutter, in other words, or only a small one for the fold). Now I can set up a master layout just for that spread because multiple master pages can include different outer margins. The obvious use—to have a special master for chapter openers—is also wonderful.

Multiple master pages allows you to have a master page for each scenario you'll encounter.

📖 Q **One of the most widely publicized PageMaker 6.0 improvement areas has been its handling of color. Read on to find out how our online designer panel feels about the implementation of these features.**

Dave: Color facilities in general are much nicer, especially the ability to specify tints whenever you like, and to choose whether to import process color names. The ability to delete unused colors is great (I wish there were some way to highlight unused styles).

Jim: About the command to remove unused colors, Adobe continues to show support for commercial printers and service bureaus by building in features that are most useful for the folks who have to produce the final output. They show that it's not just a feature list item by thoughtfully putting it not only in the Define Colors dialog, but also in the Print Colors dialog box, which is where I'll probably make major use of it.

PageMaker has, for some time, had excellent spot color handling. The ability to redefine a color as tint of another has

The ability to delete unused colors is great (I wish there were some way to highlight unused styles).

been a great help with misnamed, but equal, colors. TrapMaker built in gives PageMaker a strong trapping tool for multicolor jobs. Now they've added the ability to manage RGB images—which was always a problem for all players in the past. You can't easily tell it's an RGB image until you print it and find out it's sep'ing out incorrectly.

By choosing color profiles that are close to or match your actual devices, you can produce very good color with very little effort. Watch out, though. Some of the Generic color profiles, as you might expect, produce generic-looking color seps.

Dave: The fact that the colors that come off my printer are close to what I see on-screen is little short of magnificent. But I'd still like to be able to make a specific calibration setup for my printer.

TrapMaker built in gives PageMaker a strong trapping tool for multicolor jobs. Now they've added the ability to manage RGB images—which was always a problem for all players in the past.

Jim: Right. The remaining downside of the color management stuff is that it still doesn't seem to acknowledge that my GTO 4 color does not print exactly like the same model GTO 4 color that my competitor uses. My Canon 700 does not print exactly like the Canon 700 that my competitor uses. My Deskjet 550 doesn't print exactly like yours…and on and on. The current color management stuff gets you close—but people need to understand that there are limitations and it is not the final version of what Color Management really needs to look like.

What it needs to be is kind of like handing out a PPD for my Lino that reflects its specific, customized capabilities. I need the ability to produce a color profile for my GTO or my CLC 700 that I can give to customers to plug into PageMaker. Then their versions of PageMaker know how to display the image on-screen to reflect how my equipment will reproduce it.

Pantone Hexachrome support makes high-fidelity color available to the masses. While the great majority of folks won't get a chance to use this feature, PageMaker 6.0 is the first mainstream application to let us make good use of our ability to run stochastic screening.

Customers give me a transparency or an RGB scan and say, "Print this." In the past, they then ask, "Why did my colors go flat? Why didn't the proof 'pop' like the original?"

The answer used to be the limitations of the CMYK color gamut. The answer now is, if you're very concerned about color matching, or we find that the furnished transparencies are suitable, we can suggest hi-fi color as an alternative to give the printed piece more vibrancy and reproduce a wider range of colors than previously available—as long as you did your job in PageMaker.

Pantone Hexachrome support makes high-fidelity color available to the masses.

And now there's integrated trapping—PC and Mac! The computer that I do most of my work on is a PC, although by necessity I work on both because as a commercial printer and service bureau we must work with anything. I've been impressed all along with the quality of traps produced by the TrapMaker Addition introduced for Version 5.0 of Macintosh PageMaker. There were severe constraints put on the fellow who originally made the addition, and it still did a great job. With TrapMaker now built right into PageMaker, I expect it to work better still. And I'm pleased to see it now on both platforms instead of just on the Mac side.

Ⅰ Q. Those who design large projects, involving lots of text that may need to be cleaned up or otherwise massaged, had a lot to say about PageMaker 6.0's

scripting, tagging, and enhanced search and replace capabilities.

Phil: Real tags are going to be a big help. Being able to do advanced search and replace on a formatted text file offers *many* more possibilities than the previous route of editing only in Word for direct import into PageMaker.

Kathleen: PageMaker Tags allow it to compete with XPress in the automation game. It was silly before—PageMaker had the better long-document tools in general but XPress had flexible tagging, so it got a lot of that work regardless of which tool the user preferred.

Enhanced search and replace will also be very helpful. The ability to Copy/Paste into the dialogs was inevitable—late, but gratefully received. And the addition of Set Width to the attributes you can search for or replace was a stroke of genius.

Dave: Yes, the reorganized Find and Change dialog is nice—the new way that attributes are handled, dividing text attributes and paragraph attributes. And, of course, what's most important is that there are so many more things you can search for. For example, as Kathleen says, the

> *PageMaker Tags allow it to compete with XPress in the automation game.*

ability to search for every space in a selection that has a set width of 100 percent and replace with spaces set at 90 percent.

Kathleen: Being able to script the Story Editor—there's another productivity enhancement.

Dave: The ability to script Find and Change is marvelous. I have this idea for a script and maybe Ray will work on it. Basically, in laying out books, I often get into the situation where I need to squeeze some space out of a single line in a paragraph. A good way to do this is to shorten the word spacing for just that stretch of text. And the best way to do that is to change the

> *...the addition of Set Width to the attributes you can search for or replace was a stroke of genius.*

width of the space bands. You could do that with a script, and apply the change to selected text by double-clicking on that item in the Script palette.

Q **Several enhancements have been made to PageMaker's printing capabilities, including the ability to quickly set up standard printing routines, or styles, and to print side-by-side "reader spreads."**

Kathleen: For output services (and for users), restoring the ability to query

> *The ability to script Find and Change is marvelous.*

the printer will make an enormous difference—in the past, the need to set up precisely accurate PPDs was a disaster. Direct support for Scitex CT, DCS 2.0, and JPEG will make it easier for output operators to control work flow, especially in a mixed (for example, Scitex/desktop) operation.

The alert that warns of missing fonts in placed EPS files is also great. And an effective Printer Styles function should save some wasted output—those reduced pages, missing crop marks, and wrong PPD situations.

Phil: Right. Printer styles are now an actual menu item. We all know about the printer styles, don't we? Very handy things. I use 'em in QuarkPrint all the time; couldn't live without 'em. Now they're in PageMaker for real.

The ability to print a reader spread—on paper big enough, of course—is something PageMaker has always lacked, unless the Manual-Tile workaround worked, which it didn't always do.

Dave: Last evening, after I turned in my first Top Ten list, I realized I'd failed to include one of PageMaker 6.0's really neat features: the fact that it checks EPS files to make sure that the fonts you need are loaded. Wonderful!

When I get a job ready for the service bureau, I might have hundreds of EPS files. So, with this feature I can organize my fonts so that I have only the ones I think are used opened, then print. If I've missed any fonts, this feature will tell me.

Right, printer styles are now an actual menu item…very handy things… couldn't live without 'em…

The Features part of the Print dialog box is great for my HP 560C. I had to really screw around to print to it from PageMaker 5.0 via HP's PostScript software. Now I just choose the options I want. You get to choose the type of paper, quality of the print job, density of the ink, how long to wait between pages (to allow the ink to dry). These are now available via the Features panel. With PageMaker 5.0, you had to write your own ALBEFORE.PS file.

Q PageMaker has for some time been able to import a variety of file formats, and this capability has been extended in several important ways.

Kathleen: The new Photo CD import filter will help many people who use this technology. It has the capability to acquire, sharpen, and color-manage Photo CD images without leaving PageMaker. It's almost as powerful and flexible as PhotoShop, and should go a long way toward improving photos for the many users who don't invest in PhotoShop (and any users who believe PCD images ought to be ready to go straight from the disc).

Dave: The ability to save in PageMaker 5.0 format is nice—it will save a whole slew of complaints on the forum!

Jim: Save As PageMaker 5.0 was very useful in the early days while PageMaker 6.0 was in beta, but will also be a great feature—one that's lacking from Quark—even after PageMaker 6.0 is released. There are always those folks out there who don't upgrade for six months or so and this allows us to keep them happy, while still using the version that's best for us. Of course, saving in Version 5.0 form will cause the loss of such Version 6.0 features as masking and grouping.

Kathleen: Smoother compatibility will help in the transition as well, like the gradual segue toward common controls in Illustrator, PageMaker, and PhotoShop. It's also nice to have an XPress converter and access to some PhotoShop plug-ins.

The Adobe Table utility also is a good enhancement. The ability to add colors to the table would be nice, as would be a more accessible interface (I'd like it to look and work a lot more like Excel, in fact). While it is still far from the table-building facility in FrameMaker with its straddle heads and other niceties, it's great to have any method, even a stand-alone, that outputs an EPS file instead of a PICT and that provides for most useful controls over the type, at least.

Q **No matter how fancy the feature list gets, often the most important aspect of a program are little things that you spend all day with—the details of the user interface.**

Dave: They used a small font in the palettes. I begged for that for PageMaker 5.0 but it was too late, so I'm glad to see it here. Not only that, the palettes remember where you left them!

Phil: Yes, I agree that is a good one, that palettes stay where you put 'em from work session to work session.

Also, baseline leading has been fixed. This was the screen-draw problem, where your descenders disappeared until you made the screen redraw. Major hassle: enough to cause almost everybody to not use baseline leading. Now it's fixed: Hallelujah!

Kathleen: Guide Manager. Hurrah, hurray—at last there's a logical and easy way to use a Swiss grid system in Page-Maker for all the dinosaur designers who still rely on them. Once again we can spec (think of) type in terms of size/leading/measure as we always did before DTP came along, because you can define columns by width directly, not only by adding and subtracting crazy numbers to arrive at margin widths.

…baseline leading has been fixed… Hallelujah!

PART X

Appendixes

A ▲ Installation

B ▲ Rescue!

C ▲ Keyboard Shortcuts

D ▲ New Tagging Language

E ▲ Resource Guide

F ▲ What's on the CD?

Appendix A

Installation

FIRST, LET'S TALK about system requirements—
what you absolutely must have as well as what
you really should have. Then we will move on to
the actual installation. ▶ ▶ ▶

System Requirements

What is the lowest-level machine that can run PageMaker? You can run it on a 486 machine, although something with a bit more zip is recommended. At least a VGA display will be required, although you will be a more successful (and certainly a more efficient) designer if you have a higher resolution display.

Official Specifications

Here are the *minimum* and recommended requirements published by Adobe for a Windows 95 setup:

▶ 486 processor, Pentium recommended

▶ Windows 95

▶ 8M of RAM, recommended 16M (assuming you use the default settings for virtual memory and have color management turned off)

▶ At least 24M of available hard disk space for installation, 40M recommended, plus an additional minimum of 25M of hard drive space for virtual memory, 50M recommended

▶ VGA display, recommended high-resolution 24-bit or greater Super VGA or XGA

▶ High-density floppy drive, CD-ROM recommended

▶ Mouse or other pointer

You can run PageMaker 6.0 as a 32-bit application under Windows 3.1, and here are the *minimum* and recommended requirements for that kind of setup:

▶ 486 processor, Pentium recommended

▶ Windows 3.1 with Win32s installed (Win32s 1.30a Dynamic Link Libraries come with PageMaker); PageMaker requires 1.30a or later (preferably Version 1.30a-167)

▶ 10M of RAM, recommended 16M

▶ At least 24M of available hard disk space for installation, 40M recommended

▶ VGA display, recommended high-resolution 24-bit or greater Super VGA or XGA

▶ High-density floppy drive, CD-ROM recommended

▶ Mouse or other pointer

TIP ▶ Butcher That RAM Hog!

PageMaker 6.0 takes a lot of RAM; there's no doubt about it. It's a big graphics program, after all. Unfortunately, the requirements are right on the cusp of what you might call the "natural" break points for installed RAM. A lot of people who bought machines with 8M RAM are just short enough on chips to make this RAM situation particularly frustrating.

You can do one thing to reduce RAM requirements by about 2M. Turn off the color management. Set it off by default by starting PageMaker with no document open and going to Preferences. Make sure Color Management is off, which it should be by default anyway.

Making Yourself More Efficient

If you are using PageMaker in a business environment, you really should consider doing whatever it takes to optimize your hardware. It's not just PageMaker. It's all the other graphics programs you are likely to be working with as you produce your pages—Photoshop, Illustrator, FreeHand. All these graphics programs seem to suck up computing power, kind of like a black hole. And when you are on deadline, it's best to avoid black holes.

Working with a color monitor is best. If you can't afford a color monitor and will be working with photographic material or anything more than line art, at least get a grayscale monitor.

A two-page display, especially if it's color, is very helpful. Fortunately, prices continue to drop, so this is less painful than it used to be.

Get the biggest hard disk you can manage. In the last edition, I suggested that 1/2G wouldn't be too much. Now the standard has reached a full gigabyte.

RAM? Well, RAM is like money. You can never have too much of it. If possible, exceed the requirements listed previously, especially if you will be using Photoshop.

Installing PageMaker

It's almost embarrassing to give instructions for such an easy installation process. That's one of the reasons the information resides here in an appendix.

PageMaker 6.0's CD-ROM has a Windows 95 AUTOSTART file on it. So when you put the CD in and close the drive door on the CD, it will launch an introduction screen from which you can install PageMaker 6.0, ATM 3, Photoshop LE, Acrobat Distiller PE, and view the multimedia "welcome" tour or other information files.

This is only a Windows 95 feature. Refer to the "Getting Started" manual that comes with PageMaker 6.0.

> **TIP** ▶ **The Shift Key Can Save You Time**
>
> You can prevent the AUTOSTART file from running if you hold down the Shift key as you insert the CD-ROM.

Installation Options

Once you begin the installation process, you will have three basic options to choose from (see table A.1).

TABLE A.1   Installation Choices

Option	What You Get
Easy Install	This option takes over and does a maximum installation of the basic program, including Adobe Table, Kodak Precision Color Management System, the Plug-ins that come with the program, import filters for graphics and text, the tutorial and sample files, templates, color libraries, and utilities.
	If you have the Deluxe CD-ROM version, the Easy Install will load you up with all the goodies, including Acrobat Reader and Distiller.
Minimum Install	This option allows you to install the bare minimum set of files needed to run PageMaker—good for installing on a laptop computer, for example.
Custom Install	Using this option, you can choose among all the files that come with PageMaker. You can custom design your initial installation or use this option for an after-the-fact installation of filters or other items that you decided not to include in your initial installation.

Performing the Installation

The following list includes the basic steps for getting PageMaker 6.0 onto your hard disk and ready to roll (along with some advice about managing the changeover process if you are upgrading from Version 5.0):

1. Start clean. Shut down any applications that are running and turn off any virus detection.

> **TIP** ▶ **Use the Special Upgrade Tool to Save Your 5.0 Settings**
>
> Take special note: Version 6.0 ships with a utility to convert many of your customized PageMaker 5.0 materials to be used with PageMaker 6.0. Run the utility after you complete this installation process.

Also, note that PageMaker 6.0 has significantly changed its file location setup. Almost everything in Version 6.0 will be stored right in the application folder, making it a lot easier to have two versions of PageMaker installed at the same time, and easier to manage the complex number of supporting files PageMaker 6.0 uses to achieve its power. This also will help the installation run smoother on networks.

2. Preserve your older versions of PageMaker, in any case, whether you will keep PageMaker 5.0 installed or not. Collect them all, because the company has a policy, maintained again with this latest upgrade of making new versions of PageMaker compatible with the previous version only. In other words, you can convert your 4.0 and 5.0 files with 6.0, but 6.0 can't read your older files. You never know when you will need to breathe new life into a publication you did a few years back with an older version of PageMaker.

   If you have not kept old versions, there is help for you because Adobe makes available a special conversion utility that will convert 3.0 files into a format that more recent versions of PageMaker can read. The converter is on the PageMaker CD-ROM in the TECHINFO folder.

   It's a good sign for the future that PageMaker 6.0, for the first time, will have some new backware compatibility, because it will save in the 5.0 format.

3. Begin with Disk One—or your CD-ROM! PageMaker has been available for some time now in both floppy and deluxe CD-ROM versions.

   If you do not have a CD-ROM drive, as you might expect, begin the installation process by slipping Disk One into your floppy drive.

   Whichever media you are using, start the Install program. (You might, for example, use the Run command from the Start button and use Browse to locate the install file on your floppy or CD-ROM.) On the CD, the Installer is in \PM6\DO (PM6SETUP.EXE).

4. Choose installation options. You will have a series of choices to make before the installation begins in earnest.

   Choose your language when prompted to do so.

   From a pop-up menu, you have a choice to make from the three options already described in the previous section. You can perform an Easy Install, a Minimum Install, or a Custom Install. There's also a button to allow you to change the folder where PageMaker will be installed.

   Then you reach the main window of the installation program.

5. Next, you need to provide the serial number of your PageMaker package. You'll find it on your disks and on a sheet of stickers that comes inside your envelope of disks. The installer also asks for your name and company, but the serial number's the main thing.

TIP ▶   **Uprading Your PageMaker Serial Number**

An upgrade does *not* come with a new PageMaker serial number. Use the old number from your previous version. There will be a READ THIS FIRST card in the package that has the serial numbers for Photoshop LE and Distiller PE. These will be needed if you install these programs.

---

6. Choose from the list of filters the ones you will need for your page assembly tasks. The choices include a wide variety of word processor and graphics formats you may need to import into your PageMaker publications.

7. Now select which dictionaries you would like to have installed for use in PageMaker. You can select just one or you can pick several. Remember that PageMaker allows you to establish a dictionary on a paragraph-by-paragraph basis. Depending on the content of your publications, it may make perfect sense to install more than one dictionary.

8. Assuming you will be using a PostScript printer, pick the PostScript Printer Description (PPD) files you will be needing. Click the first one you want and then you can choose multiple files by holding down the Ctrl key while clicking your additional choices.

   If you are installing from the Deluxe CD-ROM version of PageMaker 6.0 that came in your package, don't forget to select the PPD for Acrobat Distiller, or you won't be able to use that program for your electronic publishing.

   If you don't find your printer on this list, it's possible that you will need to contact the manufacturer for help in obtaining a PPD. Also, it may be that your printer doesn't have PostScript capability and therefore wouldn't be included on this list of PostScript Printer Description files.

   As the Windows 95 program from Microsoft does not have a very large variety of PS printers in its install routine, PageMaker has included PPD an INF files to help with this situation. After installing PageMaker 6, run the Windows 95 printer Installer Wizard and if your printer is not listed, click the Have Disk button and navigate to the PM6/RSRC/USENGLSH/PPD4 folder and select the PM6PRINT.INF file. You will find more printers listed here that can be installed via this INF file and the PPD you should have selected during the installation. If your printer isn't listed here, you can also go the the Adobe web page (**www.adobe.com**) and check through a list of additional INF/PPD files available for downloading.

9. Next, choose the device profiles for the Kodak Color Management System that has been built into PageMaker. My advice is to pick them all unless you are sure that you won't ever be receiving input from or sending output to any of the items on this list.

10. PageMaker will tell you if you have selected more options than you have space for on your hard disk. You may need to go to a custom installation to try to save space by putting your options on a slimming diet.

11. The floppy version of PageMaker's installation comes on a number of disks. You'll need to feed them into your floppy drive as they are requested by the installer.

    If you have the CD-ROM, go get a cup of joe and relax for a few minutes while all the work is done for you.

12. When the installer lets you know it's done...well, you're done! Just re-activate any programs or utilities that you might have shut down for the install process (antivirus program, for example). You'll probably need to restart your machine to get them back up and running.

13. PageMaker will give you the opportunity to register in several different ways. You can cancel if you are reinstalling and have already registered. But if you haven't registered yet, do it. It's one of the best ways to get information about program and filter updates. Don't forget to say you want to get Adobe Magazine. It's a great source of information about PageMaker and about other important desktop publishing tools, including Adobe PostScript fonts.

    If you have a modem, the easiest option is probably the online registration. You can also have the registration program print out a form that you can mail in to Adobe.

14. Take a moment to go through the ReadMe information included in the installation. The ReadMe files include last-minute news, and it's the natural order of the universe that information that didn't make the printed documentation is exactly the information you need to save yourself from a nuclear meltdown.

Appendix B

Rescue!

LIKE MANY, IF not all, software packages, PageMaker is most likely to choke when you have the most at stake. It's the perversity of computers in modern life. Voodoo meets high tech. Well, that siren you hear as you enter this appendix is not because you were speeding on the fabled Information Superhighway. It's the response to your 911 call. It's rescue for when PageMaker goes bad. ▶ ▶ ▶

Preventing Problems In the First Place

The best route to rescue? Stay out of harm's way in the first place. This list sums up a conservative approach to working with PageMaker:

Break the Book into Pieces

It's a basic fact of life for any computer program. The bigger the files, the harder you are stretching the software—and the more you have at risk if anything does go bad. The feature chart might say you can do 999 pages in PageMaker, but that's no reason to try it. Break your publication into chapter-size bites and use the Book command. You'll work more efficiently in chapter-size chunks anyway, because the program won't be churning so hard to manage all those pages, and you'll be able to navigate the document much faster.

Along the same lines, there is a practical limit to the number and size of files you can store in PageMaker. The Feature chart says you are only limited by your memory, but once again that's no reason to tiptoe on the edge of disaster. Use the linking capability of PageMaker and store large graphics files on your hard disk where PageMaker can find them. There's no need to have your graphics elements stored completely inside PageMaker as well as on your hard disk.

Take It Easy on Resources

Here's a related axiom to "The bigger the files, the harder you are stretching the software." Danger increases in direct proportion to your proximity to the edge of your computer resources. If you try to work in a low memory situation or with little head room on your hard disk, you're asking for trouble because you leave little room for error. Likewise, if you are having repeated crashes—perhaps because of conflicts with TSR utilities or device drivers, or problems in your SCSI chain—you are bound to trigger file corruption problems for whatever publications you happen to be working in at the time of a crash.

Use Save As or Save Smaller

Before shutting down from a session, use the Save As command. Saving your publication under a new version name gives you a backup of sorts.

The Save As command (or the Save Smaller option in Preferences) reduces your publication to its smallest possible disk size and cleans up (to some extent) any problems caused by the mini-saves that temporarily bloat a working PageMaker file.

Edit Asterisked Styles

When you Place a word processor file, you bring in new paragraph styles in the process. The imported style definitions are marked with an asterisk in the Style palette. This marking convention indicates that PageMaker hasn't fully digested them. Ctrl+click each one (or double-click in Style definition) and click OK to give PageMaker a chance to store that new style in its optimum form.

Stick with EPS and TIFF

PageMaker can import armloads of different graphic file types. However, the conservative approach, and the one that will help you avoid troubles at service bureau output time, is to use only EPS and TIFF files for graphics. These are the most robust file formats you have available to you, and they are the ones most likely to be widely accommodated by any service bureau environment.

Use Place and Link

Rely on PageMaker's Place and Link technology. OLE, so familiar in other Windows applications, must seem like an obvious and convenient mechanism to build a workgroup publishing environment or to expand the capabilities of your one-person PageMaker publishing system. As tempting as OLE may be, use Place and Link anyway. Place and Link follows a standard workflow path, one that everyone in the DTP world has worked with for years. Place and Link also make your publication independent from supporting publications, a stand-alone and less complicated environment, and the stronger for it, too.

Ohmigosh, Back Up!

This should have been the first step, but you knew that already, right? If you do frequent backups, you will never have to worry about losing the manuscript for your Great American Novel when PageMaker goes bad.

When PageMaker Goes Bad

It *will* happen, inevitably. You *will* have a problem, and it *will* occur at the worst possible time.

Stay calm. Take a deep breath, and follow the steps in this section. Keep in mind that these suggestions are not in any precise order. A lot depends on what kind of problems you are experiencing, so proceed with ingenuity and flexibility, and if your problems persist, try repeating some of the steps. Your difficulties could be caused by a combination of underlying problems:

```
Internal error: Bad Record Index.
Cannot lock block.
Cannot Open Files.
```

These error messages all suggest what PageMaker veterans call a *Bad RIX error*— bad record index.

Don't confuse this index business with the kind of index you create when building a book. The PageMaker index that has gone bad in this case is an internal file structure index—the kind of index common in databases. PageMaker files—if you were to examine them in low-level digital form—are closer to database files than to word processor files. Those are the links, locks, blocks, and records being referred to in these error messages.

Assuming you can get PageMaker up and running with your bad file, try a diagnostic recompose first.

Performing a Diagnostic Recompose

PageMaker comes with a built-in file cleanup utility that performs five cleanup operations on your publication. The utility does repairs in the style sheet and cleans up the story, indexes, and links. Then it recomposes the text in the entire document. In other words, it tries to fix bad record links, locks, indexes, and records.

To force a diagnostic recomposition of your publication, start by making absolutely sure you have selected the Pointer and nothing else. Double-clicking the Pointer tool in the toolbox works every time.

Hold down the Shift+Ctrl keys while choosing Type, Hyphenation. PageMaker beeps at you once, twice, or three times:

▶ One beep means the recompose turned out just fine and there was nothing to fix.

▶ Two beeps means the recompose found and repaired one or more minor problems.

▶ Three beeps means trouble. Get out the backups. PageMaker could not complete the recompose because it hit some serious problems. If you get two or three beeps, try it again. It can't hurt.

When the recompose has been completed and you have heard your beeps, use the Save As command immediately to preserve the newly cleaned file with a new file name.

Other Things to Try Inside PageMaker

If you can get your publication open, in addition to a diagnostic recompose, try these other steps:

Do a Slide Show

Run through each page of the publication, using the Shift+Go To Page command on the Layout menu. PageMaker will go to page one and flip through each page one-by-one. This gets PageMaker to look at the elements on each page, doing a mini-save after each page turn. In the process, it allows the program to find all the page elements, or, at least that's the hope.

Find the Problem Element (The Links Command Option)

Open up the Links dialog box by choosing File, Links. Look through the list of page elements for anything that has a questionable link. There will be a UN symbol next to the item or perhaps a question mark. Unlink any such linked files and do a Save As, preferably under a new name.

If this doesn't work, unlink everything in the publication. You can go back through the publication and re-link each item if need be. It'll be a pain, but it may well be a better option than having to rebuild the publication from scratch.

Find the Problem Element (The One-By-One Option)

Go through the publication and select each item on each page using the Pointer tool. One-by-one, use the Link Info command from the Element menu on each item. If you get an error, that element may be the source of your problem. Delete it, choose Save As, and replace it. Just because you found one doesn't mean you've solved the whole problem. Check every element to be sure.

Find the Defective Paragraph Style

Styles are one kind of record that can go bad in PageMaker. Find a bad one by Ctrl+clicking on each style in the Style palette. If it gives you an error message, you've hit pay dirt. As with problem elements, there could be more than one bad style, so you may have to repeat this procedure to find all the problems.

Once you identify a style gone bad, go to Define Styles and create a brand-new style with a new name and use that style on any text formatted with the bad one. Now go to the Story Editor and use Change to replace all occurrences of the bad style with the new one. If things are really bad, you may need to use Find and apply the new style on a paragraph-by-paragraph basis. Once you've replaced all the bad style occurrences with the new style, delete the new style's evil twin.

Save As for All Linked Files

Use the Save As command option to try to create a new, clean copy of your publication. PageMaker will not be able to copy any linked files it can't find, and that's fine because those are the files most likely to be causing a problem.

Try to Place Your Text

As a last-gasp effort, open PageMaker with a new, blank publication and try to import the text from your broken document using the PageMaker Story Filter, available whenever you use the P̲lace command to work with a PageMaker document. (You will need to install the PageMaker story filter, if you didn't already do so.)

Try to Export Your Text

Use the E̲xport command to rescue your text. As with the Story Filter option we've just discussed, this means losing all your specially tuned typography but it's still going to be less bother than retyping the entire text. In some cases, depending on the current stage of your work, you might be better off going back to the word processor file you originally placed in PageMaker.

Copy Page Elements

Open a new PageMaker publication and copy each page element from the damaged publication into the new one. You'll want to have both publications open side-by-side to make these as painless as possible. Also, using Select A̲ll (Ctrl+A) with the Pointer tool selected will reduce the tedium level a bit.

You can drag copy items from publication to publication. Or, you can select items and Copy and Paste them into the new publication.

Try File Operations at the Desktop Level

You have a list of options to try from the Desktop if the PageMaker publication won't open:

Look for a Temp File in the TEMP Folder

If your computer freezes up while you are in PageMaker, chances are good that you will find a temp file somewhere. The program does a mini-save every time you turn a page or print, storing the short save information in a temporary file. Look in the folder you have designated in Windows as your TEMP folder. You might also try a Find File search for TMP. Open any temp files you locate, and you might just find the work you thought you lost, preserved during a mini-save.

Make a Copy

If you simply cannot open a file, your hard disk may have a glitch. Copy the file and then try to open the copy.

Run Diagnostics and Repairs

Use any of the utilities designed to repair and rebuild files, Norton Utilities being one good example. They might not work, but it's worth a try.

Try to Open from Inside PageMaker

If a publication does not open with a double-click, get PageMaker up and running and try using the Open command instead.

Shrink Your PageMaker Window

If the problem is a damaged graphic or graphic link, maybe you can get the file to open if it doesn't have to draw the screen. Size your PageMaker window way down so that it is maybe one-inch square. Then try to open the file. The pages will be too small for PageMaker to try to draw the text or graphics. Once you've at least got the file open, you will be able to use some of the other repair techniques in this appendix.

Trash PageMaker Defaults

Rename the PM6.CNF file, located in the PM6/RSRC/USENGLSH folder. You should keep a backup for this anyway. Save it right there and name it something obvious so you don't forget what it is. PageMaker will automatically rebuild a new defaults file when you relaunch the application, although you will lose all your program defaults and will need to reset them. It's a small price to pay, though, to save hours of hard work on a publication.

Open It Any Way You Can

Open the defective PageMaker file with a word processor. Things will look a mess, but you will at least be able to get your text, mixed in with a lot of garbage characters that need to be edited out, but that's better than retyping the text and building from complete ground zero.

TIP ▶ **More Information and Tips**

The TECHINFO directory on the CD-ROM has tech notes and other information. Also, the home page (**www.adobe.com**) often updates a PageMaker 6 Top 10 Issues PDF file for both Mac and Windows.

Appendix C

Keyboard Shortcuts

PAGEMAKER'S KEYBOARD SHORTCUTS will often be faster than mousing around. In fact, this comprehensive and unabridged list of shortcuts could put jets on your fingers. ▶ ▶ ▶

Help

You can get a handy graphic layout of all these keyboard shortcuts by accessing PageMaker help.

Help	Keyboard Shortcut
Help	F1
Help cursor	Shift+F1 and click on menu item

Tools

Tool	Keyboard Shortcut
Magnifying tool	Ctrl+space bar+click or drag Shift+F8
Reducing tool	Ctrl+Alt+space bar+click F9
Pointer	Ctrl+space bar (slight tap only) (toggles current tool and Pointer)
Text tool	Shift+F2
Oval (or Ellipse) tool	Shift+F3
Rectangle tool	Shift+F4
Diagonal Line tool	Shift+F5
Constrained Line	Shift+F6
Polygon	Shift+F7
Rotate	Shift+F9
Cropping tool	Shift+F11
Tool palette	No longer has a shortcut
Master Pages palette	Ctrl+H
Edit master page	Ctrl+click on master page name
New master page	Ctrl+click on [None] in palette
Remove master objects, keep ruler guides	Alt+Shift+[None]
Remove master object, keep column guides	Ctrl+Shift+[None]
Scripts palette	Ctrl+F9

Express Preferences

Most of the items in the Toolbox give you rapid access to Preferences dialog boxes.

Preference Item	Tool
Document Setup	Alt+double-click pointer
Type Specifications	double-click Text
Paragraph Specifications	Alt+double-click Text
Fill and Line	double-click Oval (Ellipse)
Rounded Corners	double-click Rectangle
Custom Line	double-click Line
Polygon Specifications	double-click Polygon
100% zoom	double-click Magnifying Glass
Fit in Window	Alt+double-click Magnifying Glass
Preferences	double-click Pointer

File and Program Management

Action	Keyboard Shortcut
Close all open publications	Shift+[Close]
Save all open publications	Shift+[Save]
Links	Ctrl+Shift+D
New	Ctrl+N
Open	Ctrl+O
Close	Ctrl+W
Place	Ctrl+D
Auto/Manual text icon (toggle)	Ctrl+loaded text cursor
Semiauto text icon	Shift+loaded text cursor
Print	Ctrl+P
Printer Style (save)	Ctrl+Style (OK button) in the Print dialog box

continues

File and Program Management (continued)

Action	Keyboard Shortcut
Save	Ctrl+S
Lock	Ctrl+L
Unlock	No shortcut
Revert to last mini-save	Shift+Revert
Open a copy	Shift+Recent Pubs

Layout

Action	Keyboard Shortcut
Select all	Ctrl+A
Undo	Alt+Backspace or Ctrl+Z
Clear	Delete
Copy	Ctrl+C
Cut	Ctrl+X
Paste	Ctrl+V
Power Paste	Ctrl+Shift+P
Guides on/off	Ctrl+J
Rulers on/off	Ctrl+R
Snap to guides	Ctrl+Shift+5
Snap to rulers	Ctrl+Shift+Y
Send to back	Ctrl+B
Send back (one layer)	Ctrl+9
Bring to front	Ctrl+F
Bring forward (one layer)	Ctrl+8
Place	Ctrl+D
Links	Ctrl+Shift+D
Insert one page	Ctrl+Shift+'

Graphics

Action	Keyboard Shortcut
Restore proportions	Shift+drag corner handle
Proportional stretch	Shift+drag handle
"Magic Stretch" (resizes 1 bit TIF, PCX, BMP to [printer resolution])	Ctrl+drag handle of bitmap
Proportional magic stretch (resizes bitmap proportionally to [printer resolution])	Ctrl+Shift+drag handle
Group	Ctrl+G
Ungroup	Ctrl+U

To defer text recomposition while adjusting the text boundary around a graphic, hold down the space bar while adjusting. The text recomposes when the space bar is released.

Adjusting Graphics or Text Blocks

Action	Keyboard Shortcut
Select multiple objects	Shift+click each
Select object behind others	Ctrl+click (each click selects the next object back)
Select multiple behind others	Ctrl+Shift+click
Constrain move vertically or horizontally	Shift+drag
Multipaste (without dialog box)	Shift+[Multiple paste]
Edit OLE object	double-click object
Edit non-OLE object	Alt+double-click object
Choose Editor	Shift+Alt+double-click object

View, Layout

Action	Keyboard Shortcut
25 percent size	No longer has a shortcut command
50 percent size	Ctrl+5
75 percent size	No longer has a shortcut command
Actual size	Ctrl+1
200 percent size	Ctrl+2
400 percent size	No longer has a shortcut command
Fit in Window	Ctrl+O
100 percent/Fit window (toggle)	Click right mouse button
200 percent/100 percent (toggle)	Shift+click right mouse button
Set all pages to same view	Ctrl+Alt+any view
Change page to fit in window	Shift+click page icon
Show entire pasteboard	Shift+Ctrl+W
Reduce view	Ctrl+Magnifying Glass
Mask	Ctrl+6
Mask & Group	Shift+Mask
Unmask & Ungroup	Shift+Unmask
Unmask	Ctrl+7
Align object	Ctrl+4

View, Story Editor

Action	Keyboard Shortcut
Close all open publications	Shift+[Close]
Edit story/edit layout	Ctrl+E
Edit story	Triple-click text block with Pointer tool
Close all open stories in current publication	Shift+[Close story]

Action	Keyboard Shortcut
Cascade open story windows for all open publications	Shift+[Cascade]
Tile open story windows for all open publications	Shift+[Tile]

View, Selecting and Redrawing Page

Action	Keyboard Shortcut
Redraw current page	Shortcut for Current view
Redraw page in high resolution	Ctrl+Shift+F12
Force redraw	Ctrl+F12
Go to page	Ctrl+/
Cycle through pages	Shift+[Go to Page] (click the mouse to stop)
Next page	F12
Previous page	F11

View, Scrolling

Action	Keyboard Shortcut
Scroll with grabber hand	Alt+left mouse button
Constrained grabber hand	Shift+Alt+left mouse button

Control Palette

Action	Keyboard Shortcut
Display/hide	Ctrl+'
Activate Control palette	Ctrl+' (Toggles capability to type characters into palette instead of Layout or Story Editor)
Changing measurements in Control palette	Shift+F12

continues

Control Palette (continued)

Action	Keyboard Shortcut
Paragraph/character view (toggle)	Ctrl+Shift+`(grave)
Go to next option	Tab
Go to previous option	Shift+Tab
Choose reference point on proxy	pad numbers
Display last valid value for option	Esc
Apply changes and return to layout	Enter
Apply changes, focus stays in palette	Shift+Enter
On/off option	space bar
Select different unit of measure (for current option)	Shift+F12

Power Nudging

To nudge by ten times the normal amount, press the Ctrl key and click the nudge button or press arrow keys.

Selecting a Style, Font, or Track

Type the first few characters of the style, font, or track name to select it from the list.

Styles Palette

Action	Keyboard Shortcut
Display/hide Styles palette	Ctrl+Y
Edit style	Ctrl+click style name in palette list
Define new style	Ctrl+click No Style in palette list
Define styles	Ctrl+3

Colors Palette

Action	Keyboard Shortcut
Display/hide Colors palette	Ctrl+K
Edit color	Ctrl+click color name in palette list
Define new color	Ctrl+click Registration (Opens the Edit Color dialog box with an empty name. Does not affect Registration.)
Toggle spot/process	Ctrl+Alt+Shift+click color name

Type Formatting

Font Size

Action	Keyboard Shortcut
Increase one point size	Ctrl+Shift+>
Increase to next standard size	Ctrl+>
Decrease one point size	Ctrl+Shift+<
Decrease to next standard size	Ctrl+<

Alignment

Action	Keyboard Shortcut
Align left	Ctrl+Shift+L
Align right	Ctrl+Shift+R
Align center	Ctrl+Shift+C
Justify	Ctrl+Shift+J
Force justify	Ctrl+Shift+F

Leading, Width, Track

Action	Keyboard Shortcut
Auto leading	Ctrl+Shift+A
Normal width	Ctrl+Shift+X
No track	Ctrl+Shift+Q

Case

Action	Keyboard Shortcut
All caps	Ctrl+Shift+K

Position

Action	Keyboard Shortcut
Subscript	Ctrl+\
Superscript	Ctrl+Shift+\

Type Style

Action	Keyboard Shortcut
Bold	Ctrl+Shift+B or F6
Italic	Ctrl+Shift+I
Underline	Ctrl+Shift+U or F8
Strikethrough	Ctrl+Shift+S
Normal	Ctrl+Shift+space bar or F5
Reverse	Ctrl+Shift+V

All Character Attributes

Action	Keyboard Shortcut
Type Specs dialog box	Ctrl+T

Paragraph Formatting

Action	Keyboard Shortcut
Define styles	Ctrl+3
Paragraph specs	Ctrl+M
Hyphenation (Layout view)	No longer has a shortcut command
Discretionary hyphen	Ctrl+ - (hyphen)
Indents/tabs (Layout view)	Ctrl+I
Drag lower left indent marker only	Shift+drag indent in Indents/Tabs dialog box

Text Editing

Selecting

Action	Keyboard Shortcut
Select word	Double-click with Text tool
Select paragraph	Triple-click with Text tool
Edit story/edit layout	Ctrl+E

Insertion Point

Action	Keyboard Shortcut
Up one line	Up arrow or pad 8
Down one line	Down arrow or pad 2
Up one screen	Page Up or pad 9
Down one screen	Page Down or pad 3
To beginning of line	Home or pad 7
To end of line	End or pad 1
To beginning of sentence	Ctrl+Home or Ctrl+pad 7
To end of sentence	Ctrl+End or Ctrl+pad 1
To beginning of story	Ctrl+Page Up or Ctrl+pad 9

continues

Insertion Point (continued)

Action	Keyboard Shortcut
To end of story	Ctrl+Page Down or Ctrl+pad 3
Left one character	Left arrow or pad 4
Right one character	Right arrow or pad 6
Left one word	Ctrl+left arrow or Ctrl+pad 4
Right one word	Ctrl+right arrow or Ctrl+pad 6
Up one paragraph	Ctrl+up arrow or Ctrl+pad 8
Down one paragraph	Ctrl+down arrow or Ctrl+pad 2

Search and Replace (Story Editor Only)

Action	Keyboard Shortcut
Find	Ctrl+F
Find next	Ctrl+G
Change	Ctrl+9
Reset attributes to "any"	Alt+click Attributes
Spelling	Ctrl+L

Indexing

Action	Keyboard Shortcut
Show index (for current publication only)	Ctrl+[Show index]
Copy book list to all book publications	Ctrl+[Book]
Copy existing topics for new entry	Ctrl+OK in the Select Topic dialog box

Remove entries (In Show Index Dialog Box)

Remove all index entries	Ctrl+Alt+Shift+Remove

Action	Keyboard Shortcut
Remove entries (In Show Index Dialog Box)	
Remove all cross-referenced entries	Ctrl+Shift+Remove
Remove all page-referenced entries	Ctrl+Alt+Remove
Remove entries since last Accept	Alt+Add x-refs
Restore Entries (In Show Index Dialog Box)	
Restore since last "Accept"	Alt+Remove
Highlight text, then:	
Create index entry	Ctrl+;
Create fast index entry	Ctrl+Shift+;
Create proper name index entry	Ctrl+Shift+Z

Kerning

Click the insertion point at one end of text to be selected, hold Shift, and press one of the cursor movement shortcuts.

Action	Keyboard Shortcut
Kern apart .01 em	Ctrl+Shift+pad plus sign
Kern together .01 em	Ctrl+Shift+pad minus sign
Kern apart .04 em	Ctrl+pad plus sign or Ctrl+Shift+Backspace
Kern together .04 em	Ctrl+pad minus sign or Ctrl+Backspace
Kern more than two characters	shortcuts above [selected text]
Clear manual kerning	Ctrl+Shift+0 (zero)
Set text to No Track	Ctrl+Shift+Q

Special Characters

For a complete list of Windows characters, see the Character Map utility included with Microsoft Windows 95. You can copy characters from this utility to the Clipboard and paste them into publications.

PageMaker has its own keyboard shortcuts for the most frequently used special characters.

Action	Keyboard Shortcut
▶ Bullet	Ctrl+Shift+8
© Copyright	Ctrl+Shift+O (the letter)
¶ Paragraph	Ctrl+Shift+7
" Open double quote	Ctrl+Shift+[
" Close double quote	Ctrl+Shift+]
' Open single quote	Ctrl+[
' Close single quote	Ctrl+]
® Registered trademark	Ctrl+Shift+G
§ Section	Ctrl+Shift+6
… Ellipses	Alt+0133
En space	Ctrl+Shift+N
Em space	Ctrl+Shift+M
Thin space	Ctrl+Shift+T
Nonbreaking (hard) space	Ctrl+Shift+H
- Discretionary (soft) hyphen	Ctrl+-
- Nonbreaking hyphen	Ctrl+Shift+-
/ Nonbreaking slash	Ctrl+Shift+/
–En dash	Ctrl+=
— Em dash	Ctrl+Shift+=
Page # on master pages	Ctrl+Shift+3
New line or soft return	Shift+Enter

Metacharacters

You can't type certain characters or markers into the Find, Change, or Indexing dialog boxes. You must type them as character pairs called *metacharacters*. Those that can only be entered in the Find What edit box are marked with *. A ^ stands for caret (not Ctrl).

Action	Keyboard Shortcut
*Inline graphic	^g
Index marker	^;
Page # marker	^3
Proper name index entry (Can only be entered in the Change To edit box.)	^z
Paragraph end (carriage return)	^p
New line (soft return)	^n
Discretionary (soft) hyphen	^-
Nonbreaking hyphen	^~ (tilde)
*Computer-inserted hyphen	^c
En dash (–)	^=
Em dash (—)	^_ (underscore)
Nonbreaking slash	^/
*Unspecified (wild) character	^?
Caret (^)	^^
Registered trademark (®)	^r
Copyright (©)	^2
Section (§)	^6
Paragraph (¶)	^7
Bullet (▶)	^8
Open double quote (")	^{
Close double quote (")	^}

continues

(continued)

Action	Keyboard Shortcut
Open single quote (')	^[
Close single quote (')	^]
Tab	^t
Thin space	^<
En space	^>
Em space	^m
Nonbreaking space	^s
*White space, tab, (any space)	^w

Power Shortcuts

Special Commands

Action	Keyboard Shortcut
OK all open dialog boxes	Shift+OK or Shift+Enter
Cancel all open dialog boxes	Shift+Cancel or Shift+Esc
List installed filters, dictionaries, Plug-ins	Ctrl+[About PageMaker]
Save print settings without printing	Shift+Done (Print button)

Compressing TIFFs In Place Dialog Box

To compress or decompress a TIFF before placing it, press keys for two or more seconds and click OK in the Place dialog box. (PageMaker creates a new TIFF file in the same directory as the original.)

Action	Keyboard Shortcut
Moderate compression	Ctrl+Alt+OK
Maximum compression	Ctrl+Alt+Shift+OK
Decompression	Ctrl+OK

Action	Moderate	Maximum	Decompression
B/W	_P.tif	_L.tif	_U.tif
Palette color	_P.tif	_L.tif	_U.tif
Gray/color	_D.tif	_M.tif	_U.tif

Recomposing Text

Recomposition refigures line breaks and hyphenation throughout a publication.

Diagnostic recomposition refigures line breaks and hyphenation, and also looks for such items as bad styles, links, and index topics. When diagnostics are complete, the results are indicated as follows:

1 beep = No problems found

2 beeps = Problems found and fixed

3 beeps = Problems could not be fixed

To initiate recomposition, select the Pointer tool, make sure nothing is selected on the page, then:

▶ For global recomposition, press Shift+[Hyphenation]

▶ For diagnostic global recomposition, press Ctrl+Shift+[Hyphenation]

Appendix D

PageMaker's New Tagging Language

PUT THE POWER of PageMaker's tagging codes to work, using this unabridged list of tagging commands. You will find lots of information on putting tags to work in Chapter 28, "Automating PageMaker." ▶▶▶

Character Level Formatting Tags

Attribute	Tag	Tag Abbreviation
Font	<font "font name">	<f "fontname"> You can also use this command to establish the character set PageMaker should use. Between the closing bracket and the closing quote after the font name, type **Win** or **Mac**, or if for DOS type **OEM** (Original Equipment Manufacturer).
Type size	<size ###>	<s###>
Set width	<horizontal ###>	<h###>
Manual pair	kerning	<kern ###> <k###>
Range kerning	<letterspace ###>	<l###>
Plain text		<p>
Bold		<b>
Italic		<I>
Outline		<o>
Shadow		<¯>
Underline		<u>
Strikethrough		<x>
Superscript		<+>
Subscript		<->
All caps	<call>	<ca>
Small caps	<csmall>	<cs>
Reverse	<creverse>	<cr>
Baseline shift	<cbaseline ###>	<cb###>
Leading	<cleading ###>	<cl###>

X

Appendixes

Attribute	Tag	Tag Abbreviation
Linebreaks	<cnobreak #>	For #, **t** (or true) = lines can break; **f** (for false) = lines not permitted to break
Small caps size	<cssize###>	<css###>
Superscript/ subscript size	<c+size ###>	<c+s###>
Superscript position	<c+position ###>	<c+p###>
Subscript position	<c-position ###>	<c-p###>
Tracking	<ctrack ###>	<ct###> ### = name of a track, which can be in form of following abbreviations: **none** for No Track **-2** or **vt** for Very Tight **-1** or **t** for Tight **0** or **n** for Normal **1** or **l** for Loose **2** or **vl** for Very Loose
Color (custom)	<c-colortable ("name" # ####)>	<c-c...> Defines custom colors to be applied with <ccolor...:\> tag. Place each defined color between parentheses. "name" = name of the color inside quotes. # field = color model = **O** for CMYK, and **1** for RGB. #### field = percentages of R, G, and B, or C, M, Y, and K colors.
Color (existing)	<ccolor "name">	<cc"colorname"> "name" = the name of the color between quotes. Color must be defined with <c-colortable...> tag or a color previously defined in publication. Following abbreviations acceptable for predefined colors: **p** or **none** for paper **k** for black **b** for blue **g** for green **r** for red

Paragraph Level Formatting Tags

Attribute	Tag	Tag Abbreviation
Left indent	<gleft ###>	<gl###>
Right indent	<gright ###>	<gr###>
First line indent	<gfirst ###>	<gf###>
Tabs	<gtab(<###> <align#><"leader">)>	<gt(<###><align><"leader">)> Set of parentheses = tab in the paragraph. <###> = tab position (distance from the left edge of the text block) and must be included for each tab. Other fields are optional and if not included will go to current default. <align#> = tab alignment; **1** for Left, **2** for Right, **3** for Center, **4** for Decimal. <"leader"> = string of tab leader characters (such as periods, hyphens, or underscores).
Alignment	<galignment #>	<ga#> # = **1** for Left, **2** for Right, **3** for Center, **4** for Justify, **5** Force Justify
Leading grid	<ggrid ###>	<gg###>
Language	<g& "dictionary name">	
Space before	<g+before ###>	<g+b###>
Space after	<g+after ###>	<g+a###>
Autoleading percentage	<g% ###>	
Leading method	<gmethod #>	<gm#> # = **1** for proportional leading; **2** for top of caps leading; **3** for baseline leading.
Word spacing	<gwordspace ### ### ###>	<gw### ### ###> ### = Minimum, Desired, and Maximum spacing, in that order.

Attribute	Tag	Tag Abbreviation
Letter spacing	<gspace *### ### ###*>	<gs*### ### ###*> ### = Minimum, Desired, and Maximum spacing, in that order.
Pair kerning above	<gpairs *###*>	<gp*###*>
Hyphenation	<ghyphenation *# ### #*>	# = preferred hyphenation method (type **O** for Off, **1** for Manual Only, **2** for Manual Plus Dictionary, **3** for Manual Plus Algorithm). You may also set a new hyphenation method with the tags <g0>, <g1>, <g2>, and <g3>. ### = Hyphenation Zone. # = Limit Consecutive Hyphens To setting.
Keep together	<gktogether>	<gkt>
Keep begin	<gkbegin>	<gkb> Works with <gkend> and sets range of paragraphs to keep together on same page or column.
Keep end	<gkend>	<gke> Works with <gkbegin> and sets range of paragraphs to keep together on same page or column.
Keep with next	<gknext *###*>	<gkn*###*>
Widow control	<gkwidow *###*>	<gkw*###*>
Orphan control	<gkorphan *###*>	<gko*###*>
Page break	<g+page>	<g+p>
Column break	<g+column>	<g+c>
Include in TOC	<gcontents>	<gc>

Attribute	Tag	Tag Abbreviation
Rule Above	<gbabove *### # ### ### ### "Color" ### #*>	First field = **Col** for width of column, or **Text** for width of text. Second field = **T** for a transparent line, **F** for an opaque line. Next three fields = left indent, right indent, and distance from baseline, in that order. "Color" = rule color. *###* following "Color" = weight (12 for a 12-point line). Final *#* = type of line: **1** for solid, **2** for dashed, **3** for squared, **4** for dotted.
Rule Below	<gbbelow>	[same as Rule Above]
Define paragraph style	<@*###*=definition>	*###* = name of the style. Characters "@," , "-," or "=" not permitted in style name. Include after the equal sign all the tags needed to define style formatting; separate defining tags with vertical bar character (|) rather than "<" and ">". Any unspecified attributes will be formatted with default values. Paragraph definition tag must be followed by a paragraph return.
Set Next Style	<@-next "*###*">	<@-n "*###*"> *###* = name of the Next Style. Only used in conjunction with "<@*###*=...>" tag.
Apply paragraph style	<@*###*:>	*###* = name of style to apply This tag inserted within paragraph will be adopted only for character-level attributes, as overrides to the existing paragraph style.
Set Based On style	<@-parent "*###*">	<@-p "*###*"> *###*= name of the Based On style. Only used in conjunction with "<@*###*=...>" tag.

Special Character Tags

Special Character	PageMaker Tag
Em space	<m>
En space	<n>
Thin space	<t>
Word space	<w>
Non-breaking space	<!w>
Em dash	<\>
En dash	<\->
Soft return	<r>
Page number	<\d>
Discretionary hyphen	<d>
Non-breaking hyphen	<\!->
Non-breaking slash	<\!/>
Any ASCII character	<\#[type the ASCII number]>

Note: If you want characters @, < , and > to appear in your text, you must place a backslash (\) immediately before them. The characters are read as codes in the Tag language if the backslash is not present.

Appendix E Resource Guide

Product	Manufacturer	Address
AA Celler AA Shadow	Integrated Software, Inc.	475 Park Avenue S. New York, NY 10016 (212) 545-0110
America Online	America Online	8619 Westwood Center Dr. Vienna, VA 22182 (800) 227-6364
ATM/PostScript fonts Illustrator Photoshop PageMaker	Adobe Systems	1585 Charleston Road Mountain View, CA 94039 (800) 833-6687 (415) 961-4400
Before&After	PageLab, Inc.	1830 Sierra Gardens Dr., Suite 30 Roseville, CA 95661 (916) 784-3880
Bookends Pro 3.1	Westing Software	134 Redwood Ave. Corte Madera, CA 94925 (415) 435-9343
Capture	Mainstay	591-A Constitution Ave. Camarillo, CA 93012 (805) 484-9400
CompuServe	CompuServe	5000 Arlington Centre Blvd. P.O. Box 20212 Columbus, OH 43220 (800) 848-8199 (614) 457-8600
ConversionsPlus	DataViz	55 Corporate Dr. Trumbull, CT 06611 (203) 268-0030
CREF (Computer Ready Electronic Files Booklet)	Scitex Graphic Arts Users Assn.	P.O. Box 2345 Brentwood, TN 37027 (800) 858-0489
DesignKit	Logic Arts Corporation	11475 Chickahominy Branch Dr. Glen Allen, VA 23060 (804) 266-7996
DocuComp	MASTERSOFT Adobe	8737 E. Via de Commercio Scottsdale, AZ 85258 (800) 624-6107

Product	Manufacturer	Address
DTP Forum Font Catalog (CD-ROM)	(see CompuServe)	CIS: **GO DTPFORUM**
FontMinder	Ares Software Corporation	565 Pilgrim Drive, Suite A Foster City, CA 94404 (800) 783-2737 (415) 578-9090
Fræmz, Arrowz, and Starz	ShadeTree Marketing	5515 N. 7th St. Suite 5-144 Phoenix, AZ 85014 (602) 279-3713
GalleyOops	Sundae Software	11801 Ojai Rd. Ojai, CA 93023 (805) 933-2152
HiJaak Graphics Suite	Inset System	71 Commerce Dr. Brookfield, CT 06804 (800) 374-6738 CIS: **GO INSET**
LaserCheck	Systems of Merritt	2551 Old Dobbin Dr. E. Mobile, AL 36695-3732 (205) 660-1240
Object Series (and other digital stock photo art)	PhotoDisc	2013 Fourth Avenue, Suite 402 Seattle, WA 98121 (206) 441-9355
PageTools	Extensis Corporation	55 SW Yamhill 4th Floor Portland, OR 97204 (800) 796-9798 (503) 274-2020 Internet: **extensis@aol.com**
PIXymbols Shadowkey	Precision Type	47 Mall Dr. Commack, NY 11725-5703 (516) 864-1067 Fax (800) 248-3668
POSTools	Azalea Software	P.O. Box 16745 Seattle, WA 98116-0745 (800) 48A-SOFT (206) 932-6028

X

Appendixes

Product	Manufacturer	Address
Publish Magazine	Integrated Media, Inc.	510 Second St. San Francisco, CA 94107 (800) 656-7495
QuarkXPress	Quark, Inc.	1800 Grant Street Denver, CO 80203 (800) 788-7835 (303) 894-8888
SNR (batch search and replace)		Thomas A. Lundin 16267 Hudson Ave. Lakeville, MN 55044 (612) 431-5805 CIS: **70523,262**
Sonar Bookends 3.5 [p]Sonar TOC 2.1	Virginia Systems, Inc.	5509 West Bay Court Midlothian, VA 23112 (804) 739-3200
Step-by-Step (newsletter)	Step-by-Step Publishing (Dynamic Graphics)	6000 N. Forest Park Dr. Peoria, IL 61614-3592 (800) 255-8800
StuffIt Expander	Aladdin Systems, Inc.	165 Westridge Drive Watsonville, CA 95076 (408) 761-6200 **Internet: aladdin@well.sf.ca.us**
[T-26]		361 West Chestnut Street First Floor Chicago, IL 60610
ThePage (newsletter)	The Cobb Group	P.O. Box 35160 Louisville, KY 40232 (800) 223-8720
TransverterPro	TechPool Studios	1463 Warrensville Center Road Cleveland, OH 44121 (800) 543-3278 (216) 291-1922 (sales)
Treacyfaces		P.O. Box 26036 West Haven, CT 06516-8036 (203) 389-7037
Word Excel	Microsoft Corporation	1 Microsoft Way Redmond, WA 98052 (206) 882-8088

Product	Manufacturer	Address
WordPerfect	WordPerfect Corporation (Novell)	1555 N. Technology Way Orem, UT 84057 (800) 453-1267
Zephyr Specs	Zephyr Design	SuperSnap 800 Fifth Avenue, Suite 296 Seattle, WA 98104 (206) 545-0319 (800) 685-3547

Appendix F

What's on the CD?

THE CD-ROM INCLUDED with *Special Edition Using PageMaker 6 for Windows 95,* includes several dozen scripts and utilities to ease your desktop publishing labors—free fonts and font specimen files, some free high-resolution stock photos, and a collection of tools for Web publishing. Each of the following sections covers a folder with roughly the same name on the CD-ROM. (I've abbreviated names where necessary to stay within the eight-character limit, in case you are running PageMaker under Windows 3.x.) ▶ ▶ ▶

Several of the folks listed below are making special offers for sale of stock photos and fonts to readers of this book.

PhotoDisc

The PhotoDisc people have provided a mini-sampler of stock photos from their well-known Object Series. You'll find here a pig, a light bulb, a mask, and other items you can use to dress up your publication.

Naturally, aside from giving you some free images, the folks at PhotoDisc did this so you would try out their product; you'll find an Acrobat file to give you a look at the rest of their product line.

To view the Acrobat PDF file on the CD, you need to have installed the Adobe Acrobat Reader Software that came with PageMaker 6.0 (and which is also available for downloading from Compuserve (**GO ADOBEAP**), America Online (keyword **Adobe**), and the Adobe Web page (**http://www.adobe.com**).

Simply double-click on the COOLSTUFF.PDF file on the CD-ROM. If Acrobat is installed correctly, it will launch and display the contents of this file.

Precision Type

Precision Type distributes the products of many different font foundry products and thus have access to a huge array of fonts. They've put together for this CD-ROM the most comprehensive encyclopedia I've ever seen of Symbol and Pi fonts—everything from checkers and chess to sign language, from dingbats to road signs. They've also included a free typeface for you.

You will find an Adobe Acrobat PDF file in the PRECTYPE folder on the CD-ROM. To view the Acrobat PDF file on the CD, you need to have installed the Adobe Acrobat Reader software that came with PageMaker 6.0 (and which is also available for downloading from Compuserve (**GO ADOBEAP**), America Online (keyword **Adobe**), and the Adobe Web page (**http://www.adobe.com**).

Simply double-click on the PTREADME.PDF file on the CD-ROM. If Acrobat is installed correctly, it will launch and display the contents of this file.

In the DISPLAYS folder, you will find additional PDF files. Double-click on the INDEX.PDF file to bring up an index of fonts available from Precision. Click (once) on any font in the list, and it will display a sample of that font for you.

There is also a FREEFONT folder which contains (ta-da!!) a free font from Precision Type. In the FC-INVE1 folder, you will find a PostScript type 1 font which can be installed via ATM (Adobe Type Manager). Run ATM's Control Panel, click the Add button, then navigate to the FC-INVE1 folder on the CD, select the FC-Inverserif font, and click on the add button again.

[T-26]

Carlos Segura, the experimental type designer, has assembled for you a specimen collection of the dozens of fonts that find a home at his foundry. Browsing through it will give you a much better idea of what this grunge type stuff is all about. He's also offering a discount on purchase of fonts for readers of this book.

Treacyfaces

Joe Treacy has also put together an electronic specimen collection of his foundry's typefaces, in addition to a free font, for you.

In the TREACY folder on the CD-ROM, you will find a program file called TFSHOW.EXE. This is an "electronic specimen collection" that will display the Treacyfaces catalog of fonts.

There is also a free font from Treacyfaces here that you can install with ATM (Adobe Type Manager). The font is Treacyfaces Habitat Regular. To install, run the ATM Control Panel, click on the Add button, navigate to the TREACY folder on the CD-ROM, select the TFHabitat-Regular font, and click on the Add button again.

Scripts By Ray

Ray Robertson slam-dunked more than six dozen scripts to make your day go faster and easier. Turn to Chapter 28, "Automating PageMaker," for directions on installing them and putting them to work. Ray's already blushing over the praise he's received for the work, so I won't mention that Chapter 28 is also where you'll find the brass plaque I erected in his honor.

SNR

Thomas Lundin has been programming the premier batch search-and-replace program for some years now, hailed by desktop publishers who have been using Ventura and QuarkXPress. Now that PageMaker has a tagging language, you'll hail it, too.

Open the README.TXT and README2.TXT files in Windows NotePad for information on using the SNR program files.

There's good news about SNR if you feel a bit intimidated by working in plain old DOS. Tom promises a Windows version. Here's the note he sent me:

```
Since it's clear that I won't be able to have a Win version
ready in time for publication, I chose to add an "advance or-
der" option for the Windows version: readers who select to
register in advance for the Win version will receive the DOS
version right away, and will be shipped the Win version upon
completion (which I estimated in the order form as 1Q [the
first quarter of] '96, to give me a little breathing room).
They can still choose to register for just the DOS version if
they want; it's a little cheaper. The Win registration option
will give them both DOS and Win versions of SNR for the price
of Win alone; in addition, the Win version is specially priced
"for a limited time"--after it's officially released, the
price will go up a bit. I figure this will give a little extra
value for their patience.
```

ZIP and StuffIt

There's one main compression format you are likely to encounter as you assemble files of elements for a desktop publishing project—ZIP files.

WinZip makes it easy to zip files without going to the DOS command line to run PKZip. You can point-and-click right in Windows.

To install the WinZip program on the CD-ROM, go to the ZIPSTUFF folder, then to the WINZIP60 folder. Then double-click on the WINZIP95.EXE filename to launch the WinZip installer. Follow the instructions on the screen to complete the installation.

Graphics Converters

In order to perform your Web publishing work, you'll need to convert your DTP graphics elements to JPEG and GIF files. PaintShop Pro and VuePrint will do the job for you. In addition, they are handy for working on bitmapped graphics files if you don't own Photoshop. (For EPS conversions, you'll need to use a commercial program. There's no shareware EPS converter available for Windows users, at least not as we go to press.)

To install PaintShop Pro, go to the GRAPHICS/PSP folder on the CD-ROM and run the SETUP.EXE program. Then follow the instructions on the screen to install PaintShop Pro to your hard disk. See the README.TXT file for additional information on PaintShop Pro.

To install VuePrint, go to the GRAPHICS/VUEPRINT folder on the CD-ROM and run the VUEPRO42.EXE file. This is a Windowws installer program. Follow the instructions on the screen to complete the installation.

Web Editing Tools

Once you've run HTML Author on your PageMaker files, you'll probably want to do some fine-tuning on your Web pages. For that, you'll need a good HTML editor. Give these three programs a try: HTMLed, HTMLWriter, and HoTMetal.

To install HoTMetal, copy the HOTMLNEW.EXE file from the CD-ROM to a temporary folder on your hard disk and run the file there. It will self-extract a number of files to that folder, including a README.WRI and INSTALL.TXT files with further instructions for installing the program.

HTMLed can be run directly from the CD-ROM (double-click on the HTMLED.EXE program name). Or you can copy the file to your hard disk and run it from there. See the HELP.TXT file for additional information about HTMLed.

To install HTMLWriter, go to the HTMLWRIT folder on the CD-ROM (in the WEBEDIT folder) and see the README.TXT file.

Index ▶ ▶ ▶

SYMBOLS

* (asterisk), 176
! (exclamation point), link status code, 774
$ (dollar sign) tag code, 736
^ (caret) tag code, 735
+ (plus sign), link status code, 774
- (hyphen), link status code, 774
< (less than sign) tag code, 734
> (greater than sign) tag code, 734
? (question mark)
   link status code, 774
   Show Index dialog box, 473
\ (backslash) tag code, 736
... (ellipsis), keyboard shortcut, 858
© (copyright symbol), keyboard shortcut, 858

A

AA Celler (Integrated Software, Inc.), address, 872
AA Shadow (Integrated Software, Inc.), address, 872
AAs (Author's Alterations), defined, 604
About PageMaker command (Help menu), 193, 686

Acquire command (File menu), 267
Acrobat
   home page, 753
   files (electronic publishing), 744-745
      creating, 760-764
      Distiller program, 761-762
   fonts, 761
   linking table of contents and index, 762-763
Action mode, Proxy (Control palette), 334-335
Actual Size, keyboard shortcut, 850
Add Cont'd Line Plug-in, 687
Add Index Entry dialog box, 460
   Promote/Demote button, 465
   Sort boxes, 463-464
   X-Ref Override check boxes, 466
Add Word dialog box, 218
Additions, see Plug-ins
Adobe Acrobat, 744-745
   Distiller program, 50, 761-762, 812
   files
      creating, 760-764
      installing
      fonts, 761
      linking table of contents and index, 762-763
      PDF, 39
   home page, 753
   Reader program, 50, 812-813
   World Wide Web (WWW), 811-812

Adobe Systems, 249
   address, 872
Adobe Table (editor), 405
   opening, 408
   tables
      data entry, 412
      formatting text, 417-418
      navigating cells, 412-413
      selecting cells, 412-413
      setup, 411-412
Adobe Type Manager (ATM), 672-673
Align command, 787
Align Objects command (Arrange menu), 37, 348
Align/Distribute feature, 819
aligning, 348-349
   headlines, companion column headlines, 373-376
   keyboard shortcuts, 348, 853
   master pages
      baselines, 309-311
      Snap to Rulers, 312
   objects, keyboard shortcut, 850
   tag, 866
   text, 117-136, 190
      alerts, 123
      baseline alignment, 393-394
      centered, 118
      Control palette, 119
      flush left, 118
      flush right, 117
      hyphenating, 126-135, 132
      justification, 118, 120-126, 135-136

letter spacing, 124
paragraph spacing
    attributes, 122
Paragraph Specifications
    dialog box, 118
readability, 120, 125-126
word spacing, 122
types, 790
undoing, 350
see also formatting
**American National Standards
Institute (ANSI), finding
character numbers, 225**
**American Standard Code for
Information Interchange, *see*
ASCII**
anchors, 758
**ANSI (American National
Standards Institute), finding
character numbers, 225**
AppleScript, 729
application defaults, 274
    see also permanent defaults;
    program-level default
**Apply button (Control
palette), 333**
Ares FontMinder, 677-678
Arrange menu commands
Align Objects, 37, 348
Bring to Front, 243
    keyboard shortcut, 243
Group, 38, 346
Lock Position, 355
Remove Transformation, 446
Send to Back, 243
    keyboard shortcut, 243
Ungroup, 346
Unlock, 355
**arrow keys, nudging objects,
330**
**Arrowz (ShadeTree
Marketing), address, 873**
art, scanning
into PageMaker, 266-267
memory problems, 267
see also drawing objects;
    graphics
**ASCII (American Standard
Code for Information
Interchange), 198-199, 700**
characters
    finding, 225
    tags, 869

dictionaries
    creating, 220
    importing, 220
files, importing, 198-199
**ATM (Adobe Type Manager),
672-673**
attributes, selecting, 84-86
    see also formatting
**audience of book, defining for
publications, 648-650**
**Author's Alterations (AAs),
defined, 604**
**Autoflow (inserting pages
automatically), 444**
**AutoFlow command (Layout
menu), 186**
**AutoFlow text placement icon,
186**
Autoleading, 96-100

B

backgrounds
graphics, 264
inserting behind text, 399-402
backslash (\ ) tag code, 736
backups (files), 321, 839
sending to service bureaus,
    595
**backwards compatibility, 14,
52, 833**
CleanSweep Plug-in, 687
PM5 Custom Settings
    program (PM5FILES.EXE),
    221
**bad record index error
message, 839-840**
**Balance Columns dialog box,
316**
Balance Columns Plug-in, 687
**banding graphics, preventing,
587-589**
**Based On Style function, 172,
178-179**
baselines, 108
alignment
    master pages, 309-310
    text, 393-394
grids, creating, 297
leading, 825
measurements, changing, 109
shifting, 92, 108

**batch processing, tagging,
738-739**
**Before&After (PageLab, Inc.),
address, 872**
bidding process, 657-658
bid forms, developing, 628
bindery services, 631
paper specifications, 628-631
bindery services, 631, 668
case bound books, 631
defined, 631
die cutting, 631
embossing, 631
foil stamping, 631
inserting, 631
perfect bound books, 631
stuffing, 631
tipping, 631
**bitmapped graphics, *see*
resolution-dependent**
bleeder tabs
creating, 485-486
defined, 485
printer setup, 568
bluelines, defined, 614
boldface formatting
index entries, 462-463
keyboard shortcut, 854
tag, 864
see also formatting
bond paper, 629
book binders, defined, 631
**Book command (File menu),
440-441**
Book dialog box, 440-441
book list
building, 440-444
composing, 440
    for indexes, 474-475
copying to all publications,
    441
organizing files, 442-444
prefix numbering chapters,
    443-444
renumbering pages
    automatically, 441
**Bookends Pro (Westing
Software), address, 872**
borders in tables, 418-420
breaks
columns, 147
line, 146
page, 147
brightness, graphics, 263

Bring to Front command (Arrange menu), keyboard shortcut, 243
brochures
    designing, 784-793
    see also Build Booklet Plug-in
budgeting for publications, 650-651
Build Booklet Plug-in, 50, 579-583, 687
built-in templates, opening, 283
bullets, 143
    keyboard shortcut, 858
Bullets and Numbering Plug-in, 143, 687
buttons, Control palette
    Apply button, 333
    nudge buttons, 331-332

C

cameras, process cameras, 634-641
capitalization
    automatic, 99-100
    index entries, 473-474
    initial caps, 388
        drop caps, 389-392
        hanging caps, 388-389
        raised caps, 388
    letter size, adjusting, 99
    keyboard shortcut, 854
    tag, 864
captions, inserting in text wrap boundaries, 386
Capture (Mainstay), address, 872
caret (^) tag code, 735
carriage return symbol, 368
Cascade command (Window menu), 15, 209
cascading style application, 165
case bound books, 631
Case command, Type Specifications dialog box, 99
Cell menu commands (Adobe Table)
    Delete, 414
    Group, 414
    Insert Above, 414
    Insert After, 414
    Insert Before, 414
    Insert Below, 414
    Row/Columns Size, 416
    Ungroup, 414
cells (tables)
    borders, 419-420
    fills, 419-420
    grouping, 414
    navigating, 412-413
    selecting, 412-413
center Proxy point (Control palette), 336
centering pages before printing, 563-564
Change command (Utilities menu), 29, 223
Change dialog box, 223
chapter-level table of contents, creating, 452-453
chapters
    breaking book into, 838
    list, *see* book list
    see also indexes; table of contents
Character Map (Windows 95), 225
Character mode (Control palette), 33-34
characters
    formatting, tags, 864-865
    symbols
        carriage return, 368
        keyboard shortcuts, 858
        metacharacters, keyboard shortcuts, 859-860
        special character tags, 869
CHARSET.PT6, *see* **templates, character map**
check boxes on forms, 435
checklists, 583
Choose Editor dialog box, 777
CIE (Commission Internationale de l'Eclairage) color model, 531
Circle tool, keyboard shortcut, 846
circles
    drawing, 235
    moving, 238-239
    None attribute, 244
    resizing, 239
    reversing (knockout), 244
CleanSweep Plug-in, 687
clearing, keyboard shortcut, 848
Close All Stories command (Story menu), 206
Close command (File menu), 17
    Adobe Table, 408
Close Story command (Story menu), 30, 205
closing, keyboard shortcut, 847
CMS (Color Management System), 65
CMYK color, 47
coated book paper, 629
coated stock paper, 630
codes, tagging, 730
coding index entries, 456, 458-460
    copying entries from master topic list, 464-465
    cross-references, 466-468
    each occurrence of word, 468-470
    formatting text, 462-463
    highlighting text, 465-466
    keyboard shortcuts, 460, 856-857
    levels, 461
    location reference, 460
    multiple entries at one location, 464-465
    names, 469-470
    opening codes, 473-474
    page ranges, 462
    Promote/Demote button, 465
    rotating topic levels, 465
    selecting topics from topic list, 461
    sorting, 463-464
    topics, 460
collated printing, 559
color, 821
    additive, 500
    Black, 502, 504, 520
    CMYK (cyan, magenta, yellow, black), 496, 500-503
    converting RGB to CMYK, 47
    consistent definitions, 512-513
    copying, 514
        between PageMaker and other applications, 514-515
        between publications, 515

correction, 599
creating, 505, 520
custom, 508
   defining, 36
DCS files, 524
defining, 503-512
editing, 47
files, CIE Lab TIFF, 531
fill patterns, 523
Focoltone, 502
gamut alarms, 501
GCR (gray component
   replacement), 503
graphics, 263
halftones
   gray percentage, 636-641
   process color, 638-640
   screen angles, 638-640
   screening color, 637-641
high-fidelity, 497-504
hue, 507
importing
   EPS graphics, 514-515
   FreeHand 5.0 EPS files,
      515
knockouts, 511-512
libraries, 48, 507-510
   adding notes, 516
   COLOR folder, 516
   creating, 515-516
   Pantone Hexachrome, 508
lightness, 507
management systems, 47, 65,
   502, 505
   CMS (Kodak Precision
      Color Management
      System), 530
   converting systems,
      500-503
   described, 531-532
   device profiles, 531-532
   settings, 533-536
matching systems, 502-503,
   528
   calibrated, 492
   DIC (Dainippon), 508
   Focoltone, 508
   MUNSELL, 508
   Pantone, 492
   Pantone(r), 509
   TOYOpc, 509
   TRUMATCH, 509
memory colors, 611-612
merging, 513

mini-defaults, 515
models
   CMYK (cyan, magenta,
      yellow, black), 506
   HLS (hue, lightness,
      saturation), 506-507
   RGB (red, green, blue),
      506
   selecting, 506-507
monitor display, 500
   calibrating, 536
   comparisons to printing
      press, 492-494
naming, 510, 519
None, 503, 519
objects (PageMaker)
   Colors palette, 522
   Fill and Line dialog box,
      522
   overprinting, 524
overprinting, 511-512
Pantone, 502
Paper, 504, 519, 630
paragraphs
   rules, 153
   styles, 520
Precision Transforms, 532
printers, 611-613
printing, 528, 535
   halftones, 528
   image files, 529
   inks, 529
   mechanicals, 529
   proofs, 529
   selecting paper, 528
   trapping, 530
printing processes
   expense, 498-499
   selecting, 499
process color, 496-498,
   505-506
   traditional, 496
proofing documents, 667-668
   in controlled light, 612
Registration, 504, 520
removing, 47
   Remove Unused feature,
      513, 526
reproduction
   accuracy, 530-532
   device-dependency,
      531-532
restoring, 525
RGB (red, green, blue),
   500-503

saturation, 507
selecting, 35-36, 505-506
separations, 76, 600
   composite proofs, 612-613
   laminate proofs, 613
   printing, 572
   proofing on laser printers,
      610
service bureaus, consulting,
   528-530
spot color, 494-496, 505-506
   accuracy, 494
   creating, 495
   editing, 506
   overlays, 496
   press plates, 495
subtractive, 500
swatches, 494, 503
   defining non-PageMaker,
      510
   selecting, 510
tables, 419-420
tag, 865
templates, 515
text, 520-522
   finding and replacing, 369
   readability, 521-522
TIFF graphics, 524
tints, 523
   defining, 510
   naming, 511
   object-level tints, 47
trapping, 537-539
   automatic, 547-550
   avoiding problems,
      543-546
   CMYK (cyan, magenta,
      yellow, black), 544
   design problems, 544-546
   framing, 544
   kiss fit, 542-543
   mechanical, 539-540
   object-level, 540-541
   raster, 541
   service bureaus, 541
   spot colors, 544
TRUMATCH, 502
WYSIWYG (What You See Is
   What You Get), 492
see also Color palette
Color dialog box, options,
   570-574
COLOR folder, 516
Color palette, 35-36, 47, 276
   colors list, 518-519

defining colors, 503-504
Fill command, 519
keyboard shortcut, 853
Line command, 519
slider bars, 505
**Color palette command
(Window menu), 35**
column guides, 287
copying, 297-298
master page guides, 291
deleting, 291, 297-298
displaying, 291
Guide Manager Plug-in, 292
defining grids, 295-297
grid libraries, 292-295
hiding, 291
locking, 290
moving, 290
to back/front, 291
setting, 288-289
**Column Guides dialog box,
288**
columns
breaks, 147
tag, 867
databases, *see* records
tables
deleting, 414
inserting, 414
resizing columns, 415-417
tabbed columns, 428-429
width, resizing automatically,
295
commands
Align, 787
Arrange menu
Align Objects, 37, 348
Bring to Front, 243
Group, 38, 346
Lock Position, 355
Remove Transformation,
446
Send to Back, 243
Ungroup, 346
Unlock, 355
Cell menu (Adobe Table)
Delete, 414
Insert Above, 414
Insert After, 414
Insert Before, 414
Insert Below, 414
Group, 414
Row/Columns Size, 416
Ungroup, 414

Control palette, Skew, 790
Edit menu
Edit Original, 207, 255, 776
Edit Story, 28, 205
Multiple Paste, 350
Paste Special, 256
Select All, 27, 214
Undo, 164, 238, 320
Edit menu (Adobe Table)
Edit Adobe Table Object,
407
Insert Object, 407
Element menu
Define Colors, 36, 503,
518
Fill, 242
Fill and Line, 242
Image, 266
Image Control, 263
Line, 240
Link Info, 200
Link Options, 200
Mask, 357
Polygon Settings, 24
Text Wrap, 381
File menu
Acquire, 267
Book, 440-441
Close, 17
Create Adobe PDF, 39, 50,
744, 760
Document Setup, 277
Export, 208, 732
Import Text, 412
Links, 200, 773, 841
New, 12, 274, 277
Place, 184, 251
Preferences, 58
Print, 30
Printer Styles, 31, 577
Recent Publications, 15, 50
Revert, 170, 222, 238, 321
Save, 14
Save As, 14
Templates, 15
File menu (Adobe Table)
Close, 408
Save Copy As, 408
Guides and Rulers menu,
Snap to Ruler, 312
Help menu, About
PageMaker, 193, 686
Layout menu
AutoFlow, 186
Copy Master Guides, 291

Entire Pasteboard, 23
Go To Page, 17
Guides and Rulers, 19-20
Insert Pages, 279
Preferences, 19
Sort Pages, 446
View, 18
Multiple Paste, 786
scripts, 711-712
Start menu, Settings, 217
Story menu
Close All Stories, 206
Close Story, 30, 205
Type menu
Choose Paragraph, 28
Define Styles, 35
Edit Tracks, 104
Expert Kerning, 103
Font, 27, 87
Hyphenation, 127, 840
Indents/Tabs, 136
Size, 27
Type Specs, 27
Utilities menu
Change, 29, 223
Create Index, 457, 474
Create Table of Contents,
449
Create TOC, 448
Find, 29, 223
Index Entry, 460
Open Template, 15, 283
PageMaker Plug-ins, 37-38
Show Index, 470-471
Spelling, 29
Spelling command, 215
Window menu
Cascade, 15, 209
Color palette, 35
Tile, 15, 209
Toolbox, 24, 82
see also scripts
**Commission Internationale de
l'Eclairage color model, 531**
**CommissionPlus (DataViz),
address, 872**
**companion column graphics,
hanging indents, 360-362**
**companion column headlines,
369-370**
alignment, 373-376
converting text into graphics,
371-372
hanging indent method, 371

multiple text block method,
370
opposing indent styles,
372-373
compiling
indexes, 457
formatting style, 475-477
table of contents, 449-450
see also indexes; table of
contents
**Compose to Printer option
(Document Setup dialog
box), 13**
composites
color proofs, 612-613
proofing tool, 607
compressing files
graphics, 261-263
JPEG compression, 263
keyboard shortcuts, 262,
860-861
LZW compression, 263
computers
DOS/Windows-based, reading
Macintosh floppy disks, 696
Macintosh, reading DOS
floppy disks, 696
concordances
creating with Sonar
Bookends, 456
defined, 454
see also indexes
Constrained Line tool, 24
keyboard shortcut, 234-235,
846
constraining
graphics, 235
magic stretch, 258-259
ovals, 235
rectangles, 235
resizing, 239
with Shift key, 326-330
**context-sensitive Help
(Shift+F1), 40**
Control palette, 31-35, 330-331
aligning text, 119
buttons
Apply, 333
nudge buttons, 331-332
case (capitalization), 99
Character mode, 33-34
commands, Skew, 790
cropping objects, 338-340
flipping objects, 341-342

indents, 145-146
keyboard shortcuts, 851-852
leading, 95
Magic Stretch, 339
moving, 32
multiple objects, 337
objects, 32-33, 338
navigating, 85, 111-112
nudge buttons, 32-33, 60,
111-112
Object mode, 32-33
Paragraph mode, 34-35
paragraphs
spacing, 150
styles, 34-35, 163
Proxy, 333-334
center point, 336
locking or sliding, 334-335
readout, positioning graphics
or text, 326
rotating objects, 343-345
scaling objects, 338-340
sizing objects, 33
proportionally, 340
skewing objects, 340-341
styles, 98
instant styles, 170
merging, 174
superscripts/subscripts, 110
text
editing, 111-112
formatting, 33-34
Text mode, 32
text-entry boxes, 331-332
type size, 89-90, 788
typeface, selecting, 87-88
typesetting, 85-86
**Copy button (Define Styles
dialog box), 174-175**
**Copy Master Guides command
(Layout menu), 291**
copying
colors, 514
documents, damaged, 842
graphics, 256-257
guides (layout grids), 297-298
from master pages, 291
index entries from master
topic list, 464-465
keyboard shortcut, 848
master pages, 303, 308
**copyright symbol (©),
keyboard shortcut, 858**
**corners on drawings,
rounding, 236**

cover stock (paper), 629
**Create Adobe PDF command
(File menu), 39 , 50, 744, 760**
**Create Color Library Plug-in,
515, 687**
**Create Index command
(Utilities menu), 457, 474**
Create Index dialog box, 474
**Create New Master Page
dialog box, 22**
**Create Table of Contents
command (Utilities menu),
449**
**Create TOC command
(Utilities menu), 448**
**CREF (Computer Ready
Electronic Files Booklet),
address, 872**
cropping
defined, 338
graphics, 259-269
with Control palette, 338-340
see also masking objects
Cropping tool, 24, 259-260
keyboard shortcut, 259, 846
**cross-column headlines,
364-366**
cross-references (indexes)
adding, 472
composing, 466-468
to another page, 482-483
see also indexes
**Ctrl+' (Control palette)
keyboard shortcut, 31, 85**
**Ctrl+ - (discretionary/soft
hyphen) keyboard shortcut,
128**
**Ctrl+/ (Go To Page) keyboard
shortcut, 17**
Ctrl+\ (subscripts), 110
**Ctrl+>/Ctrl+< (type size
adjustment), 90**
**Ctrl+? (Help command)
keyboard shortcut, 40**
**Ctrl+3 (Define Styles dialog
box) shortcut key, 171**
**Ctrl+4 (Align Objects)
keyboard shortcut, 37**
**Ctrl+8 (moving object to front
by one layer) keyboard
shortcut, 243**
**Ctrl+9 (moving object to back
by one layer) keyboard
shortcut, 243**

Ctrl+A (Select All) keyboard shortcut, 27, 214
Ctrl+D (Place command) keyboard shortcut, 184
Ctrl+E (Edit Story) keyboard shortcut, 28, 205
Ctrl+F (Find) keyboard shortcut, 223
Ctrl+G (Find Next) keyboard shortcut, 228
Ctrl+H (Change) keyboard shortcut, 223
Ctrl+I (Indents/Tabs) keyboard shortcut, 136
Ctrl+J (keyboard shortcut), 787
Ctrl+K (Define Colors) keyboard shortcut, 35
Ctrl+L (spell checker) keyboard shortcut, 215
Ctrl+M (Choose Paragraph) keyboard shortcut, 28
Ctrl+S (Save) keyboard shortcut, 14
Ctrl+Shift+\ (superscripts) keyboard shortcut, 110
Ctrl+Shift+K (all caps) keyboard shortcut, 99
Ctrl+Shift+M (em space) keyboard shortcut, 97
Ctrl+Shift+N (en space) keyboard shortcut, 97
Ctrl+Shift+P (power paste) keyboard shortcut, 190
Ctrl+Shift+T (thin space) keyboard shortcut, 97
Ctrl+spacebar (magnify view) keyboard shortcut, 19
Ctrl+T (Type Specifications) keyboard shortcut, 27, 84
Ctrl+V (Paste) keyboard shortcut, 190
Ctrl+W (Close Story) keyboard shortcut, 30, 205
Ctrl+X (Cut) keyboard shortcut, 190
Ctrl+Y (Styles palette) keyboard shortcut, 163
cursor, four-arrow, 238
Custom Line dialog box, 241
cut-in headlines (run-in), 366-367
losing style coding, 367-368
retaining style coding, 368-369

cutting
graphics, 256-257
keyboard shortcut, 848

D

data encoding, print options, 566
databases
fields, 421
importing as tables, 424-425
records (columns), 421
DCS (Desktop Color Separation) files, 251
DDE (Dynamic Data Exchange), scripts, 729-730
deadlines, setting for publications, 651-652
debugging scripts, 726
decks (headlines), 366
decompressing files, keyboard shortcuts, 860-861
defaults, 55-58
backups (files), 67
documents, 274
graphics, 276
master pages, 300
mini, 65-68
palettes, positioning, 276
PANOSE font substitution technology, 682-683
program-level (application defaults), 274
restoring, 56
publication-level (temporary defaults), 56, 65, 274
scripts, 727
sets, 68
setting, 57
styles, removing, 711
tables, 420
tabs, 140-141
type, 276
see also scripts
Define Colors command (Element menu), 36, 503, 518
Define Colors dialog box, 503, 511
Define Styles command (Type menu), 35
Define Styles dialog box, 169-170
Copy button, 174-175

defining
layout grids, guides, 295-297
palettes, 276
Delete command (Cell menu; Adobe Table), 414
deleting
guides (layout grids), 291, 297-298
index entries, 472
pages, 445-446
undoing, 283
tables, columns or rows, 414
tabs, bleeder tabs, 486
Design Class options (Expert Kerning), 103
designing
brochures, 784-793
grids, 784
fonts, 795-805
sketching, 792
types, 795-805
DesignKit (Logic Arts Corporation), address, 872
Desktop Color Separation (DCS) files, 251
desktop publishing
color separations, 76
concepts, 71-72
imposition, 77-78
outputting, 76
page layout, 73-76
planning, 70-71
printing services, contacting, 72
trapping, 76
developing book concepts, 652-654
diagnostic recompose, 840
Diagonal Line tool, keyboard shortcut, 846
dialog boxes
Add Index Entry, 460
Promote/Demote button, 465
Sort boxes, 463-464
X-Ref Override check boxes, 466
Add Word, 218
Balance Columns, 316
Book, 440-441
Change, 223
Choose Editor, 777
closing multiple, 109

Color, options, 570-574
Column Guides, 288
Copy/Paste, 823
Create Index, 474
Custom Line, 241
Define Colors, 503, 511
Define Styles, 169-170
Document, Proof check box, 607
Document Setup, 12, 277
    Number of Pages box, 279
Edit Color, 47, 503, 511, 520
Edit Styles, 169-170
Expert Kerning, 103
Export, 194
Fill and Line, 522
    options, 242-243
Font Matching Preferences, 681
Hyphenation, 127
Image Control, 263
Indents/Tabs ruler, 141
Index Entry, Page Range option buttons, 462
Index Format, 475
Links, 769
    Retain Cropping Data check box, 775-776
    symbols, 773
Multiple Paste, 350
PANOSE alert, 680
Paragraph Specifications, 28, 147, 240
Place, 252
Place Document, 184-185
Polygon Settings, 236
Polygon Specifications, 24
Preferences, 58-61
    keyboard shortcuts (options), 847
    More Preferences, 61-64
Print, 30-31, 49, 558
    options, 558-561, 565-568
Remove Pages, 445
ruler-style, 136
scripts, 730
Select Topic, 461
Show Index
    ? (question mark), 473
    codes, 473
Spacing Attributes, 122, 155
Spelling, 216, 218
sticky, 349
Story Importer, 199

Table Setup, 411
Text Wrap, 381
Translation Options, 703
Type Specifications, 27, 84
dictionaries (spelling checker)
adding, 129-130
capitalization, 218
converting non-PageMaker to ASCII format, 222
custom (personal), 217
    printing, 219
Dictionary Editor, 130, 217-223
    adding to menus, 217
Dictionary list box, 218
disabled, 221
editing, 217-223
exporting format, 221
hyphenation, algorithms, 220
importing, 220-221
    format, 221
    overwriting previous, 220
languages, 217
misspelled words, deleting, 218
multiple, 130
shared group, 218
word lists, installing, 221
words
    adding, 218-219
    deleting, 219
    hyphenated words, 129-130
Dictionary list box, 218
die cutting, defined, 631
disks
floppy
    reading DOS disks in a Macintosh, 696-697
    reading Macintosh disks in Windows machines, 696
hard disks, 831
space, saving, 766
display (screen display)
magnification, 321
    keyboard shortcuts, 322-323
    toggling, 322-323
redrawing screen, 324-325
    forced redraw, 374
    screen resolution, 324-325
Display PPD Name (printer drivers), 64
displaying, *see* **viewing**

Distiller program
defined, 761
installing, 761-762
distribute space (split justification), 363-364
distributing objects, 349-350
DocuComp (MASTERSOFT Adobe), address, 872
Document dialog box, Proof check box, 607
Document Master (master pages), 21, 300
Document Setup command (File menu), 277
Document Setup dialog box, 12-14, 277
    All Linked Files button, 14
    Compose to Printer option, 13
    Files Required for Remote Printing button, 14
    Number of Pages box, 279
    Numbers button, 12
documents
appearance, 110
creating, 50, 274-277
    from templates, 274
default settings
    graphics, 276
    type, 276
electronic publishing, 50
formatting, 275-276
    changing setup results, 281-283
    copying before changing, 281-283
    default settings, 274
    gutters, 279
    margin settings, 279-280, 282
    numbering first page, 278-279
    numbering pages, 278-279
    page number styles, 280-284, 282
    page size, 277-278
    print orientations, 277-278
    title page unnumbered, 278-280
layout grids, designing, 276
navigating, keyboard shortcuts, 851
open, maximum number, 15
pages
    deleting, 445-446

double-sided, 282
  inserting, 444-445
  inserting automatically,
    279-284
  single-sided, 282
  sorting, 446-448
printing
  double-sided, 279
  resolution, 280
swapping between Windows
  and Macintosh, 682
updating linked, 200
see also publications
dollar sign ($) tag code, 736
dot gain, 641
  adjusting for multiple inks,
    644
  correction software, 644
  defined, 267
  edit contrast/lightness,
    643-644
**double-sided pages, printing,
  279, 282**
dragging and dropping
  copying between
    publications, 16
  graphics, 256
    drawing objects, 238
    from Library palette, 257
  scripts, 711
draw images, *see* **resolution-
  independent graphics**
drawing objects, 234
  circles, 235
  fills, 242, 244
  flipping, 341-342
  layers, 243
    stacking order, 243
  lines, 234-235
    Fill and Line dialog box
      options, 242-243
    hairlines (fine), 241-242
    positioning, 235
    quick lines, 240-245
    reverse, 241
    transparent, 241, 245
    width settings, 241
  moving, 238-239
  None attribute, 244
  ovals, 235
  page rules on master page
    grids, 307
  polygons, 236-237

rectangles, 235
  around text, 395-398
  rounding corners, 236
resizing, 239
  handles, 238-239
  reversing (knockout), 244
squares, 235
  around text, 395-398
  rounding corners, 236
tools, keyboard shortcuts, 234
see also graphics
**drivers, printers, selecting
  and setup, 554-557**
Drop Cap Plug-in, 687
drop caps, 389
  creating
    as text wrap graphic,
      390-391
    with Drop Caps Plug-in,
      389-390
drop shadows, 394-395
**DTP Forum Font Catalog,
  online address, 873**
**dummy copies of documents,
  614-615**
duplex printing, 568-569
**duplicating master pages, 303,
  308**
**Dynamic Data Exchange
  (DDE), scripts, 729-730**
**dynamic page cross-
  referencing, 482-483**

E

**Edit Adobe Table Object
  command (Edit menu;
  Adobe Table), 407**
**Edit Color dialog box, 47, 503,
  511, 520**
Edit menu commands
  Edit Original, 207, 255, 776
  Edit Story, 28, 205
  Multiple Paste, 350
  Paste Special, 256
  Select All, 27, 214
  Undo, 164, 238, 320
**Edit menu commands (Adobe
  Table)**
  Edit Adobe Table Object, 407
  Insert Object, 407

**Edit Original command (Edit
  menu), 207, 255, 776**
**Edit Story command (Edit
  menu), 28, 205**
**Edit Styles dialog box,
  keyboard shortcuts, 169-171**
**Edit Tracks command (Type
  menu), 104**
Edit Tracks Plug-in, 106
editing
  color, 47, 506
    keyboard shortcut, 853
  dictionary entries (spelling
    checker), 130, 217-223
  files, 692
    EPS, 692-694
  finding and changing, 228
  graphics
    backdrops, 264
    before importing, 258
    brightness, 263
    color, 263
    filtering, 266
    imported, 255-256
    line screen settings, 264
    resolution-dependent,
      263-266
  indexes, 457
    adding cross-references,
      471-472
    capitalizing entries,
      473-474
    codes, 472-473
    consolidating entries, 471
    deleting entries, 472
    entries, 471-472
    saving work, 472
    Show Index command,
      470-471
  linked objects, 776-777
  master pages, 303
    keyboard shortcut, 302
  PPD file code, 557
  styles, 169-171
    imported, 838
    keyboard shortcut, 852
  table of contents, 452-453
  tables, 46
  text, 28-30, 111-112
    flipped, 345
    keyboard shortcuts,
      855-856
    rotated, 345
    skewed, 345

editors
Adobe Table, 405
data entry, 412
formatting text, 417-418
navigating cells, 412-413
opening, 408
selecting cells, 412-413
table setup, 411-412
Story Editor, black diamond
marker, 460
Table Editor, 409-410
elbows (drawing objects), 234
**electronic publishing (World
Wide Web), 50**
Acrobat files, 744-745
creating, 760-764
Distiller program, 761-762
fonts, 761
linking table of contents
and index, 762-763
converting
documents to Web pages,
747-750
graphics files to JPEG and
GIF files, 750-751
future outlook, 747
guidelines, 751-754
HTML (HyperText Markup
Language), 745-747
HTML Author Plug-in
content of Web page,
755-756
exporting publications to
World Wide Web,
759-760
hypertext links, 758
paragraph styles, 756-758
problem spotter report,
754-755
running, 754-764
Web sites, 753-754
Element menu commands
Define Colors, 36, 503, 518
Fill, 242
Fill and Line, 242
Image Control, 263
Line, 240
Link Info, 200
Link Options, 200
Mask, 357
Polygon Settings, 24
Text Wrap, 381

**Ellipse tool, keyboard
shortcut, 846**
see also drawing objects
**ellipsis (...), keyboard
shortcuts, 858**
em dash, 228
tag, 869
em space, 92
keyboard shortcuts, 363, 858
tag, 869
embedding
objects, 778-780
text in graphics files, 586
see also linking
embossing, defined, 631
**emulsion settings (printing),
571**
en dash, tag, 869
en space, 92
keyboard shortcuts, 858
tag, 869
**Entire Pasteboard command
(Layout menu), 23**
**EPS (Encapsulated PostScript)
files, 45, 249, 251, 815**
converting, 45
to JPEG and GIF files,
750-751
editing, 692-693
embedding text in, 586
fonts, 824
nesting, 586
previewing translated, 703
printing with embedded TIFF
files, 252
see also files, graphics; TIFF
files
**EPS Font Scanner Plug-in, 49,
681, 687**
**error detection, PostScript
error checker, 608**
**error messages, bad record
index, 839-840**
**exclamation point (!), link
status code, 774**
**Expert Kerning, Design Class
options, 103**
**Expert Kerning command
(Type menu), 103**
**Expert Kerning dialog box,
103**
Expert Kerning Plug-in, 103

**Export command (File menu),
208, 732**
Export dialog box, 194
exporting
tables as stand-alone graphics,
408-409
text, 194
troubleshooting, 842

F

F1 key (Help), 846
**F11 (step backward through
pages) keyboard shortcut, 17**
**F12 (step through pages)
keyboard shortcut, 17**
feathering, 312
felt surface paper, 629
fields (databases), 421
File menu commands
Acquire, 267
Book, 440-441
Close, 17
Create Adobe PDF, 39, 50,
744, 760
Document Setup, 277
Export, 208, 732
Links, 200, 773, 841
New, 12, 274, 277
Place, 184, 251
Preferences, 58
Print, 30
Printer Styles, 31, 577
Recent Publications, 15, 50
Revert, 170, 222, 238, 321
Save, 14
Save As, 14
Templates, 15
**File menu commands (Adobe
Table)**
Close, 408
Import Text, 412
Save Copy As, 408
files
Adobe Acrobat files
(electronic publishing),
744-745
creating, 760-764
Distiller program, 761-762
fonts, 761

linking table of contents and index, 762-763
backups, 839
    sending to service bureaus, 595
colors, CIE Lab TIFF, 531
compressing
    cross-platform (Macintosh/DOS) sharing, 701
    keyboard shortcut, 262
    utilities, 694, 701
    WinZip compression program (CD-ROM), 878
converting
    direct connections, 697
    DOS to Macintosh, 696
    Macintosh to DOS, 696
    MacBinary, 697
    modems, 697
    networks, 698-699
    PageMaker files from DOS to Macintosh, 702
    utilities, 693
damaged, saving, 200
dictionary (spelling checker), 218-219
editing, 692
EPS (Encapsulated PostScript) files, 45, 249
    converting, 45
    previewing translated, 703
    printing translated, 703
fonts, 674-675
graphics files
    compressing, 261-263
    converting between Macintosh and DOS format, 699-700
    converting to JPEG and GIF files, 750-751
    DCS (Desktop Color Separation) files, 251
    embedding text in, 586
    EPS (Encapsulated PostScript), 251, 699
    nesting, 586
    resolution-independent, 63, 248-250
    SCT (Scitex Continuous Tone) files, 251
    size alerts, 63
    TIFF (Tag Image File Format), 250-251
    translating into EPS or TIFF, 699-700

linking
    guidelines, 770
    transferring from Macintosh to DOS, 702-704
    updating linked files, 200
    viewing links, 200
PageMaker files
    sending to service bureaus, 590-591
    transferring from DOS to Macintosh, 701
PageMaker Translation Options, 702
PDF files, 39
Photo CD (PCD), 47, 699
printing, color image, 529
rebuilding, 842
saving, suggestions, 838
scripts, 711
    template, 717
submitting to service bureaus, 665-666
TEMP file, 842
text files, importing, 255-256
TIFF files (graphics), 45, 699, 732
    compression/decompression, 860-861
    importing, 515
    printing, 515
Tracking Values, creating, 106
troubleshooting problems, 842-843
Files Required for Remote Printing (Document Setup dialog box), 14
Fill command (Element menu), 242
Fill and Line command (Element menu), 242
Fill and Line dialog box, 522
    options, 242-243
fill-in blanks (forms), 436-438
fills
    graphics, 244
        drawing objects, 242
    tables, 419-420
filters (graphics)
    import filters, 51
    Photo CD Import Filter, 268
Find command (Utilities menu), 29, 223

Find & Change dialog box, new features, 823
finding and changing, 714
    batch processing (tagging), 738
    colored text, 369
    keyboard shortcuts, 856
    scripts, 717-719
    see also text, finding and changing
Fit Image preview box, 49
Flash, The (laser printer specialists), 577
flipping
    lines, 328
    objects with Control palette, 341-342
foil stamping, defined, 631
folders, SCRIPTS, 711
folding, 668
Font command (Type menu), 27, 87
Font Matching Preferences dialog box, 681
FontMinder (Ares Software Corp.), address, 873
fonts, 64-65
    Ares FontMinder, 677-678
    design issues, 795-805
    file types, 674-675
    folders, 676
    font list (Type Specifications dialog box), 86
    font managers, 675-678
    formatting, keyboard shortcuts, 853
    HTML tag, 864
    Marlett, 677
    missing, message box, 823
    organization, 675-678
    PANOSE font substitution technology, 679-680
        settings, 681-683
    PDF files, 761
    PostScript, 88, 672-674
        file types, 674
        folders, 676-677
    Precision Type sampler, 876
    rasterized, 673
    scalable, 672-673
    scanning, 49
    selecting, keyboard shortcut, 852

substituting, 679-680
  EPS graphics, 681
  permanent, 681
  recognizing simulated, 683
  temporary, 681
[T-26] sampler, 877
transferring between
  Macintosh and Windows,
  704
Treacyfaces font sampler
  (CD-ROM), 877
TrueType fonts, 672, 674
  folders, 677
Windows system, 672, 674
footers, running footers
  creating, 481-482
  defined, 477-478
  defining content, 480-481
  deleting, 482-485
  formatting, 479
  positioning, 478-479
  previewing, 481-482
  spacing, 479
footnotes, 484-485
formatting
  alignment, 363-364
    aligning to grid, 310
    automatic (master pages),
    309-310
    keyboard shortcuts, 348,
    850, 853
    undoing, 350
  attributes, finding and
    changing, 226-229
  boldface, keyboard shortcuts,
    854
  capitalization, keyboard
    shortcuts, 854
  characters, tags, 864-865
  dictionaries (spelling
    checker), importing/
    exporting, 221
  documents, 275-276
    first page numbers, 278-279
    gutters, 279
    margin settings, 279-280,
    282
    page numbers, 278-279
    unnumbered title pages,
    278-279
  fonts
    keyboard shortcuts, 853
    strikethrough, 854

footers, running footers, 479
graphics
  hanging indents, 360-362
  keyboard shortcuts, 849
headers, running headers, 479
headlines
  adding inline graphics,
    378-379
  paragraph rules, 376-378
indexes
  before compiling, 475-477
  styles, 457, 477
  text, 462-463
italicizing text, keyboard
  shortcuts, 854
justification, 363-364
  keyboard shortcut, 853
  vertical justification, 312
leading, keyboard shortcuts,
  854
numbers, hanging indents,
  360
paragraphs
  keyboard shortcuts, 855
  tags, 866-868
punctuation marks, hanging
  indents, 362-363
resizing, keyboard shortcuts,
  854
scripts, 725
style sheet options, 659-660
styles
  global, 165
  local/hard, 165-167, 170
subscripts, keyboard
  shortcuts, 854
superscripts, keyboard
  shortcuts, 854
table of contents
  entries, 450
  styles, 451-452
tables
  borders, 418-420
  color, 419-420
  column width, 415-417
  fills, 419-420
  hanging indents, 428-429
  page breaks, 410
  paragraph rules, 429-430
  row height, 415-417
  tabbed columns, 428-429
  text, 417-418
  vertical rules, 431-432

text
  alignment, 348-349
  baseline alignment,
    393-394
  boxes around or behind,
    395-398
  drop shadows, 394-395
  hanging indents, 360
  kerning, 393-394
  tracking, keyboard shortcuts,
    854
  underlining, keyboard
    shortcuts, 854
  see also tagging
forms, 435
  check box settings, 435
  fill-in blanks, 436-438
  service bureau submission
    forms, 592-599
fractions, writing, 379-381
**Fræmz, Arrowz, and Starz
(Fræmz Plug-in (ShadeTree
Marketing), 398**
  address, 873
framing, *see* **masking objects**

G

**GalleyOops (Sundae
Software), address, 873**
**GCR (gray component
replacement), 503**
GIF files
  converting PageMaker
    graphics files to, 750
  transparency, 815
**Go To Page command (Layout
menu), 17**
**goals, defining for
publications, 648-650**
grammar checker, 604-605
  see also proofing documents;
    spelling checker
graphics
  banding, preventing, 587-589
  bitmapped, 699
  constraining, 235
  conversion
    PaintShop Pro (CD-ROM),
    878
    VuePrint (CD-ROM), 878
    utilities, 700

copying between documents,
256-257
cropping, 259-269, 339-340
default settings, 276
displaying, 60
distributing, 349-350
dot gain, defined, 267
dragging and dropping, 256
from Library palette, 257
drawing objects, moving,
238-239
editing
backdrops, 264
brightness, 263
color, 263
filtering graphics, 266
imported graphics, 255-256
line screen settings, 264
files
compressing, 261-263
converting between
Macintosh and DOS,
699-700
converting to JPEG and
GIF files, 750-751
DCS (Desktop Color
Separation) files, 251
EPS (Encapsulated
PostScript) files, 815
GIF files, 815
JPEG files, 815
nesting, 586
SCT (Scitex Continuous
Tone) files, 251
size alerts, 63
fills, 242, 244
flipping, 341-342
formatting
aligning, 348-349
hanging indents, 360-362
keyboard shortcuts, 849
grouping, 345-347
keyboard shortcut, 849
importing, 251-252
editing before, 258
EPS files, 513
inline graphics, 252-255, 283
leading (Autoleading),
353-354
tagging, 736
layers, stacking order, 243
linking, 767-768
locking to page, 355-357

masking, 355-357
moving, 238-239
keyboard shortcuts, 849
tips, 585
None attribute, 244
pasting, 256-257
multiple graphics, 350-351
precision (Power Paste),
351-352
Photo CD images, 268-269, 699
photocopy quality, 264-265
positioning
Control palette readout,
326
ruler readout, 325
small graphics, 329-330
snapping to guides,
327-329
with arrow keys, 330
with Control palette,
330-340
with Shift key, 326-327
printing, 565-568
replacing, 253
resizing, 239, 258
handles, 238-239
Magic Stretch, 258-259
proportionally, 258-260
tips, 585
resolution
changing settings, 324-325
defining, 63
high-resolution, 324
resolution-dependent, 248-250
editing, 263-266
TIFF (Tag Image File
Format), 250-251
resolution-independent,
248-250
EPS (Encapsulated
PostScript) files, 249-251
reversing (knockout), 244
rotating, 343-345
tips, 587
saving in/out of publications,
255-257
scaling, 339-340
scanning
into PageMaker, 266-267
memory problems, 267
selecting, keyboard shortcuts,
849
skewing, 340-341

special effects, example, 265
TIFF files, 815
importing, 515
tips, 586
translating into EPS or TIFF
files, 699-700
vectors, 700
viewing, 260-263
keyboard shortcut (high
resolution), 261
monitor problems, 264
screen resolution, 261
World Wide Web (WWW),
814
pages, 809
wrapping text around, 381-383
see also drawing objects
**Graphics Display buttons
(Preferences dialog box), 60**
grayed out graphics, 260
**grayscale photographs,
printing, 633-641**
**greater than sign (>) tag code,
734**
greeking text, 61
**grids (layout grids), 276,
286-287**
applying, 293-294
baseline grids
alignment, 309-311
creating, 297
columns, calculating width
automatically, 295
creating, 292-293
defining, 295-297
designing, 276
guides, 286
column guides, 288-289
copying, 297-298
copying master page
guides, 291
custom, 296-297
custom ruler guides,
311-312
deleting, 291, 297-298
displaying, 291
Guide Manager Plug-in,
292-298
hiding, 291
locking, 290
margin guides, 287-288
moving, 290
moving to back/front, 291
ruler guides, 289-290

leading, 312-318
    body-copy, 310
master pages, 304-306
    page numbers, 307-308
    page rules, 307
    white space, 306
mirroring, 294-295
preview images, 294-295
reference points, 295-296
rows, calculating width
    automatically, 295
selecting, 293-294
snapping to guides/rulers, 298
**Group command (Arrange
    menu), 38, 346**
**Group command (Cell menu;
    Adobe Table), 414**
grouping, 819
graphics, keyboard shortcut,
    849
objects, 345-347
    keyboard shortcut, 346
    ungrouping, 346
table cells, 414
text, 401-402
**Guide Manager Plug-in, 37,
    44, 292, 687, 785, 825**
grid libraries
    applying grids, 293-294
    creating, 292-293
    mirroring grids, 294-295
    opening, 293
    selecting grids, 293-294
grids (layout grids)
    baseline grids, 297
    defining, 295-297
    reference points, 295-296
guides, copying or deleting,
    297-298
**guides (layout grids), 20, 37,
    44, 61, 286**
column guides, 287
    setting, 288-289
copying, 297-298
    master page guides, 291
creating, 20
custom guides, selecting,
    296-297
deleting, 291, 297-298
displaying, 291
Guide Manager Plug-in, 292
    defining grids, 295-297
    grid libraries, 292-295

hiding, 291
locking, 290
margin guides, 287
    settings, 287-288
moving, 290
    to back/front, 291
numbering, 724
ruler guides, 287
    custom, 311-312
    horizontal, 295
    setting, 289-290
    vertical, 295
**Guides and Rulers command
    (Layout menu), 19-20**
gutters
defined, 411
documents, 279

H

hairline-weight lines, 241-242
halftones, 633-641
color percentage, 636-641
creating
    with laser printers or
        imagesetters, 635-641
    with process cameras,
        634-641
defined, 635
dot gain, 641
dots, 635
process color, 638-640
screen angles, 638-640
screening color, 637-641
**handles around objects,
    graphics, 238**
hanging caps, 388-389
hanging indents
companion column
    headlines, 371
graphics, 360-362
numbers, 360
punctuation marks, 362-363
tables, 428-429
text, 360
**headers, running headers,
    477-478**
creating, 481-482
defining content, 480-481
deleting, 482-485
formatting, 479

positioning, 478-479
previewing, 481-482
spacing, 479
headlines
adding
    inline graphic, 378-379
    paragraph rules, 376-378
companion column
    headlines, 369-370
    alignment, 373-376
    converting text into
        graphics, 371-372
    handing indent method,
        371
    multiple text block
        method, 370
    opposing indent styles,
        372-373
cross-column, 364-379
cut-in heads (run-in), 366-367
    losing style coding, 367-368
    retaining style coding,
        368-369
decks, 366
kickers, 366
Help
keyboard shortcuts, 846
resources, 40-42
Help command (Ctrl+?), 40
**Help menu commands, About
    PageMaker, 193, 686**
**hiding guides (layout grids),
    291**
**high-resolution graphics,
    260-263, 324**
keyboard shortcut, 261
**high-resolution photo scans,
    599**
**highlighting text, index
    entries, 465-466**
**HiJaak Graphics Suite (Inset
    System), address, 873**
**home pages (World Wide
    Web)**
electronic publishing, 753
tags
    character formatting,
        864-865
    paragraph formatting,
        866-868
    special characters, 869
**horizontal printing (landscape
    orientation), 560**

horizontal ruler guides, 295
HTML (HyperText Markup Language), 809, 811-814
  authoring tools, 38-39
  editors, 879
  tags
    character formatting, 864-865
    paragraph formatting, 866-868
    special characters, 869
HTML Author Plug-in, 38-39, 50, 688, 744, 809, 811
  content of Web pages, 755
  converting documents to Web pages, 747-750
  exporting document to World Wide Web, 759-760
  hypertext links, 758-759
  paragraph styles, 756-758
  problem spotter report, 754
  running, 754-760
hypertext links (Web publications), 38-40, 50, 758-759
HyperText Markup Language, *see* HTML
hyphen (-), link status code, 774
hyphenation
  keyboard shortcut, 855, 858
  tags, 867, 869
Hyphenation command (Type menu), 127, 840
Hyphenation dialog box, 127

I

icons
  AutoFlow text placement, 186
  master pages, 17, 300
  page, 17
  Semiautomatic text placement, 186-187
  text placement, 185-186
Image command (Element menu), 266
Image Control command (Element menu), 263
Image Control dialog box, 263
imagesetter printing
  halftones, 635-641
  right reading, 571

  settings
    color separations, 572
    emulsion, 571
    mirror, 571
    negative, 571
    screen angle, 574
    screen frequency, 573
  settings, color, 570-574
  wrong reading, 571
Import Text command (File menu; Adobe Table), 412
importing
  databases as tables, 424-425
  dictionaries (spelling checker), 220-221
  documents
    Microsoft Word, saving before, 198
    PageMaker, 199-200
  files
    ASCII files, 198-199
    EPS files, 513-515
    FreeHand 5.0 EPS files, 515
  graphics, 251-252
    editing before, 258
  import filters, 51
    Microsoft Word, 196-198
  indexes
    codes, 197
    entries from word processors, 457-458
    master topic list, 457-458
  Read Embedded OPI Image Links check box, 515
  spreadsheets as tables, 424-425
  stories, Story Editor, 207
  table of contents, 197
  tables, 197
    as stand-alone graphics, 409
    finding and changing imported data, 427
    options, 406-407
    word processor tables, 426
  text, 192-201
    Microsoft Word, 196-198
    to tables, 412
    troubleshooting, 841
  text files, re-importing, 255-256
  TIFF files, 515
imposition, 579-583, 668
  defined, 600

indenting, 141-145
  bullets, 143
  Control palette, 145-146
  first lines in paragraphs, 142
  hanging indents, 142-143
    graphics, 360-362
    numbers, 360
    punctuation marks, 362-363
    tables, 428-429
  keyboard shortcut, 855
  tag, 866
Indents/Tabs command (Type menu), 136
Indents/Tabs Ruler, 136-137
Indents/Tabs Ruler dialog box, 141
Index Entry command (Utilities menu), 460
Index Entry dialog box, Page Range option buttons, 462
Index Format dialog box, 475
indexes, 225, 454
  book list, creating, 474-475
  coding entries, 456, 458-460
    copying entries from master topic list, 464-465
    cross-references, 466-468
    each occurrence of word, 468-470
    formatting text, 462-463
    highlighting text, 465-466
    keyboard shortcuts, 460, 856-857
    levels, 461
    location reference, 460
    multiple entries at one location, 464-465
    names, 469-470
    opening codes, 473-474
    page ranges, 462
    Promote/Demote button, 465
    rotating topic levels, 465
    selecting topics from topic list, 461
    topics, 460
  compiling, 457, 474-477
  concordances, defined, 454
  content, 664
  cross-reference, 466-468
    to another page, 482-483
  editing, 457

adding cross-references, 471-472
codes, 472-473
consolidating entries, 471
entries, 471-472
saving work, 472
Show Index command, 470-471
entries
  capitalizing, 473-474
  deleting, 472
  formatting, 462-463
  importing from word processors, 457-458
  organizing, 455
  sorting, 463-464
formatting before compiling, 475-477
keyboard shortcuts, 850-851
linking to World Wide Web pages, 762-763
master topic list
  creating, 456
  importing, 457-458
  selecting entries from, 461
placing, 477
proofreading, 605
see also herein references, 468
see/see also references, 466-468
Story Editor, 458-460
styles, 457, 477
  nested, 476
  run-in, 476
inherited style assignment, 165
initial caps, 388
drop caps, 389
  as text wrap graphic, 390-391
  Drop Caps Plug-in, 389-390
hanging caps, 388-389
raised caps, 388
inkjet printers, 612
inline graphics, 253-254, 283, 3522-355
formatting, hanging indents, 360-362
inserting in headlines, 378-379
leading (Autoleading), 353-354

Insert Above command (Cell menu; Adobe Table), 414
Insert After command (Cell menu; Adobe Table), 414
Insert Before command (Cell menu; Adobe Table), 414
Insert Below command (Cell menu; Adobe Table), 414
Insert Object command (Edit menu; Adobe Table), 407
Insert Pages command (Layout menu), 279
inserting
backgrounds behind text, 399-401
binding services, 631
keyboard shortcut, 848
pages in documents, 444-445
  automatically, 279-284
  keyboard shortcut, 444
  undoing, 283
screens behind text, 399-401
tables, columns or rows, 414
insertion point, keyboard shortcuts, 855-856
installation
dictionaries, word lists, 221
options, 832
palettes, 276
Plug-ins, 686
procedures, 832-835
scripts, 717
serial numbers, 833-834
system requirements, 830-831
internal links, 766
internal locations, defined, 758
italicizing text
index entries, 462-463
keyboard shortcut, 854
tag, 864
see also formatting

J-K

JPEG files, 815
compression, 263
converting PageMaker graphics files to, 750
justification, 363-364
keyboard shortcut, 853

vertical justification, 312
see also formatting
Kai Krause home page, 753
kerning text, 46, 92, 97, 100-103, 393-394
automatic, 102, 125-126, 132
keyboard shortcuts, 857
manual, 101-103, 131
tag, 864
keyboard
arrow keys, nudging objects, 330
F1 key (Help), 846
Shift key, positioning text or graphics, 326-327
keyboard shortcuts
Alt+Ctrl+spacebar (reduce view), 19
capitalization, 99
  all caps, 99
Change (Ctrl+H), 223
clearing, 848
closing documents, 847
compressing files, 262
Control palette, 31, 85
copying, 848
cutting, 190, 848
drawing tools
  Constrained Line tool, 235
  Line tool, 235
  Toolbox, 234
editing master pages, 302
F11 (step backward through pages), 17
F12 (step through pages), 17
files, compression/decompression, 860-861
finding, 223, 228
fonts, selecting, 852
formatting
  alignment, 37, 348, 853
  attributes, 98
  bold formatting, 854
  capitalization, 854
  centering text (Shift+Ctrl+C), 118
  flush left text, 117
  flush right text, 118
  fonts, 853
  italicizing, 854
  justification, 118, 853
  leading, 854

paragraphs, 855
resizing, 854
strikethrough, 854
subscripts, 854
superscripts, 854
tracking, 854
underlining, 854
graphics
adjusting, 849
bringing to front, 243
grouping, 849
sending to back, 243
viewing in high resolution, 261
grouping objects, 346
Help, 40, 846
contextsensitive, 40
hyphenation, 128
indenting, 136
indexing, 459-487, 850-851
coding entries, 856-857
entries, 460
inserting, 848
pages in documents, 279, 444
linking, 847
locking, 847
magnification, 19, 322-323
masking objects, 357, 850
minimizing, 850
navigating documents, 851
nudging objects, 852
opening documents, 847
palettes
Color palette, 853
Control palette, 851-852
Styles palette, 163, 852
pasting, 190, 848
power pasting, 190
placing, 184
Preferences dialog box
options, 847
printing, 847
redrawing screen, 324, 374
reverting, 847
rulers on/off, 848
saving, 14, 847
scrolling, 851
search and replace, 856
selecting
paragraphs, 28
Select All, 27, 214, 848

spacing, 97
em spaces, 363
special characters, 858
metacharacters, 859-860
special commands, 860-861
spell checker (Control+L)
Story Editor, 28, 205, 446, 850-851
closing, 30, 205
styles, selecting, 852
subscripts, 110
superscripts, 110
tabs, 136
text
kerning, 857
moving insertion point, 855-856
recomposition, 861
selecting, 855
Text tool, 82
toggling guides display, 291
Toolbox, Cropping tool, 259
tools, list, 846
turn guides off, 787
type specifications, 84
undoing mistakes, 238, 320, 848
views, 850
Keyline Plug-in, 395-398, 688
kickers (headlines), 366
knockout graphics, 244
lines, 241
see also paper; reversing objects
knockouts (color), 511-512
Kodak Color Management System, installing device profiles, 835
Kodak Monitor Installer, 536
Kodak Precision Color Management System (CMS), 65

L

laid paper, 629
laminate color proofs, 613
landscape orientation (horizontal printing), 560
languages, spelling checker dictionaries, 217

laser printers (PostScript printers), 558
advantages, 554
cartridges
cleaning, 575
recycling, 577
color proofing
color printers, 611
color separations on laser printers, 610
composite proofs, 612-613
in controlled light, 612
laminate proofs, 613
memory colors, 611-612
comparisons to non-PostScript printers, 569
fixative sprays, 575
foil embossing, 577
halftone printing, 635-641
high-resolution output, 574-576
optimizing output, 574-577
options
bleeding tabs, 568
data encoding, 566-568
downloadable fonts, 567-568
duplex printing, 568-569
graphics handling, 565-568
imagesetting color, 570-574
page independence, 568
PostScript error checking, 567-568
printing to disk, 565-568
paper
iron-on, 577
special, 576-577
parameter settings, 558-561
photocopying output, 576
phototypesetter, 576
proofing tools
composites, 607
Proof check box (Document dialog box), 607
thumbnails, 606
renting for impositions and bleeds, 576
settings
blank pages, 560
book printing, 560
both pages, 560
centering pages, 563-564

collating pages, 559
copy number, 559
even pages, 560
non-printing objects, 560
odd pages, 560
orientation, 560
page range, 559
paper size, 561-564
paper source, 561
printer's marks, 562-564
proofs, 559
reader's spreads, 560
registration marks, 562-564
reverse order, 559
scaling images, 564
thumbnails, 564
tiling images, 564
setup, 554-557
styles, 577-578
toner adjustments, 575
warming up, 575
laser proofs, 667
laser spots, 635
LaserCheck (Systems of
Merritt), 608-610
address, 873
layers
graphics, stacking order, 243
moving objects to back/front
by one layer, 243
layout grids, 276, 286-287
applying, 293-294
baseline grids
alignment, 309-311
creating, 297
columns, calculating width
automatically, 295
creating, 292-293
defining, 295-297
designing, 276
guides, 286
column guides, 287-289
copying, 297-298
copying master page
guides, 291
custom, 296-297
custom ruler guides,
311-312
deleting, 291, 297-298
displaying, 291
Guide Manager Plug-in,
292-298
hiding, 291

locking, 290
margin guides, 287-288
moving, 290
moving to back/front, 291
ruler guides, 287, 289-290
leading grids, 312-318
body-copy, 310
master pages, 304-306
page numbers, 307-308
page rules, 307
white space, 306
mirroring, 294-295
preview images, 294-295
reference points, 295-296
rows, calculating width
automatically, 295
selecting, 293-294
snapping to guides/rulers,
298
Layout menu commands
Copy Master Guides, 291
Entire Pasteboard, 23
Go To Page, 17
Guides and Rulers, 20
Insert Pages, 279
Preferences, 19
Sort Pages, 446
View, 18
Layout Problems check boxes
(Preferences dialog box), 59
Layout view
finding and changing, 717
spelling, 217
LBOs (lines, boxes, ovals), 234
leading, 93-96, 155-158
Autoleading, 96-100
baseline, 158
body-copy, master pages, 310
graphics, inline graphics,
353-354
grids, 312
keyboard shortcut, 854
mini-defaults, 158
proportional, 158
top of caps, 158
leaning objects (skewing),
340-341
less than sign (<) tag code, 734
libraries
color, 507-510
adding notes, 516
COLOR folder, 516
creating, 515-516

grids
applying, 293-294
creating, 292-293
mirroring grids, 294-295
opening, 293
preview images, 294-295
selecting, 293-294
Plug-ins, Zephyr Specs,
689-690
styles, 179-180
Library palette, 179-180
creating, 257
dragging and dropping
graphics, 257
opening, 257
Line command (Element
menu), 240
Line End function (Type
Specifications dialog box),
107
line screen
dot gain, 641
adjusting for multiple inks,
644
correction software, 644
edit contrast/lightness,
643-644
guidelines, 643
output line screen setting,
641-643
scanning resolution, 641-643
settings, 264
Line tool, 24
keyboard shortcut, 234-235
lines
drawing, 234-235
Fill and Line dialog box
options, 242-243
flip effect, 328
hairline (fine), 241-242
pixel-edge effect, 328
positioning, 235
quick lines, 240-245
reverse, 241
transparent, 241, 245
width, 316, 241
Link dialog box, Retain
Cropping Data check box,
775-776
Link Info command (Element
menu), 200
Link Options command
(Element menu), 200

linking
  advantages
    saving disk space, 766
    team collaborations on
      documents, 767
    updating work, 767
  breaking links, 773-780
  control, 769
  defined, 765
  editing linked objects,
    776-777
  finding unlinked elements,
    841
  graphics, 767-768
  guidelines, 770
  in PageMaker, 770-771,
    777-778
    suggestions, 839
  indexes, 762-763
  internal links, 766
  keyboard shortcut, 847-848
  OLE (Object Linking and
    Embedding), 766, 771-772,
    778-779
  relinking, 776
  retain cropping feature,
    775-776
  table of contents, 762-763
  updating links, 773-780
  see also embedding
**Links command (File menu),
  200, 773, 841**
Links dialog box, 769
  symbols, 773
loading
  dictionaries, word lists, 221
  options, 832
  palettes, 276
  Plug-ins, 686
  procedures, 832-835
  scripts, 717
  serial numbers, 833-834
  system requirements, 830-831
**location references (indexes),
  460**
**Lock Position command
  (Arrange menu), 355**
locking, 819
  Control palette, Proxy, 334-335
  graphics, 355-357
  guides (layout grids), 290
  keyboard shortcut, 847
LZW file compression, 262
  see also compressing files

M

Macintosh
  AppleTalk, 698
  operating systems, 696-697
macros, *see* scripts; tagging
Magic Stretch (resizing), 13
  from Control palette, 339
  graphics, 258-259
magnification, 321
  keyboard shortcuts, 322-323
  toggling, 322-323
Magnifying Glass tool, 19, 24
  keyboard shortcut, 846
Manual text icon, 185-186
margin settings
  documents, 279-280, 282
    gutters, 279
  guides, 287-288
    copying master page
      guides, 291
    deleting, 291
    displaying, 291
    Guide Manager Plug-in,
      292-298
    hiding, 291
    locking, 290
    moving, 290
    moving to back/front, 291
**Mask command (Element
  menu), 357**
masking, 820
  keyboard shortcut, 357, 850
  objects, 355-357
  text, 401-402
  troubleshooting, 586
  see also cropping
**master page grid, *see* layout
  grids**
master page icons, 17
Master Page palette, 44
master pages, 21-22
  alignment, snap to rulers, 312
  applying, 22, 300-302
    to one page, 301
  creating, 21, 302
    keyboard shortcut, 302
  defined, 299-300
  Document Master, 21, 300
  duplicating, 303, 308
  editing, 303
    keyboard shortcut, 302

  guides, margin guides,
    287-288
  icons, 300
  layout grids, 304-306
    leading grids, 312-318
    page numbers, 307-308
    page rules, 307-316
    white space, 306
  multiple, 821
  navigating, 22
    between, 300
  [None] listing, 304
Master Pages palette, 22, 300
  keyboard shortcut, 846
master topic list (indexes)
  creating, 456
  importing, 457-458
  selecting entries from, 461
measurements
  em space, 92
  en space, 92
  picas, 90-92
  points, 90-92
  setting, 58-59, 92
  tagging, 736
meetings, preliminary
  materials needed, 655-656
  prepress issues, 656-657
  production issues, 656-657
memory colors, 611-612
**metacharacters, keyboard
  shortcuts, 859-860**
Microsoft Corporation
  address, 874
  Microsoft OLE (Object Linking
    and Embedding), 771-772
  Microsoft Word, importing,
    196-198
mini-defaults, 65-68, 275
  colors, 515
  leading, 158
  scripts, 727
  see also publication defaults;
    temporary defaults
mini-reverting, 321
**minimizing, keyboard
  shortcut, 850**
mirror printing, 571
mirroring
  grids, 294-298
  objects, 341-342
modems, 809
  converting files, 697

molding text, 384-386
monitors, 831
  calibrating, 536
  viewing graphics, 264
mouse, insertion point
  keyboard shortcuts, 855-856
moving
  graphics
    drawing objects, 238-239
    keyboard shortcuts, 849
    tips, 585
  guides (layout grids), 290
    column guides, 288
    to back/front, 291
  objects
    with Control palette, 337
    with X and Y coordinates, 338
  see also navigating;
    positioning
Multerer, Boyd, 292
multiple master pages, 44
Multiple Paste command (Edit menu), 350, 786
Multiple Paste dialog box, 350

N

names, index entries, 469-470
navigating
  documents, keyboard
    shortcuts, 851
  master pages, 300
  table cells, 412-413
  see also moving
negative printing, 571
nested style, indexes, 476
nesting files, graphics, 586
networking Macintoshes and PCs, 698-699
New command (File menu), 12, 274, 277
Next Style function, 172
non-printing objects, printing, 560
[None] listing (master pages), 304
None attribute, drawing objects, 244
normal resolution, graphics, 261

nudging
  buttons, 32-33, 60, 111-112
    Control palette buttons, 331-332
  objects, 330
  power nudging, keyboard shortcut, 852
numbering
  chapters in book list, 443-444
  lists, 143
pages, 278-279
  first page, 278-279
  master pages, 307-308
  renumbering in book list, 441
  styles, 280, 282
  tag, 869
  title pages, 278-279
numbers
  formatting, hanging indents, 360
  tagging, 736

O

Object Linking and Embedding, *see* **OLE; OLE 2.0**
Object mode (Control palette), 32
Object Series (PhotoDisc), address, 873
object-oriented graphics, *see* **resolution-independent graphics**
objects
  alignment, 37-38, 44, 348-349
    keyboard shortcut, 850
    Snap commands, 20
  colors
    applying to imported objects, 524-526
    applying to PageMaker drawn objects, 522-524
    assigning, 35-36
    removing, 47
  controlling, 31-33
  distributing, 44, 349-350
  edges, 724
  embedding, 778-780
  graphics
    clipping, 45
    importing, 45

  grouping, 38, 45, 345-347
    ungrouping, 45, 346
  layers, 243
    moving, 788
    stacking order, 45, 243
  LBOs (lines, boxes, ovals), 234
  linking, 778-779
    editing linked objects, 776-777
  locking to page, 45, 355
    unlocking, 45
  masking, 45, 355-357
    troubleshooting, 586
  moving, 32-33
  multi-sided, drawing, 45
  nonprinting, 48
  numbering layered, 724
  object-level tints, 47
  OLE (Object Linking and Embedding), transferring between Macintosh and DOS, 703
  pasting
    multiple objects, 350-351
    power pasting, 351-352
  photographs, PhotoDisc sampler, 876
  resizing handles, 238
  rotating, 26-27, 789
  sizing, 33
  text blocks, 182
    selecting, 191
  trapping, 48, 540-541
OLE (Object Linking and Embedding)
  embedding objects, 778-780
  linking objects, 771-772, 778-779
  tables
    creating, 407
    opening, 407
    saving, 408
    updating, 408
OLE 2.0 (Object Linking and Embedding), 52
online services, addresses, 872
Open Template command (Utilities menu), 15, 283
Open Template Plug-in, 688
opening
  Adobe Table Editor, 408
  index entry codes, 473-474

keyboard shortcut, 847
libraries, 257
grids, 293
tables, OLE, 407
templates, 284
PageMaker, 283
operating systems
Macintosh, 696-697
Windows 95, 696
OPI (Open Prepress Interface), 49
orientations (printing)
documents, 277-278
settings, 560
orphans, 147-157
outlines, tag, 864
Oval tool, 24, 25
keyboard shortcut, 234, 846
ovals
drawing, 235
moving, 238-239
None attribute, 244
resizing, 239
handles, 239
reversing (knockout), 244
see also drawing objects
overlays, creating notes, 504
overprinting (color), 511-512

P

[p]Sonar TOC 2.1 (Virginia Systems, Inc.), address, 874
Page Break Before command (Paragraph Specification dialog box), 147
page breaks
tables, 410
tag, 867
page icons, 17
page size (documents), 277-278
PageMaker
files, sending to service bureaus, 590-591
home page, 753
new features, 817-825
Align/Distribute, 819
baseline leading, 825
colors, 821
Copy/Paste into dialog boxes, 823

EPS files (fonts), 824
Find & Change dialog box features, 823
grouping, 819
Guide Manager, 825
locking, 819
masking, 820
master pages, 821
missing fonts message, 823
scripting, 823
searching and replacing, 823
Story Editor, scripting, 823
tagging, 823
templates, opening, 283
PageMaker 5.0, backwards compatibility, 14
PageMaker Plug-ins command (Utilities menu), 37, 38
PageMaker Plug-ins list (Utilities menu), 15
PageMill (Web page authoring tool), 747
pages
deleting, 445-446
undoing, 283
designing, 44-46
double-sided, 282
inserting, 444-445
automatically, 279-284
keyboard shortcut, 444
undoing, 283
multiple master pages, 44
numbering, 278-279
master pages, 307-308
renumbering in book list, 441
styles, 282
tag, 869
redrawing, keyboard shortcuts, 851
single-sided, 282
sorting, 446-448
title pages, unnumbered, 278-279
PageTools (Extensis Corp.), address, 873
paint graphics, *see* resolution-dependent graphics
PaintShop Pro (CD-ROM), 878
palettes
Color palette, 276
keyboard shortcut, 853

Control palette, 330-331
Apply button, 333
cropping objects, 338-340
flipping objects, 341-342
keyboard shortcuts, 851-852
locking or sliding Proxy, 334-335
Magic Stretch, 339
moving multiple objects, 337
moving objects with X and Y coordinates, 338
nudge buttons, 331-332
Proxy, 333-334
Proxy center point, 336
rotating objects, 343-345
scaling objects, 338-340
sizing proportionally, 340
skewing objects, 340-341
text-entry boxes, 331-332
defining, 276
installing, 276
Library palette, 179-180
dragging and dropping graphics, 257
Master Pages palette, 300
keyboard shortcut, 846
positioning, default settings, 276
Scripts palette, 51, 277, 708, 710-713
keyboard shortcut, 846
Styles, 711
keyboard shortcut, 852
Tool palette, keyboard shortcut, 846
PANOSE (font substitution), 64-65, 679-680
settings
defaults, 682-683
substitution frequency, 681
swapping documents between Windows and Macintosh, 682
PANOSE Alert dialog box, 680
paper
bond, 629
coated book, 629
coated stock paper, 630
color, 630
cover stock, 629
felt surface paper, 629
grain, 631

ink holdout, 629
laid paper, 629
opacity, 630
selecting for publication,
  628-631
size, 630
weight, 630
woven, 629
paper graphics, 244
lines, 241
paper source, 561
**paragraph marks, keyboard
  shortcut, 858**
**Paragraph mode (Control
  palette), 34-35**
**paragraph rules, tables,
  429-430**
**paragraph specifications,
  keyboard shortcut, 847**
**Paragraph Specifications
  command (Type menu), 28**
**Paragraph Specifications
  dialog box, 28, 240**
aligning text, 118
indents, 145
Keep Lines Together
  command, 147
Keep With Next command,
  147
Page Break Before command,
  147
Paragraph Space settings, 150
paragraphs, 116-117
breaks
  columns, 147
  controlling, 146-149
  lines, 146
  page, 147
formatting
  alignment, 34
  keyboard shortcuts, 855
  tags, 866-868
indenting, 141-145
  bullets, 143
  Control palette, 145-146
  first lines, 142
  hanging indents, 142-143
leading, 155-158
line length options, 131-132
  priority order, 132-133
orphans, 147-157
rules, 152-155
  colors, 153

selecting, 214
spacing, 150-151
  measurements, 151
  rules, 155
styles, 34-35
  assigning automatically,
    164-165
  asterisk (*), 176
  augmenting, 165-167
  Based On function, 172
  cascading, 172
  colors, 520
  consistency, 175
  copying, 174-175
  defining, 169-171
  editing, 169-1771
  identifying, 167-168
  importing, 175-176
  instant, 170
  libraries, 179-180
  menus, 163
  merging, 173-174
  mimicking, 172
  naming, 178
  Next Style function, 172
  No style, 170
  overriding, 165-167
  page breaks, 178
  palettes, 163
  removing, 170
  search and replace, 167
  style sheets, 176-180
  tables of contents, 178
  tags, 868
tab characters, 138
tab stops, 136-138
tables, 138
widows, 147-157
**Paragraphs dialog box, Rules
  command, 792**
**Paragraph Specifications
  dialog box, Column Break
  Before command, 147**
**Paste Special command (Edit
  menu), 256**
Pasteboard, 23
pasting
graphics, 256-257
keyboard shortcut, 848
objects
  multiple objects, 350-351
  power pasting, 351-352

**PCL-based printers,
  disadvantages, 554**
**PDF (Portable Document
  Format) files, 39-40, 50,
  744-745**
creating, 760-764
Distiller program, installing,
  761-762
fonts, 761
linking table of contents and
  index, 762-763
perfect bound books, 631
permanent defaults, 274
  see also application defaults;
    program-level defaults
**personal dictionary, *see*
  dictionaries, custom**
Photo CD Import Filter, 268
Photo CDs, 268-269
scans, 599
**photocopying graphics,
  improving quality, 264-265**
**PhotoDisc photographs
  sampler (CD-ROM), 876**
photographs
importing, 47
PhotoDisc sampler, 876
printing in halftones, 633-641
scanning
  into PageMaker, 266-267
  memory problems, 267
Photoshop, home page, 753
**Photoshop-compatible filters,
  266**
picas, 90-92
pixel-edge effect, 328
**PIXymbols (Precision Type),
  address, 873**
**Place command (File menu),
  184, 251**
Place dialog box, 252
Read Tags feature, 196
Retain Format feature, 196
**Place Document dialog box,
  184-185**
placing
graphics, tips, 585
indexes, 477
planning publications, 661
audience, 648-650
bidding, 657-658
budget, 650-651
color elements, 664

deadline, 651-652
developing book concept, 652-654
goals, 648-650
graphics
    organizing, 660-661
    placing, 663
index content, 664
preliminary meeting
    materials, 655-656
    production issues, 656-657
prepress issues, 656-657
schedule, 651-652
setup
    books, 661-662
    design grids, 661
    master pages, 661
    preferences, 662-663
special effects, 664
style sheets, 658-659
    formatting, 659-660
testing new book concept, 654-655
text, 658
    editing, 660
    placing, 663
Plug-ins
    Add Cont'd Line, 687
    Balance Columns, 687
    Build Booklet, 50, 579-583, 687
    Bullets and Numbering, 143, 687
    CleanSweep, 687
    Create Color Library, 515, 687
    Drop Caps, 389-390, 687
    Edit Tracks, 106
    EPS Font Scanner, 49, 681, 687
    Expert Kerning, 103
    Guide Manager, 37, 44, 292, 687
        copying guides, 297-298
        defining grids, 295-297
        deleting guides, 297-298
        grid libraries, 292-295
    HTML Author, 38, 688, 744, 809, 811
        converting documents to
            Web pages, 747-750
        content of Web page, 755
        exporting documents to
            Web pages, 759-760
        hypertext links, 758-759

paragraph styles, 756-758
problem spotter report, 754
running, 754-760
installing, 686
Keyline, 395-398, 688
listing installed plug-ins, 686
Open Template, 688
Pub Info, 168, 599, 688
running, 686
Running Headers/Footers, 478-487, 688
Sonar Bookends, 456-457
third-party
    Arrowz, 691
    bar codes, 692
    ExecuTable, 691
    Extensis PageTools, 690-691
    Fræmz, 398, 691
    GalleyOops, 691
    Starz, 691
    Zephyr Specs, 689-690
Trapping, 48
Update PPD, 688
Plug-ins submenu, 686
plus sign (+), link status code, 774
PM5 Custom Settings program, converting PageMaker 5.0 dictionaries, 221
PM6/RSRC/LINGUIST/PRX/ USENGLSH, shared dictionaries file, 218
pointer
    four-arrow, 238
    insertion point, keyboard
        shortcuts, 855-856
Pointer tool, 24, 25
    dragging and dropping, 16
    keyboard shortcut, 846
points, 90-92
Polygon Settings command (Element menu), 24
Polygon Settings dialog box, 236
Polygon Specifications dialog box, 24
Polygon tool, 24
    keyboard shortcut, 234, 846
polygons
    adjusting settings, 237
    drawing, 236-237

moving, 238-239
None attribute, 244
resizing, 239
reversing (knockout), 244
see also drawing objects
Portable Document Format (PDF), 50
portrait orientation (vertical printing), 560
positioning
    graphics
        Control palette readout, 326
        ruler readout, 325
        small, 329-330
        snapping to guides, 327-329
        with arrow keys, 330
        with Control palette, 330-340
        with Shift key, 326-327
    palettes, default settings, 276
    text
        Control palette readout, 326
        ruler readout, 325
        small, 329-330
        snapping to guides, 327-329
        with Control palette, 330-340
        with Shift key, 326-327
    see also moving
POSTools (Azalea Software), address, 873
PostScript, 249
    error checkers, 608
    fonts, 88, 672-674
        kerning, 102
    printers, *see* laser printers
Power Paste, 351-352
PPD (PostScript Printer Discription) files, 834
    editing code, 557
Precision Transforms (PT), 532
Precision Type font sampler (CD-ROM), 876
Preferences command (File menu), 19, 58
Preferences dialog box, 58-61
    Control palette
        measurements, 60

Graphics Display buttons, 60
Layout Problems check
  boxes, 59-60
Measurements option, 59
More Preferences, 61-64
  Turn Pages When
    Autoflowing, 62
options, keyboard shortcuts,
  847
preflight meetings, 620
  goals, 623-624
  preparations, 621
  samples, 622-623
  prepress strategies, 624-626
prepress strategies, 48-50
**PrePRESS Main Street home
  page, 754**
press check, 615-616
**Print command (File menu),
  30**
**Print dialog box, 30-31, 49,
  558**
  Features button, 49
  options, 558-561, 565-568
  reader's spreads, 49
print shop
  bidding process, 621
    bid forms, 628
    binder services, 631
    paper specifications,
      628-631
  line screen recommendations
    adjusting for multiple inks,
      644
    dot gain, 641
    dot gain correction
      software, 644
    editing contrast/lightness,
      643-644
    guidelines, 643
    output line screen setting,
      641-643
    scanning resolution,
      641-643
  preflight meeting, 620
    goals, 623-624
    preparations, 621-623
    prepress strategies,
      624-626
    samples, 622-623
  proofing documents, 668
  LaserCheck, 608-610
**Printer Styles command (File
  menu), 31, 577**

printers
  color printers, 611
    composite, 612-613
  drivers
    Display PPD Name, 64
    selecting, 554-557
    setup, 554-557
  imagesetters
    color separations, 572
    color settings, 570-574
    emulsion settings, 571
    mirror setting, 571
    negative setting, 571
    right reading, 571
    screen angle, 574
    screen frequency, 573
    wrong reading, 571
  installing PPD (PostScript
    Printer Description) files,
    834
  laser printers (PostScript), 558
    advantages, 554
    cleaning cartridges, 575
    fixative sprays, 575
    foil embossing, 577
    halftone printing, 635-641
    high-resolution, 576
    high-resolution output,
      574-575
    iron-on paper, 577
    optimizing output, 574-577
    paper selection, 576-577
    parameter settings, 558-561
    photocopying output, 576
    phototypesetter, 576
    proofing tools, 606-607
    recycling cartridges, 577
    renting for impositions and
      bleeds, 576
    toner adjustments, 575
    warming up, 575
  non-PostScript printers,
    comparisons to PostScript
    (laser) printers, 569
  options
    bleeding tabs, 568
    data encoding, 566-568
    downloadable fonts,
      567-568
    duplex printing, 568-569
    graphics handling, 565-568
    page independence, 568
    PostScript error checking,
      567-568
    printing to disk, 565-568

PCL-based, disadvantages, 554
settings
  centering pages, 563-564
  paper size, 561-564
  paper source, 561
  printer's marks, 562-564
  registration marks, 562-564
  resolution, 13
  scaling images, 564
  thumbnails, 564
  tiling images, 564
setup
  blank pages, 560
  book printing, 560
  both pages, 560
  collating pages, 559
  copy number, 559
  even pages, 560
  non-printing objects, 560
  odd pages, 560
  orientation, 560
  page range, 559
  proofs, 559
  reader's spreads, 560
  reverse order, 559
styles, 577-578
  creating, 49
printer's marks, 510, 562
printing, 30-31, 48-50
  checklists, 583
  color, 528, 535
    expense, 498-499
    halftones, 528
    inks, 529
    selecting paper, 528
    selecting processes, 499
    trapping, 530
  color image files, 529
  color matching systems, 528
  dictionaries, custom
    (personal), 219
  documents
    double-sided, 279
    orientations, 277-278
    resolution, 280
  fitting to paper, 49
  graphics
    EPS (Encapsulated
      PostScript) file, 252
    screen resolution, 261
  keyboard shortcut, 847
  mechanicals, 529
  methods, 528
  nonprinting objects, 48

photographs in halftones, 633-641
printer's marks, 510
service bureaus, consulting, 528-530
thumbnail sketches, 792
TIFF graphics files, 515
to disk, 565-568
process cameras, 634-641
process color, 638-640
program-level defaults, 56, 274
programming interactivity, scripts, 728-730
programs, Distiller, 761
Proof button (tracking), 105
Proof check box (Document dialog box), 607
proofing documents
at print shop, 668
color proofing, 667-668
color printers, 611
color separations on laser printers, 610
composite proofs, 612-613
in controlled light, 612
laminate proofs, 613
memory colors, 611-612
copy proofing, 666-667
grammar checker, 604-605
indexes, 605
laser printer problems, 607-608
laser proofs, 667
composites, 607
Proof check box (Document dialog box), 607
thumbnails, 606
LaserChecker, 608-610
on-screen, 608
PostScript error checker, 608
print shop
blueline, 614
dummy copies, 614-615
inspecting film, 614
press check, 615-616
swatches of ink and varnish, 613-614
proofreaders, hiring, 605-606
signing off documents, 606
spelling checker, 604-605
table of contents, 605
tips, 606

proofs, checklists, 583
Proximity dictionary, 217
see also dictionaries
Proxy (Control palette), 333-334
center Proxy point, 336
locking or sliding, 334-335
PT (Precision Transforms), 532
Pub Info Plug-in, 168, 599, 688
publication-level defaults, 274
publications
color, 47-48
copying to another publication, 16
creating, 12-14
defaults, 56, 65
acccessing, 26
sets, 68
loading, 15-17
navigating, 17
planning, 661
assembling graphics, 660-661
audience, 648-650
bidding, 657-658
books, 661-662
budget, 650-651
color elements, 664
deadline, 651-652
design grids, 661
developing book concept, 652-654
editing text, 660
goal, 648, 648-650
index content, 664
master pages, 661
placing graphics and text, 663
preference settings, 662-663
preliminary meeting materials, 655-658
prepress issues, 656-658
production issues, 656-658
schedule, 651-652
special effects, 664
style sheet formatting, 659-660
style sheets, 658-659
testing new book concept, 654-655
text, 658
saving, 14

viewing, 18-19
see also documents
Publish Magazine Inc. (Integrated Media), address, 874
publishing
binding, 668
electronic publishing
Acrobat files, 744-745
converting documents to Web pages, 747-750
converting graphics files to JPEG and GIF files, 750-751
creating Adobe Acrobat files, 760-764
future outlook, 747
guidelines, 751-754
HTML (HyperText Markup Language), 745-747
running HTML Author Plug-in, 754-7664
Web sites, 753-754
folding, 668
imposition, 668
proofing documents
at print shop, 668
color, 667-668
copy proofing, 666-667
laser proofs, 667
service bureaus, submitting files to, 665-666
punctuation marks, hanging indents, 362-363

Q

QuarkXPress (Quark, Inc.), address, 874
question mark (?)
link status code, 774
Show Index dialog box, 473
quick lines, 240-245
quotation marks, 62, 229
keyboard shortcuts, 858
scripts, 725
tagging, 736
typographer's, 380-381

R

raised caps, 388
raster images, *see* **resolution-dependent graphics**
Read Tags (Place dialog box), 196
reader's spreads, printing, 560
Recent Publications command (File menu), 15, 50
recomposing text, 840
  keyboard shortcuts, 861
records (databases), 421
Rectangle tool, 24-25
  keyboard shortcut, 234, 846
rectangles
  drawing, 235
    around text, 395-398
    rounding corners, 236
  moving, 238-239
  None attribute, 244
  resizing, 239
  reversing (knockout), 244
redrawing
  pages, keyboard shortcut, 851
  screen, 324-325
    keyboard shortcut, 324, 374
Reducing tool, keyboard shortcut, 846
reference points
  layout grids, 295-296
  selecting with Proxy (Control palette), 333-334
registered trademark symbol (®), keyboard shortcuts, 858
Remove Pages dialog box, 445
Remove Transformation command (Arrange menu), 446
removing, *see* **deleting**
renting laser printers, 576
replacing
  colored text, 369
  graphics, 253
  keyboard shortcuts, 856
  see also text, finding and changing
resizing
  cropping objects, defined, 338
  graphics, 258
    drawings, 239

    Magic Stretch, 258-259
    proportionally, 258-260
    tips, 585
  handles, 238, 239
  keyboard shortcut, 854
  scaling objects, defined, 338
  windows, PageMaker, 843
  with Control palette, 338-340
resolution
  documents, printing, 280
  graphics
    changing settings, 324-325
    high-resolution, 324
    viewing, 261
  screen resolution, 324-325
resolution-dependent graphics, 248-250
  editing, 263-266
  inline graphics, 253-257
  TIFF (Tag Image File Format), 250-251
resolution-independent graphics, 248-250
  EPS (Encapsulated PostScript) files, 249-251
    printing problems, 252
Retain Format (Place dialog box), 196
reversing objects, 244
  lines, 241
  see also knockout graphics; paper
Revert command (File menu), 170, 222, 238, 321
reverting, 320-321
  keyboard shortcut, 847
  mini-revert, 223, 321
RGB color, 47
Rich Text Format (RTF) files, 700
right reading, 571
Rotate tool, keyboard shortcut, 846
rotating
  graphics, tips, 587
  objects
    with Control palette, 343
    with Rotation tool, 344-345
Rotation tool, 24, 27, 344-345, 789
Row/Columns Size command (Cell menu; Adobe Table), 416

rows (tables)
  deleting, 414
  height adjustments, 415-417
  inserting, 414
  width, calculating automatically, 295
RTF (Rich Text Format) files, 700
ruler guides, 287
  copying, 297-298
    master page guides, 291
  custom, 311-312
  deleting, 291, 297-298
  displaying, 291
  Guide Manager Plug-in, 292
    defining grids, 295-297
    grid libraries, 292-295
  hiding, 291
  horizontal, 295
  locking, 290
  master page grids, 307
  moving, 290
    to back/front, 291
  setting, 289-290
  vertical, 295
ruler-style dialog box, 136
rulers, 19-20, 37, 59
  custom, 59
  readout, positioning graphics or text, 325
  snapping to guides/rulers, 298
  toggling on/off, keyboard shortcut, 848
  vertical rules, 398-399
Rules command (Paragraphs dialog box), 792
run-in headlines (cut-in), 366-367
  losing style coding, 367-368
  retaining style coding, 368-369
run-in style, indexes, 476
running footers/headers, 477-478
  creating, 481-482
  defining content, 480-481
  deleting, 482-485
  formatting, 479
  positioning, 478-479
  previewing, 481-482
  spacing, 479
Running Headers/Footers Plug-in, 688

S

Save command (File menu), 14
Save dialog box, 14
Save As command (File menu), 14
Save as Type list, 14
Save Copy As command (File menu; Adobe Table), 408
saving
disk space, 766
files
backups, 321
suggestions, 838
graphics, in/out of
publications, 255-257
indexes, edits, 472
keyboard shortcut, 847
options, 61
scripts, 718
suggestions, 838
tables
as stand-alone graphics,
408-409
OLE, 408
scaling objects
defined, 338
printing, 564
with Control palette, 338-340
scanning images
dot gain, 267
into PageMaker, 266-267
memory problems, 267
scanning resolution, 641-643
**scheduling publications,
651-652**
**Scitex Continuous Tone (SCT)
files, 251**
screen display
magnification, 321
keyboard shortcuts,
322-323
toggling, 322-323
redrawing screen, 324-325
forced redraw, 374
keyboard shortcut, 324
screen resolution, 324-325
printing graphics, 261
**screens, inserting behind text,
399-401**
Script Guide, 718

scripts, 708, 823, 877
alternatives, 739
benefits, 709
commands, 711-712
comments, 722-723
debugging, 726
defaults, 727
mini-defaults, 727
dragging and dropping, 711
external, 728-730
AppleScript, 729
DDE (Dynamic Data
Exchange), 729-730
dialog boxes, 730
finding and changing, 717-719
formatting, 725
fractions, 719-720
installing, 717
interactivity, 728-730
language, 720
spelling, 722
limitations, 727-728
measurements
changing, 712-713
overriding, 724
multiple commands, 722
organizing (subfolders), 711
parameters
empty, 721-722
separating, 721
pre-packaged (CD-ROM)
Crops, 714
Find/Change, 714
Graduated Screens, 714
Guides to Object, 715
instructions, 714
Measurement System, 715
Place Text, 716
Split Objects, 716
Straighten Rounded
Corners, 716
Zeropoint of Object, 716
queries, 729
relational page positions,
723-724
reverting, 726
running, 710-711
saving, 718
mini-save, 726
screen redrawing, 725
spell checking, 726
stopping, 725
template file, 717

text
ASCII (American Standard
Code for Information
Interchange), 725
quotation marks, 725
troubleshooting, 725-727
writing, 717-719
zero point, 723
see also commands; tagging
SCRIPTS folder, 711
**Scripts palette, 51, 277, 708,
710-713**
commands, 711-712
keyboard shortcut, 846
see also palettes
**scrolling, keyboard shortcut,
851**
**SCT (Scitex Continuous Tone)
files, 251**
search and replace, 823
keyboard shortcuts, 856
see also text, finding and
changing
**see references (indexes),
466-468**
**see also references (indexes),
466-468**
**see also herein references
(indexes), 468**
**Select All command (Edit
menu), 27, 214**
Select Topic dialog box, 461
selecting
grids in libraries, 293
guides, custom, 296-297
keyboard shortcut, 848
color, 853
fonts, 852
graphics, 849
styles, 852
text, 855
reference point, 333
table cells, 412-413
**Semiautomatic text icon,
186-187**
**Send to Back command
(Arrange menu), 243**
separations (color), 600
creating notes, 504
service bureaus
prepress services
color correction, 599
color separations, 600

high-resolution photo
scans, 599
imposition, 600
trapping, 599-600
rates, negotiating lower rates,
591-592
sending
backup files, 595
files, 590-591
original art, 595
submission forms, 592-599
submitting files to, 665-666
**Settings command (Start
menu), 217**
shadowing text, 394-395
tag, 864
**Shadowkey (Precision Type),
address, 873**
**Shift key, positioning text or
graphics, 326-327**
**Shift+Ctrl+C (centering text),
118**
**Shift+Ctrl+F (force
justification), 118**
**Shift+Ctrl+J (justifying text),
118**
**Shift+Ctrl+L (flush left text),
117**
**Shift+Ctrl+R (flush right text),
118**
Shift+F2 (text tool), 82
**Shift+Go To Page command,
17**
shortcut keys, Define Styles
dialog box (Ctrl+3), 171
shortcut keys, *see* keyboard
shortcuts
**Show Index command
(Utilities menu), 470-471**
Show Index dialog box
? (question mark), 473
codes, 473
**Show Loose/Tight Lines
command (Preferences
dialog box), 123**
**simultaneous forced left/right
alignment, 363-364**
single-sided pages, 282
**Size command (Type menu),
27**
sizing
cropping objects, defined,
338

graphics, 239-240, 258
Magic Stretch, 258-259
proportionally, 258-260
tips, 584-585
scaling objects, defined, 338
windows, PageMaker, 843
with Control palette, 338-340
**Skew command (Control
palette), 790**
skewing
objects with Control palette,
340-341
text, 392-393
**Small Caps option (Type
Specifications dialog box),
99**
**smart quotes (quotation
marks), setting, 380-381**
**Snap commands (Layout
menu), 20**
**Snap to Ruler command
(Guides and Rulers menu),
312**
**snapping to guides/rulers,
298, 327-329**
**SNR (Search N Replace)
program (CD-ROM), 877**
address, 874
**soft (discretionary) hyphens,
128**
soft return, tag, 869
**software, printer driver setup,
554-557**
**Sonar Bookends 3.5 (Virginia
Systems, Inc.), 456, 457**
address, 874
see also Plug-Ins
**Sort Pages command (Layout
menu), 446**
sorting
document pages, 446-448
index entries, 463-464
spacing
em spaces, keyboard shortcut,
363
graphics, inline graphics,
353-354
keyboard shortcuts, 858
tags, 866
**Spacing Attributes dialog box,
122, 155**
**special characters, keyboard
shortcuts, 858**

special effects
fractions, writing, 379-381
graphics, example, 265
headlines
companion column
headlines, 369-376
cross-column, 364-366
cut-in heads (run-in),
366-369
decks, 366
formatting, 376-379
kickers, 366
initial caps, 388
drop caps, 389-392
hanging caps, 388-389
raised caps, 388
text
baseline alignment,
393-394
boxes around or behind,
395-398
drop shadows, 394-395
grouping, 401-402
kerning, 393-394
masking, 401-402
molding, 384-386
skewing, 392-393
spinning, 392-393
vertical rules, 398-399
word wrap, 381-383
customizing, 383-384
inserting captions in
boundaries, 386
inside a shape, 386-387
**specialty lists, constructing,
452-453**
**spelling checker, 215-222,
604-605, 666-667**
Alternate Spellings option,
216
capitalization, 218
dictionaries (spelling
checker)
adding, 129-130
adding words, 218-219
capitalization, 218
converting non-PageMaker
to ASCII format, 222
custom (personal), 217,
219
deleting misspelled words,
218
deleting words, 219

Dictionary Editor, 130, 217-223
Dictionary list box, 218
disabled, 221
editing, 217-223
exporting format, 221
hyphenated words, 129-130, 220
importing, 220-221
languages, 217
multiple, 130
shared group, 218
word lists, 221
ignoring words, 216
keyboard shortcut, 856
Layout view, 217
replacing words, 216
scripts, 726
selecting text, 216
Show Duplicates option, 216
see also dictionaries
Spelling command (Utilities menu), 29, 215
Spelling dialog box, 216, 218
see also spelling checker
spinning text, 392-393
split justification, 363-364
spreadsheets, importing as tables, 424-425
squares
drawing, 235
around text, 395-398
rounding corners, 236
moving, 238-239
None attribute, 244
resizing, 239
reversing (knockout), 244
stacking order, object layers, 243
Start menu commands, Settings, 217
Starz (ShadeTree Marketing), address, 873
Step-by-Step (Step-by-Step Publishing), address, 874
sticky dialog boxes, 349
storing graphics in/out of publications, 255-257
Story Editor, 28-30, 204-211
black diamond marker, 460
coding indexes in, 458-460
customizing, 62-63
exiting, 205-206

flipping pages in Layout view, 206
keyboard shortcuts, 446, 850-851
navigating, 212, 214
opening, 205-209
preferences
Display Marks option, 211
fonts, 211
scripting, 823
search and replace, keyboard shortcuts, 856
stories
importing, 207
new, 207
styles, identifying, 167
text
clearing, 214
copying, 214
cutting, 214
dragging and dropping, 214
formatting, 215
pasting, 214
selecting, 213-214
unplaced text, 208-209
toggling Story Editor/Layout view, 206
windows
cascading, 209
opening, 206
tiling, 209
viewing, 209
see also indexes
Story Importer, 199-200
damaged files, saving, 200
setting document length, 200
Story Importer dialog box, 199
Story menu commands
Close All Stories, 206
Close Story, 30, 205
strikethrough
keyboard shortcuts, 854
tag, 864
stuffing, bindery service, 631
StuffIt Expander (Aladdin Systems, Inc.), address, 874
style sheets, 162
creating, 176-180
formatting, 659-660
setup, 658-659

Style submenu (Type menu), 164
styles, 171
applying, 162-168
automatically, 164-165
asterisk (*), 168, 176
adopting, 198
augmenting, 165-167
Based On function, 172
cascading, 172
style application, 165
consistency, 175
copying, 174-175
defining,169-171
editing, 169-171
imported styles, 838
finding defective styles, 841
formatting, local/hard, 165-167, 170
identifying, 167-168
importing, 175-176
indexes, 457, 477
nested, 476
run-in, 476
inherited style assignment, 165
instant, 170
keyboard shortcuts, 166
libraries, 179-180
merging, 173-174
mimicking, 172
naming, 178
Next Style function, 172
No style, 170
overriding, 165-167
page breaks, 178
page numbers, 280
paragraphs, tags, 868
plus sign (+), 168
printers, 577-578
reference lists, 168
removing, 170
search and replace, 167
selecting, keyboard shortcut, 852
style sheets, 162, 176-180
table of contents, 178, 451-452
tables, 433-434
tags, 195-196
Undo command (Edit menu), 164

Styles palette, 163, 711
    keyboard shortcut, 852
    placement, 163
    sizing, 163
subdecks (headlines), 366
submenus
    Plug-ins, 686
    Style (Type menu), 164
subscripts, 109
    customizing, 110
    keyboard shortcut, 854
    tag, 864-865
    writing fractions, 379-381
superscripts, 109
    customizing, 110
    keyboard shortcut, 854
    tag, 864-865
    writing fractions, 379-381
symbols
    carriage return, 368
    keyboard shortcuts, 858
    linking, 773
system requirements, 830
    reducing RAM requirements,
    831

T

**[T-26] font sampler (CD-ROM),
877**
    manufacturer's address, 874
Table Editor, 409-410
    see also Adobe Table
table of contents
    constructing, 448
        chapter-level or specialty
        lists TOC, 452-453
    editing, 452-453
    entries
        compiling, 449-450
        defining, 448-449
        formatting, 450
    linking to Web pages,
        762-763
    nonprinting items, 449
    placing (inside/outside of
        publication), 451
    proofreading, 605
    style adjustments, 451-452
Table Setup dialog box, 411

tables
Adobe Table (editor), 405
    opening, 408
as stand-alone graphics
    exporting, 408-409
    importing, 409
    saving, 408-409
    updating, 409
cells
    grouping, 414
    navigating, 412-413
    selecting, 412-413
columns
    deleting, 414
    inserting, 414
    width adjustments,
        415-417
data entry, 412
default settings, 420
editing, 46
formatting
    borders, 418-420
    color, 419-420
    fills, 419-420
    hanging indents, 428-429
    page breaks, 410
    paragraph rules, 429-430
    tabbed columns, 428-429
    vertical rules, 431-432
importing
    databases, 424-425
    finding and changing
        imported data, 427
    options, 406-407
    precoding imported data,
        433-434
    spreadsheets, 424-425
    word processor tables,
        197, 426
OLE (Object Linking and
    Embedding)
    creating, 407
    opening, 407
    saving, 408
    updating, 408
rows
    deleting, 414
    height adjustments, 415-
        417
    inserting, 414
setup, 411-412
styles, 138

Table Editor files, 409-410
tabs, 138-139
text
    formatting, 417-418
    importing, 412
transferring between
    Macintosh and DOS, 703
tabs
    bleeder tabs
        creating, 485-486
        defined, 485
        printer setup, 568
    characters, 138
    default settings, 140-141
    leaders, 139-140
    precision, 139
        multiple, 140
    tab stops, 136-145
        setting, 137-138
    tables, 138-139
    tag, 866
**Tag Image File Format (TIFF)
files, 250-251**
    compressing, 261-263
tags, 708-709, 730-731, 823
    alternatives, 739
    batch processing, 738-739
    benefits, 709
    codes, 735
    exporting text, 733
    HTML (HyperText Markup
        Language)
        character formatting,
            864-865
        paragraph formatting,
            866-868
        special characters, 869
    inline graphics, 736
    macros, 737-738
    mathematical operators, 736
    measurements, 736
    numbers, 736
    placing text, 733
    procedures, 732-733
    quotation marks, 736
    tables, 434
    tag alert, 734
    Tagged Text file format, 732
    translating codes literally,
        736
    see also scripts

Target printer resolution setting (Document Setup dialog box), 13
teasers (kickers), 366
TEMP file, 842
Template command (Save as Type list), 14
templates
    character map (CHARSET.PT6), 225
    colors, 515
    creating, 14, 283
    opening, 284
        PageMaker template, 283
    scripts, 717
Templates command (File menu), 15
temporary defaults (publication-level), 274
    see also mini-defaults; publication defaults
testing book concept, 654-655
text
    alignment, 117-136, 190, 348-349, 790
        alerts, 123
        baseline alignment, 393-394
        centered, 118
        Control palette, 119
        flush left, 118
        flush right, 117
        force justification, 118, 135-136
        hyphenating, 126-135
        justification, 118, 120-126
        letter spacing, 124
        paragraph spacing attributes, 122
        Paragraph Specifications dialog box, 118
        readability, 120, 125-126
        Type menu, 119
        word spacing, 122
    attributes, 84-86
        setting, 82-83
    baseline, 108
    blocks, 182
        finding lost, 192
        positioning, 189-190
        rethreading (linking), 191-193
        selecting, 191

    sizing, 189-190
    threads, 182
    unthreading (unlinking), 190
    codes, tagging, 730
    colors, 520-522
    defaults, mini-defaults, 83
    dictionary (spelling checker)
        adding text, 129-130
        hyphenated words, 129-130
    editing, 28-30, 111-112
        flipped, 345
        keyboard shortcuts, 855-856
        rotated text, 345
        skewed text, 345
    embedding in graphics files, 586
    exporting, 194
        troubleshooting, 842
    files
        backups, 208
        converting, 700-701
        importing, 255-256
        translation utilities, 701
    finding and changing, 222-229
        adding entries to indexes, 225
        capitalization, 225-226
        Change All option, 227
        colored text, 369
        editing during, 228
        formatting attributes, 226-229
        special characters, 224-225
        text box entries, 224
        undoing, 222
        Whole Word option, 225
    fitting on lines, 316
    flipping, 341-342
    formatting, 27-28, 33-34, 85
        boxes around or behind, 395-398
        distributing, 349-350
        drop shadows, 394-395
        hanging indents, 360
        justification, 121-122, 133-135, 363-364
        kerning, 46, 102-103, 125-126, 393-394, 857
        scripts, 725
        see also tags

    greeking, 61
    grouping, 401-402
    hyphenating
        algorithms, 220
        manual, 128-129
        preventing, 130
        tildes (~), 218
    importing, 192-201
        ASCII files, 198-199
        import filters, 192
        local (hard) formatting, 196
        Microsoft Word, 196-198
        tagging styles, 195-196
        troubleshooting, 841
        viewing import filters, 193
    indexes
        formatting, 462-463
        highlighting entries, 465-466
    inserting
        backgrounds/screens behind, 399-401
        new text, 83
    line length options
        automatic kerning, 132
        hyphenation, 132
        letter spacing, 132
        manual kerning, 131
        priority order, 132-133
        tracking, 131
        width, 131
        word spacing, 132
    locking to page, 355
    masking, 355-357, 401-402
    molding, 384-386
    pasting
        multiple pasting, 350-351
        power pasting, 351-352
    placement, 185-186
        AutoFlow, 186
        column guides, 188-190
        custom, 187
        dragging, 185
        icons, 185-186
        manual, 185
        pausing, 188
        semiautomatic, 186-187
    positioning
        Control palette readout, 326
        ruler readout, 325
        small text, 329-330
        snapping to guides, 327-329

with Control palette, 330-340
with Shift key, 326-327
recomposing, 840
keyboard shortcuts, 861
resizing with Control palette, 788
rotating, 343-345
scripts, quotation marks, 725
selecting, 27, 83, 191-192
keyboard shortcuts, 855
Pointer tool, 28
skewing, 340-341, 392-393
spell checking, 215-222
see also spelling checker
spinning, 392-393
tables
formatting, 417-418
importing, 412
tool, 82
tracking, 103-104
windowshades, 189
wrapping, 381-383
customizing word wrap, 383-384
inserting captions in boundaries, 386
inside a shape, 386-387
see also Story Editor
Text mode (Control palette), 32
text placement icons, 185-186
Text tool, 24-25, 27, 35, 82
keyboard shortcut, 846
Text Wrap command (Element menu), 381
Text Wrap dialog box, 381
text-entry boxes (Control palette), 331-332
ThePage (The Cobb Group), address, 874
thermal dye sublimation printers, 612
thin space
keyboard shortcuts, 858
tag, 869
thumbnail pages, 790, 792
printing, 564
proofing tool, 606
TIFF (Tag Image File Format) files, 45, 250, 251, 815
clipping path support, 45
compressing, 261-263
keyboard shortcuts, 860-861

converting to JPEG and GIF files, 750-751
decompression, keyboard shortcuts, 860-861
Tile command (Window menu), 15, 209
tiling images, printing, 564
tints
defining, 510
naming, 511
tipping, bindery service, 631
title page, unnumbered, 278-279
TOC, *see* **table of contents**
toggling magnification, 322-323
Tool palette, keyboard shortcut, 846
see also palettes
Toolbox
Constrained Line tool, 24
keyboard shortcut, 234-235
Cropping tool, 24, 259-269
keyboard shortcut, 259
keyboard shortcuts, 234, 846
Line tool, 24
keyboard shortcut, 234-235
Oval tool, 24
keyboard shortcut, 234
Polygon tool, 24
keyboard shortcut, 234
publications defaults, accessing, 26
Rectangle tool, 24
keyboard shortcut, 234
Rotation tool, 24, 344-345, 789
Toolbox command (Window menu), 24, 82
tools
Magnifying Glass, 24
Pointer, 24
Text, 24, 82
World Wide Web (WWW), 814-815
topic list (indexes)
creating, 456
importing, 457-458
selecting entries from, 461
topics, indexes, 460
tracking, 103-104, 131

copying among fonts, 105-106
editing settings, 104-106
keyboard shortcut, 854
Proof button, 105
tag, 865
Tracking Values file, creating, 106
transferring files, *see* **files, converting**
Translation Options dialog box, 703
transparency, graphics, 815
lines, 241, 245
TransverterPro (TechPool Studios), address, 874
trapping, 76, 512, 537-539, 599
automatic
parameter settings, 549-550
technical specs, 547-548
avoiding problems, 543-546
design problems, 544-546
framing, 544
kiss fit, 542-543
mechanical, 539-540
object-level, 540-541
process colors, 544
raster, 541
service bureaus, 541
spot colors, 544
Trapping Plug-in, 48
Treacyfaces font sampler (CD-ROM), 877
address, 874
troubleshooting
error messages, bad record index, 839-840
file cleanup utility, 840
scripts, 725-727
suggestions
backups, 839-840
breaking book into pieces, 838
checking all page elements, 840-841
copying damaged pages to new document, 842
editing imported styles, 838-839
exporting text, 842
files, 842, 843
finding defective styles, 841
finding unlinked elements, 841

graphics files, 839
importing text, 841-842
linking in PageMaker, 839
saving, 838
Turn Pages When Autoflowing (More Preferences dialog box), 62
tutorials, Welcome program (PageMaker CD), Disk-Based Training, 40
TWAIN module, 267
type
design issues, 795-805
points, 90-92
reverse styling, 98
sizes, 88-93
tag, 864
specifications, keyboard shortcut, 847
styles, 97-98
compared to paragraph styles, 165-166
width adjustments, 106-107
see also fonts; formatting, text
Type menu
aligning text, 119
Expert Tracking submenu, 104
Font command, 87
Leading submenu, 96
Size submenu, 89
Style submenu, 164
Type menu commands
Choose Paragraph, 28
Define Styles, 35
Edit Tracks, 104
Expert Kerning, 103
Font, 27
Hyphenation, 127, 840
Indents/Tabs, 136
Size, 27
Type Specs, 27
Type Specifications dialog box, 27, 84
Case command, 99
font list, 86
leading, 95
Line End function, 107
Small Caps option, 99
superscripts/subscripts, 110
type sizes, 88
Type Specs command (Type menu), 27

typefaces
readability, 93
selecting, 86-88
typesetting, 46
professional, 110
typographer's quotes, setting, 380-381

U

underlining text
index entries, 462-463
keyboard shortcut, 854
tag, 864
Undo command (Edit menu), 164, 238, 320
undoing mistakes, 320-321
alignment, 350
deleting pages, 283
distributing objects, 350
inserting pages, 283
keyboard shortcut, 238, 320, 848
moving guides (layout grids), 290
Ungroup command (Arrange menu), 346
Ungroup command (Cell menu; Adobe Table), 414
ungrouping objects, 346
Uniform Resource Locators (URLs), 758
see also World Wide Web
Unlock command (Arrange menu), 355
Update PPD Plug-in, 688
see also Plug-ins
updating
links, 773-780
tables
as stand-alone graphics, 409
OLE, 408
URLs (Uniform Resource Locators), 758
see also World Wide Web
utilities
batch search and replace, 693
file compression, 694, 701
file conversion, 693
graphics conversion, 700
indexes/citation lists, 693

proofing, 693
text file translation, 701
see also Plug-ins
Utilities menu commands
Change, 29, 223
Create Index, 457, 474
Create TOC, 448-449
Find, 29, 223
Index Entry, 460
Open Template, 15, 283
PageMaker Plug-ins, 15, 37-38
Show Index, 470-471
Spelling, 29, 215

V

vector images, *see* **resolution-independent graphics**
vertical justification, 312
vertical printing (portrait orientation), 560
vertical ruler guides, 295, 398-399
tables, 431-432
View command (Layout menu), 18
viewing
graphics, 260-263
keyboard shortcut (high resolution), 261
monitor problems, 264
screen resolution, 261
guides (layout grids), 291
keyboard shortcuts, 850
Story Editor window, 209
keyboard shortcuts, 850-851
thumbnail pages, 790
VRML (Virtual Reality Modeling Language), 747
VuePrint (CD-ROM), 878

W

Welcome program (PageMaker CD), Disk-Based Training, 40
widows, 147-157

width, keyboard shortcut, 854
Window menu commands
  Cascade, 15, 209
  Color palette, 35
  Tile, 15, 209
  Toolbox, 24, 82
windows, resizing, 843
**WinZip file compression
  program (CD-ROM), 878**
word wrap, 381-383
  customizing, 383-384
  inserting captions in
    boundaries, 386
  inside a shape, 386-387
  molding text, 384-386
**WordPerfect Corporation,
  address, 875**
World Wide Web, 808
  authoring tools, PageMill, 747
  electronic publishing, 50
    Adobe Acrobat files,
      744-745, 811-812
    converting documents to
      Web pages, 747-750
    converting graphics files
      to JPEG and GIF files,
      750-751
    creating Adobe Acrobat
      files, 760-764
    future outlook, 747
    guidelines, 751-754
    HTML (HyperText Markup
      Language), 745-747
    running HTML Author
      Plug-in, 754-764
    sites, 753-754
  graphics, 815
  files, 814
  HTML (HyperText Markup
    Language), 809, 811-814
  HTML tags
    character formatting,
      864-865
    paragraph formatting,
      866-868
    special characters, 869
  internal locations, 758
  modems, 809
  PageMaker 6.0, 811-814
  pages, 38-39, 50
    constructing, 38-39
    designing contents,
      810-811
    graphics, 809

  tools, 814-815
  URLs (Uniform Resource
    Locators), 758
wove paper, 629
writing scripts, 717-719
wrong reading, 571
**WYSIWYG (What You See Is
  What You Get), color, 492**

X-Y-Z

X (link status code), 774

**Yahoo! Directory home page,
  754**

**Zephyr Specs (Zephry Design),
  address, 875**
zero point, 723
Zoom tool, 46

PLUG YOURSELF INTO...

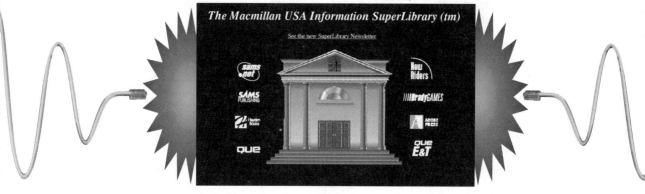

The Macmillan USA Information SuperLibrary (tm)

See the new SuperLibrary Newsletter

THE MACMILLAN
INFORMATION SUPERLIBRARY™

Free information and vast computer resources from the world's leading computer book publisher—online!

FIND THE BOOKS THAT ARE RIGHT FOR YOU!
A complete online catalog, plus sample chapters and tables of contents!

- **STAY INFORMED** with the latest computer industry news through our online newsletter, press releases, and customized Information SuperLibrary Reports.

- **GET FAST ANSWERS** to your questions about QUE books.

- **VISIT** our online bookstore for the latest information and editions!

- **COMMUNICATE** with our expert authors through e-mail and conferences.

- **DOWNLOAD SOFTWARE** from the immense Macmillan Computer Publishing library:
    - Source code, shareware, freeware, and demos

- **DISCOVER HOT SPOTS** on other parts of the Internet.

- **WIN BOOKS** in ongoing contests and giveaways!

TO PLUG INTO QUE:

WORLD WIDE WEB: **http://www.mcp.com/que**

FTP: ftp.mcp.com

Complete and Return this Card
for a *FREE* Computer Book Catalog

Thank you for purchasing this book! You have purchased a superior computer book written expressly for your needs. To continue to provide the kind of up-to-date, pertinent coverage you've come to expect from us, we need to hear from you. Please take a minute to complete and return this self-addressed, postage-paid form. In return, we'll send you a free catalog of all our computer books on topics ranging from word processing to programming and the internet.

Mr. ☐   Mrs. ☐   Ms. ☐   Dr. ☐

Name (first) [＿＿＿＿＿＿＿＿＿＿＿＿] (M.I.) ☐   (last) [＿＿＿＿＿＿＿＿＿＿＿＿＿＿＿＿＿]

Address [＿＿＿＿＿＿＿＿＿＿＿＿＿＿＿＿＿＿＿＿＿＿＿＿＿＿＿＿＿]

[＿＿＿＿＿＿＿＿＿＿＿＿＿＿＿＿＿＿＿＿＿＿＿＿＿＿＿＿＿]

City [＿＿＿＿＿＿＿＿＿＿＿] State [＿＿] Zip [＿＿＿＿＿＿]

Phone [＿＿＿＿＿＿＿＿] Fax [＿＿＿＿＿]

Company Name [＿＿＿＿＿＿＿＿＿＿＿＿＿＿＿＿＿＿＿＿＿＿＿＿＿]

E-mail address [＿＿＿＿＿＿＿＿＿＿＿＿＿＿＿＿＿＿＿＿＿＿＿＿＿]

Please check at least (3) influencing factors for purchasing this book.

Front or back cover information on book .... ☐
Special approach to the content .... ☐
Completeness of content .... ☐
Author's reputation .... ☐
Publisher's reputation .... ☐
Book cover design or layout .... ☐
Index or table of contents of book .... ☐
Price of book .... ☐
Special effects, graphics, illustrations .... ☐
Other (Please specify): _____ ☐

How did you first learn about this book?

Saw in Macmillan Computer Publishing catalog .... ☐
Recommended by store personnel .... ☐
Saw the book on bookshelf at store .... ☐
Recommended by a friend .... ☐
Received advertisement in the mail .... ☐
Saw an advertisement in: _____ ☐
Read book review in: _____ ☐
Other (Please specify): _____ ☐

How many computer books have you purchased in the last six months?

This book only .... ☐   3 to 5 books .... ☐
books .... ☐   More than 5 .... ☐

4. Where did you purchase this book?

Bookstore .... ☐
Computer Store .... ☐
Consumer Electronics Store .... ☐
Department Store .... ☐
Office Club .... ☐
Warehouse Club .... ☐
Mail Order .... ☐
Direct from Publisher .... ☐
Internet site .... ☐
Other (Please specify): _____ ☐

5. How long have you been using a computer?

☐ Less than 6 months   ☐ 6 months to a year
☐ 1 to 3 years   ☐ More than 3 years

6. What is your level of experience with personal computers and with the subject of this book?

	With PCs	With subject of book
New	☐	☐
Casual	☐	☐
Accomplished	☐	☐
Expert	☐	☐

Source Code ISBN: 0-7897-0610-5

7. Which of the following best describes your job title?

Administrative Assistant .... ☐
Coordinator .... ☐
Manager/Supervisor .... ☐
Director .... ☐
Vice President .... ☐
President/CEO/COO .... ☐
Lawyer/Doctor/Medical Professional .... ☐
Teacher/Educator/Trainer .... ☐
Engineer/Technician .... ☐
Consultant .... ☐
Not employed/Student/Retired .... ☐
Other (Please specify): _____ ☐

8. Which of the following best describes the area of the company your job title falls under?

Accounting .... ☐
Engineering .... ☐
Manufacturing .... ☐
Operations .... ☐
Marketing .... ☐
Sales .... ☐
Other (Please specify): _____ ☐

9. What is your age?

Under 20 .... ☐
21-29 .... ☐
30-39 .... ☐
40-49 .... ☐
50-59 .... ☐
60-over .... ☐

10. Are you:

Male .... ☐
Female .... ☐

11. Which computer publications do you read regularly? (Please list)

_____
_____
_____
_____
_____
_____
_____
_____
_____
_____

Comments: _____
_____
_____

Fold here and scotch-tape to mail.

Licensing Agreement

The CD-ROM included with Special Edition Using PageMaker 6 for Windows 95 contains several dozen scripts and Utilities to ease your desktop publishing labors, free fonts and font specimen files, some free high-resolution stock photos, and a collection of tools for Web publishing. See Appendix F, "What's on the CD?," for more information.